THE JACOBEAN AND
CAROLINE STAGE

THE JACOBEAN
AND
CAROLINE STAGE

PLAYS AND PLAYWRIGHTS

BY

GERALD EADES BENTLEY

VOLUME III

36247

OXFORD
AT THE CLARENDON PRESS
1956

Oxford University Press, Amen House, London E.C.4

GLASGOW NEW YORK TORONTO MELBOURNE WELLINGTON
BOMBAY CALCUTTA MADRAS KARACHI CAPE TOWN IBADAN

Geoffrey Cumberlege, Publisher to the University

PRINTED IN GREAT BRITAIN

PREFACE

THESE three long overdue volumes present the second aspect of a study of the Jacobean and Caroline stage; Plays and Playwrights now follow the study of Dramatic Companies and Players set forth in two earlier volumes. A final instalment will treat Theatres and Theatrical Customs and provide a comprehensive index for all six volumes.

Since this study of Plays and Playwrights is intended for reference purposes and not—grisly thought—for consecutive reading, it is especially incumbent upon me to set forth here the principles of inclusion and selection I have tried to follow and the pattern for the ordering of the rather scattered and varied material under the individual plays—a pattern often obscured by the vast difference between the number of facts and comments extant concerning a well-known play like *A Game at Chess* as compared with those for an obscure one like Peter Heylyn's *Doublet, Breeches, and Shirt*.

Generally speaking, I have tried to consider all plays, masques, shows, and dramatic entertainments which were written or first performed in England between 1616, the last year covered by Sir Edmund Chambers in *The Elizabethan Stage*, and the closing of the theatres in 1642. I have consciously allowed no exceptions to this rule of inclusion, though I fear there may have been inadvertent omissions. On the other hand, I have often included pieces which do not properly fall within these limits when I thought I could render a service to scholars who might use the book regularly. A few plays written before 1616 are to be found here because they were omitted or (as later studies have shown) misdated by Sir Edmund Chambers; I have constantly envisaged these volumes for use in connexion with his. A larger number of plays written after 1642 have been included because they have often been misdated before 1642, or because they have never been discussed and might be thought at first glance to date before the closing of the theatres. The plays performed abroad in the Jesuit school for English boys at St. Omer (commonly called St. Omers in England in the seventeenth century) have been included, though not fully discussed, because of the confusion which has arisen from occasional references to the manuscripts as if they were compositions for performance in England.

Other plays outside the period have been included—generally with the scantiest discussion possible, or none at all—when it seemed that for one reason or another notice of them would be helpful to scholars using this book. The earlier plays of dramatists who wrote both before and after 1616 (such as Jonson and Fletcher) have been merely listed with references to *The Elizabethan Stage*. Similarly, plays written after 1642 by Caroline dramatists (such as Davenant, Killigrew, Jordan, and Tatham) have been given brief notice, since there is no standard reference work for the later period. Thus there are entries of some kind for about 1,200 plays, though less than 800 of them were actually written in England between 1616 and 1642.

Though the collection and discussion of material for these three volumes on Plays and Playwrights has gone on at intervals over a span of a quarter of a century, most of the individual accounts were written during the years 1944–50, and the first few hundred pages of manuscript were sent to the publishers in 1951. One of the tribulations arising from a consideration of some two hundred and twenty authors and 1,500 or more plays over such a protracted period has been the regular appearance of new studies after my material had been assembled, organized, and frequently written up; consequently there were endless revisions and alterations, often requiring the scrapping of a cherished analysis and the substitution of a cross-reference. Obviously it was necessary to call a halt before utter frustration set in. Reluctantly, therefore, I set an arbitrary limit for the consideration of new publications. Studies printed after the end of 1950 I have sternly ignored—except where my stern resolution melted before such a monumental achievement as the second volume of Sir Walter Greg's *A Bibliography of the English Printed Drama to the Restoration*. Even Sir Walter has been curtailed, for I had referred to him in literally hundreds of biographies and play discussions under the familiar title of 'Dr. Greg',

used with unique respect for half a century by grateful
Elizabethan scholars. Perhaps it was only indolence which
prevented me from replacing a doctorate with a knighthood,
but I find a nostalgic satisfaction in keeping the old title with
its accumulations of admiration and gratitude.

In the smaller units of the study, dramatists are listed in
alphabetical order, with the anonymous plays at the end of
the alphabet in volume five. The biography of each author is
preceded by a scanty bibliography, consisting mostly of titles
which have been used in an abbreviated form in the account
of the playwright's life and works. Many studies consulted
have been ignored in these short bibliographies because they
had nothing to contribute or because they have been super-
seded. Sometimes I have included unpublished dissertations,
mostly American, and for this practice I must apologize to
readers outside the United States. American libraries can
usually borrow such manuscripts, or microfilm copies of them,
and consequently unpublished theses can often be helpful to
American scholars. A few such dissertations which I consulted in manuscript have been published after my terminal
date for bibliography, 1950. An example is Gwynne Blakemore
Evans's *The Plays and Poems of William Cartwright.*

Collected editions, listed in chronological order, appear at
the end of the biographies. They are followed by discussions
of the individual plays of the dramatist, marshalled alpha-
betically, not chronologically as in *The Elizabethan Stage.*
These play discussions will be most frequently consulted,
I suspect, by scholars seeking facts about particular plays,
not studying the entire work of a playwright. For such readers
I hope the alphabetical order will be more convenient,
especially for dramatists so prolific as Jonson, Massinger,
Middleton, Shirley, Brome, Fletcher, Davenant, Heywood,
Jordan, or Anon.

In the heading for each play is given the date of first production, as nearly as I can determine it. Since a play comes
into full existence only when it is performed, this date is more
important than the date of composition; for most Jacobean
and Caroline plays, however, production seems to have
followed shortly after the dramatist's completion of his

manuscript. Where the play was not produced in its own time, as in the case of Jonson's *May Lord* or Thomas May's *Antigone*, I have fallen back on a date of composition.

After the title and date of the play are listed the manuscripts—if any are known to exist—and then such modern editions as have appeared. Generally speaking, I have listed only those modern editions which provide discussions and annotations of the play; simple reprints are ignored except for occasional plays likely to be unavailable to scholars in any other form.

Following the modern editions comes a brief bibliography of books and articles on the play up to and including the year 1950. All these bibliographies are selective, and for the better-known plays, like Jonson's, highly selective. Finally, in these preliminary lists, there are set out in chronological order all the seventeenth-century records I can find bearing on the performance, publication, and reputation of the play —performance licences, Stationers' Register entries and transfers, court performance records, bills, and payments, title-pages, contemporary comments, Lord Chamberlain's lists, notices in diaries, letters, and accounts, revisions, repertory lists, manuscript lists, allusions, and quotations. These dated records I have tried to make full and complete for the seventeenth century; performances and revisions in the eighteenth, nineteenth, and twentieth centuries have been listed only when they came to hand, mostly from modern editions of Jacobean and Caroline plays, but I have made no organized search of theatrical annals for the years after 1700.

Perhaps my system of transcribing seventeenth-century title-pages in these lists requires comment, since it is a compromise. Full bibliographical transcription seemed supererogatory if not presumptuous after the appearance of Sir Walter Greg's *A Bibliography of the English Printed Drama to the Restoration*; bibliographers will always use his work rather than mine. On the other hand, short titles would frequently have been inadequate for the discussions which follow and which often make use of details from early title-pages. Under these circumstances a compromise was devised which will, I hope, be serviceable. Every word and punctuation mark of a title-page, except for mottoes and imprints, is transcribed in the spelling of the original. Italics and initial capitalization follow the original, but other typographical variations and lineation are ignored. Since most of my transcriptions were made before the appearance of Sir Walter's first volume, and all before the appearance of his second, all of them—except for perhaps a dozen inaccessible examples—come from the originals, and all have been checked from more than one copy where duplicates were known in the British Museum, the Bodleian, the Cambridge University Library, the Huntington, the Folger, the Newberry, Harvard University Library, the University of Chicago Library, or Princeton University Library. Since my purpose was historical rather than bibliographical, variants and manuscript notes have generally been recorded only when they seemed significant for my discussion of the play.

These bibliographies and lists preceding each play are the basic sources for the discussions which follow and should be noted before the discussion is read, for I have constantly assumed familiarity with them. I hope that their stark listing in this fashion will make them more readily usable by scholars who may wish simply to review the facts. The material in the various transcriptions will be indexed in volume six and can thus, I hope, be reassembled by scholars wishing to use it for conclusions I did not have space for or did not see.

The discussions of individual plays vary markedly in length, depending upon the extent of the material available, or the complexity of the problems involved, or what seemed to me the mistaken conclusions in previous discussions. I have tried to avoid the popular error of considering the plays as non-dramatic literary documents, and to keep them in their proper theatrical context; hence the frequent references back to the purely theatrical materials of volumes one and two, to the repertory to which a play belonged, and to the state of the company for which it was written.

Since the setting of these plays in their theatrical context has been my primary task, and one which has taken far more space than was originally intended, I have tried to suppress my comments on literary and dramatic values in the plays —not always successfully. At first I proposed also to refrain from any speculation and to limit myself strictly to the evidence at hand. So much confusion has been caused by the unsupported guesses and hunches of F. G. Fleay, W. J. Lawrence, and others, that one is strongly impelled to suppress all comments which cannot be supported by solid evidence. Yet no scholar who has worked extensively in the field of sixteenth- and seventeenth-century drama can have failed to be struck by the number of good guesses of Fleay and Lawrence amid all their absurdities—guesses for which sound evidence has eventually been found or which have led to illuminating discoveries. These men had so much experience with the plays and the theatrical records of the time that at their best they instinctively, or subconsciously, set up for themselves limits of probability more precise and valid than less experienced scholars can set with fully developed arguments. The confusion has been caused by the failure of the unwary to distinguish between demonstrated facts and informed (though often erroneous) guesses. For my own part I have tried to be scrupulous in branding all speculation as such, whether my own or other men's. Hence the frequent repetition of such phrases as 'This is pure speculation', 'This is a mere guess'.

Most of the work on these volumes has been done in the great research libraries, and I cherish pleasant memories of many months spent in the British Museum, the Bodleian, Cambridge University Library, the Huntington Library, the Folger Shakespeare Library, and the Houghton and Widener Libraries at Harvard. For shorter but equally pleasant periods I have enjoyed the courtesies of the libraries at the Victoria and Albert Museum; Trinity, St. John's, and Emmanuel Colleges, Cambridge; Worcester College, Oxford; the New York Public Library; Yale University Library; and the Newberry Library. To the librarians and assistants at these great collections I am indebted for their hospitality and for many acts of kindness. Perhaps I have too often taken for granted similar kindnesses in the libraries of the universities to which I have been attached, Chicago and Princeton.

Hospitality for the parting guest is often achieved, but courtesy towards an inescapable member of the family requires Christian forbearance.

Much of the research time and travel required for work of an exacting kind in such widely scattered centres has been provided by a Huntington Library Research Fellowship, a Guggenheim Fellowship, a Fulbright Research Fellowship at Cambridge, and by the Research Committee of Princeton University. Without their aid the material here assembled and discussed could not have been collected; for pleasures as well as opportunities I am indebted to them.

Three research assistants have helped me at various times in checking bibliography, transcriptions, deductions, and proof. Professor Frank Wadsworth, Professor R. J. Schoeck, and Dr. H. K. Miller, Jr., have cheerfully and competently waded through oceans of typescript and fished out many an error. I am grateful to them for their conscientious help and for their friendship.

Like the first two volumes of this study, these three display on every page the handiwork of my wife, who has read with me in all the libraries and manuscript repositories, revised all the copy, typed all the versions, checked all the manuscript, scrutinized all the proof, and charmed all the assistants. 'Gratitude is but a lame sentiment. . . .'

G. E. B.

Princeton
November 1954

PLAYS AND PLAYWRIGHTS

M. A.

(?—?)

That a man with these initials wrote a play is known only from Abraham Hill's notice of a manuscript play called *Tereus with a Pastoral* written by M. A. (See below, Middleton, *The Conqueror's Custom*.) No seventeenth-century dramatist with these initials is known to me, and Maurice Atkins is my only guess among seventeenth-century writers. The initials reversed could refer to Anthony Munday, but this would seem to be twisting the evidence.

Tereus with a Pastoral (?)

(Lost)

This title is thirty-fourth in the list of manuscript plays found among the papers of Abraham Hill. (See Middleton, *The Conqueror's Custom*.) The list seems to have been Hill's record of the stock of some bookseller, set down between 1677 and 1703, but it is notable that nearly all the identifiable plays and playwrights in the list are Jacobean and Caroline.

In his list Hill records the manuscript as follows:

Tereus with a pastoral   M. A.
   Actors. Agnostus Eupathus &c
   Actors Mufti Nassuf &c

This rather enigmatic set of notes might indicate one play or two. J. Q. Adams in his discussion of Hill's list (*Library*, Fourth Series, xx [1939], 93–94) is inclined to think that 'a single dramatic manuscript in two parts' is recorded because Hill customarily listed plays separately and because one author's initials are used. Perhaps this is the best interpretation of the listing because of the repetition of the term 'Actors'. In the two other instances where Hill noted names in the dramatis personae he did not repeat 'Actors', though in one instance he gave three names. In any event, neither *Tereus* nor any of the character names is familiar from other seventeenth-century records.

JOHN ADSON

fl. 1620–40

Adson was a musician and composer and perhaps an occasional actor. (See above, ii. 343–4.) He has sometimes been listed as a dramatist (Hazlitt, *Manual*, p. 3) because of the titles 'Mr Adson's

Masque' and 'Adsonn's Masque' in the *Catalogue of Manuscript Music in the British Museum* (iii. 174). The manuscript volume referred to (Add. MS. 10444) is labelled on the parchment cover 'Masques & other Tunes   Treble', and the second half of the volume is headed 'Bassus'. The music in the volume is mostly titled with masque designations: 'The Queenes Masque the first', 'The Prince's Masque', 'A Masque at Fryers', 'Hampton Court Masque', 'The Amazons Masque', 'Lincolnes Inne Masque', and so on. The catalogue dates the volume 'After 1635?' There is no evidence that Adson ever wrote a play.

Adson's Masque

Not a dramatic production, as has sometimes been implied, but a piece of music, perhaps written for a masque.

WILLIAM AINSWORTH (Aynsworth)
c. 1607–71

William Ainsworth may be only the transcriber of a Latin play and not a dramatist at all. The Emmanuel College MS. of *Clytophon* carries at the end the inscription 'Gulielmus Bretonus possessor. Gulielmus Ainseworthus Scriptor.' The name has several times been misread as *George* Ainsworth; see *Retrospective Review*, xii (1825), 27; Hazlitt, *Manual*, p. 44; Fleay, *Biog. Chron.* i. 23.

William Ainsworth was admitted sizar at Emmanuel College 11 July 1622 and matriculated in the same year. There are no records of his further University associations or degrees, but he is later called M.A. He was probably curate of Ripponden in Yorkshire in 1630 and lecturer at St. Peter's, Chester. From 1647 to 1650 he was curate of Lightcliffe, Yorkshire, and in 1648 vicar of South Kirkby. He was prebendary of York in 1660, vicar of Hooten Pagnel from 1661 to 1662, and Master of Charterhouse in Hull in 1661. At an unknown date he became vicar of Sculcoates, where he was buried 19 April 1671. He is presumably the author of *Triplex Memoriae*, 1650, three sermons, and *Medulla Bibliorum, the Marrow of the Bible*, 1652. (*Alumni Cantab.* i. 10.)

The only seventeenth-century William Breton at Cambridge was the son of Robert Breton of Barwell; he was admitted pensioner 2 July 1618 at Emmanuel, where he was later a Fellow. He received degrees of B.A. 1621/2, M.A. 1625, and B.D. 1632. He was rector of Clapton, Northamptonshire, from 1631 to 1658 and died 17 August 1658. (*Alumni Cantab.* i. 212.)

The fact that this William Breton and William Ainsworth were together at Emmanuel College, the present repository of the manuscript, in the 1620's, probably from 1622 to about 1630, suggests that they are probably the two referred to in the manuscript of *Clytophon*.

Clytophon (1622?–30?)

MS.: Emmanuel College, Cambridge, MS. 3. 1. 17.

Clytophon is the fifth play in the Emmanuel College MS. After the epilogue comes the inscription:

> Gulielmus Bretonus possessor.
> Gulielmus Ainseworthus Scriptor.

If William Ainsworth was the author of this play, he probably wrote it during his Cambridge residence between 1622 and about 1630. In the somewhat more likely event that he was only the transcriber, the play could have been written almost any time before Ainsworth's departure from Cambridge about 1630. Even as transcriber, however, Ainsworth is likely to have been interested in a play produced during his own residence or shortly before.

Since the transcriber, or author, of the manuscript and the original owner were both Emmanuel men, and since the manuscript was deposited in the Emmanuel College Library, the play was presumably produced there.

Hazlitt suggests (*Manual*, p. 44) that the play was 'probably founded on Achilles Tatius'.

THOMAS ATKINSON
1599–1639

Atkinson was born in August 1599 and entered the Merchant Taylors' School as a Londoner in 1608. In 1615 he was elected a Merchant Taylor scholar to St. John's College and matriculated at Oxford 13 October 1615. At Oxford he took degrees of B.A. 12 May 1619, M.A. 26 April 1623, and B.D. 12 May 1630, and he served as Proctor of the University in 1629. Presumably he was the Thomas Atkinson who made a speech to Charles and Henrietta Maria and their nephews, Charles and Rupert of the Palatinate, as they passed St. John's College entering Oxford on 29 August 1636. Archbishop Laud says the speech was 'very brief and very much approved of by his Majesty afterwards to me'. (*The Autobiography of Dr. William Laud*, ed. 1839, pp. 200–1.)

Atkinson was inducted to the living of South Warnborough, Hampshire, 20 January 1637/8, a living which he exchanged shortly after with Peter Heylyn for Islip, near Oxford. On 6 February 1638/9 he was buried in St. John's College Chapel, a fact suggestive of a close connexion with the college. His will was proved at Oxford 21 February 1639/40. (*Alumni Oxon.* i. 42; Simmonds, *Merchant Taylor Fellows*, p. 17; *D.N.B.*)

Besides *Homo*, Atkinson wrote two Latin poems against Andrew Melvin, 'Andrei Melvini Anti-Tami-Cunicategoria' and 'Melvinus delirans'. There is a copy of the former in Folger MS. 2203.1.

Homo (1615–21)

MS.: B.M. Harleian 6925.

The play in the Harleian MS. is dedicated

> Reverendo viro M^ro Guilielmo
> Laud S. S. Theol. Doct: et
> Coll: D^l Ioan: Bapt: præ-
> sidi dignissimo

Since Laud was elected President of St. John's 10 May 1611 and resigned 17 November 1621, the dedication must fall within this period. Halliwell-Phillipps and Fleay dated the play 1612, apparently because Laud took office in this year, but the reasoning baffles me. Harbage dates it *c.* 1634–9 (*P.M.L.A.* liii [1938], 625, and *Annals of the English Drama 975–1700* [1940], p. 106), but again I fail to understand why. The dedication of the play and the facts of Atkinson's career would indicate a date between his matriculation and the resignation of Laud, 1615–21.

The dramatis personae given in the manuscript is:

Homo
Prologus

Iupiter		Tempus	
Epimetheus		Prometheus	
Anoetus	Epim:	Hedone Prom: uxor	
Metanoetus	famuli	Hesychia	Pro: famulæ
Penia		Techne	

Homo
Epilogus

This dramatis personae resembles those of Blencowe's *Mercurius*, Crowther's *Cephalus et Procris*, and Bellamy's *Iphis* (q.v.). All four plays were written by men of the Merchant Taylors' School and St. John's College, and three of them are dedicated to presidents of St. John's. Do they represent a standard St. John's exercise?

H. B.

fl. 1642–60

These initials appear as those of the author on the Bodleian MS. of *The Female Rebellion*, which has been attributed to Henry Burkhead (q.v.).

The 'H. H. B.' on the title-page of the 1659 edition of *The World's Idol, or Plutus the God of Wealth*, a translation from Aristophanes, might refer to the same man. The British Museum *Catalogue of Printed Books* says that 'H. H. B.' was Henry Burnell (q.v.), but on what grounds I do not know.

T. B.

fl. 1632–3 ?

These initials appear on the title-page of *The Country Girl*, entered in the Stationers' Register in 1640 and published in 1647, and they are also signed to the dedication of *The Rebellion of Naples*, printed in 1649. The 'T. B.' of *The Country Girl* was expanded to Thomas Brewer by Archer in his play-list of 1656. Kirkman in his play-lists of 1661 and 1671 credited the play to Anthony Brewer. Later writers have generally preferred Anthony Brewer— T for Tony! There is no serious evidence to connect either of these men with either play.

Before venturing on an attempt to identify T. B., it is salutary to consult the British Museum *Catalogue of Printed Books* under B., T. Of the many publications with only the initials T. B. on the title-page as author, there are about fifty 1600–90, i.e. of such a date that any one of them might conceivably have been written by a man who had a work entered in the Stationers' Register in 1640 and published in 1647. Further examination of titles and title-page comments and later expansions shows that at least ten different T. B.s must be involved. It is well to wait for solid evidence before proposing candidates for T. B.

The Country Girl (1632–3 ?)

Anon. 'The Countrie Girle', *The Retrospective Review*, Second Series, ii (1828), 14–23.

Oliphant, E. H. C. 'Problems of Authorship in Elizabethan Dramatic Literature', *Mod. Phil.* viii (1911), 422.

1640, 18 Nov. S.R. 'Abell Roper   Entred for his Copie vnder the hands of Doctor Wykes & Mr Man warden a Play called The Country Girle'. (Greg, *Bibliography*, i. 54.)

1647. The Covntrie Girle. A Comedie, As it hath beene often Acted with much applause. Never Printed before. *By* T. B. . . . 1647.

1677. The Country Innocence: Or, The Chamber-Maid Turn'd Quaker. A Comedy. With Alterations and Amendments. As it is now Acted at the Theatre-Royal. Written by *John Leanerd*. . . . 1677. (Very slightly adapted from *The Country Girl*; only the last two acts have been materially altered.)

Certain allusions in the prologue suggest a *terminus a quo* for the play. After a series of questions about the dubious appeal of such a homespun title and the suggestion of several current popular appeals which the play does not have, the prologue continues:

> *None of these?*
> *Alas poor Girle, where's then, thy hope to please?*
> *What can she sing? and, like the Northern Lasse,*
> *(That brave blithe Girle) hope to procure a passe?*
> *Or, can she fight?—If so so stout, so bold*
> *A brave Virago, like the Girle, worth Gold.*
> *Or is she one, that once a Countrey Maide,*
> *Crack'd in the carriage, is come to Trade,*
> *And set up some new Leaguer?*

The 'Northern Lasse' is, of course, the title character, the singing country girl Constance, in Brome's play of that name. *The Northern Lass* (q.v.) was licensed for performance by the King's company 29 July 1629; its success probably prompted the printing of the ballads entered in the Stationers' Register in January 1631/2, September 1632, and July 1633. Brome's comedy was printed in 1632 with commendatory verses by Ben Jonson, Thomas Dekker, John Ford, and others.

The 'Girle, worth Gold' is presumably Heywood's Bess Bridges, certainly a stout, bold, brave Virago, the heroine of *The Fair Maid of the West, or A Girl Worth Gold* (q.v.), published in 1631 'As it was lately acted before the King and Queen, with approved liking', and with a cast of Queen Henrietta's men dating about 1630. These two plays seem to have been associated in the popular mind, for St[ephen] Br[ome's] commendatory verses for *The Northern Lass* have the lines:

> *Not a Good woman, nor a Girle worth Gold,*
> *Nor twenty such (whose gaudy shewes take hold*
> *Of gazing eyes) shall in acceptance thriue*
> *With thee, whose quaintnesse is superlatiue.*

The prologue's 'Countrey Maide' who would 'set up some new Leaguer' might be a reference to Marmion's *Holland's Leaguer* (q.v.), which was acted for six consecutive days at the Salisbury Court in December 1631, but the description fits more aptly Nicholas Goodman's tale of *Holland's Leaguer: or an Historical Discourse of the Life and Actions of Dona Britannica Hollandia*, entered in the Stationers' Register 20 January 1631/2 and published in 1632. This publication, with a frontispiece of the famous bawdy house, Holland's Leaguer, tells the story of a country girl who comes to town, marries, becomes the mistress of a Jesuit, and eventually takes over the bawdy house, Holland's Leaguer. The aptness with which the prologue references fit this story is rather striking.

These concentrated allusions to theatrical affairs of 1631 and 1632 indicate that the prologue, and presumably the play, were written in 1632 or very soon thereafter. One allusion might be misapplied, but not three, especially when one of them is so specific as that to *Holland's Leaguer*. The date of the play, then, appears to be about 1632 or 1633.

E. H. C. Oliphant thought that the play was revised by Massinger:

> His [T. B.'s] work was evidently done early, and an examination of the play has convinced me that Massinger revised it, his share being parts of I, 1, the greater part of I, 2, . . . II, 2, parts of III, 1, IV, 1 (which is corrupt and perhaps of mixed authorship), the first 8 speeches of IV, 2, parts (perhaps all) of V, 1, and parts of V, 2, the rest of the play being the original author's. This is nothing more than a personal view. (*Mod. Phil.* viii [1911], 422.)

The final sentence impresses me more than the rest of the quotation. These rationalizations of stylistic impressions involve too many obscure reactions and faint memories to be trusted much. In the present instance it may be significant that most of the scenes in which Oliphant thought he saw Massinger's style are scenes which involve actions rather like those at Lady Allworthy's house in *A New Way to Pay Old Debts*. I see no evidence that T. B.'s work was done early. Much of the dialogue and the structure is crude, but Caroline playwrights could be just as incompetent as Elizabethans. It is, moreover, quite notable that many of the situations, characters, and attitudes are similar to those found in comedies written by Shirley, Massinger, and Brome in the late twenties and thirties. We have noted that the prologue at least must date in or after 1632 because of the allusions. Massinger was, at this time, regular dramatist for the dominant

King's company, probably under contract. The play seems much too crude for this company, and plays performed by them and published 1620–60 nearly always boasted the distinction on the title-page. It is a little difficult to imagine Massinger deserting the King's men at the Blackfriars to revise a crude play for an inferior company in 1632 or 1633.

The Country Girl has sometimes been accredited to Thomas Brewer because it was assigned to him in Archer's advertisement list appended to his edition of *The Old Law*, 1656. The attributions of this list have no authority: Archer assigns *The Chances*, *The Roman Actor*, and *A Trick to Catch the Old One* to Shakespeare when the correct authors were easily ascertainable from title-pages.

A more popular attribution has been that of Kirkman in his advertisements of 1661 and 1671 to 'Ant. Brewer'. Fleay (*Biog. Chron.* i. 34) explains this—apparently seriously—as an expansion of T[ony] B[rewer] of the title-page. The name Anthony Brewer appears on the 1655 title-page of *The Lovesick King* (see *Elizabethan Stage*, iii. 237), but this author is not otherwise known, unless he was the 'Anth Brew' who appears in the manuscript stage directions for *The Two Noble Ladies* (see above, ii. 388–9). I cannot take any of these attributions seriously; in the present state of our information we know only that *The Country Girl* is said by the publisher to have been written by a man whose initials were T. B. but who is otherwise unknown.

John Leanerd's *The Country Innocence, or the Chambermaid Turned Quaker*, 1677, is an adaptation of *The Country Girl*. Montague Summers says (*The Playhouse of Pepys*, p. 413) that the first three acts of Leanerd's play are 'little more than a condensed adaptation' of *The Country Girl*, but that the last two acts are considerably altered, Langbaine and Genest to the contrary notwithstanding.

Garrick's play of the same title, produced in October 1766, has nothing to do with this play, but is an incredibly flat revision and expurgation of Wycherley's *Country Wife*.

The Rebellion of Naples, or the Tragedy of Massenello
(1647–9)

The initials 'T. B.' are signed to the dedication of this play, which was printed in 1649. According to the dedication, this T. B. was a companion and 'cousen' of John Caesar, of Hyde Hall, Hertfordshire, with whom he had travelled 'through divers

Countries' and suffered much. There is no way to tell whether
he is the same T. B. as the author of *The Country Girl*. The title-
page says that the play was 'WRITTEN By a Gentleman who was
an eye-witnes where this was really Acted upon that bloudy
Stage, the streets of NAPLES *Anno Domini* MDCXLVII'. In any
case it was written beyond the limits of this study.

THOMAS BARKER

The Bloody Banquet, published in 1639 as by 'T. D.', was assigned
to 'Thomas Barker' in Edward Archer's *Catalogue of all the Plaies*
appended to his 1656 edition of *The Old Law*. The other mid-
century advertisements do not go beyond 'T. D.' Since no
Thomas Barker is known, Archer's attribution has been generally
ignored. See below, Thomas Drue, *The Bloody Banquet*.

— BARNES
fl. 1624

Nothing whatever is known of this man save that he wrote a play
called *The Madcap* which was licensed for performance by Prince
Charles's (I) company in 1624.

Fleay (*Biog. Chron.* i. 30) listed this play under Barnaby Barnes,
author of *The Devil's Charter*, but queried his own attribution
because nothing was known of Barnaby Barnes after 1607. This
was quite a proper doubt, since it was later discovered that
Barnaby Barnes was buried in 1609. (Chambers, *The Elizabethan
Stage*, iii. 214.) Fleay also suggested (ibid.) that the play might
have been written by the 'little Will Barne' who was an actor in
1 *Tamar Cam* in 1602, but since nothing else is known of this
lad, his adult activities can be only a pleasant fancy.

A William Barnes contributed commendatory verses to Tatham's *Fancies Theatre*, 1640, but there is nothing about them to
suggest a theatrical connexion. The carpenter, Thomas Barnes,
who posed as a player to baffle his victims (see above, ii. 358–9),
does not seem a likely candidate.

The Madcap (1624)
(Lost)

1624, 3 May. 'For the Prince's Company; A New Play, called,
  The Madcap: Written by *Barnes*.' (Adams, *Herbert*, p. 28.)

The only record of this lost play is its entry by Sir Henry Herbert. The company for which the play was licensed, never one of the most distinguished, was at this time in a state of decline, acting, apparently, at the lowly Red Bull. (See above, i. 205–10.) The fact that the great majority of the plays of the company's ascertainable repertory of this period were never printed is suggestive.

William Heminges's *The Coursing of a Hare* (q.v.), licensed for the company at the Fortune in March 1632/3, has the sub-title *The Madcap*. This fact could conceivably indicate some connexion with Barnes's play, but, since next to nothing is known of either play, speculation seems idle.

ROBERT BARON
1630–58

Beck, Edmund. *Robert Barons Leben und Werke* (1915).
Slagle, Kenneth C. 'Robert Baron, Cavalier Poet', *N. & Q.* clxix (1935), 254–6.
Smith, G. C. Moore. 'Robert Baron, Author of *Mirza, a Tragedie*', *N. & Q.*, Eleventh Series, ix (1914), 1, 22, 43, 61, 206.

Since Robert Baron was twelve years old when the theatres were closed, he cannot possibly have written any of the plays properly considered in this volume. So many plays, or revisions of plays, have been attributed to him, however, that it may be convenient to have a few of the bare facts of his career listed.

He was baptized at Norwich 22 July 1630, the son of Robert Baron who became mayor of Norwich. He was admitted to Caius College, Cambridge, 22 July 1645, and to Gray's Inn 23 October 1646. He was a precocious youth. His *Cyprian Academy* was published in 1647, with his portrait inscribed 'Ætat. suæ 17', and several of the writers of commendatory verses remark on his extreme youth. He died at Norwich in 1658.

Baron's acknowledged dramatic works are:

Deorum Dona, a masque dated 1647 and printed with a separate title-page as part of *The Cyprian Academy*, 1647.
Gripsius and Hegio, or The Passionate Lovers, a three-act pastoral, printed with a separate title-page as part of *The Cyprian Academy*, 1647.
Mirza, A Tragedy, [1647?, 1655?].

Baron's carefree plagiarism has made his work a happy hunting-ground for those who like to attribute authorship on the basis of parallel passages.

JOHN BARRETT
c. 1599–?

The only evidence of a playwright of this name is to be found in the manuscript diary of Sir Symonds D'Ewes, who was entered at St. John's College, Cambridge, in May 1618 and left in September 1620. (*Autobiography and Correspondence of Sir Symonds D'Ewes*, i. 107, 147.) Though the diary has not been printed, extracts and summaries are found in the anonymous *College Life in the Time of James the First as Illustrated by an Unpublished Diary of Sir Symonds D'Ewes*, 1851. One passage, under the date 1620 (p. 99) reads:

> After an interval of a month from the first Act belonging to the Bachelor's Commencement came 'the latter Act'. The Tripos on this occasion was a friend of Symonds, 'one Sir Barret' [i.e. Dominus, or Bachelor of Arts] of St. John's, the author of the Latin Comedy, which had been acted in the Hall at the preceding Christmas.

Though there were a number of Barretts at St. John's in the seventeenth century, only one—two, if Venn is wrong in suggesting that the entries are for the same man—was a contemporary of D'Ewes. The scanty record of this man is as follows:

> Barrett, John. Matric. pens. from St. John's, Easter 1614.
> Barrett, John. Matric. pens. from St. John's, Easter 1615. One of these (if really two) B.A. 1618/19; M.A. 1622. Fellow 1625. (*Alumni Cantab.* i. 96.)

Since this man was a recent B.A. at the time of the 1620 commencement and not yet a M.A. entitled to be called 'Mr.', he is evidently Sir Symonds's friend who wrote the Latin comedy performed in the Hall at St. John's during the Christmas celebrations of 1619–19/20.

There is no evidence as to the name of Barrett's Latin comedy. It would help tidy up Jacobean dramatic history if one could assign him the anonymous Latin comedy *Stoicus Vapulans*, which was produced at St. John's for the Christmas celebrations of 1618. Unfortunately for neatness, not only are the extracts from D'Ewes clearly dated in *College Life*, but the anonymous editor indicates that D'Ewes reported *Stoicus Vapulans* as the Christmas comedy of 1618 and Barrett's play as of the Christmas preceding the Bachelor's Commencement in the spring of 1620.

THOMAS BASKER

A misprint for Thomas Barker repeated by Langbaine, Baker, and others.

SIMON BAYLIE

fl. 1620–40

The man is known as a dramatist only from the appearance of his name in the Durham Cathedral Library MS.: 'The Wizard by Simon Baylie.' In his edition of the play Professor De Vocht discusses various other Baylies of literary interest but finds no Simon.

The registers of the Merchant Taylors' School record two men of the name in the admission record of 1653–4:

Simon Baylie, eld. son of *Simon*, merchant taylor, b. in Martin's Outwich, 18 Sep. 1644. (Charles J. Robinson, *A Register of the Scholars admitted into Merchant Taylors' School*, i. 217.)

This boy matriculated from St. John's at Oxford in July 1662, and was rector of St. Mary's, Romney Marsh, Kent, in 1674. (*Alumni Oxon.* i. 91.) He is the only seventeenth-century Simon Baylie recorded at Oxford or Cambridge. Unless all who have examined *The Wizard* have been misled into dating it too early, however, the Merchant Taylors' scholar cannot have written the play. It is notable that his father had the same name. The father or the grandfather of a boy born in 1644 would better fit the dates suggested for the play.

The Wizard (*c*. 1620–40 ?)

MSS.: Durham Cathedral Library MS. Hunter 77; B.M. MS. Add. 10306.

Edition: *The Wizard A Play by Simon Baylie.* Edited—for the first time—from the Durham and London Manuscripts, with Introduction and Notes by Henry De Vocht. *Materialien* (1930).

Greg, W. W. *Dramatic Documents from the Elizabethan Playhouses* (1931), pp. 344–6.

The two manuscripts of the play are discussed in detail by De Vocht. He demonstrates that neither can be the author's original, and that neither can have been copied from the other (op. cit., pp. lxxxi–xc), conclusions which seem valid from his evidence but which postulate the preparation of at least four manuscripts of the play, a surprising number considering its obscurity.

De Vocht dates the play 1614–25 (op. cit., pp. lvii–lviii), between *Albumazar*, which Baylie has imitated, and *The Elder Brother*, in which De Vocht thinks Fletcher imitated Baylie. It is true that the resemblances between the action of *The Wizard* and *The Elder Brother* are too close for chance (op. cit., pp. xlii–xlvi), but De Vocht is misled by his conviction that *The Wizard* is a 'play with a purpose' as set forth in his section called 'The Wizard and its *Message*' (pp. lxix–lxxii). His dating of the play 'results from a consideration of its significance in the history of the struggle against witchcraft, by which without doubt it was called into existence' (p. lviii). This humourless conviction, which requires the priority of Baylie's play, is rationalized by a contention that the old-man-in-love-with-a-young-woman episodes are integral in *The Wizard* but an unnecessary and irrelevant plot quirk in *The Elder Brother* and therefore imitated from Baylie by Fletcher (pp. xlvii–liv). The contention is doubly unconvincing: (1) such irrelevant and unnecessary episodes are almost standard in the last third of a Fletcher play; (2) if Fletcher had to have a source for such material, it was available in a dozen printed plays. The notable resemblance between the two plays is not in these episodes at all, but in the elder-and-younger-brothers-as-wooers situations. Since Fletcher was notably fertile and Baylie an unknown, and since Fletcher's play was printed and Baylie's was not, it seems more likely that Baylie was the imitator.

Greg says: 'The play may from internal evidence be assigned to *c.* 1620–40, but there is nothing to show that the manuscript may not be later.' (Op. cit., p. 345.) He does not cite the internal evidence, and I can find nothing very definite, but the general impression seems sound.

Both manuscripts of the play show a number of revisions, which De Vocht lists in detail but does not account for very well. William van Lennep, Curator of the Theatre Collection in the Harvard Library, writes me that his study of a photostat of the B.M. MS. reveals that 'its revisions were made between 1663 and 1687, perhaps with production in mind'.

Miss Eleanore Boswell has made the best statement of the history of the B.M. MS.:

There remains one curious bit of evidence for the clue to which I am indebted to Dr. Greg, a pencilled note in a modern hand on the flyleaf of *The Wizard*, Brit. Mus. Add. MS. 10306. It has been erased, but most of it has been retraced and this part runs 'formerly in possession

of Cartwright presented by him to Dulwich College then in Garrick's
... there. ....' This manuscript was purchased by the Museum in the
Heber sale in 1836, the Catalogue of which contains the following
description: 'The Wizard, A Comedy, *written before* 1640. This MS.
was presented by Cartwright the Player, with his Collection of Old
Plays, to Dulwich College. *It was afterwards sold in the Garrick Collection.*' And it was. Thorpe the bookseller bought it at the Garrick sale
on 3 May 1823. ('Young Mr. Cartwright', *M.L.R.* xxiv [1929], 141–2.)

THOMAS BEARD

He was not a dramatist, though he has sometimes been mistakenly listed as such.

An Evangelical Tragedy

This piece is not a play, though it is carefully divided into acts
and scenes. The title in the manuscript (B.M. MS. Royal 17 D
xvii) describes the work fairly: 'An Evangelical Tragœdie A Har-
monie of the passion of our Lord Iesus Christe paraphrastically
expounded according to the Fower Euangelistes:' The dedication
to King James is signed 'Tho: Beard Minister of the word'.

FRANCIS BEAUMONT
1584 or 1585–1615/16

The collaboration of Beaumont and Fletcher had ended before
the beginning of the period covered here. In 1613 or 1614 Beaumont married Ursula Isley and probably retired to Kent. He died
6 March 1615/16. See Fletcher for the plays published in the
Beaumont and Fletcher folios.

SIR JOHN BEAUMONT
1582 or 1583–1627

Gayley, Charles Mills. *Beaumont, the Dramatist* (1914), passim.
Grosart, Alexander B., ed. *The Poems of Sir John Beaumont*,
     Fuller Worthies' Library (1869).

John Beaumont was the second son of Francis Beaumont,
Justice of the Common Pleas, and elder brother of Francis Beaumont, the dramatist. He was born, probably at the family seat
of Grace Dieu in Leicestershire, in 1582 or 1583, according to later

statements of his age. With his two brothers he entered Broad-
gate's Hall, Oxford, in February 1596/7, but did not take a degree,
probably going from the University to the Inner Temple. (Grosart,
pp. xix–xxi; Gayley, pp. 25–36.) His early publication, *The Meta-
morphosis of Tobacco*, 1602, has a dedication to Michael Drayton,
and other associations led Grosart to think that John Beaumont
was one of the circle at the Mermaid (op. cit., pp. xxii–xxvii); at
any rate, both John and Francis Beaumont were lifelong friends
of Drayton. (Gayley, pp. 42–44.) At an unknown date John
Beaumont married a sister of George Fortesque. At the death of
his elder brother, Sir Henry, he came into his father's estates,
some of which seem later to have been alienated because of John's
recusancy. (See Gayley, pp. 59–61.)

John Beaumont was patronized by George Villiers, eventually
Duke of Buckingham, and his work was introduced by Villiers to
the King. In 1626 he was made a baronet (Grosart, p. xlv), and
much of his verse suggests his standing at court. He died in 1627
and was buried 29 April 1627 in Westminster Abbey. (Grosart,
p. xlviii.) Two years after his death much of his verse was collected
and published by his son under the title *Bosworth Field: with a
Taste of the Variety of Other Poems, left by Sir John Beaumont,
Baronet, deceased*. The volume was dedicated to Charles I and
contained commendatory verses by Ben Jonson, Michael Drayton,
and others.

The Theatre of Apollo (1624/5)

MS.: B.M. MS. Royal 18 A lxx.

*Edition: The Theatre of Apollo, an entertainment written by Sir
John Beaumont in 1625*. W. W. Greg., ed. (1926).

This short entertainment or device of less than 200 lines—not
a masque, as Greg points out in his introduction, since it does
not include dancing—was written to be performed before King
James I, and the B.M. MS. was evidently intended for presentation
to him. The beauty of the elaborate title-page is spoiled by a note:

> *Before prepared to be offered to the
> sacred* Maiesty *of our deceased
> Souereigne* King IAMES.

> *And now presented to the Roiall
> handes of our* Gracious Lord, King
> CHARLES, *heire of the Kingdoms,
> Vertues, and glories of his Father.*

This statement, Greg points out, indicates that the piece was prepared before the death of King James on 27 March 1625. Certain lines in the entertainment itself, noted by Greg, show that the marriage of Charles with Henrietta Maria had already been arranged and that the expected audience knew Buckingham would be Charles's proxy. After praise of Prince Charles, the lines continue:

> And though yet absent, still my thoughtes adore
> Thy heav'nly *Nymphe*, borne to inritch this *Shore*.
> *Shee* must increase our ioys, crowne our desires,
> And ioyne *her* flames, vnto *Apolloes* fires.

> *Chorus*
>
> .   .   .   .   .
>
> *And thy Nimphe, that coms from farre,*
> *When shee sees her Charles his Starre;*
> The Duke of   *Shall with ioy receiue that* guide,*
> Buckingham   *That shall make her Charles his Bride.*

Thus *The Theatre of Apollo* must have been written between 12 December 1624, when the marriage treaty was ratified, and 27 March 1625; January or February 1624/5 seems a likely date to Greg. (Op. cit., p. ix.)

Sir John Beaumont's authorship, according to Greg, is indirectly indicated in the manuscript. Apollo (James) holds a laurel to crown 'that *Muse*, that best should sing his praise', and the presenter says:

> Yet still the *Laurell* standes, as due to none,
> But her, whom greatest *Villiers* brought vnknowne,
> Before *Apollo's* throne, and made her sing
> With heave'nly tunes, the greatnes of his *King*.

Opposite the second and third lines are written '*Beaumonts Muse*'. Beaumont was a protégé of Buckingham, whom he praised and to whom he directed much of his verse, and a loyal admirer of James. I am a little uneasy at the picture of James, as Apollo, crowning the muse of the author, but I have no better interpretation of this obscure piece, and bow to Greg's authority.

THOMAS BEEDOME

A friend and writer of commendatory verses for dramatists Nabbes, Glapthorne, and May, but not a dramatist himself.

CHRISTOPHER BEESTON *alias* HUTCHINSON
c. 1575–1638

Beeston began his career in the theatre as an actor, and in the late Jacobean period and during most of the Caroline he was the most prominent theatre manager in London. (See above, ii. 363–70, for his career.) He has not heretofore been noticed as a dramatist, but the entry copied by Malone from Herbert's office-book shows that he was at least a 'play doctor'. If he did such a revision once, it is not unlikely that, as a theatre manager for over twenty years, he did it on other unrecorded occasions.

Unnamed Play (1631/2)
(Lost?)

1631/2, 12 Jan. 'For allowing of an ould play, new written or forbisht by Mr. Biston, the 12th of January, 1631,—£. 1 0 0.' (*Variorum*, i. 424 n.)

This note, which Malone took from Herbert's manuscript, was missed by Adams in his edition of *The Dramatic Records of Sir Henry Herbert*. Malone had also published it earlier in his 1790 edition (i, pt. 1, 406, n. 2) and in his 1813 edition (ii. 398, n. 9).

In January 1631/2 Beeston was manager of Queen Henrietta's men at the Phoenix theatre and principal owner of the theatre. Presumably he revised the play for that company. There is no clue to what the play was, but the size of Herbert's fee and the wording indicate that the revision was extensive.

DAUBRIDGCOURT BELCHIER (Belcher, Belgier, Beltcher)
c. 1581–1621

Daubridgcourt Belchier, the son and heir of William Belchier, or Belcher, of Guilsborough, Northamptonshire, matriculated at Corpus Christi College, Cambridge, 2 March 1597/8 and after eight terms migrated to Oxford, where he received his B.A. as of Christ Church 8 February 1600/1. (*Alumni Oxon.* i. 102.) From Oxford he went to the Middle Temple, where he was admitted 29 June 1601, to share a chamber with Henry Martyn. (Hopwood, *Middle Temple Records*, i. 414.) He was apparently still there 2 June 1603 when John Hodder was admitted to share his chamber in the

place of Henry Martyn, but on 2 May 1605 his place was surrendered to William Savage. (Ibid. ii. 440, 454.)

Anthony à Wood, in recording Belchier's B.A., notes *Hans
Beer-Pot* and continues, 'Which translation was made at *Utrecht*,
in 1617, about which time he wrote several Poems and other
Translations, but whether publish'd, I cannot tell. He died in the
Low-countries in 1621.' (*Fasti Oxon.*, ed. 1721, i. 158.)

Hans Beer-Pot, His Invisible Comedy of See Me and See Me Not (> 1617)

1618, 3 June. S.R. 'Barn: Alsope. . . . Entred for his Copie vnder
the hand[es] of m^r Tavernor and m^r Swinhowe warden A poeme
called see me and see me not. by Dabridgcourt Belgier.' (Greg,
Bibliography, i. 30.)

1618. Hans Beer-Pot His Invisible Comedie of *See me, and See
me not*. Acted In the Low Countries, by an honest Company of
Health-Drinkers . . . 1618.

Though no author's name appears on the title-page, the dedication to Sir John Ogle, Knight, '*Collonell of our English Regement
of* Foot, vnder the Lordes, the Estates generall of the Vnited
Prouinces, and Lord Gouernor *of the Towne and Garrison of
Vtreicht*' is signed and dated 'Vtriecht from my lodging the 14. of
Nouember, 1617 . . . Dabridgcourt Belchier'. The attribution of
the play to Thomas Nashe by Phillips and Winstanley suggests
that they had not read the dedication, though Langbaine had.

The frequent statement that the piece is a translation from the
Dutch is clearly contradicted by the praise of Elizabeth and her
great captains, as Schelling pointed out. (*Elizabethan Drama*, ii.
257 and n. 1.) It is also contradicted by the lament that knight-
hoods are now given to boobies and not to men of desert as in
the good old days, and by the boast in the dedication that the
piece is the work of sixteen days—no feat if it is only a translation.

Hans Beer-Pot is not a dialogue about the respective merits of
horse and foot, as it has sometimes been described, though the
subject is discussed. Langbaine made the best characterization of
it as an interlude, for it is an irregular sort of entertainment
evidently intended for a specialized audience. The author recognizes its irregularity in the dedication when he says that it is
neither comedy nor tragedy 'as wanting first the iust number of
Speakers; Secondarily, those parts or Acts it should haue, which
should bee at the least fiue'. He says it is a plain dialogue between
three persons in only three acts, and in the prologue he repeats

the statement that it is neither comedy nor tragedy. All this has very much the tone of an educated man apologizing for a show which served well enough for its intended audience, but which was not designed for the sophisticated London reading public.

There are nine characters who wander in and out, identifying themselves, morality fashion, and indulge in various more or less amusing dialogues. The play is so incoherent that it is almost impossible to follow at times, but some of the scenes have possibilities as farce. The author's gratuitous assurance in the dedication that no real people are reflected on, suggests that some Dutch personalities of Utrecht may be imitated and possibly some English soldiers. Though the piece was obviously not intended for London theatres, it is not difficult to imagine its performance as a show 'by an honest Company of Health-Drinkers' to entertain English officers in a camp.

There is little evidence of date save that it must have been written before the dedication of 14 November 1617. The references to Elizabethan times are to the good old days. A date not long before the dedication seems plausible.

HENRY BELLAMY
1604– < 37

Henry Bellamy, son of Robert, a merchant tailor, was born 27 July 1604. He entered the Merchant Taylors' School in 1611 and matriculated at Oxford from St. John's College 9 November 1621. His B.A. was granted 16 May 1625, his M.A. 28 April 1629, and his B.D. 18 December 1637. In 1638 he became vicar of St. Giles in the Suburbs in Oxford. (*Alumni Oxon.* i. 104.)

Iphis (1622–6? or 1628–32?)

MS.: Oxon. Bodley MS. Latin Misc. e. 17 (old Malone MS. 43).

Morgan, Louise B. 'The Latin University Drama', *Sh. Jahr.* xlvii (1911), 79–81.

1660, 29 June. S.R. An entry to Humphrey Moseley includes:

> The History of King Stephen. ⎫
> Duke Humphrey. a Tragedy. ⎬ by Will: Shakspeare
> Iphis & Iantha, Or a marriage ⎪
>   without a man. a Comedy. ⎭

(Greg, *Bibliography*, i. 68–69.)

The vellum-bound and beautifully written Bodleian MS. of the play is dedicated to 'Ornatissimo doctissimoque viro M^{ro} Guilielmo Juxon Ł Ł D^{ri} et coll: Divi Joan: Bapt: præsidi dignissimo', and Falconer Madan suggested that this was the presentation copy. (*Summary Catalogue of Western Manuscripts in the Bodleian Library, 24331–31000*, p. 626.) Inside the back cover is the inscription, 'Ex Dono Rev.^{di} Bartini Gutteridge amico suo Thomae Percy. Julij 8. 1758.' Madan noted that the Percy sale catalogue called attention to the S.R. entry, and he pointed out that the description there would fit this play. Bellamy's name is both found on the cover of the manuscript and signed to the dedication, 'Henricus Bellamy'.

The play was presumably performed during Juxon's presidency of St. John's 10 December 1621 to 5 January 1632/3. Since he is called Doctor of Laws, it must date after his D.C.L. degree, 12 December 1621. (Wood, *Fasti Oxon.*, Bliss ed., i. 398.) Juxon was Vice-Chancellor of the University from 22 July 1626 to 24 July 1628 (ibid., pp. 425, 429, 438), and Bellamy would surely have included that title in his dedication had it been appropriate at the time of presentation. Thus the play would presumably date 1622–6 or 1628–32. The former period seems slightly preferable, since Bellamy might well have alluded to Juxon's former dignity as Vice-Chancellor in the later period.

Miss Louise Morgan gives the dramatis personae and a scene-by-scene synopsis of the play.

SIR WILLIAM BERKELEY (Barclay, Bartlet [?], Bartley)
1606?–77

Sir William Berkeley, the Governor of Virginia who put down the Bacon Rebellion, was the fourth son of Sir Maurice Berkeley, of Bruton, Somerset, the brother of Lord Berkeley of Stratton, and the first cousin of Thomas Killigrew, the dramatist, and of Henry Jermyn, the favourite of Queen Henrietta Maria. (R. C. Bald, *Library*, Fourth Series, xvii [1937], 395–426; Harbage, *Killigrew*, pp. 37–38.) He was born at Hanworth, near London, and the date of his birth has been variously given as 1606, 1608, and 1609. The most specific record is Daniel Lysons's quotation from the Hanworth parish registers: 'Henry, son of Sir Maurice Berkeley, Knight, baptized Dec. 8, 1600 . . . William, July 16, 1608.' (*An Historical Account of those Parishes in the County of Middlesex, which are Not Described in the Environs of London* [1800], p. 101.) This record, however, contradicts the record of his matriculation at Oxford from Queen's College, 14 February 1622/3, which says that he was then 'aged 17'. (*Alumni Oxon.* i. 114.) Though he matriculated from Queen's College, his B.A. was granted from St. Edmund Hall 10 July 1624. (Ibid.) On 3 May 1624 he had been admitted to the Middle Temple (C. H. Hopwood, *Middle Temple Records*, ii. 690), but presumably he did not long remain in London, for he was made a Fellow of Merton College in 1625 and received his M.A. from Oxford 10 July 1629. (*Alumni Oxon.* i. 114.) The Merton fellowship he continued to hold until he was expelled by the Parliamentary Visitors in 1646, but he probably left Oxford not long after receiving his M.A., for Anthony à Wood says: 'In 1630 he travelled into various countries, and at his return was much valued for his experience and knowledge in many matters.' (*Athenæ Oxonienses*, Bliss ed., iii. 1111.)

Bald (op. cit., p. 396, n. 3) points out that most of the accounts of Berkeley are wrong in assuming that he was appointed one of the Commissioners for Canada in 1632, and that the *D.A.B.* has confused his appointment to the Privy Chamber with an appointment to the Privy Council. (Ibid., p. 397, n. 1.) Berkeley was made a Gentleman of the Privy Chamber in 1632 (Harbage, *Cavalier Drama*, p. 116), a courtly post (see *Eliz. Stage*, i. 43–44, and n. 1, p. 43) in which he was at one time and another a colleague of the courtier dramatists Walter Montagu and Sir John Suckling. His standing at court is suggested by the approval in 1638 of his scheme for the registration of aliens and by the grant to him and his brother of the reversion of the office of Clerk of the Treasury of the Court of Common Pleas. (*C.S.P. Dom., Charles I*, ccclxxx. 20, and cccciv. 52.)

The fact that Suckling included Berkeley in his 'A Sessions of the Poets' seems to suggest that the future Governor of Virginia had more of a literary reputation in 1637 than we can see reason for. In stanza 4 when he is introducing all the candidates for the laurel, Suckling includes

> *Selwin* and *Walter* [i.e. Waller], and *Bartlets* both the brothers;
> *Jack Vaughan* and *Porter*, and divers others.

A later stanza is devoted entirely to William:

> To *Will Bartlet* sure all the wits meant well,
> But first they would see how his snow would sell:
> *Will* smil'd and swore in their judgements they went lesse,
> That concluded of merit upon successe.
>
> (*Fragmenta Aurea*, 1646, A₄ and A₄ᵛ.)

Perhaps this inclusion indicates personal friendship more than literary reputation, for Suckling and Berkeley had both been Gentlemen of the Privy Chamber for several years, and George Garrard coupled their names when he wrote to Sir Thomas Wentworth, 7 February 1637/8, that they had both written plays for the court and for Blackfriars. (See below.) Perhaps the spelling 'Bartlet' does not refer to William Berkeley and his brother John, but it is similar to other spellings of the name, and I can think of no more plausible candidates for Suckling to include in his group. The allusion to 'snow' I cannot explain. It might refer to some scheme for which the courtier Berkeley was seeking patronage, but the context and Bartlet's reply to the wits suggests reference to literary efforts.

Berkeley was in the royal force which marched to the border in the First Bishops' War, and he was in the large group knighted by Charles at Berwick in July 1639 (Shaw, *The Knights of England*, ii. 206–7), shortly after the signing of the Treaty of Berwick. As a loyal cavalier, Sir William was again with the King in the north the following year, negotiating with the Scots. In August 1641 he was commissioned Governor of Virginia, and in a few months he had sailed for America. (Bald, op. cit., pp. 397–8.)

Berkeley's American career is a significant one, but not for the Caroline drama. In spite of Parliament, he governed Virginia for the King until the Parliamentary fleet arrived to depose him, when he retired to his plantation. At the Restoration he took over the governorship again. After the Bacon Rebellion he returned to England in broken health. He was buried at Twickenham 9 July 1677. (*D.A.B.* and *D.N.B.*)

Cornelia (> 1662)
(Lost)

MS.? Professor Bald understood the entry for this play in *Biographia Dramatica* to indicate that a manuscript of the play was then, or had recently been, in existence. This appears to be a mistaken inference. (See R. C. Bald, 'Sir William Berkeley's *The Lost Lady*', *Library*, Fourth Series, xvii [1937], 398. I can find no 1825 edition of *Biographia Dramatica*.)

1662, 1 June. 'Cornelia a New Play, sir W. Bartleys' is in Sir Henry Herbert's 'List of plays acted by the Kings Companie at the Red Bull and the new house in Gibbon's Tennis Court near Clare Market'. (Adams, *Herbert*, pp. 116–18.)

1662[-3 ?]. In his record of expenses at plays 'At the New Theatre
in Lincolnes Jnne fields' Edward Browne entered 'Cornelia . . .
I 6'. (W. W. Greg, 'Theatrical Repertories of 1662', *Gentleman's Magazine*, ccci [1906], 69–72, from B.M. MS. Sloane 1900,
fols. 65–60 [*sic*].)

The play is now lost. It is possible to doubt whether Herbert's
'sir W. Bartley' was the Governor of Virginia, but it seems likely
that he was, especially as Professor Bald has pointed out (*Library*,
Fourth Series, xvii [1937], 399) that he was in London to appear
before the Council for Foreign Plantations on 5 August 1661 and
sailed for Virginia again in September 1662, in which time he may
well have arranged for and seen the production of *Cornelia* by the
King's company at Gibbon's Tennis Court. Whether the play was
a product of Sir William's days as a Caroline courtier or of his
enforced leisure in Virginia there is at present no evidence. Professor Bald likes the idea of composition in Virginia, but Professor
Harbage has noted (*Killigrew*, pp. 72–73) that a passage in III. 2
of Killigrew's *The Parson's Wedding* refers to a play at the theatre
written by a gentleman recently knighted with many others in
the north. The description fits Berkeley, but the date seems too
late for a reference to *The Lost Lady*. Harbage therefore suggests
a pre-Restoration performance of *Cornelia*. The conjecture is
tempting, but the list of literate gentlemen knighted in the north
is a long one, and other plays by courtiers may be lost like
Cornelia, even another play by Berkeley.

That the play was witty and not very enthusiastically received
at the performance in 1662 is asserted in a verse letter about
London theatrical activities printed by Professor Hotson from
a B.M. MS.:

> For Cornelia they all doe say
> There was abundance of witt in the play
> Indeed t' had soe much t' was the worse for 't
> For t' was to witty for *the* vulgar sort
> And they who'd have poetts their Benefactors
> Say witt *wi*thout mony's naught for *the* Actors.

(*Commonwealth and Restoration Stage*, p. 246, from B.M. Add. MS.
34217, fol. 31*b*.)

The Lost Lady (1637–8)

MS.: Lambarde Collection, Folger Shakespeare Library. Incomplete, ending at v. 2, line 124. In the hand of a scribe and

corrected by the author, it was apparently intended for Queen Henrietta Maria and later belonged to her.

Edition: Reprinted in the tenth volume of Dodsley's *A Select Collection of Old English Plays* (1744).

Bald, R. C. 'Sir William Berkeley's *The Lost Lady*', *Library*, Fourth Series, xvii (1937), 395–426.

1637/8, 7 Feb. 'Two of the King's Servants, Privy-Chamber Men both, have writ each of them a Play, Sir *John Sutlin* and *Will. Barclay*, which have been acted in Court, and at the *Black Friars*, with much Applause.' (Garrard to Wentworth in Ireland, *Strafforde's Letters*, ii. 150.)

1637/8, 2 Mar. 'Imprimatur. Tho. Wykes March. 2. 1637. Printed at London. 1637.' (Statement on $O_2{}^v$ of the folio of 1638.)

1637/8, 5 Mar. S.R. John Okes entered 'a Play called The Lost Ladie'. (Greg, *Bibliography*, i. 47.)

1638, 26 Mar. 'At the Cocpit the 26th of march . . . The lost ladie.' First entry in a list of King's men's plays acted 'before the king & queene this [present] yeare of our lord 1638.' (Adams, *Herbert*, p. 76.)

1638. The Lost Lady A Tragycomedy. Imprinted at London. Anno MDCXXXVIIJ. (F_1.)

1638, 24 Sept. S.R. John Okes's rights in 'the Play called The lost Ladie. by mr Wm. Berkeley' transferred to John Colebey. (Greg, *Bibliography*, i. 49.)

1638. The Lost Lady A Tragycomedy. Imprinted at London by *Jo. Okes*, for *John Colby* . . . 1638. (F_2.)

1639. A second issue of F_2 with the date reset.

1640, 5 Sept. S.R. John Colebey transferred his rights in the play to Richard Roiston. (Greg, *Bibliography*, i. 53.)

1660/1, 19 Jan. 'Saterday the 19. Jan. The Lost Lady.' appears in a list of plays performed by 'the Kings Companie at the Red Bull and the new house in Gibbon's Tennis Court near Clare Market', 1660–2. (Adams, *Herbert*, p. 117.)

1668/9, *c.* 12 Jan. In 'A Catalogue of part of His Mates Servants Playes as they were formerly acted at the Blackfryers & now allowed of to his Mates Servants at ye New Theatre' occurs the title, 'The Lost Lady'. (A. Nicoll, *A History of Restoration Drama 1660–1700*, 3rd ed., pp. 315–16.)

The letter of George Garrard to Wentworth suggests that the play was new. He says it was acted at Blackfriars (which is evidence that it belonged to the King's company) and that it had already been performed at court. We know that the King's men performed fourteen plays at court between 30 September 1637 and 3 February 1637/8, but Suckling's *Aglaura* is the only one known by title. (See above, i. 57–58.) Presumably Berkeley's *The Lost Lady* is another, and the performance of 26 March 1638 was at least the second one at court.

The manuscript of the play in the Lambarde collection at the Folger Shakespeare Library seems to be one transcribed from a prompt copy for Henrietta Maria at the author's direction (see Bald, op. cit., pp. 405–12), for it has many corrections in Berkeley's hand, and a note on the first page indicates that it belonged to the Queen. The manuscript has a 'Prologue To the King'.

Professor Bald has determined that F_1, of which the only known copy is at the Folger, was extensively corrected by the scribe of the manuscript, apparently at Berkeley's direction, and that F_2 was set up from a copy of F_1 which he had corrected. Ten of the eleven examined copies of F_2 contain manuscript corrections in Berkeley's hand (ibid., pp. 412–19)—evidently the courtly author was very proud of his brain-child.

The play evidently had more appeal than a modern reader would think likely, for there are various records of it after the closing of the theatres. Dorothy Osborne wrote on 10 July 1654 of an amateur performance at Knowlton in Kent in which she was to play the title-role (*The Letters from Dorothy Osborne to Sir William Temple*, ed. E. A. Parry, p. 255); Pepys saw it on the 19th and 28th of January 1660/1; it is in the list of plays allotted to Killigrew for performance at the Theatre Royal in 1668/9 (Nicoll, *A History of Restoration Drama*, pp. 315–16); and on 30 June 1673 Thomas Vere and John Wright entered in the Stationers' Register the transfer of the rights in this play with several others from Anne Oakes (Greg, *Bibliography*, i. 73).

SAMUEL BERNARD
c. 1591–1657

Samuel Bernard, of Berkshire, matriculated from Magdalen, Oxford, 3 July 1607 at the age of sixteen. He received his degrees of B.A. 25 October 1610, M.A. 5 June 1613, B.D. 8 February 1620/1, and D.D. 15 March 1638/9. He was incorporated at Cambridge in 1622. In 1612 he became Usher at Magdalen School, and he was Master from 1617 to 1625. Under date of 28 April 1625, Peter Heylyn says in 'Heylyn's Own Memoranda': 'My deare friend and *fidus Achates* Mr Allibond made Schoolmaster of Magdalen College in the place of Mr. Barnard.' (John Rouse Bloxam, ed., *Memorial of Bishop Wayneflete* [1851], p. xviii.) Bernard was licensed to preach 6 July 1621, became vicar of Croydon, in Surrey, in 1624, and continued until sequestered in 1643. He became rector of Tarring, Sussex, in 1629, of Hollingbourne in 1637, and of Buxted St. Margaret, Sussex, in 1638. He died 5 August 1657 and was buried in Farley Church. (*Alumni Oxon.* i. 115.)

All Bernard's plays date from the period of his schoolmaster career at Magdalen School. Apparently Bernard was also a poet; one of the lost manuscripts of his plays is said to contain poems also.

Andronicus Comnenus (1617/18)

MS.: B.M. MS. Sloane 1767, fols. 18–66, entitled 'Tragœdia Andronicus Commenius'.

Morgan, Louise B. 'The Latin University Drama', *Sh. Jahr.*, xlvii (1911), 78.

The B.M. MS. is carefully divided into acts and scenes with a prologue and epilogue, a total of about 2,300 lines. The manuscript gives no indication of author or date, but the play is probably the one referred to by W. D. Macray:

1617. . . . In this year and in the two years following plays written by Samuel Bernard the schoolmaster were performed. The particulars are learned from the description of the original MSS. (of which the present place of deposit is not known) found in the Sale Catalogue of the library of his son, Charles Bernard, serjeant-surgeon to Queen Anne, in March 1710/11, p. 217, lot 674 of books in folio. From a priced copy of the Catalogue in the Bodleian Library (Crynes 701) it appears that the MSS. were sold for 10s. On Jan. 23, 1616/17, ' Julius et Gonzaga, tragoedia nova,' was acted in the President's house; Jan. 26, 1617/18, 'Andronicus, tragoedia,' in the Hall; Jan. 27, 1618/19 'Phocas, tragoedia nova,' also in the Hall. The cost for the second of these performances (which included an unknown comedy) is entered in the Bursars' accounts for 1618. . . . And the cost in 1618 was verily costly: 'diversis per billas pro comoedia et tragoedia, ultra 22^{li}. 17^s. 4^d. deduct. ex batellis, 24^{li}. 9^s. 5^d. ' It would seem from this that the expense was divided between *domus* and its members. Another copy of the three tragedies, 'et alia quaedam poemata,' was sold at the same sale for 2s., p. 218, lot 925 of books in quarto. (*A Register of the Members of St. Mary Magdalen College, Oxford*, iii. 45–46.)

Miss Louise Morgan, who first noted that the British Museum

play was probably the one referred to in the Magdalen records, says of it:

The play in question is well written, and has unusual virility, with almost no lengthy soliloquies, and a number of short speeches and broken lines. The *Personae* are:

Alexius Protosebastus
Alexius Commenus, Imperator
Andronicus Commenus, Imperator
Isaacius Angelus, Imperator
Lapardas } nobiles ex familia imperatoria
Commenus }
Johannes } filij Andronici
Manuell }
Maria Cæsarissa, Soror Alexij Commeni
Theodosius Patriarcha
Salmanazar Maurus, Satellites.

. . . The plot proceeds along historical or pseudo-historical lines entirely. (Loc. cit.)

The Magdalen accounts indicate a rather elaborate production and suggest that the play was presented by the college and not by the boys of Magdalen School.

Julius et Gonzaga (1616/17)
(Lost)

The existence of this lost play was pointed out by W. D. Macray:

1617. . . . In this year and in the two years following plays written by Samuel Bernard the schoolmaster were performed. The particulars are learned from the description of the original MSS. . . . On Jan. 23, 1616/17, 'Julius et Gonzaga, tragoedia nova,' was acted in the President's house. (*A Register of the Members of St. Mary Magdalen College, Oxford,* iii. 45. See *Andronicus Comnenus* for the complete entry.)

Macray suggests that the 1617 entry in the Bursar's accounts refers to the production of this play, 'Hoby, pro diversis per billam in tragoedia per pauperes scholares, 8ˢ.' (Ibid.)

It is evidently to this performance of *Julius et Gonzaga* that Peter Heylyn refers in 'Heylyn's Own Memoranda':

1616[/17] March 8. My English Tragedy cal'd Spurius was acted privatly (as Mr White's and Mr Bernard's plaies were) in the president's lodgings. (*Memorial of Bishop Wayneflete,* ed. John Rouse Bloxam [1851], p. xiv.)

Since Bernard had for several years been Usher at Magdalen School and was about to become Master, one would conjecture that the tragedy was performed by the boys of the school.

Phocas (1618/19)
(Lost)

The play is known only from the entry in W. D. Macray's *A Register of the Members of St. Mary Magdalen College, Oxford,* iii. 45. (See *Andronicus Comnenus* for the complete entry.)

1617. . . . In this year and in the two years following plays written by Samuel Bernard the schoolmaster were performed. The particulars are learned from the description of the original MSS. . . . On . . . Jan. 27, 1618/19, 'Phocas, tragoedia nova,' also in the Hall.

'In the Hall' presumably means in Magdalen College hall before the members of the college, but whether by undergraduates or by the boys of Magdalen School one cannot tell.

Henslowe records seven rather profitable performances of a play of this name in 1596, and in 1598 he lent money to his company to buy the manuscript and four others from Martin Slater. (*Henslowe's Diary,* i. 30, 42, 86.) Greg notes that 'Phocas, a centurion, was elected Emperor of Constantinople in 606, and was deposed and killed by Heraclius in 610'. (Ibid. ii. 180.) It is not likely that there was any connexion between Henslowe's play and that of the learned schoolmaster.

JOHN BLENCOWE (Blencoe, Blencow, Blenkow, Blincou)
1608/9– < 1648

According to the records of the Merchant Taylors' School, Blencowe was born 29 January 1608/9 and entered that institution in 1620/1. (C. J. Robinson, *A Register of the Scholars Admitted into Merchant Taylors' School, 1562 to 1874,* i. 103.) He became a Merchant Taylor Fellow in 1627 and matriculated at Oxford as a plebe from St. John's College 13 November 1629 and received his degree of B.C.L. 25 June 1633. There seems to be some contradiction about his later career at St. John's, for Simmonds says that he resigned his fellowship on his marriage in 1638 (*Merchant Taylor Fellows of St. John's College, Oxford,* p. 21), but Foster says in *Alumni Oxon.* (i. 138) that he was expelled from his fellowship by the Parliamentary Visitors in 1648. The *D.N.B.* says that the man expelled was a Fellow of New College, and it may be that the records concern two different Blencowes.

A man of these names was vicar of Abergwelly, Carmarthon, in 1638. Wood says he 'did afterwards publish *St. Michael's Combate with the Devil*, a serm. on the 9*th* verse of St. Jude's epistle, Lond. 1640, qu. and perhaps other things.' (*Fasti*, Bliss ed., i. 468.) According to the *British Museum Catalogue of Printed Books* (xx. 580) the title-page says the alternative title of the sermon was 'Moses his Funerall' and that it was preached at St. Paul's.

Mercurius sive Literarum Lucta (1629–38 ?)

MS.: St. John's College, Oxford. MS. 218.

The following note is found in the St. John's College MS.:

This MS was deposited in the Library of St. John's College, Oxford, by Messrs. Crawley Arnold and Co., solicitors, 1 Dean's Yard, Westminster, S.W., together with the MS of Joseph Crowther's Latin play on Cephalus and Procris [q.v.], subject to the liability of restoration to them set out in the latter MS. Both MSS were received on 24 December, 1915.

W. H. Stevenson
Jany. 20, 1916   Librarian

The play has neither prologue nor dramatis personae, but at the beginning there is a 'Fabulae Argumentum', and at the end an epilogue followed by 'Finis. Joannes Blenkow'. The characters in order of entrance are: Jupiter, Mercurius, Cupido, Clotho, Lachesis, Atropos, Charon, Saturnus, Astrae, Pax, Simplicitas, and Otium. Boas summarizes the plot, which he thinks is original. (*M.L.R.* xi [1916], 298–301.) The play is divided into acts and scenes and runs to about 1,000 or 1,100 lines. It concludes with a compliment to St. John's and its founder, an indication that it was at least intended for performance at St. John's.

Various facts connect this play and Joseph Crowther's *Cephalus et Procris*: the two manuscripts were found together and deposited together; the authors were contemporaries at the Merchant Taylors' School and contemporaries at St. John's, Oxford; the plays, both unusually short, are about the same length, with similar small casts of mythological characters; both seem more literary than theatrical. The texts proper of the two plays are not written in the same hand, but each has speech prefixes and stage directions added in a different hand and different ink. These revising hands and inks in the two manuscripts are quite similar and may be identical. These considerations would suggest that the history of *Mercurius* may be like that of *Cephalus et Procris*, about which somewhat more can be inferred.

WILLIAM BONEN (Bowen)
fl. 1623

Since the name appears three times as Bonen and only once as Bowen, all apparently referring to the same man, Bonen is the more likely choice. In any case, nothing is known of him save that in the autumn of 1623 Sir Henry Herbert licensed two of his plays, one for the Lady Elizabeth's company and one for the Palsgrave's company.

The Cra . . . Marchant, or Come to My Country House
(1623)
(Lost)

1623, 12 Sept. 'For the Lady Elizabeth's Players; a new Comedy, called, *The Cra . . . Marchant, or Come to my Country house*; Written by William Bonen. It was acted at the Red Bull, and licensed without my hand to itt; because they were none of the *four* Companys.' (Adams, *Herbert*, p. 25.)

1623, 12 Sept. 'For the lady Eliz:' Players. September
A new Comedy called the Cra Marchant [or come to my Cuntry] houss contayninge 9 sheetes may bee acted [this 12th Septr. 1623] Written by William Bonen
It was acted at the Red Bull & licensed without [my hande to itt because] they were none of the foure companys.' In the margin is '3. o. o.' The bracketed words were written in by Halliwell-Phillipps to replace those cut off the sheet. (Folger Shakespeare Library, in the MS. Scrap-Book of J. O. Halliwell-Phillipps, labelled *Theatres of Shakespeare's Time*, p. 53.)

1653, 9 Sept. S.R. 'The Crafty Merchant. or the Souldred Citizen by Shakerly Marmion' entered for Moseley with a number of other plays. (Greg, *Bibliography*, i. 61).

1660, 29 June. S.R. 'The Sodered Citizen. a Comedy. by Shakerley Marmion', entered S.R. for Moseley with a number of other plays. (Ibid., p. 69.)

c. 1710–50. The twenty-seventh item in Warburton's list of play manuscripts allegedly burnt by his cook is 'The [Marchants

Sacrifice *crossed out*] Crafty Marchat [*sic*] C Shack. Marmio[n].'
(See W. W. Greg, *Library*, Third Series, ii [1911], 231.)

First, the various entries which have been associated with this
play need to be disentangled. Since Herbert's manuscript office-
book is not extant, there is no foundation for even a guess as to what
'Cra . . . Marchant' might have been. Several scholars have guessed
The Crafty Merchant, and working on from that guess have identified the play with the one entered in the Stationers' Register in
1653 as *The Crafty Merchant, or The Soddered Citizen*. Probably
there was never a play with the combination of title and sub-title
which Moseley entered. The lost manuscript of *The Soddered Citizen* (q.v. under Clavell) has now been recovered, and it has nothing to do with a crafty merchant. Furthermore it has a cast of
actors showing that it was performed by the King's company and
not the Lady Elizabeth's, as Bonen's 'Cra . . . Marchant' was.
Probably Moseley was entering two plays, *The Crafty Merchant*
and *The Soddered Citizen*, under one title. If so, the first may have
been Bonen's play wrongly attributed, but only if we accept the
guess 'crafty'.

Moseley's second entry in 1660 is a curious duplication of part of
his first. One can only suggest that he may have forgotten the entry
of 1653. Again he asserts Marmion's authorship, which would be
very dubious for the play Herbert entered. In the first place it
would contradict Herbert, a man generally more knowledgeable
than publishers so far as plays were concerned, and in the second
it would attribute to Marmion a play licensed while he was still
at Oxford, where his M.A. was granted 7 July 1624. (*Alumni Oxon.*
iii. 971.)

The presence of the title in Warburton's list cannot be taken as
additional information, since it was probably derived from Moseley's entry and does not indicate possession of a manuscript. (See
W. W. Greg, 'The Bakings of Betsy', *Library*, ii [1911], 255-9.)

We are brought back then to Herbert's entry as our only source
of information on Bonen's play. Even this entry shares the confusion which dogs *The Cra . . . Marchant, or Come to My Country
House*. The Lady Elizabeth's company does not seem to have been
at the Red Bull in 1623. It has been suggested that the sentence
about the Red Bull rightly belonged to the next entry and was
misplaced by Chalmers in copying Herbert's manuscript. I accepted this explanation once (see above, i. 206–7), but since then I
have seen the independent transcript of Herbert's manuscript in
a nineteenth-century hand which has been cut up and pasted into

Halliwell-Phillipps's scrap-books. The version of 'The Cra . . . Marchant' entry in this transcript displays several variants from Chalmers's transcript but still keeps the Red Bull sentence. Now I can only suggest that Herbert meant that some unauthorized company had originally acted the play at the Red Bull and that he was now giving the play his official approval for acting by the Lady Elizabeth's men. Perhaps the unusually large fee of £3— not noted in Chalmers's transcript—was intended to cover some irregularity. There are still too many uncertainties for an entirely satisfactory explanation.

Two Kings in a Cottage (1623)
(Lost)

1623, 19 Nov. 'For the Palsgrave's Players; a new Tragedy, called, *Two Kings in a Cottage*; Written by Bonen.' (Adams, *Herbert*, p. 26.)

1623, 19 Nov. 'For the Palsgraves Players   November
A new Tragedye called 2 kings in a cottage written by Bowen this 19ᵗʰ 1623—1ˡⁱ.' (Folger Shakespeare Library, in the MS. Scrap-Book of J. O. Halliwell-Phillipps entitled *Fortune*, p. 149.)

The second version of Herbert's licence comes from an independent transcript of his office-book in a nineteenth-century hand. This transcript, perhaps that of Craven Ord, has been cut up and pasted into appropriate sections of Halliwell-Phillipps's scrapbooks, now preserved in the Folger Shakespeare Library. Its slight variations from Chalmers's transcript in *A Supplemental Apology for the Believers in the Shakspeare-Papers* show Chalmers's substantial accuracy and add the fee paid by the Palsgrave's company, the normal one for licensing a new play at this period. (See Adams, *Herbert*, pp. 17, 26.)

When *Two Kings in a Cottage* was licensed for the Palsgrave's men, that company was engaged in a desperate attempt at survival after the destruction of their repertory in the Fortune fire of 9 December 1621. (See above, i. 141–2 and 149–51.) Most of the phenomenal number of plays licensed for them in this period are now lost, probably an indication of the inferior quality of the plays.

WILLIAM BOWER

Schelling's misprint for William Bonen (or Bowen) (q.v.).

WILLIAM BOWYER

See J. W., *The Valiant Scot.*

ROGER BOYLE, BARON BROGHILL, FIRST EARL OF ORRERY

1621–79

Clark, William Smith, II, ed. *The Dramatic Works of Roger Boyle, Earl of Orrery*, 2 vols. (1937), i. 1–60.

The first Earl of Orrery was a figure of the Restoration and not of the Caroline theatre. He is included here because of the possibility that he was the author of the play called *The General*, produced in Ireland 1636–40 with a prologue by James Shirley.

Roger Boyle, fifth son of Richard, Earl of Cork, was born at Lismore Castle in Ireland 25 April 1621. By royal patent issued at Westminster 30 November 1627 he became Lord Boyle, Baron of Broghill in the Kingdom of Ireland. Two years later his father moved to Dublin and Lord Broghill was entered at Trinity College, Dublin, 9 May 1630.

In February 1635/6, with his elder brother, Lord Kynelmeaky, he left for London in the charge of a tutor, M. Isaac Marcombes, and in March they set out for the Continent. They stayed at Geneva from April 1636 through September 1637. In the next year they were in France and Italy, and various letters show their interest in plays at this time. (Clark, i. 7–8.) They returned to London 4 March 1638/9. Here Broghill seems to have stayed, with brief interludes for the campaigns in the north and visits to his father's seat at Stalbridge in Dorset, until he returned to Ireland in October 1641, where he served for the next year in the Irish wars.

His later Restoration career is not of significance here. He died at Castlemartyr in Ireland, 16 October 1679.

The General (1636–40 ? ; > 1664)

MSS.: Worcester College Library, Oxford. A second manuscript, from which Halliwell-Phillipps printed his text of the play, is now apparently lost. (See Clark, *Works*, ii. 827–9.)

Editions: J. O. Halliwell[-Phillipps], *A Brief Description of the Ancient & Modern Manuscripts Preserved in the Public Library, Plymouth: To which are added, Some Fragments of Early Literature*

Hitherto Unpublished. (1853), pp. 55–175. Halliwell-Phillipps does not annotate and does not say the manuscript was in the Plymouth Library. William Smith Clark, II, ed., *The Dramatic Works of Roger Boyle, Earl of Orrery* (1937), i. 101–64.

Altemira. A Tragedy . . . Written by the Right Honourable *Roger* Late Earl of *Orrery*; and Revis'd by the Honourable *Charles Boyle*, Esq. . . . 1702. (An alteration of *The General.*)

Clark, William S. 'The Relation of Shirley's Prologue to Orrery's *The Generall*', *R.E.S.* vi (1930), 191–3.

In James Shirley's *Poems &c.*, 1646, is a section entitled 'Prologves, and Epilogves; Written to severall Playes Presented in this Kingdom, and else-where'. The first prologue in this section is entitled 'A Prologue to Mr. *Fletchers* Play in IRELAND', and the next seven prologues and epilogues all have 'there' or 'Acted there', i.e. in Ireland, in their titles. The eighth is '*To a Play there, called the* Generall'. Evidently Shirley meant to indicate that he wrote only the prologue and not the play, for he distinguishes clearly between prologues and epilogues for his own plays and those written for the plays of others: the first eight are for plays of others, all but one identified by title or author; the last ten are for six plays of his own, each play identified in the title as Shirley's by such phrases as 'To his own Comedy', 'to his Comedy', 'to his Tragedy'. This distinction has often been missed, and consequently the plays of the first eight prologues and epilogues—including *The General*—have several times been mistakenly ascribed to Shirley.

Since *The General* was not written by Shirley, it has been suggested that it may have been Orrery's *The General*, first printed by Halliwell-Phillipps from the manuscript in 1853, but several times recorded in the early sixties as *The General* or *Altemira*. (See Clark, ed., i. 101–7.) Orrery's lifelong associations with Ireland, and Sir Heneage Finch's description of the play when it was performed in 1664 as 'my Lo Orerys new play calld ye Generall formerly acted in Ireland by the name of Altamira, but much alterd & improved' (ibid., p. 103), lend colour to the suggestion that the Restoration piece was the same as, or an alteration of, the pre-Civil-War play for which Shirley wrote a prologue.

Professor Clark in his eagerness to make Orrery the father of heroic tragedy goes much too far:

When all available evidence is marshalled together, it would seem to indicate conclusively that any relation between the play for which

Shirley's prologue was written and the drama by Orrery of the same name is really based upon a hypothesis so far-fetched as to be ruled even out of the realm of possibility. (*R.E.S.* vi [1930], 193.)

It is true that his summary of the record of Broghill's life during the years Shirley was in Ireland—about November 1636 to April 1640 (see Shirley)—seems to indicate that he could not have been in Ireland when Shirley was, but Clark ignores the possibility that *The General* could have been written by the noble young play-reader during his continental travels or during his man-about-town days in London and sent to Ireland, or that Broghill after his return to Ireland could have taken the manuscript of the play Shirley knew, revised it into his rhymed tragi-comedy, and passed it off as his own. Such a procedure would be far from unique in Restoration theatre annals. (See Alfred Harbage, 'Elizabethan-Restoration Palimpsest', *M.L.R.* xxxv [1940], 287–319.) Clark himself observes that the play was planned—as the stage directions and structure show—for a Caroline rather than a Restoration type of stage; he also notes marked influence of the Caroline plays of Davenant and Suckling. (*Dramatic Works*, i. 65–70, 101; ii. 767–8.) All this he interprets as evidence of the author's reminiscence of the theatre before the wars, failing to see that it could equally well indicate original composition before the wars. *The General* might well repay a careful search for remnants revealing an original version 1636–40, whether Orrery's or another's.

It is, of course, entirely possible that, as Clark thinks, *The General* of Shirley's prologue is not related to Orrery's play, but it would be a curious coincidence that of less than a score of plays known to have been written for Irish production 1636–63 (La Tourette Stockwell, *Dublin Theatres and Theatre Customs 1637–1820* [1938], pp. 4–30), two should be named *The General* and should be wholly unrelated.

WILLIAM BOYLE
fl. 1600

Logically Boyle has no place in this volume, for there is no evidence that he wrote plays in our period, or even that he was alive after 1600. He is included because he is not listed as a dramatist or even indexed in *The Elizabethan Stage*, and because there are Jacobean and Caroline records of his one known play.

The only extant record of the man is found in *Henslowe's Diary*: lent vnto me W birde the 9 of februarye [1599/1600] to paye for a new booke to will: Boyle. cald Jugurth xxx^s w^c if yo^u dislike Ile repaye it back. (*Henslowe's Diary*, i. 118.)

Bird was at this time a member of the Lord Admiral's company, which Henslowe financed, and the play, therefore, must have been bought for that company.

Fleay's conjecture, 'I think Boyle, who is utterly unknown elsewhere, is merely a *nom de plume* for Bird himself' (*Biog. Chron.* i. 33), is one of his most irresponsible. The payment through Bird, as agent for the company, is one of Henslowe's standard procedures.

Jugurth, King of Numidia (1599/1600, 1624?)

MS.: Bodleian MS. Rawl. poet. 195, is a folio volume composed of six manuscripts, of which the fourth is entitled 'IUGURTHA or THE FAITLESS [*sic*] COSEN GERMAN A TRAGEDY'.

1599/1600, 9 Feb. See entry quoted above from *Henslowe's Diary*.
1624, 3 May. 'An Old Play, called, *Jugurth, King of Numidia*, formerly allowed by Sir George Bucke.' (Adams, *Herbert*, p. 28. In note 5 on this page, Adams adds: 'Elsewhere Chalmers writes (*S. A.* 203): "On the 3d of May, 1624, Sir Henry Herbert states, that he had licensed, without a fee, *Jugurth*, an old play, allowed by Sir George Bucke, and *burnt, with his other books.*"')

The original play of *Jugurth* for which Henslowe advanced thirty shillings was evidently purchased for the Lord Admiral's men, a company which Henslowe regularly financed and of which William Bird (*alias* Borne) was a member. This company became Prince Henry's company at the accession of James I and the Palsgrave's company after the death of Prince Henry. (See above, i. 135–6.) Bird was an active member of the troupe from 1597 until about two years before Herbert's licence. (See above, ii. 379–80, and Chambers, *Eliz. Stage*, ii. 303, and chapter xiii, part xix, *passim*.) These facts suggest that the *Jugurth, King of Numidia* which Herbert licensed without fee in 1624 was the same play as Boyle's *Jugurth* of 1599/1600, for Sir George Buc was Deputy Master of the Revels at the time Henslowe paid for the play, and he was active in the office as Deputy or Master until 1622. (See Adams, *Herbert*, pp. 7–8.) The fire to which Herbert referred was probably the Fortune fire of 9 December 1621, in which the repertory of the Palsgrave's men was destroyed. (See above, i. 141–51.) Chalmers's transcript of Sir Henry Herbert's entry would indicate that the fire was one which burned Buc's books, but it is noteworthy that Chalmers's quotation is not direct, and there is no good evidence for Buc's fire. (See Adams, *Herbert*, p. 10, n. 1.) Moreover it was not customary for the Master of the Revels to keep copies of the plays he licensed; it was usual for him to write his licence on the company's manuscript, which was kept in the company archives. (See Middleton's *A Game at Chess*, Massinger's *Believe as You List*, Mountfort's *The Launching of the Mary*, Glapthorne's *Lady Mother*, Anon., *The Second Maiden's Tragedy* [Greg, *Dram. Doc.*, p. 264], and Beaumont and Fletcher's *The Honest Man's Fortune* [ibid., p. 288].)

It may well be this play to which Edmund Gayton referred in his *Pleasant Notes upon Don Quixot*, 1654. Speaking of the demands of the popular theatre audiences he says:

> I have known upon one of these *Festivals*, but especially at *Shrove-tide*, where the Players have been appointed, notwithstanding their bils to the contrary, to act what the major part of the company had a mind to; sometimes *Tamerlane*, sometimes *Jugurth*, sometimes the Jew of *Malta*, and sometimes parts of all these, and at last, none of the three taking, they were forc'd to undresse and put off their Tragick habits, and conclude the day with the merry milk-maides. (See above, ii. 690–1.)

Since Gayton more than once speaks of the Red Bull and the Fortune and their actors, it is not unlikely that he was referring to the Fortune play of *Jugurth, King of Numidia*, and his remarks suggest the character of the play.

The play in the Bodleian MS. is in what appears to be a late seventeenth-century hand. Of the six pieces in the manuscript, four are later than the Restoration, and a fifth is Chappell's *Susenbrotus* (q.v.). *Jugurtha, or the Faithless Cousin German* is unfinished, ending its formal numbering at IV. 1, though there are three or four sketched-in scenes following, and, after a break of three pages, four smaller pages of rough unintegrated material. The play is crude, and parts of it—such as the clown scene in IV. 1 —sound like pre-Restoration material incorporated into a later play. On the verso of the second folio is a list of characters:

Men

Iugurtha	partner in the Kingdome of Numidia Supposed Sonn of Monstabales and adopted Son Mysipsa [?] late King of Numidia & ffather to the Brothers

Atherball   partner in the Kingdome of Numidia Brother to
                 Hyempsall in love with Seraphina
Hyempsall   partner in the Kingdome of Numidia in Love with
                 Seraphina
Marius   The Roman Consull
Calphurnius   his Generall
Nabdalsa   Generall of Iugurtha's Army

Women

Octavia   Marius Daughter in Love with & beloved by Iugurtha
Seraphina   Sister to Iugurtha in Love with Hyempsall
Lysandra   Seraphina's Woman of Honour and Confident to
                 Atherball

Scane Thala or thereabouts

The play begins 'Actus primus Scen̄ a pallace'. These various
features suggest a Restoration rather than a Jacobean or a Caroline,
much less an Elizabethan, play. *Jugurtha, or the Faithless Cousin
German* might be an incomplete and inexpert Restoration adaptation of Boyle's old play, but it does not seem much more closely
related to the earlier *Jugurth* than that.

RICHARD BRATHWAIT (Braithwaite, Brathwaite, Brathwayte, Braythwait, Braythwayte)
1588–1673

Black, Matthew Wilson. *Richard Brathwait. An Account of His
Life and Works* (1928).
Haslewood, Joseph, ed. *Barnabae Itinerarium, or Barnabee's Jour-
nal*. The seventh edition: to which are prefixed an account of
the author, now first discovered (1818).
——A New Edition Carefully Revised by W. Carew Hazlitt (1876).

Since Brathwait's portrait—reproduced as a frontispiece in
Black—is inscribed 'Anº 1626 Æᵗ 38', he must have been born in
1588, presumably at his father's manor-house of Burneshead Hall,
near Kendal in Westmorland. He matriculated at Oxford from
Oriel College 22 February 1604/5 (Clark, ed. *Register of the Univ. of
Oxford*, ii. Part 2, p. 279), where Anthony à Wood says he remained
for three years, but there is no record that he took a degree.
Apparently he spent a short time at Cambridge (Black, pp. 16–20)
and then, shortly before his father's death, entered Gray's Inn 11
May 1609—'Richard Brathwaite, son of Thomas B., of Burnside,

Westmoreland, Esq.' (Foster, *Register of Admissions to Gray's Inn,*
p. 121.) There is no record of the length of time he spent at Gray's
Inn, but according to statements in his works Brathwait disliked
the law and spent much of his time at taverns, playhouses, and the
court, in the company of the wits of London. *The Golden Fleece,*
the first of his long series of publications, appeared in 1611.

On 4 May 1617 Brathwait married Frances, daughter of James
Lawson of Nesham. (Black, pp. 35–36.) Nine children of this
marriage are recorded in the Kendal Parish Register from March
1617/18 to February 1630/1 (Black, p. 36), but Brathwait seems
to have been much in London in the earlier years, and Professor
Black thinks he was a prisoner in the Fleet about 1618. (Black, pp.
36–37.)

At an unknown date Brathwait took up residence at his father's
manor of Burneshead, where Wood says (*Athenæ Oxon.*, 1721 ed., ii.
516) 'he became Captain of a Foot-Company in the Trained-bands,
a Deputy-Lieutenant in the County of *Westmorland*, a Justice of
Peace and a noted Wit and Poet'. His first wife died 7 March
1633/4, and in 1639 he married Mary Crofts, daughter of Roger
Crofts of Kirtlington, Yorkshire, and for many years seems to
have resided principally at the manor of Catterick which she
brought him. (Black, pp. 42–43, 47.)

There is no record that Brathwait saw active service in the wars,
but he was fined £1,150 in 1650, and later some of his estates were
sequestered. (Black, pp. 47–50.) He died 4 May 1673 and was
buried in the parish church at Catterick, where a memorial tablet
was set up to him, his wife, and his son Strafford. (Black, pp. 58–59.)

Though Brathwait was a prolific writer of satires, characters,
poems, criticism, courtesy-books, essays, tales, and histories (Black,
pp. 159–69, lists fifty publications from 1611 to 1662 which he
accepts as genuine Brathwait, besides twenty-odd attributions
which he rejects), and though Thomas Nabbes dedicated his
Unfortunate Mother, 1640, to him, the evidence that Brathwait
wrote for the stage is tempting but dubious. His non-dramatic
works are filled with allusions to players and playhouses, and at
least one autobiographical passage makes a direct claim to dramatic writing:

Yet amidst these dis-relishing studies, whereto I was rather enforced than enclined: I bestowed much precious time (better spent
then in Tavernes and Brothells) in reviving in mee the long-languish-
ing spirit of Poetrie, with other Morall Assayes; which so highly delighted mee, as they kept mee from affecting that loose kind of libertie,
which through fulnesse of meanes, and licentiousnesse of the age, I

saw so much followed and eagerly pursued by many. This moved mee sometimes to fit my buskin'd Muse for the Stage; with other occasionall Presentments or Poems; which being free-borne, and not mercenarie, received gracefull acceptance of all such as understood my ranke and qualitie. For so happily had I crept into *Opinion* (but weake is that *Happinesse* that is grounded on *Opinion*) by closing so well with the temper and humour of the time, as nothing was either presented by mee (at the instancie of the noblest and most generous wits and spirits of that time) to the *Stage*; or committed by mee to the *Presse*; which past not with good approvement in the estimate of the world. Neither did I use these *private Solaces* of my pen, otherwise than as a *play* onely to the *imagination*: rather to allay and season more serious studies; than account them any fixt imployment. (*A Spiritual Spicerie*, 1638, S_{11}–S_{12}.)

Other passages, possibly autobiographical in character (see Black, pp. 23–27), claim experience in the writing of court masques. Since many plays and entertainments of Brathwait's time have been lost, and many others were anonymously published, it is possible that plays and masques from his pen have been lost or are still unidentified. The man was not notable, however, for his strict accuracy, and it may well be that *Mercurius Britannicus* and *Tragi-Comoedia* are all the dramatic writing he ever accomplished.

Cornelianum Dolium

See T. R.

Mercurius Britannicus, or The English Intelligencer (1641)

Edition: Mercurius Britannicus. *A Collection of Scarce and Valuable Tracts* (Somers Tracts), ed. Sir Walter Scott, 1809–15, v (1811), 444–61.

Black, Matthew Wilson. *Richard Brathwait. An Account of His Life and Works* (1928), pp. 75–78.

N.D. [1641?] Mercurivs Britannicus. Judicialis Censura; Vel, Curialis Cura. Febris Judicialis. Sententia navalis. Tragi-comoedia *Lvtetiæ*.

N.D. [1641?] [Another edition] 'Editio secunda.'

1641. [Another edition with changed title.] Mercurius Britanicus, or The English intelligencer. A Tragic-Comedy, at Paris. Acted with great Applause. Printed in the yeare, 1641.

1641. [Another edition] Printed in the yeare, 1641.
1641. [Another edition] Printed in the yeare, 1641.
1641. [Another edition] 1641.
 (See Woodward and McManaway, *English Plays 1641–1700*,
 Nos. 142–7. Editions distinguished by collation.)
1656. 'Mercurius Brittanicus, *Brathwat*', in 'An exact and perfect
 Catalogue of all *Playes* that are Printed', appended to Rogers
 and Ley's edition of *The Careless Shepherdess*, 1656.

There seems to be no adequate discussion of the authorship of
this piece. Dr. Greg points out (*Edinburgh Bibliographical Society
Transactions*, ii. Part 4 [1946], 308–9) that it was first attributed
to Brathwait in the play-list of Rogers and Ley printed with their
edition of *The Careless Shepherdess*, 1656, and that the attributions
of anonymous plays in this list usually carry little weight. Anthony
à Wood (*Athenæ Oxon.*, Bliss ed. iii. 987) credited the play to
Brathwait, but Dr. Greg points out that Wood owned a copy of
Rogers and Ley's list in which the *Mercurius Britannicus* entry
is marked. Later bibliographers and biographers of Brathwait have
simply accepted the attribution without discussion. Brathwait's
authorship seems likely enough, but it ought to be examined.

Mercurius Britannicus is not an acting play and probably was
never intended to be. Essentially it is one of the great spate of
political pamphlets of the forties, though written in dramatic form.
Though it is strongly Royalist in sympathies, it is an indictment
of the judges who convicted Hampden in the ship-money case.
Most of the individuals can be identified.

Since Ægon, one of the characters, is enthusiastic about the
Triennial Parliament Bill, introduced in January 1640/1, passed
and signed by the King in February (Gardiner, ix. 262–3, 290),
and describes the celebration of the Bill in the country, and since
another character in the play is the ghost of Coriolanus, i.e.
Strafford (executed 12 May 1641; ibid., p. 369), the play must
have been written in the year of publication.

In spite of the statement on the title-page, it is highly unlikely
that the play was acted—or ever intended to be. The structure is
unwieldy, almost no action is provided, and probably no company
would have dared attempt such matter.

Woodward and McManaway (loc. cit.) worked out the number
and order of the editions as listed above. Black comments on the
texts: 'It seems likely that the book appeared first in Latin, and
was translated—very badly—by some unscrupulous person. The
second editions, in Latin and English, are much better, and

contain a warning "To the Reader" that they are "the only genuine edition[s]" '. (Op. cit., p. 76, n. 26.)

Tragi-Comoedia . . . Regicidium (1648/9–65)

1665. Tragi-Comoedia, Cui in titulum inscribitur Regecidium, Perspicacissimis Judiciis acuratiùs perspecta, pensata, comprobata; *Authore* Ri. Brathwait, *Armigero, utriúsque Academiæ Alumno...* 1665.

This piece follows very much the lines of *Mercurius Britannicus*. The judges tried are those of Charles I instead of Hampden. It is Brathwait's only other known dramatic work, but it falls well beyond the closing of the theatres.

WILLIAM BRETON

Not a dramatist, as has sometimes been assumed, but only the seventeenth-century owner of the manuscript of *Clytophon*, probably written by William Ainsworth (q.v.).

ANTHONY BREWER
fl. 1617?

Nothing is known of a playwright called Anthony Brewer save that his name appears on the title-page of the only edition of *The Lovesick King*, 1655. Miss M. Hope Dodds has presented an interesting case that he was the 'Anth Brew:' whose name appears in the manuscript stage directions of *The Two Noble Ladies* (*M.L.R.* xix [1924], 158–68.) Since no more is known about the actor than about the playwright, the identification must remain, until more facts are discovered, only an interesting speculation.

Chetwood quotes four lines from 'an old poem, call'd *Steps to* PARNASSUS', which he assumes apply to the author of *The Lovesick King*.

> Let *Brewer* take his artful pen in hand,
> Attending Muses will obey command,
> Invoke the aid of *Shakespear's* sleeping clay,
> And strike, from utter darkness, new-born day.

(Introduction to *The Love-Sick King, A Select Collection of Old Plays* [1750] A₃.)

I do not know what the poem is, and the quotation, if accurate, may or may not refer to the dramatist.
See also T. B., *The Country Girl.*

The Lovesick King (1617?)

Editions: Included in W. R. Chetwood's *A Select Collection of Old Plays* (1750); A. E. H. Swaen, *Anthony Brewer's The Love-Sick King*, edited from the Quarto of 1655, *Materialien* (1907).

Chambers, E. K. *The Elizabethan Stage* (1923), iii. 237.
Dodds, M. Hope. ' "Edmond Ironside" ' and "The Love-Sick King" ', *M.L.R.* xix (1924), 158–68.
Swaen, A. E. H. 'The Date of Brewer's "Love-Sick King" ', *M.L.R.* iv (1908), 87–88.

1655, 20 June. S.R. Entered for John Sweeting 'a booke called The Loue sick King. an English Tragicall History wth the life & death of Cartis Mundy the faire Nunne of Winchester. Written by Anthony Brewer Gen^t. (Greg, *Bibliography*, i. 64.)
1655. The Love-sick King, An English Tragical History: *with* The Life and Death of *Cartesmunda*, the fair Nun of *Winchester*. Written by *Anth. Brewer* Gent. . . . 1655.
1662, 16 July. S.R. John Sweeting and Clement Punge, executors of John Sweeting, assigned to Robert Horne twenty-four titles, including '[15] The Louesick King, wth: the Life & Death of Curtis Mundy, by Anth: Brewer'. (Greg, *Bibliography*, i. 70.)
1680. 'This Play [*The Lovesick King*] was likewise reviv'd by the Actors of the King's House in the Year 1680. and acted by the Name of the *Perjur'd Nun.*' (Langbaine, *An Account of the English Dramatick Poets*, 1691, p. 31.)
1680. An edition of this year under the title *The Perjur'd Nun* has been frequently referred to (*Biographia Dramatica*, 1812, ii. 394; Hazlitt, *Handbook*, p. 60; *C.B.E.L.* i. 641; Woodward and McManaway, *English Plays 1641–1700*, p. 16, &c.), but W. W. Greg points out (*T.L.S.*, 10 August 1946, p. 379, and *Library*, Fifth Series, i [1946], 85) that the existence of this alleged edition has never been confirmed.

Sir Edmund Chambers gingerly assigned a date of c. 1607 to this play, following the evidence set forth by A. E. H. Swaen in his edition (though Swaen's subsequent article suggests a later date). This evidence (Swaen ed., pp. vi–ix) seems to me negligible: chiefly that Osric and Hoffman, used as character names in *The*

Lovesick King, may have been taken from *Hamlet* and *Hoffman*. The names are not so strange as this implies, and in any case their use is no real capitalization of Shakespeare's and Chettle's plays and therefore no indication of proximity in date. The apparent allusion to Anthony Munday, 'I shall love Mondays vein to poetize as long as I live' (line 548), is not tied to the satirization of Munday in *The Case Is Altered*, for Munday lived until 1633 and published a number of pieces after 1607 and as late as 1623. There is no reason to connect this play with the lost *History of Richard Whittington* (S.R. 1604/5) simply because it concerns the merchant hero of another English city. The most direct dating evidence, which Swaen minimizes but Sir Edmund gives more weight, is the fact that Thornton sings four lines of a song (lines 539–42) which Merrythought sings in *The Knight of the Burning Pestle*, III. 599–602. Miss Dodds (op. cit., p. 162) notes further that the version which Thornton sings is not the original but Merrythought's adaptation. The play therefore would seem to date not earlier than the production of *The Knight of the Burning Pestle* in 1607, and possibly not earlier than its first printing in 1613.

The principal discussion of the play is Miss Dodds's, in 1924. She elaborates Fleay's observation (*Biog. Chron.* i. 34) that the play has so much reference to Newcastle, its history, heroes, and places, that it must have been prepared for production there, since no other audience would have been interested in such a multitude of references. She notes in addition many similarities between this play and *Edmond Ironside*, which was not printed until 1927, as well as apparent anachronistic borrowings from it. Finally she points out that the king is received in Newcastle and praises the town (Act IV, lines 1625 ff.) and that there are numerous unnecessary compliments for the Scots. Putting these observations together she concludes that the play was prepared by someone familiar with *Edmond Ironside* for a visit of James I to Newcastle. Though her case is not conclusive, it seems to me very good. The only two recorded visits of James to Newcastle were in 1603 and 1617, and the first was probably too unexpected and short to have been the occasion for the preparation of a play. Miss Dodds, therefore, on the basis of her earlier arguments, dates the piece 1617, a date for which the evidence is inadequate, but more persuasive than for the earlier years previously assigned.

From a study of the structure and method of *The Lovesick King* and from some of its stage directions, Miss Dodds concludes that the play—unlike *Edmond Ironside*, from which it is partially derived—is an actor's play. This conclusion seems to me well

founded. Her further conclusion that the 'Anth. Brewer' of the
1655 title-page is the 'Anth Brew:' of the manuscript stage
directions of *The Two Noble Ladies* is worth consideration, but
since no facts about the company of *The Lovesick King* are known
and since 'Anth Brew:' is recorded in only one place, the identification can be only tentative.

THOMAS BREWER
fl. 1623

Nothing is known of the life of Thomas Brewer, whose name
appears on the title-pages of several Jacobean and Caroline publications—*The Life and Death of the merry Deuill of Edmonton. With
the pleasant prancks of Smug the Smith*, 1631; *The Weeping Lady:
or London like Niniuie in Sack-cloth*, 1625; &c.

The Country Girl and *The Rebellion of Naples* have sometimes
been attributed to him because of the initials T. B. (q.v.) on the
title-page or signed to the dedication. There is no valid reason for
assigning either to the author of *A Knot of Fools*.

A Knot of Fools (> 1623)

1623, 28 Aug. S.R. 'A Booke Called, *A Knott of fooles: or Come
laughe and spare not* by THOMAS BREWER' entered. (Arber, iv.
103.)
1624. A knot of Fooles. Bvt, Fooles, or Knaues, or both, I care
not, Here they are; *Come laugh and spare not* . . . 1624.
1658. A knot of Fooles. But, Fooles, or Knaues, or both, I care
not, Here they are; *Come laugh and spare not* . . . 1658.

There is no name on either title-page, but the address is signed
'Tho. Brewer'. The first stanza of 'To the Reader' suggests the
character of the piece.

> *Kind Reader (cause I'de finde thee so,*
> *I so enstile thee) I haue here*
> *(I will not call't a* Puppit-show:
> *Though those and these, come something neare,*
> *Compar'd with iudgment) Such a sight,*
> *As for thy* Cost *returnes* Delight.

A Knot of Fools is a semi-dramatic satire in dialogue. First the
fools meet and have twelve numbered speeches with suggested
action, though no stage directions. Then Democritus seems to
enter and deliver a number of satiric verses, each classified under a

proverbial head, one of which, *Much ado about nothing*, has sometimes been quaintly called a Shakespeare allusion. Finally Democritus withdraws to sleep, and Pride comes in and tells the story of
Sesostris.

A Knot of Fools is certainly not a play, but it could possibly
have had some sort of occasional presentation. There is no indication of date.

On 20 May 1613 the King's men were paid for performing
fourteen plays at court, one of which was 'the knott of ffooles'.
(*Eliz. Stage*, iv. 180.) It does not seem likely that Brewer's unsophisticated piece could have been performed by such a company
for such an audience.

FRANCIS BRISTOWE

fl. 1635

The existence of a writer named Francis Bristowe is known only
from Hazlitt's statement that he knew of the manuscript of a
tragedy translated by him. The only seventeenth-century Francis
Bristowe recorded at Cambridge matriculated from St. John's in
1676. The following entry at Oxford could conceivably refer to the
translator:

> Bristow, Francis, of co. Hereford, gent. Christ Church, matric.
> 6 April, 1582, aged 16. (*Alumni Oxon.* i. 183.)

If the St. John's man made the translation, he was about 69 at
Hazlitt's date.

King Freewill (1635)

(Lost?)

W. C. Hazlitt records a manuscript (*A Manual for the Collector
and Amateur of Old English Plays* [1892], p. 125) described as:

> King Freewill: A tragedy, translated from the French by Francis
> Bristowe, 1635.
> A MS. in private hands.

The title suggests that the original play was the *Tragedia di
F. N. B. intitolata, Libero arbitrio*, 1546, of Francesco Negri of Bas-
sano, which was translated into French and published in 1558,
presumably by Jean Crespin, under the title *Tragédie du Roy
Franc-Arbitre*. (P. L. Jacob, *Bibliothèque Dramatique de Monsieur de Soleinne* [1843–4], iv. 121, Nos. 4697–4701.) An English

translation by H. Cheeke had been printed in 1589 with the title
A certayne tragedie entituled Freewyl, wrytten first in Italian.

There is a manuscript translation of Francesco Negri's play
at the Folger Shakespeare Library (411202) which says on the
title-page, 'Translated by Henry Cheeke', but it has front material
not found in the Cheeke edition of 1589, and the few random lines
I have compared are not at all the same as the corresponding
lines in Cheeke's printed translation. There is nothing on the
Folger MS. to indicate whose it was or that it might be the one
Hazlitt saw.

ALEXANDER BROME (Broom, Broome)
1620?–66

Brooks, John Lee. *Alexander Brome: His Life and Works.* Unpublished dissertation, Harvard, 1932.

Alexander Brome was a song-writer and editor whose connexions with the drama are his composition of a youthful play, *The
Cunning Lovers*, his editing of Richard Brome's *Five New Playes*,
1653, and perhaps of the *Five New Playes* of 1659, and the composition of verses for a few dramatic publications—the Beaumont
and Fletcher Folio, 1647, Cartwright's *Comedies, Tragi-comedies*,
1651, and Richard Brome's *Jovial Crew*, 1652.

Mr. John Lee Brooks finds that according to Brome's will he
was born in the parish of Evershott in Dorset and bred at West
Milton in the same county. (Op. cit., p. 326.) He thinks that Brome
came to London before he was eighteen and probably became a
clerk in some lawyer's office, but did not enter Gray's Inn for
formal training until 1648. (Joseph Foster, *Register of Admissions
to Gray's Inn*, p. 249.) Later, in February 1658/9, he was admitted
to Lincoln's Inn. (*Records of the Honorable Society of Lincoln's Inn*,
i. 280.) Brooks found that he married the widow of the bookseller
Thomas Whitaker some time between 6 October 1649 and 2 January
1651/2. (Op. cit., p. 45.)

Most of his life Brome appears to have been active as a lawyer
as well as a poet and editor. In 1675 Phillips spoke of him as 'an
Atturny of the Mayors Court, yet Poetically addicted, a Man of
Law and Poetry at once'. (*Theatrum Poetarum*, ii. 6.) When he
saw him at the Royal Oak Tavern, Pepys spoke of him as 'Alexander Brome the poet . . . a merry and witty man', and on the
news of his death called him 'Alexander Brome, the great song-
maker'. (*Diary*, 10 April 1663 and 3 July 1666.) In 1687 Winstanley

called him 'our English *Anacreon*'. (*Lives of the Most Famous English Poets*, p. 171.)

Brome's portrait appears in his *Songs and Other Poems*, 1661. Brooks distinguished three separate engravings in various copies of this edition and the edition of 1664. Brome was buried at St. Stephens, Walbrook, 4 July 1666.

John Lee Brooks has shown Brome's importance as a song-writer, an anthologist, and an active Royalist (*Alexander Brome*, passim), but he found nothing to connect him with the stage or theatrical affairs beyond the title-page of *The Cunning Lovers* and his editorship of Richard Brome's plays. Neither did he find any-thing definite about his life—beyond the statement in the will of the place of his birth and breeding—before the Civil War. Considering how much of his own affairs appears in Brome's verse and the amount of miscellaneous reference to him by other Commonwealth and Restoration writers, this is odd. Perhaps his name on the title-page of the 1654 edition of the play is a misattribution.

The Cunning Lovers (1632–9)

Brooks, John Lee. *Alexander Brome: His Life and Works.* Unpub-lished Harvard Ph.D. dissertation, 1932.

1639, 10 Aug. 'The Cunning Louers' is one of the forty-five plays of the repertory of the King and Queen's Young Company protected by the Lord Chamberlain against other companies. (See above, i. 330–1.)

1654. The Cunning Lovers. A Comedy. As it was Acted, with great Applause, by their Majesties Servants at the private House in *Drury Lane*. Written by Alexander Brome, Gent. . . . 1654.

This play does not fit easily into the career of Alexander Brome as it is known now. He does not mention it anywhere in his writings (Brooks, p. 22), and—if his generally accepted birth-date is correct—he cannot have been more than nineteen years old when it was written, even if we make the purely arbitrary assumption that the play had been just completed when the Lord Chamberlain certified it as part of the repertory of Beeston's company.

No evidence as to the date of the play's composition or first per-formance has been offered, and we can only conclude that it had to be written and accepted for performance before 10 August 1639. The nearer that date we assume composition, the less implausible Alexander Brome's authorship becomes. In August 1639 Richard Brome was dramatist for the King and Queen's Young Company at

the Cockpit, and there may be some connexion between this fact
and young Alexander Brome's composition of a comedy for the
company.

Langbaine said of the sources of the play:

Part of the Plot is borrow'd; as the Duke of *Mantua's* shutting up
his Daughter in the Tower, and his being deceiv'd by her, and Prince
Prospero, is taken from a Story in the Old Book of the *Seven Wise
Masters*; but which the Reader may find better related in the *For-
tunate Deceiv'd*, and *Unfortunate Lovers*: in the Fifth Novel of the
Deceiv'd Lovers. (*An Account of the English Dramatick Poets*, p. 32.)

Miss Mary Augusta Scott also lists *The Cunning Lovers* as one of
the four plays whose plots derive from *The Fortunate, the Deceived,
and the Unfortunate Lovers*, 1632. (*Elizabethan Translations from
the Italian*, p. 103.)

RICHARD BROME (Broome)
c. 1590?–1652 or 1653

Allen, Herbert F. *A Study of the Comedies of Richard Brome,
Especially as Representative of Dramatic Decadence* (1912).

Andrews, Clarence Edward. *Richard Brome: A Study of His Life
and Works* (1913).

Cook, Elizabeth. 'The Plays of Richard Brome', *More Books*, xxii
(1947), 285–301.

Faust, E. K. R. *Richard Brome. Ein Beitrag zur Geschichte der
englischen Litteratur* (1887).

Guardia, C. E. 'Richard Brome as a Follower of Ben Jonson',
Bulletin of Louisiana State University, xxxi (1939), 59 ff.

Thaler, Alwin. 'Was Richard Brome an Actor?' *M.L.N.* xxxvi
(1921), 88–91.

No records of the early life of Richard Brome have been found,
and no non-theatrical records of his later life. In the last known
piece from his pen, the dedication to Thomas Stanley of the 1652
edition of *The Jovial Crew*, Brome speaks of the edition as '*this
Issue of my* Old age', and later in the same dedication he says,
'*You know, Sir, I am old, and cannot cringe.*' More than a decade
before, in the prologue to *The Court Beggar* (q.v.), which was
probably written in 1639 or 1640, he had spoken of himself as
'*the Poet full of age and care*'. These references and the fact that he
was called 'man' in 1614 (see below) are the only indications of
the probable time of his birth, which is customarily set at about
1590. It should be recognized, however, that such methods of

dating are only acts of desperation. There is no definite fact in Brome's career to make a birth-date of 1575 or 1595 impossible.

Brome first appears as a servant of Ben Jonson, and it was in this capacity and in that of a disciple of the laureate that he was chiefly known to the seventeenth century. His name is first found in the Induction to *Bartholomew Fair* (1614), written by Jonson himself:

> But for the whole *Play*, will you ha' the truth on 't? (I am looking, lest the *Poet* heare me, or his man, Master *Broome*, behind the Arras) it is like to be a very conceited scuruy one, in plaine English. (Lines 6–9.)

Andrews suggested (op. cit., p. 2) that Jonson was also referring to Brome when he spoke of 'my man' in Epigram CI, *Inviting a Friend to Supper*:

> How so ere, my man
> Shall reade a piece of VIRGIL, TACITVS,
> LIVIE, or of some better booke to vs.
> (Lines 20–22.)

It would be pleasant to accept this as an allusion to the future dramatist because it would establish something of his relationship to Jonson and his claim to learning. Unfortunately, though the epigram must have been written before 1616, there is no other clue to its date, and at any date Jonson may have had another man.

Jonson refers again to the fact that Brome had been his servant in the title of his verses for *The Northern Lass*, 'To my old Faithful Servant . . . Mr. *Richard Brome*', and again in the first lines of the poem,

> I had you for a Servant, once, Dick Brome;
> And you perform'd a Servants faithful parts.

Brome himself records the relationship in the verses he wrote for the Beaumont and Fletcher Folio of 1647:

> *Why, what are you (cry some) that prate to us?*
> *Doe not we know you for a flashy Meteor?*
> *And stiled (at best) the Muses' Serving-creature?*
> *Doe you controll? Y' have had your Jere: Sirs, no;*
> *But, in an humble manner, let you know*
> *Old Serving-creatures oftentimes are fit*
> *T' informe young masters . . .*
>
> *. . . even then, when He,*
> *That was the Master of his Art and Me,*
> *Most knowing Jonson . . .*
> (Lines 54–60 and 95–97.)

These lines of Brome imply that he had been often twitted about his menial relationship to Jonson, and so he had. Jonson himself, in his first flush of anger at the failure of *The New Inn* at Blackfriars and the great success of Brome's *Lovesick Maid* (q.v.) at the same theatre a few weeks later, had written in his *Ode to Himself* of 'Broomes sweeping' and 'his Masters Meale'. Thomas Randolph in his reply to Jonson spoke of 'what Broome swept from thee'. Not long after, William Heminges in his *Elegy on Randolph's Finger* wrote of the funeral cortège:

> for sent by Iohnson as some Authors say
> Broome went before and kyndly sweept the way.
> Next heathen Broome. . . .
> (ed. G. C. Moore Smith, lines 111–13.)

In *Jonsonus Virbius* R. Brideoake, evidently with the contretemps at Blackfriars and the *Ode to Himself* in mind, wrote to Jonson:

> Though the fine *Plush* and *Velvets* of the *age*
> Did oft for sixepence damne *thee* from the Stage,
> And with their *Mast* and *Achorne*-stomacks, ran
> To t'h nastie sweepings of *thy* Servingman.

And the anonymous author of the address to the reader of *Five New Playes* of 1659 felt it necessary to defend Brome against those who had belittled him because he was Jonson's servant:

> And yet there are a sort (one would wonder there should be) who think they lessen this *Author's* worth when they speak the relation he had to *Ben. Johnson.*

Both Brome himself and his contemporaries also recognized that he was a dramatic disciple of Jonson's. Brome wrote in the prologue for the revival of *The City Wit* that the play

> was written, when
> It bore just judgement, and the seal of *Ben.*

The Weeding of the Covent Garden was published in 1658 as 'A Posthume of Richard Brome, An Ingenious Servant, and Imitator of his Master . . . *Ben.* Johnson'. C. G. in his verses for *The Antipodes* begins, 'Ionson's alive!' and concludes:

> But stay, and let me tell you, where he [Jonson] *is,*
> He sojournes in his Brome's *Antipodes.*

John Hall wrote for the 1652 edition of *The Jovial Crew*:

> You do not invade;
> But by great *Johnson* were made free o' th' *Trade.*
> So, that we must in this your *Labour* finde
> Some Image and fair Relique of *his* Minde.

And John Tatham's commendatory verses for the same play begin:

> There is a Faction (Friend) in Town, that cries,
> Down with the *Dagon-Poet, Johnson* dies,

and conclude:

> there is
> Some hope left us, . . .
> . . . that their sense
> May be conformable to *Ben's* Influence;
> And finding here, *Nature* and *Art* agree,
> May swear, thou liv'st in Him, and he in Thee.

The first record of Brome as a playwright appeared in 1623 in the office-book of the Master of the Revels when Sir Henry Herbert licensed *A Fault in Friendship* for Prince Charles's (I) company. Though probably several of Brome's undated plays belong to the intervening years, there is no other definite date in his dramatic career—unless we assume that he was the Lady Elizabeth's man of the June 1628 warrant (see above, ii. 389–90)—until *The Lovesick Maid* was licensed for the King's men at Blackfriars in February 1628/9. For this, the leading London troupe, Brome wrote at least four more plays in the next five years: *The Northern Lass, The Queen's Exchange, The Novella,* and *The Late Lancashire Witches* (with Heywood). Brome does not seem quite the man for the fashionable Blackfriars, and it is somewhat surprising that his association with them lasted so long. Perhaps his reiterated objections to the courtier dramatists and the cavalier plays in his later prologues, epilogues, and verses have some connexion with his supersedence at Blackfriars.

Before 1635 Brome wrote for a time for the Red Bull theatre, as is known from C. W. Wallace's discussion of his Salisbury Court contract, but none of the plays he wrote for this theatre can now be identified. This Salisbury Court contract is our only really first-hand information about Brome's life, and it is a central document in seventeenth-century theatrical history, though its importance has often been unrecognized. Unfortunately it is known only from some grossly inadequate remarks of C. W. Wallace, who found the relevant documents (presumably the records of a suit for breach of contract) but never published them or revealed their exact location. His only published statement appeared in 'Shakspere and the Blackfriars', a popular article published in *The Century Magazine*, lxxx (1910), 742–52:

Yet another set of documents assists here in understanding certain relations of the poet to the theater. Richard Brome, former servant to

Ben Jonson and his literary disciple, in 1635 made a contract with Salisbury Court theater to write three plays a year for three years at a salary of 15s. a week, plus the first day's profits from each new play as a benefit. In 1638, it was agreed that the contract should be continued seven years longer at a salary of 20s. a week for Brome's exclusive services. But the rival theater, the Cockpit, lured him away with a better offer, and the new contract was not signed. The most interesting new items here are, the limit of three plays a year and the special provision that Brome should not be allowed to publish any of his own plays without the consent of the company. (Op. cit., p. 751.)

A little more information about these documents was elicited from Professor Wallace by C. E. Andrews when he was preparing his *Richard Brome*.

Professor Wallace has been so generous as to send me some further facts regarding this contract, from his hitherto unpublished notes. He states that Brome, previous to the contract, was with the Red Bull Company. The contract is dated July 20, 1635. The amount of the benefit of the first night on one occasion was estimated at 5£ or upwards. Brome was to give his exclusive services to the company. One play he wrote for them, the *Sparagus Garden*, was so popular that the estimated profits to the company were 1000£. In the three years during which Brome was writing for the Salisbury Court Theatre, he had written, besides numerous songs, epilogues, and revisions of scenes in revived plays, but six of the nine plays agreed on in the contract. He had also written a play or two for the Cockpit, contrary to contract.

Though Professor Wallace states in the article quoted above that the second contract was not signed, he writes me that Brome, on this new contract, which is dated August, 1638, delivered one play the following winter after Christmas, and another before Easter, 1639, which the company refused to accept. 'Then he went to the Cockpit with Beeston, where he met with better favor, about which details are not given.' (Andrews, *Richard Brome*, pp. 14–15.)

Professor Wallace died in 1932 without publishing his documents or revealing the location of the originals.

The primary significance of these documents is in their revelation of actual customary relations between a playwright and an acting company, relations which have been so frequently and so fantastically imagined for Shakespeare. To the student of Brome, the documents reveal his popularity—in the case of *The Sparagus Garden* surely exaggerated for the purposes of a lawsuit—and the fact that he wrote six plays for the King's Revels company and Queen Henrietta's company at Salisbury Court and one or two for Queen Henrietta's men, or more probably Beeston's Boys, at the Cockpit, as well as unidentified revisions, prologues, epilogues, and songs, between July 1635 and August 1638. Only four of these plays, *The Sparagus Garden*, *The Queen and Concubine*, *The Antipodes*, and *The English Moor*, can be certainly identified now. Brome's transfer to the Cockpit, under the management of William Beeston, is foreshadowed or recorded in his note at the end of *The Antipodes* and in the epilogue to *The Court Beggar*. Presumably he continued to write for this company and playhouse until the closing of the theatres, but only *The Court Beggar* and *The Jovial Crew* can be confidently assigned to this association.

It may be that Brome's odd connexion with the manuscript of Fletcher's *Monsieur Thomas* is related to his association with the Cockpit company. This comedy was published in 1639 (S.R., 22 January 1638/9) as 'Acted at the Private House in *Blacke Fryers*', but it is not in the repertory list of the King's men 7 August 1641 (see above, i. 65–66), and it is in the repertory of the King and Queen's Young Company at the Cockpit on 10 August 1639 under the title 'Fathers owne sonne.' (Ibid., pp. 330–1.) Brome wrote commendatory verses for the 1639 quarto, and he signed the dedication to Charles Cotton in which he says that he (Brome) has been the 'unworthy preserver' of the play. Evidently there was some confusion about the ownership of the piece, and Brome may have been acting as Beeston's agent.

Brome must have died in 1652 or early 1653. He wrote a dedication for the 1652 edition of *The Jovial Crew*, but in the address to the readers of *Five New Playes*, 1653, Alexander Brome says, '*for the* Author *bid me tell you, that, now he is dead, he is of* Falstaffs minde*'.

Brome has been conjectured to be the editor of *Lachrymæ Musarum*, a collection of elegies on the death of Henry, Lord Hastings, son of the Earl of Huntingdon, which was published in 1649 as 'Collected and set forth by R. B.' One of the poems in the volume (E$_7$^{v}–E$_8$^{v}) is signed 'Ric. Brome', and this man was evidently the dramatist, since he says of his Muse,

> . . . by thy dictates, I
> Never spilt Ink, except in Comedie;

The writer of this poem was apparently the editor of the volume, since he says that his poem is the last in the volume, a fact which only an editor would know. As the book is printed, Brome's poem does not come last, but it is followed by an editorial note saying that it was intended to be last, but that the following poems came in late. These facts taken together make it almost certain that the 'R. B.' who edited *Lachrymæ Musarum* was indeed the dramatist. Perhaps an interregnum connexion between Brome and the Huntingdons might be found.

Presumably we have a list of Brome's friends in the names of those who wrote commendatory verses for his publications—Ben Jonson, St[ephen?] Br[ome], Thomas Dekker, John Ford, Robert Chamberlain, John Hall, James Shirley, John Tatham, Alexander Brome. Brome himself wrote verses for the Beaumont and Fletcher Folio, for Tatham's *Fancies Theatre*, Nabbes's *Microcosmus*, Marmion's *Cupid and Psyche*, Humphrey Mill's *A Night's Search*, Jordan's *Poetical Varieties*, and Cavendish's *Variety*, and for the 1639 edition of Fletcher's *Monsieur Thomas*.

Collected Editions

1653. Five New Playes, (*Viz.*)

The { Madd Couple well matcht. Novella. Court Begger. City Witt. Damoiselle.

By *Richard Brome* . . . 1653.

1659. Five new Playes, *Viz.* The English Moor, or The Mock-Marriage. The Love-Sick Court, or The Ambitious Politique. Covent Garden Weeded. The New Academy, or The New Exchange. The Queen and Concubine. By Richard Brome . . . 1659.

1873. The Dramatic Works of Richard Brome Containing Fifteen Comedies Now First Collected in Three Volumes (1873).

The Antipodes (1638)

Edition: G. P. Baker, ed., in C. M. Gayley, *Representative English Comedies*, iii (1914), 417–543.

Andrews, C. E. *Richard Brome* (1913), pp. 112–34.
Davis, Joe Lee. 'Richard Brome's Neglected Contribution to Comic Theory', *Stud. Phil.* xl (1943), 520–8.
Faust, E. K. R. *Richard Brome* (1887), pp. 55–60.

1639/40, 19 Mar. S.R. Entered for Constable 'three Playes called.
Sparagus garden. The Antipodes. & Witt in a Madnes. [by Ric
deleted]'. (Greg, *Bibliography*, i. 52.)

1640. The Antipodes: *A Comedie.* Acted in the yeare 1638. by
the Queenes Majesties Servants, at *Salisbury* Court in Fleet-
street. The Author *Richard Brome* . . . 1640. [Variants in the
quarto have been noted in the Huntington Library copies and
in a note by G. P. B. in the Harvard copy.]

1647/8, 17 Feb. S.R. The administrators of the estate of Alice
Constable, widow of Francis Constable, transferred to Richard
Thrale twenty copyrights, including '14. Sparagus garden a
play. 15. The Antipodes. a play. 16. Witt in a Madnes. a play.'
(Greg, *Bibliography*, i. 58.)

1661, 26 Aug. '. . . to the Theatre, and saw "The Antipodes",
wherein there is much mirth, but no great matter else.' (Diary
of Samuel Pepys.)

1662. 'The Antipodes' appears in a list of plays performed by
'the Kings Companie at the Red Bull and the new house in
Gibbon's Tennis Court near Clare Market', 1660–2. (Adams,
Herbert, p. 118.)

1681, 11 Apr. S.R. Dorothy Thrale, administratrix of Richard
Thrale, assigned the three plays of the 1647/8 entry, with
thirty-nine other titles, to Benjamin Thrale. (Greg, *Bibliography*, i. 74.)

The Antipodes was one of the plays which Brome wrote under
his contract with the Salisbury Court theatre (see above, iii. 52–53),
though this one was prepared for Queen Henrietta's company,
which had come to that theatre after the plague of 1636–7 (see
above, i. 236–42), instead of for the King's Revels, which had
occupied the theatre when his original contract was drawn up.
One might guess that all three of the plays licensed by Constable
in 1639/40 were written under Brome's Salisbury Court contract—
which included a clause that Brome would not publish his plays
(see above, iii. 53)—and that Brome, after his break with the
company some time subsequent to Easter 1639, turned them over
to the publisher in a pique.

The Antipodes in particular bears witness not only to the terms
of the contract but to factors which caused it to be broken. It
will be recalled that Brome agreed to write plays exclusively for
the Salisbury Court theatre, that when the contract was ter-
minated he went to the Cockpit theatre, and that he was accused
of violating his agreement by writing one or two plays for that

theatre before the expiration of the contract. (See above, iii. 53.) *The Antipodes* is a play which Brome had intended for the King and Queen's Young Company under the governorship of William Beeston at the Cockpit but which the Salisbury Court managers had forced him to give them according to the stipulations of his contract. These facts Brome himself recorded in a signed note printed in small type at the conclusion of the 1640 edition of the play:

> Courteous Reader, *You shal find in this Booke more then was presented upon the* Stage, *and left out of* Presentation, *for superfluous length (as some of the* Players *pretended) I thoght good al should be inserted according to the allowed* Original; *and as it was, at first, intended for the* Cock-pit Stage, *in the right of my most deserving Friend Mr.* William Beeston, *unto whom it properly appertained; and so I leave it to thy perusal, as it was generally applauded, and well acted at* Salisbury Court.   *Farewell*, Ri. Brome.

Fleay, with his usual eye for theatrical detail, noted (*Biog. Chron.* i. 40) that in the play Brome took a fling at the boy company of the King's Revels, for whom he had written during the first year or so of his contract with the Salisbury Court, in the lines,

a Play,
Compos'd by th' Divell, and acted by the Children
Of his blacke Revelles.   (II, 5)

The Antipodes is one of Brome's cleverest and most entertaining comedies, and one would suppose that it had been presented with some success. That it was at least not a failure can be deduced from the allusion in the epilogue to *The Court Beggar* a year or so later:

> And let me tell you he [the author] has made pretty merry Jigges that ha' pleas'd a many. As (le'me see) th' *Antipodes*, and . . .

More allusions to the comedy might have been expected, but national troubles tended to diminish theatrical talk in the years before the outbreak of war.

There is a rather superficial consideration of the possible sources and analogues of the play and of the objects of satire in Andrews's *Richard Brome*, pp. 112–34.

The Apprentice's Prize (c. 1634?)

with Thomas Heywood

(Lost)

1654, 8 April. S.R. 'M^r. Mosely. Entred for his Copies Two plaies called. The Life & Death of S^r. Martyn Skink. wth ye warres of ye Low Countries. by Rich. Broome. & Tho: Heywood. & The Apprentices Prize, &c.' (Greg, *Bibliography*, i. 62.)

This title is known only from the Stationers' Register entry. Since the only extant collaboration of Heywood and Brome was *The Late Lancashire Witches* (q.v.), which they wrote for the King's men in 1634, this play is generally listed as written for the same company at about the same date. Fleay's suggestion (*Biog. Chron.* i. 41) that all three plays of the Brome–Heywood collaboration were Brome's revisions of old plays by Heywood is improbable in the case of *The Late Lancashire Witches*, the only one for which there is any evidence.

Though it is assumed that Moseley indicated that both plays were by Heywood and Brome, his entry might mean that only the first was.

The Careless Shepherdess

Brome has sometimes been suggested as the author of the prologues and epilogues and the praeludium of Goffe's *Careless Shepherdess*. See under Goffe and Thomas Randolph.

Christianetta, or Marriage and Hanging Go by Destiny (> 1634?)

with George Chapman

(Lost)

1640, 4 Aug. S.R. Entered for Crooke 'six Playes vizt. Christianetta. The Iewish gentleman. A new Academy or Exchange. The love sick Co^rt. The Covent Garden. and The English Moore or mock Marriage by M^r. Rich: Broome.' (Greg, *Bibliography*, i. 53.)

c. 1677–1703. 'Christianetta or Marriage & hanging goe by destiny Chapman & Brome.' (J. Q. Adams, 'Hill's List of Early Plays in Manuscript', *Library*, Fourth Series, xx [1939], 71–99. See Middleton, *The Conqueror's Custom*.)

The identical first titles and the common attribution to Brome can leave little doubt that the publisher, Crooke, and the bibliophile, Abraham Hill, had seen manuscripts of the same play, possibly the same manuscript, in spite of the fact that Hill added a sub-title and a collaborator. Hill's list of plays seems to have been set down from some bookseller's stock between 1677 and 1703, though most of the identifiable plays and playwrights are Jacobean and Caroline. (See Middleton, *The Conqueror's Custom*.) Hill's attribution of authorship to Chapman as well as Brome was presumably based on something he saw on the manuscript, since there is no evidence that he owned or read the plays in the list.

Assuming that Hill was right in his designation of Chapman as collaborator, the play would have to date before Chapman's death in May 1634. The title sounds rather like those Herbert was licensing for the Fortune and the Red Bull companies in 1623 and 1624, when Brome collaborated with young Johnson on *A Fault in Friendship* for the Prince's company, probably at the Red Bull. Accordingly I should like to guess at the date as some time in the twenties before Brome began writing for the King's men. This is sheer unsupported conjecture.

The City Wit (*c.* 1629? and 1637–9?)

Faust, E. K. R. *Richard Brome* (1887), pp. 49–53.

1653. The City Wit, Or, The Woman wears the Breeches. A Comedy . . . 1653. (Separate title-page in *Five New Playes*, 1653.)

1659, 11 June. S.R. Richard Marriott assigned to Humphrey Moseley twenty-one titles of which the last was 'Five new Playes. viz! The mad Couple well Matcht. The Novella: The Court Beggar. The Cittie Witt. The Damoiselle. by Rich: Broome.' (Greg, *Bibliography*, i. 67.)

1661, 6 July. 'S., [i.e. Saturday] "City Witt," and "Tu quoque" againe.' (From Wood's record of plays seen at Oxford. Andrew Clark, *The Life and Times of Anthony Wood*, i. 405.)

1661, 10 July. 'W., [i.e. Wednesday] in the morning, "The City Witt," 6*d*; in the afternoone, "The poore man's comfort" a tragi-comedy, 6*d*.' (Ibid., p. 406.)

There is no external evidence of when or by whom this satiric comedy of intrigue was produced. The prologue, however, gives a few hints as to its history. This prologue is printed with some confusion in the 1653 edition, a confusion perhaps derived from

the state of the playhouse manuscript from which it was set up
—see, for instance, the prompter's warning at the beginning of
Act II. Actually there seem to be two prologues run together. The
first begins, 'Quot quot adestis, salvete, salvetote', introduces
the schoolmaster, and ends, apparently incomplete, with the line
'Ile nothing speak but figures, strayns & tropes'. The second
begins, 'Quot quot adestis Salvete salvetote', introduces the
schoolmaster, discusses the fact that the performance is a revival,
and ends:

> So with the salutation I first brought yee,
> Quot quot adestis, salvete salvetote.

The lines on the revival are suggestive:

> . . . exercise your Judgement with your wit,
> On this our Comedy, which in bold Phrase,
> The Author sayes has past with good applause
> In former times. For it was written, when
> It bore just Judgement, and the seal of Ben.
> Some in this round may have both seen't, and heard,
> Ere I, that beare its title, wore a Beard.

The player reading the prologue says that the performance is a
revival on the authority, not of the players, as was usual, but of
the author. Such a distinction implies that the original performance was not given by this company. The last two lines
indicate that the original performance was given in the boyhood
of the prologue actor, and they might be interpreted to mean that
that performance had taken place in this same theatre. The line
about the approval of Ben indicates that the play was written
before Jonson died, in August 1637, and it would seem to imply
that Jonson was dead at the time of the revival.

The unusually large number of characters who are boys or
women—eight—and the importance of their roles suggest that
the comedy was written for a boy company, since adult companies presumably would not have had enough competent boys
for the parts. All these inferences may be reconciled by the hypothesis that *The City Wit* was one of Brome's earlier compositions
for the King's Revels company at Salisbury Court, a theatre
which they first occupied in 1629. (See above, i. 283 ff.) In this
case, the revival would have been a production of Queen Henrietta's men, who performed at the Salisbury Court with Brome as
their poet 1637–9. (See above, iii. 53.) Fleay (*Biog. Chron.* i. 36)
suggested the year 1629 on the evidence of a ballad entitled 'The
Woman would wear the Breeches' which was entered in the

Stationers' Register 26 November 1629 (Arber, iv. 222), but since the title is proverbial, the ballad and the play may be unrelated. Mr. Andrew J. Walker noted that the ballad in II. 2, is stanza 4 of 'The Knight and the Shepherd's Daughter' (F. J. Child, *The English and Scottish Popular Ballads*, 5 vols., ii. 457–77) and that it was registered as a broadside ballad in 1624. (*Popular Songs and Broadside Ballads and the English Drama, 1559–1642*, Harvard MS. thesis, p. 350.)

The large number of songs written for the part of Crack suggests that Brome had an unusually good singing-boy in mind when he wrote the play. Ronald Bayne pointed out (*C.H.E.L.*, 1932 ed., vi. 228–9) the very effective use of Latin tags and paraphrases for comic effect and wondered how well the audience could follow them.

George Powell's *A Very Good Wife*, 1693, is an amalgamation of Middleton's *No Wit No Help like a Woman's*, Shirley's *Hyde Park*, and Brome's *Court Beggar* and *The City Wit*.

The Masque at Coleoverton

See Anon.

The Court Beggar (1639–40)

Faust, E. K. R. *Richard Brome* (1887), pp. 39–48.

1653. The Court Begger. A *Comedie*. Acted at the *Cock-pit*, by his Majesties Servants, *Anno* 1632. Written by Richard Brome . . . 1653. (Separate title-page in *Five New Playes*, 1653.)

1659, 11 June. S.R. Richard Marriott assigned to Humphrey Moseley twenty-one titles, of which the last was 'Five new Playes. vizͭ The mad Couple well Matcht. The Novella: The Court Beggar. The Cittie Witt. The Damoiselle. by Rich: Broome.' (Greg, *Bibliography*, i. 67.)

The theatre-wise Fleay noted long since (*Biog. Chron.* i. 40–41) that the production statement on the title-page of this play states an impossibility, though some of his less canny successors have continued to accept it. Fleay suggested that the compositor of the 1653 collection copied the statement by mistake from the title-page of *The Novella*. This is an excellent guess. There are two forms of separate title-pages in this volume, one for *The Novella* and *The Court Beggar* with the imprint 'Printed for RICHARD MARRIOTT, and / THO. DRING', and the other for *The City Wit*

and *The Damoiselle* with the imprint 'Printed by T. R. for *Richard
Marriott*, and *Thomas | Dring*'. A *Mad Couple Well Matched* has
no separate title-page. Now the first two—*The Novella* and *The
Court Beggar*—not only have the same imprint, but, except for
the titles and the single word '*Black-Friars*' or '*Cock-pit*', they
are identical, line for line, type face for type face, rule for rule,
including the Latin motto which the other plays do not have.
Fleay's guess at the compositor's confusion in the light of these
facts seems more than plausible.

That there was confusion and that *The Court Beggar* was not
produced by the King's men or in 1632 are inescapable facts.
Most obviously, the King's men never acted at the Cockpit. Moreover, the play is full of allusions to events after 1632, most of
them events of 1638 and 1639. The prologue begins with a reference to the love-and-honour plays of the thirties and continues
with a reference to the plays spectacularly produced with scenery,
such as Henry Killigrew's *Pallantus and Eudora or The Con-
spiracy*, produced 1635, Cartwright's *Royal Slave*, 1636/7, and
Habington's *Queen of Aragon*, 1640:

> *Wee've cause to fear yours, or the Poets frowne*
> *For of late day's (he know's not (how) y' are grown,*
> *Deeply in love with a new strayne of wit*
> *Which he condemns, at least disliketh it,*
> *And solemnely protests you are to blame*
> *If at his hands you doe expect the same;*
> *Hee'l tread his usuall way, no gaudy Sceane*
> *Shall give instructions, what his plot doth meane;*
> *No handsome Love toy shall your time beguile*
> *Forcing your pitty to a sigh or smile,*
> *But a slight piece of mirth. . . .*

Line 16 of this prologue refers to '*the Poet full of age and care*',
a description which would be much more appropriate for Brome
in 1640 than in 1632. Lines 21–26 refer (as do later lines in Act II,
sig. P_4, and in the epilogue) to the courtiers' plays, which were
given to the players and not written for profit:

> *Yet you to him* [the poet] *your favour may expresse*
> *As well as unto those whose forwardnesse*
> *Make's them your Creatures thought, who in a way*
> *To purchace fame give money with their Play,*
> *Yet you sometimes pay deare for't, since they write*
> *Lesse for your pleasure than their own delight.*

The most notable of the plays which were written by courtiers,

admired at court, and given to the rival King's men for production
at Blackfriars were Sir William Berkeley's *Lost Lady*, produced
1637–8, Suckling's *Aglaura*, 1637 and 1638, which Brome ridiculed
elsewhere, Carlell's *Arviragus and Philicia*, 1636, and his *Passionate Lovers*, 1638, and Habington's *Queen of Aragon*, 1640. The
Earl of Newcastle, Davenant, and Killigrew were also courtier-
playwrights, but there is no indication that the plays of the first
were admired at court, and the other two were not in the habit
of giving anything away.

At the beginning of Act III there are clear references to the
First Bishops' War of 1639 and apparently to the gaudy cavalry
troop of Suckling and Goring:

> *Doct.* Here set him downe. Unbind him, and unblind him.
>
> (*Ferdinand brought in a chaire bound and hooded, &c.*)
>
> *Fer.* Am I then taken prisoner in the North?
> Wounded, disarm'd and bound? I shall be ransom'd
> To which of your rebelliously usurp'd
> Castles ha' you brought me? you sir *Presbiter*,
> That better can *pugnare* than *orare*,
> And so abjure all duty and allegiance—
> *Men.* Hee takes you for a Northerne Pastor Mr. Doctor.
> *Doct.* No matter what, let him run out his fancy.
> *Fer.* You were best to use me well; and like a souldier
> Order will else be tane (though you know none.)
> *Doct.* You shall have all best usage sir.
> *Fer.* And use my horse well too, and let my horse and armor
> Be decently preserv'd and seene forth-comming
> At my redemption.
> *Doct.* With all best care sir.
> *Fer.* For I shall soone be sent for, or fetch'd off
> With ruine of your countrey 'bout your eares.
> *Doct.* You shall have all content the countrey yeilds sir.
> *Fer.* I shall have Oat-bread, Ale, and Bag-pipes, shall I?
> *Doct.* If you'l be merry sir.
> *Fer.* Merry! why not? come let's ha' cards; and you and I to
> cribbage
> For an od hundred pound, I meane not Scotch,
> But sterling English pieces, where's your money?
> All gone in Ammunition, and charge Military.
> *Doct.* I'le finde you money enough.
> *Fer.* O here's a third man, let's then to Gleeke.
> *Men.* Crown Gleeke sir, if you please.
> *Fer.* Crown Gleeke! no more?
> You seeme to be a thrifty Covenanter
> To play but at crowne Gleeke, whole piece Gleeke or nothing.

In I. I, the proposed

> new project
> For buylding a new Theatre or Play-house
> Upon the *Thames* on Barges or flat boats

sounds very much like a satiric allusion to Davenant's project of
a large new theatre to be built in Fleet Street, a proposal suggested 26 March 1639 and abandoned 2 October of the same year.
(See Adams, *Shakespearean Playhouses*, pp. 424–31.) This proposal
is expected

> To helpe the watermen out of the losse
> They've suffer'd by Sedans,

a statement which indicates that sedan chairs had been in use for
some time. Sir S. Duncombe is said to have introduced them into
England in 1634 (*Encyclopœdia Britannica*, 11th ed., xxiv. 576),
and Brome had already ridiculed them as a new and strange thing
in his *Sparagus Garden*, which was acted at Salisbury Court in
1635.

The line in Act II (sig. P_4), 'as idle as the Players going to Law
with their Poets', sounds like a reference to the suit of the pro-
prietors of the Salisbury Court theatre against Brome for violation
of his contract in 1639—the presumptive source of C. W. Wallace's
information. (See above, iii. 52–53.) And the reference on the same
page to Courtwit's project

> to procure a Patent for my selfe to have the onely priviledge to give
> instructions to all the actors in the city, (especially the younger sort)
> the better to enable them to speake their parts emphatically and to
> the life,

sounds very much like a reference to Davenant's patent of 27 June
1640 to be governor of the King and Queen's Young Company
at the Cockpit. (See above, i. 334–5.) Indeed it might be worth
detailed consideration whether the character Courtwit is not
intended as a caricature of Davenant throughout.

Finally, the epilogue is most explicit in its references to the
affairs of the King and Queen's Young Company at the Cockpit
under William Beeston:

> There's wit in that now. But this small Poet vents none but his
> own, and his by whose care and directions this Stage is govern'd, who
> has for many yeares both in his fathers dayes, and since directed
> Poets to write & Players to speak till he traind up these youths here
> to what they are now. I some of 'em from before they were able to say
> a grace of two lines long to have more parts in their pates then would
> fill so many Dry-fats. And to be serious with you, if after all this, by

the venemous practise of some, who study nothing more than his destruction, he should faile us, both Poets and Players would be at losse in Reputation.

The man 'by whose care and directions this Stage is govern'd' was William Beeston, who had been sworn governor of the company 5 April 1639 and who had worked with the company at the Cockpit in his father's time, i.e. before October 1638, when his father, Christopher Beeston, died. (See above, ii. 370–4.) 'These youths here' are the boys of the King and Queen's Young Company or Beeston's Boys, who had begun acting at the Cockpit in 1637 and continued there until the theatres were closed. (See above, i. 324–5.) The allusion to the venomous practice of some who might make Beeston 'faile us' sounds as if it might refer to Beeston's imprisonment of 4 May 1640 and the company's short suppression. (See above, i. 332–3.)

Finally, near the conclusion of the epilogue are references to Brome's plays 'th' *Antipodes*' and '*Tom Hoyden* o' *Tanton Deane*', that is, *The Antipodes* of 1638 and *The Sparagus Garden* of 1635.

It seems to me that this unusual multiplicity of references to events of 1635, 1636, 1637/8, and especially of 1638, 1639, and perhaps of 1640, leaves no ground at all for thinking that this is a play of 1632 and good grounds for thinking that it must have been written in 1639 or 1640. The references to the company of Beeston's Boys are sufficiently clear to demonstrate that this was not a play of the King's company, as the 1653 title-page says.

The play of the Restoration actor-playwright, George Powell, entitled *A Very Good Wife* (1693), is a rather intricate amalgamation of Middleton's *No Wit No Help like a Woman's*, Shirley's *Hyde Park*, and Brome's *City Wit* and *Court Beggar*. The plagiarism was first pointed out by Genest. (*Some Account of the English Stage*, ii. 50.)

Covent Garden Weeded

See *The Weeding of the Covent Garden, or The Middlesex Justice of Peace*.

The Damoiselle, or The New Ordinary (1637–8 ?)

1653. The Damoiselle, or The New Ordinary. A Comedy . . . 1653. (Separate title-page in *Five New Playes*, 1653.)
1659, 11 June. S.R. Richard Marriott assigned to Humphrey

Moseley twenty-one titles, of which the last was 'Five new Playes. viz? The mad Couple well Matcht. The Novella: The Court Beggar. The Cittie Witt. The Damoiselle. by Rich: Broome.' (Greg, *Bibliography*, i. 67.)

There is little to tell who acted this sentimental comedy, or when. Fleay (*Biog. Chron.* i. 36) noted the allusive prologue:

> Our Playmaker (*for yet he won't be calld*
> *Author, or Poet*) nor beg to be installd
> Sir Lawreat) . . .
> . . . bids me tell you, That though he be none
> Of those, whose towring Muses scale the Throne
> Of Kings . . .
> . . . nor does claime
> Lawrell, but Money; Bayes will buy no Sack.

The sneer at aspirants for the laureateship would be most pointed after Jonson's death in August 1637, and before Davenant was given his pension in December 1638. Fleay did not note that the sneer at playwrights who called themselves authors would also apply to Davenant. So far as I know, Ben Jonson had been the first to allow this rather pretentious designation—'The Author B. Ionson'—on the title-pages of his plays, with *The Silent Woman*, 1620, and *The New Inn*, 1631. Jonson, of course, was privileged in the mind of Brome, but Davenant had imitated him with the same designation on the title-pages of *The Platonic Lovers*, 1636, and *The Wits*, 1636; so had Massinger with *A New Way to Pay Old Debts*, 1633, and especially Nabbes with *Hannibal and Scipio*, 1637, *Microcosmus*, 1637, *Tottenham Court*, 1638, *The Bride*, 1640, and *The Unfortunate Mother*, 1640, and Lewis Sharpe with *The Noble Stranger*, 1640. Probably the last three came after Brome wrote the prologue. Davenant and Nabbes were both offensive to him for their pretensions.

The line, 'whose towring Muses scale the Throne', could apply to various dramatists of the time of Charles I, but it would be particularly pointed for the love-and-honour plays and the masques of Davenant. These remarks in the prologue, then, point to 1637 or 1638 when Davenant was manœuvring to succeed Jonson as laureate and after he had imitated Jonson in styling himself author on the title-pages of plays. Brome was still writing under his contract for the Salisbury Court in these years, and the company at that theatre then was Queen Henrietta's men. (See above, i. 236 ff.) It should be remembered, however, that Brome was charged with writing a play or two for the Cockpit players—

the King and Queen's Young Company at this time—in violation
of his contract (see above), and this might be one of those plays.

The English Moor, or The Mock Marriage (1637)

MS.: Lichfield Cathedral Library. See below, 1637–52.

1640, 4 Aug. S.R. 'M^r. Crooke. Entred for his Copies . . . six
Playes vizt. Christianetta. The Iewish gentleman. A new Academy or Exchange. The love sick Co^rt. The Covent Garden.
and The English Moore or mock Marriage by M^r. Rich: Broome.'
(Greg, *Bibliography*, i. 53.)

1637–52. Lichfield Cathedral Library owns a manuscript of the
play dedicated 'To the thrice honourable William Lord Seamor
Earle of Hertford Lord Beauchampe, &c.'. The dedication concludes, 'In this tender of my service, to the constancy of your
noble nature I am an humble petitioner, that your Lordship
according to your wonted vertue will please to preserue in your
good opinion, amongst the faithfullest of your Seruants Your
Lordships Humblest Richard Brome.' (B. M. Wagner, *T.L.S.*,
4 October 1934.)

1658. The English Moor, Or The Mock-Marriage: A Comædy as
it was often acted with general applause by her Majesties Servants . . . 1658. (Separate title-page in *Five New Playes*, 1659.)

1659. [Another issue.] With the attribution 'By Richard Brome'
and the imprint 'Printed in the year, 1659'.

c. 1677–1703. 'The painted Lady.' (Ninth entry in Hill's list. See
below, Middleton, *The Conqueror's Custom*.)

The title-page statement about production shows that *The
English Moor* was another of the plays written by Brome under
his contract with the Salisbury Court theatre, 1635–9. (See above.)
Queen Henrietta's company performed at that theatre from 1637
until, presumably, the closing of the theatres in 1642. (See above,
i. 238–45.) The highly allusive prologue for the play fixes the date
very closely, and within the term of Brome's contract:

> *Most noble, fair and curteous, to ye all*
> *Welcome and thanks we give, that you would call*
> *And visit your poor servants, that have been*
> *So long and pitiless unheard, unseen.*
> *Welcome, you'l say your money that does do,*
> *(Dissembling is a fault) we say so too.*
> *And your long absence was no fault of your,*
> *But our sad fate to be so long obscure.*

Jove and the Muses grant, and all good Men,
*   We feel not that extremity again:*
The thought of which yet chills us with a fear
*   That we have bought our liberty too dear:*
For should we fall into a new restraint,
*   Our hearts must break that did before but faint.*
You noble, great and good ones, that vouchsafe
*   To see a Comedy, and sometimes laugh*
Or smile at wit and harmless mirth, As thus
*   ye have begun to grace and succour us;*
Be further pleas'd (to hold us still upright,
*   For our relief, and for your own delight)*
To move for us to those high powers whom we
*   submit unto in all humility,*
For our proceeding, and we'le make it good
*   To utter nothing may be understood*
Offensive to the state, manners or time,
*   We will as well look to our necks as climb.*
*   You hear our sute, obtain it if you may;*
*   Then find us money and we'le find you play.*

As Fleay noted (*Biog. Chron.* i. 39–40), the 'poor servants, that
have been So long and pitiless unheard, unseen' are, as the title-
page shows, the players of Queen Henrietta's company who, like
the other London companies, had been silent for nearly seventeen
months because of the protracted plague-closing of 1636–7. (See
above, ii. 661–5.) The tone of the prologue is quite similar to that
of Randolph's *Praeludium*, which was prepared for the reopening
at this theatre after the long plague-closing in November 1630
(see Bentley, *Joseph Quincy Adams Memorial Studies*, pp. 775–83),
and the wording is not unlike that of the company's petition to
be allowed to play again, a petition which they submitted to the
Privy Council 24 September 1637. The players complained that
because of the plague

they have for a long time, almost to their vtter vndoing (having noe
other Imployment nor meanes to maintain themselves and their
families) been restrayned from vsing their quallity, And therefore
humbly besought their Lo^pp^s to bee restored to their former Liberty.
(See above, ii. 664.)

Lines 15–26 of the prologue—'You noble, great and good ones',
through 'We will as well look to our necks as climb'—seem to
indicate that the company had also been suppressed, or feared to
be suppressed, because of political comments in their plays.
Nothing is known of any such restraint or threat.

Professor J. Q. Adams made the tentative suggestion that the manuscript play, 'The painted Lady', which Abraham Hill listed, apparently as in the stock of some Restoration London bookseller, might be this play. (See *Library*, Fourth Series, xx [1939], 83.) It is true that Milicent, painted black, is a prominent feature of *The English Moor*, and that plays of the time were sometimes known under a variety of titles, but so little is known of Hill's list that the identification must remain only the vaguest of guesses.

A Fault in Friendship (1623)
With — Johnson
(Lost)

1623, 2 Oct. '"For the Prince's Companye; a new Comedy, called *A Fault in Friendship*: Written by *Young* Johnson, and Broome." (These were the *Son*, and Servant of Ben Jonson.)' (Adams, *Herbert*, p. 26, from George Chalmers, *A Supplemental Apology*, p. 215. The parenthetical comment is Chalmers's.)

This entry from the lost office-book of the Master of the Revels is our first evidence that Ben Jonson's servant, Richard Brome, was a playwright. The Prince's company was one of the weaker troupes in London at this time and seems to have been performing at the Red Bull theatre. (See above, i. 205–8.) This play, like most of the repertory of the company in this period (ibid., pp. 214–17), has been lost—an indication that the repertory as a whole was not very distinguished.

A fair amount of nonsense has been written about this play, beginning with Chalmers's parenthetical comment noted above. There is nothing in Herbert's entry to indicate that '*Young* Johnson' was the son of Ben. Others have carried the illusion farther, christened the imagined son Ben Jr., and assembled a life and a work or two for him. There is no evidence that Jonson had a son Ben who grew to manhood or any other son who was alive in 1623. Malone was confused by a pseudonym of 1672 and did not understand that it was the laureate himself and not a namesake son who obtained the reversion of the Mastership of the Revels in 1621. Gifford gave his imagination play in the confusion. (See below, Ben Jonson, Jr., and Mark Eccles, *R.E.S.* xii [1936], 257–72.) It is conceivable, of course, that '*Young* Johnson' was an unknown son of Ben, but it is rather more likely that he was one of the scores of other London Johnsons.

The fact that this play was licensed in 1623, five and a half years before the next certainly dated play of Brome's, suggests that several of his undated plays were probably written between 1623 and 1629, a probability not recognized by Fleay and Andrews.

The Jewish Gentleman (> 1640)
(Lost)

1640, 4 Aug. S.R. 'M^r. Crooke. Entred for his Copies ... six Playes vizt. Christianetta. The Iewish gentleman. A new Academy or Exchange. The love sick Co^rt. The Covent Garden. and The English Moore or mock Marriage by M^r. Rich: Broome.' (Greg, *Bibliography*, i. 53.)

The Stationers' Register entry provides our only information about this play. One might have guessed that, since Andrew Crooke licensed six of Brome's plays together about a year after Brome had broken his contract with the Salisbury Court theatre (see above), these were Salisbury Court plays which Brome sold in violation of his contract after he left that theatre for the Cockpit. It cannot be demonstrated, however, that even a majority of the six were old Salisbury Court plays.

The Jovial Crew, or The Merry Beggars (1641)

Edition: Giles Floyd, *A Critical Edition of Brome's A Jovial Crew, with Introduction, Textual Notes, and Glossary*. MS. Ph.D. Thesis, University of Iowa (1943).

Faust, E. K. R. *Richard Brome. Ein Beitrag zur Geschichte der englischen Literatur* (1887), pp. 83–89.

1652. A Joviall Crew: Or, The Merry Beggars. Presented in a Comedie, At The Cock-pit in Drury-Lane, in the yeer 1641. Written by *Richard Brome* . . . 1652.

1661, 25 July. 'To the theatre, and saw "The Joviall Crew," (the first time I saw it) and indeed it is as merry and the most innocent play that ever I saw, and well performed.' (Diary of Samuel Pepys.)

1661, 27 Aug. 'Hence my wife and I to the Theatre, and there saw "The Joviall Crew," where the King, Duke and Duchess, and Madame Palmer, were, and my wife, to her great content,

had a full sight of them all the while. The play full of mirth.'
(Ibid.)

1661, 1 Nov. 'To the Theatre, to "The Joviall Crew."' (Ibid.)

1661. [Another edition.] With the addition 'And since, acted by
his Majesties Servants, at the *New Theatre* in *Vere*-Street, 1661'.

1661/2, 21 Jan. 'Jouiall Crew. 21. Jan.' appears in a list of performances of plays by 'the Kings Companie at the Red Bull
and the new house in Gibbon's Tennis Court near Clare Market',
1660–2. (Adams, *Herbert*, p. 118.)

1662[–3 ?]. In his record of expenses at plays 'At the New Theatre
in Lincolnes Jnne fields', Edward Browne entered 'Joviall
Crew . . . 1 6'. (W. W. Greg, 'Theatrical Repertories of 1662',
Gentleman's Magazine, ccci [July 1906], 69–72, from B.M. MS.
Sloane 1900.)

< 1663. Downes lists 'The Jovial Crew' as one of the old stock
plays acted by the King's company after the opening of the new
Drury Lane theatre in 1663. (*Roscius Anglicanus*, ed. Summers,
p. 8.)

1668/9, 11 Jan. 'Abroad with my wife to the King's playhouse,
and there saw "The Joviall Crew"; but ill acted to what it
was heretofore, in Clun's time, and when Lacy could dance.'
(Diary of Samuel Pepys.)

1684. [Another edition.]

1731. 'A New Book of Songs to the Jovial Crew.'

1731. A comic opera revision, 'As it is Acted at the Theatre-
Royal, by His Majesty's Servants . . . With the Musick prefix'd
to each Song.' Other editions in 1732, 1760, 1761, 1764, 1767,
1774, 1780, and 1781.

1792. 'Airs Songs and Duettos from The Jovial Crew.'

The explicit statement on the title-page of the first edition that
the comedy was performed at the Cockpit in 1641 indicates that
Brome wrote it for his friend William Beeston and the King and
Queen's Young Company, who performed at that theatre in 1641.
(See above, i. 335.) Brome's friendship for Beeston and his com-
pany had been expressed before in his *Antipodes* (q.v.) and *Court
Beggar* (q.v.); presumably he had been under contract to Beeston
since 1639. (See above, iii. 52–53.)

Brome's statement, in the dedication to Thomas Stanley in the
1652 edition, that the play '*had the luck to tumble last of all in
the Epidemicall ruine of the* Scene' probably means that it was performed on the last day the company acted before they were suppressed by Parliament's order, 2 September 1642. The statement

could possibly mean that *The Jovial Crew* was the last new play written for the company, but an opening date in April 1641 seems plausible for it (see below), and this leaves sixteen months before the closing of the theatres, which seems too long a period for the Cockpit company to have been without a new piece. The statement might also be interpreted to mean that *The Jovial Crew* was the last of Brome's compositions for the Cockpit, but since Brome in 1635 estimated that he could compose three plays a year, a sixteen-month blank seems unlikely.

There are suggestions that the play was planned to open 25 April 1641, or thereabouts. In the first scene Oldrents marvels that his steward, Springlove, has brought in his accounts ahead of the reckoning date:

> *Old.* But why, *Springlove,*
> Is now this expedition?
> *Spr.* Sir, 'Tis duty.
> *Old.* Not common among Stewards, I confess,
> To urge in their Accompts before the day
> Their Lords have limited. . . .
> 'Tis yet but thirty daies, when I give forty
> After the half-year day, our *Lady* last.

That is, the accounting year began as usual on Michaelmas Day, and the half-yearly accounts were closed on Lady Day (25 March). Springlove was allowed forty days of grace to make up his accounts, or until about 5 May, but here he is after only thirty days, or about 25 April. This same date is suggested later in the scene when Oldrents says, ''Tis well-nigh *May*'.

The edition of 1652 was evidently sponsored by the author, for it has his dedication to Thomas Stanley, and it provides commendatory verses by John Hall, J. B., James Shirley, John Tatham, and Alexander Brome. The verses are all addressed to Brome. Three of the poets—Hall, J. B., and Shirley—take the occasion to sneer at William Cartwright's recent *Comedies, Tragicomedies, with Other Poems*, which was issued in 1651 with fifty-two—in some copies more—sets of commendatory verses. None of the poets says much about Brome or *The Jovial Crew*.

Early popularity was probably denied to this gay and captivating comedy by the troublesome times in which it appeared—Brome speaks in the prologue of 'these sad and tragick daies' —and by the closing of the theatres before it was two years old. Pepys's records and the lists of Restoration and eighteenth-century revivals, adaptations, and imitations show what it might have attained earlier. Professor Nicoll points out that 'Dance's

The Ladies Frolick (D.L. 1770) is but another of the many eighteenth-century versions of Brome's *The Jovial Crew'*. (*A History of Late Eighteenth Century Drama*, p. 113.)

There had been earlier beggar and gipsy plays, such as Fletcher's *Beggars' Bush*, Middleton and Rowley's *Spanish Gipsy*, and Jonson's *Gipsies Metamorphosed*. There is little evidence of Brome's indebtedness to *The Beggars' Bush*, but he does seem to have used *The Spanish Gipsy* and bits of *The Gipsies Metamorphosed*. (See E. K. R. Faust, *Richard Brome*, pp. 83–89, and Giles Floyd, MS. thesis, pp. xlvii–lxvi.) Both were easily accessible to Brome: the masque was printed in folio and in duodecimo in 1640; *The Spanish Gipsy* belonged to Beeston's Boys, the company for which Brome was writing, in 1639 (see above, i. 330–1), and he presumably could use the manuscript in the archives at the Cockpit theatre.

The Late Lancashire Witches (1634)
with Thomas Heywood

Editions: L. Tieck, ed., '*Die Hexen in Lancashire*', in *Shakspeare's Vorschule* (1823), i, pp. xxxviii–xlii and 251–420; J. O. Halliwell, '*The Lancashire Witches*', in *The Poetry of Witchcraft* (1853), pp. 145–239.

Andrews, C. E. 'The Authorship of *The Late Lancashire Witches*', *M.L.N.* xxviii (1913), 163–6. Reprinted in his *Richard Brome*, pp. 48–53.

Clark, Arthur Melville. *Thomas Heywood: Playwright and Miscellanist* (1931), pp. 120–7.

Martin, R. G. 'Is *The Late Lancashire Witches* a Revision?' *Mod. Phil.* xiii (1915), 253–65.

Notestein, Wallace. *A History of Witchcraft in England from 1558 to 1718* (1911), pp. 146–60.

1634, 20 July. 'Players peticõn   A peticõn of the Kings Players
             about ye Witches   complayning of intermingleing
some passages of witches in old playes to ye priudice of their designed Comedy of the Lancashire witches, & desiring a prohibition of any other till theirs bee allowed & Acted. Answered p[er] Reference to Blagraue in absence of Sr H. Herbert. / Iuly 20. 1634.' (*M.S.C.* ii, Part iii, 410.)

1634, 28 Oct. S.R. 'Ben: ffisher: Entred for his Copy vnder the hands of Sr. Henry Herbert & mr Rothwell warden a Play called The Witches of Lancasheire &c.' (Greg, *Bibliography*, i. 44.)

1634. The late Lancashire VVitches. A well received Comedy, lately Acted at the *Globe* on the *Banke-side*, by the Kings Majesties Actors. Written, by Thom. Heyvvood, and Richard Broome. . . . 1634.

1635, 10 July. Under the heading 'At our Act besides ye playes at ye Kings armes other things were to be seene for money', Thomas Crosfield, a Fellow of Queen's College, Oxford, lists ten entertainments about the town, including 'The witches of Lancashire over against ye *Kings* Head, their Tricks, Meetings'. (*Crosfield's Diary*, p. 79.)

1637, 27 Mar. S.R. Assigned with seventy-nine other books from Fisher to Young is '27. The witches of Lancashire   the play.' (Greg, *Bibliography*, i. 46.)

1642, 14 June. S.R. Half the interest of Robert Young in these eighty titles is assigned to Benjamin Fisher, including '27. The witches of Lancasheire   the play.' (Ibid., p. 54.)

1644, 22 July. S.R. Entered to Mr. James Young, 130 titles 'the wch. apperteyned to Mr Robte. young, his late father deceased', including '[65] [his part] of the Witches of Lancasheire.   a play.' (Ibid., p. 55.)

This play was written to exploit the interest in the Lancashire women accused of witchcraft in 1633. There was much curiosity when several of them were brought to London. The prologue refers to

> *The Project unto many here well knowne;*
> *Those Witches the fat Iaylor brought to Towne.*

The epilogue indicates that the trial was not yet over.

> *Now while the Witches must expect their due*
> *By lawfull Iustice . . .*
> *. . . what their crime*
> *May bring upon 'em, ripeness yet of time*
> *Has not reveal'd.*

The contention of Andrews (*Richard Brome*, pp. 48–53), using evidence collected by Fleay (*Biog. Chron.* i. 301–3), that the piece is a play of Heywood's written about 1612 to exploit the first Lancashire witch scare of that year and then revised by Brome in 1634 for the King's men's play on the later Lancashire witches, seems reasonable at first glance. There are serious difficulties about this interpretation, however. If Brome revised for the King's company a Heywood play written in 1612 or 1613, that troupe must have had the manuscript. Now Heywood was an active member and a leader of Queen Anne's company from 1603 to 1619. (See above, ii. 472–3, and *Eliz. Stage*, ii. 229–40.) Not only were all his assignable plays of that period written for Queen Anne's men, but as one of the active leaders of the organization he was completely associated with its interests. He would no more have written a play for the rival King's company than William Shakespeare, whose position with the King's company was similar, would have written a play for Queen Anne's. The revision theory is well refuted on other grounds by Robert Grant Martin (*Mod. Phil.* xiii [1915], 253–65).

Since Fleay and Andrews wrote, further doubt of their notion of a revision rather than a collaboration has been raised by the appearance of the King's players' petition to the Lord Chamberlain about this play. The King's men say definitely that it was another company which was having an old play revised to exploit the interest in the Lancashire witches of 1634. Possibly they might have been brazen enough to ask that another company be forbidden to do precisely what they were doing themselves, but it does not seem likely, for Sir Henry Herbert was no fool. Incidentally, the play to which the King's men objected was probably *Doctor Lambe and the Witches*, hastily prepared for the Salisbury Court theatre. (See above, i. 40–42.)

Heywood was not exclusively connected with Queen Henrietta's men at this time, as Fleay thought, for he wrote *A Challenge for Beauty* (q.v.) for the King's men about this time, and his other collaborations with Brome, *The Apprentice's Prize* and *The Life and Death of Sir Martin Skink*, may have been prepared for the same troupe. Altogether, it seems practically certain that Heywood and Brome worked together in 1634 on *The Late Lancashire Witches*. The contradictions and loose ends of the play are easily accounted for by the haste which the petition shows was required.

The composition of the play can be dated with some precision. The petition shows that it was not quite completed—or at least had not yet been 'allowed & Acted'—on 20 July 1634, but the publisher, Ben Fisher, had his manuscript of it on 28 October following.

Andrews attempts (op. cit., pp. 50–53) to assign their respective parts to Brome and Heywood, but since he assumes revision and assigns to Heywood what seems to be old material and to Brome all new material and revisions, his assignments are ill grounded.

The character of the material, the summer date of production, and the statement on the title-page all show that the play was written for performance at the Globe and not Blackfriars.

'The witches of Lancashire' which Thomas Crosfield reported

at Oxford, among the other entertainments which came to town at the Act time, was probably a puppet-show of some sort, since he seems to distinguish it from the plays and lists it with such things as rope-dancing, 'The lion', 'The Camells', 'The water-workes', and 'A person with a cloven foot'. It does indicate the popularity of the subject if not of the play. Of the same sort are Thomas Nabbes's reference in *Tottenham Court* (I. 2, B$_2$^{v}),

how many doubles shee [a hare] made, and mock't his Worships hope of a better dinner so long, till hee thought in his conscience she was a *Lancashire* Witch,

and Thomas Shadwell's in *The Humorists* (Act v, sig. K$_1$),

I am the Son of a *Lancashire* Witch, if thou art not an errant stink-ing Fellow then.

The Life and Death of Sir Martin Skink (c. 1634?)
with Thomas Heywood
(Lost)

1654, 8 Apr. S.R. 'M^r. Mosely. Entred for his Copies Two plaies called. The Life & Death of S^r. Martyn Skink. wth y^e warres of ye Low Countries. by Rich. Broome. & Tho: Heywood. & The Apprentices Prize, &c.' (Greg, *Bibliography*, i. 62.)

Nothing of this play is known beyond the entry in the Sta-tioners' Register. Since the only extant collaboration of Brome and Heywood was on *The Late Lancashire Witches* (q.v.) for the King's men in 1634, it is generally assumed that this collaboration occurred about the same time and for the same company. Fleay suggested (*Biog. Chron.* i. 41) that all three of the Brome–Heywood collaborations were revisions of old Heywood plays by Brome. This is apparently wrong in the case of *The Late Lancashire Witches* (q.v.), and here there is no evidence at all.

One might doubt that this play was written for the King's men on the grounds that the title sounds more like those in vogue at the Red Bull and the Fortune.

The Lovesick Court, or The Ambitious Politique (c. 1632–40)

Harbage, Alfred. *Cavalier Drama*, pp. 158–9.

1640, 4 Aug. S.R. Entered for Crooke 'six Playes vizt. Chris-tianetta. The Iewish gentleman. A new Academy or Exchange.

The love sick Co^{rt}. The Covent Garden. and The English Moore
or mock Marriage by M^r. Rich: Broome.' (Greg, *Bibliography*,
i. 53.)

1658. The Love-sick Court. Or The *Ambitious Politique*. A
Comedy Written by Richard Brome . . . 1658. (Separate title-
page in *Five New Playes*, 1659.)

The prologue for the play indicates that it was not one of
Brome's first, and that the producing company was not one of the
major London troupes.

> *A little wit, lesse learning, no Poetry*
> *This Play-maker dares boast: Tis his modesty.*
> *For though his labours have not found least grace,*
> *It puffs not him up or in minde or face,*
>
> .   .   .   .   .   .
>
> *Sometimes at poor mens boards the curious finde*
> *'Mongst homely fare, some unexpected dish,*
> *Which at great Tables they may want and wish:*
> *If in this slight Collation you will binde*
>   *Us to believe you' have pleasd your pallats here,*
>   *Pray bring your friends w' you next, you know your cheer.*

The play is quite unlike Brome's usual vein and is, in fact,
fairly characteristic of the cavalier drama which he so frequently
scorned. (See Harbage, pp. 158–9.) Since this mode was not congenial to Brome, indeed many of his prologues would lead one to
think it was intolerable to him, it seems likely that *The Lovesick
Court* was a reluctant imitation, or possibly a satirization, of those
plays. It would accordingly date from the thirties when they were
in vogue.

Fleay's guess (*Biog. Chron.* i. 36) at the date as about 1629 is
based only on the similarity of the title to *The Lovesick Maid*,
Brome's lost play, which was licensed 9 February 1628/9.

The Lovesick Maid, or The Honour of Young Ladies
(1628/9)
(Lost)

1628/9, 9 Feb. 'Very soon, indeed, after the ill success of Jonson's
piece [*The New Inn*], the King's Company brought out at the
same theatre [Blackfriars] a new play called *The Love-sick
Maid, or the Honour of Young Ladies*, which was licensed by
Sir Henry Herbert on the 9th of February, 1628–9, and acted
with extraordinary applause. This play, which was written by

Jonson's own servant, Richard Brome, was so popular that
the managers of the King's Company, on the 10th of March,
presented the Master of the Revels with the sum of two pounds,
"on the good success of *The Honour of Ladies*;" the only
instance I have met with of such a compliment being paid
him.' (Adams, *Herbert*, p. 32, from Malone, *Variorum*, i. 421.)

1629, 6 May. 'Hemings. A Warr^t for paym^t of Ten pound[es]
vnto Iohn Hemings for a Play called y^e
Loue sick maid Acted before his Ma^{ty} on Easter Munday [i.e.,
6 April]. May 6th 1629.' (*M.S.C.* ii, Part iii, 349.)

1641, 7 Aug. 'The louesick maid' appears in the list of King's
men's plays which the Lord Chamberlain forbade any printer
to publish without the consent of the players. (See above, i.
65–66.)

1653, 9 Sept. S.R. In a list of forty-one plays entered to Humphrey
Moseley, the second and third are:

Witt in Madnesse
The Louesick Maid, or the honour of Young ⎫ Rich: Brome.
Ladies. by   ⎭

(Greg, *Bibliography*, i. 60–61.)

It is strange that a play which roused so much enthusiasm at
Blackfriars and which reached the hands of a reputable publisher
like Moseley should have been lost. Possibly some member of the
audience which made Brome's play so profitable for the King's
men as to jar them into unaccustomed—though probably not
uncalculated—benevolence ordered a copy which may yet be
found. Though there are no known references to the character of
the play, the title suggests one of the love-and-honour concoctions
which Davenant, Ford, and Massinger were supplying for the
Blackfriars audience in the late twenties and early thirties.

The comparison of the success of this play with the failure of
Jonson's *New Inn* (q.v.) at the same theatre three weeks before
(licensed 19 January 1628/9) was, of course, inevitable because
of the relationship between Jonson and Brome, but Jonson
insured it by his angry *Ode to Himself*, in the earlier versions of
which the following sneers at popular theatrical taste appear:

> Noe doubt A Mouldye Tale,
> Lyke Pericles, and stale
> As the Shriues Crustes; & Nastye as his fish,
> Scrapps out of euery dishe;
> Throwne forth; and rackt in to the Common tubb
> may keepe vpp the play Clubb:

> Broomes sweeping doe as well
> Thear as his Masters Meale,
> For whoe the Relish, of thes guests, will fitt;
> Needes sett them, but the Almes Baskett, of witt.
> (George Bremner Tennant, ed., *The New Inn* [1908], p. xxiii.)

The allusions to Brome and his master were dropped in the version which Jonson published with the 1631 octavo of *The New Inn*, but copies of the original must have circulated—it is the version which John Benson printed with Jonson's translation of Horace in 1640—and J. C.'s reply to Jonson's *Ode* published with the original in Benson's 1640 edition of the translation of Horace seems to refer to this stanza and to Brome's success:

> Let him who daily steales
> From thy most precious meales.
> (Since thy strange plenty findes no losse by it)
> Feed himselfe with the fragments of thy wit.

Certainly Jonson's disciple, Thomas Randolph, knew the original. His reply to Jonson's *Ode* uses the same stanza form and in some places is a rather clever line-for-line imitation of the original, often rearranging the same words. The end of his third stanza and the beginning of his fourth read,

> Yet if they will have any of thy store,
> Give 'em some scraps, and send them from thy door.

> And let those things in plush,
> Till they be taught to blush,
> Like what they will, and more contented be
> With what Broome swept from thee.
> (*Poetical and Dramatic Works of Thomas Randolph*, ed. W. C.
>   Hazlitt [1875], ii. 582.)

But, however hurt the ailing laureate was at the contrast between his own failure and his servant's success at Blackfriars, the estrangement did not last, as witness the revisions in the *Ode* when it was published with *The New Inn* in 1631 and Jonson's commendatory verses for the 1632 quarto of Brome's *Northern Lass*, also produced by the King's men. The title of the verses suggests a desire to make amends:

> To my old Faithfull Seruant: and (by
> his continu'd Vertue) my louing Friend:
> the Author of this Work, M. RICH. BROME.
>   (*Ben Jonson*, viii. 409.)

Gifford, in his eagerness to defend Jonson, confuses the order of the variants of the *Ode* and discovers a plot to embroil Jonson

with Randolph. (See Tennant ed., *The New Inn*, pp. xxi–xxix.)
It was not so difficult to rouse Jonson's ire as Gifford imagined.

A Mad Couple Well Matched (1637?–9)

1639, 10 Aug. 'A mad couple well mett' is one of the plays listed
as the property of the King and Queen's Young Company at
the Cockpit under the governorship of William Beeston and
forbidden to all other companies by the Lord Chamberlain.
(See above, i. 330–1.)

1653. 'A Mad Couple Well Match'd' is the first play in *Five New
Playes*, but there is no separate title-page for it as there is for
the four other plays in the volume.

1659, 11 June. S.R. Richard Marriott assigned to Humphrey
Moseley twenty-one titles, of which the last was 'Five new
Playes. vizt The mad Couple well Matcht. The Novella: The
Court Beggar. The Cittie Witt. The Damoiselle. by Rich:
Broome.' (Greg, *Bibliography*, i. 67.)

1667, 20 Sept. '. . . by coach to the King's playhouse, and there
saw "The Mad Couple," which I do not remember that I have
seen; it is a pretty pleasant play.' (Diary of Samuel Pepys.
Pepys may have seen James Howard's *All Mistaken, or The
Mad Couple* instead of Brome's play.)

1677. The Debauchee: or The Credulous Cuckold, A Comedy.
Acted at His Highness the Duke of York's Theatre . . . 1677.

Though the play was in the repertory of Beeston's Boys in 1639,
it was not necessarily written for them, for a number of the plays
in that company's repertory had originally been written for Queen
Henrietta's company when they were at the Cockpit but kept at
the theatre when Queen Henrietta's men left and later acted there
by Beeston's Boys. The number of women and boys in the cast
of this play suggests, however, that it was written for a boy rather
than an adult company, i.e. Beeston's Boys. The play cannot
certainly be dated after the abrogation of Brome's contract with
the Salisbury Court theatre in 1638/9, for Brome is said to have
violated his contract by writing a play or two for the Cockpit.
(See above.)

Thus it is only likely, but by no means certain, that Brome
wrote *The Mad Couple* for the King and Queen's Young Company
at the Cockpit after he had broken with the Salisbury Court in
1638/9. A reference in III. 1, to sedan chairs as a usual means of
conveyance suggests a date after 1635, for in *The Sparagus Garden*

of that year Brome had ridiculed sedan chairs as an absurd innovation. Fleay (*Biog. Chron.* i. 39) suggested a reference to Glapthorne's *Ladies' Privilege* in III. 1, but it seems to me more like a proverbial allusion. I do not know why he thought the play dated 1636.

The Debauchee of 1677 is an alteration of Brome's *A Mad Couple Well Matched*. Though the play was published anonymously, it was probably written by Aphra Behn.

The New Academy, or The New Exchange (> 1640)

1640, 4 Aug. S.R. Crooke entered 'six Playes vizt. Christianetta. The Iewish gentleman. A new Academy or Exchange. The love sick Co^{rt}. The Covent Garden. and The English Moore or mock Marriage by M^r. Rich: Broome.' (Greg, *Bibliography*, i. 53.)

1658. The New Academy, Or, the New Exchange. By Richard Brome . . . 1658. (Separate title-page in *Five New Playes*, 1659.)

There is no external evidence concerning this rather dull comedy save the Stationers' Register entry of 1640. Fleay (*Biog. Chron.* i. 38–39) could find 'no definite note of time in this play', but guessed that it might have been written for the King's company about 1628, 'as it has neither Prologue nor Epilogue'!

I can only suggest that the new 'Academy' in Act IV is very much like Shirley's School of Compliment in his play, *The School of Compliment*, which was licensed for the Cockpit 11 February 1624/5 and printed in 1631. If Brome's play had been written as a rival attraction, it would date 1625, but such evidence is too slight to warrant any conclusion.

The Northern Lass (1629)

Nicholson, B. 'The Date of *Northward Ho, A Chaste Maid*, and *The Northern Lass*', *N. & Q.*, Fourth Series, xi (1873), 317–19; reply 386.

1629, 29 July. '*The Northern Lass*, which was acted by the King's Company on the 29th of July, 1629.' (Adams, *Herbert*, p. 32.)

1631/2, 2 Jan. S.R. 'Received of *ffrancis Coules* for ballades belonging to the partners in that stock . . . 6^s . . . 9 *The Louely northerne Lasse.*' (Arber, iv. 234.)

1631/2, 24 Mar. S.R. 'Nich: Vavasor Entred for his Copy vnder

the hands of S^r. Henry Herbert & m^r Islip warden a Comedy
called the Northerne Lasse by m^r Broome.' (Greg, *Bibliography*,
i. 41.)

1632, 3 Sept. S.R. 'ffrancis Grove   Entred for his Copy a Ballad
called *Loves Solace or sweet is the last* [? *lass*] *that loves me.*'
(Arber, iv. 249.)

1632. The Northern Lasse, A Comœdie. As it hath beene often
Acted with good applause, at the Globe, and Black-Fryers. By
his Maiesties Servants. Written by Richard Brome . . . 1632.

1633, 8 July. S.R. 'John Wright and the rest of the Partners in
Ballads. Entred for their Copies these Ballads hereafter men-
cioned being entred since the 30th. of July 1632. to the Eighth
of July 1633 . . . *The Northerne Lasse or sweet is the lasse that
loues me.*' (Arber, iv. 273.)

1638, 29 Nov. 'At the Cocpit the 29th of november   The northern
las.' (From a bill presented by the King's company for plays
acted 'before the king & queene this [present] yeare of our lord
1638'. (Adams, *Herbert*, p. 77.)

1638, 28 Dec. 'At Richmount the 28 of desember the ladie Elsa-
beths berthnight & our day lost at our house   The northern
las.' (Ibid.)

1653, 9 July. S.R. Mary Vavasour, widow of Nicholas, assigned
to Humphrey Moseley her husband's rights in 'a booke or Copie
called The Northerne Lasse, written by M^r. Rich: Broome'.
(Greg, *Bibliography*, i. 60.)

1662, 4 Apr. 'northerne Lasse. 4. Aprill.' appears in a list of performances of plays by 'the Kings Companie at the Red Bull
and the new house in Gibbon's Tennis Court near Clare Market',
1660–2. (Adams, *Herbert*, p. 118.)

1663. [Another edition.] As it hath been Acted with great Applause, at the Theatre-Royal. By His Majesties Servants.
Written by Richard Brome . . . 1663.

1667, 14 Sept. 'To the King's playhouse to see "The Northerne
Castle" [probably *The Northern Lass*], which I think I never
did see before. Knipp acted in it, and did her part very extraordinary well; but the play is but a mean, sorry play; but the
house very full of gallants. It seems, it hath not been acted
a good while.' (Diary of Samuel Pepys.)

1668/9, *c.* 12 Jan. In 'A Catalogue of part of His Ma^{tes} Servants
Playes as they were formerly acted at the Blackfryers & now
allowed of to his Ma^{tes} Servants at ye New Theatre' occurs the
title 'The Northern Lasse'. (A. Nicoll, *A History of Restoration
Drama 1660–1700*, 3rd ed., pp. 315–16.)

1684. [Another edition.] As 'tis Acted at the Theatre-Royal . . .
1684.
1706. The Northern Lass, or, The Nest of Fools. A Comedy. . . .
The Sixth Impression. . . . 1706.
1717. [Another edition.]

The popularity of this play is variously attested. The number
of editions indicates its appeal to readers. The two performances
within a month in 1638 before the same courtly audience indicate
its contemporary theatrical success. And it must be remembered
that most records of court performances by even so well known
a company as the King's men have been lost (see above, i. 94–100),
and that therefore there may have been other performances before
royalty. The three ballad entries in the Stationers' Register seem
to indicate efforts to capitalize on the success of the play. The
most unequivocal evidence of its popularity occurs in the apolo-
getical prologue to T. B.'s *The Country Girl* (q.v.), which sets up
The Northern Lass and its singing heroine as a standard of success.
After naming several popular appeals which his play does not
have, the author says:

> *None of these?*
> *Alas poore Girle, where's then, thy hope to please?*
> *What can she sing? and, like the Northern Lasse,*
> *(That brave blithe Girle) hope to procure a passe?*

Brome was proud of the success of his play and issued it—his
first known publication—with a collection of commendatory front
matter. There are verses by Ben Jonson, F. T., St[ephen] Br[ome],
John Ford, Thomas Dekker, and another F. T. Brome dedicated
the play to Richard Holford, Esquire, from whom he says he has
received 'real favours'. This dedication has one rather cryptic
phrase. Brome says that his Northern Lass gained many lovers
and friends and lived prosperously 'until her late long Silence,
and Discontinuance (to which she was comppell'd) gave her justly
to fear their losse and her own decay'. Fleay (*Biog. Chron.* i. 37)
asserted that this long silence referred to the plague closing of
1631. But that closing cannot have lasted for more than fifteen
or sixteen weeks and probably for less. (See above, ii. 658–9.) The
period does not seem very long as compared to the eight months'
closing in 1625 and seven in 1630. (Ibid., pp. 654–8.) Furthermore,
Brome's play was licensed for printing on 24 March 1631/2, and
presumably he wrote his dedication about that time. This was
nine and a half months after the end of the plague closing of
1631, which occurred not later than 10 June. The term 'late' does

not seem very apt so long after. Could the phrase, 'to which she was comppell'd', refer to some action applying to this play alone? There seems to be no material in it which could be called offensive. It is true there is a reference to *A Game at Chess* and Gondomar in the last scene, but it does not seem censorable; the notorious Spanish match was five or six years in the past when the play was written.

Jonson's praise of Brome in his verses for the quarto made up for his sneers three years before in his *Ode to Himself*. The commendatory verses by the 'rogue' Dekker insist on the closeness of the author's relationship to Brome: they are addressed to 'my Sonne Broom', the second line refers to Brome as Dekker's 'Son and Friend', and the last eight lines play on the idea that the Northern Lass, Brome's daughter, is therefore Dekker's granddaughter. The lines are more intimate than Jonson's and would be appropriate for a collaborator, but there is no record of such collaboration.

Most plays of the King's company published in this period mention only the Blackfriars theatre on the title-page (see above, i. 30, n. 6), whereas the 1632 quarto of this play records that it was acted at 'The Globe and Black-Fryers'. Probably it was acted first at the Globe, since it was licensed in July, the middle of the Globe season. The character of the play, almost ballad-opera in type, seems more appropriate to the Globe than to Blackfriars.

Edward F. Rimbault says that Dr. Wilson wrote music for *The Northern Lass* of which 'one or two pieces exist in MS in the Music School, Oxford'. (*Bonduca*, ed. for the Musical Antiquarian Society, London [1842], p. 11.) There are records of several eighteenth-century productions of the play. (Nicoll, *A History of Early Eighteenth Century Drama*, pp. 47, 129, 130, 131.)

The Novella (1632)

Sharpe, Robert Boies. 'The Sources of Richard Brome's *The Novella*', *Stud. Phil.* xxx (1933), 69–85.

1641, 7 Aug. 'The Nouella' appears in the list of King's men's plays which the Lord Chamberlain forbade any printer to publish without the consent of the players. (See above, i. 65–66.)

1653. The Novella, A *Comedie*. Acted at the *Black-Friers*, by his Majesties Servants, *Anno* 1632. Written by Richard Brome . . .

1653. (Separate title-page for the second piece in Moseley, Marriott, and Dring's edition of *Five New Playes*, 1653.)

1659, 11 June. S.R. Richard Marriott assigned to Humphrey
Moseley twenty-one copyrights, of which the last is 'Five new
Playes. vizt The mad Couple well Matcht. The Novella: The
Court Beggar. The Cittie Witt. The Damoiselle. by Rich:
Broome. One 3ᵈ parte.' (Greg, *Bibliography*, i. 67.)

1668/9, *c.* 12 Jan. In 'A Catalogue of part of His Maᵗᵉˢ Servants
Playes as they were formerly acted at the Blackfryers & now
allowed of to his Maᵗᵉˢ Servants at yᵉ New Theatre' occurs the
title 'The Novella'. (A. Nicoll, *A History of Restoration Drama
1660–1700*, 3rd ed., pp. 315–16.)

The play evidently achieved some popularity in the repertory
of the King's men, for they took pains to have the Lord Chamberlain protect it for them in 1641, though they did not include
Brome's *Queen's Exchange* or his *Weeding of the Covent Garden*.
(See above, i. 65–66.) The intrigue plot and the disguises are
rather complicated, but they might well be titillating on the
Blackfriars stage, as would the innocent courtesan, the Novella.

Robert Boies Sharpe thinks that Brome took much of his
material, especially about the Venetian courtesans, from *Coryat's
Crudities*, 1611, Fynes Moryson's *Itinerary*, 1617, and the manuscript of the still unpublished fourth part of the *Itinerary*. (Op.
cit.) A few of the details do seem to come from these sources,
especially *Coryat's Crudities*, but no plot material. Sharpe has
grossly exaggerated his case. However, his notation of the custom
of throwing perfume balls by gallants and courtesans demolishes
Fleay's contention (*Biog. Chron.* i. 38) that the lines, 'Some Night-
walkers, that throw / Balls at their Mistresses' (I. 1), are references
to Shirley's *The Ball* and his revision of Fletcher's *Night-Walker*.

The Queen and Concubine (1635–9?)

Koeppel, Emil. 'The Queen And Concubine. A Comedie By
Richard Brome', *Quellen und Forschungen*, lxxxii (1897), 209–
18.

1659. The Queen and Concubine. A Comedie By *Richard Brome*
. . . 1659. (Separate title-page in *Five New Playes*, 1659.)

No external evidence concerning this long and confused tragi-
comedy has been cited. Fleay (*Biog. Chron.* i. 39) suggested that
the play was written for the King's Revels company because at
the end of v. 7, when Lodovico sends the citizens of Palermo

away to the curate to prepare to entertain the King, Andrea says
as they leave,

> Come then, let's away,
> No longer Brothers of the Bench wee'l be,
> But of the Revels for his Majesty.

The punning allusion is sufficiently conspicuous to be deliberate
and probably would not have been used in the play of any competing company. Moreover, the association of Brome with the
King's Revels company was much closer than Fleay knew, for
after he wrote Wallace discovered that Brome signed a contract
with the King's Revels company, 20 July 1635, to write three plays
a year for them for three years, and that he did write six plays
for them in the period 1635–8 and two more after this contract
expired. (See above.) Fleay knew of Brome's association with the
company only through the title-page of *The Sparagus Garden*.

Presumably, then, the play dates from the term of Brome's
association with the King's Revels company, 1635–9. During
fifteen months of this time the theatres were closed because of
the plague (see above, ii. 661–5), but Brome might have written
plays for their use on the road.

Koeppel pointed out (op. cit.) that Greene's *Penelope's Web* is
the source of the play, followed closely in parts, but with additions
and elaborations elsewhere.

The Queen's Exchange [The Royal Exchange] (? 1631–2 ?)

Nicholson, B. 'R. Brome's "Queen's Exchange," 1657, and
"Royal Exchange," 1661', *N. & Q.*, Seventh Series, vii (16
February 1889), 126–7.

1656, 20 Nov. S.R. Entered for Randolph Taylor 'a Comedy
called The Queens Exchange Acted with generall Applause at
ye Blackfry^rs. by his Majesties Servants written by Mr Rich:
Brome'. (Greg, *Bibliography*, i. 65.)

1657. The Queenes Exchange, A Comedy Acted with generall
applause at the *Black-Friers* By *His* Majesties *Servants*.
Written By Mr. Richard Brome . . . Printed for *Henry Brome*
. . . 1657.

1661. The Royall Exchange . . . 1661. [A reissue of sheets of the
1657 edition with a new title-page.]

When Henry Brome published this tragi-comedy in 1657, he
said in the preface that '*when 'twas written, or where acted, I know*

not', yet on the title-page of the same edition there appeared the statement, presumably at his direction, 'Acted with generall applause at the *Black-Friers* By *His* Majesties *Servants*'. Perhaps the title-page is right and Brome secured additional information after he wrote his preface, but one cannot escape the troublesome thought that 'acted by His Majesty's Servants at the Blackfriars' was probably the best advertising a play could have in 1657 or for several decades before. The tragi-comedy has a number of effective scenes, but in places it seems too naïve in its technique for a sophisticated Blackfriars audience.

Fleay asserted (*Biog. Chron.* i. 37) that the date was fixed by Jeffrey's statement in II. 2, 'The King we make no doubt of, we have pray'd / For him these seven years.' It is true that casual statements of this kind frequently refer to the current year in Jacobean and Caroline plays, regardless of their setting in time and place, and that the seventh year of Charles I was 1631-2, but one would like some confirmation.

Henry Brome's title of *The Royal Exchange* was only a fraudulent attempt to sell the remaining sheets of the 1657 edition; it does not increase one's confidence in his statement about the performance of the play on the 1657 title-page.

The Royal Exchange

See *The Queen's Exchange*.

The Sparagus Garden (1635)

Miles, Theodore. 'Place-Realism in a Group of Caroline Plays', *R.E.S.* xviii (1942), 428-40.

1639/40, 19 Mar. S.R. Constable entered 'three Playes called. Sparagus garden. The Antipodes. & Witt in a Madnes. [by Ric *deleted*].' (Greg, *Bibliography*, i. 52.)

1640. The Sparagvs Garden: *A Comedie*. Acted in the yeare 1635, by the then Company of Revels, at *Salisbury* Court. The Author *Richard Brome* . . . 1640.

1647/8, 17 Feb. S.R. The administrators of the estate of Alice Constable, widow of Francis Constable, transferred to Thrale twenty copyrights, including '14. Sparagus garden a play. 15. The Antipodes. a play. 16. Witt in a Madnes. a play.' (Greg, *Bibliography*, i. 58.)

1681, 11 Apr. S.R. Dorothy Thrale, administratrix of Richard

Thrale, assigned the same three plays with thirty-nine other titles to Benjamin Thrale. (Ibid. i. 74.)

The Sparagus Garden was a spectacularly popular play, if any confidence can be placed in a lawsuit statement quoted indirectly and vaguely by C. W. Wallace to the effect that the company made a profit of £1,000 on the play. (See above, iii. 53.) Such a phenomenal return would put this comedy in a class with Middleton's *Game at Chess* (see above, i. 9–14), but I suspect gross exaggeration here. There are numerous allusions from contemporaries to *A Game at Chess*, but the only one I have found to *The Sparagus Garden*, besides the commendatory verses to the quarto, is the one in the long epilogue to Brome's *Court Beggar*, presumably written by the author himself:

And let me tell you he [the author] has made many prety merry Jigges that ha' pleas'd a many. As (le'me see) th' *Antipodes*, and (oh I shall never forget) *Tom Hoyden o' Tanton Deane*. Hee'l bring him hither very shortly in a new Motion, and in a new paire o' slops and new nether stocks as briske as a Body-lowse in a new Pasture.

The play was one of the series with Marmion's *Holland's Leaguer*, produced December 1631, Shirley's *Hyde Park*, April 1632, Brome's *Weeding of the Covent Garden*, 1632, Nabbes's *Covent Garden*, 1632/3, and Nabbes's *Tottenham Court*, 1633, which made explicit use of particular places in London. (See Miles, op. cit.) In this play the third act is given up to largely irrelevant scenes concerning the conduct of the currently popular Asparagus Garden in the suburbs.

The Sparagus Garden is basically a comedy of intrigue, like others of Brome's plays, but it was probably the farcical satire which, along with the garden scenes, made the play popular. There are several references to the new sedan chairs and one brief discussion of *The Knight of the Burning Pestle* (II. 2), which was probably appearing at the Phoenix about this time. (See the two 1635 quartos of *The Knight of the Burning Pestle* and the court performance of 1635/6 listed in Adams, *Herbert*, p. 56.)

This is one of the four plays—*The Sparagus Garden*, *The Northern Lass*, *The Antipodes*, and *The Jovial Crew*—which were published with dedications and commendatory verses and therefore presumably the only ones printed with the consent and co-operation of the author. *The Late Lancashire Witches* is the only other play of his which appeared in his lifetime, but it is without author's front matter. *The Sparagus Garden* is dedicated to William, Earl of Newcastle, a patron of Ben Jonson and James

Shirley and here called 'Governour to the Prince his Highnesse'. It may be significant that Brome notes especially Newcastle's position in the establishment of the young Prince Charles. When Brome signed his contract as playwright for the Salisbury Court theatre in July 1635 (see above), he had recently been connected with the Red Bull theatre. The occupants of that theatre in 1634 and later were Prince Charles's (II) company. (See above, i. 309 ff.) Possibly Newcastle's 'favourable *Construction* of [Brome's] poore *Labours*' indicates some contact between the two in the affairs of Prince Charles's company.

Commendatory verses, which say little, were furnished for the play by C. G. (Charles Gerbier? See Andrews, *Richard Brome*, pp. 21–22) and by R. W.

Tom Hoyden o' Tanton Deane

A ghost title. Tom Hoyden is a low-comedy character in Brome's *Sparagus Garden* who is referred to as a popular hit in the epilogue to Brome's *Court Beggar*. One or two scholars have mistakenly taken the name as a play title because it occurs with *The Antipodes*, and it has thus crept into play lists.

The Weeding of the Covent Garden, or The Middlesex Justice of Peace (1632 and *c.* 1642)

Miles, Theodore. 'Place-Realism in a Group of Caroline Plays', *R.E.S.* xviii (1942), 428–40.

1640, 4 Aug. S.R. Entered for Crooke 'six Playes vizt. Christianetta. The Iewish gentleman. A new Academy or Exchange. The love sick Co^{rt}. The Covent Garden. and The English Moore or mock Marriage by M^r. Rich: Broome.' (Greg, *Bibliography*, i. 53.)

1658. The Weeding of the Covent-Garden. Or the *Middlesex-Jvstice* of Peace. A Facetious *Comedy*. A *Posthume* of Richard Brome, an Ingenious Servant, and Imitator of his Master, that famously Renowned Poet *Ben. Johnson*...1658. (Separate title-page in *Five New Playes*, 1659.)

This play belongs to a small group which exploited the vogue for place realism in the early thirties (see Miles, op. cit.); they all feature explicit descriptions of and comments upon particular places in London. The five are Marmion's *Holland's Leaguer* (produced December 1631), Shirley's *Hyde Park* (April 1632), Brome's

Weeding of the Covent Garden (1632), Nabbes's *Covent Garden* (1632/3) and *Tottenham Court* (1633), and Brome's *Sparagus Garden* (1635). *The Weeding of the Covent Garden* opens with very precise comments on features of the new buildings in Covent Garden, as if the two characters on the stage were viewing them, but there is little such place particularity after the first scene.

From the references in Nabbes's *Covent Garden*, whose title-page says that it was 'Acted in the Yeare MDCXXXII [i.e. 1632/3— see under Nabbes] By the *Queenes* Majesties Servants', it is clear that Brome's play antedated Nabbes's, as Fleay saw (*Biog. Chron.* i. 37–38). Nabbes is most anxious to disclaim indebtedness to Brome and makes several clear references to the earlier play in the prologue to his *Covent Garden*:

> *Doe not expect th' abuses of a* Place;
> *Nor th' ills sprung from a Strumpets painted* face
> *To be exprest. Our* Author *doth not meane*
> *With such vile* stuffe *to clothe his* modest Scæne.
> *Nor doth he brand it with a* Satyres *marke*;
> *But makes a* Justice *wiser then his* Clerke.
> *His* Rusticks *likewise will pretend to* Wit:
> *So all the* Persons *which wee counterfeit.*
> *He justifies that 'tis no borrow'd* Straine,
> *From the invention of anothers* braine.
> *Nor did he steale the* Fancie. *'Tis the same*
> *He first intended by the* proper Name.

These references to Brome's setting in the first line, to his prostitutes, Bettie, Frank, and Madge, and to Dorcas's prostitute-disguise in the second, to Justice Cockbrain in lines 5 and 6, to the Covent Garden idea in lines 10 and 11, and to the title in the last line, together with his repeated protests against accusation of imitation, make it impossible to doubt that Nabbes was referring to *The Weeding of the Covent Garden*. One might add that he protests too much and thereby makes it clear enough that his *Covent Garden* was written to help a rival company exploit the popular interest in the great building development in Covent Garden, whose dramatic appeal Brome had discovered.

Nabbes's references to the details of Brome's play, which he clearly expected his audience to recognize, indicate that Brome's comedy was quite recent, i.e. 1632, and none of the references in the play itself contradicts this date. Fleay thought that certain allusions in the play established 1632 definitely (*Biog. Chron.* i. 37–38), but it is very doubtful if Mihil is referring to Prynne's *Histriomastix* in IV. 2, and there were other proclamations of restraint besides the one of 1632 which Mihil might possibly have intended in II. I. (See Norman G. Brett-James, *The Growth of Stuart London*, passim.) None the less, Nabbes's prologue is so particular and explicit that it could not refer to a play more than a few months old and therefore establishes 1632 as the date for *The Weeding of the Covent Garden*.

There is no external evidence that *The Weeding of the Covent Garden* was produced by the King's men, but it seems probable. The company which produced Brome's comedy must have been a rival of Queen Henrietta's men, who produced Nabbes's competing *Covent Garden*. The London companies competing with that troupe in 1632 were the King's men, the King's Revels, and Prince Charles's (II) company. (See above, i, *passim*.) The King's men were by far the strongest of these competitors. Furthermore Brome is known to have been writing for that troupe for at least three years, and he worked for them again in 1634 when he collaborated with Heywood on *The Late Lancashire Witches* (q.v.). His work for the King's Revels is not known to have begun until 1635. One hesitates to assign the play to the King's company, however, because it does not appear in the list of plays protected for them by the Lord Chamberlain in 1641 (See above, i. 65–66.) The play was revived in 1641 or 1642 (see below), presumably by the original company, and it seems likely that if they had just revived or intended to revive it, the King's men would have asked the Lord Chamberlain to protect the play, for it had not yet been published. Moreover, the seven women's roles in this play seem too many for an adult company. The evidence is not clear. Did Brome begin writing for the King's Revels company—which had plenty of boys for such a cast—earlier than has been supposed? Did he write the play for Prince Charles's (II) company?

We know from one of the prologues that there was a revival of *The Weeding of the Covent Garden*, probably in 1641 or 1642. The play was published with two prologues and two epilogues. The second prologue begins:

> *'Tis not amisse ere we begin our Play,*
> *T' intreat you, that you take the same surveigh*
> *Into your fancie, as our Poet took,*
> *Of* Covent-Garden, *when he wrote his Book.*
> *Some ten years since . . .*

and it concludes:

> *The Play may still retain its former grace.*

This revival had to occur, of course, before the closing of the theatres in September 1642, and probably even 1641 would have been close enough to the play's tenth anniversary to allow the statement of age.

Wit in a Madness (1635 ?–9)
(Lost)

1639/40, 19 Mar. S.R. Entered for Constable 'three Playes called. Sparagus garden. The Antipodes. & Witt in a Madnes. [by Ric *deleted*.]' (Greg, *Bibliography*, i. 52.)

1647/8, 17 Feb. S.R. The administrators of the estate of Alice Constable, widow of Francis Constable, transferred to Richard Thrale twenty copyrights, including '14. Sparagus garden a play. 15. The Antipodes. a play. 16. Witt in a Madnes. a play.' (Ibid., p. 58.)

1681, 11 Apr. S.R. Dorothy Thrale, administratrix of Richard Thrale, assigned the same three plays with thirty-nine other titles to Benjamin Thrale. (Ibid., p. 74.)

The play is not extant, and I know of no allusions to it beyond the three entries in the Stationers' Register. *The Antipodes* and *The Sparagus Garden*, with which it was registered, were both written under Brome's contract with the Salisbury Court theatre, a contract which Brome broke after Easter 1639. (See above.) There is evidence of bad feeling at the time the contract was broken, and apparently there was a lawsuit. Since one of the terms of the contract was that Brome would not publish the plays he wrote for the Salisbury Court, it seems a plausible guess that all three of these plays are Salisbury Court plays given to the publisher with some spite after the contract was broken early in 1639. If so, the play was written for the King's Revels company 1635–7 or Queen Henrietta's company 1637–9.

Of course it is possible that *Wit in a Madness* was not written by Brome.

SIR GEORGE BUC (Buck, Bucke)
1562 or 1563–1622

Bald, R. C. 'A Revels Office Entry', *T.L.S.*, 17 March 1927, p. 193.

Eccles, Mark. 'Sir George Buc, Master of the Revels', in *Thomas Lodge and Other Elizabethans*, edited by Charles J. Sisson (1933), pp. 409–506.

The only evidence for a playwright of this name is found in the entry in Abraham Hill's list of plays in manuscript (see Middleton, *The Conqueror's Custom*):

the ambitious brother   G. Buc

The best-known man of the name is Sir George Buc, who received his patent of reversion of the Office of Master of the Revels in 1603, was active in the office at least as early as 1606, and was Master from 1610 to 1622. (Eccles, 'Sir George Buc', pp. 434, 462–4, 481–2.) This man was born in 1562 or 1563 (ibid., p. 420), studied law at Thavies Inn, the New Inn, and the Middle Temple in the middle eighties, served against the Armada, was a member of Parliament in 1593 and 1597, and acted in various capacities about the court before he obtained the reversion of the Mastership of the Revels. (Ibid., pp. 420–1, 424–37.) He was removed from office when he became mad in 1622 and died 31 October of that year. (Ibid., pp. 481–4.)

Buc was the author of *The Baron, or Magazin of Honour*; *A Commentary upon the New Roulle of Winchester* (same as *The Baron*?); *The Third Universitie of England*, 1615; *The History of the Life and Reigne of Richard the Third*, 1646, and several poems, treatises, and accounts.

J. Q. Adams in his discussion of the titles in Hill's list (*Library*, Fourth Series, xx [1939], 94–95) thinks it unlikely that the Master of the Revels should have written this play and suggests that Hill mistook Buc's signature to the licence at the end of the manuscript as an author's signature, or that some other George Buc was intended.

Considering the amount of literary work of different kinds which Buc composed and the large proportion which was never published, together with the record of the quantity of manuscript in his possession at the time of his death (Eccles, pp. 494–5), it seems to me that the most plausible interpretation of Hill's note is that he had seen the manuscript of an unrecorded play by the Master of the Revels. It is noteworthy that the form of the name copied by Hill, 'G. Buc', was Sir George Buc's usual signature. (Ibid., pp. 456, 462, and Greg, *Dram. Doc.*, p. 264.)

The Ambitious Brother (1582?–1622?)
(Lost)

This title is thirty-ninth in the list of manuscript plays found among the papers of Abraham Hill. (See Middleton, *The*

Conqueror's Custom.) The list seems to have been Hill's record of some bookseller's stock, set down between 1677 and 1703, but it is notable that nearly all the identifiable plays and playwrights are Jacobean and Caroline.

The title does not appear elsewhere, and the only clue to its date is Hill's assignment of authorship to G. Buc. If Hill were correct and the Buc intended were the Master of the Revels, then the play would date some time between 1582, when Buc was about twenty, and his death in 1622. If one accepts J. Q. Adams's suggestion (*Library*, Fourth Series, xx [1939], 94–95) that Hill was confused and Buc was simply the signer of the licence, not the author, then the play would date between the first of his known licences for the press in 1606 and his removal from office in 1622. The suggestion (ibid.) that the play might have been a dramatization of Buc's *Historie of the Life and Reigne of Richard the Third* is pure speculation.

HENRY BURKHEAD

fl. 1640–5

Henry Burkhead is known only as the author of *The Tragedy of Cola's Fury, or Lirenda's Misery*. One of the writers of commendatory verses for the play, William Smyth, calls the author his '*loving and respected friend Mr.* Henry Burkhead *Merchant*'. Anthony à Wood says, 'I find one *Henry Burkhead* who wrote a Tragedy called *Cola's Fury, or Lirenda's Misery* . . . but the said *Burkhead* was no Academian, only a Merchant of *Bristol*'. (*Athenæ Oxon.*, 1721 ed., ii. 1007.) I know of no evidence for the Bristol association; possibly Wood invented it.

Burkhead was presumably an Irish patriot, since the whole matter of his play is the treachery and cruelty of the Angoleans (the English) and the virtues of the Lirendans (the Irish).

Cola's Fury or Lirenda's Misery (1645 ?)

Harbage, Alfred. *Cavalier Drama*, pp. 178–9.

1646. A Tragedy of Cola's Fvrie, or Lirenda's Miserie. Written by Henry Burkhead, 1645. Printed at Kilkenny, 1645. And are to be sold at the signe of the white Swanne, in Kilkenny, M.DC.XLVI.

The play is a crude and diaphanously veiled account of Irish

affairs. The dedication to Edward Somerset, Lord Herbert, says
that the subject is drawn from records of foreign countries and
is 'fitly applyable to the distempers of this kingdome' and that
Lord Herbert has come, with great danger, 'to appease the raging
fury of our intestine harmes'. Lirenda is Ireland, and the Angoleans are English. In the British Museum copy of the play, a
number of the names in an incomplete dramatis personae have
been identified in an old hand. Unfortunately the first few letters
of nearly every name have been trimmed away, and the ink is
badly faded, but what remains seems to be:

rsons	Pitho	llnie (?)	Ruffus
alass	Berosus	Read	
Ch. Coote	Cola	ston	Abner
ongan	Belfrida	ldlae (?)	Caespilona
nwall	Cephalon	sle	Lysana

These fragmentary identifications and the action of the play
suggest that the characters were probably meant to represent the
following men: Pitho, Sir William Parsons; Berosus, Sir John
Borlase; Osirus, the Earl of Ormonde; Cola, Sir Charles Coote;
Cephalon, Sir Nicholas Barnwall; Abner, Thomas Preston;
Lysana, Lord Lisle. A little study of the play and of the Rebellion
of 1641 would probably enable one to identify most of the characters. The transparency of the allegory is indicated by the lines
of Dora in the first act:

> we are departed from our home, under
> the conduct of a happy leader, to whom
> as to the publique good we owe the tender
> of life, estate and fortune, for royal *Carola*
> his just prerogative, wrested from him
> by an elected crew of shameless *Round-heads*;
> wherefore lets once again confirme our vow
> in his defence, that is most deere to us.

The action opens with events about the beginning of the revolt
late in 1641 and ends with the truce proclamation of September
1643. It is not unlikely, therefore, that the rather unusual statement of authorship on the title-page means that Burkhead composed the play in 1645. Strictly speaking, it ought not to be
included in this volume.

The Female Rebellion (c. 1658)

MSS.: Bodleian MS. Tanner 466, fols. 174 seq.; University of
Glasgow, MS. Hunterian 635.

Edition: 'The Female Rebellion. A tragi-comedy [in five acts, partly in prose and partly verse] from a MS. in the Hunterian Museum, University of Glasgow. [Edited by A. S., i.e. Alexander Smith, with notes partly by J. P. Collier] pp. 88. *Privately printed: Glasgow*, 1872. . . . *Only 50 copies printed.*' (*British Museum Catalogue of Printed Books.*)

This play, which survives in two manuscripts and Alexander Smith's edition of 1872, is inscribed in the Bodleian MS., 'H. B.', which a contemporary hand has identified as the initials, and the hand as the autograph of Henry Birkhead, presumably the Oxford poet and scholar from whose bequest the Oxford professorship of poetry was founded. (See *D.N.B.*)

Professor Harbage notes that the conception of antiquity displayed in *The Female Rebellion* seems much too naïve for a classics scholar like Birkhead. (*T.L.S.*, 8 November 1934, p. 775, and *Cavalier Drama*, pp. 179 and 189, n. 18.) Since the allegorical treatment of contemporary events is much like that in *Cola's Fury*, Harbage suggests that Henry Birkhead, the Latin poet, may have been confused with Henry Burkhead, the merchant. He points out that the events treated in *The Female Rebellion* are not those subsequent to 1680, as the editors of the 1872 text thought, but those of the last years of the Interregnum, nearer to the events of *Cola's Fury*, but well beyond the period under discussion here.

HENRY BURNELL
fl. 1641

His play *Landgartha* is the principal item in our knowledge of Henry Burnell. J. T. Gilbert recorded in the *D.N.B.* that the Burnells were an Anglo-Irish family with estates in Leinster and that Henry appears to have been the son and heir of Christopher Burnell of Castleknock, near Dublin, and to have married the daughter of the Earl of Roscommon. He added that Henry Burnell was a member of the Irish Confederation in 1642. One of the three sets of commendatory verses for *Landgartha* is entitled 'Patri suo Charissimo operis Encomium' and signed 'Eleonora Burnell'.

In his commendatory verses for *Landgartha* 'Io. Bermingham' says that Burnell had never been in England. The prologue says that the author's first play 'met with too much spite' and that this is his second. It is presumably this reference to an unknown play of Burnell's which led Harbage to list *The Toy* and *The Irish Gentleman* as 'Possibly Burnell, H.' (*Annals of the English Drama, 975–1700*, p. 112.) For these plays, now lost, Shirley wrote prologues when he was in Ireland, but there is no indication that Burnell was the author of either.

The *British Museum General Catalogue of Printed Books* lists as by Henry Burnell a translation from Aristophanes, *The World's Idol, or Plutus the God of Wealth*, published in 1659 as by 'H. H. B.', on what authority I do not know.

Landgartha (1639/40)

Stockwell, La Tourette. *Dublin Theatres and Theatre Customs* (1938), pp. 17–22.

1639/40, 17 Mar. 'This Play was first Acted on *S. Patricks* day, 1639. with the allowance of the Master of the Revels.' (1641 quarto, K_1^v.)

1641. Landgartha. A Tragie-Comedy, as it was presented in the new Theater in *Dublin*, with good applause, being an Ancient story, *Written by* H. B. . . . Printed at *Dublin*, Anno 1641. (The dedication is signed '*Henry Burnell*'.)

The date of the play is conveniently fixed by the statement about performance at the end of the quarto, a date which probably means 1639/40, however, rather than the 1638/9 often assumed. The epilogue says that the author spent less than two months on the play.

Though Burnell's cousin, John Bermingham, says in his commendatory verses for the play that Burnell was never in England, various contemporary influences are apparent. Bermingham himself compares Burnell's work to Jonson's, and the author makes his armed prologue call attention to the armed prologue of 'The best of English Poets for the Stage', i.e. in *Poetaster*. Other similarities to Jonson are less discernible than Bermingham and probably Burnell himself fondly imagined. Various characters and situations suggest Fletcher, as does the author's indignant statement about the essentials of tragi-comedy at the end of the play, but the most pervasive influence apparent is the effeminacy of the courtier dramatists, epitomized in the title and in the dedication 'To all faire, indifferent faire, vertuous, that are not faire and magnanimous Ladies'. This effeminate tone of the play is often ludicrously in contrast with the chronicle material on which it is based.

Langbaine (*An Account of the English Dramatick Poets*, p. 42) suggested Krantzius, Saxo Grammaticus, and Josephus Magnus as the sources of the Danish history which is the basis of the play; Chetwood (*General History of the Stage* [1749], p. 52, n. *a*] suggested Saxo Grammaticus.

— BURROUGHS

fl. > 1646

Nothing is known of this man save that the last of the forty-nine plays entered in the Stationers' Register to Robinson and Moseley in September 1646 is said to be by 'm^r Burroughes'.

The Fatal Friendship (> 1646)

1646, 4 [*or* 4–15] Sept. S.R. Added to a list of forty-eight plays entered to Robinson and Moseley is 'The fatall friendship. by m^r Burroughes'. (Greg, *Bibliography*, i. 56–57.)

1672/3, 30 Jan. S.R. Number 97 in a list of 105 titles transferred from Humphrey Robinson as executor of Humphrey Robinson to John Martyn and Henry Herringman is 'Burroughs fatall frendship. halfe'. (Ibid., pp. 72–73.)

1683, 21 Aug. S.R. Number 104 in a list of 360 titles transferred from Sarah Martin, relict of John Martin, to Robert Scott is 'Burroughes fatall freindship'. (Ibid., p. 75.)

The play is known only from the three entries in the Stationers' Register. The original list of forty-nine plays entered in 1646 contains forty-six plays known to have belonged to the King's company; of the remaining three, Carlell's *Spartan Ladies* may well have been theirs (see above, i. 117), and the other two, Killigrew's *Princess* and this play, cannot be associated with any other company. It seems not unlikely, therefore, that Moseley had secured a section of the repertory of the King's company of which *The Fatal Friendship* was a part. He was at this time preparing the Beaumont and Fletcher Folio which was published the next year; indeed the majority of plays in this list are plays issued in that volume. The King's men certainly had a close connexion with the Beaumont and Fletcher Folio, for the ten leading members of the company signed the dedication.

ROBERT BURTON
1576/7-1639/40

Jordon-Smith, Paul. *Bibliographia Burtoniana* (1931), *passim*.
—— (ed.). *Robert Burton's Philosophaster, with an English Trans-lation of the Same. Together with His Other Minor Writings in Prose and Verse* (1931), pp. ix–xii and 239–78.

The Anatomist was born at Lindley Hall in Leicestershire, the fourth child of Ralph and Dorothy Burton. He says he was at school in Nuneaton and Sutton-Coldfield in Warwickshire. In 1593 he went to Brasenose College, Oxford, but in 1599 he was elected student of Christ Church. He took degrees of B.A. in 1602, M.A. in 1605, and B.D. in 1614. Though he remained for the rest of his life at Christ Church, where he was tutor and librarian, he held three livings, St. Thomas, Oxford, from 1616, Walesby from 1624 to 1631, and Segrave in Leicestershire from about 1630. He contributed verses to eighteen collections of Oxford verse from 1603 to 1638, and a poem and preface to the 1617 edition of Rider's *Dictionary*.

The first edition of the famous *Anatomy of Melancholy* appeared in 1621. Burton continued to revise and reissue the book until his death, 25 January 1639/40. He was buried in Christ Church Cathedral, where the famous monument to him was erected by his brother William.

Philosophaster (1606, 1615, 1617/18)

MSS.: W. A. White Library. (This is the manuscript formerly in the possession of William Edward Buckley and edited by him for the Roxburghe Society in 1862. See below.)

Folger Shakespeare Library MS. 1828.2. 'Philosophaster Comædia noua Scripta A° domini 1606 Alterata, reuisa, perfecta Anno domini 1615. Acta demū et publicè exhibita Academicis In aula Ædis Christi, et a studiosis ædis Christi Oxōn alumnis, Anno 1617 Februarij die decimo sexto, die lunæ ad horā sextā pomeri-dianā. Auctore Roberto Burton sacræ Theologiæ Baccalaureo atcɩ, Ædis Christi Oxōn alumno 1617   Osuna scena, opidū Andalusiae In Hispaniæ Bœtica.' On the fly-leaf of the manuscript is the inscription, 'Liber W^{mi} Burton Lindliaci Leicestrêsis de Falde com: Staff: 1618: ex dono fratris mei Robti Burton Authoris'.

Editions: [William Edward Buckley, ed.], *Philosophaster Comoedia, Nunc primum in lucem producta. Poemata, Antehac sparsim edita, Nunc in unum collecta.* Auctore Roberto Bvrtono, S. Th. B. Roxburghe Club (1862).

Paul Jordan-Smith, *Robert Burton's Philosophaster, with an English Translation of the Same. Together with His Other Minor Writings in Prose and Verse* (1931).

Since this play, according to the author's statement, was written in 1606, it does not properly belong in this volume. It is included because the first performance took place after 1616 and because there is no mention of the play in *The Elizabethan Stage*, in conjunction with which this volume is likely to be used.

The essential information about the composition, revision, and performance of the play is given by Burton himself with rare consideration for future historians; indeed, Burton repeats the information about the performance at the end of the 'Actorum Nomina', and again at the end of the epilogue, in the first instance even giving the detail, 'It began about five at night and ended at eight'.

The White MS. gives the cast for the Christ Church performance of 16 February 1617/18, a cast with ten of the same actors who had performed in the Christ Church performance of Holyday's *Technogamia* three days before. (See Cavanaugh ed., pp. 114–16.) At least three plays were given at Christ Church in this year, since Goffe's *Courageous Turk* (q.v.) was also performed by the college in the following September.

The two manuscripts of the play, one of which was Burton's own and the other a presentation copy to his brother, are both said to be holograph, but I can find no record that they have ever been collated.

The resemblance of the play to Jonson's *Alchemist* has several times been noted and much exaggerated. The alchemy in Burton's play is very slight, and presumably he was able to note practices of the time as well as Jonson. It may be, however, that Burton feared someone would charge him with imitating Jonson, for, as Bullen pointed out in the *D.N.B.*, certain lines in the prologue are suggestive.

> Si quid pervulgatum hâc fabulâ fuerit
> Absoletum [*sic*], si quid quod minus arriserit,
> Emendicatum e nuperâ scenâ aut quis putet,
> Sciat quod undecim abhinc annis scripta fuit.

Mr. Geoffrey Tillotson has pointed out that *The Alchemist* was acted in Oxford in 1610 (*T.L.S.*, 20 July 1933), a performance which could have reminded Burton that critics might carp at him.

at Cambridge in 1612. (Clark, *Register . . . Oxford*, II. ii. 301, and II. iii. 301; *Alumni Cantab.* i. 291.)

Carew was admitted to the Middle Temple 6 August 1612 (*Middle Temple Records*, ii. 552–3), but seems not to have remained for long, for he is soon found in the entourage of Sir Dudley Carleton, the English Ambassador at Venice. Carleton had married the niece of Sir Matthew Carew, and their correspondence suggests that Sir Matthew looked to the influential diplomat as a patron; the senior Carew was in serious financial difficulties from 1612 to his death in 1618. (Dunlap, ed., pp. xvii–xxix.) The date at which Thomas Carew joined his kinsman, perhaps as secretary, is not clear, but Dunlap suggests with some plausibility that he arrived in the autumn of 1613 and stayed with Sir Dudley until his return to London in December 1615. (Ibid., pp. xviii–xix.) Carleton took young Carew with him on his next embassy to The Hague in March 1615/16, but because of some unspecified indiscretion Carew was sent home in August 1616. (Ibid., pp. xx–xxviii.) Probably it was at this time that the young man began his career at court, for he is reported as an attendant at the creation of the Prince of Wales in November 1616. (Ibid., pp. xxix–xxx.)

In 1619 he went to France in the train of Sir Edward Herbert, and he may have remained with him until 1624, but there are no records of his whereabouts in these years. Except for undatable references to his currency in literary and courtly groups, the next definable event in Carew's life is recorded in the Lord Chamberlain's warrant for him to be sworn a Gentleman of the Privy Chamber Extraordinary on 6 April 1630 (ibid., pp. xxxi–xxxv), and Dunlap suggests that at about the same time he became Sewer in Ordinary to the King. On 18 February 1633/4 his masque, *Coelum Britannicum*, was danced by the King and fourteen of the great lords of the court. Presumably he followed the court regularly during the thirties, though there are few specific records of his presence. He was with the King on the expedition against the Scots in the spring and early summer of 1639. (Ibid., pp. xxxvi–xlii.) Nothing more is known of him until his burial at St. Dunstan's-in-the-West 23 March 1639/40. (Ibid., pp. xxxvi–xliii.)

Though Carew's only extant dramatic piece is *Coelum Britannicum*, his associations with plays and playwrights were various: he appears to have been an intimate of Suckling, Killigrew, and Davenant; he wrote commendatory verses for Thomas May's *The Heir*, 1622, for Davenant's *Just Italian*, 1630, and for Davenant's *The Wits*, 1636; he wrote a judicious reply to Jonson's indignant verses on the reception of *The New Inn*. (Dunlap, ed., pp. 92, 95, 97, and 64.) Even more suggestive of dramatic activity are the 'Foure Songs by way of *Chorus* to a play, at an entertainment of the King and Queene, by my Lord Chamberlaine' published in the *Poems*, 1640. (Ibid., pp. 59–62.) The piece for which these songs were written is unknown. Thomas Killigrew appropriated the first for his *Cicilia and Clorinda*, explaining that it was written by Carew 'and sung in a Masque at *White-hall, Anno* 1633'. (*Comedies and Tragedies*, 1664, p. 309.) This sounds like a confusion with *Coelum Britannicum*, which had been produced in February 1633/4. The four songs are followed in the *Poems*, 1640, by two '*Songs in the Play*', possibly, though not necessarily, intended for the same production. Fleay suggested (*Biog. Chron.* ii. 239) that some of these songs were written for Shirley's *Arcadia*, but his reasons are inadequate.

The 'Wyburd' manuscript at the Bodleian (MS. Don. b. 9) contains, among other poems apparently by Carew, 'The prologue to a Play presented before the King and Queene, att an Entertanement of them by the Lord Chamberlaine in Whitehall hall' and 'The Epilogue to the same Play'. (Dunlap, ed., pp. lxix, lxxi, and 127–8.) The titles sound as if the prologue and epilogue might belong to the same performance as the 'Foure Songs', but one cannot be sure. At least these various dramatic associations and fragments suggest that Carew's dramatic activities went beyond *Coelum Britannicum*, that perhaps a play or masque by him is now lost or unidentified.

The seventeenth-century allusions to Carew, mostly non-dramatic, are considered by Dunlap. (Op. cit., pp. xlvi–li.) He reproduces as a frontispiece Van Dyck's portrait, now in the Royal collection at Windsor, of Thomas Killigrew and an unknown, probably Carew.

Coelum Britannicum (1633/4)

Editions: Poems, Songs, and Sonnets: Together with a Masque, with a seven-page life, edited by T. Davies (1772); *The Poems and Masque of Thomas Carew*, edited by Joseph Woodfall Ebsworth (1893); *The Poems of Thomas Carew*, edited by Arthur Vincent (1899); *The Poems of Thomas Carew with his Masque Coelum Britannicum*, edited with an introduction and notes by Rhodes Dunlap (1949).

Brotanek, Rudolf. *Die Englischen Maskenspiele* (1902), pp. 363 *et passim*.

Evans, Willa McClung. *Henry Lawes, Musician and Friend of Poets* (1941), pp. 79–89.

Nicoll, Allardyce. *Stuart Masques and the Renaissance Stage* (1938), pp. 101–4 *et passim*.

Reyher, Paul. *Les Masques anglais* (1909), *passim*.

Simpson, Percy, and C. F. Bell. *Designs by Inigo Jones for Masques & Plays at Court* (1924), pp. 17–19 and 83–88.

1633, 28 Dec. A warrant to the Surveyor for 'A scene to bee made in yᵉ banquetting house for the Kings Masque at Shrouetide next'. (Lord Chamberlain's Warrant Books. *Malone Society Collections*, ii, Part iii [1931], 361.)

1633/4, 9 Jan. 'There are two Masques in Hand, the first of the Inns of Court, which is to be presented on *Candlemas-day*; the other the King presents the Queen with on *Shrove-Tuesday* at Night.' (Mr. Garrard to the Lord Deputy, *Strafforde's Letters*, i. 177.)

1633/4, 24 Jan. (i.e. 3 February 1633, Venetian style). 'The king is preparing a very stately and solemn masque in return for the entertainment given him by the queen a few days ago at Somerset House.' (*C.S.P., Venetian, 1632–6*, p. 190. The Queen's entertainment was *The Faithful Shepherdess* [see above, i. 38–39], given at Somerset House 6 January 1633/4. *The Triumph of Peace* by James Shirley followed, but that was given *for* the King and Queen by the Inns of Court. *Coelum Britannicum* is the masque given *by* the King.)

1633/4, 14 Feb. (See Shirley, *The Triumph of Peace*.)

1633/4, 18 Feb. 'On Shrovetusday night, the 18 of February, 1633, the Kinge dancte his Masque, accompanied with 11 lords, and attended with 10 pages. It was the noblest masque of my time to this day, the best poetrye, best scenes, and the best habitts. The kinge and queene were very well pleasd with my service, and the Q. was pleasd to tell mee before the king, "Pour les habits, elle n'avoit jamais rien vue de si brave".' (Adams, *Herbert*, p. 55.)

1633/4, 18 Feb. 'for the Masque of his Ma eod — 00–00–06.' (Mildmay's Accounts, p. 178.) '. . . att nighte was pformed his Maᵗˢ: Masque of Lordes et att Whitehall.' (Mildmay's Diary, p. 5ᵛ. See above, ii. 676.)

1633/4, 27 Feb. 'On *Shrove-Tuesday* at Night, the King and the Lords performed their Masque. The Templers were all invited and well placed, they have found a new way of letting them in by a turning Chair, besides they let in none but such as have Tickets sent them beforehand, so that now the keeping of the Door is no trouble, the King intends to have this Masque again in the *Easter* Holydays.' (Mr. Garrard to the Lord Deputy, *Strafforde's Letters*, i. 207.)

1633/4, ? March. Weber is probably wrong in thinking that two undated and unaddressed letters of Viscount Falkland were addressed to Carew and concern *Coelum Britannicum*. The letters are extremely vague, but there is one apparent reference to the Queen as a performer. She had no part in Carew's masque. (Kurt Weber, *Lucius Cary, Second Viscount Falkland* [1940], pp. 61–63.)

1634. The accounts of the Gentleman of the Robes contain a number of items for the costuming of *Coelum Britannicum*. (See Reyher, op. cit., pp. 516–18.)

1634. *Cœlum Britanicum*. A Masque *at* Whitehall in the Ban-qveting-Hovse, on Shrove-Tvesday-Night, the 18. of *February*, 1633 . . . 1634. [See Dunlap, pp. lx–lxi, for variants.]

1638? MS. B.M. Harl. 4931. fol. 28 contains two pages of a synopsis headed:

> An: 1638.   The Designe.   This was acted in Germany, before ye Earle of Arundel, w^n he went to Vienna in behalf of ye Paulsgraue.

There follows a synopsis of *Coelum Britannicum*. (Transcribed with minor inaccuracies by Dunlap, op. cit., pp. 274–5.)

1639/40, 23 Mar. S.R. A book 'called The workes of Thomas Carew Esqr. late Sewer to his Ma^{ty}. being Poems & Masques' was entered to Thomas Walkley. Since the date of entry is that of Carew's funeral, it seems likely that his death prompted the collection. (Greg, *Bibliography*, i. 52.)

1640 [< 29 April, the date of Matthew Clay's imprimatur; > 26 June, when Humphrey Mildmay bought a copy] *Cœlum Brit-tanicum*. A Masqve at Whitehall in the Banquetting house, on *Shrove-Tuesday-night*, the 18. of *February*, 1633. The Inventors. *Tho: Carew. Jnigo Iones* . . . 1640. (A separate title-page for the reprint of the 1634 edition which concluded Walkley's volume, itself entitled *Poems*.)

1640. [Another issue.] (See Dunlap, p. lxv.)

1642. *Coelum Brittanicum*. A Maske at White-hall in the Ban-quetting House, on *Shrove-Tuesday-night*, the 18. of *February*, 1633. The Inventors. *Tho. Carew. Inigo Iones* . . . 1642. (Separate title-page in the second edition of the *Poems*.)

1650, 8 June. S.R. Walkley's rights in Carew's *Poems* were assigned to H. Moseley. (Greg, *Bibliography*, i. 59.)

1651. Separate title-page, identical with 1642 edition, in the third edition of the *Poems* which was brought out by Moseley.

1651. [Another issue.] (See Dunlap, pp. lxvii–lxviii.)

1667, 19 Aug. S.R. Ann Moseley's rights in 'Poems wth a maske by Thomas Carewe Esqr' assigned with eight others to Henry Herringman. (Greg, *Bibliography*, i. 71.)

1670, 22 Nov. Herringman licensed *Poems*, etc., for publication in Michaelmas Term. (Arber, *The Term Catalogues, 1668–1709*, i. 62.)

1670. The mask has a separate title-page in the fourth edition of the *Poems* brought out by Herringman. Though the second issue of this edition is dated 1671, the masque is dated 1670 in both issues.

1673. *The Works of Sr William D'avenant K^t* . . . 1673, published by Herringman, contains *Coelum Britannicum*.

Coelum Britannicum is one of the most elaborate of Inigo Jones's productions, but Carew's efforts are not particularly distinguished. The extent of the degeneration from Jonson's greatest productions and the elaborateness of the spectacle are suggested by the fact that there are eight antimasques, including monsters, vices, country people, gipsies, the five senses, Picts, Scots, and Irish. The chief spectacles were cloud machines, and a mountain which rose from beneath the stage until it filled the entire scene. Its sensational effect is recorded in the masque itself, lines 968–71:

This strange spectacle gave great cause of admiration, but especially how so huge a machine, and of that great height could come from under the Stage, which was but six foot high.

There is some confusion about the composer of the music for *Coelum Britannicum*. In the 1640 and 1642 editions of the *Poems* the last page contains, as usual, the names of the chief masquers, beginning with the King, together with 'The names of the young Lords and Noblemens Sonnes'; on the verso of this leaf is the statement, 'The Songs and Dialogues of this Booke were set with apt Tunes to them, by M^r. *Henry Lawes*, one of his Majesties Musitians'. This statement has often been taken to refer to the music for the masque, but Dunlap thinks (op. cit., pp. 276–7) that later editors were correct in assuming that it referred to the *Poems* as a whole. He adds that Mr. Percy Young thinks Grove, Pulver, and Greg in their attribution of the music to Henry Lawes were misled by Rimbault, who made this ascription on the evidence of 'detached pieces in Playford's various publications'. Mr. Young thinks William Lawes the more likely composer. (Ibid.)

The synopsis of the masque in Harl. 4931 adds several interesting details to the quarto. Though Arundel did make a trip to Germany, it was in 1636, and such an elaborate piece as *Coelum Britannicum* was certainly not staged for him there. Brotanek (op. cit., p. 206 n.) suggests that 'The Designe' has been confused by the writer of the date and note with the allegorical drama which William Crowne says (*A True Relation of All the Remarkable Places and Passages Observed in the Travels of . . . Thomas Lord Howard*, 1637) Arundel saw in Germany. This seems likely, for the date and note on 'The Designe' are in a different hand and ink from the title and synopsis. The details of the synopsis show that it was written by an eyewitness and not derived from the printed text. Dunlap says that the hand is not Carew's.

The source of Carew's masque is Giordano Bruno's *Spaccio de la Bestia Trionfante*, 1584; Dunlap analyses the indebtedness. (Op. cit., pp. 275–6 and 278–82.) The relationship of the masque to other courtly spectacles is discussed by Brotanek, Reyher, and Nicoll, and several of Jones's designs and sketches are described or reproduced by Nicoll and by Simpson and Bell. Certain expenditures for the masque from the Audit Office records are transcribed by Simpson and Bell (*Designs*, pp. 17–19) and by Reyher (op. cit., pp. 516–18).

It is perhaps worth noting that two of the 'young Lords and Noblemens Sonnes' who took part in the masque were Lord Brackley and Mr. Thomas Egerton, who played the roles of the two brothers in Milton's *Comus* at Ludlow Castle in the following September.

Unknown Play (1630 ?–1639/40)
(Lost ?)

Several pieces printed in Carew's *Poems*, 1640, suggest that he wrote a play which has been lost. Under the general title, 'Foure Songs by way of *Chorus* to a play, at an entertainment of the King and Queene, by my Lord Chamberlaine', appear four songs, followed by two others headed, '*Songs in the Play*'. (Dunlap, ed., pp. 59–64.)

Fleay (*Biog. Chron.* ii. 239) suggests that at least some of these songs belong in Shirley's *Arcadia*, but there is little to recommend his suggestion. Thomas Killigrew used one of the songs in his *Cicilia and Clorinda*, but acknowledged that it was Carew's 'and sung in a Masque at *White-hall, Anno,* 1633'. This statement seems to be intended to refer to *Coelum Britannicum,* but the songs do not belong in that masque.

In the 'Wyburd' manuscript (see Dunlap, p. lxix), with a number of other Carew poems, several of them not found elsewhere, occurs 'The prologue to a Play presented before the King and Queene, att an Entertanement of them by the Lord Chamberlaine in Whitehall hall' and 'The Epilogue to the same Play'. The similarity of the title to the general title for the four songs in the *Poems* suggests that all belong to the same play and that it was probably Carew's own composition. The repeated word 'entertainment' suggests a masque rather than a play, but masques did not have prologues and epilogues, and the words would be more appropriate to a play than to a masque. The last lines of the epilogue, if taken literally, would indicate an entertainment with scenery after a banquet.

The lost piece presumably was written between Carew's attainment of a position at court in 1630 and his death in March 1639/40.

LODOWICK CARLELL (Carlel, Carliell, Carlile, Carlill)
1601 or 1602–75

Gray, Charles H. *Lodowick Carliell, His Life, A Discussion of His Plays, and 'The Deserving Favourite', A Tragi-Comedy . . .* (1905). Harbage, Alfred. *Cavalier Drama* (1936), pp. 95–104.

Professor Gray presented evidence in his biography of the courtier-dramatist that he generally signed his name 'Carlile' or 'Carliell', and Gray accordingly uses the second spelling throughout. But on the title-pages of his works the name is invariably spelled 'Carlell', and nearly all historians and scholars have used that spelling. It seems to me only confusing, therefore, to adopt the 'i' spelling at this late date, even though the author did like it.

The dramatist came from a border family living at Brydekirk in Dumfriesshire (Gray, pp. 14–18), where he was born in 1601 or 1602, according to the allegation for his marriage which said he was twenty-four in July 1626. (Ibid., p. 22.) He was the third son of Robert Carlell, Laird of Brydekirk, a huntsman of James I. (Ibid., pp. 23–26.) Nothing is known of the early youth or education of Lodowick, but he was in London and possessed of some court influence by November 1621. On the 11th of that month the Marquis of Buckingham wrote Lord Cranfield to forward the application of Lodowick Carlell for the wardship of Walter Mild-may's son. The letter concludes with a phrase which indicates that the young Scot was already known at court: 'the King favours him.' (Ibid., p. 27.) Gray suggests that the youth may have been presented to the King on his visit to nearby Dumfries in 1617.

Carlell was married 11 July 1626 to Joan Palmer, daughter of William Palmer, gentleman, of St. James's Park, at St. Faith's in London. (Ibid., p. 22.) The residence of the bride's father suggests that he may have been a professional colleague of Carlell, for at some unknown date before 1629 the dramatist became huntsman for the King. There are numerous payments to him as huntsman, harrier, and master of the bows from 1630 to 1635 (ibid., pp. 28–29), and on the 1629 title-page of *The Deserving Favourite* he is styled 'Gentle-man of the BOVVES, and Groome of the King *and Queenes Priuie Chamber*'. Before February 1636/7 he had become one of the keepers of the royal park at Richmond (ibid., pp. 29–31), a position in which he was evidently very active, for in the prologue to the second part of *The Passionate Lovers*, produced in 1638, he speaks of his hunting and gamekeeping activities as occupying 'Not some, but most fair days throughout the yeer'.

Carlell's dramatic activities, which were carried on from 1622 to 1638, seem to have been mostly the leisure productions of a cour-tier and huntsman. Probably his first production was *Osmond the Great Turk*, written under unknown circumstances and produced by the King's men in 1622. His principal plays, *The Deserving Favourite*, *Arviragus and Philicia*, Parts I and II, and *The Passion-ate Lovers*, Parts I and II, were all produced for the court and were acted at court before they were performed by the King's men at Blackfriars. *The Fool Would Be a Favourite* and *The Spartan Ladies* are not known to have had court performances, but it may be that the records are missing.

There is no record that Carlell followed the King during the wars, but he appears to have retained his post as huntsman, for in January 1649/50 he was concerned with the appointment of a keeper for St. James's Park. (Ibid., pp. 38–39.) Gray notes a family tradition that he rented Richmond Park from the city of London. Shortly after the Restoration, in September 1660, he and his son were made lodge-keepers at Petersham, possibly as a reward for services during the interregnum. (Ibid., pp. 39–40.)

A few years after the Restoration, Carlell translated Corneille's *Héraclius* and expected it to be produced, but he was disappointed. He died in the parish of St. Martin's-in-the-Fields and was buried at Petersham 21 August 1675. (Ibid., pp. 42–43.) Gray reprints extracts from the wills of the dramatist and of his wife as well as one or two other documents of minor interest concerning his affairs. (Ibid., pp. 169–77.)

There are singularly few literary allusions to Carlell. Dekker dedicated his *Match Me in London* to him in 1631, but I know of nothing else before the late seventeenth-century bibliographers.

Arviragus and Philicia, Parts I and II (1635–1635/6)

MSS.: Bodley MS. Eng. misc. d. 11. (See letter from B. M. Wagner, *T.L.S.*, 4 October 1934, p. 675.) Petworth House MS., owned by Lord Leconfield, reported in *Hist. MSS. Com.*, Sixth Report, Appendix, 1877, p. 312. (See ibid.)

Harbage, Alfred. *Cavalier Drama* (1936), pp. 97–99.
Mills, Laurens J. *One Soul in Bodies Twain* (1937), pp. 362–6. Synopsis.

1635, Nov.–May 1636. 'The King sate yesterday at Van Dyke's for the Prince of Orange, but y^r Mat^y hath forgate to send me the mesure of the picture; his howse is close by Blake Friers, where the Quene saw Lodwick Carlile's second part of Arviragus and Felicia acted, wch is hugely liked of every one, he will not faile to send it to your Mat^y.' (Charles, Prince Palatine, to the Queen of Bohemia, *Hist. MSS. Com.*, Northumberland MSS., App. to the Third Report, p. 118, No. 132. For the date, see above, i. 48, nn. 3 and 4.)

1635/6, 16 Feb. 'The Second part of *Arviragus and Philicia* playd at court the 16 Febru. 1635, with great approbation of K. and Queene.' (Adams, *Herbert*, p. 55.)

1636, 18 and 19 Apr. 'The first and second part of *Arviragus and Philicia* were acted at the Cockpitt [Whitehall], before the Kinge and Queene, the Prince, and Prince Elector, the 18 and 19 Aprill, 1636, being monday and tusday in Easter weeke.' (Ibid., p. 56.)

1636, 18 Apr. 'Easter munday at the Cockpitt the firste parte of Arviragus.' (Ibid., p. 75, from a bill presented by the King's men for plays acted at court 1636–7.)

1636, 19 Apr. 'Easter tuesday at the Cockpitt the second parte of Arviragus.' (Ibid.)

1636, 26 Dec. 'The first part of *Arviragus*, Monday Afternoon, 26 Decemb.' (Ibid., p. 57, from a list of plays presented at Hampton Court 1636–7.)

1636, 26 Dec. 'S^t. Stephens day at Hampton Court. the first pte of *Arviragus*.' (Ibid., p. 76, from a bill presented by the King's men for plays acted at court 1636–7.)

1636, 27 Dec. 'The second part of *Arviragus*, tusday 27 Decemb.' (Ibid., p. 57, from a list of plays presented at Hampton Court 1636–7.)

1636, 27 Dec. 'S^t. Johns Day at Hampton Court. the second parte of Arviragus.' (Ibid., p. 76, from a bill presented by the King's men for plays acted at court 1636–7.)

1638, 26 Oct. 'Iohn Crooke. & Rich: Serger. Entred for their Copie vnder the hands of Mr Clay & m^r Mead warden A play called Arviragus & Philicia. first & Second pts.' (Greg, *Bibliography*, i. 49.)

1639. Arviragvs and Philicia. As it was acted at the Private House in *Black-Fryers* by his Majesties Servants. *The first and second Part* . . . 1639. [After the epilogue of Part II is '*Imprimatur*, Math. Clay. Octob. 26. 1638'.]

1668/9, *c.* 12 Jan. In 'A Catalogue of part of His Ma^{tes} Servants Playes as they were formerly acted at the Blackfryers & now allowed of to his Ma^{tes} Servants at ye New Theatre' occur the titles:

Arviragus & Philitia 1st pt.
Arviragus & Philitia 2d pt.

(Nicoll, *A History of Restoration Drama*, 3rd ed., pp. 315–16.)

Prince Charles's letter to his mother, perhaps the first notice of the play, and the only contemporary one to name the author, is undated, but it must have been written after the Prince came to England in November 1635, and before the theatres were shut up for the long plague closing on 12 May 1636. (See above, ii. 661–5.) The performance seen by the Queen at Blackfriars—presumably a private one arranged for her—could have taken place either before or after the court performance of 16 February 1635/6. Prince Charles's remark on the popularity of the play is amply verified by the records of the court performances.

The play is one of the exemplars of the courtier productions which so annoyed Richard Brome and others of the professional playwrights. These plays by amateur dramatists were written with the courtly audience primarily in mind and, if Brome is to be trusted, were often given to the companies free or even with a gift of money. (See the prologue to *The Antipodes* and the prologue and epilogue to *The Court Beggar*.) They are characterized by their posturing, their intricate love-plots, and their interminable length.

Arviragus and Philicia is really a ten-act play broken in the middle. Langbaine says of the source:

Several of our Historians speak of the Actions of this Illustrious Prince. See *Matth. Westmonast.* A.D. 44. pag. 93. *Galf. Monumetens.* lib. 4. c. 16. *Pol. Vergil.* lib. 2. *Grafton.* Part 7, p. 77. (*An Account of the English Dramatick Poets*, p. 46.)

There was a revival of the play at Lincoln's Inn Fields about 1672, for which Dryden wrote a prologue which Langbaine says was spoken by Hart.

The Deserving Favourite (c. 1622 < > 1629)

Edition: Charles H. Gray, ed., *Lodowick Carliell . . . and 'The Deserving Favourite', A Tragi-Comedy reprinted from the original edition of 1629 with Introduction and Notes* (1905).

Harbage, Alfred. *Cavalier Drama* (1936), pp. 96–97.

1629. The Deseruing Fauorite. As it was lately Acted, first before the Kings Maiestie, and since publikely at the *Black-Friers*. By his Maiesies [*sic*] Seruants. *Written by* Lodovvicke Carlell, *Esquire*, Gentle-man of the Bovves, and Groome of the King *and Queenes Priuie Chamber. At London* . . . 1629.

1652/3, 7 Mar. S.R. John Rhodes's title in 'The Deseruing Fauourite Written by Lodowick Carlell Esqr. formerly printed in the name of Mathew Rhodes his Brother, but for the vse & benefite of the said Iohn Rhodes,' was assigned to Moseley. (Greg, *Bibliography*, i. 60.)

1659. The *Deserving* Favorite. A *Tragi-Comedy*. As it was presented before the King and Queenes Majesties at *White-Hall*, and very often at the Private house in *Black-Friers*, with great Applause. *By his late* Maiesties *Servants. Written by Lodowick Carlell*, Esq ; . . . 1659.

1668/9, c. 12 Jan. In 'A Catalogue of part of His Ma^{tes} Servants Playes as they were formerly acted at the Blackfryers & now allowed of to his Ma^{tes} Servants at ye New Theatre' occurs the title 'The Deserveing ffavorett'. (A. Nicoll, *A History of Restoration Drama 1660–1700*, 3rd ed., pp. 315–16.)

The Deserving Favourite is Carlell's first printed play, though probably not his first dramatic composition. The courtier's attitude which the professional dramatists found so offensive is expressed several times in the front matter. The title-page emphasizes the fact that the play was not written for the common theatre, but was performed first at court and only later came to the Blackfriars. Carlell's dedication to two of the Gentlemen of the King's Bedchamber expresses the same condescending attitude:

... this Play, which know at first was not design'd to trauell so farre as the common Stage, is now prest for a greater iourney, almost without my knowledge.

The prologue before the King opens with the lines,

> Doe not expect strong Lines, nor Mirth, though they
> Iustly the Towne-wits, and the Vulgar sway.

Most explicit of all is 'The Printers Epigrammaticall Epistle to the *Vnderstanding Reader*', signed I[ohn] R[hodes]:

> Vnknowne to'th Author this faire Courtly Piece
> Was drawne to'th *Presse*; not for a Golden Fleece,
> As doe our *Midan* Mimickes of these Times,
> Who hunt out Gaine, with *Reasons* losse in *Rhimes*,
>
> .   .   .   .
>
> He with a new, choyce, and familiar Straine
> Strikes full Conceit deepe in the Master-Veyne,
> Stoopes not for drosse; his *profit* was his *pleasure*,
> Ha's (for his Friends) ransackt the *Muses* Treasure.

In the play of an author so disdainful of the commercial theatre, it is odd to find one of the few casts of pre-Restoration publication. All the named roles except servants are assigned to seven adult and three boy actors of the King's company. (See above, i. 84–85.) Since both Carlell and the printer of the first quarto say that the play came to the press without the knowledge of the author, this cast might be taken as evidence that the manuscript came from the playhouse, but the quarto shows none of the characteristics of a prompt copy.

In his edition of the play Charles H. Gray contended that a source of *The Deserving Favourite* was Castillo Solórzano's *La duquesa de Mantua* (pp. 57–68). The similarities between the two narratives are really not very striking, and most if not all of them could be found in other romances and plays of the sixteenth and early seventeenth centuries. Moreover, Solórzano's tale first appeared in the collection entitled *La Huerta de Valencia*, which was published in Spain in 1629, the year of the publication of *The Deserving Favourite*. It would be surprising if an untranslated Spanish tale were put to use so promptly, and there is no evidence to show that Carlell's play was not written *before* 1629.

The statements on the title-page, in the dedication, and in the printer's epistle are equally compatible with hypotheses either that the play was a very recent production or that it was six or eight

years old. The only evidence offered for date is Gray's proposed
source, and that seems to me untenable. At present one can be
certain only that the play was written not later than 1629. But,
since Carlell was twenty-seven in that year and since he probably
would not have written a play much before he was twenty, one
might set an inferior date at about 1622.

The Fool Would Be a Favourite, or The Discreet Lover
(1625 ?–42 ?)

Edition: Allardyce Nicoll, ed., *The Fool would be a Favourit: or
The Discreet Lover (1657) By Lodowick Carlell* (1926).

Mills, Laurens J. *One Soul in Bodies Twain* (1937), pp. 366–9.

1653, 9 Sept. S.R. Entered for Moseley, with other plays, 'The
Discreet Louer, or the Foole would bee a Fauourite. by . . . Lod:
Carlel.' (Greg, *Bibliography*, i. 60–61.)

1657. At the end of his edition of Middleton's *Two New Playes*,
Humphrey Moseley prints a number of titles under the heading
'These Books I do purpose to Print very speedily', including:

241   The Spartan Ladyes
242. The Discreet Lover or the
        Fool would be a Favorite }By *Lodowick Carlell* Gent
243. *Osman* the Great *Turk* or the
        Noble Servant

1657. The Fool Would be a Favourit: Or, the *Discreet Lover*. A
Trage-Comedy. *Written by Lodowick Carlell*, Gent. *London* . . .
1657. (Separate title-page in *Two New Playes*, 1657.)

1657. Two New Playes. *Viz*. 1. The *Fool* would be a Favourit: or,
The Discreet *Lover*. 2. *Osmond*, the Great Turk: or, The Noble
Servant. As they have been often acted, by the Queen's Majesty's
Servants, with great applause. *Written by* Lodowick Carlell, Gent.
. . . 1657. (Joint title-page of 1657.)

The Fool Would Be a Favourite is the only one of Carlell's extant
plays with a comic element; here not only is it prominent, but it
gives the play its title. This unusual pandering to popular taste
and the absence of any record of court performance suggest that
the play may have been written originally for a popular audience
rather than for Carlell's customary courtly one.

The production statement on the title-page of *Two New Playes*
is explicit, but there is some reason to think that it may be inaccurate, It seems likely that the other of the *Two New Playes, Osmond*

the Great Turk (q.v.), belonged to the King's company at Black-friars, as did *The Deserving Favourite, Arviragus and Philicia, The Passionate Lovers*, and probably *The Spartan Ladies*. This is not proof that the statement that *The Fool Would Be a Favourite* was performed by the Queen's men is erroneous, but it is reason for uncertainty.

I know of no external evidence to date the play, and I recognized no internal evidence. Professor Allardyce Nicoll said in the introduction to his edition of the play, 'It is not known when either of the two plays was performed, but the year 1638 may be suggested as the possible date of production for the former [i.e., *The Fool*].' Presumably he based this statement on his discussion of date in the introduction to *Osmond* (pp. x-xi), but the evidence is not valid. Harbage's suggestion (*Cavalier Drama*, pp. 99–100) of 1637–8 because Queen Henrietta's men were not known as 'the Queen's Majesty's Servants' before 1637 and because Carlell said in the prologue to *The Passionate Lovers*, Part II (1638), that he would write no more plays, is untenable. He is mistaken about the change in designation of the company (see above, i. 250–9), and dramatists' promises to retire from the stage are, as he recognizes, highly unreliable.

John Downes, Restoration book-keeper and prompter, says in his *Roscius Anglicanus*:

> This being the last New Play that was *Acted* in *Lincolns-Inn* Fields, yet there were sundry others done there, from 1662, till the time they left that House: *As Love's Kingdom*, Wrote by *Mr. Fleckno: The Royal Shepherdess*, by *Mr. Shadwell*: *Two Fools well met*, by *Mr. Lodwick Carlile*: (Montague Summers, ed., p. 31.)

No such play by Lodowick Carlell is known. Summers suggested in a note (ibid., p. 202) that Downes blundered either by antedating James Carlisle's *The Fortune Hunters, or, Two Fools Well Met* by twenty years or more, or by giving an inaccurate title to *The Fool Would Be a Favourite*.

Heraclius, Emperor of the East (1663)

Summers, Montague. *The Playhouse of Pepys* (1935), pp. 359–60.

1663/4, 10 Mar. S.R. John Starkey entered 'a booke or coppy intituled *Heraclius, Emperor of the East*, A Tragedy, written in French, by Monsieur de Corneille, Englished by Lodowick Carlill Esqr.' (*A Transcript of the Registers of the Worshipful Company of Stationers, 1640–1708*, ed. Eyre, ii. 339.)

1664. Heraclius, Emperour Of the East. A Tragedy. Written in French by *Monsieur de Corneille*. Englishrd [*sic*] by *Lodowick Carlell*, Esq; . . . 1664. (On the verso of the title-page is '*March 9*, 1664. Imprimatur *Roger L'Estrange*.')

Corneille's play was not printed in French until 1647. Carlell says in the 'Advertisement' prefixed to the 1664 edition that his translation was prepared for the players but rejected by them. Summers (loc. cit.) reconstructs the circumstances.

Osmond, the Great Turk, or The Noble Servant (1622?)

Edition: Allardyce Nicoll, ed., *The Tragedy of Osmond the Great Turk, or the Noble Servant (1657)*, 1926.

Chew, Samuel. *The Crescent and the Rose* (1937), pp. 488–9.
Harbage, Alfred. *Cavalier Drama* (1936), pp. 99–101.
Rice, Warner G. *Turk, Moor, and Persian in English Literature, 1550–1660.* Harvard MS. thesis (1926), pp. 366–8.

1622, 6 Sept. 'Item 6 Sept., 1622, for perusing and allowing of a new play called *Osmond the Great Turk*, which Mr. Hemmings and Mr. Rice affirmed to me that Lord Chamberlain gave order to allow of it because I refused to allow at first, containing 22 leaves and a page. Acted by the King's players . . . 20s.' (Transcript by Malone from Sir John Astley, written by Malone in his copy of *Biographica Dramatica*, quoted by W. J. Lawrence in *T.L.S.*, 29 November 1923, p. 820.)

1653, 9 Sept. S.R. Moseley entered a number of plays, including 'Osman, [*sic*] the Great Turke, or The Noble seruant. both by Lod: Carlel.' (Greg, *Bibliography*, i. 60-61.)

1657. At the end of his edition of Middleton's *Two New Playes*, Humphrey Moseley prints a number of titles under the heading 'These Books I do purpose to Print very speedily', including the following:

241   The Spartan Ladyes
242. The Discreet Lover or the
         Fool would be a Favorite } By *Lodowick Carlell* Gent
243. *Osman* the Great *Turk* or the
         Noble Servant

1657. The Famous Tragedy of Osmond The great Turk, Otherwise called the *Noble Servant. Written by Lodowick Carlell*, Gent. . . .
1657. (Separate title-page in *Two New Playes*, 1657.)

1657. Two New Playes. *Viz.* 1. The *Fool* would be a Favourit: or, The Discreet *Lover*. 2. *Osmond*, the Great Turk: or, The Noble *Servant.* As they have been often acted, by the Queen's Majesty's Servants, with great applause. *Written by* Lodowick Carlell, Gent. . . . 1657. (Joint title-page.)

1668/9, *c.* 12 Jan. In 'A Catalogue of part of His Ma^{tes} Servants Playes as they were formerly acted at the Blackfryers & now allowed of to his Ma^{tes} Servants at ye New Theatre' occurs the title 'Osmond ye Great Turke'. (A. Nicoll, *A History of Restoration Drama 1660–1700*, 3rd ed., pp. 315–16.)

c. 1677–1703. 'Osmand the Turk or the Ottoman custome' is the eighteenth title in Abraham Hill's list of plays. (J. Q. Adams, 'Hill's List of Early Plays in Manuscript', *Library*, Fourth Series, xx [1939], 71–99. See Middleton, *The Conqueror's Custom.*)

The chief problem concerning this tragedy is to decide how many of the above notices pertain to the same play. It has been doubted that the licence for the stage refers to Carlell's play because he was only twenty or twenty-one at the time, because the joint title-page of the 1657 edition says that the play was acted 'by the Queen's Majesty's Servants', not the King's, and because he is said to imply in the dedication to *The Deserving Favourite*, printed in 1629, that it was his first composition. The first and third objections are negligible: other dramatists have written plays at twenty or twenty-one, and Carlell shows himself no master of his craft in this play; the dedication of *The Deserving Favourite* simply says that the approval of the dedicatees has persuaded the author to 'continue to wast more paper'. Nothing here indicates a first play; the dedication says only that it will not be his last.

The difficulty about the two companies is more serious. I see only two possibilities: either the title-page is inaccurate, or the 1622 licence does not apply to Carlell's play, for it seems highly improbable that the Queen's men should have taken a play away from the most successful and influential troupe of the time. For various reasons I think an error in the 1657 title-page the more probable of the two alternatives. The identical phrasing of the titles is suggestive. Equally suggestive of Carlell's authorship of the King's men's play is the fact that the licence was secured by the intervention of the Lord Chamberlain, which was pretty surely an indication of court influence, an exceedingly rare commodity among playwrights. Carlell, however, did have court influence at this time, as is demonstrated by a letter of 11 November 1621 from the Marquis of Buckingham to Lord Cranfield asking a grant of wardship for Carlell and adding the significant phrase, 'the King favours him'. (Gray, *Lodowick Carliell*, p. 27.)

There is material in Carlell's play as we have it which might have alarmed a censor, and there is evidence of cuts. Melchoshus's speech in Act I might well have been thought a reference to James's difficulties in raising benevolences in 1622. (See Gardiner, *History of England, 1603–42*, iv. 294–5.)

> You see, doggs, it is not with us, as with your ruin'd Maister; who when he pleaded with his best eloquence, as I have heard, to make his greedy Subjects open their Cofers for their own safety, could not prevail with them: for they both base and foolish, rather chose to perish with their Idols, than to relieve the generall necessity. (1657 ed., A_3.)

This speech is as close to political events in England as the one in Massinger's *The King and the Subject* which so offended Astley's successor, Sir Henry Herbert, and King Charles in 1638. (See Adams, *Herbert*, pp. 22–23.) There is also evidence of derangement in the text of *Osmond*, a derangement which certainly indicates the deletion of something, and possibly of lines which Astley found objectionable. For instance, at the end of Act II there is a sudden cry of 'Fire, fire, fire'. Calibeus inquires anxiously, 'What noise is that, ha, fire!' Here a violent action is prepared for, and we learn in the next act that there has been a fire which provided cover for a rape. Yet in the text as we have it now, Calibeus's inquiry is followed by the entrance of two characters who are already on the stage and the utterly irrelevant line, 'My Lord, I'le to the Court this morning'. Whereupon the act concludes.

Another reason for thinking that Carlell was the author of the 1622 *Osmond* and that the 1657 title-page is wrong is that all his other assignable plays were the property of the King's men—*The Deserving Favourite*, the two parts of *Arviragus and Philicia*, the two parts of *The Passionate Lovers*, and probably *The Spartan Ladies* (q.v.). This fact does not *require* the assignment of *Osmond* to the troupe at the Blackfriars, but it makes it consistent with the author's general practice and with the custom of most of the courtier dramatists of the time.

Altogether, then, it seems likely that Carlell wrote *Osmond the Great Turk* in 1622, when he was twenty or twenty-one, that he gave it to the King's company, who had trouble licensing it, and that he secured the influence of the Lord Chamberlain and thus persuaded Astley to grant the licence, with the possible concession of certain omissions shown by the state of the present text. The statement

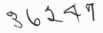

on the 1657 title-page is therefore presumably wrong, or possibly applies only to *The Fool Would Be a Favourite*.

Whether or not Abraham Hill had a manuscript of Carlell's play, it is impossible now to tell. As Professor Adams pointed out in his article on Hill's list, the sub-title could refer to the suicide of the heroine.

Langbaine noted (*An Account of the English Dramatick Poets*, pp. 47–48) that the action was based on the taking of Constantinople in 1453, and that the story was that of Mahomet and Irene, for which he suggests several sources. Warner G. Rice (loc. cit.) is somewhat more particular in his analysis of the relation of the material of the play to Knolles's *Generall Historie of the Turks*, which had appeared in editions of 1603 and 1610.

The title of the play is odd. Osmond is the Noble Servant, but he is a Tartar and not the Great Turk.

The Passionate Lovers, Parts I and II (1638)

Harbage, Alfred. *Cavalier Drama* (1936), pp. 101–3.
Simpson, Percy, and C. F. Bell. *Designs by Inigo Jones for Masques & Plays at Court* (1924), p. 118.

1638, 10 July. 'At Sumerset-house the 10th of July & our day—lost at our house mr Carlels play the first part of the pasionate louers'. (From a list of plays acted by the King's company at court, 1638–9, Adams, *Herbert*, p. 76.)

1638, 18 Dec. 'At the Cocpit the 18th of desember m Carlels play agayne the first part of . . . The pasionate louers.' (Ibid., p. 77.)

1638, 20 Dec. 'At the Cocpit the 20th of desember the 2d part of . . . The pasionate louers.' (Ibid.)

1638, 27 Dec. 'At the Cocpit the 27 of desember the 2d part agayne of the pasionate louers.' (Ibid.)

1641, 7 Aug. 'The 1st & 2d pt of ye Passiont louer.' (In a list of King's company plays which the Lord Chamberlain forbade the printers to publish without the company's consent. See above, i. 65–66.)

1646, 4 Sept. S.R. Robinson and Moseley entered, with other plays, 'The passionate Louer [*sic*] [1st. & 2d. parts. *added*] . . . by Mr Carlile.' (Greg, *Bibliography*, i. 56–57.)

1655. The Passionate Lovers, A *Tragi-Comedy. The First and Second Parts*. Twice presented before the King and Queens Majesties at *Somerset-House*, and very often at the Private

House in *Black-Friars*, with great Applause, *By his late* Majesties *Servants. Written by Lodowick Carlell*, Gent. . . . 1655.
1655. [Another issue.]
1672/3, 30 Jan. S.R. 'Passionate Louers. [*sic*] halfe' transferred with 104 other titles from the estate of Humphrey Robinson to John Martin and Henry Herringman. (Greg, *Bibliography*, i. 72–73.)
1683, 21 Aug. S.R. 'Passionate Lover. [*sic*]' transferred with 359 other titles from the estate of John Martin to Robert Scott. (Ibid., p. 75.)

The Passionate Lovers is similar to Carlell's previous court darling, *Arviragus and Philicia*, and is probably an attempt to repeat that success. The action and emphasis are similar, and like its predecessor *The Passionate Lovers* is really a ten-act play performed in two parts. Harbage notes (loc. cit.) that the isolated performance of the first part on 10 July 1638 suggests that the second part was not yet finished. This seems very likely, for in this case we have good evidence that the performance was isolated and not simply the only one recorded, since the record comes from a bill of the company for all their performances at court in the 'yeare of our lord 1638'.

Harbage also notes (ibid.) Carlell's implication that the plot of Part I, at least, was suggested by the King. In the epilogue addressed to the sovereign the author says:

> If what hath been presented to your sense
> You do approve, thank your own influence;
> Which moving in the story that you told,
> Infus'd new heat into a brain grown cold.

This is not a unique instance of Charles's active interest in the court drama. He had previously furnished the plot for Shirley's *Gamester* (q.v.), and he several times participated in censorship. (See Davenant's *The Wits*, Massinger's *The King and the Subject*, and above, i. 333.)

Inigo Jones prepared scenes and costumes for the court performance. (See Simpson and Bell, *Designs*, p. 118.)

The edition of 1655 was dedicated to Mary, Duchess of Richmond and Lennox, by the former King's actor, Alexander Gough. During the interregnum Gough also brought to the publishers, and wrote dedications for, editions of *The Widow* and *The Queen*.

Alexander Brome published verses on the play in his *Songs and Other Poems*, 1661, but he says that he never saw it and did not know the author well.

The Spartan Ladies (1634)
(Lost)

1634, 1 May. 'To a Newe play Called the spartan Lady: 1 . . . 00–
01–03.' (From the Account-Book of Sir Humphrey Mildmay,
B.M. Harl. MS. 454, 176ᵛ. The Diary entry [6ᵛ] is 'after dynner
att a play alone'. See above, ii. 676.)

1646, 4 Sept. S.R. Robinson and Moseley entered, with other plays,
'Spartan Ladies . . . by Mʳ Carlile'. (Greg, *Bibliography*, i.
56–57.)

1657. '241 The Spartan Ladyes . . . By *Lodowick Carlell* Gent.'
(Advertised by Humphrey Moseley in Middleton's *Two New
Plays* under the heading 'These Books I do purpose to Print
very speedily.')

1668/9, c. 12 Jan. 'Plays Acted at the Theatre Royall.
    A Catalogue of part of His Maᵗᵉˢ Servants Playes as they
were formerly acted at the Blackfryers & now allowed of to his
Maᵗᵉˢ Servants at yᵉ New Theatre. . . .
                            The Spartan Ladyes.'
(Printed by Nicoll, *A History of Restoration Drama*, 3rd ed.,
pp. 315–16, from L.C. 5/12, p. 212.)

1672/3, 30 Jan. S.R. 'Spartan Ladys. halfe'. (Transferred from
the estate of Humphrey Robinson to John Martin and Henry
Herringman with 104 other titles. Greg, *Bibliography*, i. 72–73.)

1683, 21 Aug. S.R. 'Spartaine Ladies.' (Transferred from the
estate of John Martin to Robert Scott. Ibid., p. 75.)

Though the play is lost, it can be dated from the fact that Sir
Humphrey Mildmay called it 'Newe' in May 1634. This fact ne-
gates W. W. Greg's suggestion (*Library*, Third Series, ii [1911],
240, n. 1) that *The Spartan Ladies* was simply another title for
Carlell's *The Deserving Favourite*, for *The Deserving Favourite* was
published in 1629, and a theatre habitué like Sir Humphrey would
not have designated as new a play which was five years old and
possibly more.

Since Mildmay does not name the theatre at which he saw the
play, there is no direct evidence that it was performed by the
King's men, but there is a good amount of evidence suggesting
that it probably was. (See above, i. 117.)

Mildmay's is the only one of six listings of the title which gives
it in the singular; it seems likely, therefore, that the plural was
used by Carlell.

THOMAS CARLETON (*alias* Medcalf)
fl. 1614–25

This man wrote three Latin plays, two of which are lost, for performance at the English College at Douai in 1619, 1620, and 1623. In 1619 he was Professor of Rhetoric there. Father McCabe notes (*T.L.S.*, 15 August 1935, p. 513) that he was at the college as student, teacher, and priest from 1614 until 1625.

Actio . . . de Henrico 8° (1623)
(Lost)

A play with this title, now lost, was performed in the English College at Douai 10 October 1623. (William H. McCabe, *T.L.S.*, 15 August 1935, p. 513.)

Fatum Vortigerni Seu miserabilis vita et exitus Vortigerni regis Britanniae una complectens aduentum Saxonum siue Anglorum in Britanniam (1619)

MS: B.M. MS. Lansdowne 723, folios. 1–42.

Churchill, G. B., and W. Keller. 'Die lateinischen Universitäts-Dramen Englands in der Zeit der Königin Elisabeth', *Shakespeare Jahrbuch*, xxxiv (1898), 258–64.
McCabe, William H. 'Fatum Vortigerni', *T.L.S.*, 15 August 1935, p. 513.

This play has been several times examined and assigned various conjectural dates. Father McCabe points out that it was written by Thomas Carleton (Medcalf) and produced at the English College at Douai 22 August 1619. He says that 'the whole treatment of the Vortigern-Roxina situation is a transparent Catholic commentary on that of Henry VIII and Anne Boleyn'.

Tragaedia de Emma Angliae Regina ac Matre Hardi-Canuti Regis (1620)
(Lost)

A Latin tragedy, now lost, produced at the English College at Douai 8 September 1620. (William H. McCabe, *T.L.S.*, 15 August 1935, p. 513.)

JOHN CART
fl. 1625?

W. J. Lawrence suggested that John Cart, known only as the author of a ballad, may have been the author of *The Two Merry Milkmaids*, 1620. Mr. Lawrence's own phraseology indicates how casual a guess this suggestion is:

> The author [of the dialogue song, *The Cunning Age*, S.R. 1629] was one John Cart, of whom we know nothing, and, idle as it may be, I feel disposed to speculate whether this man was the ' J. C.' who wrote the play of *The Two Merry Milkmaids*, printed in 1620, and usually assigned without any particular reason to John Cumber [e.g. by Lawrence himself in 1922], the actor, who is not known to have written anything. (*Pre-Restoration Stage Studies* [1927], p. 98.)

WILLIAM CARTWRIGHT
1611–43

Anon., 'Cartwright's Poems and Plays', *The Retrospective Review*, ix (1824), 160–72.

Boas, F. S. 'The William Cartwright of the Beaumont and Fletcher First Folio', *M.L.R.* xxv (1930), 81–82.

Danton, J. Periam. 'William Cartwright and his *Comedies, Tragi-Comedies, With Other Poems* . . . 1651', *Library Quarterly*, xii (1942), 438–56.

Evans, Gwynne B. '*Comedies, Tragi-Comedies, with Other Poems, By Mr. William Cartwright (1651) A Bibliographical Study*', *Library*, Fourth Series, xxiii (1942), 12–22.

—— *The Life and Works of William Cartwright*, 3 vols. Unpublished Harvard Dissertation (1940).

Goffin, R. Cullis. *The Life and Poems of William Cartwright* (1918).

Cartwright was christened on 26 December 1611 at Ashchurch, near Tewkesbury, the son of William Cartwright, a gentleman of Northway (Goffin, p. xii), who later, according to Anthony à Wood (*Athenæ Oxon.*, Bliss ed., iii. 69), became an innkeeper at Cirencester. After studying with Henry Topp at Cirencester, the boy became a King's Scholar at Westminster. In 1628 he was entered as a gentleman commoner at Christ Church, Oxford, where he remained for the rest of his life, proceeding B.A. in 1632 and M.A. in 1635. (*Alumni Oxon.* i. 245.) In 1638 he took orders and in 1642 became Reader in Metaphysics to the University. (Goffin, p. xvii.) After active hostilities began Cartwright was elected a member of the University Council of War, and in September 1642, when Lord Say entered Oxford, he was imprisoned because of his Royalist activities. He was shortly released, and after Edgehill he preached before the King when His Majesty lodged at Christ Church. (Goffin, p. xxiv.) In April 1643 Cartwright was appointed Junior Proctor by the University. (Ibid., p. xxiv.) Wood says that he died on 29 November of this year and was buried two days later (*Athenæ Oxon.*, Bliss ed., iii. 70), but the registers of Christ Church Cathedral record that he was buried in the church on 7 December 1643. (Goffin, p. xxvi.)

Wood calls Cartwright 'the most noted Poet, Orator, and Philosopher of his time' (op. cit. iii. 69), and the fifty-odd commendatory poems prefixed to the *Works* of 1651 (surpassing even the number in the Beaumont and Fletcher Folio of 1647) testify to his great reputation, especially at Oxford, where his Metaphysical school and his preaching were very popular. Several of the poets of the 1651 collection record their admiration for Cartwright's unusual combination of talents, as poet-preacher-philosopher. To the modern mind it seems a little curious that this darling of the Oxford dons, the eloquent preacher, the inspiring lecturer in philosophy, should have been a playwright, but it is characteristic of the Caroline scene that on his way to the rostrum and the pulpit he should have dallied on the stage. His four plays are all academic or private productions, though three of them eventually reached the London stage.

Cartwright's contemporary reputation is somewhat surprising to twentieth-century readers. In addition to the fifty-odd commendatory poems for the 1651 edition, there are more than a score of allusions to him between his death and 1700, and Sir Richard Baker lists him with Shakespeare, Fletcher, Jonson, Beaumont, Massinger, and eight or nine others who made poetry 'never more resplendent' than in their time. (*A Chronicle of the Kings of England*, 1660, p. 503.)

The poet, playwright, and preacher should not be confused—as he has been sometimes—with either of the two London actors of the same name. (See above, ii. 402–5.)

Collected Editions

Comedies, Tragi-Comedies, With other Poems, By Mr *William Cartwright*, late Student of *Christ-Church* in *Oxford*, and Proctor of the University . . . 1651. (Contains *The Lady Errant, The Royal Slave, The Ordinary, The Siege*, and *Poems*.)

The Life and Works of William Cartwright, ed. Gwynne Blake-more Evans. 3 vols. Unpublished Harvard Dissertation (1940).

The City Cozener

See *The Ordinary*.

The Lady Errant (1628–43)

Evans, Gwynn Blakemore, ed. *The Life and Works of William Cartwright*. Unpublished Harvard Dissertation, 1940, i. 47–66.

1648, 4 May. S.R. Humphrey Moseley entered 'a booke called Poems & Playes (vizt.) The Seige or Loues Convert, The Lady Errant, The Citty Cozener or The Ordinary. being TrageComedies by M^r. [*altered from* W^m.] W^m: Cartwright.' (Greg, *Bibliography*, i. 59.)

1651. The Lady-Errant. A Tragi-Comedy. Written by Mr William Cartwright, Late Student of *Christ-Church* in Oxford, and Proctor of the *Vniversity* . . . 1651. (Separate title-page in *Comedies, Tragi-comedies, with other Poems*, 1651.)

Except for a passing reference to Lucasia in John Berkenhead's verses for the 1651 collected edition, I can find no contemporary external evidence concerning this play; conjectures must be made from the text itself.

Notable is the highly abnormal fact that half the characters are women, and that women have far more lines than the men. The explanation of this unusual plan of the play is found in the prologue:

> *Yet if you will conceive, that though*
> *The Poem's forc'd, We are not so;*
> *And that each Sex keeps to it's Part,*
> *Nature may plead excuse for Art.*
>
> *As then there's no Offence*
> *Giv'n to the Weak or Stubborn hence,*
> *Being the Female's Habit is*
> *Her owne, and the Male's his:*
> *So (if great things may steer by less)*
> *May you the same in looks express:*
> *Your Weare is Smiles, and Gracious Eyes;*
> *When ere you frown 'tis but disguise.*

Such a performance, with women in the female roles, would

necessarily have been a private one in Cartwright's time; both the number and the prominence of the female roles indicate that Cartwright prepared the play for a production with actresses and did not merely adapt it for them. Fleay's suggestion (*Biog. Chron.* i. 48) that it was performed before the Elector Palatine and Prince Rupert has nothing to recommend it, but he is right in noting that the play was not performed at court; the second stanza of the prologue makes this clear:

> *We cannot here complain*
> *Of want of Presence, or of Train;*
> *For if choice Beauties make the Court,*
>   *And their Light guild the Sport,*
> *This honour'd Ring presents us here*
> *Glories as rich and fresh as there;*
> *And it may under Question fall,*
> *Which is more Court, This, or* White-Hall.

Such an assembly of ladies, if not at court, would presumably have been in some great house, and the occasion might have been a wedding. Though the plot of the play does not seem specially designed for a wedding, the last stanzas of the epilogue suggest some such occasion:

> *But Sleep beginning now to shed*
>   *Poppies on every Bed,*
> *Love stay'd his hands, and said our Eyes*
>   *This Night were made his Prize:*
> *And now (instead of Poppies) flings*
> *These wishes on you from his wings.*
>
> *The Calm of Kingdoms new made Friends,*
> *When both enjoy their Hopes, and Ends,*
>   *The like in you Create,*
>   *And make each Mind a State:*
> *The thoughts of Princes, when they do*
> *Meet Princes to coyn Princes too,*
>
> *Possess your Breasts with Fire and Youth,*
>   *And make each dream a Truth:*
> *The Joyes of Friendship after Fight,*
>   *Of Love's first happy Night,*
> *Of Lords return'd, make you still greet,*
>   *As when you first did meet.*
> *And, quitted thus from Grief and Fear,*
> *Think you enjoy a* Cyprus *here.*

The prologue and the stage directions make specific and detailed

K

references to the setting, as in *The Royal Slave*, from which Professor Allardyce Nicoll concluded that the play was intended to be acted with scenery. (*Stuart Masques*, p. 139.) There is, however, another possible explanation. In all his plays Cartwright has written stage directions more specific and descriptive than those in most Caroline plays, but only *The Royal Slave* and *The Lady Errant* make specific use of the setting beyond the normal Caroline practice. There is, however, a striking difference between the two. The stage directions in *The Royal Slave* are so pointed and boastful in their references to the sets, and especially to the change of sets, that the presence and character of the scenery would be perfectly clear even if we had none of the external evidence. In *The Lady Errant* there is no description, no advertising, and no real change of scenery noted or required. The wording of the stage directions, their casualness, and especially the use of the definite article rather than the indefinite as in *The Royal Slave*, suggest to me the use of a real and not a painted setting. For example:

I. I. Cosmeta, Pandena, (Rhodia between them) *busily discoursing in the Myrtle Grove.*

I. 4. *Eumela goes to Florina and Malthora who are sate in the Grove.*

III. I. Olyndus *to* Lucasia *in the Grove.*

III. 2 [near end]. *They fight, and wound each other dangerously, and then retire,* Charistus *to* Lucasia's *Myrtle, and* Olyndus *to the next adjoyning, and leaning there speak.*

III. 5, line 16. *They rise amaz'd, the Princess repairs to the Tree where* Charitus *bled, and* Eumela *to the Tree where her* Olyndus *bled.*

III. 6. *They leave their Trees, and repair to* Machessa.

IV. 3. *She draws the hangings and shews 'em.*

Further, at the beginning of the last scene (v. 8) there is an elaborate tableau with nine lines of directions for the placing of the characters, as in the last scene of *The Royal Slave*, but here there is not one word of the setting. I should hazard the guess, therefore, that *The Lady Errant* was played—or intended to be played—in a garden before a grove, with a painted cloth stretched between two trees for the revelation of IV. 3. Such a setting would account for the distinctive character of the play's stage directions among the Cartwright plays and would be compatible with the odd designation of the seated audience in the prologue:

> *This honour'd Ring presents us here*
> *Glories as rich and fresh as there:*

Gwynne Blakemore Evans suggests (op. cit., pp. 48–49) that the opening lines of the epilogue indicate a rivalry between this play and Randolph's Cambridge pastoral play, *Amyntas*. The lines are:

> *Though we well know the Neighbouring Plain*
> *Can strike from Reeds as high a Strain,*
> *And that the Scrip, and Crook*
> *May worse our Poet's Book;*
> *Like Fayries yet we here could stay*
> *Till Village Cocks proclame the Day:*

Evans's suggestion seems to me a very apt and ingenious explanation of the lines, but I hesitate to accept it in the absence of any evidence of date or of circumstances of production. It requires the assumption that *Amyntas* was also produced before this same audience.

The play has been variously dated between 1634 and 1637—all without significant evidence except for Moseley's statement in his address 'To the Reader' before the 1651 edition:

> *We have not yet told you He was a* Divine, *some body will like his* Poems *the worse for it; but such will mistake both Him and his Book: for as here is nothing his* Function *need blush at, so here is but one Sheet was written after he entred* Holy Orders; *some before He was twenty years old, scarce any after five and twenty.*

The address as a whole seems rather knowledgeable, but Moseley was, after all, trying to sell books, not write history. The winning frankness of 'but one Sheet' is not quite what it seems when one notes that twelve pages of the poems are dated in the titles 1640, 1638, 1638, 1640, 1641, 1641. I see no good evidence to date the play more accurately than after Cartwright's matriculation and before his death, that is 1628–43.

There is no known comprehensive source for the play, though there are several familiar situations. Evans's statement is fair:

> In the case of *The Lady Errant* it is impossible to point to any specific source, though Cartwright seems to have taken hints from the *Ecclesiazusae* and *Thesmophoriazusae* of Aristophanes, Erasmus's 'The Assembly or Parliament of Woman', and perhaps Fletcher's *The Sea-Voyage*. These are woven together with strands of Amazonian legend and pygmy lore. (*Summaries of Theses, 1940*, Harvard University [1942], p. 344.)

The play was prepared for revival in the Restoration. Professor T. W. Baldwin, of the University of Illinois, owns a copy of the *Comedies, Tragi-comedies*, 1651, in which *The Lady Errant* and *The Ordinary* are marked as prompt copies. *The Lady Errant* shows various cuts and alterations and bears the licence of Sir Henry

Herbert to the Duke's Company, dated 9 March 1671. (Evans, *Life and Works*, pp. 40–41, 52–53.)

Thorn-Drury noted in his edition of *Parnassus Biceps* (p. 177) that the ode from III. 4 was set to music by Dr. Colman (for the original performance?) and that poem and music were printed in Playford's *Select Musicall Ayres, And Dialogues*, 1652. The verses alone also appear in *Parnassus Biceps*, 1656, and Cotgrave's *Wits Interpreter*, 1655.

Love's Convert

See *The Siege*.

The Ordinary, or The City Cozener (1634–1634/5)

Editions: Ancient British Drama (1810), iii. 142–78; Robert Dodsley, ed., *A Select Collection of Old Plays* (1825–7), x. 167–268.

Ballmann, Otto. 'Chaucers Einfluß auf das englische Drama', *Anglia*, Bd. xxv, Neue Folge Bd. xiii (1902), 1–85.

Evans, Gwynne Blakemore, ed. *The Life and Works of William Cartwright*. Unpublished Harvard Dissertation, 1940, i. 112–54.

Gerber, Friedrich, *The Sources of William Cartwright's Comedy, The Ordinary* (1909).

1648, 4 May. S.R. Humphrey Moseley entered 'a booke called Poems & Playes (Viz^t.) The Seige or Loues Convert, The Lady Errant, The Citty Cozener or The Ordinary. being Trage-Comedies by M^r. [*altered from* W^m.] W^m: Cartwright'. (Greg, *Bibliography*, i. 59.)

1651. The Ordinary, A Comedy, Written by William Cartwright, *M.A. Ch. Ch. Oxon*. . . . 1651. (Separate title-page in *Comedies, Tragi-comedies*, 1651.)

The play is dated from a speech by Moth, the Chaucerian antiquary, in III. 1:

> I *Robert Moth*, this tenth of our King
> Give to thee *Joan Potluck* my biggest crumpe Ring:
> And with it my Carcasse entire I bequeathen
> Under my foot to Hell, above my head to heaven:

The tenth regnal year of Charles I began 27 March 1634 and ended 26 March 1635. On the separate title-page for *The Ordinary* in the 1651 collection, Cartwright is called '*M.A. Ch. Ch. Oxon.*', whereas on the title-pages of the other three plays in the volume he is called, with various spellings, 'Late Student of Christ-Church in Oxford, and Proctor of the Vniversity'. Fleay took this fact as evidence that the play was presented on the occasion of the award of Cartwright's M.A. (*Biog. Chron.* i. 47–48.) Cartwright was indeed popular at Oxford in his later years, but it seems scarcely plausible that Christ Church would have gone to such lengths to celebrate his Master's degree; author designations in other University manuscripts tend to give the author's degrees at the time the copyist wrote, not at the time of first performance.

The prologue and epilogue of the play emphasize the author's inexperience and show an oddly deferential attitude toward the audience—not quite obsequious enough for a royal audience, but much more respectful than was usual for a University audience. Perhaps the play was performed before some visiting dignitaries at Oxford.

Like so many of the cheating comedies, *The Ordinary* is full of reminiscences. Evans goes so far as to say, 'Indeed *The Ordinary* is little more than an overt imitation of the Jonsonian comedy of humours and in particular of *The Alchemist*', and he goes on to list seven more Jonsonian productions and twelve other plays 'which may be supposed to have contributed their share'. (Op. cit., p. 344.) Gerber finds a number of other parallels, most of them very dubious, to Peele, Shakespeare, Middleton, Shirley, and Beaumont and Fletcher. He demonstrates very clearly, however, that many of the speeches of Moth are derived from Chaucer, a number of them paraphrases or even quotations from *The Canterbury Tales, Troilus and Criseyde, The Legend of Good Women, Boethius,* and *The Book of the Duchess.* A number of these borrowings had been pointed out before by Ballmann. (Op. cit., p. xiii.) Miss Margery Fisher finds imitations of Middleton's *A Fair Quarrel, Michaelmas Term, The Mayor of Quinborough, Your Five Gallants,* and *The Phoenix. (R.E.S.* xv [1939], 293 n.)

Cartwright was obviously a widely read man, and *The Ordinary* is not an example of fresh observation, but neither is it a scissors-and-paste job, as some of the scholars might lead one to believe. For Cartwright, Jonson was the model poet, as his verses in *Jonsonus Virbius* and the remarks of his contemporaries in their commendatory verses indicate; the comedy of humours, therefore, and especially *The Alchemist,* seem to be models rather than sources for the play. In his character of Moth, the antiquary, Cartwright has clearly amused himself by working in as many quotations from or paraphrases of Chaucer as he could. It is at least doubtful that he had direct reference to the other plays mentioned. Scenes of cheating and of tavern life have a certain amount of similarity in scores of Jacobean and Caroline realistic comedies; scholars sometimes forget that many of them can also be duplicated in the records of cases in Chancery.

The comedy was not forgotten after its first performance, as most University plays were. Langbaine noted that a dialogue from the play was reprinted in Cotgrave's anthology, *Wits Interpreter*, 1655, and Evans noted two others in this anthology and three more in *The Marrow of Compliments*, 1655.

The play was prepared for a Restoration performance. Professor T. W. Baldwin of the University of Illinois has a copy of *Comedies, Tragi-comedies*, 1651, in which *The Lady Errant* and *The Ordinary* have been marked as prompt copies, and *The Ordinary* bears Sir Henry Herbert's licence for production dated 15 January 1671. A prologue and an epilogue, presumably for this revival, are printed in *A Collection of Poems Written upon Several Occasions*, 1673; I have not seen the edition of 1671. (Evans, *Life and Works*, pp. 40–41; 115–18.)

Miss Willa McClung Evans discusses Henry Lawes's music for Priscilla's song, 'Com O Com I brooke noe staye', in III. 2, and its contribution to the effect of the scene. (*Henry Lawes, Musician and Friend of Poets* [1941], p. 113 and n. 7.)

The Persian Slave

See *The Royal Slave*.

The Royal Slave [*The Persian Slave*] (30 August and 2 September 1636; 12 January 1636/7)

MSS.: B.M. Add. MS. 41616; Petworth House (see *Hist. MSS. Com.*, Sixth Report, Appendix, p. 307); Folger Shakespeare Library MS. 7044; Bodleian MS. Arch. Seld. B. 26; Library of the Duke of Bedford.

Evans, Gwynne Blakemore, ed. *The Life and Works of William Cartwright*. Unpublished Harvard Dissertation, 1940, i. 67–112.

Evans, Willa McClung. *Henry Lawes, Musician and Friend of Poets* (1941), pp. 122–35.

Rice, Warner G. 'Sources of William Cartwright's *The Royall Slave*', *M.L.N.* xlv (1930), 515–18.

Simpson, Percy. *Proof-Reading in the Sixteenth, Seventeenth, and Eighteenth Centuries* (1935), pp. 83–84.

1636, 15 July. Letter of Archbishop Laud. (See below.)

1636, 30 Aug. Diary of Thomas Crosfield. (See below.)

1636, 4 Sept. George Garrard to Viscount Conway. (See below.)

1636, 8 Sept. Thomas Reade to Secretary Windebank. (See below.)

1636, 26 Sept. George Evelyn to his father. (See below.)

1636/7, 11 Jan. Edward Rossingham to Sir Thomas Puckering. (See below.)

1636/7, 12 Jan. 'The 12th. of January the new play from Oxford. the Royall slave.' (From a bill of the King's company for plays presented before the King and Queen in 1636 and 1636/7. Adams, *Herbert*, pp. 75–76.)

1636/7, 12 Jan. '*The Royal Slave*, on thursday the 12 of Janu.— Oxford play, written by Cartwright. The king gave him forty pounds.' (Ibid., p. 57.)

1637, 4 Apr. Payment of production expenses in the Lord Chamberlain's Warrant Book. (See below.)

1639. The Royall Slave. *A* Tragi-Comedy. Presented to the King and Queene by the Students of *Christ-Church* in Oxford. *August* 30. 1636. Presented since to both their Majesties at *Hampton-Court* by the Kings Servants. *Oxford* . . . 1639.

1640. The Royall Slave . . . *The second Edition* . . . 1640.

1651. The Royall Slave . . . The Third Edition . . . 1651. (Separate title-page in *Comedies, Tragi-comedies, with other Poems,* . . . 1651.)

1668/9, *c.* 12 Jan. 'The Royall Slaue' is one of a number of plays listed in 'A Catalogue of part of His Ma^tes Servants Playes as they were formerly acted at the Blackfryers & now allowed of to his Ma^tes Servants at ye New Theatre'. (Nicoll, *History of Restoration Drama*, 3rd ed., pp. 315–16.)

The Royal Slave is the third of a series of three plays produced at Oxford for the visit of the King, the Queen, and the two Princes of the Palatinate, 29, 30, and 31 August 1636. On the night of the 29th they saw Strode's *The Floating Island* (q.v.) in Christ Church Hall; on the afternoon of the 30th Wilde's *Love's Hospital* (q.v.) in St. John's Hall; and on the night of the 30th Cartwright's *Royal Slave*, again in Christ Church Hall.

The visit, carefully and generously planned by Archbishop Laud, then Chancellor of Oxford, was a great success and was described by a number of contemporaries. (See below, Strode's *Floating Island*.) *The Royal Slave* was clearly the climax of the visit. George Garrard wrote to Viscount Conway, 4 September 1636, that:

The play [*Love's Hospital*] over, their Majesties returned to Christ-church to supper, then had another play, the Persian Slave, excellently written by a young Master of Arts, one Cartwright. Generally liked, and the Lord Chamberlain so transported with it, that he swore mainly he never saw such a play before. (*C.S.P., Dom., 1636–7*, p. 114.)

Thomas Crosfield, Fellow of Queen's College, recorded in his diary, '. . . & after supper a Comedy vizt ye Royall Slave was acted wth good applause of King & Queene.' (*Crosfield Diary*, p. 92.) George Evelyn, brother of the diarist, wrote to his father a full description of the festivities on 26 September 1636, in which he said of Cart-wright's triumph:

The play [*Love's Hospital*] being ended, he went to Christ-church; and, after supper, to another play, called the Royal Slave, all the actors performing in a Persian habit, which play much delighted his Majesty and all the nobles, commending it for the best that ever was acted. (William Bray, ed., *The Diary and Correspondence of John Evelyn* [1870], i. 423–4.)

Archbishop Laud confirms the success of the play in his account:

The Play ended, the King and the Queen went to Christ Church, retired and supped privately, and about eight o'clock, went into the Hall to see another Play, which was upon a piece of a Persian story. It was very well penned and acted, and the strangeness of the Persian habits gave great content; so that all men came forth from it very well satisfied. And the Queen liked it so well, that she afterwards sent to me to have the apparel sent to Hampton Court, that she might see her own players act it over again, and see whether they could do it as well, as it was done in the University. . . . And by all men's confession, the players came short of the University actors. (*Autobiography*, pp. 207–8.)

Anthony à Wood has apparently taken part of his record of the performance from Laud, but he adds some very interesting details:

The Play ended, the King and the Queen went to Christ Church, retired and supped privately, and about 8 of the clock went into the Common Hall there to see another Comedy called 'The Royall Slave', made by Mr. Will. Cartwright of that House. It contained much more variety than that of 'Passions calmed' [Strode's *Floating Island*; q.v. for his description of its sets]. Within the shuts were seen a curious Temple, and the Sun shining over it, delightful forests also, and other prospects. Within the great shuts mentioned before, were seen villages, and men visibly appearing in them, going up and down, here and there, about their business. The Interludes thereof were represented with as much variety of scenes and motions as the great wit of Inigo Jones (well skilled in setting out a Court Maske to the best advantage)

could extend unto. It was very well pen'd and acted, and the strangeness of the Persian habits gave great content. All men came forth very
well contented, and full of applause of what they had seen and heard.
'It was the day of St. Felix,' (as the Chancellor observed) 'and all
things went happy.' (*History and Antiquities of Oxford*, ii, Book I,
411–12.)

A play received with such enthusiasm by the court could not be
forgotten. Three days after the departure of the royal guests and
the court there was another performance:

On Friday in the afternoon (Sept. 2) was acted according to the
Chancellor's appointment, 'The Royall Slave,' in Christ Church Hall,
before the University and Strangers, and the next day in the afternoon, 'Passions calmed.' Both which were acted very quietly and
gave great content. (Wood, op. cit. ii, Book I, 412.)

Though there is no cast of the play, so far as I know, Langbaine
says that Richard Busby, later the famous birching Headmaster
of Westminster, played in it and proved himself 'a second *Roscius*.'
(*An Account of the English Dramatick Poets*, pp. 53–54.) The authors
of *The Record of Old Westminsters* (i. 148) say that he 'acted the
part of Cratander in Cartwright's Royal Slave at Ch. Ch. Aug. 30,
1636, with great success'. Probably most of the members of the
cast were Christ Church men, but Archbishop Laud's letter of 15
July 1636 suggests that some may not have been:

Indeed, if Christ Church men will say, they will have no actors but
of their own House, let them bear the charge of their own Plays, in
God's name: but if they will take any good actors from any other
College or Hall, upon trial of their sufficiency to be as good, or better
than their own; then I see no reason in the world, but that the whole
University should contribute to the charge. And I pray see it ordered,
and let your successor follow you accordingly. (*Autobiography*, p. 196.)

In addition to the University performances of the play there was
also a request performance given by professional actors at court,
as we saw in Laud's account above. Laud says further:

I caused the University to send both the clothes, and the perspec-
tives of the stage; and the Play was acted at Hampton Court in
November following. And by all men's confession, the players came
short of the University actors. Then I humbly desired of the King and
the Queen, that neither the Play, nor clothes, nor stage, might come
into the hands and use of the common players abroad, which was
graciously granted. (*Autobiography*, pp. 207–8.)

Anthony à Wood has virtually the same account, except that he
says the request and not the performance came in November, and

he adds that Cartwright went to London for the performance. (*Hist. and Antiq. Oxon.* ii, Book I, 412–13.)

In spite of Laud's superior sources of information, his version of the date seems to be wrong; Wood's statement that the letter, not the performance, came in November fits the other records of the play better. The King's men presented a bill for twenty-two plays performed at court between April 1636 and February 1636/7, in which the only performance of *The Royal Slave* is dated 12 January 1636/7, at Hampton Court (see above, i. 51); and Sir Henry Herbert in recording this performance under the same date says, 'Oxford play, written by Cartwright. The king gave him forty pounds.' (Adams, *Herbert*, p. 57.) Neither Herbert's identification of the play nor the King's reward would seem to be appropriate for a second London court performance.

It may be noted that both Laud and Wood say that the Queen borrowed the play costumes and sets in order to see a performance by 'her own players'. Now these words would presumably mean Queen Henrietta's company, which had performed for a number of years at the Cockpit theatre under the management of Christopher Beeston, yet the record shows a performance by the King's company. The reason that the Queen did not have the play performed by her own company is probably that by the time the sets and costumes got to London she had no company. Beeston seems to have broken the Queen's men during the protracted plague of 1636–7; there is no record of the company after the Queen's visit to Oxford in August 1636, and her new company was not active before the autumn of 1637. (See above, i. 236–41.)

Though the official record of Sir Henry Herbert and the players' formal bill presented to the Lord Chamberlain seem conclusive as to the company and the date of the professional performance of *The Royal Slave* at court, there is a disturbing discrepancy in a letter dated 11 January 1636/7 written by Edward Rossingham to Sir Thomas Puckering:

Upon Twelfth-night, the Royal Slave, which had been acted at Oxford before their majesties the last summer, was acted by the king's players at Hampton Court. These players had procured from the university all their apparel and the scenes, which the university did not altogether approve of; yet they lent them, but with a letter to my lord chamberlain, that because they had provided that entertainment only for their majesties against their coming to Oxford, they humbly besought, that what they had done for the entertainment of their majesties might not be made common upon a stage. And this was the request of the university in general. (Birch, *Charles I*, ii. 266.)

In spite of his general information, Rossingham is clearly wrong about the date, for both the bill of the King's men and Sir Henry Herbert's record show that the play they acted at Hampton Court on Twelfth Night was *The Elder Brother*. (See above, i. 51.) I can suggest only that the spectacular revival of *The Royal Slave* might have been intended for Twelfth Night but postponed, and that Rossingham reported an event he had not seen.

Elaborate preparations for the performance at Hampton Court were made. The Lord Chamberlain's warrant for the payment for these preparations shows that the Londoners intended to outdo the University and suggests that additions to the spectacle were provided:

Wheras ye Charge of ye alterations, reparacõns & addition which were made vnto ye scene, Apparell & propertyes that were imployed for the setting forth of ye new Play called the Royall slaue, which was lately Acted & presented before his Ma^{tye} at Hampton Court, together wth the Charge of Dancers and composers of Musique which were vsed therin, amount to ye sume of One Hundred fifty fower pound*es* appearing by the billes of ye seuerall persons imployed therin . . . [pay] vnto ye seuerall persons heerafter named (vizt) to Peter Lehuc Property-maker the sume of 50^{ll} to George Portman Painter the sume of 50^{ll} & Etienne Nau & Sebastian la Pierre for themselues & twelue Dancers the sume of 54^{ll}, amounting in ye whole to ye aforesayd sume of 154^{ll} to bee payd vnto them wthout Account imprest or other Charge to bee sett vpon them or their Executors for ye same or any part therof. And this shall bee y^r warr^t. Aprill 4. 1637. (From the Lord Chamberlain's Warrant Book 5. 134. *M.S.C.* ii. 382–3.)

The £54 for the dancers would of course have been a necessary expenditure for a London performance which was identical with the Oxford one, but the £100 to painters and property-makers would not. The Lord Chamberlain's warrant expressly mentions 'ye alterations, reparacõns & addition which were made vnto ye scene, Apparell & propertyes', and the sums paid the painter and property-maker are large enough to suggest more than the repair of damage done in the shipment from Oxford.

The number of extant manuscripts and editions of the play, as well as the allusions to the Oxford performance, testify to its renown. No doubt most readers sought the text of the play as a substitute for, or memento of, the great Oxford spectacle. This, at any rate, seems to be implied in a letter from Thomas Reade of New College to his uncle, Secretary Windebank, who had probably attended the original performances, both at Oxford and at Hampton Court. The letter, dated 8 September 1636, is somewhat cryptic, but the remarks would fit *The Royal Slave* and not any other play I know.

[Reade] Has obtained all the acts of the comedy, from stem to stern of it, as he may say, which even without scenery will probably please. Scholars in a university cannot attain courtly elegance, but who shall forbid them to imitate ? The rest of the productions of the university muses are still unpublished. What was formerly in print he commits to Windebank, not as to the Antistarchus of the university, but to their Maecenas. (*C.S.P., Dom., 1636–7*, p. 117.)

Long after Cartwright's death the play was remembered. In the Collier controversy at the end of the century *The Royal Slave* takes its place in the amusingly perverted dramatic history written by George Ridpath (?):

Thus we see that our Universities formerly condemn'd the Stage, and that they came afterwards to countenance them, must without doubt be ascribed to the Influence of K. *Charles* I. and A. Bishop *Laud*; for I find on *Aug.* the 30th. 1636. the Students of *Christ-Church* in *Oxford* presented a Tragi-comedy call'd, *The Royal Slave, to the K. and Queen*, which was afterwards presented again to their Majesties at *Hampton-Court*. (*The Stage Condemned* [1698] p. 208.)

Later in his treatise (pp. 212–14) Ridpath (?) summarizes and comments upon the play.

The work which attracted so much gossip and attention in its time is by no means one of the best Caroline plays. It is stilted and dull, but, as Thomas Reade implied in his apology for it, it is clearly designed to appeal to the current court taste. (See also Alfred Harbage, *Cavalier Drama*, pp. 142–3 *et passim*.) Its spectacle is not irrelevant to the action but rather approximates the masque usage. Baskervill noted that 'the regularly placed masque scenes and antic dances in Cartwright's *Royal Slave* of 1636 foreshadow heroic opera with its elaborate scenery'. (*The Elizabethan Jig and Related Song Drama*, p. 161.)

The best study of the sources of the play, as of other aspects, is found in the Harvard manuscript thesis of Gwynne Blakemore Evans, *The Life and Works of William Cartwright*, 1940 (chap. iv, pp. 67–112). He notes that the Persian law or custom upon which the typical tragi-comedy reversal is based probably comes ultimately from Dion Chrysostom, and that details of the military plot come from Persian history. He finds even more use of the Greek romance of Theodorus Prodromus called *Rhodanthes et Dosicles Amorum*. The somewhat irrelevant IV. 3 is much like *The Beggars' Bush*, probably too like to be accidental. The resemblances between Cartwright's play and Massinger's *Bondman* noted by Warner G.

Rice (*M.L.N.* xlv [1930], 515–18) are largely inherent in the situations. Evans thinks that Rice has overstated Cartwright's indebtedness to Massinger, and I agree.

The variations in the texts of the play which I have noticed are not significant. They consist mostly in the omission of one or more of the prologues or epilogues and, especially in the manuscripts, of the set descriptions. The B.M. MS., which he thinks may have been a presentation copy for the court, is described by Greg. (*Dramatic Documents*, pp. 363–4.) The Folger MS. is the one advertised by Dr. Rosenbach. (*English Plays to 1700* [1940], Item 65.) A Harvard copy of the 1651 edition is inlaid, and in the margin are G. Thorn-Drury's notes of collation with the Bedford MS.

Miss Willa McClung Evans discusses (loc. cit.) the music of the Lawes brothers for this and for the other plays of the Oxford series.

The Siege, or Love's Convert (1628–43)

Evans, Gwynne Blakemore, ed. *The Life and Works of William Cartwright.* Unpublished Harvard Dissertation, 1940, i. 155–73.

1648, 4 May. S.R. Humphrey Moseley entered 'a booke called Poems & Playes (vizt.) The Seige or Loues Convert, The Lady Errant, The Citty Cozener or The Ordinary. being Trage-Comedies by M^r. [*altered from* W^m.] W^m: Cartwright.' (Greg, *Bibliography*, i. 59.)

1651. The Siedge: Or, Love's Convert, A Tragi-Comedy. Written by Mr William Cartwright, Late Student of *Christ-Church in* Oxford, and Proctor of the *Vniversity* . . . 1651. (Separate title-page in *Comedies, Tragi-comedies, with other Poems*, 1651.)

There is no evidence that this play was ever acted. Evans seems inclined to think that the commendatory verses of W. Towers in the 1651 edition indicate that *The Siege* was acted in London and not liked. (Evans, op. cit., pp. 156–7.) These verses are extremely obscure, and I find no evidence that they refer to *The Siege* at all, much less to its London failure. Evans thinks that the verses of Joseph Howe confirm the unsuccessful production, but Howe recounts what would have happened *if* the play had been acted, so that his verses really furnish evidence that there was no London production.

Cartwright's dedication to King Charles says that the author was about to destroy the play when the King ordered him not to, and that it was revised before publication. Evans suggests that the royal intervention must have taken place at the time of Charles's visit to Oxford in 1636, but it could equally well have occurred in London, or in Oxford after hostilities had begun. There is no considerable evidence for date.

Prefixed to the play is the 'Occasio Fabulæ' in Greek, from Plutarch's Life of Cimon, and on the same page a translation 'Which is done out of Greek into French by Mr *Jaques Amiott*, thus:' This is the source of the early part of the play. Langbaine said that part of the comic plot came from the *Decameron*, but Evans points out that the similarity is not very marked. He finds a German analogue in Pauli's *Schimpf und Ernst* and suggests that Cartwright may have seen a Latin or English version now lost. (Op. cit., pp. 162–5.)

WILLIAM CAVENDISH, Viscount Mansfield, Baron Ogle, and Earl, Marquis, and Duke of Newcastle
1593–1676

Firth, C. H., ed. *The Life of William Cavendish, Duke of Newcastle, to which is added the True Relation of My Birth, Breeding, and Life.* By Margaret, Duchess of Newcastle. (Second edition, N.D.)

Perry, Henry Ten Eyck. *The First Duchess of Newcastle and Her Husband as Literary Figures* (1918).

The great Duke of Newcastle was only incidentally and occasionally a playwright, but he wrote two plays before the closing of the theatres and three more and a dramatic translation afterwards.

William Cavendish, the second son of Sir Charles Cavendish, was baptized 16 December 1593 (Perry, op. cit., pp. 7–8). He was sent to St. John's College, Cambridge (*Alumni Cantab*. i. 311), but according to his duchess showed much more interest in sport than in learning. (Firth ed., pp. 104–5.) The groundwork for his great skill and learning in the art of equitation had already been laid. In 1612 he went abroad for a year with Sir Henry Wotton, Ambassador to Savoy, and after his return attended regularly at court. About 1618 he married Elizabeth Basset, a Staffordshire heiress (Firth ed., p. 3, n. 2), and established his residence at Welbeck Abbey. In 1620 he was created Viscount Mansfield, in 1628 Baron Cavendish of Bolsover and Earl of Newcastle, and in 1629 Baron Ogle. (Perry, pp. 11–14.)

Just when Newcastle became a friend and patron of Ben Jonson is not clear, but Jonson's epitaph on Newcastle's mother, who died in 1629, seems to indicate some knowledge of the household (*Ben Jonson*, viii. 399–400), and Jonson's extant letters to Newcastle in the early thirties indicate fairly regular association. (Ibid. i. 210–14.) For Newcastle's extravagant entertainments of King Charles at his estates of Welbeck and Bolsover in the summers of 1633 and 1634 Jonson wrote his last royal entertainments. (See below.)

In 1637/8, after several years of application, Newcastle was made tutor to the young Prince Charles. (Perry, pp. 14–20.) At the time of the First Bishops' War he raised a troop of horse called Prince Charles's troop and took them to the border, and the Duchess says that he loaned the King £10,000 at this time. (Firth ed., p. 6.) During this expedition a quarrel with the Earl of Holland, General of the Horse, caused Newcastle to send him a challenge, but Holland did not appear at the rendezvous, and the King composed the difference. (Firth ed., p. 7 and n. 5.)

In 1641 Newcastle was involved in the Army Plot; upon its exposure in Parliament he resigned his governorship of the Prince in May of that year and retired to the country. (Ibid., p. 8 and n. 1.) His retirement lasted only a few months, for in January 1641/2 the King ordered him to Hull to take command there and protect for the Crown the military supplies assembled for the recent campaign. He was forestalled by the recalcitrance of the mayor of Hull, and recalled for examination by the House of Lords. (Firth ed., p. 9, n. 1.) Again the Earl retired to the country, only to be called once more by the King in June 1642, when he was given command in the counties of Northumberland, Cumberland, Westmorland, and Durham. (Op. cit., pp. 10 ff.)

It is possible that the Earl took James Shirley with him at this time, for Anthony à Wood says in his account of Shirley:

When the Rebellion broke out, and he [i.e. Shirley] thereupon forced to leave *London*, and so consequently his Wife and Children, . . . he was invited by his most noble Patron *William* Earl (afterwards Marquess and Duke) of *Newcastle* to take his Fortune with him in the Wars, for that Count had engaged him so much by his generous liberality towards him, that he thought he could not do a worthier act, than to serve him, and so consequently his Prince. (*Athenæ Oxonienses*, 1721 ed., ii. 376–7.)

Here we reach the beginning of the Civil War, and Newcastle's later activities are of less significance for this study. He remained in command of the forces in the north for about two years and was created Marquis of Newcastle 27 October 1643. (Firth ed., p. 30 and n. 1.) After the disastrous defeat at Marston Moor in July 1644, Newcastle fled to the Continent, where he spent the next sixteen years in exile. Eventually he joined the Queen at Paris and there in December 1645 married, as his second wife, Margaret Lucas, who became famous as the 'scribbling' Duchess of Newcastle. From about 1649 until the Restoration he lived at Antwerp, where he established his famous riding school, and his first work on horsemanship was published there in 1658.

At the Restoration Newcastle returned with the King and succeeded in regaining the greater part of his sequestered estates, though because of his habitual extravagance he was heavily in debt. He was created Duke of Newcastle in 1665, and thereafter he lived much on his estates, largely absorbed in the training of horses. He died in 1676 and was buried in Westminster Abbey.

In such an active political career, literature could not have had a major part, yet Newcastle was widely known as a patron of letters and not unknown as a dramatist. Langbaine said of him:

> No Person since the Time of *Augustus* better understood Dramatick Poetry, nor more generously encourag'd Poets; so that we may truly call him our *English Mecaenas*. (*An Account of the English Dramatick Poets* [1691], p. 386.)

He was a patron of Jonson, Brome, Shirley, Davenant, Dryden, Shadwell, Flecknoe, and Hobbes.

Newcastle's notoriety as a dramatist was partly a product of the hatred of his political enemies. In February 1644/5 *Mercurius Britanicus* said:

> First, Enter *Newcastle*; one that in time of peace tired the stage in *Black-Fryers* with his *Comedies*; and afterwards, one that trode the stage in the *North* with the first *Tragedies*. (Hotson, *Commonwealth and Restoration Stage*, p. 20.)

A few weeks later the same Parliamentary news-sheet called him:

> A great pretender to Wit, a Member of Blackfryers colledge, a Stage-player, one that hath left off his *Comicall* Sockes to act Tragedies of Crueltie in the North. (12 March to 18 March, No. 27.)

About 1645 a Parliamentary pamphleteer fulminated,

> And for *Newcastle*, He's but a *Counterfeit Marquis*; at best but a *Play-wright*; one of *Apollo's Whirligigs*; one that when he should be fighting, would be *fornicating* with the *Nine Muses*, or the Deane of *York's* daughters. (*The Character of an Oxford Incendiary*, N.D.)

Still another hostile writer sneered at Newcastle's dramatic interests:

But the Earle of *Newcastle*, the brave Marquesse of *Newcastle*, which made the fine playes, he danced so quaintly, played his part a while in the North, was soundly beaten, shew'd a paire of heels, and *exit* Newcastle. (Hotson, op. cit., p. 20.)

How much of the noble lord's dramatic publication was his own unaided composition and how much the willing assistance of more experienced playwrights, it is probably now impossible to determine. Anthony à Wood said that

Our Author *Shirley* did also much assist his generous Patron *William* Duke of *Newcastle* in the composure of certain Plays, which the Duke afterwards published. (*Athenæ Oxonienses*, 1721 ed., ii. 378.)

There is some indication that this was true in the case of *The Country Captain* (q.v.).

Captain Underwit

See *The Country Captain*.

The Country Captain (1639–41)

MS.: B.M. MS. Harl. 7650 (formerly Add. MS. 5001).

Edition: A. H. Bullen, ed., *Captain Underwit* [i.e. *The Country Captain*] in *A Collection of Old English Plays* (1883), ii. 315 ff. (From the B.M. MS.)

Forsythe, Robert Stanley. *The Relations of Shirley's Plays to the Elizabethan Drama* (1914), pp. 419–29.
Perry, Henry Ten Eyck. *The First Duchess of Newcastle and Her Husband as Figures in Literary History* (1918), pp. 102–12.

1641, 7 Aug. 'The Country Captaine' is in a list of plays belonging to the King's men which the Lord Chamberlain forbade the printers to publish without the company's consent. (See above, i. 65–66.)
1639–49? B.M. MS. Harl. 7650. (See Greg, *Dramatic Documents*, pp. 362–3.)
1646, 4 Sept. S.R. In a long list of plays entered as their copies by Robinson and Moseley are:

Country Captaine⎫
Varieties [*sic*] ⎬ by my Lord of Newcastle

(Greg, *Bibliography*, i. 56–57.)

1649. The Country Captaine A Comoedye Lately Presented By his Majesties Servants at the Blackfryers. In 'Sgrave Van Haghe. Printed by Samuell Broun English Bookeseller at the Signe of the English Printing house in the Achter-ome. Anno 1649. (Separate title-page in the following.)

1649. The Country Captaine, And the Varietie, Two Comedies, Written by a Person of Honor. Lately presented by His *Maiesties* Servants, at the *Black-Fryers*. London, Printed for *Hum: Robinson* at the *Three-Pidgeons*, and *Hum: Moseley* at the *Princes Armes* in St. *Pauls* Church-yard. 1649.

1661, 26 Oct. '. . . my wife and I to the Theatre, and there saw "The Country Captain," the first time it hath been acted this twenty-five years, a play of my Lord Newcastle's, but so silly a play as in all my life I never saw, and the first that ever I was weary of in my life.' (Diary of Samuel Pepys.)

1661, 25 Nov. '. . . to the Theatre, and there saw "The Country Captain," a dull play.' (Ibid.)

1661, 13 Dec. 'The Cuntry Captaine 13. [Decemb.]' appears in a list of performances by 'the Kings Companie at the Red Bull and the new house in Gibbon's Tennis Court', 1660–2. (Adams, *Herbert*, p. 117.)

1667, 18 May. In a warrant for payment for performances of plays before royalty at court or at the Theatre Royal occurs the item: 'May 18 The Country Capt. at ye Theatre . . . £10.' (Nicoll, *History of Restoration Drama*, 3rd ed., pp. 305–6.)

1667, 14 Aug. '. . . to the King's playhouse, and there saw "The Country Captain," which is a very ordinary play. Methinks I had no pleasure therein at all.' (Diary of Samuel Pepys.)

1668, 14 May. '. . . then into the [King's] playhouse again, and there saw "The Country Captain," a very dull play, that did give us no content, and besides, little company there, which made it very unpleasing.' (Ibid.)

1668/9, c. 12 Jan. In 'A Catalogue of part of His Mates Servants Playes as they were formerly acted at the Blackfryers & now allowed of to his Mates Servants at ye New Theatre' is found 'Country Captaine / The Variety.' (A. Nicoll, *A History of Restoration Drama*, 3rd ed., pp. 315–16, from L.C. 5/12, p. 212.)

1672/3, 30 Jan. S.R. 'Country Captaine, halfe,' transferred from the estate of Humphrey Robinson to John Martin and Henry Herringman with 104 other titles. (Greg, *Bibliography*, i. 72–73.)

c. 1680. Welbeck Abbey MS. of a 'Prologue or Epilogue To The Country Captain' by Thomas Shadwell for a revival of the play 'after forty yeares'. (*Welbeck Miscellany*, No. 2 [1934], p. 50.)

1683, 21 Aug. S.R. 'Country Capt:' transferred from the estate of
John Martin to Robert Scott with 359 other titles. (Greg,
Bibliography, i. 75–76.)

When Bullen in his *Collection of Old English Plays* reprinted
the play from the B.M. MS., he did not know that it had been
printed before, and he did not know the name of the author. He
followed Halliwell[-Phillipps], *A Dictionary of Old English Plays*,
in entitling it *Captain Underwit*, and he proposed James Shirley as
author. The manuscript in the British Museum is, however, Newcastle's *Country Captain*, though it shows a number of minor
variations from the version printed at The Hague in 1649.

It is not surprising that Newcastle gave his play to the King's
company at Blackfriars, for that troupe performed most of the
plays written by courtiers. The date of the Lord Chamberlain's
letter listing the play as part of the repertory of the company
provides us with a *terminus ad quem*. In III. 3 there is a reference
to the Great Ship which was common talk in 1637 and 1638.
(See Thomas Heywood's pamphlet *A True Description of His
Majesties Royall Ship Built . . . at Wooll-witch*, 1637.) Even later
are the events referred to in I. I in the reference to the 'league
at Berwick and the late expedition', an evident allusion to the
First Bishops' War and the Treaty of Berwick, which was signed
18 June 1639. (See Gardiner, *History of England*, ix. 1–40.) This
last allusion indicates production not earlier than the last half
of 1639.

The opening lines of the prologue are clearly intended to refer
to a recent elaborate production:

> Gallants, I'le tell you what we doe not meane
> To shew you here, a glorious painted Scene,
> With various doores, to stand in stead of wit,
> Or richer cloathes with lace, for lines well writ;
> Taylors and Paynters thus, your deare delight,
> May prove your Poets onely for your sight.

This description would fit the production of Habington's *Queen
of Aragon* (q.v.), which took place in April 1640, with clothes and
scenery furnished by the Lord Chamberlain. There may, however,
have been other such productions now unknown, and the allusion
is not certain enough for one to say with assurance that *The
Country Captain* was produced after April 1640.

Dr. Forsythe argued for a much earlier date (op. cit.), but he
was led astray by his eagerness to identify *The Country Captain*
with the lost *Looke to the Ladie*, entered in the Stationers' Register

as Shirley's on 11 March 1639/40. Since that title (q.v.) has now been found in a list dated about 1619 or 1620, all possibilities of identification disappear.

What connexion did James Shirley have with the play? That he had something to do with it has been frequently asserted and seems likely enough from his known associations with Newcastle and that nobleman's rank and inexperience. When Bullen published the play without knowledge of what it was or of Newcastle's connexion, he cited many similarities to Shirley's work and summarized that 'it is absolutely certain . . . that *Captain Underwit* is a comedy of Shirley's'. (Ed. cit., preface.) The most direct evidence of Shirley's part in the play is the appearance of the dicing song at the beginning of Act IV in Shirley's *Poems &c.*, 1646, where it is entitled 'A Catch' but printed as a rebus with pictures of the dice. How much of the play is his composition is a matter of speculation. Firth's statement that Newcastle 'wrote many passages, and doubtless conceived the plan of the play, but to fit it for the stage he had to call in the aid of an expert dramatist, and owed more to his assistant than he owned' (*The Life of William Cavendish, Duke of Newcastle*, 2nd ed., N.D., p. xviii) is only a guess.

The hand of the manuscript of *The Country Captain* at the British Museum is, according to R. W. Haworth (*R.E.S.* viii [1932], 203), the same as that of the original hand in the Worcester College MS. of James Shirley's *The Court Secret*.

The Humorous Lovers (1667)

1677. The Humorous Lovers. A Comedy, Acted by His Royal Highnes's Servants. Written by His Grace the Duke of Newcastle . . . 1677.

See Henry Ten Eyck Perry, *The First Duchess of Newcastle and Her Husband as Figures in Literary History* (1918), pp. 145–50.

A Pleasant and Merry Humour of a Rogue (1655–60?)

Edition: 'A Pleasante & Merrye Humor off a Roge', edited by Francis Needham, *Welbeck Miscellany*, No. 1 (1933).

This short piece was first published by Francis Needham in 1933 from the manuscript in the hand of the first Duke of Newcastle at Welbeck Abbey. Needham says that in the manuscript this piece of eleven scenes 'follows closely on a prologue written at Antwerp (where Newcastle was living from 1649 to 1660), and immediately before a piece which appears from internal evidence to date from shortly after the Restoration. It may therefore be taken as having been composed while Newcastle was in exile, probably between 1655 and 1660.' (Op. cit., pp. vii–viii.) Most of this short play was incorporated into *The Triumphant Widow.* (Ibid., pp. v–vi.)

Sir Martin Mar-All, or The Feigned Innocence (1667)
with John Dryden

See Henry Ten Eyck Perry, *The First Duchess of Newcastle and Her Husband as Figures in Literary History* (1918), pp. 150–2.

The Triumphant Widow, or The Medley of Humours (1674–5)

See Henry Ten Eyck Perry, *The First Duchess of Newcastle and Her Husband as Figures in Literary History* (1918), pp. 156–65.

The Variety (1641–2 ?)

Elson, J. J., ed. *The Wits* (1932), pp. 204–9 and 387–8.
Perry, Henry Ten Eyck. *The First Duchess of Newcastle and Her Husband as Figures in Literary History* (1918), pp. 113–17.

1646, 4 Sept. S.R. In a list of forty-nine plays entered as their copies by Robinson and Moseley are the following:
  Country Captaine⎱
  Varieties [*sic*]   ⎰ by my Lord of Newcastle.
(Greg, *Bibliography*, i. 56–57.)
1649. The Varietie, A Comoedy, Lately presented by His Majesties Servants at the *Black-Friers* . . . 1649. (Separate title-page in the following.)
1649. The Country Captaine, And the Varietie, Two Comedies, Written by a Person of Honor. Lately presented by his *Majesties* Servants, at the *Black-Fryers* . . . 1649. (Joint title-page.)
1659. 'To my Lord of *Newcastle*, on his *Play* called *The Variety*. He having commanded to give him my true opinion of it.' (Title of verses by Richard Brome printed in *Five New Playes*, 1659.)
1661, 10 Dec. In the 'List of plays acted by the Kings Companie at the Red Bull and the new house in Gibbon's Tennis

Court near Clare Market' is 'The Dancinge Master Decemb.
10'. (Adams, *Herbert*, p. 117 and n. 2.)

1661/2, 11 Mar. Later in the same list is 'The Frenche dancinge
Master'. (Ibid.)

1662, 21 May. '. . . to the Theatre to "The French Dancing
Master." . . . The play pleased us very well; but Lacy's part,
the Dancing Master, the best in the world.' (Diary of Samuel
Pepys.)

1668/9, *c.* 12 Jan. In 'A Catalogue of part of His Ma^{tes} Servants
Playes as they were formerly acted at the Blackfryers & now
allowed of to his Ma^{tes} Servants at ye New Theatre' are found
'Country Captaine / The Variety'. (Nicoll, *A History of Restoration Drama*, 3rd ed., pp. 315–16, from L.C. 5/12, p. 212.)

1672/3, 30 Jan. S.R. 'Varieties [*sic*], halfe,' transferred from
the estate of Humphrey Robinson to John Martin and
Henry Herringman with 104 other titles. (Greg, *Bibliography*,
i. 72.)

1683, 21 Aug. S.R. 'Varieties [*sic*]' transferred from the estate
of John Martin to Robert Scott with 359 other titles. (Ibid.,
pp. 75–76.)

The publishers evidently considered both *The Variety* and *The
Country Captain* as the noble lord's compositions for the Blackfriars, but *The Country Captain* is found in the company's repertory list of 7 August 1641, while *The Variety* is not. At first glance
this might suggest that *The Variety* was not a play of the King's
men, but it was listed as an old Blackfriars play in 1668/9 (see
above), and in February 1644/5 *Mercurius Britanicus* sneered at
Newcastle as 'one that in time of peace tired the stage in *Black-
Fryers* with his *Comedies*', indicating by the use of the plural that
Newcastle had had more comedies than *The Country Captain* produced by the King's men. It may be that the play came into the
repertory after the list of 7 August 1641 was made.

There are various contemporary allusions in the play, but only
two seem identifiable and indicative of date. In i. 2 Newman says,
'That makes Van Trumpe so troubled with the wind colicke', an
allusion to the Dutch admiral who became familiar in England
after his defeat of the Spanish fleet in the Downs in October 1639.
In i. 1 Jeerer says, 'With what devotion you look at the seven
of Spades and the eight of Diamonds at cribbish.' The *O.E.D.*
gives the first mention of Suckling's game of Cribbage as in Brathwaite's *English Gentleman*, 1630, but this is an error. The name
does not occur in the editions of 1630 or 1633, but it has been

added to the list of faculties required by different card games in the edition of 1641, p. 126. These various allusions and listings of the play indicate a date between October 1639 and the closing of the theatres in September 1642. The absence of the title, though the play was still new, from the company repertory of August 1641 suggests a date of 1641-2.

After the closing of the theatres—apparently during the interregnum—a droll was made from two scenes of this comedy and entitled *The Humours of M. Galliard*. This piece is thought to have been the same as *The French Dancing Master*, in which Lacy made such a hit after the Restoration and in which role his portrait was painted, but Elson suggests that Pepys may have been referring to Cavendish's play under the droll title. (Elson, op. cit., p. 388.) The character of the French Dancing Master is one of those portrayed on the title-page of *The Wits*, along with Falstaff, the Hostess, the Changeling, Clause, Simpleton, and Bubble of *Tu Quoque*.

JOHN CAYWORTH
c. 1594– < 1637

Cayworth was admitted as a sizar at Emmanuel College, Cambridge, 12 April 1610. He received his B.A. in 1613/14 and his M.A. in 1617, and was ordained deacon 17 December 1615 and priest 22 September 1616. From 1622 to 1637 he was rector of Suffield, Norfolk. (*Alumni Cantab.* i. 312.)

Enchiridion Christiados (Christmas, 1636)

MS.: B.M. MS. Add. 10311.

This piece is not dramatic at all, but since it has several times been described as a masque or an entertainment, it is included here to avoid confusion.

The manuscript is all in one hand, presumably that of the author. The title-page proper (not the pasted-in parchment square which precedes it) reads:

Enchiridion Christiados / A twelve Dayes Taske / or / Twelve Ver-
Incarnation
dicts, and Visions / Upon Christ his Nativity   / So Numbred,
Circumcision &c
and Natur'd for the Time: / And / Presented for a Christmas Maske /
To the right wor^{ll}: and worthy / Gentleman M^r. Will: Paston esq^r /

the now high Shrieffe of Norfolk / And to the Noble, and Vertuous / Ladye with him. / Tamen est Laudanda Voluntas

The dedication on folio 5 begins:

Syr, As tis my Fashion, Every Christmas, to bring forth some Byrth; my Folly, to Christen itt; so Tis my Presumption to make you Godfather to this,

and is signed 'Joh. Cayworth'. Though the composition which follows is divided into twelve 'acts' separated by visions, there is no dialogue and no characterization. The acts are: 1. Incarnation, 2. Nativity, 3. Circumcision, 4. Baptism, 5. Fasting, 6. Temptation, 7. Agony, 8. Death, 9. Burial, 10. Descent, 11. Resurrection, 12. Ascension. Cayworth used 'masque' for his annual composition in a very special sense.

Since William Paston was High Sheriff of Norfolk 1636–7, the Christmas of 1636 was the only one occurring during his term of office.

ROBERT CHAMBERLAIN (Chamberlaine, Chamberleyne)
1607– < 40

Robert Chamberlain is an obscure Caroline figure who made a collection or two of anecdotes and epigrams and wrote one comedy. He was born in 1607 at Standish in Lancashire, the son of Richard Chamberlain. (*Athenæ Oxonienses*, ed. Bliss, ii. 675.) He became a clerk to Queen Henrietta Maria's Solicitor General, Peter Ball, to whom he dedicated his *Nocturnal Lucubrations*, and to various members of whose family he wrote verses printed in that volume. In 1637 he was sent by Ball to Exeter College, Oxford (ibid.), and his *Nocturnal Lucubrations*, 1638, carries the title-page statement, 'Written by Rob: Chamberlain of Exeter College in Oxford'. In 1637 he had published a collection—now very rare—called *A New Book of Mistakes*. In 1639 was issued the equally rare *Conceits, Clinches, Flashes, and Whimzies, Newly Studied*, and in 1640 an enlarged edition under the title *Jocabella, or a Cabinet of Mistakes*. His only other known publication is the comedy *The Swaggering Damsel*, published in 1640. The prologue to the play says that it is '*the Primrose of the Authors Spring*'. There are no records that he ever received a degree from the University and no clues to his existence after 1640.

It seems to me unlikely that he was the Robert Chamberlain

whose verses 'Balaam's Asse Cudgeld' appeared in 1661 and who wrote verses for Leonard Blunt's 'Asse upon Asse', 1661.

Perhaps a little may be inferred about the man from his friends. *The Swaggering Damsel* is dedicated to Thomas Kendall, and Chamberlain says, 'J have beene long the unworthy object of your many favours'. He wrote commendatory verses for Nabbes's *Spring's Glory*, 1638, and others which were written for Nabbes's *Bride*, 1640, but published in *Jocabella*; for Thomas Rawlins's *Rebellion*, 1640, for John Tatham's *Fancies Theatre*, 1640, and for Humphrey Mills's *A Night's Search*, 1640. For Chamberlain's own publications, verses were written by C. G. of Oxford, T. R., Thomas Nabbes, H. Harris, Thomas Rawlins, E. B., and M. R. The clearest association here is with Rawlins and Nabbes. The latter was an Exeter College man, but long before Chamberlain's time; the association with both men seems to be one of 1638-40 and suggests London, implying that Chamberlain did not stay long at Oxford.

The Swaggering Damsel (> 1640)

1640, 2 Apr. S.R. Andrew Crooke entered 'a Comedy called The swagering Damosell by Mr Chamberleyne. And a Tragedy called The Prisoner [*sic*] by M^r killegrey.' (Greg, *Bibliography*, i. 52.)
1640. The Swaggering Damsell. A Comedy. Written by *R. C.* . . . . 1640.

Though the author's name does not appear on the title-page of the quarto, it is found in the Stationers' Register entry, and the dedication to Thomas Kendall found in some copies is signed 'Rob. Chamberlain'. The commendatory verses by T. Rawlins, H. Harris, and E. B. all mention the author's name. In some copies (e.g. one of the two at the Huntington and one of the two at the Folger) two additional sets of commendatory verses, one signed C. G. and one M. R., are found.

There is no external evidence concerning the play. In the light of the date of Chamberlain's other compositions it seems probable that it was composed not long before the date of publication. There is no indication of the acting company, though it is likely enough that the comedy was acted. Chamberlain's association with Nabbes (see below) and the fact that his play was licensed with Killigrew's *Prisoners*, a Phoenix play, offer a faint suggestion that the play may have been written for that theatre. The repeated references to the ladies in the prologue would be more appropriate for a private theatre like the Phoenix than for a public theatre. In IV. I Trash says, 'If old sir *Plenteous* doe not take pitty upon me, I must even go and drive Wheele-barrowes in Lincolnes-Inne-fields. for ought I know.' Such a reference would be especially apt in a theatre close to Lincoln's Inn Fields, as the Phoenix was, but of course it could have been said anywhere in London.

WILLIAM CHAMBERLAINE (Chamberlayne)
1619 or 1620–1688/9 or 1689/90

Parsons, A. E. 'A Forgotten Poet: William Chamberlayne and "Pharonnida"', *M.L.R.* xlv (1950), 296–311.

William Chamberlaine was a physician of Shaftesbury, Dorset-shire, who wrote the poems *Pharonnida*, 1659, and *England's Jubilee*, 1660, and the play *Love's Victory*. His birth-date is derived from his monument in Holy Trinity churchyard, Shaftes-bury, which says that he died 11 January 1689[/90?], at the age of seventy.

Love's Victory (< 1642)

Editions: [S. W. Singer, ed.] *Pharonnida; an Heroic Poem in Five Books by William Chamberlayne* (3 vols., 1820), iii. 105–223; with notes and an introduction by Charles K. Meschter (Bethele-hem, Pa., 1914).

Anon., 'Love's Victory: a Tragi-Comedy, by William Chamber-layne, of Shaftesbury in the County of Dorset', *Retrospective Review*, i (1820), 258–71. Includes synopsis.

1658. Loves Victory: A Tragi-Comedy. By *William Chamberlaine* Of *Shaftsbury* in the County of *Dorset* . . . 1658.
1678. Wits Led By The Nose, or A Poet's Revenge . . . 1678. [An anonymous adaptation of *Love's Victory*.]

The play was not produced before the wars, for the author says in his dedication to Sir William Portman,

Nor shall I repent to have rowz'd it from its so long lying dormant, it being then in the embryo, when with us, War first made the present Age unhappy, so may have something to excuse the roughness of its style, its production being whilst I sacrificed to Minerva *in the Temple of* Mars.

And in his address to the reader, the author repeats,

Though this imperfect embryo was begot
Whilst Clamorous wars wilde fury was so hot
It dry'd up Helicon. . . .

The play has sometimes been confused with the anonymous *Love's Victory* (q.v.), the manuscript of which is now in the collections at the Huntington Library; Halliwell-Phillipps quoted copiously from it in his *Brief Description of the Ancient and Modern MSS. Preserved in the Public Library at Plymouth*, 1853, when it was in the possession of Sir E. Deering, Bt. The anonymous manuscript play is quite different from Chamberlaine's *Love's Victory*.

GEORGE CHAPMAN
c. 1560–1634

Chapman was an Elizabethan playwright, and there is no reliable evidence that he ever did any unaided dramatic composition after 1616. He is included here, therefore, simply as the occasional collaborator of Jacobean and Caroline playwrights.

George Chapman—who in his own time was at least as well known as a poet and translator as he was as a dramatist—was born in Hertfordshire in or about 1560. He does not appear as a writer until the publication of *The Shadow of Night* in 1594, or as a playwright until his employment by Henslowe in 1595 or 1595/6. For Henslowe he wrote the very popular *Blind Beggar of Alexandria*, as well as a number of other plays. About 1600 he began writing for the children at Blackfriars, and he continued to give most of his plays to them until 1608, when he stopped, or at least drastically curtailed, his dramatic writing. He was a protégé of Prince Henry from 1603 until the Prince's death in 1612; thereafter the Earl of Somerset became his patron. His translations of Homer began to appear in 1598 and continued until 1624, though they culminated in 1615 and 1616. His later life is very obscure, and there is no clear indication of any connexion with the stage. He died in London 12 May 1634 and was buried at St. Giles-in-the-Fields, where a monument by Inigo Jones was erected to his memory.

Collected Editions

The Comedies and Tragedies of George Chapman [edited by R. H. Shepherd], 3 vols. (1873).

The Works of George Chapman, edited by R. H. Shepherd, 3 vols. (1874–5).

[Another edition] (1892).

[Another edition] (1903).

The Plays and Poems of George Chapman. The Tragedies, edited by Thomas Marc Parrott (1910).

The Plays and Poems of George Chapman. The Comedies, edited by Thomas Marc Parrott (1914).

All Fools

See *The Elizabethan Stage*, iii. 252.

Alphonsus, Emperor of Germany

See Anon.

The Ball

See James Shirley.

The Blind Beggar of Alexandria

See *The Elizabethan Stage*, iii. 251.

Bussy D'Ambois

See *The Elizabethan Stage*, iii. 253.

Chabot, Admiral of France

See James Shirley.

Charlemagne, or The Distracted Emperor

See *The Elizabethan Stage*, iv. 5.

The Conspiracy and Tragedy of Charles, Duke of Biron

See *The Elizabethan Stage*, iii. 257–8.

Christianetta, or Marriage and Hanging Go by Destiny

See Richard Brome.

Eastward Ho!

See *The Elizabethan Stage*, iii. 254–6.

The Fatal Love, A French Tragedy

See *The Elizabethan Stage*, iii. 259–60.

The Fount of New Fashions, or The Isle of Women

See *The Elizabethan Stage*, iii. 252–3.

The Gentleman Usher

See *The Elizabethan Stage*, iii. 251.

Sir Giles Goosecap

See *The Elizabethan Stage*, iv. 15–16.

An Humorous Day's Mirth

See *The Elizabethan Stage*, iii. 251.

May Day

See *The Elizabethan Stage*, iii. 256.

The Middle Temple and Lincoln's Inn Masque

See *The Elizabethan Stage*, iii. 260–2.

Monsieur D'Olive

See *The Elizabethan Stage*, iii. 252–3.

'a pastoral tragedy'

See W. W. Greg, *Henslowe's Diary*, i, pp. xlix, 110; ii. 249–50.

The Revenge of Bussy D'Ambois

See *The Elizabethan Stage*, iii. 258–9.

Revenge for Honour

See Henry Glapthorne.

Rollo, Duke of Normandy, or The Bloody Brother

See John Fletcher.

The Second Maiden's Tragedy

See *The Elizabethan Stage*, iv. 45.

Two Wise Men and All the Rest Fools

See Anon.

The Wars of Pompey and Caesar

See *The Elizabethan Stage*, iii. 259.

The Widow's Tears

See *The Elizabethan Stage*, iii. 256–7.

The Will of a Woman

See *The Elizabethan Stage*, iii. 252–3.

A Tragedy of a Yorkshire Gentlewoman and Her Son

See *The Elizabethan Stage*, iii. 259–60.

JOHN CHAPPELL
c. 1590– < 1632

John Chappell was a scholar of Trinity College, Cambridge, in 1605. He graduated B.A. 1607/8, M.A. 1611, and was made a Fellow in 1610. According to Innes (*Fellows of Trinity College, Cambridge*, p. 29), the first payment to him as a Fellow was made in 1612 and the last in 1618. This would suggest that he left Cambridge not long after his ordination, which took place 26 July 1618. He became rector of Earnham in Lincolnshire in 1618 and of Glooston, Leicestershire, in 1632. He was perhaps the Master of Dedham School, Essex, 1612–13. (*Alumni Cantab.* i. 324.)

The suggestion that this Fellow of Trinity was the author of the Trinity College play *Susenbrotus* comes from G. C. Moore Smith. (*College Plays*, p. 101.) The Trinity College Senior Bursar's Accounts show the following entries:

1615–1616

Extraordinaries

. . . . . .

Item to Mʳ Chappell for coales & other necessar*ies* for the
   Comedy to be acted at Court by oʳ Mʳ his appoyntm*ent*   xˢ
Item to Mʳ Chappell going to the Court to see the Comed:
   acted by oʳ Mʳ his appoyntm*ent*   vˡⁱ
(*M.S.C.* ii, Part ii. 173.)

Though none of the entries in the Bursar's accounts is dated by month or day, these two follow entries concerning Shrovetide and presumably refer to the preparation of the Trinity play for its command performances and the expenses incurred in taking it to Royston. It is possible, of course, that Chappell's connexion with the play was not that of author.

Susenbrotus or Fortunia (12 March 1615/16)

MSS.: Bodleian Rawlinson MS. Poet. 195, fol. 79 ff.; Bridge-water MS. entitled 'Fortunia'.

Morgan, Louise B. 'The Latin University Drama', *Shakespeare Jahrbuch*, xlvii (1911), 77.

Miss Morgan says of the two manuscripts of the play, 'The existence of a Bridgewater ms. of this same play, under the title *Fortunia*, was pointed out to me by Mr. G. C. Moore Smith—the latter ms. is much more legible, and, in part, is fuller than the Bodleian, but one corrects the other very conveniently.' (Op. cit.) She gives the dramatis personae, apparently from the Bridge-water MS., for it has numerous minor variations from that in the Bodleian.

The date of the play is fixed by the letter in IV. 3, which is subscribed '12 die Martij 1615', a date which fits well enough with the King's presence at Royston, for he arrived back from New-market on 16 March 1615/16. (Nichols, *James I*, iii. 133 and 135.) Though the Bodleian MS. bears the endorsement, 'Susenbrotus

Comœdia. Acta Cantabrigiæ in Collegio Trin. cora*m* Rege Jacobo
& Carolo principe. Anno 1615', other evidence makes it clear
enough that the play was performed before them at Royston and
not at Cambridge. John Chamberlain wrote from London to Sir
Dudley Carleton on 27 March 1616, '. . . after the king's coming
to town, who came the 16th. . . . As the king came from New-
market, he had a play at Royston, acted by some of the younger
sort of our Cantabrigians. He had heard it commended, and so
would needs have it, bearing their charges.' (Birch, *James I*, i.
394–5.) Chamberlain wrote again in his next letter to Carleton,
dated 6 April 1616, 'I send you here a proper piece of heraldry,
being a part of the play or shew our young Cambridge scholars
presented to the king at Royston.' (Ibid., p. 397.) Performance at
Royston seems to be confirmed by two extracts made by G. C.
Moore Smith from Trinity College Senior Bursar's Accounts (see
above). That *Susenbrotus* was the play performed by the Trinity
College men at Royston is at least compatible with the dialogue
of the prologue between Cantabrigia and Aulicus and with that of
the epilogue between Cantabrigia and Trina.

P. CLARETUS
fl. 1623–55

The man is unidentified. His name is affixed to two St. Omers
plays, *Innocentia Purpurata seu Rosa Candida et Rubicunda*, acted
1623, and *Homo Duplex sive Funestum Corporis et Animae Duel-
lum tragoedia*, acted 1655. See William H. McCabe, *Revue de
littérature comparée*, xvii (1937), 362 and 369.

Innocentia Purpurata seu Rosa Candida et Rubicunda
(26 October 1623)

MS.: Stonyhurst MS. A VII 50 (2), pp. 2–31.

McCabe, William H. 'The Play-List of the English College of
St. Omers 1592–1762', *Revue de littérature comparée*, xvii (1937),
355–75.
—— 'Notes on the St. Omers College Theatre', *Philological
Quarterly*, xvii (1938), 225–39.

Father McCabe suggests that the Stonyhurst play is that acted
in the Jesuit College for English boys at St. Omers on 26 October
1623 ('Play-List', p. 362) and perhaps revived 16 August 1629

(ibid., pp. 365–6). He gives the cast of characters for the three-act play in the Stonyhurst MS.

JOHN CLAVELL
1601–1642/3

Pafford, J. H. P., and W. W. Greg, eds., *The Soddered Citizen*, Malone Society Reprints (1936), pp. xiii ff.

John Clavell was born 11 May 1601, presumably at his father's house called the Mansion House, near Sherborne in Dorset. He matriculated at Brasenose College, Oxford, 19 November 1619, but there is no record that he took a degree. On his father's death in 1623 he became administrator of the estate. Not long after, he became a highwayman—if his own account is to be accepted, this desperate move was dictated by great necessity—and was involved in a number of robberies, for several of which he was convicted and sentenced to death 30 January 1625/6. The case had some public notice at the time, for Joseph Mead, the letter-writer of Christ's College, Cambridge, informed his correspondent, Sir Martin Stuteville:

> Mr Clavell a gentleman a knights eldest son a great highway robber & of Posts was together with a souldier his companion arraigned at [*sic*] condemned on munday last (Ian 30) at the Kings bench barre. He pleaded for himselfe that he neuer had stricken or wounded any man, neuer taken any thing from their bodyes as ringes & neuer cutt their girts or saddles or done them whom he robbed any corporall violence. He was with his companion repriued & sent these following verses to the King for mercy & hath obtained it. (Pafford and Greg, eds., p. xiv, from B.M. MS. Harley 390, fol. 11b.)

In spite of his reprieve and of the pardon which was promised as part of the coronation celebrations, Clavell's final pardon was not entered on the Patent Rolls until 22 November 1627, and in the meantime he had presumably remained in prison. While in prison he wrote a long poem which was printed for Richard Meighen in 1628 with the title *A Recantation of an ill led life. Or a discouerie of the High-way Law. With vehement dissuasions of all (in that kind) Offenders. As also many cautelous Admonitions and full Instructions, how to know, shun, and apprehend a Theefe.* This poem was published twice in 1628 and again in 1634. The publisher says that Clavell was no longer in London in 1634; he later appears in Ireland as a physician. A Bodleian MS. dated 1636 preserves Clavell's own account of some of his cures there.

He died 17 February 1642/3. (Pafford and Greg eds., pp. xiii–xviii.)

The Soddered Citizen was probably accepted (or commissioned?) by the King's men because of Clavell's notoriety, for he is frequently referred to in commonplace books, and his *Recantation* was widely known.

Clavell's portrait is reproduced by Pafford and Greg from the second edition of his *Recantation*.

The Soddered Citizen (c. 1630)

MS.: In the private collection of Lieutenant-Colonel E. G. Troyte-Bullock, of Zeals House, Mere, Wiltshire.

Edition: *The Soddered Citizen*, edited by J. H. P. Pafford and W. W. Greg, Malone Society Reprints (1936).

[1653, 9 Sept.] S.R. Among several plays entered for Moseley is 'The Crafty Merchant. or the Souldred Citizen by Shakerly Marmion'. (Greg, *Bibliography*, i. 60–61.)

1660, 29 June. S.R. Among several plays entered for Moseley is 'The Sodered Citizen. a Comedy. by Shakerley Marmion'. (Ibid., pp. 68–69.)

Neither Moseley entry necessarily refers to this manuscript play. The first one probably indicates an attempt to register two separate plays for a single fee. The matter is confused by the fact that on 12 September 1623 Sir Henry Herbert licensed for the Lady Elizabeth's company a play called 'The Cra. . . Marchant' and said it was by William Bonen (q.v.). It may be that Moseley simply guessed at authorship in both cases, or that the play he had was not the same as the one Herbert licensed. In any event, the manuscript play under discussion has nothing to do with a crafty merchant; it is not the play Herbert licensed, for it was acted by the King's company; and it appears to have been written by neither Bonen nor Marmion.

The editors of the play note that the prologue makes most unusual assertions about the author:

> Ould Sarum's Playne, Gads, Sutors hill
> Our Poett rang'd, that course prou'd ill;
> Better resolu'd, hee makes accompt
> To sollace, on Parnassus Mount,:
> But in your Censures, danger lyes,
> Which are, as then were, Hue, & cryes,

> And yett the Plott, & language, all,
> Hee his owne proper Coyne, may call,
> Has robbd noe Authors, in him, thefte
> Vnpardonable, that Trade lefte,
> Hee's honest growne, . . .

Three separate times in these lines the audience is informed that the author of this play has been a thief, twice they are told that he has reformed, and once that since he has left his trade of thieving further theft would be unpardonable. The places named in the first couplet indicate that the author was a highwayman. Such accomplishments are not usual for Jacobean and Caroline playwrights. Clearly the King's men, performers of the play, were exploiting the fact that the play was written by a reformed thief, and the rest of the prologue suggests that the company expected more response to be elicited by the character of the author than by the quality of the comedy.

The editors of the play were greatly assisted in their search for a literary highwayman by the fact that the names 'Iohn Clauell' and 'Clauell' are scribbled on fol. 2ª of the manuscript. John Clavell's career and dates fit the allusions of the play so well that there can be little doubt that he was the author—or at least the advertised author—of *The Soddered Citizen*. Additional evidence of his authorship can be seen in lines 2809–18 near the end of the play:

> *Vnder*: . . . him didst thou force
>   By th' Cheate of his first fortunes, to fly out,
>   And pillage on the Roade, for livelyhood,
>   Then didst thou seize him, . . .
> 2. *Com̃*: But hee lives still, ?
> *Vnder*: All humble thankes vnto our gratious Queene
>   That ask'd his pardon & our Kings that gaue it
>   liues, but hee's turnd Poett.

These lines fit not only the events of Clavell's career, but his assertion in *A Recantation of an ill led Life* that the Queen's intercession with the King gained his pardon for him. Finally, Clavell had some acquaintance with the Blackfriars—where *The Soddered Citizen* was presumably produced—for in the first edition of his *Recantation*, near the beginning, he says:

> You must not looke from me to haue the straine
> Of your *Black-friers* Poets, or the vaine.
> Of those high flying men, whose rare Muse brings
> Forth births, that Gossipt are by Lords and Kings.

The play was performed by the King's company, as is indicated by the cast given on fol. 3ᵇ of the manuscript. All the twelve named actors of the cast are well-known members of the company (see above, i. 84–85), and even the anonymous thirteenth, 'John: Shanks Boy', relates to the known activities of the popular comedian of the troupe, John Shank. (See above, ii. 563.)

The make-up of this cast for a performance by the King's men indicates a date for *The Soddered Citizen* somewhat earlier than that fixed on by Pafford and Greg in their edition of the manuscript. They date the play 1632–3 because of their analysis of the careers of the members of the cast, because of the watermarks in the paper, of which there are many examples 1623–37 but the most around 1633, because one set of corrections in the manuscript is in the hand of 'Jhon' who was book-keeper of the company at least from 1625 to 1631, and because an almost illegible date which appears to be 1633 accompanies the name 'Iohn Clauell' in the scribbles on the manuscript. These reasons are not convincing to me: their analysis of the cast omits important information, unavailable to them but of crucial value; the watermarks make the date 1633 possible, not probable; 'Jhon's' hand is more compatible with 1630 than with 1633; and there is, finally, no reason to take the date with the 'Clauell' scribble as a date of production—it is much more probably the date of scribbling.

The most conclusive evidence that 1633 is too late for the play is the fact that Richard Sharpe, who played the romantic lead and delivered the prologue and epilogue, was buried 25 January 1631/2. (See above, ii. 571.) Almost equally convincing is the fact that John Thompson, who was young enough to be assigned the role of the girl Miniona in *The Soddered Citizen*, had by October 1632 become the father of two daughters. Alexander Gough, who was assigned the role of Fewtricks, a boy whose small size is repeatedly referred to in the play, was nineteen years old in August 1633. (See above, ii. 447, 599–600.) All these facts about the members of the cast demand an earlier date than 1633 for *The Soddered Citizen*. For a *terminus a quo*, the career of John Honyman is relevant. He was assigned the minor adult role of Sly in *The Soddered Citizen*, but he had played the female lead in Massinger's *The Picture*, which was licensed for performance 8 June 1629. This fact suggests, though it does not necessarily prove, that the cast of *The Soddered Citizen* is somewhat later than that of *The Picture*. All in all, a production date of about 1629 or 1630—as early as possible in the careers of Thompson and Gough—would best fit the cast recorded in the manuscript. This date would also be nearer the appearance in 1628 of Clavell's poem, *A Recantation*, and therefore more compatible with the actors' obvious attempt to exploit the reputation of the highway-man-poet.

The manuscript of the play is damaged so that a number of lines are lost or illegible. The first and last folios are almost entirely gone, and the next to the last reveals only a few letters down the inner margin. (Pafford and Greg ed., pp. vi–vii.) The hand seems to be that of a professional scribe, not the author. Corrections and alterations are made in five different hands, one of which is that of ' Jhon', the well-known scribe for the King's company, who wrote in a number of additions. (Ibid., pp. viii–ix.)

The play itself is a poor thing, confused and contradictory, which must have caused the company some embarrassment. It is the construction and characterization which are worst; the verse, while undistinguished, is not so bad as one might have expected from a highwayman.

JOHN CLEVELAND
1613–58

There are no known dramatic works of the poet John Cleveland and not even any direct assertion that he wrote any, but a satiric manuscript poem upon him seems to imply that he did. The poem, first noted by S. V. Gapp (*P.M.L.A.* xlvi [1931], 1078–9), appears to refer to Cleveland's Cambridge days.

> UPON MR. CL. WHO MADE A SONG AGAINST DD[rs]
> Leaue of, vaine Satyrist, & doe not thinke
> To staine our reuerend Purple with thy inke.
>
> .   .   .   .   .
>
> Must now thy Poems be made fidlers notes
> Puft with tobacco through their sutty throats ?
> Shake of that ill fac't crew, Ar't in a vaine ?
> Putt on thy socks, & tread the stage againe.
> Had they bin on, (as all have thought more meet,)
> They had done service to thy stinking feet.
> (Bodleian MS. Tanner 465, fol. 44.)

If this refers to a play by Cleveland, it was presumably a college play. Cleveland was at St. John's, Cambridge, from 1634 to *c.* 1643.

JA. CO.

This is a ghost name derived from a careless reading of the fragments of an anonymous play called *Romanus* (q.v.) in the Harleian MSS. (4628) at the British Museum. Part of the play is written on the back of a legal document concerning a plaintiff named James Cobbes, and his name appears elsewhere in the miscellaneous collection of documents of which *Romanus* is a part. Presumably this is the source of the Ja. Co.

JAMES COBBES

The anonymous fragmentary manuscript play *Romanus* (q.v.) is found in a collection of miscellaneous documents (B.M. Harleian MS. 4628), some of which concern James Cobbes, and at the end of the last document in the collection the name James Cobbes is scribbled several times. The name does not appear, however, on the play manuscript, and there is no indication that James Cobbes wrote the play.

SIR ASTON COKAYNE (Cockaine, Cochaine, Cockayn, Cokain)
1608–83/4

Aston Cokayne was the son of Thomas Cokayne and his wife Anne, half-sister of Philip, first Earl of Chesterfield. He is himself authority for the statement that he was born at Elvaston and baptized at Ashbourne in Derbyshire, 20 December 1608. (*D.N.B.* xi. 224, and *A Chain of Golden Poems*, 1658, p. 184.) He was sent to the Chenies School in Buckinghamshire and to Trinity College, Cambridge (*A Chain of Golden Poems*, pp. 138, 11, 194, 237–8), about 1624, but there is no record of his admission at Cambridge. (*Alumni Cantab.* i. 362.) He says that thereafter he entered one of the Inns of Court (*D.N.B.*) and in 1632 left England for a tour of France and Italy. (*A Chain of Golden Poems*, p. 93.) Miss K. M. Lea has noted that he enrolled as a student at Padua 11 October 1632. (*M.L.R.* xxiii [1928], 47, from H. F. Brown, *Inglesi e Scozzesi all' Università di Padova, 1618–1765*, p. 113.) He was back in England in July 1633. His *Trappolin* (q.v.) was a result of this Italian stay. His translation *Dianea* must have been the result of a later visit, for the author's epistle is dated from Venice 25 October 1635. After his return to England he was married at an unknown date to Mary, daughter of Sir Gilbert Knyveton, and a son was born to them in May 1636. (*D.N.B.*)

Cokayne succeeded to his father's estate of Pooley Hall on 26 January 1638/9 and was created a baronet by King Charles 10 January 1641/2, though there was later some confusion about the creation. His activities during the Civil War and interregnum are not known except that he had to compound for his estate. He died a ruined man, as is shown by his will, in lodgings in Derby, in February 1683/4. Anthony à Wood sums up Cokayne's reputation as he found it a few years after his death:

> This person, I say, mostly lived at Pooley, and sometimes in the great city, was esteemed by many an ingenious gent. a good poet and a great lover of learning, yet by others a perfect boon fellow, by which means he wasted all he had. (*Athenæ Oxonienses*, Bliss ed. iv. 129.)

Cokayne's interest in dramatic affairs is shown by some of his miscellaneous verse. He was a friend of Massinger, whom he may have known through his aunt, the Countess of Chesterfield, for Massinger in a manuscript poem addressed her as 'my Lady and M:ʳˢ.' (Cruickshank, *Massinger*, pp. 211–12.) For the publication of Massinger's *Emperor of the East*, 1632, and his *Maid of Honour*, 1632, Cokayne wrote commendatory verses, and he referred to the dramatist as 'my good friend Old *Philip Messinger*' in his verses to Charles Cotton about the confusion of Beaumont and Fletcher in the folio of 1647. (*A Chain of Golden Poems*, 1658, pp. 91–93 and 217.) This poem shows a knowledge of the compositions of the 'twin dramatists' which most stage historians lacked in the next two centuries. He wrote verses on Massinger and Fletcher's burial in the same grave (*A Chain of Golden Poems*, p. 186), a theatrically allusive *Praeludium* for Brome's *Five New Playes*, 1653, and commendatory verses for the 1647 Beaumont and Fletcher Folio. Verses on Randolph's *Muses' Looking-Glass* appear in *A Chain of Golden Poems*, but were not published with Randolph's play. He also wrote verses to the actor John Honyman. (Ibid., p. 140.) Cokayne was evidently one of the gentlemanly patrons of the drama who were prominent in the audiences at the Blackfriars and Cockpit in the thirties.

Collected Editions

Small Poems of Divers Sorts (1658). (Contains *The Obstinate Lady, Trappolin*, and *A Masque*.)

A Chain of Golden Poems (1658). (*Small Poems* with a cancel title-page.)

Poems (1662). (Another issue of *Small Poems* with cancel title-page and *The Tragedy of Ovid* added.)
[Another issue] (1662).
The Dramatic Works of Sir Aston Cokain [J. Maidment and W. H. Logan, eds.] (1874).
Poems by Sir Aston Cokaine, A. E. Cokayne, ed. (1877).
Aston Cokain's Dramen, Hermann Spaemann, ed. (1923).

A Masque (6 January 1639/40)

1658. A Masque *Presented at* Bretbie *in* Darbyshire *On Twelfth-Night*. 1639. (In *Small Poems of Divers Sorts*, 1658.)
1658. [Another issue. Under cancel title-page, *A Chain of Golden Poems*.]
1662. [In *Poems*. Two issues.]
1669. [In *Choice Poems of Several Sorts*.]

Bretbie was the estate of Philip Stanhope (1584–1656), first Earl of Chesterfield, who was the half-brother of Sir Aston's mother; there are various poems to members of the family in Cokayne's collected works.

The masque is rather simple, but fitted to the celebration of the Earl and Countess and their household. There is an antimasque of satyrs, and the two sons of the Earl and Countess are introduced into the action, seeking their parents.

The Obstinate Lady (> 1642)

1656, 29 Sept. S.R. Entered for William Godbid 'a booke entituled The Obstinate Lady by A. C.' (Greg, *Bibliography*, i. 65.)
1657. The Obstinate Lady: *A New Comedy* Never formerly Published: The Scene London. Written by Sir Aston Cockayn . . . 1657.
1658. [In *Small Poems of Divers Sorts*.]
1658. [Another issue. With cancel title-page, *A Chain of Golden Poems*.]
1662. [In *Poems*, two issues.]
1669. [In *Choice Poems of Several Sorts*.]

The 1657 edition of *The Obstinate Lady* was unauthorized. In his 'Apology to the Reader' in *A Chain of Golden Poems*, 1658, Sir Aston says:

These poor trifles (courteous Reader) had not now become so troublesome to the World, if it had been in my power to have prevented them: for at my going once out of *London*, I left them with a friend of mine, who dying, they were dispersed into divers hands. Mr. *William Godbid* got my *Obstinate Lady*, and though he found it with the last leaf torn out, wherein my conclusion to the play with the Epilogue were; he procured some acquaintance of his to supply the defect at the end, and so Printed it. And though that Comedy, be very much of it writ in number, he put it forth as if the most part of it were prose. Here you have that defect much amended, and my own conclusion and Epilogue added.

Of the production of the play there is no record, but, as Fleay noticed (*Biog. Chron.* i. 72), the repeated references to the theatres as in operation indicate that it was composed not later than 1642. Most precise is the exchange in II. 1:

> *Van.* You frequent plays, do you not?
> *Lor.* They are most commonly my afternoon's employment,

and Lorece's statement in III. 2:

> I at any time will carry you to a play, either to the Black Friar's or Cockpit,

and Phylander's boast, IV. 1:

> I'll challenge him
> By such sure circumstances, and set the papers
> On public places by the play-bills.

Perhaps there is a precise time reference in Lorece's reply to Vandona in II. 1:

> The King of Spain hath his gold there, of which the Hollanders took a great prize when they won the silver fleet,

but Lorece's extended description of his trip to the Antipodes, of which these lines are a part, is intended to show ignorance and paradox, and it is not clear how literally these lines are intended to be taken. Fleay (loc. cit.) dated the play 'c. 1631' but gave no reasons.

Langbaine's statement,

> Sr. *Aston's Obstinate Lady*, seems to be Cousin-German to *Massinger's Very Woman*; as they that will compare *Don John*, *Antonio*, and *Almira*, with *Carionil* and *Lucora* in this Play, may easily perceive (*An Account of the English Dramatick Poets*, 1691, p. 69),

has been frequently repeated, not always with acknowledgement. Where Hazlitt got his information that 'There is a tradition that the serving-man, Jaques, was a study from life in the Ashborne district' (*Manual*, p. 169), I do not know.

The Tragedy of Ovid (1658?)

1662. *Poems* . . . Whereunto is now Added The tragedy of Ovid. Intended to be Acted shortly . . . 1662.
1662. [Another issue.]
1669. [In *Choice Poems of Several Sorts*.]

The play can be dated by Sir Aston's own statement in his 'Apology to the Reader' in *A Chain of Golden Poems*, 1658:

Lastly, I have made some progress into a Play, to be called the Tragedy of *Ovid*, which (if my *Obstinate Lady*, and *Trappolin* take) I may be encouraged to perfect, and present to you hereafter, with some other things that are not yet put into method, fit for the Press.

Trappolin, Supposed a Prince (1633)

Lea, K. M. 'Sir Aston Cokayne and the "Commedia dell' Arte"', *M.L.R.* xxiii (1928), 47–51.
Summers, Montague. *The Playhouse of Pepys* (1935), pp. 243–5.

1657, 4 May. S.R. William Godbid entered 'a booke called Poems of divers sorts together with a famous Italian Play entituled Trappolin by Sʳ Aston Cockaine'. (Greg, *Bibliography*, i. 65.)
1658. *Trappolin creduto Principe.* or Trappolin Suppos'd a Prince. An Italian Trage-Comedy. The scene part of *Italy*. Written by Sir *Aston Cokain* . . . 1658. (Separate title-page in *Small Poems of Divers Sorts*, 1658.)
1658. [Another issue. Under cancel title-page, *A Chain of Golden Poems*.]
1662. [In *Poems*.]
1662. [Another issue.]
1669. [In *Choice Poems*.]

Sir Aston indicates the source for his play and the place of composition in the prologue:

> Gallants, be 't known as yet we cannot say
> To whom you are beholding for this play;
> But this our Poet hath licens'd us to tell,
> Ingenious Italy hath lik'd it well:
> Yet is it no translation; for he nere
> But twice in Venice did it ever hear;

and in the epilogue:

> . . . *for here it was not writ*
> *In sweet repose and fluencies of wit;*
> *But far remote, at* Rome *begun, half made*
> *At* Naples, *at* Paris *the conclusion had.*

These remarks indicate that Sir Aston had based his play on a performance he had attended and not on a written text, for he does not say that he has read the play, but that he heard it twice. Miss K. M. Lea has shown that what he saw was a performance of the *Supposed Prince* play of the Comedia dell' arte, a piece which is extant in nine versions and whose action is that of Cokayne's play. Moreover, one of these versions uses for its title the sub-title of the English play, 'Il Creduto Principe'. Miss Lea has even shown that the company Sir Aston saw was the one called 'Affezionati', for he used the stage names of five of these actors for the names of his characters and assigned to others roles commonly assumed by members of the troupe. (Op. cit., pp. 49–50.)

The specific places which Sir Aston names in his epilogue set the date of the composition of the play. He started his French and Italian tour in July 1632, and on 11 October 1632 entered the University of Padua as a student. (Ibid., p. 47, from H. F. Brown, *Inglesi e Scozzesi all' Università di Padova, 1618–1765*, p. 113.) He is quite definite about the details of his return to England in the verses to his son printed in *Poems*, where he says that he came back by way of Rome, Naples, and Paris, landing at Dover in July 1633. The sequence of cities can scarcely be accidental, and we therefore have evidence from the author's own writings that the play was written on his way home from Italy in 1633, after he had seen the Affezionati company twice play his farce plot in Venice.

The opening of the prologue indicates that Cokayne intended to have the play produced, but that the audience was not to know his name. There is no evidence that it was produced in the Caroline theatre, but I know of no good reason for concluding that it was not.

Nahum Tate's farce, *A Duke and No Duke*, an alteration of *Trappolin*, was produced at the Theatre Royal in November 1684 and achieved some popularity. Later versions were printed or acted in 1720, 1732, 1733, 1757, 1758, and 1818. (See Summers, *The Playhouse of Pepys*, p. 245.) This later popularity of at least the basic situations of Cokayne's play makes it seem unlikely that it lay unacted during the last eight or nine years of the Caroline theatre.

FRANCIS COLE
fl. 1641

A Francis Cole is said to have been the author of a prologue and epilogue for a play which was part of the entertainment furnished for Prince Charles when he visited Cambridge in March 1641/2. (Cooper, *Annals of Cambridge*, iii. 321–3.) According to John Payne Collier, a pamphlet with the prologue and epilogue appeared in 1642:

> Mr. Douce is in possession of a tract with the following title:—'The Prologue and Epilogue to a comedie presented at the Entertainment of the Prince his Highnesse, by the Scollers of Trinity Colledge, in Cambridge, in March last, 1641. By Francis Cole.' London, 1642, 4to. It is preceded by a wood-cut, of a person in a black suit, including a cloak, with a paper in his hand. (*H.E.D.P.*, 1831 ed., iii. 443 n.)

Apparently no one else has seen this tract.

There are no records of a Francis Cole at Trinity in the seventeenth century in *Alumni Cantab.* The only Coles recorded at Trinity at dates which might be related to Prince Charles's visit are Nathaniel, who commenced B.A. in 1629/30 and M.A. 1633, and Robert, who was admitted in 1637 and was granted a B.A. in 1641. (*Alumni Cantab.* i. 367.) A Francis Cole received his B.A. at Oxford in 1632/3. (*Alumni Oxon.* i. 300.)

P. COUF

See Anon., *Sanguis Sanguinem*.

ABRAHAM COWLEY (Cooley)
1618–67

Loiseau, Jean. *Abraham Cowley, sa vie, son œuvre* (1931).
—— *Abraham Cowley's Reputation in England* (1931).
Nethercot, Arthur H. 'Abraham Cowley as Dramatist', *R.E.S.* iv (1928), 1–24.
—— *Abraham Cowley, the Muse's Hannibal* (1931).
Sprat, Thomas. 'An Account of the Life and Writings of Mr Abraham Cowley', *The Works of Mr. Abraham Cowley* (1668), A_1–e_2^v.

Wallerstein, Ruth. 'Cowley as a Man of Letters', *Transactions of the Wisconsin Academy of Sciences, Arts and Letters*, xxvii (1932), 127–40.

Though there is no record of the birth or baptism of Abraham Cowley, other accounts show that he was born in 1618. He began writing verse at a very early age, in imitation of Spenser, he says, and he speaks of the poems which he 'wrote at *School* from the age of ten years, till after fifteen'. (*Poems*, 1656, Preface, a_3^v.) Five of these schoolboy poems were published in *Poetical Blossoms*, 1633, when Cowley was a King's Scholar at Westminster School; his portrait appears in the volume inscribed '*Ætat: suæ 13 Anno 1633*'. Since Cowley was born in 1618, there is a discrepancy here. Nethercot suggests that the manuscript was in circulation in 1631, marked '*Ætat: suæ 13*', and that the '1633' was added at the time of publication. (*Cowley*, pp. 22–23.) When Cowley entered Westminster or when he became a King's Scholar is unknown; his name appears for the first time in a list of King's Scholars which is dated 7 July 1630, where it is last and presumably latest. (Loiseau, *Abraham Cowley, sa vie, son œuvre*, p. 21.) While still at school he wrote the pastoral play, *Love's Riddle*.

In 1636 Cowley failed of election to a Trinity College scholarship from Westminster, but on 30 March 1636 [1637?] the Master and Seniors of Trinity ordered for him the reversion of a 'dry chorister's place', 'and that the Colleadge shall allow him the benefitt thereof, till it fall, or that he be chosen scholler att the election of schollers next following'. (Loiseau, op. cit., p. 44, n. 4.) He matriculated 21 April 1636 and was admitted Scholar at Trinity 14 June 1637.

While an undergraduate at Trinity he wrote, in addition to non-dramatic poetry, the Latin comedy *Naufragium Joculare*, which was acted at Trinity 2 February 1637/8. At Cambridge he was an intimate of the poets Richard Crashaw and Robert Cresswell, and of William Hervey. (Nethercot, *Cowley*, pp. 43–53.) He received his B.A. degree in 1639–40 and became a minor Fellow of Trinity in 1640; there is no record of his appointment as a major Fellow and no accounts of fellowship payments to him in the Bursar's books before the Restoration. (*Alumni Cantab.* i. 407; Innes, *Fellows of Trinity College, Cambridge*, p. 33.)

In March 1641/2 Cambridge entertained and honoured the young Prince Charles on his journey to York. Part of the University entertainment, as on many similar occasions, was a new comedy acted at Trinity. Cowley says that the play was the product of one week's effort, and, even allowing for great exaggeration, one gets the impression of notable collegiate admiration for young Cowley. He says that after the performance he revised the play (possibly for professional performance ; he had a good precedent in his predecessor at Westminster and Trinity, Thomas Randolph), but that the revision was lost. (*Poems*, 1656, Preface, a_1ᵛ.)

Even before hostilities began, Cambridge was much more subject to Parliamentary domination than Oxford, and on 17 August 1642 Oliver Cromwell and other commissioners were given military authority for the town. (Cooper, *Annals of Cambridge*, iii. 324–36.) Many of the colleges were despoiled and the students persecuted, and on 8 April 1643 Cowley and a number of other Fellows were formally dispossessed. Before this date Cowley had probably fled from Cambridge, for his earlier works show a strong anti-Puritan feeling, and in 1642 and 1643 several violently anti-Puritan pieces appeared which have been attributed to him with varying degrees of probability. (Nethercot, *Cowley*, pp. 82–89.)

For an unknown period Cowley was at the Royalist headquarters at Oxford. Sprat implies that he was there two years ('An Account of the Life . . .', *Works*, 1668, A_2ᵛ–a_1), and probably at Oxford he became secretary to Baron Jermyn and consequently attached to the court of Queen Henrietta Maria. He was with the court on the Continent during most of the period of the war and the Commonwealth ; Sprat says for twelve years. There he wrote *The Mistress*, published in 1647, and attained sufficient reputation to make profitable the unwarranted use of his name and works in England. In 1648 *The Four Ages of England, or the Iron Age* was published in London with his name on the title-page, and in 1650 *The Guardian*. Cowley himself said that he did not write the former and that the latter was published 'without my consent or knowledge'. (*Poems*, 1656, Preface, a_1–a_1ᵛ.) His principal activities in France must have been political. Sprat says that for five years he 'cypher'd and decypher'd with his own hand, the greatest part of all the Letters that passed between their Majesties, and managed a vast Intelligence in many other parts: which for some years together took up all his days, and two or three nights every week'. He went on various missions for the exiled court, and in 1651 he spent some time in the island of Jersey. (Nethercot, *Cowley*, pp. 128–35.)

In 1654 Cowley was back in London, apparently as a Royalist agent, and there on 12 April 1655 he was arrested by Cromwell's soldiers and imprisoned. He was eventually released on a bail of

£1,000 and may have made some sort of a compromise, for he
included in the Preface to his *Poems*, 1656, a statement of his
reconciliation to the Commonwealth, his resolve to write no more
poetry, and his hope to seek quiet and seclusion in America.
(Nethercot, *Cowley*, pp. 142–67.) For a year or so he studied
medicine in retirement and was granted an M.D. by Oxford on
2 December 1657. (Loiseau, op. cit., p. 123, n. 31.)

After Cromwell's death Cowley went back to France and became Jermyn's secretary again, though there were difficulties
about the political statement he had made in his Preface to
Poems, 1656. (Nethercot, *Cowley*, pp. 179–93.) He returned with
the exiles in 1660, and in January 1660/1 Charles ordered him
reinstated in his Trinity fellowship, though he did not receive the
mastership of the Savoy for which he long petitioned.

Alexander Davenant said in a suit of 1691 that Cowley was an
adviser and literary assistant of Sir William Davenant at Lincoln's Inn Fields, and that he held half a share of stock in the
enterprise as compensation; another party to the suit says that
Cowley was Davenant's partner from the beginning. He certainly
held half a share in the theatre, for he bequeathed it to John
Hervey in his will. (Nethercot, *Cowley*, pp. 200–2 and 296–7.)
Cowley's Restoration theatrical activity, therefore, may be only
inadequately represented by his revision for Davenant's enterprise of his old comedy, *The Guardian*. Under its new title, *The
Cutter of Coleman Street*, the play was produced at Lincoln's Inn
Fields on 16 December 1661, with Betterton and Nokes in the
cast. Though its first reception was disappointing, Downes says
it ran for a week. (*Roscius Anglicanus*, p. 25; Nethercot, *Cowley*,
pp. 202–8; Summers, *The Playhouse of Pepys*, pp. 227–30.)

In 1663 Cowley retired from city life and his campaigns for
court preferment to Barn Elms, and two years later to Chertsey.
Here he finished his botanical writings and probably composed
most of his essays. Here he died 28 July 1667. He was buried in
Westminster Abbey.

Collected Editions

So far as I know the bibliography of the collected editions of
Cowley's works has never been worked out in adequate bibliographical detail, and the editions are much too numerous and too
complicated for proper treatment here. A very hasty and superficial survey indicates that *The Works of Mr. Abraham Cowley*, 1668,
1669, 1672, 1674, 1678, 1680, 1681, 1684, 1688, does not include plays.

The edition of 1693 and the following eighteenth-century editions add *Cutter of Coleman Street*.

In 1681 appeared an independent publication titled *The Second Part of the Works of Mr. Abraham Cowley* and containing *Love's Riddle* and *Naufragium Joculare*. This collection was reissued under various titles in 1682, 1684, 1689, 1700, 1708, 1711, and 1721.

The matter is nicely complicated by the fact that these two independent publications are often found bound together. Later eighteenth- and early nineteenth-century editions are variously related to the seventeenth-century ones, but none appears to be complete.

The only really complete collection of the plays appears to be:

> *The Complete Works in Verses and Prose of Abraham Cowley.* Edited by A. B. Grosart. (The Chertsey Worthies' Library.) 2 volumes (1881).

Cutter of Coleman Street

See *The Guardian*.

The Guardian (12 March 1641/2)

(Revised as *Cutter of Coleman Street*)

MSS.: The prologue and epilogue alone are found in the following manuscripts: B.M. Harl. MS. 6918, fol. 25ᵛ, Egerton MS. 2725, fol. 31, and Egerton MS. 2623; Bodleian Douce MS. 357 and Rawlinson Poet. 26, fol. 138.

Editions: The play is printed in the editions of Cowley's works in 1707–8, 1710–11, 1721, 1777, 1809, 1881, and 1905–6.

Nethercot, Arthur. 'Abraham Cowley as Dramatist', *R.E.S.* iv (1928), 16–23.

1641/2, 21 Mar. 'From yᵉ Regenthouse his Highnes went to Trinity College, where after dinner he saw a Comedy in English, & gave all sighnes of great acceptance which he could, & more then yᵉ University dared expect. The Comedy ended, he took Coach in yᵉ Court & returned to Newmarket.' (Joseph Beaumont to his father, Cooper, *Annals of Cambridge*, iii. 321.)

1650. The Guardian; A Comedie. Acted before Prince Charles His *Highness* At Trinity-Colledg in *Cambridge*, upon the twelfth of *March*, 1641. Written by Abraham Cowley . . . 1650.

1663. Cutter of Coleman-Street. A Comedy. The Scene *London*, in the year 1658. Written by Abraham Cowley . . . 1663.

1668, 5 Aug. 'So home to dinner, and thence out to the Duke of
York's playhouse, and there saw "The Guardian"; formerly
the same, I find, that was called "Cutter of Coleman Street"; a
silly play.' (Diary of Samuel Pepys.)

1668, 9 Aug. In a warrant for payment for performance of plays
before royalty by the Duke's company occurs the item, 'Aug: 9,
1668 The Guardian . . . 10.' (Allardyce Nicoll, *A History of
Restoration Drama*, 3rd ed., p. 309.)

1672, 17 Nov. In a warrant for payment for performance of plays
before royalty by the Duke's company occurs the item, '[Nov.]
17 Y^e Guardian . . . 10.' (Ibid.)

1674/5, 8 Jan. In a warrant for payment for performances of plays
before royalty by the Duke's company occurs the item, 'Jan. 8
Y^e Guardian K. & Q. . . . 20.' (Ibid., p. 310.)

1693. *Cutter of Coleman Street* in *The Works of Mr. Abraham
Cowley*, 1693.

1700. *Cutter of Coleman Street* in *The Works of Mr. Abraham
Cowley*, 1700.

The date of the performance of the play is set both by the
statement on the title-page and by Cutter's remarks to Tabytha as
he persuades her to marry him because of the vision he has had
(V. I):

And the vision told me, sister *Tabytha*, that this same day, the
twelfth of March, in the yeer of grace 1641, at this same holy place, by
a holy man, we two, who are both holy vessels, should be joyned
together in the holy band of Matrimony.

Moore Smith notes that the prologue and epilogue of the play
appear in Douce MS. 375, where they are entitled 'The Prologue
and Epilogue in a Comedy made by ye Poet Aquila p^rsented att
ye Entertainm^t of the Princes Highñss by the Schollars of
Trinity Colledge in Cambridge March 1641', and adds, 'At the
side, explanatory of "ye Poet Aquila", is written "Pooly",
probably for "Cooly."' (*College Plays*, p. 90.)

In the Senior Bursar's Accounts at Trinity College the following
entry refers to the unusual expenses in the presentation of the play:

1641–42 / Extraordinaries
To Mr Willis for D^s Cooleys Comœdy   lxv^li xvj^s
(*Malone Society Collections*, ii, Part ii [1923], 174.)

The visit of the Prince and the University celebrations of which
the presentation of Cowley's comedy at Trinity was a part are

described in a letter written from Peterhouse by Joseph Beaumont, 21 March 1641/2. Of this part of the festivities he says:

> From ye Regenthouse his Highnes went to Trinity College, where after dinner he saw a Comedy in English, & gave all sighnes of great acceptance which he could, & more then ye University dared expect. The Comedy ended, he took Coach in ye Court & returned to New-market. (Cooper, *Annals of Cambridge*, iii. 321.)

The reason that the University could not have expected a very enthusiastic reception for the play is indicated in the lines in the prologue addressed to Prince Charles:

> Accept our hastie zeal; a thing that's play'd
> Ere 'tis a Play, and acted ere 'tis made.

And in the epilogue:

> The Play is done, . . .
> In which if our bold wishes should be crost,
> 'Tis but the life of one poor week that's lost.
> Though it should fall beneath your present scorn,
> It could not die sooner then it was born.

Cowley wrote of the occasion and his subsequent attitude towards the play in his Preface in *Poems*, 1656. He says that on his recent return to England—he had left, probably, in 1644 (Nethercot, *Cowley*, pp. 90–92)—he had found *The Iron Age* published with his name on the title-page, and continues:

> So that I esteem my self less prejudiced by it, then by that which has been done to me, since almost in the same kinde, which is, the publication of some things of mine without my consent or knowledge, and those so mangled and imperfect, that I could neither with honor acknowledge, nor with honesty quite disavow them. Of which sort, was a *Comedy* called *The Guardian*, printed in the year, 1650. but made and acted before the *Prince*, in his passage through *Cambridge* towards *York*, at the beginning of the late unhappy War; or rather neither *made* nor *acted*, but *rough-drawn* onely, and *repeated*; for the haste was so great, that it could neither be *revised* or *perfected* by the *Author*, nor *learnt without-Book* by the *Actors*, nor set forth in any measure tolerably by the *Officers* of the *College*. After the *Representation* (which, I confess, was somewhat of the *latest*) I began to look it over, and changed it very much, striking out some whole parts, as that of the *Poet* and the *Souldier*; but I have lost the *Copy*, and dare not think it deserves the pains to write it again, which makes me omit it in this publication, though there be some things in it which I am not ashamed of, taking in the excuse of my age and small experience in humane conversation when I made it. But as it is, it is onely the hasty

first-sitting of a *Picture*, and therefore like to resemble me accordingly. (*Poems*, 1656, Preface, a₁ᵛ.)

After its Cambridge performance the play was acted, according to Cowley, '*several times after privately during the troubles, as I am told, with good approbation, as it has been lately too at* Dublin'. (Preface, *Cutter of Coleman Street*, 1663.) When the Restoration theatres were opened, the author revised it for performance at Lincoln's Inn Fields, where Pepys saw the opening, 16 December 1661, under the new title, *Cutter of Coleman Street*. Pepys says:

After dinner to the Opera, where there was a new play, Cutter of Coleman Street, made in the year 1658, with reflections much upon the late times; and it being the first time, the pay was doubled, and so, to save money, my wife and I went into the gallery, and there sat and saw very well; and a very good play it is—it seems, of Cowley's making. (Hazlitt, *Manual*, pp. 56–57.)

The plot and most of the characters in the revision are basically the same as in *The Guardian*, but Cowley has reorganized the scenes, reset the play in the London of 1658, and rewritten most of the dialogue, working in copious allusions to the experiences of the characters during the wars and the Commonwealth. This new background of experience makes the dialogue better than in *The Guardian*, but when Cowley transformed Captain Blade and Colonel Cutter and Dogrel into the real or pretended veteran Cavaliers, Colonel Jolly, Cutter, and Worm, he offended some members of the Restoration audience, who accused him of writing '*abuse and Satyre against the Kings party*'. (Preface, *Cutter of Coleman Street*.)

Love's Riddle (1633–6?)

Editions: The play is found in the editions of Cowley's works in 1707–8, 1710–11, 1721, 1777, 1809, 1881, and 1905–6.

1637/8, 14 Mar. S.R. Entered to Mr. Seile 'a Pastorall Comedy called Loues Ridle. by Abr: Cowley whilst he was Kings scholler in Westʳ: [shcoole *sic added*]'. (Greg, *Bibliography*, i. 47.)

1638. Loves Riddle. A Pastorall Comædie; Written, At the time of his being Kings Scholler in *Westminster* Schoole, by *A. Cowley* . . . 1638.

1681. *Loves Riddle* in *The Second Part of the Works*, 1681.

1682. *Loves Riddle* in *The Second Part of the Works*, 1682.

1684. *Loves Riddle* in *The Second Part of the Works*, 1684.

1689. *Loves Riddle* in *The Second and Third Parts of the Works*, 1689.

1689. [Another issue.]
1700. *Loves Riddle* in *The Second and Third Parts of the Works*, 1700.

The precise date of the composition of *Love's Riddle* cannot be fixed, and there is no evidence that it was ever produced in its original form. Since the title-page of the 1638 edition says, 'Written, At the time of his being Kings Scholler in *Westminster* Schoole', the play must have been written between about 1630, the approximate time of Cowley's election as King's Scholar (Loiseau, *Abraham Cowley, sa vie, son œuvre*, p. 21; Nethercot, *Cowley*, pp. 12–13), and his appointment to the reversion of a 'dry chorister's place' at Trinity College, Cambridge, 30 March 1636, after his failure, a month or so before, to be elected to a Trinity scholarship. (Nethercot, *Cowley*, pp. 36–40.) Whatever the inadequacies of the play, it is a surprising performance for a schoolboy at any stage of his career, and Nethercot is probably right in his suggestion that it was written late in Cowley's residence at Westminster. (Ibid., pp. 32–33.) The years 1633–6, Cowley's fifteenth to eighteenth years, probably include the composition date of the play.

Because of Cowley's great reputation in the seventeenth century and the undeniable precocity of this schoolboy achievement, much has been written about the sources of *Love's Riddle*. Most of it is irresponsible and sometimes ridiculous guess-work. The best discussions are Greg's (*Pastoral Poetry and Pastoral Drama*, pp. 362–5) and Nethercot's ('Cowley as Dramatist', pp. 2–6). Because of the parallel between Cowley's precocious career at Westminster and Trinity with Randolph's very similar one some twelve years earlier, it is inevitable that the influence of *Amyntas* and *The Jealous Lovers* should have been proclaimed. There are a number of similarities, but most of them consist of material fairly common in such a conventional form as the pastoral drama, in which Cowley's principal achievement was the 'manner in which borrowing, reminiscence, and tradition were interwoven and combined'. (Greg, *Pastoral Poetry & Pastoral Drama*, p. 362.)

The Young Ladies Miscellany; or, Youth's Innocent and Rational Amusement, 1726, by Daniel Bellamy, the elder, contains an adaptation of *Love's Riddle* called *The Rival Nymphs*, prepared 'for the *Diversion* and *Improvement* of the Young Ladies of Mrs *Bellamy's* Boarding-School'. I have not seen the first edition of 1723.

Naufragium Joculare (2 February 1636/7)

Editions: The play is found in *The Second Part of the Works of Mr. Abraham Cowley*, 1681, 1682, 1684, and *The Second and Third Parts of the Works of Mr. Abraham Cowley*, 1689, 1693, 1700, and the editions of 1707–8, 1710–11, 1721, 1809, and 1881.

Nethercot, Arthur H. 'Abraham Cowley as Dramatist', *R.E.S.* iv (1928), 8–16.

1637/8, 14 Mar. S.R. Entered to Mr. Seile 'a Latyn Comedy called Naufragiũ Ioculare. by Abra: Cowley'. (Greg, *Bibliography*, i. 47.)

1638. Navfragivm Iocvlare, *Comœdia*: Publicè Coram Academicis Acta, in Collegio S S. et individuæ Trinitatis. 4°. Nonas *Feb.* An. Dom. 1638. Authore *Abrahamo Cowley*. Mart. — *Non displicuisse meretur Festinat, Lector, qui placuisse tibi. . . .* 1638.

1675, 14 Apr. S.R. Assigned by Ann Seale, widow, to Andrew Clarke and Charles Harper 'A Latine Comedy called Naufragium Ioculare by Abra: Cowley', with thirty-five other titles. (Ibid., p. 74.)

There has been some confusion about the date of this play, derived from the title-page of the first edition: '4°. Nonas *Feb.* An. Dom. 1638.' Moore Smith (*College Plays*, pp. 70 and 90) and Nethercot (*Cowley*, p. 64; 'Cowley as Dramatist', p. 10) and others have interpreted this date as Old Style, making it 2 February 1638/9. Other evidence, however, indicates that the performance was in 1637/8, not 1638/9. On 12 May 1638 Robert Cresswell wrote from Trinity College, Cambridge, to Viscount Falkland about his room-mate and former schoolmate at Westminster as follows:

I humbly thank yo[r] L[d]ship for this & other vndeserued courtesyes ther, wher I had only that & my boldnes to authorize my welcome. The like obligation I must acknowledg in the behalf of my ingenious chamber fellow [Mr. Cowley], albeit now absent. He hath been as yett a Poett in Decimo sexto, but is now enlarging the Edition:—An English Pastorall & a Latin Comedy prsented here: We have as yett receiued neither them nor himselfe. (Kurt Weber, *Lucius Cary, Second Viscount Falkland*, pp. 125–6.)

Cresswell here indicates not only that the Latin comedy, i.e. *Naufragium Joculare*, had already been performed, but that its publication was imminent. Since the printer had registered the book two months before, on 14 March 1637/8 (Greg, *Bibliography*,

i. 47), all the facts fit together to demonstrate that the date on the title-page is New Style and that the play was presented in February 1637/8, not 1638/9. For once Fleay was right and his successors wrong, for he said of the date of the performance, 'Not 1638–39'. (*Biog. Chron.* i. 74.)

Cowley's sources were probably in large part Plautine, but some of his material had been used by Heywood in *The English Traveller* and *The Captives*. Neither seems likely to have been so familiar to Cowley as Plautus, especially *The Captives*, which was not published until the nineteenth century. (See Nethercot, 'Cowley as Dramatist', pp. 10–14.) As Nethercot points out, various previous plays had had satiric school scenes which Cowley might have seen in London (ibid., p. 12), but such scenes are so obvious for academic comedy that source-hunting seems vain. Cowley's predecessor at Westminster and Trinity, Thomas Randolph, had used them in *The Drinking Academy*, and so no doubt had many of Randolph's predecessors.

Genest (x. 64) pointed out that the prologue seems to indicate that Cowley himself had a role in the performance, as the author of a play commonly did at Cambridge. (See Moore Smith, *College Plays*, pp. 74–88.)

There is no record of any other performance, but the play continued to be read. Pepys records on 19 February 1660/1 that he 'spent the evening in reading of a Latin play, the "Naufragium Joculare" '. It was translated by Charles Johnson in 1705 as *Fortune in Her Wits*, and in 1740 Daniel Bellamy, the younger, asserted that he had used the comedy for the sub-plot of his *The Perjur'd Devotee; or, The Force of Love*. (Nethercot, 'Cowley as Dramatist', pp. 14–15.)

There is a synopsis of the play in Nethercot's article on Cowley, pp. 10–14.

ROBERT COX (Coxe)
1604?–55?

Robert Cox, the famous player and writer of drolls, was an actor before the closing of the theatres (see above, ii. 414–15), but there is no indication that he ever wrote anything before that time. Indeed his fame was attained wholly through the drolls, which were brought into existence by the abolition of the regular performances. (See Langbaine, *An Account of the English Dramatick Poets* [1691], pp. 89–90; Hyder Rollins, *Stud. Phil.* xviii [1921], 307–9, and xx

[1923], 59–60; J. J. Elson, ed., *The Wits or Sport upon Sport* [1932], pp. 11–18 *et passim*.)

— CROUSE

A misreading of Cruso (q.v.).

JOSEPH CROWTHER (Crouther, Crowder)
c. 1610?–89

He was the son of Thomas Crowther, of Blackwall, Middlesex. C. J. Robinson indicates that he entered the Merchant Taylors' School in 1615: 'Joseph Crowther b. 12 Jan. 1604 (1606 or 1608).' (*A Register of the Scholars Admitted to the Merchant Taylors' School, 1562–1874*, i. 90.) This record, whichever year of birth is accepted, does not agree with the Oxford statement that he was sixteen when he matriculated 20 October 1626, a plebe from St. John's College. He was elected a Fellow in 1628 and granted the degrees of B.A. 30 April 1629, M.A. 9 May 1633 (incorporated Cambridge 1634), B.D. 15 March 1638/9 (incorporated Cambridge 1640), and D.D. 2 August 1660. In 1640 he was vicar of Great Dunmow, Essex, from which he was sequestered in 1646, and he was ejected from his St. John's fellowship in 1648, when the Visitor's Register says, 'Mr. Crowder, in France'. (Montagu Burrows, *The Register of the Visitors of the University of Oxford, 1647–1658*, p. 164.) After the Restoration he was Regius Professor of Greek from 1660 to 1665 and Principal of St. Mary's Hall 1664–89. He was prebendary of Stratford and chaplain to James, Duke of York. Bliss says (Wood's *Fasti*, Bliss ed. ii. 237, n. 6) that he officiated at the marriage of James and Lady Anne Hyde. He died in the Fleet 16 December 1689 and was buried in St. Paul's Cathedral, of which he was a prebendary and chorister. Administration of his estate was granted at Oxford 27 January 1689/90. (Wood's *Fasti*, Bliss ed. ii. 236–7, and *Alumni Oxon.* i. 359.)

Cephalus et Procris (1626–8)

MS.: St. John's College, Oxford, MS. 217 P. 3587.

Boas, F. S. 'Recently Recovered Manuscripts at St. John's College, Oxford', *M.L.R.* xi (1916), 298–301.

With the St. John's College MS. of the play is the following note:

This MS. was found in London among some old legal papers in a lawyer's office in 1914, together with the MS. of John Blencowe's 'Mercurius, sive Literarum Lucta.' Through the exertions of the Rev. H. D. Elam, formerly Andrews Scholar (B.A. 1873), they were deposited in the College Library by Messrs. Crawley Arnold & Co., solicitors, 1 Dean's Yard, Westminster, S.W., on 24 December, 1915, subject to the condition that they shall be restored to the owners' representatives (if they should be discovered), on demand from Messrs. Crawley Arnold and Co. or their representatives. / W. H. S. / Librarian
    January 20, 1916.

The manuscript has no title, but Boas called it *Cephalus et Procris* from the subject (op. cit., p. 299), and it is presumably from Boas that the author of the manuscript supplement to H. O. Coxe's *Codicum MSS qui in collegiis oxoniensibus hodie adservantur* (1852) got his title of *Cephalus and Procris*.

The play is about 1,100 or 1,200 lines in length. The manuscript gives neither prologue nor epilogue, but there is a synopsis by scenes. Speech prefixes and stage directions have been added in a second hand and in ink very like, if not identical with, that in Blencowe's *Mercurius* (q.v.). The brevity of the play, its small mythological cast, and its literary character do not suggest a public collegiate performance. The dramatis personae are given on fol. 2ᵛ:

> Aurora
> Cephalus
> Procris
> Alumna Procridis
> Charinda ⎫ ancillæ
> Damalis ⎰
> Eumetis senex
> Phorus servus
> Diana
> Venatores 3
> Nymphæ 2

The manuscript can be fairly closely dated from the dedication, which is signed 'Josephᵘˢ Crowther':

> Ornatissimo doctissimoqᵘᵉ viro
> Guilielmo Iuxon LL Dʳⁱ et
> Coll:ⁱʲ Divæ Joan: Bapt: Præsidi
> Almæqᵘᵉ Academiæ Oxon:ˢⁱˢ
> Procancellario dignissimo.

Juxon was President of St. John's from 10 December 1621 to 5 January 1632/3, but he was Vice-Chancellor of the University only from 22 July 1626 to 24 July 1628. The dedication was written, therefore, between these latter dates, and presumably the play as well, though it could have been composed before Juxon's election. Boas thinks (op. cit.) that the congratulatory tone of the dedication suggests that it was written soon after Juxon's election and that 'Academica infantia' implies Crowther's freshman year, 1626–7.

AQUILA CRUSO
c. 1595–1660

The Emmanuel College MS. of *Euribates Pseudomagus* makes the attribution, 'Authore. Mr Crouso. Caij Colle: Cantabr:' Unfortunately there were several Crusos at Gonville and Caius College, Cambridge, in the seventeenth century, all of them from a Flemish family at Norwich: Aquila, c. 1595–1660; John, c. 1618–81; John, c. 1645–?; and Francis, 1651/2–1717. (John Venn, *Biographical History of Gonville and Caius College*, i. 209, 304, 414, 436.) The *D.N.B.*, apparently unaware of other Crusos, attributes the play and five military books to the first John. Venn points out that the attribution of the military books is dubious because the first was published in 1632, the year John was admitted to the college at the age of fourteen. He might also have pointed out that it would have been difficult for this John to have aquired extensive military experience while a scholar and Fellow at the college, 1632–44. The military man was probably the unrecorded grandfather of Francis Cruso, who is referred to as 'the grandson of my ancient friend Captain Cruso'. (Venn, op. cit. i. 436.) Venn agrees with the *D.N.B.*, however, in attributing the play to the first John; he gives no reason.

G. C. Moore Smith, also without reason, assigns the play to Aquila. (*College Plays*, p. 90.) On the basis of the available evidence, Aquila seems somewhat more likely than the other Crusos to have been the author of the play. His association with the college was the earliest and the longest, and his position as Fellow for eighteen years and Greek lecturer in 1619 seems most likely to have been acknowledged in 'Mr.'

Aquila Cruso, son of John, a Fleming of Norwich, was admitted, aged fifteen, as a scholar at Gonville and Caius College, 18 August 1610, tutor Mr. Oliver Naylor. He took his degrees, B.A. 1613/14, M.A. 1618, B.D. 1626, and was a Fellow of the college 1616–34.

He was rhetoric prelector in 1618, Greek lecturer in 1619, and ordained in June 1620. He was University preacher in 1623, rector of Sutton, Sussex, in 1633, and prebendary of Chichester in 1637. He was buried at Sutton 13 November 1660. (Venn, op. cit. i. 209.) Venn notes that two exercises of his were published with others by R. Watson in 1665, and that Watson speaks highly of Cruso's learning. (Ibid.)

Euribates (1616?)

MS.: Emmanuel College, Cambridge, MS. 3. 1. 17.

The play is entitled simply *Euribates* in the Cambridge MS., but the principal character is called 'Euribates Pseudomagus'. At the end of the play appears the statement 'Authore. Mr Crouso. Caij Colle: Cantabr:' and, after another flourish, 'Thom. Holbech'. Venn lists three Thomas Holbechs at Cambridge (*Alumni Cantab.* ii. 387), but only one was there in the seventeenth century before the Restoration. This man was admitted pensioner at Emmanuel in 1622, B.A. 1625-6, M.A. 1629, B.D. 1636. Later he was Master of the college and Vice-Chancellor of the University. Since he was at the University when Cruso was, and a member of the college now owning the manuscript, he was probably the man who copied out *Euribates*.

Moore Smith says of the play only, 'Query, acted at Caius in 1615/16?' (*College Plays*, p. 90), and in his chronological table of college plays he lists it under '1616?'. Apparently he selected this date because the only records in the college accounts concerning plays are those listed under the year 1615-16 (Michaelmas to Michaelmas), for repairing glass in the hall windows 'broken at the Comedie', and stone work by Mr. Lucye's chamber 'broken downe at ye comedie'. (*M.S.C.* ii, Part ii. 227.)

P. CUFF

See Anon., *Sanguis Sanguinem*.

JOHN CUMBER
?-1623

W. J. Lawrence, following Fleay (*Biog. Chron.* i. 42–43), thought that John Cumber, the actor (see above, ii. 417–18), was the 'I. C.'

named on the 1620 title-page as the author of *A Pleasant Comedy Called The Two Merry Milkmaids, or The Best Words Wear the Garland*. (*T.L.S.*, 23 March 1922, p. 191.) This identification is a plausible guess, but nothing more. (See I. C.)

J. D.
fl. 1639

Nothing is known of this man save that his initials appear on the 1640 title-page of *The Knave in Grain, New Vampt*. The fact that the play is evidently a revision makes it possible that J. D. was the reviser rather than the original author. If one were forced to name a candidate, more plausible nominations would be found among hack dramatists and actors than among poets.

The Knave in Grain, New Vampt (*c.* 1638?)

Adams, J. Q. 'Hill's List of Early Plays in Manuscript', *Library*, Fourth Series, xx (1939), 84–86.

Bald, R. C. 'The Foul Papers of a Revision', *Library*, New Series, xxvi (1945), 43–50.

Smith, Captain Alexander. *A Compleat History of the Lives and Robberies of the Most Notorious Highwaymen* (1719), ii. 217–26.

1639, 18 June. S.R. Entered for John Okes 'a Play called The knave in Graine or Iack Cottington'. (Greg, *Bibliography*, i. 51.)

1639, 22 Oct. S.R. Assigned to John Nicholson 'by vertue of a note vnder the hand & seale of Iohn Okes a Play called A knave in graine new vampt'. (Ibid.)

1640. The Knave in Graine, New Vampt. A witty Comedy, Acted at the *Fortune* many dayes together with great *Applause*. *Written by* J. D. *Gent. London*: Printed by *J. O.* and are to be sold by *John Nicholson* . . . 1640.

1654. 'Behold and view the very Picture of the Salutation-Taverne reform'd; an *Andaluzian*, and a *Manchegan* in the Spanish mode, passing Punctilios upon one another. I wonder it scap'd our Pencill men, especially when they had so many Signes to alter. A *Knight-Errant* and a Bedlam exactly drawn, in the liveliest postures of the *Madrid Salutados*, would have been as magnetick and beneficiall to the house, as the Renouned pieces of *John a Green*, or *Mul-sack*.' (Edmund Gayton, *Pleasant Notes upon Don Quixote* [1654], p. 129.)

1654/5, 7–14 Feb. '. . . a Company of young *Citts* that met the last week to act a *Comedy*, called *Knavery in all Trades*, but putting

down their Half *Crowns* apiece the first *meeting* for a *stock*, and
to engage each Person to the performance of his Part, the chief
of them, who was to act the *Knave in grain*, having his Part
studdied before-hand, having taken about 30. s. of his fellow
Actors money, made an *Exit* instead of an *Entrance*, and so is
gone to *Holland.*' (*Mercurius Fumigosus*, 7–14 February 1654/5,
as reprinted by Hyder Rollins, *Stud. Phil.* xviii [1921], 318.)
c. 1677–1703. 'mull sack or the looking glass the Bachelor or the
Hawk' is the twelfth title in Abraham Hill's list of plays. (J. Q.
Adams, op. cit., p. 73. See Middleton, *The Conqueror's Custom*.)

The 'New Vampt' of the title apparently means 'revised', as in
the case of *The Whore New Vampt* (q.v. under Anon.). The only
text of *The Knave in Grain, New Vampt*, is in such a confused
state that Professor Bald contends with good evidence that it was
set up from the foul papers of a revision. (Op. cit.) He attempts to
make a partial disentanglement of the original material and the
additions. He finds, roughly, that the revisions were intended to
make the central figure of the principal action, Julio, into the
leading character in the secondary action as well, and to add a
number of rogue episodes to this secondary action.

This reconstruction of the history of the play is complicated
and in part contradicted by Professor Adams's consideration of
the title of one of the lost manuscript plays in Abraham Hill's
list, 'mull sack or the looking glass the Bachelor or the Hawk'.
He notes that Mull Sack was the alias of the notorious cheat,
pick-pocket, and highwayman, Jack Cottington, and that in the
original entry of *The Knave in Grain* in the Stationers' Register,
18 June 1639, John Okes gave the play the sub-title 'or Iack
Cottington'. Adams suggests that the play which Okes entered
was in part about Jack Cottington or Mull Sack, but that,
frightened by the trouble about *The Whore New Vampt* in September 1639 (see above, i. 314–15), he transferred his play to
John Nicholson and that somebody had the manuscript revised
to eliminate the Cottington material by cutting a number of the
cheating episodes and changing Cottington's name to Julio. Presumably some of these eliminated episodes gave point to the
cheating terms of Hill's title, 'looking glass' and 'hawk'. Professor Adams concludes that:

if the manuscript listed by Hill was *The Knave in Graine, or Jack
Cottington*, it must have represented the original version of that play
and not the much altered text that has come down to us. (Op. cit.,
p. 86.)

This hypothesis involves a deal of conjecture, but there is support for it in a passage Adams did not note. His only evidence that there ever was a play about Jack Cottington is found in the single Stationers' Register entry of 18 June 1639, which could conceivably be simply an attempt to get through two manuscripts for one fee. Edmund Gayton, however, shows in a passage in his highly allusive *Pleasant Notes upon Don Quixote*, 1654, that there *was* a play about Cottington or Mull Sack, that it was popular, and, presumably, that it included tavern scenes. (See the passage quoted above.) All this suggests *The Knave in Grain*. One scene in the extant text of that play is conspicuously labelled 'The Taverne Sceane' (F_4^v, though misplaced); the play's popularity is indicated by the highly unusual statement on the title-page, 'Acted at the *Fortune* many dayes together'; and finally one can have some confidence in Gayton since he seems to have been more conversant than most educated men in the late Caroline period with the low theatres, the Red Bull and the Fortune, and their popular clowns, Andrew Cane and Richard Fowler. (See above, ii. 691.) Thus, though one cannot definitely establish Adams's conjecture that *The Knave in Grain, New Vampt*, was a play involving Jack Cottington which had been revised before publication in order to eliminate reference to him, it is made much more plausible by Gayton's reference.

The obscure address 'To the Generous Reader' which has been prefixed to the quarto is mostly concerned with the prevalence of knaves in all walks of life and with repeated assertions that no particular individual is represented in the play. Such protests against identification always make one suspect that identification was intended, and the suspicion would be well grounded if this play really is a revised piece about Jack Cottington.

If the original Knave play concerned Jack Cottington, it probably was produced not very long before the Stationers' Register entry, for Cottington was only forty-five when he was executed in April 1659, and it does not seem likely that he was notorious enough to be the subject of a play very long before he was twenty-five, in 1639. (See 'MUL-SLCK [misprint for SACK], *the* Chimney-Sweeper, *alias* John Cottington, *a Murderer and Highwayman*', in Captain Alexander Smith, op. cit.) Professor Bald's contention (op. cit., p. 43) that the repeated references to a leaguer suggest proximity to Marmion's *Holland's Leaguer* (q.v.) of December 1631 does not seem to me convincing. In *A Knave in Grain* the term is used to mean a brothel without particular reference, and I see no essential relation to *Holland's Leaguer*.

Professor Bald has also suggested in his edition of Middleton's *Hengist, King of Kent; or The Mayor of Queenborough*, pp. xli–xlii, that the last scene in *The Knave in Grain*, in which Julio cheats the clown of the money held in his mouth, was so similar to the cheating scene in v. 1 of *Hengist* as to indicate imitation, and that both Middleton and J. D. borrowed the episode from an old play. I see no striking similarity between the two scenes beyond the fact that both involve the swindling of a boastful bumpkin. Such scenes must have been almost daily occurrences in London, and the rogue literature of the time often records them. Bald's other suggestion of source (op. cit., p. 44) is more persuasive, namely, that Valentius's prosecution of an intrigue with a doctor's wife by pretending to be a madman is closely modelled on *The Changeling*. Here the similarity is marked. J. D. must have derived his information from a performance of *The Changeling*, not a printed text, for though the play was first produced in 1622, it was not published until 1653.

T. D.

See Thomas Drue.

ROBERT DABORNE (Dauborne, Daubourne, Dawborne)
?–1628

Robert Daborne was an early Jacobean dramatist, but there is no reliable evidence that after 1616 he wrote anything for the stage or had any connexion with theatrical activities. On 20 March 1615/16 he was witness to the agreement between the players at the Hope and Alleyn and Meade (see above, i. 199 n.), but well before 24 July 1618 he had become a minister, for on that date his *An Assize Sermon* was entered in the Stationers' Register. This transformation was known to the theatrically knowledgeable William Heminges, son of the manager of the King's company, for in his *Elegy on Randolph's Finger, c.* 1632, Heminges eliminated Daborne from the group of poets accompanying the cortège to Hell:

> Dauborne I had forgott, and lett ytt bee,
> hee dyed Amphybion by thy [the ?] Ministrye.
> (Moore Smith ed., lines 61–62.)

Thus 1617 seems to be about the latest date when Daborne could possibly have been indulging in secular theatrical activities, and

there is no real evidence for such activities after 20 March 1615/16.
See *The Elizabethan Stage*, iii. 270–2, for his earlier activity.

Unnamed Play
with Field, Massinger, and Fletcher
(Lost)

See *The Elizabethan Stage*, iii. 272.

The Arraignment of London (*The Bellman of London* ?) with
Tourneur
(Lost)

See *The Elizabethan Stage*, iii. 272.

A Christian Turned Turk

See *The Elizabethan Stage*, iii. 271.

Machiavel and the Devil
(Lost)

See *The Elizabethan Stage*, iii. 272.

The Owl
(Lost)

See *The Elizabethan Stage*, iii. 272.

The Poor Man's Comfort (1610 < > 1617)

Baldwin, T. W. *The Organization and Personnel of the Shake-spearean Company* (1927), p. 424.

Swaen, A. E. H. 'Robert Daborne's Plays', *Anglia*, xxi (1899), 373–440.

MS.: B.M. MS. Egerton 1994, fols. 268–92. (W. W. Greg, *Dramatic Documents*, pp. 311–14.)

1655, 20 June. S.R. John Sweeting entered 'a booke called The Poore mans Comfort, a Tragicomedie written by Robert Dawborne, m^r. of Arts'. (Greg, *Bibliography*, i. 64.)

1655. The Poor-Mans Comfort. A Tragi-Comedy, As it was divers times Acted at the *Cock-pit* in *Drury lane* with great applause. Written by Robert Dauborne Master of Arts . . . 1655.

1661, 10 July. 'W., in the morning, "The City Witt," 6*d*; in the afternoone, "The poore man's comfort" a tragi-comedy, 6*d*.' (Plays seen at Oxford by Anthony à Wood. Andrew Clark, *The Life and Times of Anthony Wood* [1891–1900], i. 406.)

1662, 16 July. S.R. In a list of titles assigned by the executors of John Sweeting to Robert Horne is '[16] The Poore mans Comfort, a Tragi Comedy by Robt Dawborn'. (Greg, *Bibliography*, i. 70.)

This play has several times been dated *c.* 1617, but without adequate evidence. It is true that the Cockpit in Drury Lane, in which the 1655 title-page says that the play was acted, was first used in that year, but there is no reason to think that the title-page referred to the first performance; title-pages generally refer to the latest performances. The text contains the names of two actors, 'Enter 2 Lords, Sands, Ellis' (found in the quarto but not in the manuscript), but these men are likely to have performed in a revival, and in any case the identity of the actors referred to is most uncertain. Ellis Bedowe, Ellis Guest, Ellis Worth; Gregory Sanderson, James Sands, and Thomas Sands are all possibilities. The prologue for the play is signed 'Per E. M.', and W. J. Lawrence (*M.L.R.* xxv [1930], 211) was certain that the initials stood for Edward May and that the prologue was written for a revival by Queen Henrietta's men at the Cockpit in 1635. The speculation is interesting, but the evidence is practically nil.

Professor T. W. Baldwin thinks that the play was written for Queen Anne's company in 1617 (op. cit., p. 424) because 'Some suit from porters hall' must in his opinion refer to the difficulties about the Porter's Hall theatre. This seems to me a very dubious interpretation of the passage, but I cannot say that it is impossible. In the present state of the evidence I think we can say only that the play presumably was written after 1610, when Daborne seems to have begun to write for the theatres, and not later than 1617, which seems to be the latest date he could have taken orders if before July 1618 he was to be ordained, to preach an assize sermon, and to prepare it for the press.

The manuscript of the play which was transcribed by 'P. Massam' appears to be of little importance. (See W. W. Greg, *Dramatic Documents*, pp. 311–14.) A. E. H. Swaen records in his edition a few of the variants noted in a hasty collation.

The She Saint
(Lost)

See *The Elizabethan Stage*, iii. 272.

SIR WILLIAM DAVENANT (Dabenett, Daunett, D'Avenant, D'avenant, Davenaunte, Davenett, Davinant, Dennant, Devenet, Devenett)
1605/6–68

Harbage, Alfred. *Sir William Davenant, Poet Venturer, 1606–68* (1935).

Hotson, Leslie. *The Commonwealth and Restoration Stage* (1928), *passim*.

Nethercot, Arthur H. *Sir William D'avenant, Poet Laureate and Playwright-Manager* (1938).

Summers, Montague. *The Playhouse of Pepys* (1935), pp. 1–64.

William Davenant, fourth child and second son of John Davenant, vintner, and Jane (Shepherd) his wife, was baptized at St. Martin's, Carfax, Oxford, 3 March 1605/6. His father was a respectable tavern-keeper of Oxford who ran the tavern known since 1666 as 'The Crown'; before his death he became mayor of Oxford. Though William eventually adopted an aristocratic apostrophe and hinted at a Lombard origin, the family had been English for many generations. (Nethercot, *D'avenant*, pp. 9–17.) According to a widely accepted tradition, William Shakespeare stood godfather for the child. The story, later tolerated if not encouraged by Sir William, that he was the illegitimate son of Shakespeare can be neither confirmed nor disproved; there is rather good testimony that Shakespeare was a friend and regular visitor of the family. (Chambers, *Shakespeare*, i. 572–6.)

Young Davenant was for a time in the Oxford grammar school of Edward Sylvester and apparently for a year or so was a pupil of Daniel Hough, of Lincoln College, though there is no record of Davenant at the University. (Nethercot, pp. 23–27.) When he was sixteen his father, then mayor, died, leaving him little money and advising that William 'being now arrived to 16 yeares of age, shall be put to prentice to some good marchant of London or other tradesman' and that this be done 'within the compasse of three moneths after my death'. (Halliwell-Phillipps, *Outlines*, 6th ed. [1886], ii. 46–48.) Though William did go to London, and apparently within the specified time, it was not to an apprenticeship.

Appropriately enough his first recorded act in London was to purchase fine raiment and thus become involved with a tailor named Urswick, with whose services, bills, and lawsuits he was troubled for the next fifteen years. (Nethercot, pp. 433–41 *et passim.*) Aubrey says that he became page to the Duchess of Richmond (*Brief Lives*, i. 205) and later attached to the household of Fulke Greville, Lord Brooke, who continued as his master or patron until Greville's death in 1628. (Nethercot, pp. 46–64.) Some time early in this period the young Davenant had been married, for William, son of William and Mary Davenant, was baptized at St. James, Clerkenwell, 27 October 1624. Mary Davenant, though she bore her husband at least two children, remains a very shadowy figure; not even the date of her death is known.

What was probably Davenant's first play, the unacted tragedy *Albovine*, was written in this period, though not printed until 1629. His next, *The Cruel Brother*, like nearly all his Caroline pieces, was acted by the King's men at the Blackfriars.

Before 1628 Davenant had had some unknown military experience, and in this year he was seeking more, first a commission and later permission for a wild exploit to blow up the powder magazines at Dunkirk. At this time he was living in the Middle Temple with Edward Hyde, the future Earl of Clarendon, and here, presumably, he first became attacheu to his boon companion, Sir John Suckling. (Nethercot, pp. 65–71.)

In the late twenties Davenant's complimentary verses show that he was addressing himself to a large number of prospective patrons, but eventually he became largely dependent upon Endymion Porter and Henry Jermyn. (Ibid., pp. 72–79.) Some time in this period Davenant contracted syphilis and in 1631 and 1632 was dangerously ill from the disease and the mercury poisoning resulting from its treatment. The consequent disfigurement of his nose became a sort of Davenant badge and the butt of all the London wits for the rest of his life. (Ibid., pp. 90–96.) In February 1632/3, on his way back to London after a long period of recuperation in the country, he stabbed a hostler or tapster named Thomas Warren at Braintree, and the man died in a few days. Davenant fled, apparently to Holland, and seems to have been convicted of murder in his absence. The King was petitioned for pardon, and though the full pardon seems not to have been granted until 1638, Davenant was back in London before the end of 1633, his property still sequestrated. (Ibid., pp. 100–7 and 443–7.)

Davenant's masque for the Queen, *The Temple of Love*, was pro-

duced at court, after a great deal of anticipation, on 10 February
1634/5, and he was the principal writer of masques for the remainder of the reign. His Blackfriars plays of this period were
calculated to appeal to the courtly group, and on at least one
occasion the Queen attended one at Blackfriars, probably a private performance. (See above, i. 48, n. 5.)

In 1638 *Madagascar; with Other Poems* appeared, King Charles
granted him a full pardon for the murder of Thomas Warren, and,
after much skirmishing with Thomas May and James Shirley, he
was made poet laureate in succession to Ben Jonson. Though the
term 'laureate' itself was not used in the grant, he was given
the same annual pension that Jonson had enjoyed. (Nethercot,
pp. 144–50, 163–7.)

On 26 March 1639 Davenant was granted the King's patent to
erect a large theatre near the Three Kings Ordinary in Fleet Street
in which to present music, musical presentments, scenes, dancing,
and plays, but by some unknown means the project was stopped,
and six months later Davenant surrendered his patent. (Adams,
Shakespearean Playhouses, pp. 424–31.) Davenant did not, however, lose his chance at theatre management. The King and
Queen's Young Company, or Their Majesties Servants, popularly
known as Beeston's Boys, had presented at the Cockpit or Phoenix
in Drury Lane an unlicensed play dealing with the King's Scottish
difficulties, and on 3 May 1640 the company was suppressed and
the manager, William Beeston, together with two principal actors,
was jailed. The company was allowed to act again in a few days,
and on 27 June Davenant was appointed governor of the company in Beeston's place. (See above, i. 332–5.) There are no
records of Davenant's activities in this ideal preparation for his
Restoration career, but his training cannot have lasted long, for
in less than a year he had fled London.

Davenant was in the field with the King in both Bishops'
Wars. In the first he was one of the paymasters under the Earl
of Newport, commander of the ordinance, and in the second he
served in some unspecified capacity with the artillery. (Nethercot,
pp. 182–8.) In May 1641 he was involved in the Army Plot with
Percy, Billingsley, Jermyn, and Suckling, and fled London, but
he was captured and returned, and it was expected he would be
sentenced to death. He was, however, admitted to bail in July.
He does not appear to have returned to the Cockpit, for Beeston
is again listed as governor in 1641. (See above, i. 335, and Nethercot, pp. 182–98.)

For a year there are no records of Davenant's activities, but in

July 1642 he was at The Hague with the Queen, and later, perhaps at her request, he was made lieutenant-general of the ordinance on the staff of the Earl of Newcastle. Later he was with the King's army in and about Oxford, and he was knighted by the King at the siege of Gloucester in the late summer of 1643. (Nethercot, pp. 198–207.) In 1643 and 1644 he was frequently in Holland on Royalist missions, and in the middle forties he was generally active as a royal messenger and supply officer. (Ibid., pp. 209–33.) In June 1646 he was a member of the Queen's commission which brought Prince Charles to Paris from Jersey.

In 1649 Charles II commissioned Davenant treasurer of Virginia, and he prepared to go to America with a group of artisans recruited from Paris prisons. Before he started the poet had the *Preface to Gondibert* published in Paris. In Jersey his appointment was changed to Lieutenant-Governor of Maryland, and he sailed for the New World on 3 May 1650, only to be captured in the Channel and imprisoned in Cowes Castle (ibid., pp. 251–65), where he finished as much of *Gondibert* as he ever published. He was transferred to the Tower of London about the time *Gondibert* was published, setting off the famous controversy. Not until October 1652 was the poet given the freedom of the Tower, i.e. London, which he used to marry the widow of Sir Thomas Cademan. He was pardoned by Cromwell in August 1654. (Ibid., pp. 268–94.)

In 1655, six months after the death of his second wife, Davenant returned to France, married Henrietta Maria du Tremblay, and brought her back to London. In 1655/6 he formed a company to build a structure for representations and shows and seems to have made several attempts at production which were foiled by his creditors. (Ibid., pp. 295–302.) In May 1656 he began his famous series of operatic performances in the hall at the back part of Rutland House (Hotson, *Commonwealth and Restoration Stage*, pp. 133–63), and by July 1658 had succeeded in transferring his enterprise to the old Cockpit theatre in Drury Lane. This astonishing series of historic performances demonstrates Davenant's resourcefulness; it placed him in a most advantageous position for the revival of the drama at the Restoration. (Hotson, pp. 133–63, and Nethercot, pp. 297–336.)

In August 1659 Davenant was arrested again, possibly in connexion with the premature uprising of the Royalists, but he was soon released. After the Restoration he again brought forward his old patent of 1639 for a theatre and company and drafted an order for a censorship of plays and a monopoly of London acting in two theatres controlled by Killigrew and himself. After pre-

DAVENANT PLAYS AND PLAYWRIGHTS 197

liminary difficulties and a short period of amalgamation, these two companies became established, one as the King's company under Killigrew at, successively, the Red Bull, Gibbon's Tennis Court, and finally the Theatre Royal in Bridges Street, and the other as the Duke's company under Davenant at the Salisbury Court and Lisle's Tennis Court or the Duke's Theatre. (Hotson, pp. 197–223, and Nethercot, pp. 337–57.)

Davenant had Lisle's Tennis Court remodelled to provide a stage equipped for the regular use of movable scenery and manager's quarters for his family and for the actresses he had contracted to support, and here he managed the Duke's company until his death. In general his troupe was better managed and better trained than the King's company. At the Duke's or Lincoln's Inn Fields theatre he presented those adaptations of Shakespeare's plays which have occasioned so many pious lamentations —*Hamlet, The Law against Lovers, The Rivals, Macbeth,* and *The Tempest.* (Nethercot, pp. 357–403.)

Sir William Davenant died in his quarters at the theatre 7 April 1668 and was buried in Westminster Abbey on the 9th. *The Works of S*ʳ *William D'avenant K*ᵗ were published four years later with a portrait by Faithorne. (Nethercot, pp. 409–19, and Harbage, *Davenant,* pp. 166–70.)

Collected Editions

*The Works of S*ʳ *William D'avenant K*ᵗ *Consisting of Those which were formerly Printed,* And *Those which he design'd for the Press*: Now Published Out of the Authors Originall Copies. *London*: Printed by *T. N.* for *Henry Herringman . . .* 1673.

The Dramatic Works of Sir William D'Avenant, with Prefatory Memoir and Notes. Eds. J. Maidment and W. H. Logan (1872–4), 5 vols.

Albovine, King of the Lombards (1626?)

Harbage, Alfred. *Sir William Davenant, Poet Venturer, 1606–68* (1935), pp. 225–8. Includes synopsis.

Morgenroth, Hugo. *Quellenstudien zu William Davenants Albovine* (1911).

Nethercot, Arthur H. *Sir William D'avenant, Poet Laureate and Playwright-Manager* (1938), pp. 52–54, 82–83.

Summers, Montague. *The Playhouse of Pepys* (1935), pp. 6–9.

1629. The Tragedy of Albovine, King of the Lombards: By W^m. D'auenant . . . 1629.

1639, 27 July. S.R. The Court of the Stationers' Company granted Benson leave to print an impression of 1,500 copies of the play 'wch was printed in Anno 1629. & neuer entred & therefore in the disposall of this Co^{rt} . . .'. (Greg, *Bibliography*, i. 51.)

1651, 3 May. S.R. *Albovine* is one of four plays in a list of thirty-six titles assigned to Richard Marriott from his father John Marriott. (Ibid., p. 59.)

1652/3, 7 Mar. S.R. *Albovine* was assigned to Humphrey Moseley by Richard Marriott. (Ibid., p. 60.)

1673. *Albovine* was printed in the Davenant folio, Part ii, Fff₄ᵛ– Kkk₁ᵛ.

There is no indication of performance on the title-page of the quarto or in the folio, and no prologue or epilogue, and the title occurs in no Caroline theatrical records. Since none of the eight writers of commendatory verses for the first quarto mentions production, it seems fairly clear that the play was never acted.

Nethercot points out that two different writers of verses in the fifties speak of the play as Davenant's first. (Op. cit., p. 52, n. 24.) If they knew whereof they spoke, the play must date several months before 12 January 1626/7 when Sir Henry Herbert licensed *The Cruel Brother* to the King's men (Adams, *Herbert*, p. 31), but not too long before, for the author was not quite twenty-one at that time. Harbage prefers to reverse the order of the plays (op. cit., p. 222), because he thinks *Albovine* superior to *The Cruel Brother* and because he believes Davenant would have preferred to publish his second play first. Neither reason is very impressive.

Davenant's source for his tragedy probably was Belleforest's *Histoires Tragiques* and not Paulus Diaconus (Killis Campbell, *J.E.G.P.* iv [1902], 22–23; Morgenroth, op. cit., pp. 11 ff.), as Harbage points out (op. cit., pp. 225–6), but the story is found in several places. Various Shakespearian echoes have been noted. (See J. D. E. Williams, *Sir William Davenant's Relation to Shakespeare*, 1905.)

Davenant went to no little pains to attract attention with his first publication. The quarto is dedicated to the Earl of Somerset and displays commendatory verses by Henry Blount, Edward Hyde, Richard Clerk, Robert Ellice, William Habington, Roger Lorte, Thomas Ellice, and 'H: Howard'. Blount compares the play to *Sejanus* and *Catiline*, and Samuel Sheppard, twenty-two years later, compared it to *Othello* and *Catiline* in Epigram 30, Book 4, of *Epigrams Theological, Philosophical, and Romantic,* 1651.

The folio text, as Nethercot points out (op. cit., p. 54), has been altered to prose, and a number of passages have been omitted.

Britannia Triumphans (7 January 1637/8)

Harbage, Alfred. *Sir William Davenant,* pp. 76–77, 219–20.

Nethercot, Arthur H. *Sir William D'avenant,* pp. 159–61.

Nicoll, Allardyce. *Stuart Masques and the Renaissance Stage* (1937), pp. 114–16 *et passim.*

Reyher, Paul. *Les Masques anglais* (1909), pp. 204–5, 308–9.

Simpson, Percy, and C. F. Bell. *Designs by Inigo Jones for Masques & Plays at Court* (1924), pp. 102–18.

Welsford, Enid. *The Court Masque* (1927), pp. 233–5. Includes synopsis.

1637, 6 and 26 Nov. An order to the Surveyor to provide timber and iron work for the two masques, and one to Michael Oldisworth for £1400 for expenses for the Twelfth Night masque. (Lord Chamberlain's Warrant Books, *Malone Society Collections,* ii, Part iii [1931], 386.)

1637, 9 Nov. 'Here are to be two Masks this Winter, one at *Christmas,* which the King with the young Noblesse do make; the other at *Shrovetide,* which the Queen and her Ladies do present to the King. A great Room is now in building only for this Use betwixt the Guard-Chamber and Banqueting-house, of Fir, only weather-boarded and slightly covered. At the Marriage of the Queen of *Bohemia* I saw one set up there, but not of that Vastness that this is, which will cost too much Money to be pulled down, and yet down it must when the Masks are over.' (George Garrard to Wentworth in Ireland, *Strafforde's Letters,* ii. 130.)

1637, 16 Dec. 'Here are two Masks intended this Winter; the King is now in practising his, which shall be presented at *Twelfthtide,* most of the young Lords about the Town, who are good Dancers, attend his Majesty in this Business. The other the Queen makes at *Shrovetide,* a new House being erected in the first Court at *Whitehall,* which cost the King 2500 *l.* only of Deal Boards, because the King will not have his Pictures in the Banqueting-house hurt with Lights.' (Garrard to Wentworth, ibid., p. 140.)

1637/8, 8 Jan. '*Britannia Triumphans* licensed for press, Jan. 8, 1637.' (Adams, *Herbert*, p. 41.)

1637/8, 7 Feb. 'The *French* and *Spanish* Ambassadors were both at the King's Mask, but not received as Ambassadors; the *French* sat amongst the Ladies, the *Spanish* in a Box: It was performed on a *Sunday* Night, the Day after Twelfth-night, in very cold Weather, so that the House was not filled according to Expectation.' (Garrard to Wentworth, *Strafforde's Letters*, ii. 148.)

1637/8. Britannia Trivmphans: A Masque, Presented at White Hall, by the Kings Majestie and his Lords, on the Sunday after Twelfth-night, 1637. By *Inigo Iones* Surveyor of his Majesties workes, and *William Davenant* her Majesties servant . . . 1637.

As the foreword to the masque points out, there had been no masques at Whitehall for three years before *Britannia Triumphans* because of the King's fears, probably well justified, that smoke from the torches and candles would ruin the ceiling paintings in the Banqueting Hall. For *Britannia Triumphans* a temporary masquing hall was built, as Garrard notes.

The political implications of this masque are unusually specific: it is Royalist and boldly anti-Puritan and anti-democratic. Probably this feature is the reason for the long and bitter analysis of *Britannia Triumphans* in *The Stage Condemn'd* in 1698, long after one would assume that it had been forgotten.

The details of Inigo Jones's *décor* for the masque are better known than those for almost any other English masque because of the large number of his plans and sketches for the production which are still extant—Simpson and Bell describe fifty-five. Jones also gives some of the details of labour requirements of the production. At the end of the edition appear the names of the fifteen masquers, including the King.

Miss Welsford (*The Court Masque*, p. 235) notes the indebtedness of both Jones and Davenant to the first intermedio of *Guidizio di Paridi*.

Coelum Britannicum

See Thomas Carew. The masque has often been attributed to Davenant because it was printed in the Davenant folio of 1673.

The Colonel

See Davenant, *The Siege*.

The Countryman

See Anon.

The Cruel Brother (1626/7)

Harbage, Alfred. *Sir William Davenant*, pp. 51–54 and 222–5. Includes synopsis.

Nethercot, Arthur H. *Sir William D'avenant*, pp. 54–56.

Summers, Montague. *The Playhouse of Pepys*, pp. 9–11.

1626/7, 12 Jan. '*The Cruel Brother*, by William Davenant, licensed.' (Adams, *Herbert*, p. 31.)

1629/30, 10 Jan. S.R. 'The Crewell Brother written by Wm Davenant' entered to John Waterson. (Greg, *Bibliography*, i. 37.)

1630. The Crvell Brother. A Tragedy. As it was presented, at the priuate House, in the *Blacke-Fryers*: By His Maiesties Seruants . . . 1630.

1646, 31 Oct. S.R. John Waterson assigned his rights in *The Cruel Brother* and *The Just Italian* to Humphrey Moseley. (Ibid., p. 57.)

1673. Printed in the Davenant folio, Part ii, Nnn₁–Ppp₄^v.

The only indication of Blackfriars performance is that given on the title-page of the quarto; it is presumably the one for which Sir Henry Herbert licensed the tragedy, for the play does not occur in any later performance record, and there is neither prologue nor epilogue in the quarto. The quarto is dedicated to Lord Weston, Lord High Treasurer of England.

All commentators on *The Cruel Brother* have pointed out the influence of Fletcher, particularly in the similarity of the central situation to that of *The Maid's Tragedy*. Harbage suggests also *Othello*, *The Duchess of Malfi*, and *Measure for Measure* (op. cit., p. 225), but these plays represent youthful reminiscences rather than comprehensive sources.

Fleay pointed out (*Biog. Chron.* i. 101) that Wither's *Abuses Stript and Whipt* is alluded to in II. ii, and that Castruchio represents Wither in the play. There are references to several other works of Wither.

As in the case of *Albovine*, the verse of the quarto has been printed as prose in the folio edition. Both texts of *The Cruel Brother* have several prompt stage directions, but the folio text has been cut somewhat.

The Cruelty of the Spaniards in Peru (1658)

See Hotson, *Commonwealth and Restoration Stage*, pp. 156–9, and Nethercot, *Sir William D'avenant*, pp. 325–31.

The Distresses [or The Spanish Lovers?] (1639)

Harbage, Alfred. *Sir William Davenant*, pp. 214–15.
Nethercot, Arthur H. *Sir William D'avenant*, pp. 173–5.
Summers, Montague. *The Playhouse of Pepys*, pp. 26–27.

1639, 30 Nov. 'The Spanish Lovers, by William Davenant, licensed.' (Adams, *Herbert*, p. 38.)

1641, 7 Aug. 'The distresses' is in the list of plays in the repertory of the King's company which the Lord Chamberlain forbade any printer to publish without the consent of the players. (See above, i. 65–66.)

1646, 4 Sept. S.R. 'Distresses' with about forty other plays, probably all formerly in the repertory of the King's company, entered to Robinson and Moseley. (Greg, *Bibliography*, i. 56–57.)

1657/8, 12 Feb. S.R. 'The Distresses a Play by Sʳ Willm Davenant' entered to John Crooke without reference to any former entry. (Ibid., p. 65.)

1672, 14 Oct. S.R. *The Distresses* and three other plays of Davenant's assigned to Henry Herringman by Anne Moseley. (Ibid., pp. 71–72.)

1672/3, 30 Jan. S.R. Half interest in *The Distresses* and 104 other titles assigned to John Martin and Henry Herringman by Humphrey Robinson, son of Humphrey Robinson. (Ibid., pp. 72–73.)

1673. *The Distresses* is printed in the separately paged and signed section at the end of the Davenant folio, Eeee₁ᵛ–Hhhh₃ᵛ.

1683, 21 Aug. S.R. One-fourth interest in the play assigned to Robert Scott by Sarah Martin, relict of John Martin. (Greg, *Bibliography*, i. 75–76.)

Malone (*Variorum* [1821], iii. 284) deduced that *The Distresses* was probably *The Spanish Lovers* of 1639, and the identification has been generally accepted, for the title is appropriate, and Davenant was a careful preserver of his work.

It has usually been said that there is no indication of the company that performed the play, and even production has sometimes been doubted, but the appearance of the title in the King's company repertory of 1641 shows that it belonged to them, as did all the plays of Davenant which are known to have been performed before the wars. One might have guessed that this play was written for Davenant's projected theatre of 1639, or for Beeston's Boys, to whose management he was shortly to succeed, but the repertory list shows that, whatever the author's intentions may have been, the King's men got the play.

The source for the comedy has not been identified, but Summers points out its similarities to Fletcher's *Chances* and suggests that it was probably derived from Spanish comedies. (Op. cit., pp. 26–27.)

An Essay for the New Theatre

See Davenant, *The Preparation of the Athenians for the Reception of Phocion.*

The Fair Favourite (1638)

Harbage, Alfred. *Sir William Davenant*, pp. 240–1.
Nethercot, Arthur H. *Sir William D'avenant*, p. 165.

1638, 17 Nov. '*The Fair Favourite*, by William Davenant, licensed.' (Adams, *Herbert*, p. 38.)

1638, 20 Nov. 'At the Cocpit the 20ᵗʰ of november . . . The fayre favorett.' From a bill presented by the King's company for twenty-four plays acted before the court in 1638. (Ibid., pp. 76–77.)

1638, 11 Dec. 'At the Cocpit the 11ᵗʰ of desember agayne . . . The fayre favorett.' From the same bill. (Ibid.)

1641, 7 Aug. 'The faire fauorite' is in the list of plays in the repertory of the King's company which the Lord Chamberlain forbade printers to publish without the company's consent. (See above, i. 65–66.)

1646, 4 Sept. S.R. 'ffair ffavourite' with about forty other plays, probably all formerly in the repertory of the King's company, entered to Moseley and Robinson. (Greg, *Bibliography*, i. 56–57.)

1672, 14 Oct. S.R. *The Fair Favourite* and three other plays of Davenant's assigned to Henry Herringman by Anne Moseley. (Ibid., pp. 71–72.)

1672/3, 30 Jan. S.R. Half interest in *The Fair Favourite* and 104 other titles assigned to John Martin and Henry Herringman by Humphrey Robinson, son of Humphrey Robinson. (Ibid., pp. 72–73.)

1673. *The Fair Favourite* is printed in the separately paged and signed section at the end of the Davenant folio, Llll$_4$–Oooo$_4$.

1683, 21 Aug. S.R. One-fourth interest in the play assigned to Robert Scott by Sarah Martin, relict of John Martin. (Greg, *Bibliography*, i. 75–76.)

c. 1710–50. 'The fair favourit' is in Warburton's list of MS. plays. (See Greg, *The Library*, Third Series, ii [1911], 230.)

The second court performance of the play and its inclusion in the repertory of the King's company in 1641 indicate that it was not a complete failure and make one wonder why it was not published before the folio. Nethercot thinks (loc. cit.) that the Old Courtiers of the play are intended to satirize certain of the King's advisers who had fought Davenant's pardon for the murder of Thomas Warren. If so, the satire was not recognized at court or the play would scarcely have had a second performance at Whitehall in December.

There is no evidence of a Restoration performance of the play.

The First Day's Entertainment at Rutland House (1656)

See Hotson, *Commonwealth and Restoration Stage*, pp. 140–51, and Nethercot, *Sir William D'avenant*, pp. 297–308.

The History of Sir Francis Drake (1658–9)

See Nethercot, *Sir William D'avenant*, pp. 331–6 and 379–80.

The Just Italian (1629)

Harbage, Alfred. *Sir William Davenant*, pp. 202–5. Includes synopsis.

Nethercot, Arthur H. *Sir William D'avenant*, pp. 80–81.

1629, 2 Oct. '*The Just Italian*, by William Davenant, licensed.' (Adams, *Herbert*, p. 32.)

1629/30, 10 Jan. S.R. Entered with *The Cruel Brother* to John Waterson. (Greg, *Bibliography*, i. 37.)

1630. The Ivst Italian. Lately presented in the priuate house at Blacke Friers, *By his Maiesties Seruants* . . . 1630.

1673. *The Just Italian* is printed in the Davenant folio, Part ii, Kkk$_2$–Nnn$_1$.

The play was evidently a failure at Blackfriars, for the dedication and both sets of commendatory verses—presumably written

between the licence for the theatre on 2 October and the Stationers'
Register entry in the following January—speak of its hard fate
and the ignorant audience. Davenant himself in his dedication
to the Earl of Dorset speaks of the people's uncivil ignorance
which '*had depriu'd this humble worke of life*'. Will. Hopkins
repeats the caviar-to-the-general theme—

> Hence, giddy fooles; run to the noyse they make
> At *Paris* garden ...

and continues with suggestions of similar vulgar amusements.
Carew's commendatory poem is devoted almost entirely to an
indictment of the unappreciative audience, with a few concluding
lines which seem to compare the misunderstood Davenant with
the misunderstood Buckingham. This reception probably accounts
for the absence of the play from later repertories and court performance lists of the King's company and also for the prompt
publication, which suggests theatrical indifference.

Fleay (*Biog. Chron.* i. 101) thought the lines in IV. i,

> D'ye walke like *Neptune* in a maske,
> Attended on by two o' th calme Windes?

referred to Jonson's *Fortunate Isles*, but I find no such scene in
the masque, which was produced, it must be remembered, nearly
five years earlier—rather remote for an apt allusion.

The Law against Lovers (1661/2)

See Nethercot, *Sir William D'avenant*, pp. 386–8.

Love and Honour, or The Courage of Love, or The Nonpareilles, or The Matchless Maids (1634)

Editions: James W. Tupper, ed., *Love and Honour and The
Siege of Rhodes by Sir William D'Avenant*, Belles-Lettres Series
(1909); Harold Reinoehl Walley and John Harold Wilson, edd.,
Early Seventeenth-Century Plays, 1600–1642 (1930), pp. 917–81.

Harbage, Alfred. *Sir William Davenant*, pp. 229–32. Includes
synopsis.
Nethercot, Arthur H. *Sir William D'avenant*, pp. 120–2, 376–7.
Summers, Montague. *The Playhouse of Pepys*, pp. 15–19.

1634, 20 Nov. '*Love and Honour*, by William Davenant, licensed.'
Malone adds (*Variorum*, iii. 284), '*Love and Honour* was originally

called *The Courage of Love*. It was afterwards named by Sir Henry Herbert at D'Avenant's request, *The Nonpareilles, or the Matchless Maids*.' (Adams, *Herbert*, p. 36 and n. 1.)

1634, 12 Dec. 'To a play of Loue & honnor wth the :2: South-landes.' (Diary of Sir Humphrey Mildmay. See above, ii. 676.)

1636/7, 1 Jan. 'The first day of January at Hampton Court. loue and honor.' (From the bill of the King's company for twenty-two plays acted at court in 1636 O.S. See above, i. 51–52. Herbert's record of the same performance is in a slightly different form; Adams, *Herbert*, p. 57.)

1641, 7 Aug. 'Loue & honor' is in the list of plays in the repertory of the King's company which the Lord Chamberlain forbade any printer to publish without the consent of the players. (See above, i. 65–66.)

1646, 4 Sept. S.R. 'Loue & honor. by S^r W^m. Davenant' with about forty other plays, probably all formerly in the repertory of the King's company, entered to Robinson and Moseley. (Greg, *Bibliography*, i. 56–57.)

1649. Love and Honovr, Written by W. Davenant Knight. Presented by His Majesties Servants at the *Black-Fryers* . . . 1649.

1672/3, 30 Jan. S.R. Half interest in *Love and Honour* and 104 other titles assigned to John Martin and Henry Herringman by Humphrey Robinson, son of Humphrey Robinson. (Ibid., pp. 72–73.)

1673. *Love and Honour* is printed in the Davenant folio, Part ii, Ff₁^v–Mm₁^v.

1683, 21 Aug. S.R. One-fourth interest in the play was assigned to Robert Scott by Sarah Martin, relict of John Martin. (Ibid., pp. 75–76.)

The significance of this tragi-comedy in the development of the love and honour drama has often been noted, but the aptness of the title has sometimes led to the exaggeration of the seminal qualities of the play above those of other Caroline plays equally in the mode.

The play was popular after the Restoration. Pepys tells of three performances he saw (Diary, 21, 23, and 25 October 1661), and Langbaine says he had seen it several times (*An Account of the English Dramatick Poets*, p. 109). Downes records the often-repeated story that the King, the Duke of York, and the Earl of Oxford gave their coronation robes to be used in the production, which gained the company great profit and reputation (*Roscius Anglicanus*, Summers ed., pp. 21–22).

Luminalia, or The Festival of Light (1637/8)

Edition: A. B. Grosart, ed., in *Miscellanies of the Fuller Worthies' Library* (1872-6), iv. 609-30.

Brotanek, Rudolf. 'Ein unerkanntes Werk Sir William Davenant's', *Anglia Beiblatt*, xi (1900), 177-81.
Harbage, Alfred. *Sir William Davenant*, pp. 233-4.
Hooper, Edith. 'The Authorship of *Luminalia*', *M.L.R.* viii (1913), 540-3.
Nethercot, Arthur H. *Sir William D'avenant*, pp. 161-3.
Nicoll, Allardyce. *Stuart Masques and the Renaissance Stage* (1937), pp. 52, 116-17, 212.
Reyher, Paul. *Les Masques anglais* (1909), pp. 204-5.
Simpson, Percy, and C. F. Bell. *Designs by Inigo Jones for Masques & Plays at Court* (1924), pp. 115-18.
Welsford, Enid. *The Court Masque* (1927), pp. 235-40. Includes synopsis.

1637, 9 Nov. 'Here are to be two Masks this Winter, one at *Christmas*, which the King with the young Noblesse do make; the other at *Shrovetide*, which the Queen and her Ladies do present to the King. A great Room is now in building only for this Use betwixt the Guard-Chamber and the Banqueting-house, of Fir, only weather-boarded and slightly covered. At the Marriage of the Queen of *Bohemia* I saw one set up there, but not of that Vastness that this is, which will cost too much Money to be pulled down, and yet down it must when the Masks are over.' (George Garrard to Wentworth in Ireland, *Strafforde's Letters*, ii. 130.)

1637, 16 Dec. 'Here are two Masks intended this Winter; the King is now practising his, which shall be presented at *Twelfth-tide*, most of the young Lords about the Town, who are good Dancers, attend his Majesty in this Business. The other the Queen makes at *Shrovetide*.' (Ibid., p. 140.)

1637/8, 12 Jan. An order to pay Michael Oldisworth £1,400 for expenses for preparation for the masque. (Lord Chamberlain's Warrant Books, *Malone Society Collections*, ii, Part iii [1931], 386.)

1637/8, 7 Feb. 'The Queen's Mask is to be performed on *Shrove-Tuesday*, next Week after the King goes to *Newmarket* for three Weeks.' (*Strafforde's Letters*, ii. 150. Garrard's letter must be incorrectly dated. He uses the future tense, but we have several

independent records that the masque was presented on Shrove
Tuesday, and in 1637/8 Shrove Tuesday fell on 6 February.)

1637/8. Lvminalia. or The Festivall of Light. Personated in a
Masque at Court, By the Queenes Majestie, and her Ladies. On
Shrovetuesday Night, 1637. London . . . 1637.

1657/8, 6 Mar. S.R. 'Luminalia or the ffestivall Light, a Masque
at Court on Shrove Tuesday night 1637' and three other
masques 'all written by Sʳ Wiłłm Davenant' were assigned to
Humphrey Moseley by Thomas Walkley. (Greg, *Bibliography*,
i. 66.)

1667, 19 Aug. S.R. 'And also A Booke or Copie Intituled, Maskes
Playes and Poems by Sʳ Wiłłm Davenant, viz: . . . And theis
4 Maskes, vizt, Luminalia, Salmacida Tholia [*sic*] Temple of
Love, Brittannia Trivmphans' assigned to Henry Herringman
by Anne Moseley. (Ibid., p. 71.)

The authorship of this masque, long unknown, was deduced
by Brotanek from his analysis of the text; it is verified by the
Stationers' Register entries. Since all the known Whitehall
masques of the last six years of the reign were written by Davenant, his authorship seems likely enough. Miss Welsford thinks,
however (*The Court Masque*, pp. 235–6), that his part was less
than in his other masques—probably only the songs, with perhaps
the prose descriptions. She notes the formlessness of the piece
compared with his other masques and its resemblance to *Tempe
Restored* (see Aurelian Townshend), in which Inigo Jones was
responsible for everything except the verse. This is compatible
with her further observation that

in no other masque is the plagiarism so blatant and so extensive.
Luminalia is in fact nothing else but a clumsy adaptation of Francesco Cini's *Notte d'Amore*, altered to suit the form of the English
masque, and combined with an imitation of the aerial dance in
Parigi's *Triumph of Peace*.

It may be that the statement in the masque itself about the
circumstances of preparation is relevant to this plagiarism:

The Kings Majesties Masque [*Britannia Triumphans*] being performed, the Queene commanded *Inigo Jones* Surveyor of her Majesties
works, to make a new subject of a Masque for her selfe, that with high
and hearty invention, might give occasion for variety of Scenes,
strange aparitions, Songs, Musick and dancing of severall kinds; from
whence doth result the true pleasure peculiar to our English Masques,
which by strangers and travellers of judgement, are held to be as
noble and ingenious as those of any other nations: This being sud-

dainly done and shewed her Majestie, and shee approving it, the worke was set in hand, and with all celerity performed in shorter time, than any thing here hath beene done in this kind.

The implication of this statement, i.e. that the Queen did not decide to have her masque until she had seen the King's, one month before the production date, is certainly false. Garrard's letters to the Lord Deputy of Ireland show that Jones and Davenant had at least three months' warning. No doubt Jones was in a great fret, first getting his Masquing Hall finished, then preparing and mounting the King's masque, and then clearing it all away before he could set his men to work on the elaborate constructions for *Luminalia*, but he did not need to wait all this time to begin on the designs for a masque which had been commissioned and popularly discussed before Garrard could have written his letter of 9 November. Perhaps his uneasiness about the plagiarism led him to magnify and advertise the pressure of time.

The names of the masquers are given in the text. Several of Jones's sketches and designs for *Luminalia* are described by Simpson and Bell.

Macbeth (1663)

See Nethercot, *Sir William D'avenant*, pp. 391–5, and Hazleton Spencer, 'D'Avenant's *Macbeth* and Shakespeare's', *P.M.L.A.* xl (1925), 619–44.

The Man's the Master (1668)

See Harbage, *Sir William Davenant*, pp. 165–6 and 255–7, and Summers, *The Playhouse of Pepys*, pp. 163–6.

News from Plymouth (1635)

Harbage, Alfred. *Sir William Davenant*, pp. 210–13. Includes synopsis.
Nethercot, Arthur H. *Sir William D'avenant*, pp. 126–8.

1635, 1 Aug. '*News of Plymouth*, by William Davenant, licensed.' (Adams, *Herbert*, p. 36.)
1638. 'Epilogue, To a Vacation Play at the Globe', printed in *Madagascar; With Other Poems*, p. 116, is the verse which was printed with minor changes in the 1673 folio as the epilogue for *News from Plymouth*.
1641, 7 Aug. 'News from Plimouth' is in the list of plays in the

repertory of the King's company which the Lord Chamberlain forbade any printer to publish without the consent of the players. (See above, i. 65–66.)

1646, 4 Sept. S.R. 'Newes from Plymouth' was entered for Robinson and Moseley, with others. (Greg, *Bibliography*, i. 56–57.)

1672, 14 Oct. S.R. 'Newes from Plymoth' was assigned from Ann Moseley, widow, to Henry Herringman. (Ibid., pp. 71–72.)

1672/3, 30 Jan. S.R. Robinson's share in 'Newes from Plymouth' was assigned, with others, to John Martin and Henry Herringman. (Ibid., p. 72.)

1673 *News from Plymouth* is printed in the Davenant folio, Part ii, Aaaa$_1$–Eeee$_1$.

1683, 21 Aug. S.R. 'News from Plymouth' assigned with others from John Martin, deceased, to Robert Scott. (Ibid., p. 75.)

News from Plymouth is Davenant's most plebeian play, and the reason is not far to seek. All his other plays were prepared for private theatre audiences at Blackfriars and the court, Rutland House, Salisbury Court, or one of the Restoration theatres. This play was licensed in August when the Globe would have been playing, but not Blackfriars, and confirmation of the suggestion that it was licensed for the public theatre is found in the prologue for the play.

> *This House, and season, does more promise shewes,*
> *Dancing, and Buckler Fights, then Art, or Witt.*

The same indication of a performance on the Bankside is found in the sixth line of the epilogue which speaks of the departing audience as 'passing to take Boat', which a Globe audience, but no private theatre one, would do. Moreover, though the lines are entitled only 'Epilogue by *Sir Furious*' in the folio edition of the play, Davenant printed them in *Madagascar; With Other Poems*, 1638, with the title 'Epilogue, To a Vacation Play at the Globe'. In the folio version of this epilogue there are a dozen or more alterations which suggest that the play was revised for presentation before a Commonwealth or Restoration audience, but there seems to be no other evidence.

Fleay thought (*Biog. Chron.* i. 102) that *News from Plymouth* was 'evidently an alteration by Davenant from one by a superior author, who had laid the scene at Portsmouth', because of a reference to Portsmouth in I. 2. There is no other evidence for such a conjecture, and this seems inadequate.

Nethercot and others have called attention to the Jonsonian elements in the comedy—the resemblance of Sir Solemn Trifle to Sir Politic Would-Be, of Sir Furious Inland to Kastril, of Zeal and Scarecrow to Ananias and Tribulation Wholesome.

Chester Lynn Shaver has noted the multiplicity of anti-Dutch remarks in Act IV and their similarity to anti-Dutch speeches in *The Hollander* and *The Wits*. (*The Life and Works of Henry Glap-thorne*, MS. Ph.D. Dissertation, Harvard [1937], pp. 234–7.)

The Platonic Lovers (1635)

Fletcher, J. B. 'Précieuses at the Court of Charles I', *Journal of Comparative Literature*, i (1903), 145 ff.

Harbage, Alfred. *Sir William Davenant*, pp. 235–7. Includes synopsis.

Nethercot, Arthur H. *Sir William D'avenant*, pp. 128–31.

Steible, Daniel J. *A Critical Edition of William Davenant's The Temple of Love and The Platonic Lovers*. MS. Ph.D. Dissertation, University of Cincinnati (1939).

1635, 16 Nov. '*The Platonic Lovers*, by William Davenant, licensed.' (Adams, *Herbert*, p. 37.)

1635/6, 19 Jan. Herbert's licence to print, dated 19 January 1635, is on A_2^v of the first edition, 1636.

1635/6, 4 Feb. S.R. 'A Play called the Platonicke Louers by W^m. Davenant', entered to Meighen. (Greg, *Bibliography*, i. 45.)

1636. The Platonick Lovers. A Tragaecomedy. Presented at the private House in the Black-Fryers, *By his Majesties Servants*. The Authour William D'Avenant, Servant to her Majestie ... 1636.

1646, 7 Nov. S.R. 'The Platonick Lovers' was transferred with several other plays to Mrs. Mercie Meighen and Gabriell Beadell 'by consent of the said Mrs. Meighen'. (Ibid., pp. 57–58.)

1665. *Two Excellent Plays*: The Wits, A Comedie: The *Platonick* Lovers, A Tragi-Comedie. Both presented at the Private House in Black-Friers, By His Majesties Servants. *The Author*, Sir William D'Avenant, Kt. . . . 1665.

1673. *The Platonic Lovers* is printed in the Davenant folio, Part ii, Ccc_1^v–Fff_4^v.

This play belongs with Davenant's other presentation of the Queen's Platonic love fad, *The Temple of Love*, which was presented at court three or four times in February 1634/5. The prologue to the play, delivered by a veteran actor of the King's company, probably John Lowin (see above, ii. 503), indicates the source of the ideas, asserts that the play is written on order (presumably the Queen's), and implies that Davenant was not too enthusiastic about his task.

> Ours [i.e., our poet] now believes, the Title needs must cause
> From the indulgent Court, a kind applause,
> Since there hee learn't it first, and had command
> T' interpret what hee scarce doth understand.

The play evidently had no great success either at the Blackfriars or at the court, the subject probably ensuring failure at the former and the sceptical treatment of the subject failure at the latter. That the King's men did not cherish the play is suggested by its appearance in the Stationers' Register less than three months after production. The play may have been produced at court during the Christmas season 1635–6, for the plays that the King's men presented between November and April are not named, but there is a full list from 18 April 1636 to 21 February 1636/7 (see above, i. 51–52), and *The Platonic Lovers* does not appear among them, as it would have had it roused the court enthusiasm Davenant expected. Carlell's *Arviragus and Felicia* (q.v.) was the court favourite of that season. Davenant's dedication of the piece to the Queen's favourite, Henry Jermyn, contains lines which probably reflect his disappointment at the failure of the play. The phrase 'declining Fame' suggests a rather severe set-back after the triumph of the repeatedly revived masque.

> . . . When you have leisure, and can a little neglect your time, bee pleas'd to become my first Reader. If it shall gaine your liking, the severe Rulers of the Stage will be much mended in opinion; and then, it may be justlie acknowledg'd, you have recover'd all the declining Fame, belonging to
>
>

Your unfortunate
Servant,
WILLIAM D' AVENANT

The Play-House to be Let (1663)

See Nethercot, *Sir William D'avenant*, pp. 377–81.

The Preparation of the Athenians for the Reception of Phocion (1657)

See Nethercot, *Sir William D'avenant*, pp. 307–8, 325. The full title is *An Essay for the New Theatre Representing the Preparation of the Athenians for the Reception of Phocion after He Had Gained a Victory.*

The Rivals (1664)

A revision of *The Two Noble Kinsmen*. See Nethercot, *Sir William D'avenant*, pp. 388–91.

Salmacida Spolia (21 January 1639/40 [and 17–19 February?])

Editions: by W. R. Chetwood in *A Select Collection of Old Plays* (1750) and H. A. Evans in *English Masques* (1897, 1898, and 1906).

Greg, W. W. 'Paper-Saving in 1639', *The Library*, Fifth Series, ii (1948), 61.

Nethercot, Arthur H. *Sir William D'avenant*, pp. 175–80.

Nicoll, Allardyce. *Stuart Masques and the Renaissance Stage*, pp. 117–26 *et passim*.

Reyher, Paul. *Les Masques anglais*, pp. 89–90, 204–5, 310, 359–63.

Simpson, Percy, and C. F. Bell. *Designs by Inigo Jones for Masques & Plays at Court*, pp. 119–31.

Welsford, Enid. *The Court Masque*, pp. 240–2, 371–2. Includes synopsis.

1639, 5 Dec. 'The King and Queen have begun to practise their mask. A company of worse faces did I never see assembled than the Queen has got together upon this occasion; not one new woman amongst them. Lady Carnarvon conditioned, before she would promise to be of the mask, that it should not be danced upon a Sunday, for she is grown so devout by conversing with Lord Powis and the doctor that now she will neither dance nor see a play upon the Sabbath. I assure you their Majesties are not less busy now than formerly you have seen them at the like exercise.' (Algernon, Earl of Northumberland, to his sister, the Countess of Leicester, *Hist. MSS. Com.*, Appendix to the Third Report [1872], p. 79.)

1639, 30 Dec. An order to pay to Michael Oldisworth £1,400 for expenses for preparations for the masque. (Lord Chamberlain's Warrant Books, *Malone Society Collections*, ii, Part iii [1931], 391–2.)

1639/40, 23 Jan. 'The mask was performed last Tuesday night, myself being so wise as not to see it. They say it was very good, but I believe the disorder was never so great at any.' (Robert

Read to his cousin Thomas Windebank, *C.S.P., Dom., 1639–40*, p. 365.)

1639/40, 14 Feb. 'Their Majesties, with their royal children, are in perfect health, and for their recreation intend to dance again their mask this Shrovetide; the joy of her Majesty being enceinte again, advancing rather than hindering that pastime.' (Secretary Vane to Sir Thomas Roe, from Whitehall, ibid., p. 459.)

1639/40. Salmacida Spolia. *A Masqve*. Presented by the King and Queenes Majesties, at *White-hall*, On *Tuesday* the 21. day of *January* 1639 . . . 1639.

1657/8, 6 Mar. S.R. *The Temple of Love, Brittania Triumphans, Luminalia*, and 'Salmatida [*sic*] Spolia a Masque at Whitehall on Tuesday the 21th. of Ianuary 1639' were transferred from Thomas Walkley to Humphrey Moseley. (Greg, *Bibliography*, i. 66.)

1667, 19 Aug. S.R. In the list of 'Maskes Playes and Poems by Sʳ Wiłłm Davenant' assigned with others by Moseley's widow to Henry Herringman is 'Salmacida Tholia' [*sic*]. (Ibid., p. 71.)

Salmacida Spolia was the last of the great court masques before the wars, and the elaborateness of the production suggests the swan song of the Caroline court. The statement of 'credits' at the end of the edition of 1639/40 is indicative of the dominance that Inigo Jones had attained since the great days of *The Masque of Queens* and *Hymenaei*:

> The Invention, Ornament, Sceans and Apparitions, with their Descriptions, were made by INIGO IONES, Surveyor Generall of his Majesties Workes.
> What was spoken or sung, by WILLIAM DAVENANT, her Majesties Servant.
> The Subject was set downe by them both.
> The Musicke was composed by LEWIS RICHARD, Master of her Majesties Musicke.

Some forty of the sketches and designs for the masque are described by Simpson and Bell, and several of them are reproduced by Nicoll (*Stuart Masques, passim*). Chetwood's statement that 'The painting was design'd by the inimitable *Peter Paul Rubens*' (ed. 1750, p. iii) has not been substantiated.

Vane's letter to Sir Thomas Roe saying that the King and Queen proposed to have the masque repeated at Shrovetide is probably an accurate indication of intent, for Vane was in a position to know, but I have found no conclusive evidence that the intention was carried out. That there were some alterations for the intended revival is suggested by the fact that one of the Jones sketches for the masque is dated 'febyary 5 1640', nearly a month after the original production. (Simpson and Bell, *Designs by Inigo Jones*, p. 129.)

The names of the masquers, including the King and Queen, are given at the end of the text in the first edition (D_4^v). The masque was not included in the folio of 1673.

Satirical Declamations (1658?)

See Nethercot, *Sir William D'avenant*, pp. 307–8.

The Siege [or *The Colonel*?] (1629?)

Harbage, Alfred. *Sir William Davenant*, pp. 202, 228–9.
Nethercot, Arthur H. *Sir William D'avenant*, pp. 79, 171.

1629, 22 July. '*The Colonel*, by William Davenant, licensed.' (Adams, *Herbert*, p. 32.)
1629/30, 1 Jan. S.R. 'A play called The Collonell written by Wm Davenant gent' was entered to 'M^r. Eph: Dawson'. (Greg, *Bibliography*, i. 37.)
1653, 9 Sept. S.R. 'The Siege. by W^m: Dauenant' entered with many other plays to Humphrey Moseley. (Ibid., pp. 60–61.)
1672, 14 Oct. S.R. 'The Seige' with three other plays by Davenant transferred from Ann Moseley to Henry Herringman. (Ibid., pp. 71–72.)
1673. *The Siege* is printed in the Davenant folio in the separately paged section at the end of Part ii, $Hhhh_4$–$Llll_3^v$.

The Siege is generally taken to be *The Colonel* of 1629, but evidence for the identification is incomplete. There is no doubt that Davenant did write a play called *The Colonel*; he was careful to get all his plays in print; *The Siege* is the only Davenant play in print of whose early history nothing is known. Fleay said that the colonel is an important character in *The Siege* (*Biog. Chron.* i. 101), but he is by no means the leading figure. Harbage suggested (*Davenant*, p. 228, n. 10) that the leading character, Florello, was called a colonel in the original version.

There is general agreement that the text in the 1673 folio is a revision, but not much evidence has been cited besides its brevity and the prominence of the comic plot. Sir A. W. Ward thought that the comic plot had been taken from *The Humorous Lieutenant*. (*History of English Dramatic Literature*, iii. 329, n. 6.)

One of Inigo Jones's sketches for a scene, marked 'for yᵉ cokpitt for my lo chãberlin 1639', has several times been said to have been prepared for Habington's *Queen of Aragon* (q.v.), but Mr. William Grant Keith has pointed out ('John Webb and the Court Theatre of Charles II', *The Architectural Review*, lvii [1925], 51–55) that the proscenium is unlike those in other sketches for that play and suggests that the sketch may have been intended for a production of *The Siege*. Miss Boswell suggests (*The Restoration Court Stage*, p. 13) the possibility that the sketch may have been prepared for the Cockpit in Drury Lane during Davenant's brief management or for his projected theatre in Fleet Street.

The Siege of Rhodes, Part I (1656), Part II (1659?)

See Nethercot, *Sir William D'avenant*, pp. 309–18, 335–6.

The Spanish Lovers

See Davenant, *The Distresses*.

The Tempest, or The Enchanted Island (1667)

See Nethercot, *Sir William D'avenant*, pp. 398–403.

The Temple of Love (10 February 1634/5; also 11, 12, and 14 February?)

Nethercot, Arthur H. *Sir William D'avenant*, pp. 118–24.
Nicoll, Allardyce. *Stuart Masques*, pp. 106–10 *et passim*.
Reyher, Paul. *Les Masques anglais*, pp. 204–5, 238–42.
Simpson, Percy, and C. F. Bell. *Designs by Inigo Jones*, pp. 88–98.
Steible, Daniel J. *A Critical Edition of Sir William Davenant's The Temple of Love and The Platonic Lovers*. MS. Ph.D. Thesis, University of Cincinnati (1939).
Welsford, Enid. *The Court Masque*, pp. 229–33. Includes synopsis.

1634, 3 June. 'The Court affords little News at present, but that there is a Love call'd Platonick Love, which much sways there of late; it is a Love abstracted from all corporeal gross Impressions and sensual Appetite, but consists in Contemplations and Ideas of the Mind, not in any carnal Fruition. This Love sets the Wits of the Town on work; and they say there will be a Mask

shortly of it, whereof Her Majesty and her Maids of Honour will
be part.' (James Howell, *Epistolae Ho-Elianae*, ed. Joseph
Jacobs [1892], i. 317–18. Howell's dates are often faked.)

1634/5, 11 Jan. 'There is some Resolution for a Mask against
Shrovetide, the Queen and fifteen Ladies are to perform, whose
Names I will send your Lordship with this. My Lady *Northumberland* and my Lady *Carlile* are not in the Number, they have
got their Friends to excuse them, and it is not ill taken.' (Garrard to Wentworth in Ireland, *Strafforde's Letters*, i. 360.)

1634/5, 18 Jan. An order for £1,400 to be paid to Edmund Tauer-
ner for expenses in preparing the masque. (Lord Chamberlain's
Warrant Books, *Malone Society Collections*, ii, Part iii [1931],
374–5.)

1634/5, 30 Jan. 'No news there but preparations for a grand
masque of nine lords and fifteen ladies.' (Sir Thomas Roe to
Elizabeth, Queen of Bohemia, *C.S.P.*, *Dom.*, *1634–5*, p. 482.)

1634/5, 11 Feb. 'Sir Thomas Roe to Bishop Hall of Exeter. The
masque was yesternight performed with much trouble and
wearisomeness. Roe admired nothing but the Queen and her
ladies.' (Ibid., p. 510.)

1634/5, 13 Feb. [i.e. 23 February, Venetian style]. 'During these
last days of carnival there has been little room for business
amid the dances, comedies and other pleasant diversions. The
Court has been fully occupied with these and in particular with
the representation of a masque, which the queen has repeated
three times, set out with the most stately scenery, machines and
dresses.' (Anzolo Correr, Venetian Ambassador in England, to
the Doge and Senate, *C.S.P.*, *Ven.*, *1632–6*, p. 334.)

1634/5, 14 Feb. 'beinge St Vallentine was a wett day, . . . att
nighte wee both of vs wayted onn My Lady Cooke to a pretty
Masque of Ladyes.' In the margin is written, 'The Masque'.
(Mildmay's Diary; see above, ii. 677.)

1634/5. The Temple *of* Love. A Masque. Presented by the Qveenes
Majesty, and her Ladies, at *White-hall* on Shrove-Tuesday,
1634. By *Inigo Iones*, Surveyour of his Majesties Workes; and
William Davenant, her Majesties Servant . . . 1634.

1657/8, 6 Mar. S.R. 'The Temple of Love a Masque at Whitehall
on Shrove Tuesday 1634' and *Brittania Triumphans, Luminalia*,
and *Salmacida Spolia* were transferred from Thomas Walkley to
Humphrey Moseley. (Greg, *Bibliography*, i. 66.)

1667, 19 Aug. In the list of 'Maskes Playes and Poems by Sr Willm
Davenant' assigned with others by Moseley's widow to Henry
Herringman is 'Temple of Love'. (Ibid., p. 71.)

1673. *The Temple of Love* was printed in the Davenant folio, Part i, Bbb₄ᵛ–Ddd₂ᵛ.

This masque probably marks a stage in Davenant's career, for when it was published, within six weeks of the performance, his name appeared for the first time on the title-page as 'her Majesties Servant'. No doubt his dutiful handling of the Queen's favourite subject of Platonic love had something to do with his new distinction. The part of Indamora in the masque was played by the Queen and at times was evidently intended to represent Henrietta Maria. Possibly the Queen's satisfaction in playing herself also helped achieve Davenant's new distinction.

Miss Welsford points out (*The Court Masque*, p. 232) that the main entry and several of the character names in Davenant's masque were taken from a triumphal tournament prepared by Parigi for presentation at Florence in 1616 and that two of Jones's designs show a similar indebtedness. Thirty of the designs and sketches for this masque are described by Simpson and Bell, and eight of them are reproduced by Nicoll.

There is some confusion about the number and dates of the performances of *The Temple of Love*. Roe's letter indicates that it was performed on the 10th; the Venetian ambassador, if he is to be taken literally, writes that it had been performed three times before the 13th; and the 'pretty Masque of Ladyes' which Sir Humphrey Mildmay saw on the 14th was presumably still another performance of *The Temple of Love*. If these statements are accurate, there were four performances, on the 10th, 11th, 12th, and 14th of February. This seems a bit excessive, even for Henrietta Maria, but it would account for Davenant's new dignity.

The Triumphs of the Prince D'Amour (23 or 24 February 1635/6)

Nethercot, Arthur H. *Sir William D'avenant*, pp. 134–7.
Nicoll, Allardyce. *Stuart Masques*, pp. 113–14 *et passim*.
Simpson, Percy, and C. F. Bell. *Designs by Inigo Jones*, p. 101.

1635/6, 19 Feb. 'For home Passages, Prince *Rupertus* the *Palsgrave's* second Brother is lately come over, and as I hear is already sworn of the Bedchamber, and is thought will still stay here. Our famous Prince *d'Amour* invites them both to a Feast and Mask upon *Tuesday* next.' (James Howell to Wentworth in Ireland, *Strafforde's Letters*, i. 516.)
1635/6, 19 Feb. S.R. 'A maske called The Triumphs of the Prince

D'amour by W: D:' was entered to Meighen. (Greg, *Biblio-graphy*, i. 45.)

1635/6, 23 Feb. 'On Wensday the 23 of Febru. 1635, the Prince d'Amours gave a masque to the Prince Elector and his brother, in the Middle Temple, wher the Queene was pleasd to grace the entertaynment by putting of [off] majesty to putt on a citizens habitt, and to sett upon the scaffold on the right hande amongst her subjects.

'The queene was attended in the like habitts by the Marques Hamilton, the Countess of Denbighe, the Countess of Holland, and the Lady Elizabeth Feildinge. Mrs. Basse, the law-woman, leade in this royal citizen and her company.

'The Earle of Holland, the Lord Goringe, Mr. Percy, and Mr. Jermyn, were the men that attended.

'The Prince Elector satt in the midst, his brother Robert on the right hand of him, and the Prince d'Amours on the left.

'The Masque was very well performed in the dances, scenes, cloathinge, and musique, and the Queene was pleasd to tell mee at her going away, that she liked it very well.

'Henry Lause ⎱
'William Lause⎰ made the musique.

'Mr. Corseilles made the scenes.' (Adams, *Herbert*, p. 56.)

1635/6, 15 Mar. 'The *Wednesday* before [Shrove-Tuesday] the Prince of the *Temple* invited the Prince *Elector* and his Brother to a Masque at the *Temple*, which was very compleatly fitted for the Variety of the Scenes, and excellently well performed. Thither came the Queen with three of her Ladies disguised, all clad in the Attire of Citizens, Mrs. *Basset* the great Lace Woman of *Cheapside* went foremost and led the Queen by the Hand. My Lords of *Holland* and *Goring* with *Henry Percy* and Mr. *Henry Jermyn* waited on them somewhat disguised also. This done, the Prince was deposed, but since the King knighted him at *White-hall*.' (Garrard to Wentworth in Ireland, *Strafforde's Letters*, i. 525.)

1635/6. The Triumphs of the Prince D'Amovr. A Masque Presented by His Highnesse at His Pallace in the Middle Temple, the 24th of Februarie 1635 . . . 1635.

1646, 7 Nov. S.R. 'The Triumphes of Prince Damour' by 'm[r] Davenant' was entered to Mrs. Mercie Meighen and Gabriell Beadell with eighteen other books 'w[ch] did appertaine to M[r]. Meighen dec[d].' (Greg, *Bibliography*, i. 57–58.)

1673. *The Triumphs of the Prince D'Amour* is in the Davenant folio, Part i, Ddd$_3$–Eee$_2$[v].

The masque takes its title from the Christmas Prince annually elected at the Middle Temple, as at the other Inns of Court, to preside over their Christmas revels; only at the Middle Temple was he called the Prince D'Amour. In 1635 the Middle Templars decided to commission a masque in honour of the Prince Elector and Prince Rupert, visiting nephews of the King, as part of their annual festivities. Davenant says in his address to the reader that the masque was devised in great haste in three days, but that production was sadly delayed. Presumably this means that the performance had to be postponed, like the performance of Lady Hatton's masques, because the Queen was brought to bed of a daughter, Princess Elizabeth. (See Garrard's letter, *Strafforde's Letters*, i. 506–7.) Probably the discrepancy between Herbert's date for performance of the 23rd and the title-page date of the 24th indicates a further postponement, as is also suggested by Howell's announcement of the planned performance on Tuesday and Herbert's and Garrard's agreement on Wednesday as the day of actual performance. Herbert must have been confused, for Wednesday fell on the 24th.

The music for the masque was prepared by William and Henry Lawes. The part of it that survives is discussed by Edward Dent in *Foundations of English Opera*, pp. 40–41, and by Willa McClung Evans, *Henry Lawes Musician and Friend of Poets* (1941), pp. 116–19. The names of the Middle Temple masquers are given at the end of the printed text.

The Unfortunate Lovers (1638)

Harbage, Alfred. *Sir William Davenant*, pp. 237–41. Includes synopsis.

Nethercot, Arthur H. *Sir William D'avenant*, pp. 164–5, 209, 369–70.

Summers, Montague. *The Playhouse of Pepys*, pp. 21–23.

1638, 16 Apr. '*The Unfortunate Lovers*, by William Davenant, licensed.' (Adams, *Herbert*, p. 37.)

1638, 23 Apr. 'At the blackfryers the 23 of Aprill for the queene the vnfortunate lou[ers].' From a bill presented by the King's company for twenty-four plays acted before the court in 1638. (Ibid., p. 76.)

1638, 31 May. 'At the Cocpit the last of may agayne the . . . vnfortunate louers.' From the same bill. (Ibid.)

1638, 30 Sept. 'At Hamton Court the 30th of September The vnfortunate louers.' From the same bill. (Ibid., p. 77.)

1641, 7 Aug. 'The vnfortunate Louers' is in the list of plays in the repertory of the King's company which the Lord Chamberlain forbade printers to publish without the company's consent. (See above, i. 65–66.)

1643. The Vnfortvnate Lovers: A Tragedie; As it was lately Acted with great applause at the private House in *Black-Fryers*; By His Majesties Servants. The Author *William Davenaut* [*sic*], Servant to Her Majestie . . . 1643.

1645/6, 7 Mar. S.R. Entered to Moseley 'vnder the hands of S^r. Nath: Brent & both the wardens & by vertue of a note vnder the hand & seale of Mr Heiron a Tragedy called the Vnfortunate Louers &c. by W^m. Davenant'. (Greg, *Bibliography*, i. 55.)

1649 [Another issue] With the imprint, 'for Humphrey Moseley. 1649.' The sheets of the 1643 edition with a new title-page.

1659–60. In the repertory of Rhodes's company acting at the Cockpit, Downes names:

Rule a Wife and Have a Wife.	Changling.
The *Tamer* Tam'd.	Bondman.
The Unfortunate Lovers.	
Aglaura.	

(*Roscius Anglicanus*, Summers ed., pp. 17–18.)

1660, 19 Nov. 'monday the 19. No. The Unfortunate Louers' appears in a list of performances of plays by 'the Kings Companie at the Red Bull and the new house in Gibbon's Tennis Court', 1660–2. (Adams, *Herbert*, p. 116.)

1673. *The Unfortunate Lovers* is printed in the Davenant folio, Part ii, Q_1^v–X_4.

This play was Davenant's first after the long plague closing of 1636–7 and followed his three masques, *The Triumphs of the Prince D'Amour, Britannia Triumphans*, and *Luminalia*. Its popularity at court is attested by the three royal performances and by the fact that it was withheld from publication until 1643 and protected in the King's men's repertory of 1641. The performance for the Queen at Blackfriars was not unique, for she was there on three other known occasions. (See above, i. 48 and n. 5.) These performances were probably given at night when the theatre was chartered, for the players' bill for the year, now at Warwick Castle (see above, i. 60 and n. 3), lists the play with those performed at court and makes the regular charge for productions not involving the loss of an afternoon performance at the theatre. (See above, i. 48 and n. 5.)

The first edition of the play was probably not authorized by

Davenant. The dedication to the Earl of Pembroke and Montgomery is signed 'W. H.' (William Habington?), who assures his lordship that 'Had M^r. *Davenaut* himselfe beene present, hee would have elected no other Patron.'

The play was one of the first performed after the Restoration, but by Killigrew's company, not Davenant's. (Summers, p. 22.) It soon came into Davenant's repertory, and he made revisions in the text for his company's use. (Nethercot, p. 370.) Pepys saw it four times, but with no enthusiasm.

Fettiplace Bellers's *Injured Innocence*, acted at Drury Lane in February 1731/2, and published in 1732, has been said to be based upon *The Unfortunate Lovers*, but Nethercot (p. 165, n. 37) finds only the basic situations similar.

The Wits (1633/4)

Editions: Dodsley's *Collection of Old Plays* (1780), viii; Scott's *Ancient British Drama* (1810), i.

Harbage, Alfred. *Sir William Davenant*, pp. 53–54, 205–10.
Nethercot, Arthur H. *Sir William D'avenant*, pp. 108–14, 374–6.
Summers, Montague. *The Playhouse of Pepys*, pp. 12–14.

1633/4, 9 Jan. 'This morning, being the 9th of January, 1633, the kinge was pleasd to call mee into his withdrawinge chamber to the windowe, wher he went over all that I had croste in Davenants play-booke, and allowing of *faith* and *slight* to bee asservations only, and no oathes, markt them to stande, and some other few things, but in the greater part allowed of my reformations. This was done upon a complaint of Mr. Endymion Porters in December.

'The kinge is pleasd to take *faith, death, slight*, for asservations, and no oaths, to which I doe humbly submit as my masters judgment; but, under favour, conceive them to be oaths, and enter them here, to declare my opinion and submission.

'The 10 of January, 1633, I returned unto Mr. Davenant his playe-booke of *The Witts*, corrected by the kinge.

'The kinge would not take the booke at Mr. Porters hands; but commanded him to bring it unto mee, which he did, and likewise commanded Davenant to come to me for it, as I believe: otherwise he would not have byn so civill.' (Adams, *Herbert*, p. 22.)

1633/4, 10 Jan. 'The 10 of January, 1633, I returned unto Mr.

Davenant his playe-booke of *The Witts*, corrected by the kinge.' (Ibid.)

1633/4, 19 Jan. '*The Wits*, by William Davenant, licensed.' (Ibid., p. 35.)

1633/4, 22 Jan. 'To a playe att the fryers, the Witts—oo–oi–oo', in Mildmay's diary. (See above, ii. 675.)

1633/4, 28 Jan. '*The Witts* was acted on tusday night the 28 January, 1633, at Court, before the Kinge and Queene. Well likt. It had a various fate on the stage, and at court, though the kinge commended the language, but dislikt the plott and characters.' (Adams, *Herbert*, p. 54.)

1635/6, 19 Jan. In some copies of the 1636 edition (apparently all of one of the two issues of that year) opposite the title-page is '*This Play, called* THE WITTS, *as it was Acted without offence, may bee Printed, not otherwise.* 19 Ianuary 1635. HENRY HERBERT.'

1635/6, 4 Feb. S.R. Entered to Meighen 'another Play Called. the Witts by w^m. Davenant'. (Greg, *Bibliography*, i. 45.)

1636. The Witts. A Comedie, Presented at the Private House in Blacke Fryers, by his Majesties Servants. *The Authour* William D'Avenant, *Servant to Her Majestie* . . . 1636.

1638. *Madagascar; With Other Poems*, published in this year, contains a poem entitled 'To *Endimion* Porter, When my Comedy (call'd the Wits) was presented at Black-Fryars'.

1646, 7 Nov. S.R. 'The Witts' by 'm^r Davenant' with a list of other titles which had belonged to Richard Meighen entered to Mercie Meighen and Gabriell Beadell. (Ibid., 57–58.)

1665. *Two Excellent Plays*: The Wits, A Comedie: The *Platonick* Lovers, A Tragi-Comedie. Both presented at the Private House in Black-Friers, By His Majesties Servants . . . 1665.

1673. *The Wits* is printed in the Davenant folio, Part ii, X_4–Ff_1.

The Wits was Davenant's first play, so far as we know now, after four years of silence, and the first, according to the prologue ('whom, hath our long-sick-Poet wrong'd'), after his illness and long convalescence. Nethercot thinks (*D'avenant*, pp. 111–13) that Davenant had put himself into the parts of Pert and Meager, and Suckling into Pallatine the Younger. This seems too presumptuous, but there are a striking number of allusions to the Dutch, to treatment for venereal disease, and even one in Act III to 'lewd Gallants, That have lost a Nose!'

Sir Henry Herbert's entries show that the play had been in his hands in December 1633, when he had censored it so heavily as to

rouse the author's indignation and the intercession of his patron,
Endymion Porter. It is not known whether this altercation had
anything to do with the faction against the play which is referred
to in the prologue:

> *Blesse mee you kinder Stars! How are wee throng'd?*
> *Alas! whom, hath our long-sick-Poet wrong'd,*
> *That hee should meet together in one day*
> *A Session, and a Faction at his Play?*
>
> .   .   .
>
> *But 'bove the mischiefe of these feares, a sort*
> *Of cruell Spies (we heare) intend a sport*
> *Among themselves; our mirth must not at all*
> *Tickle, or stir their Lungs, but shake their Gall.*

It may be this situation to which Sir Henry Herbert refers in
his comment on the court performance: 'It had a various fate on
the stage, and at court.' It was, of course, a convention for prologues to refer to the inevitable disapproval of the carping critics
in the audience, but this one implies a determination and organization which are not usual.

The same organized opposition seems to be referred to in the
poem 'To *Endimion* Porter, When my Comedy (call'd the Wits)
was presented at Black-Fryars', which was published in *Madagascar; With Other Poems*, 1638.

> I that am told conspiracies are laid,
> To have my Muse, her Arts, and life betray'd,
> Hope for no easie Judge; though thou wert there,
> T'appease, and make their judgements lesse severe.
> In this black day, like Men from Thunders rage,
> Or drowning showres, I hasten from the stage.   (E₈–E₈ᵛ.)

Nothing more is known of the affair of *The Wits*, but a lively
afternoon at Blackfriars is suggested. Perhaps the fact that the
play was published only two years after the first performance
indicates that the King's men did not want it in their active
repertory.

A joke depending on the quarto of 1636 is printed in Robert
Chamberlain's *Conceits, Clinches, Flashes, and Whimzies*, 1639,
his *Jocabella*, 1640, and in *A Choice Banquet of Witty Jests*, 1660,
but the joke probably illustrates only the convenience of the title
for a pun rather than the popularity of the book.

After the Restoration the play was revised by the author and
acted with some frequency at his playhouse (see Nethercot, *D'aven-*

ant, pp. 374–6). It is the revised version which appears in the folio. It was last acted at Lincoln's Inn Fields 19 August 1726. (Genest, iii. 183.) Both Harbage and Nethercot note that *The Wits* was Davenant's longest acted and most frequently presented play.

ROBERT DAVENPORT (Damport)
fl. 1624–40

Very little is known of the life of Robert Davenport. The *D.N.B.* lists him as 'fl. 1623', but this date is derived from the erroneous assignment of a publication date of 1623 to Davenport's *A Crown for a Conqueror and Too Late to Call Back Yesterday*, poems which were really entered in the Stationers' Register and published in 1639.

No Robert Davenport is listed at Cambridge in the sixteenth or seventeenth centuries (*Alumni Cantab.*), and at Oxford none after the one who received a degree in 1515. (*Alumni Oxon.* i. 376.) The first appearance of the man is in the records of the Master of the Revels, where his comedy, *The City Nightcap*, and his *History of Henry the First* were licensed, the first for the Lady Elizabeth's company and the second for the King's men. None of the eight other plays which can be attributed to him with some show of evidence can be dated very accurately, though one or two of them are later than 1624.

Davenport must have been a resident of Ireland in 1634 or 1635, for his 'Dialogue between Policy and Piety' is concerned with Irish affairs, it is dedicated to John Bramhall who became Bishop of Londonderry in 1634, and the dedication is signed 'yor ... poore neighboure'. Residence outside England—possibly in Ireland—is also suggested by the opening sentence of the dedication of *A Crown for a Conqueror and Too Late to Call Back Yesterday* in 1639:

> *These Poems (true and Noble Friends) being some expence of my time at Sea, I have thus habited, to present them as my true love to you on the Land.*

The two friends to whom '*These Poems*' are dedicated are Richard Robinson and Michael Bowyer. Robinson had been a leading member of the King's company for more than twenty years. (See above, ii. 550–3.) Bowyer at the time of the publication of *A Crown* was probably also a member of the King's company, though for at least a decade he had been an actor at the Cockpit or Phoenix (ibid., pp. 385–7), where probably three and perhaps more of

Davenport's plays had been produced. Possibly this theatrical acquaintanceship was only a relic of Davenport's past, but it seems somewhat more likely that it indicates current dramatic interests.

G. Thorn-Drury owned a manuscript of Davenport's containing a character and four poems, apparently a presentation copy to the Earl of Newcastle, to whom it is dedicated. Since Newcastle is styled in the dedication 'Earle of Newcastle' and 'Lord Boulsouer & Ogle', Thorn-Drury dates the manuscript between 1629, when William Cavendish became Baron Ogle, and 1643, when he was made Marquis of Newcastle. (*A Little Ark* [1921], pp. 9–15.)

The last certain activities of Davenport date from 1639 or 1640, when he wrote commendatory verses for Nathaniel Richards's *Tragedy of Messalina* and Thomas Rawlins's *The Rebellion*. Both were published in 1640, but they were entered in the Stationers' Register in 1639. Fleay said (*Biog. Chron.* ii. 260) that the 'R. D.' who wrote commendatory verses for John Tatham's *Distracted State*, published in 1651 as written in 1641, was Robert Davenport. Both Tatham and Davenport had written verses for Rawlins's *Rebellion*, but this is scarcely enough to justify Fleay's identification.

The address to the reader which is prefixed to *A New Trick to Cheat the Devil*, 1639 (S.R., 28 March) speaks of the play as '*an Orphant, and wanting the Father which first begot it*'. Though this remark suggests that Davenport was dead, his verses for *Messalina* and *The Rebellion* in the next year seem contrariwise to indicate that he was not. The line could mean simply that Davenport was not in London—perhaps again, or still, in Ireland.

The epistle to the reader in *King John and Matilda*, published in 1655, is signed with Davenport's initials, 'R. D.', presumptive evidence that he was still alive when the play was being prepared for publication in 1654 or 1655. The epistle is highly conventional, however, and could have been written by almost anyone.

Collected Editions

The Works of Robert Davenport, now First Collected, ed. A. H. Bullen, in *A Collection of Old English Plays, New Series*, vol. iii (1890).

'A Study of the life and an edition of the works of Robert Davenport', by J. G. McManaway, listed in *Work in Progress in the Modern Humanities*, M.H.R.A., 1939, p. 49. See also *N. & Q.* clxx (1936), 295.

The Bloody Banquet

This play, which was first published in 1639 as by T. D., has several times been assigned to Robert Davenport, but see Thomas Drue.

The City Nightcap, or Crede Quod Habes & Habes (1624)

Jordan, J. C. 'Davenport's *The City Nightcap* and Greene's *Philomela*', *M.L.N.* xxxvi (1921), 281–4.

Swinburne, A. C. *Contemporaries of Shakespeare* (1919), pp. 235–49.

1624, 14 Oct. 'For the Cockpit Company; A new Play, called, *The City Night Cap*: Written by Davenport.' (Adams, *Herbert*, p. 29.)

1624, 14 Oct. 'For the Cockp: comp: A new P. call: The city Night-cap writt: by Damport 14 Oct. 1624. 1ˡⁱ.' (Halliwell-Phillipps's Scrap-Books, *Fortune*, p. 149. Folger Shakespeare Library.)

1639, 10 Aug. 'A Citty night cap' is one of a list of plays in the repertory of the King and Queen's Young Company at the Cockpit that were forbidden to all other London companies by an order of the Lord Chamberlain on this date. (See above, i. 330–1.)

1661. The City-Night-Cap: Or, *Crede quod habes, & habes*. A Tragi-Comedy. By *Robert Davenport*. As it was Acted with great Applause, by Her Majesties Servants, at the Phœnix in *Drury Lane* . . . 1661.

(?) A play without title, beginning 'Actus Primus Scena Prima Enter Mercator and Strevellus', is the second item in the volume of manuscript plays called the Lambarde volume, Folger Shakespeare Library MS. 1478.2. The piece is made up of scenes altered from Lower's *Enchanted Lovers* and Davenport's *City Nightcap*.

1680. *The Politick Whore; or, The Conceited Cuckold*, a short farce published in the collection called *The Muse of New-Market*, 1680, is made up of scenes from *The City Nightcap*.

c. 1677–1703. 'The City night cap' is the thirty-third title in Abraham Hill's list of plays in manuscript. (J. Q. Adams, 'Hill's List of Early Plays in Manuscript', *Library*, Fourth Series, xx [1939], 71–99. See Middleton, *The Conqueror's Custom*.)

The second version of Sir Henry Herbert's record of his licence for the play comes from an independent transcript of material from the office-book in a nineteenth-century hand. This transcript, perhaps that of Craven Ord, has been cut into strips and then pasted into appropriate sections of Halliwell-Phillipps's scrapbooks, now preserved in the Folger Shakespeare Library. This second version adds only the fee paid, the usual one for a new play at this time.

When Davenport wrote the play, the company performing at the Cockpit was the Lady Elizabeth's (see above, i. 184–6), and presumably he wrote it for that troupe, but when they left, the play evidently remained in the archives of the theatre and was presumably acted successively by Queen Henrietta's men and by Beeston's Boys; it belonged to the latter company in 1639.

Langbaine noticed the similarity of the Lorenzo–Abstemia plot to *Don Quixote*, Part IV, chapters 6–8 (*An Account of the English Dramatick Poets*, pp. 116–17), but the resemblance is still closer to Robert Greene's *Philomela; the Lady Fitzwater's Nightingale*. (See Jordan, op. cit.) Langbaine was right in saying that the contrasting Lodovico–Dorothea plot had been taken from the *Decameron*, vii. 7. Fleay thought (*Biog. Chron.* i. 104), reasonably enough, that Lodovico's remark in the third act, 'I intend to compose a pamphlet of all my wives vertues, put them in print, and dedicate them to the Duke, as orthodoxal directions against he marries', was intended as a dig at Overbury's *Wife*, which was reprinted for the eleventh time in 1622. He also thought that the remarks of the clown in the fourth act showed the play to have been a personal satire, but this is less evident.

The anonymous, titleless manuscript play at the Folger and *The Politic Whore* of 1680 indicate that *The City Nightcap* had more vitality than the modern reader might think.

A Dialogue between Policy and Piety (c. 1635)

MS.: 'Dialogue between Pollicy and Piety by Ro. Davenport c. 1635', MS. 1919.3, Folger Shakespeare Library.

McManaway, James G. 'MS. of Davenport's "Policy without Piety"; John Withorn: Sir John Kaye', *N. & Q.* clxx (1936), 295.

The Folger MS. looks like a presentation copy, with a double border ruled in red and occasional words in red. It is dedicated 'To the right reuerend Father in God IOHN, Lo: Bishop of London-Derry'. This dedication, which speaks of the piece as 'a

playne familliar Dialogue betweene *Piety* and *Pollicy*' and classi-
fies it 'Amongst yor Lo^{ps}. many welcomes', is signed,

At yor lo^{ps}. Comandement a seruant
and poore neighboure
Rob: :dauenport:

The Folger MS. has been dated from the elevation of John Bramhall to the see of Londonderry in 1634. Bramhall was the only
John, Bishop of Londonderry, between 1615 and 1680.

The piece is not really a play, though it begins with preliminary
descriptions as for a play. The marriage of Policy and Piety is
supervised by Hibernia with a number of general comments intended to apply to Irish affairs: 'Pollicy without Piety is much
to subtle to be sound'; 'Piety without Pollicy is still to simple to
be safe.' At the end Hibernia prepares to celebrate the marriage
with the admonition, *'But good my Merchants sell no drinck.'* The
dialogue ends with the adage, *'Obedience is no Bondage where
wee loue.'*

Davenport's obvious concern with Irish affairs and his apparent
residence in Ireland at this time offer suggestions about his life
which I have not seen pursued.

What would seem to be another manuscript of this dialogue,
dedicated to Sir John Kaye and once in the possession of John
Withorn of Broomhead, was noted by Joseph Hunter in his *Chorus
Vatum Anglicanorum* at the British Museum. See McManaway, op.
cit.

Dick of Devonshire

Davenport has been proposed as the author of this play
(James G. McManaway, 'Latin Title-Page Mottoes as a Clue to
Dramatic Authorship', *Library*, Fourth Series, xxvi [1945], 28–36),
but see Anon.

The Fatal Brothers (?)
(Lost)

1660, 29 June. S.R. In a list of eleven plays entered as his copies
by Humphrey Moseley are:
The fatall Brothers. a Tragedy.⎰ by Robt. Davenport
The Politick Queen. Or murther will out.⎱
(Greg, *Bibliography*, i. 69.)

Nothing is known of the play. Harbage assigns it to 'King's (?)' in his *Annals of English Drama*, p. 95, but I do not know on what grounds. It is true that Davenport wrote a play or two for the King's men at Blackfriars, but he wrote more for the companies at the Phoenix.

A Fool and Her Maidenhead Soon Parted
(Lost)

See Anon. Fleay suggested (*Biog. Chron.* ii. 336) that the play had been written by Davenport because it is listed between two of his plays in the repertory of the King and Queen's Young Company in August 1639. This principle of attribution was probably derived from the fact that most of the plays in the repertory are listed according to author, but the principle is not strictly followed, for Alexander Brome's *Cunning Lovers* comes between Heywood's *Love's Mistress* and his *Rape of Lucrece*. (See above, i. 330–1.)

The History of Henry I (1624)
(Lost)

1624, 10 Apr. 'For the king's company. *The Historye of Henry the First*, written by Damport [Davenport]; this 10 April, 1624, —1l.o.o.' (Adams, *Herbert*, pp. 27–28.)

1653, 9 Sept. S.R. In a long list of plays entered as his copies by Humphrey Moseley is 'Henry ye. first, & Hen: ye 2d. by Shakespeare, & Dauenport'. (Greg, *Bibliography*, i. 60–61.)

c. 1710–50. 'Henry ye 1st. by Will. Shakespear & Rob. Davenport' is the second entry in Warburton's list of plays in manuscript supposedly burned by his cook. (See W. W. Greg, *Library*, Third Series, ii [1911], 225–59.)

The fact that the title appears in Warburton's list is no assurance that he ever had the manuscript (see Greg, op. cit.), but Moseley certainly had a manuscript, and he must have had some reason for assigning it as he did. There is no evidence that Davenport began to write early enough to have collaborated with Shakespeare, and if he had, it is difficult to imagine a reason why the company should have waited eight years after Shakespeare's death to get a licence. It is not likely that the play was an old one of Shakespeare's revised by Davenport, for Herbert's fee was his usual one for a new play at that time. I have seen no reasonable suggestion as to how Shakespeare's name was connected with Moseley's manuscript. Warburton probably copied from Moseley.

Fleay made one of his cherished associations of titles for this play. (*Biog. Chron.* i. 104.) He says that *Henry I and Henry II*—

was probably a prentice work of Davenport's refashioned from an older play, perhaps *The Famous Wars of Henry I and the Prince of Wales*, by Drayton, Dekker, and Chettle, March 1598.

Greg seems to have countenanced this guess (*Henslowe's Diary*, ii. 192), but I cannot think that a company of the standing of the King's men in 1624 would have needed to make use of such an old and obscure piece, nor is it likely that they would have had one of Henslowe's manuscripts.

Henry II (?)
(Lost)

Harbage, Alfred. 'Elizabethan-Restoration Palimpsest', *M.L.R.* xxxv (1940), 310–18.

1653, 9 Sept. S.R. In a long list of plays entered as his copies by Humphrey Moseley is 'Henry y^e. first, & Hen: ye 2^d. by Shakespeare, & Dauenport'. (Greg, *Bibliography*, i. 60–61.)

The only reference to a play called *Henry II* by Davenport is in the Moseley licence. He enters the title as if it were *Henry I and Henry II*, but at other times he has listed two titles as if they were title and sub-title, apparently to save a fee, and he may have been telescoping titles here. Harbage points out (op. cit.) that the two reigns are separated by rather a long period for continuous treatment, but such considerations did not always deter Elizabethan and Jacobean dramatists.

Harbage assumes (op. cit.) that Moseley had two Henry plays and suggests that Mountfort's play, *Henry the Second, King of England; with the Death of Rosamond*, is 'a stage version of "Shakespeare and Davenport's" *Henry the Second*'. Though the evidence is very slight indeed, his general contention that a number of lost Jacobean and Caroline plays were used by Restoration writers and passed off as their own—of which the *Henry II–Henry the Second* suggestion is only a small part—is very persuasive.

King John and Matilda (c. 1628–34)

Anon. '*King John and Matilda, a Tragedy . . . Written by* Robert
Davenport, *Gent. . . .* 1655', *The Retrospective Review*, iv (1821),
87–100. Synopsis and appreciation.

Harbage, Alfred. 'Elizabethan-Restoration Palimpsest', *M.L.R.*
xxxv (1940), 310–18.

1639, 10 Aug. 'King Iohn & Matilda' is one of forty-five plays of
the repertory of the King and Queen's Young Company at the
Phoenix or Cockpit in Drury Lane protected by the Lord
Chamberlain against other companies. (See above, i. 330–1.)

1655. King Iohn And Matilda, A Tragedy. As it was Acted with
great Applause by her *Majesties* Servants at the Cock-pit in
Drury-lane. Written by Robert Davenport Gent. *London*,
Printed for *Andrew Pennycuicke*, in the Year 1655.

1662. [Another edition.]

1674/5, 13 Mar. S.R. William Cademan entered for his copies 'by
vertue of an Assignem^t vnder the hand & seale of Richard
Gammon bearing date the second day of Ianuary Last past and
alsoe an order of a Court of Assistants at a full Court held the
two & twentieth day of ffebruary Last . . . King Iohn & Matilda
A Tragedy written by William Davenport', and Heminges' *The
Fatal Contract*. (Greg, *Bibliography*, i. 74.)

King John and Matilda is one of the few pre-Restoration plays
published with a cast, and a cast introduced with an unusually
explicit statement:

The Names of the Persons in the Play, And of the Actors that first
Acted it on the Stage, and often before their *Majesties*.

This statement is probably more reliable than most such, since
Andrew Pennycuicke, the publisher, had himself been an actor in
the play according to his own statement. This cast enables us to
approach the date of the play. Pennycuicke lists none of the actors
of the female roles and only ten of those for the male roles. Since
ten is an average number of sharers in an acting troupe of the
time, and since each actor listed is honoured with the title 'M.',
it is evident that Pennycuicke listed only the sharers' parts. Thus
Hugh Clark, listed here as 'M. *Clarke*', must have been an adult
and of some importance in the company when the play was first
acted. Now, he had played the part of Sir John Belfare's daughter,
Gratiana, in Shirley's *Wedding* (q.v.) in 1626. It seems likely that

it would have taken at least two or three years after he played the role of a girl for him to have matured enough to perform as a leading adult at the time Davenport's play appeared. *King John and Matilda* can, therefore, scarcely have been performed before about 1628.

J. T. Murray said that the play must date before 1629, for John Young of the cast joined the King's Revels company in that year. (*English Dramatic Companies*, i, facing 266, n.) If this were correct, the play would date within a year or so of 1628, but unfortunately there is no evidence that Young was a member of the King's Revels company from its organization in 1629. (See above, ii. 628.) The earliest date we can assign to Young's membership in the King's Revels company is July 1634, when Thomas Crosfield listed him as a member of that troupe. (See above, ii. 688.) Christopher Goad, who played Oxford in the production of *King John and Matilda* by Queen Henrietta's men, is also in Crosfield's list of the King's Revels. These two names indicate that Davenport's play could not have been produced after July 1634, and we are left with the date of *c*. 1628–34 for the play.

Andrew Pennycuicke, who published the play and who signed the dedication to the Earl of Lindsey, says in the dedication, '*It past the Stage with generall Applause (my selfe being the last that that* [sic] *Acted* Matilda *in it*).' Since he was probably the Andreas Pennicooke christened 1 October 1620 (see above, ii. 525), he *could* have appeared in an original performance as early as 1628, but in that case he would probably have given the actors of the original female roles as well and included himself. He emphasizes 'the last' performance, and it seems a little more likely that he had the important role of Matilda in some revival. The statement before the cast that the play had been performed 'often before their *Majesties*' needs to be discounted somewhat. It may well have been performed at court, though there is no other substantiating record, but even widely discussed plays like Cartwright's and Carlell's were performed only three or four times at court, not 'often'.

In addition to the dedication, the play has an epistle 'To the knowing Reader', which is signed 'R. D.', presumably standing for Robert Davenport. It makes the usual modest disclaimers, but provides no pertinent information.

Professor Harbage makes the interesting suggestion (op. cit., pp. 317–18) that the first three epistles of Drayton's *England's Heroical Epistles* suggested to Davenport the themes of *King John and Matilda*, *Henry the Second*, and *Edward the Third*; the last two are

Restoration plays which Harbage thinks were based on lost manuscripts of Davenport's. (Op. cit., pp. 310–17.) He says:

Does it not seem likely that Davenport, acting upon the suggestion
of the volume of 1619 [i.e. Drayton's *Poems*], embarked upon the
creation of a series of neo-chronicles—centring upon the loves of the
English kings rather than upon their martial exploits, and more in
keeping therefore with the softer texture of the Fletcherian era?
(Ibid., p. 317.)

The idea is, of course, highly speculative, but it makes an interesting association. Davenport at least used an idea and a line from
Drayton's *Legend of Matilda*. (Ibid., pp. 317–18.)

Much of the material of *King John and Matilda* had appeared in
Chettle and Munday's *Death of Robert, Earl of Huntington*, as Greg
noted. (*Henslowe's Diary*, ii. 191.) A detailed comparison of the
two plays to find the extent of Davenport's utilization of the old
play might be illuminating.

A New Trick to Cheat the Devil (> 1639)

Bullen, A. H., ed. *The Works of Robert Davenport Now First Collected, A Collection of Old English Plays, New Series* (1890), iii.
337–40.

Eckhardt, Eduard. 'Robert Davenports Lustspiel *A New Trick to
Cheat the Devil*', *Anglia*, lix (1935), 394–403.

Swinburne, A. C. *Contemporaries of Shakespeare* (1919), pp. 241–9.

1639, 28 Mar. S.R. Humphrey Blunden entered 'a Booke or
Comedy called A new trick to cheat the Devill by mr Damport
[*sic*]'. (Greg, *Bibliography*, i. 50.)

1639, 10 Aug. 'A trick to cheat the Diuell:' is one of forty-five
plays of the repertory of the King and Queen's Young Company
at the Phoenix or Cockpit in Drury Lane protected by the Lord
Chamberlain against other companies. (See above, i. 330–1.)

1639 A Pleasant and Witty Comedy: Called, A New Tricke to
Cheat the Divell. *Written by R. D. Gent.* . . . 1639.

The comic sub-plot of the play incorporates in III. 1 the popular
Friars of Berwick story (see Eckhardt, op. cit.), and it is told well
enough to rouse Swinburne's delight. However much Swinburne
admired the narrative, the dramatic handling is crude and is reminiscent of that of some early-sixteenth-century farce.

The address to the reader says that *A New Trick to Cheat the
Devil* '*is a Comedy which hath bin often acted, and so well approved*',

but such statements are not necessarily indicative of any special information. This address also calls the play 'an Orphant, and wanting the Father which first begot it', a statement presumably intended to mean that the author was dead, but the address for the 1655 edition of *King John and Matilda* is signed 'R. D.'

A New Trick to Cheat the Devil is one of three plays by Davenport listed in the repertory of the Phoenix or Cockpit in 1639. The other two plays are *A City Nightcap*, which was licensed to the company at that theatre in 1624, and *King John and Matilda*, which was acted there between about 1628 and 1634. It is presumably this association with *A City Nightcap* and *King John and Matilda* which made Fleay say (*Biog. Chron.* i. 104) that *A New Trick to Cheat the Devil* was acted by Queen Henrietta's company and made Harbage say (*Annals*, p. 98) that the play was acted by Queen Henrietta's company between 1624 and 1636. There is no evidence for either statement, though neither is impossible. Queen Henrietta's men were not organized before 1625, but a play owned by the King and Queen's Young Company at the Phoenix in 1639 might, like others in their repertory, have descended to them from Queen Henrietta's men. It could equally well, however, have descended from Lady Elizabeth's men or have been written between February 1636/7 and August 1639 for the King and Queen's Young Company. One might guess that *A New Trick to Cheat the Devil* was near in date to Davenport's other datable plays, but I have seen no evidence for any date before the Lord Chamberlain protected the play for Beeston in August 1639.

The Pedlar (> 1630)
(Lost ?)

1630, 26 March. S.R. John Marriott entered 'vnder the handes of Sr Hen: Herbert and mr Bill Arristippus and The Pedler'. (Greg, *Bibliography*, i. 37.)

1630, 8 Apr. S.R. Robert Allott entered 'vnder the handes of Sr Hen Herbert and Mr Purfoote A Comedy called The Pedler by R: Davenport'. (Ibid., p. 38.)

No play of Davenport's called *The Pedlar* is now known. Possibly it was entered in the Stationers' Register but never published and the manuscript has since disappeared, as in the case of Davenport's *The Fatal Brothers*, *The Politic Queen*, *The History of Henry I*, and *The Woman's Mistaken*.

The matter is complicated, however, by the fact that identical titles, both licensed for publication by Sir Henry Herbert, are entered in the Stationers' Register 26 March and 8 April 1630 to John Marriott and to Robert Allott. Now in the case of the Marriott entry, 'The Pedler' clearly refers to Randolph's *Conceited Pedlar* (q.v.), for Marriott licensed the play with *Aristippus*, and he published the two plays together in 1630, though no author is named on the title-page. The manuscript bearing Herbert's licence which Marriott had and which he called *The Pedlar* was, then, Randolph's *Conceited Pedlar*. Was Allott's manuscript, which he also called *The Pedlar* and which was licensed by Sir Henry Herbert, simply another copy of Randolph's *The Conceited Pedlar* with no author's name on it and attributed to Davenport as a guess by Allott in his Stationers' Register entry? Perhaps it was, for Allott himself published an edition of *Aristippus* with *The Conceited Pedlar* in 1630, in addition to Marriott's. His entry of 'The Pedler by R: Davenport' is the only one which could be thought to establish his right to the Randolph play, but right he did have, for it was Allott and not Marriott who published the subsequent editions of *Aristippus* and *The Conceited Pedlar* together in 1631 and 1635.

The probability seems to be, then, that Davenport did not write a play called *The Pedlar*, but that the Stationers' Register entry of 8 April 1630 simply indicates Robert Allott's bad guess as to the author of Thomas Randolph's *Conceited Pedlar*. This probability should not be taken for certainty, however, for it requires the awkward assumption that Sir Henry Herbert licensed two different manuscripts for two publishers within a few weeks, apparently not knowing they contained the same play. Moreover, it is quite possible that there is an unrecorded transfer of Marriott's rights to Allott and that Davenport's *Pedlar* has nothing to do with the case.

The Pirate (?)

(Lost)

The existence of the play is known only because of the epigram on it which Samuel Sheppard printed in 1651.

EPIG. 19.
To Mr. Davenport *on his Play called
the Pirate.*
Make all the cloth you can, haste, haste away,
The Pirate will o'ertake you if you stay:
Nay, we will yeeld our selves. and this confesse,
Thou Rival'st *Shakespeare*, though thy glory's lesse.
(*Epigrams, Theological, Philosophical and Romantic*, 1651, p. 27 [D₂].)

I know of no evidence concerning the character or date of the play. The life of Samuel Sheppard (q.v.) affords none; he could scarcely have known Davenport or the play during Davenport's most active theatrical years. Though Sheppard's birth-date is not known, his parents were not married until April 1623.

The Politic Queen or Murder Will Out (?)

(Lost)

1660, 29 June. S.R. In a list of eleven plays entered as his copies by Humphrey Moseley are:
The fatall Brothers. a Tragedy.
The Politick Queen. Or murther will out.$\Big\}$ by Robt. Davenport.
(Greg, *Bibliography*, i. 69.)

Nothing is known of the play. Harbage assigns it to 'King's (?)' in his *Annals of English Drama*, p. 95, but I do not know on what grounds, for Davenport wrote more plays for companies at the Phoenix or Cockpit in Drury Lane than he did for the King's men. Possibly the suggestion is related to his speculation that Mountfort's *Edward the Third*, 1691, is a revision or adaptation of Davenport's lost *Politic Queen or Murder Will Out*. See 'Elizabethan-Restoration Palimpsest', *M.L.R.* xxxv (1940), 310–18.

The Woman's Mistaken (?)

(Lost)

1653, 9 Sept. S.R. Humphrey Moseley entered a long list of plays as his copies, of which one was 'The Woman's mistaken. by. Drew, & Dauenport'. (Greg, *Bibliography*, i. 60–61.)

The play is known only from Moseley's entry of his manuscript. Fleay guessed (*Biog. Chron.* i. 105), 'It was probably an early work, c. 1622, before he [Davenport] had learned to run alone', and Lawrence opined that it was probably 'brought out at the Red Bull by the Queen's men two or three years earlier [than 1622]'. (*T.L.S.*, 23 March 1922, p. 191.) Neither presents any evidence, and probably both reasoned only from their knowledge of the careers of the two men, which was, necessarily, only slight. Neither guess, however, is implausible.

It is conceivable that this play is the tragedy without title on the subject of the murder of Joan Tindall *alias* Grindall by her son in Whitechapel, licensed as by Mr. Drew in September 1624. See Drue, Unknown Play, and Dekker, *The Late Murder of the Son upon the Mother.*

ROBERT DAWES

See Anon., *Cupid's Festival.*

JOHN DAY (Daye, Dey, Deye)
c. 1574–c. 1640

Borish, M. Eugene. *John Day.* Harvard MS. Thesis, 1931.

Not much is known of the career of John Day, and what little there is mostly concerns his career before 1608. Before he begins appearing in Henslowe's Diary, our information about him comes from the records of Gonville and Caius, Cambridge:

> Dey, John: son of Walter Dey, husbandman. Born at Cawston, Norfolk. School, Ely, under Mr Spight. Age 18. Admitted, Oct. 24, 1592, sizar of his surety, Mr Fletcher, fellow. . . . He was expelled from the college for stealing a book, May 4, 1593. (*Coll. Gesta.*) (Venn, *Biographical History of Gonville and Caius College,* i. 146.)

He next appears in Henslowe's accounts 30 July 1598 and is found frequently thereafter as one of Henslowe's busiest collaborators. He wrote at least twenty-one plays before 1616, most of them for Henslowe companies and most of them lost. (See *Eliz. Stage,* iii, 284–9.) Extant are *The Blind Beggar of Bethnal Green* (1600), *Law Tricks, or Who Would Have Thought It* (1604), *The Isle of Gulls* (1606), *The Travels of Three English Brothers* (1607), and *Humour Out of Breath* (1607–8). (Ibid.)

There is a break of a full decade in our knowledge of Day's career after the appearance of *Humour Out of Breath,* which had been prepared for the King's Revels company. The ballad which celebrates the destruction of the Phoenix theatre in Drury Lane by the apprentices on 4 March 1616/17 contains the line, 'Poor Daye that daye not scapte awaye'. (*H.E.D.P.,* 1831 ed., i. 402–4.) Unfortunately the ballad is not a nineteenth-century discovery, but another of John Payne Collier's nineteenth-century compositions.

Day is next heard of in Drummond's notes of his conversations with Ben Jonson in 1618/19:

that Sharpham, Day, Dicker were all Rogues and that Minshew was one. . . .

that Markham (who added his English Arcadia) was not of the number of the Faithfull .j. Poets and but a base fellow that such were Day and Midleton. . . . (Herford and Simpson, *Ben Jonson*, i. 133, 137.)

This is the opinion one would expect Jonson to have of an irregular hand-to-mouth playwright like John Day.

There is evidence of Day's association about this time with Thomas Downton, the former player of the Admiral's–Prince Henry's–Palsgrave's company who became a vintner, presumably when he married a vintner's widow 15 Febuary 1617/18, and who died in 1625. (See above, ii. 426, 643.) The Huntington Library MS. of Day's *Peregrinatio Scholastica*—an earlier version than the more familiar one in Sloane 3150 at the British Museum—is dedicated to 'M^r: Thomas Dowtonn Gentlemann, & Brother of the Right Wo^ppf Companie of the vintners.' (M. E. Borish, *M.L.N.* lv [1940], 35–39.) In the registers of Downton's parish church, St. Giles's, Cripplegate, there is the record of the burial on 8 October 1617 of ' John Daye svant to Thomas Doughten Playe^r'. (See above, ii. 426.) The dedication must fall within the years of Downton's career as a vintner, 1617/18–1625, and the burial item surely indicates the residence of some relative of the dramatist in Downton's household. It may be that the association here is closer than we can now see, for there is an acrostic at Dulwich on 'Thomas Dowton' signed John Day. Greg doubted if the dramatist were the author (*Hens. Paps.*, pp. 126–7), but the dedication of the Huntington MS. suggests that he was, though the servant buried in 1617 is a possible author.

Most, and perhaps all, of Day's later plays are collaborations with Dekker, with whom he had collaborated at least three times in his Henslowe days. They were written for inferior companies and do not suggest much standing in the theatrical world.

Nothing further is known of Day, except for his dedication of the manuscript of his *Parliament of Bees* to William Augustine and the dedication of the edition of 1641 to George Butler. He must have been dead before the printing of *The Parliament of Bees* in 1641, for in John Tatham's *Fancies Theatre,* 1640, there is a piece entitled '*On his loving friend* M. John Day *an Elegie.*'

Collected Edition

A. H. Bullen, ed. *The Works of John Day.* 2 vols. (1881)

The Bellman of Paris
with Thomas Dekker

See Thomas Dekker.

Come See a Wonder (1623)
(Lost)

1623, 18 Sept. 'For a Company of Strangers; a new Comedy, called, *Come see a Wonder*; Written by John Deye.' (Adams, *Herbert*, p. 25, from Chalmers, *A Supplemental Apology*, p. 215. Adams points out that Chalmers probably got part of the proper entry for *Come See a Wonder* attached to another entry and that Malone's statement gives the complete information: 'Sir Henry Herbert observes that the play called *Come See a Wonder*, "written by John Daye for a company of strangers," and represented Sept. 18, 1623, was "acted at the Red Bull, and licensed without his hand to it, because they [i.e. this company of strangers] were none of the *four* companys." ' *Variorum*, iii, 224.)

No play of this name is known to be extant, but it has been plausibly suggested that *Come See a Wonder* is the same as the play called *The Wonder of a Kingdom* (q.v.), which was published in 1636 as by Thomas Dekker.

The Life and Death of Guy of Warwick
with Thomas Dekker

See Thomas Dekker.

The Noble Soldier

See Thomas Dekker.

The Parliament of Bees (c. 1634–40)

Not a play or masque, as has been often asserted, but a compiled book of twelve characters in dialogue, much of it from plays. See S. R. Golding, 'The Parliament of Bees', *R.E.S.* iii. (1927), 280–304, which seems to me completely to supersede Sir Edmund Chambers (*Eliz. Stage*, iii. 287–8) and others.

THOMAS DEKKER (Deckar, Decker, Deker, Dekkar, Dicker, Dickers, Dycher, Dychers)

c. 1572–1632

Anon. 'Thomas Dekker and the Underdog', *T.L.S.*, 31 May 1941, pp. 262, 264.

Adkins, Mary Grace Muse. 'Puritanism in the Plays and Pamphlets of Thomas Dekker', *University of Texas Studies in English* (1939), pp. 86–113.

Bang, W. 'Dekker-Studien', *Englische Studien*, xxviii (1900), 208–34.

Bullen, A. H. 'Thomas Dekker' in *Elizabethans* (1924), pp. 73–94.

Eccles, Mark. 'Thomas Dekker: Burial-Place', *N. & Q.* clxxvii (1939), 157.

Ellis-Fermor, U. M. 'Thomas Dekker', in *The Jacobean Drama* (1936), pp. 118–27.

Fluchère, H. 'Thomas Dekker et le drame bourgeois', *Le Théâtre Élizabéthain*, pp. 192–6. In *Cahiers du sud*, xx (June–July 1933).

Greg, W. W., ed. *Henslowe's Diary*, 2 vols. (1904–8), *passim*.

Gregg, Kate L. 'Thomas Dekker: A Study in Economic and Social Backgrounds', *University of Washington Publications in Language and Literature*, ii (1924), 55–112.

Hunt, Mary Leland. *Thomas Dekker. A Study* (1911).

Kupka, P. *Über den dramatischen Vers Thomas Dekkers* (1893).

Lawrence, W. J. 'Dekker's Theatrical Allusiveness', *T.L.S.*, 30 January 1937, p. 72. Reply by H. W. Crundell, ibid., 13 February 1937, p. 111.

Pierce, Frederick Erastus. 'The Collaboration of Dekker and Ford', *Anglia*, xxxvi (1912), 141–68, 289–312.

—— *The Collaboration of Webster and Dekker* (1909).

Shaw, Phillip. 'The Position of Thomas Dekker in Jacobean Prison Literature', *P.M.L.A.* lxii (1947), 366–91.

Spender, Constance. 'The Plays of Thomas Dekker', *The Contemporary Review*, cxxx (1926), 332–9.

Stoll, E. E. 'The Influence of Jonson on Dekker', *M.L.N.* xxi (1906), 20–23.

Tannenbaum, Samuel A. *Thomas Dekker (A Concise Bibliography)* (1939).

—— and Dorothy R. Tannenbaum. *Supplement to a Bibliography of Thomas Dekker* (1945).

Wilson, F. P. 'Three Notes on Thomas Dekker', *M.L.R.* xv (1920), 82–85.

Dekker several times refers to his London origin and upbringing, but no record of his christening or early life has been discovered, nor has his family been identified. He is generally said to have been born about 1572 because he speaks of 'my three-score years' in the Epistle which first appeared in the 1632 edition of *English Villainies*.

The works of Thomas Dekker show a certain amount of learning and some particular knowledge of Latin, French, and Dutch, but there are no records of his education and no sufficient grounds for conjecture. The commonly repeated statement that he must have been a soldier in the Low Countries is only an inference from his fondness for military language and persons and his acquaintance with Dutch (See Hunt, op. cit., pp. 20–24.)

Professor F. P. Wilson thinks that the dramatist may well have been the Thomas Dycker, Dykers, or Dicker whose daughters Dorcas, Elizabeth, and Anne were christened at St. Giles's, Cripplegate, on 27 October 1594, 29 November 1598, and 24 October 1602. The parish was popular with actors (see Bentley, *P.M.L.A.* xliv [1929], 789–826) and seems not an unlikely place of residence for the playwright, but there is no corroboration for the identification.

The first certain appearance of the name of the poet is in Henslowe's Diary, when he was paid, 8 and 15 January 1597/8, for his work on a play called *Phaethon*. (*Henslowe's Diary*, i. 83. Collier's note of an entry of 20 December 1597 for a prologue to *Tamburlaine* is a forgery. Ibid., p. xxxix.) There are vague suggestions that he had worked for Henslowe for several years at this time (Chambers, *Elizabethan Stage*, iii. 300–2), but the names of dramatists are not regularly recorded in the Diary until 1598. From 1598 to 1602 he was engaged in the composition of forty-four plays for Henslowe, and at least one—*Satiromastix*—for other companies. These facts are indicative of the rate of composition which was possible for Dekker in the later years for which we have no such records. Since most of these Henslowe records concern collaborations, they also provide a background for the collaborative work which is so characteristic of his dramatic activity after 1616.

The writing of *Satiromastix* made Dekker one of the principal combatants in the War of the Theatres. (See R. A. Small, *The Stage-Quarrel between Ben Jonson and the So-Called Poetasters*, 1899.) That Dekker should compose a play attacking Jonson for the Lord Chamberlain's men seems a little odd at a time when he was so fully occupied with work for the rival companies financed by Philip Henslowe. No doubt the enmity fostered by this skirmish helps to explain Jonson's classification of Dekker, in his conversations with Drummond of Hawthornden, with Sharpham, Day, and Minsheu as rogues (*Ben Jonson*, i. 133), but Dekker's hand-to-mouth existence and his hackwork for the theatres would have made him contemptible in the eyes of Ben in any case.

After the conclusion of the regular entries in Henslowe's Diary, we know of only scattered plays by Dekker—the two parts of *The Honest Whore* for Prince Henry's men in 1604 and 1605, *Westward Ho!* and *Northward Ho!* for the Children of Pauls in the same years, and *The Whore of Babylon*, again for the Prince's men, some time before 1607. This seems very leisurely composition after the proliferation of 1598–1602, and one would guess either that Dekker had unknown patronage or that many plays of these years have left no trace of their existence.

The first of Dekker's pamphlets, *The Bachelor's Banquet* and *The Wonderful Year*, appeared in 1603, and by 1606 he seems to have begun devoting most of his energies to these non-dramatic works. Before 1610 at least thirteen pamphlets had appeared, some of them of no little distinction.

Several other pamphlets and two or three plays (*The Roaring Girl*, with Middleton, *If It Be Not Good, the Devil Is in It*, and probably *Match Me in London*) appeared between 1610 and 1613, and then Dekker fell silent for a number of years. It is generally said that he spent seven years, 1613–19, in the King's Bench prison, but it would be comfortable to have more explicit evidence for this long imprisonment than the vague statement in the epistle to *Dekker His Dream* (S.R., 11 October 1619), 'Out of a long sleep, which for almost seven years together, seized all my senses, . . .', a letter to Edward Alleyn dated 12 September 1616 from the King's Bench, and the years of limited output, plus an odd reference or so to a period of seven years. (Hunt, op. cit., 165–74.)

After his release from prison Dekker probably lived in the parish of St. James's, Clerkenwell, for a 'Thomas Deckers gentleman' of this parish was presented for recusancy in 1626 and again in 1628. (Wilson, op. cit.) Since 'Thomas Decker, householder' was buried from this parish 25 August 1632, and since the poet is heard of no more after 1632, it seems likely that all three of the records of the man in St. James's, Clerkenwell, refer to the dramatist.

In his later years Dekker does not appear to have been attached to any particular company, though he wrote more for Prince Charles's men than for any other troupe—*The Witch of Edmonton*, *The Bellman of Paris*, probably *The Late Murder of the Son upon the Mother, or Keep the Widow Waking*, and perhaps *The Fairy*

Knight. Yet he also wrote for the Palsgrave's men, for the Players
of the Revels, and later perhaps for Queen Henrietta's men. He
continued to write pamphlets, and a revision of *Villainies Discovered by Lanthorn and Candlelight*, as well as *Dekker His Dream*;
Penny-Wise, Pound-Foolish; *A Rod for Runaways*; and *Wars,
Wars, Wars* all appeared after 1619, the date of his presumptive
release from the King's Bench.

One of the odd features of Dekker's later career is his repeated
collaboration with John Ford. From what little is known of the
lives of the two men and from the personal interests reflected in
their works, one would have expected them to be highly incom-
patible. Yet they wrote together five times. In 1621 they composed
The Witch of Edmonton with William Rowley, and in 1624 they
must have spent a good part of their time in conference, for in a
period of seven and a half months three plays of their joint
authorship—*The Bristow Merchant, The Fairy Knight*, and *The
Sun's Darling*—were licensed for performance, and a fourth on
which they worked with John Webster and William Rowley—
*The Late Murder of the Son upon the Mother, or Keep the Widow
Waking*—falls in the same period.

Dekker's Lord Mayors' pageants in 1628 and 1629 are work of
the type one would have expected to come in greater quantity
from this impecunious and loyal son of London. Certainly he
hoped to write at least one other one. The records of the Merchant
Taylors' company show that in 1630 Dekker offered to write a
pageant for the inauguration of Sir Robert Ducy as Lord Mayor,
but in that year the company had only a procession and no pageant.
(R. T. D. Sayle, *The Lord Mayors' Pageants of the Merchant
Taylors' Company in the 15th, 16th, and 17th Centuries* [Privately
Printed, 1931], pp. 117–23.) The revealing record is:

> Itm̃, given and paid by the consent of the Com̃ittees to
> Thomas Decker, the poett, for his service offered to the Com- } xxˢ.
> panie if any Pageants had been made, the some of
>
> (Ibid., p. 121.)

Perhaps the lost 'City Show' and the payment to Dekker by the
Grocers' Company in 1617 (see 'Proposed pageant' below) indicate more work of this sort than we now know; pageants for a
number of years during his lifetime are missing.

The administration of the estate of the Thomas Dekker, householder, who was buried from St. James's, Clerkenwell—almost
certainly the dramatist, as noted above—was renounced by his
widow Elizabeth on 4 September 1632. (See Eccles, op. cit.)

Eccles points out that renunciation of administration implies that Dekker died in debt. This implication accords with the suggestion that fear of process for debt was the reason—as Wilson had conjectured—for Dekker's recusancy in 1626 and 1628. The piling up of records of a Thomas Dekker in the parish of St. James's, Clerkenwell, all of which seem compatible with what we know of the poet, suggests that the 'Mary wife of Thomas Deckers' buried in that parish 24 July 1616 (see Wilson, op. cit.) was his first—or at least an earlier—wife.

The paucity of allusions to Dekker in seventeenth-century literature indicates that whatever his popular reputation may have been, his literary reputation was slight. I have found less than a dozen allusions. None refers to a play of Dekker's; none refers to him as a dramatist except in lists of other playwrights. His pamphlets seem to have made more impression on literary men than his plays; two of the writers of commendatory verses for Humphrey Mill's *A Night's Search*, 1640, refer to *The Bellman of London*, and R[obert] H[enderson] refers to 'an odde tractate, called, *The Gull's Horn-booke*', in *The Arraignement of the Whole Creature*, 1631, p. 180.

Collected Editions

The Dramatic Works of Thomas Dekker. [R. H. Shepherd, ed.] 4 vols. (1873).

The Non-Dramatic Works of Thomas Dekker. A. B. Grosart, ed. 5 vols. (1884–6).

Thomas Dekker. Mermaid Series. Ernest Rhys, ed. (1887). (Contains *The Shoemakers' Holiday*, 1 and 2 *The Honest Whore*, *Old Fortunatus*, *The Witch of Edmonton*.)

An Edition of the Dramatic Works of Thomas Dekker was announced by Fredson Thayer Bowers. 'Research in Progress', *P.M.L.A.* lxiii (1948), 181, No. 860.

For the forty-four plays, now mostly lost, for which Henslowe records payments to Thomas Dekker in his Diary 1598–1602, see *The Elizabethan Stage*, iii. 302–4, and for others in the Diary conjecturally assigned to him, mostly by Fleay, see ibid., pp. 300–1.

Believe It is So and 'Tis So (?)
(Lost)

This title is forty-third in the list of manuscript plays found among the papers of Abraham Hill. (See Middleton, *The*

Conqueror's Custom.) The list seems to have been Hill's record of some bookseller's stock, set down between 1677 and 1703, but it is notable that nearly all the identifiable plays and playwrights of the list are Jacobean and Caroline.

Hill's assignment of the play to Dekkèr, 'Believe it is so & tis so Th. Decker', is the only evidence I know of Dekker's authorship. Presumably Hill took the author's name from the manuscript. As J. Q. Adams points out in his discussion of Hill's list (*Library*, Fourth Series, xx [1939], 96), there is probably no connexion between this proverbial expression and Robert Davenport's title-page motto, *Crede Quod Habes et Habes*.

The Bellman of Paris (1623)
with John Day
(Lost)

1623, 30 July. 'For the Prince's Players, A French Tragedy of *the Bellman of Paris*, written by Thomas Dekkirs and John Day, for the Company of the Red Bull.' (Adams, *Herbert*, p. 24).

1623, 30 July. 'The Princes Players—A french Tragedy of the Belman of [Paris contayning 40] sheetes written by Thomas Drickers & Iohn [Day, for the company] of the Read-bull this 30 Iuly 1623. 1^{li}. o.' (Folger Shakespeare Library, in the Halliwell-Phillipps Scrap-Book entitled *Theatres of Shakespeare's Time*, p. 51.)

This play is known only from Sir Henry Herbert's allowance for Prince Charles's company at the Red Bull (see above, i. 205–9). The second version of the licence entry comes from an independent transcript in a nineteenth-century hand of material from the office-book. This transcript, perhaps that of Craven Ord, has been cut into strips and then pasted into appropriate sections of Halliwell-Phillipps's scrap-books, now preserved at the Folger Shakespeare Library. The bracketed words seem to have been inadvertently cut off the transcript and are added in a different hand. The number of sheets mentioned suggests that the play was somewhat longer than usual.

The play is one of four which Dekker wrote with various collaborators, 1621–4, all of them apparently for Prince Charles's company—*The Bellman of Paris*, *The Fairy Knight*, *The Witch of Edmonton*, and *The Late Murder of the Son upon the Mother, or Keep the Widow Waking*. Only the third is extant.

The Bloody Banquet

This play is sometimes assigned to Dekker because the title-page of the 1639 edition says 'By T. D.' See Thomas Drue.

The Bristow Merchant (1624)
with John Ford
(Lost)

1624, 22 Oct. 'For the Palsgrave's Company; A new Play, called, *The Bristowe Merchant*: Written by Forde, and Decker.' (Adams, *Herbert*, p. 30.)

1624, 22 Oct. 'For the P: comp: A new P. call: The Bristowe Marchant writt: by Forde & Decker 22 Oct. 1624. 1¹ⁱ.' (Folger Shakespeare Library, in the Halliwell-Phillipps Scrap-Book entitled *Fortune*, p. 149.)

Nothing is known of the play save Sir Henry Herbert's licence. The second of the two versions comes from an independent transcript of material from the office-book in a nineteenth-century hand. This transcript, perhaps that of Craven Ord, has been cut into strips and then pasted into appropriate sections of Halliwell-Phillipps's scrap-books, now preserved at the Folger Library.

The play is one of an unusually large number licensed to the Palsgrave's company at the new Fortune in the last half of 1623 and 1624, presumably to replenish their repertory, which was destroyed when the old Fortune burned 9 December 1621 (see above, i. 141, 149-51). It is the fourth of four collaborations by Dekker and Ford licensed in the eight months of March through October 1624—*The Sun's Darling, The Fairy Knight, The Late Murder of the Son upon the Mother or Keep the Widow Waking*, and *The Bristow Merchant*.

Several suggestions about the play have been offered, none of them convincing. Fleay (*Biog. Chron.* i. 233) thought that the play might have been a reworking of *The Bristow Tragedy*, for which Henslowe paid John Day on 4, 23, and 28 May 1602 (*Henslowe's Diary*, i. 165-7), but since both plays are lost, this is the idlest conjecture. Miss Hunt (*Thomas Dekker*, pp. 187-9) follows Bang (*Materialien*, 1908, p. vi) in his suggestion that the play may have been based on Dekker's pamphlet, *Penny-Wise, Pound-Foolish*, which tells the story of a merchant of Bristow. Bang reprinted the pamphlet in his edition of Ford. (*Materialen*, 1908, Appendix.) It has been suggested (*Elizabethan Stage*, iii. 316) that the play was the same as 'The London Merchant. a Comedy. by Iohn fforde' entered in the Stationers' Register 29 June 1660. All these suggestions are pure conjecture and add nothing to our knowledge of the play.

Britannia's Honour (29 October 1628)

Edition: *The Dramatic Works of Thomas Dekker* (1873), iv. 93–112.

1628. 'Britannia's Honor: Brightly Shining in seuerall Magnificent Shewes or Pageants, to Celebrate the Solemnity of the Right Honorable Richard Deane, At his Inauguration into the Majoralty of the Honourable Citty of *London*, on Wednesday, October the 29th. 1628. At the particular Cost, and Charges of the Right Worshipfull, Worthy, and Ancient Society of *Skinners*. . . . Inuented by Tho. Dekker . . . 1628.

The pageant consists of a preliminary glorification of London plus five shows, the third of which is a parade of fur-dressed characters—no doubt duly appreciated by the Lord Mayor's brethren of the Skinners' Company. In the first show is a French letter to Henrietta Maria, 'If her *Majestie* be pleased on the Water, or Land, to Honor These Tryumphes with her Presence'. At the end of the pageant Dekker commends Gerard Christmas and his son John Christmas, who built the works. The show is uninspired.

A City Show (?)
(Lost ?)

In Abraham Hill's list of manuscript plays the sixteenth item is 'a Citty shew on the L. Mayors day   Tho Dekker'. (See Middleton, *The Conqueror's Custom*.) The list seems to have been Hill's record of some bookseller's stock, set down between 1677 and 1703, but it is notable that nearly all the identifiable plays and playwrights of the list are Jacobean or Caroline.

It is possible that what Hill saw was one of Dekker's extant Lord Mayor's shows, *Troia Nova Triumphans*, *Britannia's Honour*, or *London's Tempe*, which may have survived in manuscript as well as in print. But it is also possible that the show is a fourth city pageant written by Dekker for one of the several years during his maturity for which no pageant is known.

Disguises, or Love in Disguise, A Petticoat Voyage (?)

(Lost)

c. 1677–1703. '[11] disguises or love in disguise, a pettycoat voyage Th. Decker.' (J. Q. Adams, *Library*, Fourth Series, xx [1939], 73.)

This title, attributed to Dekker, occurs eleventh in Abraham Hill's list of plays in manuscript. (See Middleton, *The Conqueror's Custom*.) The list seems to have been Hill's record of some bookseller's stock, set down between 1677 and 1703, but it is notable that nearly all the identifiable plays and playwrights in the list are Jacobean and Caroline.

The titles of this play are probably alternative ones. J. Q. Adams points out in his discussion of Hill's list (*Library*, Fourth Series, xx [1939], 84) that Henslowe records the performance of an anonymous new play called *The Disguises* on 2 October 1595. (*Henslowe's Diary*, i. 25.) The play in Hill's list could have been that play or a revision of it by Dekker, but there is no evidence. Note that the thirteenth play in Hill's list, also attributed to Dekker, is called 'the Welch Embassador or a Comedy in disguises'. In spite of the similarity of 'a Comedy in disguises' and 'Disguises', it does not seem likely that Hill would have confused two plays so close together on his list. Moreover, it is unusual for a play to have three titles, like this one, and identification with 'the Welch Embassador' would add a fourth. Finally, there is an extant manuscript in the Cardiff Public Library of a play entitled *The Welsh Ambassador* (see Dekker, *The Welsh Ambassador*) for which the sub-title 'A Comedy in Disguises' is appropriate, but *Love in Disguise* or *A Petticoat Voyage* is not.

In the absence of adequate evidence, I think it is safest to assume that *Disguises, or Love in Disguise, A Petticoat Voyage* is another of Dekker's many lost plays and that it is not the same as *The Welsh Ambassador* of the Cardiff MS. or 'the Welch Embassador or a Comedy in disguises' of Hill's list.

The Fairy Knight (1624)

with John Ford

(Lost?)

1624, 11 June. 'A new play, called, *The Fairy Knight*: Written by Forde, and Decker.' (Adams, *Herbert*, p. 29.)

Sir Henry Herbert's licence, Professor Adams guesses, may have been for Prince Charles's men, since the preceding entry was. The play is probably not extant, though there is a recently discovered manuscript of a play called *The Fairy Knight, or Oberon the Second.* (See Anon.) There seems good reason to believe, however, that the manuscript play is not the one by Ford and Dekker.

Fleay (*Biog. Chron.* i. 232) suggested that *The Fairy Knight* may have been a revision of *Huon of Bordeaux* of 1593, but this is only the wildest guessing. Miss Margaret Sargeaunt's suggestion (*John Ford* [1935], p. 18) that the piece may have been a masque like *The Sun's Darling* is, considering the title, authorship, and date, a somewhat more rational guess, but no more.

Gustavus, King of Sweden (? 1630–2 ?)
(Lost)

1660, 29 June. S.R. In a list of eleven plays entered to Humphrey Moseley occurs:

Gustavus King of Swethland.
The Tale of Ioconda and Astolso. a Comedy. } by Tho: Decker.
(Greg, *Bibliography*, i. 69.)

c. 1710–50. 'The King of Swedland' is the seventeenth entry in Warburton's famous list of manuscript plays allegedly burned by his cook. (Greg, *Library*, Third Series, ii [1911], 225–59.)

The existence of a play of this name is known only from Moseley's payment to establish his rights to it as recorded in the Stationers' Register. Greg (*Library*) gives good reason for thinking that Warburton copied most of his list from the Stationers' Register and may never have owned a manuscript of this or most of the other plays of his list.

A play of this title could have been written about the career of either Gustavus I (1496–1560) or Gustavus Adolphus (1594–1632). The former might have been interesting to the English because of his struggle with the papacy, but his bitter fight against the Danes would presumably have made the subject censorable in England during the reign of James, or at least during those years his Danish queen shared his throne (1603–19). Gustavus Adolphus was in any case a much more popular figure in England, as is evidenced by letters, commonplace books, and popular ballads. His English popularity began with his intervention in the Thirty Years War in 1630 and continued for some time after his death at Lützen in November 1632. A play by Dekker on the great Gustavus Adolphus could have been written between the time of his

emergence as an English hero in 1630 and Dekker's death in
August 1632.

The Life and Death of Guy of Warwick (> 1619/20)
with John Day
(Lost?)

R. S. Crane, 'The Vogue of *Guy of Warwick*', *P.M.L.A.* xxx
(1915), 125–94.

1618, 14 Oct. 'The next day I came to *London*, and obscurely
coming within More-gate, I went to a house and borrowed
money: And so I stole backe againe to *Islington*, to the signe
of the Maydenhead, staying till Wednesday, than my friends
came to meete me, who knew no other, but that Wednesday
was my first comming: where with all loue I was entertained
with much good cheere: and after Supper we had a play of the
life and death of *Guy of Warwicke*, played by the Right Honourable the Earle of *Darbie* his men. And so on the Thursday
morning being the fifteenth of October, I came home to my
house in *London*.' (*The Pennyles Pilgrimage*, 1618, in *All the
Workes of John Taylor the Water Poet*, N₄ᵛ, describing his
journey to Scotland in 1618.)

1619/20, 15 Jan. S.R. 'Iohn Trundle Entred for his copie . . .
A Play Called the life and Death of Guy of Warwicke written by
Iohn Day and Tho: Decker.' (Greg, *Bibliography*, i. 31.)

1620, 13 Dec. S.R. 'Tho: Langley Assigned ouer vnto him by Iohn
Trundle . . . [1] The Play of Guy of warwicke.' (Ibid., p. 32.)

1661. The Tragical History, Admirable Atchievments and various
events of Guy Earl of Warwick, A Tragedy Acted very Frequently with great Applause, By his late Majesties Servants.
Written by B. J. . . . 1661.

Probably two and perhaps three plays about Guy of Warwick
are covered by the above items. (See also Anon.) Bullen thought
(*The Works of John Day*, i. 11) that the play of the 1661 quarto
was much too bad for Dekker and Day, and most subsequent
writers have agreed. The play which Taylor saw presented by the
Earl of Derby's men at his festive home-coming may have been
either the Dekker and Day play, the 1661 play, or still a third.
It seems probable that the Dekker and Day work is lost, like so
many of their other plays.

*The Honest Whore, with the Humours of the Patient Man
and the Longing Wife*

with Middleton

See *The Elizabethan Stage*, iii. 294–5.

If It Be Not Good, the Devil Is In It

See *The Elizabethan Stage*, iii. 297.

The Jew of Venice (?)

(Lost)

1653, 9 Sept. S.R. Forty-one plays are entered to Humphrey
Moseley, the eighth of which is 'The Iew of Venice, by Tho:
Decker'. (Greg, *Bibliography*, i. 60–61.)

This entry in the Stationers' Register is the only record of an
English play of this name, but quite a mountain of conjecture has
been erected by identifying or associating it variously with *The
French Doctor*, *The Venetian Comedy*, *The Jew of Malta*, *The
Merchant of Venice*, and *Josephus, Jude von Venedig*. (See *Biog.
Chron.* i. 121; Greg, *Henslowe's Diary*, ii. 170–1; *Elizabethan Stage*,
iii. 301.) The plain facts are that there is no reason to connect *The
Jew of Venice* which Moseley owned in 1653 with any other play
at all. Nothing whatever is known of it or of its connexions with
any other play. Most of the plays in Moseley's list are assigned to
Caroline dramatists.

Jocondo and Astolfo

See *The Tale of Jocondo and Astolfo*.

The Late Murder in Whitechapel

See *The Late Murder of the Son upon the Mother*.

*The Late Murder of the Son upon the Mother, or Keep
the Widow Waking* (1624)

with Ford, Rowley, and Webster

(Lost)

Sisson, C. J. *Lost Plays of Shakespeare's Age* (1936), pp. 80–124.
Revised from *Library*, Fourth Series, viii (1927), 39–57,
233–59.

1624, Sept. 'A new Tragedy, called *A Late Murther of the Sonn upon the Mother*: Written by Forde, and Webster.' (Adams, *Herbert*, p. 29. No day of the month is given, but the preceding entry is dated the 3rd and the following the 15th of September.)

1624, Sept. 'A new Trag: call: a Late Murther of the sonn upon the mother writt: by Mr Forde Webster & this   Sept. 1624. 2^li.

    'The same Trag: writt: M^r. Drew & allowed for the day after theirs because they had all manner of reason.' (In the Halliwell-Phillipps Scrap-Book entitled *Fortune*, p. 149, Folger Shakespeare Library.)

From 1799 when Chalmers published Sir Henry Herbert's licence for performance in his *A Supplemental Apology for the Believers in the Shakespeare-Papers* (pp. 218–19) until 1927 when Professor Sisson published his fascinating collection of material from the contemporary suit involving the play, all that was known about this piece was its title and Herbert's attribution of authorship to Ford and Webster. The records uncovered by Professor Sisson reveal that the play was written by Thomas Dekker, William Rowley, John Ford, and John Webster, and that its sub-title was the proverbial expression, 'Keep the Widow Waking'.

The second version of Sir Henry Herbert's record of his licence for the play comes from an independent transcript of material from the office-book in a nineteenth-century hand. This transcript, perhaps that of Craven Ord, has been cut into strips and then pasted into appropriate sections of Halliwell-Phillipps's scrap-books, now preserved at the Folger Shakespeare Library. It adds the gentlemanly title for Ford and gives the fee paid, which was double the one usual at this time for licensing a new play. This double fee may be explained by an unusually large number of alterations or by the difficulties suggested by the licence of a second play on the subject by Drew. I take this second licence—which was not copied by Chalmers or Malone—to indicate that two different companies prepared plays on this topical subject at the same time; that Herbert, after hearing arguments, allowed both plays so that they could be acted in competition; that for unspecified reasons he allowed the Dekker, Rowley, Ford, and Webster play a one-day advantage. The 'all manner of reason' could refer to the reasons for allowing the second play at all, or, as J. Q. Adams once suggested to me, to the reasons for giving the Red Bull play a one-day advantage. In either case it is clear that the subject was thought to have great appeal and that two London companies were competing for the right to exploit it.

Though the Dekker, Rowley, Ford, and Webster play is not extant, not a little is known about it from Professor Sisson's researches in London record repositories. The main plot, which gave the play its primary title, was an account of the murder of Joan Tindall or Grindall by her son Nathaniel in Whitechapel, 9 April 1624. Nathaniel pleaded guilty and was sentenced, 3 September 1624, to be hanged near the house where he committed the murder. (*Lost Plays*, pp. 94–97.) The sensational nature of the crime, and perhaps also the penitence of the murderer, led to two ballads, entered in the Stationers' Register 2 July and 16 September 1624, ballads which must have made the subject even more promising for theatrical exploitation.

The secondary plot, indicated by the proverbial title, *Keep the Widow Waking*, dramatized an equally notorious affair of late July and early August of the same year, in which a young rogue, Tobias Audley, with the assistance of two prostitutes, a clergyman, and others, victimized a sixty-two-year-old widow, Anne Elsden, who was both convivial and well-to-do. By keeping Mrs. Elsden dead drunk for about five days the conspirators forced her into a marriage with Audley and made away with at least several hundred pounds worth of her property—her relatives alleged £3,000. (Ibid., pp. 82–94.)

The actors at the Red Bull theatre saw a fine opportunity in these two scandals of the moment, and Ralph Savage, apparently acting as manager of the theatre, retained Thomas Dekker and the others to get the stories on the boards of the playhouse with dispatch—a feat for which Henslowe's records show Dekker to have been eminently competent. Our knowledge of the affair comes largely from the actions which Mrs. Elsden's respectable son-in-law, Benjamin Garfield, brought against the conspirators and the theatrical folk who put her tribulations on the stage. In his deposition Dekker testified

that John Webster . . . Willm Rowly John ffoord and this deft were privy consenting & acquainted w^{t}h the making & contriuing of the sd play called keep the widow waking and did make & contrive the same vppon the instrucçons giuen them by one Raph Savage And this deft saith that he this deft did often see the said play or p^t thereof acted but how often he cannot depose. (*Library*, Fourth Series, viii [1927], 258.)

And in his answer as one of the defendants he said:

and whereas in the sayd Information, Mention is made of a Play
called by the name of Keepe the Widow waking, this Defend[t] sayth,
that true it is, Hee wrote two sheetes of paper conteyning the first Act
of a Play called The Late Murder in White Chappell, or Keepe the
Widow waking, and a speech in the Last Scene of the Last Act of the
Boy who had killed his mother w[ch] Play (as all others are) was licensed
by S[r] Henry Herbert knight, M[r] of his Ma[ties] Reuells, authorizing
thereby boeth the Writing and Acting of the sayd Play. (Ibid.,
p. 257.)

This significant testimony by one of the most experienced
dramatic collaborators of his day throws light not only on Jacobean and Caroline methods of collaboration, but clearly implies
the parts which the other collaborators had in the composition
of this piece. Evidently Rowley, Ford, and Webster each wrote
the second or third or fourth act and one part of the fifth. Dekker
and Rowley had had much experience of this sort of thing, but it
has surprised the more literary admirers of Ford and Webster to
find those poets of tragic genius lending themselves to this vulgar
phase of the show business in 1624.

The degree of vulgarity of the show at the Red Bull is indicated
by the ballad, 'keeping the widow wakeing or lett him that is
poore and to wealth would aspire gett some old rich widdowe and
grow wealthye by her, to the tune of the blazing torch'. This
ballad recounts the comic action of the play and ends:

> And you whoe faine would heare the full
> discourse of this match makeing,
> The play will teach you at the Bull,
> to keepe the widdow wakeing.

(Ibid., pp. 238–40.)

Several parties or witnesses in the actions testify that this ballad
was sung on the streets, one says that boy actors from the theatre
pointed to Anne Elsden's windows and said, 'there dwelte the
widdowe waking', and Benjamin Garfield, Mrs. Elsden's son-in-
law, said that the ballad-monger not only sang it under Mrs.
Elsden's window but when brought before a Justice of the Peace
testified that 'he was purposely sent thither to singe the said
ballad by one Holland', i.e. Aaron Holland, who built the Red
Bull theatre and was an important partner in the enterprise for a
number of years. (Ibid., pp. 248–51.)

All parties to the legal actions agree that the play was acted at
the Red Bull, and Dekker testified that he saw it several times.
There is some uncertainty about the company which occupied
the Red Bull in September 1624, but it was probably Prince

Charles's (I) company. (See above, i. 205–9.) All the testimony seems to agree that the actors made a very good thing out of the misfortunes of Nathaniel Tindall and Anne Elsden.

London's Tempe, or The Field of Happiness (1629)

Edition: Fairholt, Frederick W. *Lord Mayors' Pageants*, Percy Society, x (1844), Part ii. 37–53.

1629? London's Tempe, or *The Field of Happines*. In which *Field* are planted seuerall Trees of Magnificence, *State and Bewty, to Celebrate the Solemnity of the Right* Honorable *Iames Campebell*, At his Inauguration into the Honorable *Office of Prætorship, or Maioralty of London, on Thursday the* 29 *of October*, 1629. All the particular Inuentions, for the Pageants, Showes of Tri*umph, both by Water and land being here fully set downe, At the sole Cost*, and liberall Charges of the Right worshipfull Society of *Ironmongers*. Written by Thomas Dekker. *Quando magis Dignos licuit Spectare Triumphos?* [N.D.]

The sub-title of the pageant comes from a pun on the new Lord Mayor's name, as explained in the fifth presentation. The pageant is in no way remarkable.

According to James Peller Malcolm (*Londinium Redivivum*, ii. 45), the books of the Ironmongers' Company show that 'The sum paid for these pageants, including every expence, was 180*l*. The sea-lion and estridge were preserved, and placed in the hall [of the company]. And 32 trumpeters were employed.'

Dekker records at the end of his pageant that the constructions, like those of so many other pageants, were the inventions of Gerard Christmas.

Match Me in London (c. 1611–12?)

1623, 21 Aug. 'An Old Playe called Matche mee in London formerley allowed by Sir George Buck & now by mee freely & without fee this 21++. Augt. 1623.' (In the Halliwell-Phillipps Scrap-Book entitled *Burbage*, p. 146, Folger Shakespeare Library. This is a cutting from a transcript in a nineteenth-century hand, perhaps that of Craven Ord, of entries from Sir Henry Herbert's office-book.)

The play is included here because of the Herbert entry, which differs from that in Adams, *Herbert*, p. 25. See *The Elizabethan Stage*, iii. 297–8.

The Noble Soldier [*The Noble Spanish Soldier*], *or A Contract Broken Justly Revenged* (? 1622 < > 1631)

Editions: A. H. Bullen, ed., *A Collection of Old English Plays* (1882), i. 257–334; J. S. Farmer, ed., *Tudor Facsimile Texts* (1913).

Bowers, F. T. 'The Stabbing of a Portrait in Elizabethan Tragedy', *M.L.N.* xlvii (1932), 378–85.
Bullen, A. H., ed. *The Works of John Day* (1881), i. 25–31.
Golding, S. R. 'The Parliament of Bees', *R.E.S.* iii (1927), 280–304.
Hart, H. C. 'Notes on . . . *The Noble Spanish Souldier*', *The Academy*, xxxiv (1888), 135–7.
Koeppel, Emil. 'Zur Quellenkunde des Stuart-Dramas', *Archiv für das Studium der neueren Sprachen und Litteraturen*, xcvii (1896), 313–23.
Lloyd, Bertram. '*The Noble Soldier* and *The Welsh Embassador*', *R.E.S.* iii (1927), 304–7.

1631, 16 May. S.R. 'Iohn Iackman. Entred for his Copie vnder the hands of Sr Henry Herbert & Mr Kingston Warden a Comedy called The Wonder of a Kingdome by Tho: Decker.   vj^d
    Idem. Entred for his Copy vnder the same hands a Tragedy called The noble Spanish Souldier by Tho: Deckar.   vj^d'.
(Greg, *Bibliography*, i. 40.)
1633, 9 Dec. S.R. 'Nich: Vavasour. Entred for his Copy vnder the hands of S^r. Henry Herbert & M^r. Kingston warden A^o. dñi 1631. a Tragedy called The Noble Spanish soldior written by m^r Decker   vj^d'
(Ibid., p. 43.)
1634. The Noble Sovldier. *Or*, A Contract Broken, Justly Reveng'd. *A Tragedy. Written by* S. R. . . . Printed for *Nicholas* Vavasour . . . 1634. (The running title is *The Noble Spanish Souldier*.)

The attribution of the play to Dekker seems to me reasonable, in spite of the title-page of the 1634 quarto. The two Stationers' Register entries are explicit, and the presence of Sir Henry Herbert's name as licenser suggests that the name was on the manuscript which passed through his hands. Perhaps this seems naïve, but I find, after an analysis of Stationers' Register entries before the closing of the theatres, that sixty-nine play entries are under the hand of Sir Henry Herbert and ten under the hand of one or another of his deputies at the Revels Office. The accuracy of the attributions in these entries is far above the average for plays in the Stationers' Register. I find not one which is now generally accepted as a wrong attribution. Twenty-four omit any author's name, and one is doubtful—*Bellum Grammaticale*, a play at least forty-two years old when it was licensed 17 April 1634 and attributed to 'M^r. Spense'. This, Sir Edmund Chambers suggests (*Elizabethan Stage*, iv. 374), may be a confusion—presumably by the clerk of the Stationers' Company—with the name of the publisher, John Spenser. I cannot believe that such unusual accuracy of attribution among the Stationers' Register entries is pure chance, and therefore I suggest that manuscripts of plays licensed for publication at the Revels Office in Herbert's time were not handed on with patently false attributions, and that for some reason publishers were chary of adding fanciful guesses at authorship in the registration of manuscripts which Sir Henry or his deputies had handled, though they sometimes added them later to their title-pages.

Whether my confidence in Sir Henry Herbert is warranted or not, most scholars have accepted Dekker's authorship, at least in part. (Fleay, *Biog. Chron.* i. 128–9; *Elizabethan Stage*, iii. 300; Bertram Lloyd, op. cit.; J. Q. Adams, *Library*, Fourth Series, xx [1939], 86–88; S. R. Golding, op. cit., pp. 285–93.) The 'S. R.' of the 1634 title-page is generally assumed to be intended for Samuel Rowley because he is the only known sixteenth- or seventeenth-century dramatist with these initials. I know of no analysis which makes a good case for his work in the play (J. Q. Adams, op. cit., specifically denied it), but it is possible that Nicholas Vavasour had evidence of his original composition, collaboration, or revision. Vavasour's address, 'The Printer to the Reader', in his quarto consists mostly of the usual vague advertising claims and promises, some of which commentators have naïvely taken too literally, but at one point Vavasour is needlessly specific. 'Your Iudgement now this *Posthumus* assures himselfe will well attest his predecessors endevours to give content to men of the ablest quality.' Unfortunately '*Posthumus*', though it would apply to Dekker, who died in August 1632, might also apply to Samuel Rowley, who disappears after 1624.

A third dramatist whose collaboration in *The Noble Soldier* has been frequently asserted is John Day. Characters IV and V of Day's *Parliament of Bees*, extant in a B.M. MS. and in a revised version published in 1641, are made up of dialogue appearing also in the 1634 quarto of *The Noble Soldier*, C_1^v–C_2^v, D_3^v–E_1, and F_1^v–F_2. This fact has led to repeated assertions that Day must therefore have written the dialogue originally and that probably he was a collaborator in the play who reclaimed his own for *The Parliament of Bees*, or that, alternatively, Day worked the material from his characters into a revision of *The Noble Soldier*. This interpretation of the facts, which even Sir Edmund Chambers accepted (*Elizabethan Stage*, iii. 288, 300), seems to me oddly forgetful of the common Renaissance phenomenon of books compiled from unacknowledged sources. S. R. Golding's interpretation of the evidence seems to me much more informed and probable. He asserts that in the quarto version of *The Parliament of Bees*:

Chars. 4 and 5 and *Chars.* 2, 3, 7, 9, and 10 seem to have been lifted almost bodily—in some cases with only slight modification—from *The Noble Soldier* and *The Wonder of a Kingdom* respectively. Where the quarto of the *Bees* corresponds to passages in these plays, Dekker's craftsmanship is nearly always distinguishable; where it deviates, Day's hand is equally well marked. (Op. cit., p. 304.)

Further complications have been introduced into the history of *The Noble Soldier* by Fleay's familiar combination of a magnificent memory and an utterly undisciplined imagination. The last scene of the play is a banquet scene in which the Queen has plotted that Onælia, the King's former mistress, shall drink a poisoned cup. As the wine is poured, the Queen asks Malateste, 'Is t speeding?' To which he replies, 'As all our Spanish figs are.' (H$_2$^{v}.) Shortly thereafter the King changes cups with Onælia and is himself poisoned. According to Fleay (*Biog. Chron.* i. 128), the King is poisoned by a Spanish fig, and *The Noble Soldier* must therefore be identified with the play called *The Spanish Fig* for which on 6 January 1601/2 Henslowe made an incomplete payment for the Admiral's men to an unrecorded dramatist. (*Henslowe's Diary*, i. 153.) One is accustomed to watching Fleay on these breathless flights into the unknown, but it is sad to see W. W. Greg (*Henslowe's Diary*, ii. 220) and Sir Edmund Chambers (*Elizabethan Stage*, iii. 300), after a bit of cavilling about the difference between a fig and a cup of wine, still sufficiently dazzled by Fleay's memory to take off after him, with most of the subsequent commentators and historians in their slip-stream. There is no evidence whatever of any connexion between the two plays.

The use of identical material in parts of *The Welsh Ambassador* and *The Noble Soldier* has been several times noted and commented upon. (See Dekker, *The Welsh Ambassador*.) The relationship seems to me too close to be explained by derivation from a common source, and I am tentatively inclined to think *The Welsh Ambassador* derived from *The Spanish Soldier*, but the relationship needs closer study. (See Bertram Lloyd, op. cit.)

Fleay noted that the dramatis personae in the 1634 quarto omits Signor No, Carlo, Alonzo, Cornego, and Juanna, and though character lists in seventeenth-century quartos are often incomplete, this list of omissions seems unusually large and includes Cornego, which is a fat part. These facts, coupled with other characteristics of the play like loose ends and vague connexions, make it likely enough that *The Noble Soldier* is a revision of an earlier play. But the allusions to *Hamlet, Julius Caesar, Look about You*, and *All's Well*, which Fleay claimed to have found in *The Noble Soldier*, are either imaginary or the results of the common delusion that any use of a proverbial phrase found also in Shakespeare is necessarily an allusion to Shakespeare. Greg's idea that the earlier play was one of 1600 or thereabouts (*Henslowe's Diary*, ii. 220) is another relic of Fleay's *Spanish Fig* identification.

Quite different is another allusion vaguely noted by Fleay. This occurs at the close of a long quibbling dialogue in iv. 2 (F_4), between Baltazar, the Noble Soldier, and Cornego, the clown, a fairly important character whose omission from the dramatis personae suggests, as we noted above, that he may have been added in a revision.

> *Bal.* Woo't not trust an Almanacke?
> *Cor.* Nor a Coranta neither, tho it were seal'd with Butter; and yet I know where they both lye passing well.

Obviously this is another of the many allusions—even if the expression is proverbial—to the series of courantes or corantos issued by Nathaniel Butter and uniformly castigated for their lies by late Jacobean and Caroline dramatists, most familiarly by Jonson in *The Staple of News* (1625), a series which seems to have got properly under way in 1622. (Herford and Simpson, *Ben Jonson*, ii. 171–5; Laurence Hanson, *Library*, Fourth Series, xviii [1938], 355–84.) This familiar allusion to Butter's notoriety must have been made, therefore, between 1622 and the date of the entry of the play in the Stationers' Register 16 May 1631. We have consequently an approximate date for the revision of the play, if not for the original composition.

A final assertion of Fleay's perhaps deserves more consideration than it has received. 'I think the play is allegorical, the King being Philip 2; the Queen, his Italian possessions; and O Nœlia [*sic*] Ireland.' (*Biog. Chron.* i. 128.) It sounds fantastic, but a thorough study of the play might show it not wholly so, in which case the original version of *The Noble Soldier* would presumably be pushed back into the sixteenth century.

Northward Ho!
with John Webster

See *The Elizabethan Stage*, iii. 295–6.

Old Fortunatus

See *The Elizabethan Stage*, iii. 290–1.

Patient Grissell
with Henry Chettle and William Haughton

See *The Elizabethan Stage*, iii. 292.

Proposed Pageant? (1617)

In the very full expense accounts of the Grocers' Company for their staging of Middleton's *Triumph of Honour and Industry*, the Lord Mayor's show for the inauguration of George Bowles in 1617, appear the following entries:

BENEVOLENCES *and Rewards to Officers and others which took paines about the sayde busynesse, with other particuler charges as followeth*

	£	s.	d.
Payde and given in benevolence to Anthony Monday, gent^n, for his paynes in drawing a project for this busynesse which was offered to the Comyttee	5	0	0
Payde and given to Mr. Deckar for the like	4	0	0
	£9	0	0

(John Benjamin Heath, *Some Account of the Worshipful Company of Grocers of the City of London*, 2nd ed. [1854], p. 413.)

Fairholt (*Lord Mayors' Pageants*, Percy Society, x [1844], Part i, p. 45) interprets this as meaning that Munday and Dekker as well as Middleton had submitted pageants to the committee, that Middleton's was selected, and that Munday and Dekker were paid for their rejected pageants. I can think of no more probable explanation, though the sum seems rather high for a consolation prize.

The Roaring Girl, or Moll Cutpurse
with Thomas Middleton

See *The Elizabethan Stage*, iii. 296–7.

Satiromastix, or The Untrussing of the Humorous Poet
with John Marston?

See *The Elizabethan Stage*, iii. 293.

The Shoemakers' Holiday, or The Gentle Craft
See *The Elizabethan Stage*, iii. 291–2.

Sir Thomas Wyatt
with Webster, and possibly Chettle, Heywood, and Smith

See *The Elizabethan Stage*, iii. 293–4.

The Sun's Darling
with John Ford

See John Ford.

The Tale of Jocundo and Astolpho (?)
(Lost)

1660, 29 June. S.R. In a list of eleven plays entered to Humphrey
Moseley occurs:

Gustavus King of Swethland.
The Tale of Ioconda and Astolso. [*sic*] a Comedy } by Tho: Decker

(Greg, *Bibliography*, i. 69.)

c. 1710–50. 'Jocondo & Astolfo C. Thõ. Decker' is the twenty-
first entry in Warburton's famous list of manuscript plays
allegedly burned by his cook. (Greg, *Library*, Third Series, ii
[1911], 225–59.)

The play is known only from Moseley's entry in the Stationers'
Register. Dr. Greg (op. cit.) sets forth good reasons for thinking
that Warburton copied most of the titles in his list from the
Stationers' Register and that he may never have seen a manuscript of this or of most of the other plays which he says were
burned by his cook.

The curious use of 'The Tale' in this title might suggest that
Moseley's manuscript was a piece of prose fiction, but the further
designation, 'a Comedy', and the fact that all eleven titles are
preceded by the covering statement, 'the severall Plays following',
seem to indicate that it was a play in spite of the title.

The spelling in the Stationers' Register, 'Ioconda and Astolso', I take to be a misreading, or perhaps a perversion, of Jocundo and Astolpho, the principal characters of Canto 28 of Ariosto's *Orlando Furioso*. A misreading would be easy enough, particularly if the manuscript spelling was 'Astolfo' and the clerk of the Stationers' Company mistook the 'f' for a long 's'. This story, though not very rich in details fit for the stage, would provide a good outline for the plot of a play on the theme of the infidelity of women.

Since the play is bracketed with Dekker's *Gustavus King of Sweden*, and since nearly half the eleven plays licensed in this entry are said to be written by Caroline dramatists, it is tempting to guess that *Jocundo and Astolpho* was of approximately the same date as *Gustavus* (*c.* 1630–2 ?). The evidence is much too scanty to warrant even a guess, however, for of the eleven plays, only the anonymous *Christmas Ordinary* and *The Parliament of Love* are extant.

Troia Nova Triumphans

See *The Elizabethan Stage*, iii. 305, and R. T. D. Sayle, *Lord Mayors' Pageants of the Merchant Taylors' Company in the 15th, 16th, and 17th Centuries* (Privately Printed, 1931), pp. 96–105.

The Virgin Martyr (1620 ?)
with Philip Massinger

Koeppel, Emil. *Quellen-Studien zu den Dramen George Chapman's, Philip Massinger's, und John Ford's* (1897), pp. 82–85.

McIlwraith, A. K. 'Some Bibliographical Notes on Massinger', *Library*, Fourth Series, xi (1930), 79–81.

Ovaa, W. A. 'Dekker and The Virgin Martyr', *English Studies*, iii (1921), 167–8.

Peterson, J. M. *The Dorothea Legend: Its Earliest Records, . . . and Influence on Massinger's 'Virgin Martyr'* (1910).

Sykes, H. D. 'Massinger and Dekker's "The Virgin Martyr"', *N. & Q.*, Twelfth Series, x (1922), 61–65, 83–88.

1620, 6 Oct. 'Oct. 6, 1620. For new reforming the *Virgin-Martyr* for the Red Bull, 40s.' (Quoted from Sir Henry Herbert's office-book by William Gifford, *The Plays of Philip Massinger*, 2nd ed. i [1813], lvii n.)

1621, 7 Dec. S.R. 'Tho: Iones. Entred for his copie vnder the hands of Sr George Bucke, and Mr Swinhowe warden A Tragedy called The Virgin Martir.' (Greg, *Bibliography*, i. 32.)

1622. The Virgin Martir, A Tragedie. As It Hath Bin Divers times publickely Acted with great Applause, *By the seruants of his Maiesties Reuels*. Written by *Phillip Messenger* and *Thomas Decker* . . . 1622.

1622. [Variant.] See A. K. McIlwraith, *Library*, Fourth Series, xi (1930), 79–81.

1624, 7 July. 'For the adding of a scene to *The Virgin Martyr*, this 7th July, 1624, — £0. 10. 0.' (Adams, *Herbert*, p. 29.)

1631. [Another edition.]

1633, 24 Oct. S.R. Assigned to Mr. Mathews by Thomas Jones with twelve other books, five of them plays. (Greg, *Bibliography*, i. 43.)

1641, 28 July. S.R. Assigned to Will. Sheeres by Mr. Mathews with three other books, one a play. (Ibid., p. 54.)

1651. [Another edition.]

1660/1, 16 Feb. Pepys saw the play.

1661. [Another edition.] '*As it hath been of late Acted by his Majesties Servants with great Applause.*'

1661/2, 10 Jan. 'The Uirgin martire' occurs in the list of plays 'acted by the Kings Companie at the Red Bull and the new house in Gibbon's Tennis Court near Clare Market'. (Adams, *Herbert*, pp. 116–18.)

1662[–63 ?]. In his record of expenses at plays 'At the New Theatre in Lincolnes Jnne fields', Edward Browne entered 'Cornelia . . . 1 6'. (W. W. Greg, 'Theatrical Repertories of 1662', *Gentleman's Magazine*, ccci [1906], 69–72, from B.M. MS. Sloane 1900.)

1667/8, 27 Feb. Pepys saw the play at the King's House.

1667/8, 2 Mar. Pepys saw the play at the King's House.

1668, 6 May. Pepys again saw the play at the King's House.

The early history of the play is somewhat confused. The entry of 1620 is quoted only by Gifford, who added it to the second edition of his *Massinger*, presumably from Herbert's manuscript, now lost. He says:

Since this note first appeared [i.e. his quotation of the office-book entry of 7 July 1624], an additional proof has been discovered both of the popularity of this play, and of the practice here mentioned. Sir Henry Herbert's office-book contains a few memorandums, extracted from that of his predecessor, Sir George Buck, and among them the following, 'Oct. 6, 1620. For new reforming the *Virgin-Martyr* for the Red Bull, 40s.'

This entry shews it to have been even then an old play. Probably it was produced before the year 1609, in the time of Mr. Tylney, who was not so scrupulous in licensing plays, as his immediate successor, Buck. (Ed., *Massinger* i, [1813], lvii n.)

Gifford's interpretation that the play was an old one, probably dating from Tilney's time, seems to me almost certainly wrong. We do not have enough of Buc's entries to generalize comfortably about his practice, but his successor, Sir Henry Herbert, probably took over Buc's schedule of fees, and is certainly not likely to have lowered them. In Herbert's time 40s. would have been an unheard-of fee for examining the revisions of an old play. In the 1620's—before he doubled his fees, about 1632—Herbert's charge for reading and licensing a new play was £1. (See Herbert's licences quoted under Bonen, *Two Kings in a Cottage*; Davenport, *The City Nightcap*; Dekker, *The Bristow Merchant*; Gunnell, *The Way to Content All Women*; Heywood, *The Captive*; Massinger, *The Parliament of Love*; S. Rowley, *Richard III* and *A Match or No Match*; Shank, *Shank's Ordinary*; Anon., *The Angel King, The Dutch Painter or the French Branke*, and *The Fair Star of Antwerp*.) His charge for allowing an old play without revision was usually nothing. (See Anon., *The Peaceable King or the Lord Mendall*; Dekker, *Match Me in London*; and Shakespeare, *The Winter's Tale*, in Adams, *Herbert*, p. 25.) An old play with additions— which is what Gifford thought Buc's 40s. fee for *The Virgin Martyr* indicated—in Herbert's time cost the company only 10s. for a licence. (See ibid., pp. 29 and 32, under 7 July 1624 and 13 May 1629.) The exact duplicate of Buc's charges for *The Virgin Martyr* in 1620 is found a short time later in Herbert's charges for Drue's *Duchess of Suffolk* (1623/4) and Dekker, Webster, Ford, and Rowley's *Late Murder of the Son upon the Mother, or Keep the Widow Waking* (1624), both of which were new plays involving special difficulties for the Master of the Revels and both of which were charged for at the rate of 40s. *The Duchess of Suffolk* 'being full of dangerous matter was much reformed & for my paines this 2ᵈ Jan. 1623 I had 2 *li*'; *The Late Murder* (q.v.) involved some sort of controversy with another company about 'The same Trag:', and Herbert had to settle priority of performance.

Buc's licence for *The Virgin Martyr*, 6 October 1620, would seem to me, therefore, to indicate that at that time Dekker and Massinger's tragedy was a new play being read by Buc for the first time. The size of the fee and the phrase 'new reforming' indicate that there was censorable matter in the play, and that Buc objected to it, but that he accepted the revisions and that he charged a double fee to cover a second reading of the rejected and revised play. What was censored cannot, of course, be determined now.

The company at the Red Bull in 1620 was the company of His Majesty's Revels, successors to Queen Anne's company, for whom Dekker had previously written two or three plays. This troupe apparently still owned the play when it was published, for their name appears on the title-page of the 1622 edition, but the company appears to have broken up in 1623 (see above, i. 169–70), and the revisions of 1624 were probably for another company. Since the 1622, 1631, and 1651 editions of the play are substantially the same, the act added in 1624 must be lost.

Fleay's statement about *The Virgin Martyr* is as irresponsible as usual:

It is evidently a recasting by Massinger of an old Dekker play. The Hirtius and Spongius filth, ii. 1, 3, iii. 3, iv. 2, has not been touched by Massinger, and Dekker's hand is still discernible in bits retained in the scenes that have been rewritten. The original play was doubtless *Dioclesian*, acted at the Rose 1594, Nov. 16, but even then an old play, dating from 1591 at the latest. (*Biog. Chron.* i. 212–13.)

The guess about Massinger's revision of Dekker is based on the assumption that Buc's 1620 licence indicates an old play, an assumption we have seen to be almost surely false. There is no good reason to think that Massinger and Dekker did not collaborate in the usual way. The assertion that the *Dioclesian* of Henslowe's Diary was related to this play is sheer fancy, and most improbable on the face of it, since in *The Virgin Martyr* Dioclesian has a role of sixty-nine lines confined to the last scene of the last act.

The play acted in Dresden in 1626, 'eine Tragoedia von der Märtherin Dorothea' (Cohn, *Shakespeare in Germany*, p. cxv), may have been the Dekker and Massinger play, since the quarto of 1622 would have been easily available for touring companies.

Various attempts have been made to separate the work of Dekker and of Massinger in the play—none seems very convincing to me. Sykes (op. cit.) gives the most evidence for his impressions, and summarizes the conclusions of Boyle and Fleay.

Koeppel (op. cit.) shows that the source of the play was probably *De Probatis Sanctorum Historiis*, published at Cologne in 1576. The play was adapted by Benjamin Griffin in 1715 and published as *Injured Virtue; or, The Virgin Martyr*.

The Welsh Ambassador, or A Comedy in Disguises (*c.* 1623?)

MS.: The Cardiff Public Library. (Formerly No. 8719 in the Phillipps collection and before that the property of Joseph Haslewood.)

Edition: *The Welsh Embassador*, ed. H. Littledale and W. W. Greg. The Malone Society Reprints (1920).

Adams, J. Q. 'Hill's List of Early Plays in Manuscript', *Library*, Fourth Series, xx (1939), 86–88.
Greg, W. W. *Dramatic Documents from the Elizabethan Playhouses* (1931), pp. 279–82.
Lloyd, Bertram. 'The Authorship of *The Welsh Embassador*', *R.E.S.* xxi (1945), 192–201.
—— '*The Noble Soldier* and *The Welsh Embassador*', *R.E.S.* iii (1927), 304–7.

The large number of anticipatory stage directions in the Cardiff manuscript indicates that a prompter has prepared the piece for performance, but Dr. Greg points out (*Dramatic Documents*, p. 279) that there is no evidence of actual use as a prompt copy. He notes also that the manuscript—the anticipatory stage directions as well as text—was copied by the same scribe who prepared the Dyce MS. of Massinger's *Parliament of Love*. Since that play was licensed by Sir Henry Herbert 3 November 1624 for the Cockpit company, i.e. Lady Elizabeth's men, there is some reason to think *The Welsh Ambassador* was of approximately the same date and perhaps prepared for the same company. There is confirmation of the approximate date in lines 2161–3 of the play:

Clo: but now in [the raigne of this kinge heere in the] yeares 1621: 22 & 23 such a wooden fashion will come vpp that hee whoe walkes not wth a *Battoone* shalbee held noe gallant.

The Welsh Ambassador appears in the list of manuscript plays found among the papers of Abraham Hill (see Middleton, *The Conqueror's Custom*). The list seems to have been Hill's record of some bookseller's stock, set down between 1677 and 1703, but it is noticeable that nearly all the identifiable plays and playwrights of the list are Jacobean and Caroline. Hill's thirteenth entry reads, 'the Welch Embassador or a Comedy in disguises Tho Dekker'. Hill's entry almost certainly refers to the Cardiff play, since this sub-title is most appropriate for the action of a comedy in which from the first scene to the last Eldred, Edmond, and Penda wear two different sets of disguises, and since the huddled ending shows

their motives and characters to have been disguised as well as
their persons. Moreover, as Professor Adams pointed out (loc. cit.),
the dialogue of the play twice uses the sub-title: 'for a Comedy of
disguises letts then Arme' (line 772), and:

> I all this while
> sufferd this Comedy of welsh disguises
> still to goe on. . . .   (lines 2264–6)

The play has several times been confused with *The Welsh
Traveller* (itself sometimes miscalled *The Witch Traveller*), a play
known only from Sir Henry Herbert's licence entry of 10 May
1622. The title, however, is not appropriate for the Cardiff MS.,
since the Welshman in the play is an ambassador and not a
traveller. It does not seem likely, furthermore, that Sir Henry
would have misread the title.

Hill's attribution of 'the Welch Embassador or a Comedy in
disguises' to Thomas Dekker is interesting support for the attribution of the Cardiff play to Dekker by Bertram Lloyd, who had
apparently not seen Hill's list before his death. He found many
stylistic similarities to Dekker's work in the play and thought that
John Ford wrote III. 3 and v. 1. (*R.E.S.* xxi [1945], 192–201.)

Lloyd had previously noted (*R.E.S.* iii [1927], 304–7) so many
similarities between *The Noble Soldier* and *The Welsh Ambassador*
that he concluded the latter play to be simply a reworking of *The
Noble Soldier*. There can be little doubt that there is some close relationship between the two plays: not only are five major characters—
King, Queen or sweetheart, Wronged Lady, Prince, Noble Soldier
—the same, and the major elements of the two plots basically
identical except for the conclusions, but large sections of the
dialogue follow the same pattern, with phrases and sentences
exactly reproduced. Note *Noble Soldier* B_4^v–C_1 and *Welsh Ambassador* lines 387–407; *Noble Soldier* C_3–C_4 and *Welsh Ambassador*
lines 550–75; *Noble Soldier* D_1^v–D_2 and *Welsh Ambassador* lines
661–712. *The Noble Soldier* is the better play, it has a fuller development of the common plot elements, and it bears no trace of the
disguise plot of *The Welsh Ambassador*. These facts suggest that
The Noble Soldier may have been the prior play, but the relationship between the two needs fuller investigation.

Westward Ho!
with John Webster

See *The Elizabethan Stage*, iii. 295.

The White Moor (?)
(Lost)

In Abraham Hill's list of manuscript plays the second item is 'The white Moor   Tho Decker'. (See Middleton, *The Conqueror's Custom*.) This list seems to have been Hill's record of some bookseller's stock, set down between 1677 and 1703, but it is notable that nearly all the identifiable plays and playwrights are Jacobean and Caroline.

Though no play entitled *The White Moor* is extant, Professor J. Q. Adams points out in his discussion of the list (*Library*, Fourth Series, xx [1939], 80–81) that the story of Theagenes and Chariclea, or the white daughter of the black queen of Ethiopia, from Heliodorus' *Æthiopica*, was familiar to Jacobean and Caroline dramatists: there are records of a *Cariclia*, 1572 (*Elizabethan Stage*, iv. 146), and a *Queen of Ethiopia*, 1578 (ibid. ii. 135); the story is the source of Gough's *Strange Discovery*, published 1640; it is also the source of the anonymous manuscript play *The White Ethiopian*; Brome refers to the story at some length in his *The English Moor* (iv. 5).

The anonymous play *The White Ethiopian* (q.v.), which is extant only in a Harleian MS. at the British Museum, might possibly have been what Hill saw, but it seems unlikely, for the play of the B.M. MS. is nothing like Dekker's work. It is written in rhymed verse and is dramaturgically quite crude. The stage directions are of the literary type common with amateurs. It is difficult to imagine an old hand like Dekker displaying any one of these traits, and the combination of the three would seem to me to put his authorship quite out of the question.

The Whore of Babylon

See *The Elizabethan Stage*, iii. 296.

The Witch of Edmonton (1621, c. 1635)
with Ford and Rowley

Edition: *A Critical Edition of The Witch of Edmonton by Dekker, Rowley, and Ford, with Introduction, and Textual and Commentary Notes*. O. M. Green-Price, ed. (A dissertation at St. Hilda's College, Oxford, announced in 'Research in Progress', *P.M.L.A.* lxiii [1948], 181, No. 861.)

Bielefeld, Friedrich. *The Witch of Edmonton, by Rowley, Dekker, Ford &c. Eine Quellenuntersuchung* (1904).

Brown, Ivor. '*The Witch of Edmonton* at the Old Vic', *The Observer*, 13 December 1936, p. 15.

Hunt, Mary Leland. *Thomas Dekker, A Study* (1911), pp. 178–83.

Koeppel, Emil. *Quellen-Studien zu den Dramen George Chapman's, Philip Massinger's, und John Ford's* (1897), pp. 195–7.

M., D. L. 'The Witch of Edmonton', *The Nation and Athenaeum*, xxix (1921), 178–80.

Pierce, F. E. 'The Collaboration of Dekker and Ford', *Anglia*, xxxvi (1912), 289–312.

Sykes, H. D. 'The Authorship of The "Witch of Edmonton"', *N. & Q.* 151 (18 and 25 December 1926), 435–8 and 453–7.

West, Edward Sackville. 'The Significance of *The Witch of Edmonton*', *Criterion*, xvii (1937), 23–32.

1621, 27 Apr. S.R. 'William Butler. Entred for his Copie . . . *The wonderfull Discouery of ELIZ[ABETH] SAWYER a witch late of Edmonton*. by HENRY GOODCOALE vj^{d.}' (Arber, iv. 53.)

1621. The Wonderfull Discoverie of Elizabeth Sawyer, a Witch, late of Edmonton, her Conviction, Condemnation, and Death. Together with the relation of the Divel's Accesse to her, and their conference together. Written by Henry Goodcole, Minister of the Word of God, and her continual Visiter in the Gaole of Newgate. Published by Authority . . . 1621. (Reprinted in the Bullen–Lawrence reissue of the Dyce–Gifford, *Works of John Ford* [1895], i, pp. lxxxi–cvii.)

1621, 29 Dec. 'A warrant for allowance of xx^{tie} Marks for two plaies to the Princes Servaunts the one 27° Decembris *1621*, called the man in the moone drinks Clarrett the other the 29 of the same Moneth called the Witch of Edmonton, and for a reward for bothe xx nobles', 6 March 1621/2. (Murray, ii. 193, from MS. 515. No. 7, Inner Temple Library.)

1658, 21 May. S.R. 'Edward Blackmore Entred for his Copie . . . a booke called The Witch of Edmonton a TragiComedy by Will: Rowley &c.' (Greg, *Bibliography*, i. 66.)

1658. The Witch of Edmonton: A known true Story. Composed into A Tragi-Comedy By divers well-esteemed Poets; *William Rowley, Thomas Dekker, John Ford*, &c. Acted by the Princes Servants, often at the Cock-Pit in *Drury-Lane*, once at Court, with singular Applause. *Never printed till now.* [Woodcut of Mother Sawyer, the Black Dog, and Cuddy Banks in the pond.] . . . 1658.

c. 1677–1703. 'The Witch of Edmonton   Will. Sh.' (J. Q. Adams, 'Hill's List of Early Plays in Manuscript', *Library*, Fourth Series, xx [1939], 71–99. See Middleton, *The Conqueror's Custom.*)

The date of the play is easy to fix, since it must have been written before the performance of 29 December 1621, for which the Prince's men were paid, and after 19 April 1621, the date of Elizabeth Sawyer's execution (*Wonderful Discovery*, 1895 reprint, p. civ), which is treated in Act v of the play. The date of composition is pushed forward a bit by the authors' evident use of Goodcole's pamphlet (see Bielefeld, op. cit.), which was entered in the Stationers' Register 27 April 1621 and could scarcely have been used with such thoroughness before May. Fleay's suggestion (*Biog. Chron.* i. 231) that '*Midsummer-*Moon' in II. 1 and 'I'll never go to a Wench in the Dog-days again' in III. 1 would indicate original composition in July, is a good guess. Such topical compositions needed to be staged as soon after the event as possible.

There has been some confusion about the early performances of the play because stage historians did not know that Prince Charles's company, referred to on the title-page, had ever acted at the Cockpit in Drury Lane (*Biog. Chron.* i. 231; Murray, i. 236, n. 3), and they assumed, therefore, that Prince Charles's must be a mistake for the Lady Elizabeth's company or for Queen Henrietta's. Prince Charles's men did, however, occupy the Phoenix or Cockpit in Drury Lane about 1619–22 (see above, i. 202–5), and the payment for the court performance confirms the fact that *The Witch of Edmonton* belonged to their repertory. Since William Rowley had been a member of this company for about twelve years and an official representative as early as 1612 (see above, ii. 555–8), it is probable that he took the initiative in arranging the collaboration, though it does not necessarily follow that he wrote more of the play than Ford or Dekker. Since Rowley's familiar role was that of the simple clown (see above, ii. 556–7), it is not unlikely that he played 'Young Cuddy Banks, the Clown' in the original performances, and it has been generally assumed that he wrote the parts of the play in which Cuddy is prominent.

The 1658 edition of the play must have been printed from a manuscript prepared for a revival, for the prologue clearly refers to a revival:

> *But as the year doth with his plenty bring*
> *As well a latter as a former Spring;*

So has this Witch enjoy'd the first, and reason
Presumes she may partake the other season:
In Acts deserving name, the Proverb says,
Once good, and ever; *Why not so in Plays?*
Why not in this?

This prologue is signed '*Mr.* Bird', and the epilogue, delivered by Winifred, is signed '*PHEN.*', both of whom were actors in Queen Henrietta's company in the middle thirties. The status indicated by Bird's title, '*Mr.*', and by Ezekiel Fenn's performance of a female role suggests a revival of about 1635. (See above, i. 251–2.)

The odd statement of authorship on the title-page, 'By divers well-esteemed Poets; William Rowley, Thomas Dekker, John Ford, &c.', implies that the three dramatists had assistance in their composition. A similarly topical play prepared with equal collaborative haste three years later, presumably for the same company, was *The Late Murder of the Son upon the Mother, or Keep the Widow Waking*, written by the same three dramatists plus John Webster. The possibility that Webster also contributed to *The Witch of Edmonton* might repay investigation.

Numerous attempts to assign to the three dramatists their respective shares in the composition of the play have been made. All of them seem to me largely impressionistic, though they vary greatly in the elaborateness with which the impressions have been rationalized. Pierce (op. cit.) gives a table of his assignments compared with those of Fleay, Gifford, Rhys, Swinburne, and Ward. Sykes (op. cit.) uses the largest number of parallel passages, but the elaborateness of his division seems to me fantastic in the light of Dekker's explicit statement about the collaboration of these three dramatists on a similarly topical play three years later. (See Dekker, *The Late Murder of the Son upon the Mother, or Keep the Widow Waking*.)

The occurrence of the title in Hill's list suggests that a second manuscript of the play was extant after the Restoration, for presumably the printers of 1658 would have destroyed their copy. Hill's attribution of the play to Shakespeare may be derived, Adams suggested (op. cit.), from a confusion with *The Merry Devil of Edmonton*, several times attributed to Shakespeare.

The performances of the play by the Phoenix Society in 1921 and by the Old Vic in 1936 demonstrate its continued appeal.

Alfred Bunn's *Kinsmen of Naples* is said to be based on *The Witch of Edmonton*.

The Wonder of a Kingdom (> 1631)

Edition: Old English Plays, ed. C. W. Dilke (1814–15), iii. 1–98.

Bullen, A. H., ed. *The Works of John Day* (1881), i. 25–31.
Hunt, Mary Leland. *Thomas Dekker, A Study* (1911), pp. 183–6.
Golding, S. R. 'The Parliament of Bees', *R.E.S.* iii (1927), 280–304.

1623. 'Sir Henry Herbert observes that the play called Come See a
Wonder, "written by John Daye for a company of strangers,"
and represented Sept. 18, 1623, was "acted at the Red Bull,
and licensed without his hand to it, because they [i.e., this company of strangers] were none of the *four* companys".' (Malone,
Variorum, iii. 224. The entry seems to be garbled in Chalmers's
Apology for Believers. See Adams, *Herbert*, p. 25 and n. 6.)

1631, 16 May. S.R. 'Iohn Iackman. Entred for his Copie vnder the
hands of Sʳ Henry Herbert & Mʳ Kingston Warden a Comedy
called The Wonder of a Kingdome by Tho: Decker.' (Greg,
Bibliography, i. 40.)

1635/6, 24 Feb. S.R. 'Nich: Vavasour. Entred for his Copy vnder
the hands of Sʳ. Henry Herbert & mʳ Kingston warden (dated
the 7ᵗʰ of May 1631.) a Play called The Wonder of a Kingdome
by Tho: Decker.' (Ibid., p. 45.)

1636. The Wonder of a Kingdome. *Quod non Dant proceres, Dabit
Histrio. Written by* Thomas Dekker . . . 1636.

Fleay (*Biog. Chron.* i. 136), Greg (*Henslowe's Diary*, ii. 174–5),
and Chambers (*Elizabethan Stage*, iii. 299) think that *Come See a
Wonder* and *The Wonder of a Kingdom* are the same play, perhaps
with revisions. The similarity of the titles is suggestive, but by no
means conclusive. A more considerable suggestion of Day's connexion with the play is to be seen in the fact that Characters 2, 3,
7, 9, and 10 in his collection of twelve characters in dialogue published in 1641 under the title *The Parliament of Bees* are lifted
with suitable alterations and additions from four scenes of *The
Wonder of a Kingdom*: I. 3; III. 1; IV. 1; and IV. 2. Though the
names of the characters are all changed, much of the dialogue is
reproduced verbatim. Bullen, followed by Fleay and Hunt, thought
that Day must have been the original writer of these scenes and
that he merely reclaimed them for his *Parliament of Bees*; Chambers thinks that *The Parliament of Bees* came first, since he mis-
dates it 1608–16. (See Golding, op. cit., pp. 281–3.) The more
plausible conclusion seems to me that Day simply appropriated

suitable material where he found it, and that *The Wonder of a Kingdom* offered suitable material, as did *The Noble Soldier*. Until better evidence of Day's contribution to *The Wonder of a Kingdom* is offered, it seems to me best to accept Dekker's authorship, which is asserted not only twice in the Stationers' Register but on the title-page of the only contemporary edition as well.

Fleay (loc. cit.), followed by others, thought 'Gentili's "gift to charity" is certainly Alleyn's "God's gift" at Dulwich'. No one can say that Dekker (or Day) definitely did not have the actor Edward Alleyn in mind when he wrote his picture of a philanthropist, but I see little to suggest that he did. The charity in the play is much more extensive than Alleyn's College of God's Gift at Dulwich, and Gentili shows nothing in common with the actor except philanthropy. Gentili mentions nothing of the stage or anything connected with it; he speaks at length of his resolute bachelorhood, whereas Alleyn married Henslowe's stepdaughter in 1592, and six months after her death in June 1623 he married the daughter of John Donne as his second, or perhaps third, wife. (See above, ii. 346–9, and Greg, *Henslowe's Diary*, ii. 5.) Fleay thought that his identification of Alleyn was confirmed by the Latin motto on the title-page of the 1636 quarto of *The Wonder of a Kingdom*, 'Quod non Dant proceres, Dabit Histrio'. The Gentili story seems too much subordinated for this to apply; moreover the same Latin motto appears on the title-page of Jonson's *Every Man in His Humour*, 1601, of his *Cynthia's Revels*, 1601, of Rowley's *All's Lost by Lust*, 1633, and no doubt on divers others I do not remember.

Fleay thought that the omission of nine characters of the play from the dramatis personae of the first quarto indicated that the play had been altered, presumably in connexion with Day's work, since the omitted characters appear chiefly in scenes which Fleay claimed for Day. This is misleading, for other characters in the scenes claimed for Day are found in the dramatis personae; it is only minor ones who have been omitted, most of them characters with only generic names—broker, soldier, apothecary, &c.

Another odd connexion of the play with Rowley's *All's Lost by Lust*, in addition to the title-page motto, is the appearance of the same prologue in the first quarto of each play, with surprisingly few variants. The prologue is the usual theatrical one and not particularly appropriate to either play. Since the plays do not seem to have been published, printed, or licensed by the same stationers, it seems unlikely that a confusion could have occurred in the printing-house. It is possible that they came from the same theatre and that the company had used the same prologue for

both. If so, *The Wonder of a Kingdom* would then have been performed by Queen Henrietta's company at the Phoenix. Conceivably the Latin quotation which is found on the title-pages of
both plays was written on the manuscripts in the same theatre,
though this does not seem likely.

The play has generally been dated 1623 on the assumption that
it is the play entitled *Come See a Wonder*, which was licensed by
Sir Henry Herbert in that year as by John Day. If this identification is rejected, I know of no dating evidence before the Stationers'
Register entry of May 1631.

SIR JOHN DENHAM
1615–1668/9

Banks, Theodore Howard, Jr., ed. *The Poetical Works of Sir John
Denham* (1928), pp. 1–57.

Sir John Denham is known primarily as a poet, wit, and courtier, but he did write one play, translate an act of another, and
write a prologue for an early Restoration court performance of
Jonson's *Silent Woman*. He was the son of Sir John Denham, a
prominent lawyer and judge who lived in Essex but who was
serving, at the time of the poet's birth, as Chief Baron of the
Exchequer in Ireland. The poet was born in Dublin in 1615, but he
was brought back to England while still an infant. (Langbaine, *An
Account of the English Dramatick Poets* [1691], p. 126, and Banks,
Denham, pp. 2–3.) His early schooling is unknown, but he was
entered at Lincoln's Inn in April 1631, and at Trinity College,
Oxford, in November of the same year. Anthony à Wood says
he was examined for the B.A., but there is no record that he took
the degree. (*Athenæ Oxon.*, Bliss ed. iii. 824.) At Oxford his lifelong mania for gambling seems to have been developed. (Banks,
Denham, pp. 3–4.)

In June 1634 Denham was married to Anne Cotton in London,
and in the same year he began the study of law at Lincoln's Inn,
whence he was called to the Bar 29 January 1638/9. About this
time his father died, and Denham inherited a fair estate, which
Aubrey says he gambled away. (Ibid., pp. 4–6.) Probably Denham's literary activities began before, or shortly after, he came to
Lincoln's Inn, but his first publication was his tragedy, *The
Sophy*, in 1642.

At the beginning of the wars Denham was High Sheriff of Surrey
and Governor of Farnham Castle, but his military career was not

glorious, and he was a prisoner in London at the end of 1642. In this year the first edition of *Cooper's Hill* appeared, but little of the activities of its author are known until he again appeared a prisoner in London in January 1645/6, after the fall of Dartmouth. He was exchanged, and for a time was with Henrietta Maria in France, but he returned to take part in the negotiations between Parliament and the imprisoned King. In 1647 and 1648 he was in London, often concerned with the King's cipher correspondence. For the next four years he was with the exiled court, serving in various capacities and maintaining his reputation as a desperate gambler. (Banks, *Denham*, pp. 6–15.)

In the succeeding years before the Restoration Denham spent some time with the Earl of Pembroke at Wilton House and was occupied with minor Royalist missions, and in 1658 he returned to the Continent as guardian and companion for the Earl of Pembroke's heir. (Ibid., pp. 15–17.) Shortly after the Restoration he was made Surveyor of the Works in succession to Inigo Jones, and he received other rewards for loyalty. (Ibid., pp. 17–21.)

Denham's last years were clouded by his marriage, 25 May 1665, to Margaret Brooke, the young mistress of the Duke of York. His subsequent madness was popularly attributed to jealousy of his wife and the Duke. Denham recovered, and in January 1666/7 his wife died amid widespread rumours that she had been poisoned. Denham himself died 10 March 1668/9. (Ibid., pp. 21–26.)

Horace (> 1667)

The fifth act of Mrs. Katherine Philips's translation of Corneille's *Horace*, first published in its entirety in 1669, was translated by Denham. See P. W. Souers, *The Matchless Orinda* (1931), pp. 195, 229.

The Sophy (1641 ?)

Edition: Theodore Howard Banks, Jr., ed., *The Poetical Works of Sir John Denham* (1928), pp. 45–47 and 232–309.

Harbage, Alfred. *Cavalier Drama* (1936), pp. 131–2.

1642, 6 Aug. S.R. Thomas Walkley entered for his copy 'two bookes vizt. [1] A Tragedy called The Sophy . . . both of them by Mr Iohn Denham'. (Greg, *Bibliography*, i. 54.)

1642. The Sophy. As it was acted at the Private House in Black Friars by his Majesties Servants . . . 1642.

1649/50, 4 Feb. S.R. Humphrey Moseley entered for his copy 'all the Right & Interest of the Said M^r walkeley in a play called The Sophy a tragedy written by Mr Iohn Denham Esqr.' (Ibid., p. 59.)

1660, 12 Dec. Davenant was granted the privilege 'of reformeing some of the most ancient Playes that were playd at Blackfriers and of makeinge them, fitt, for the Company of Actors appointed vnder his direction'. Among the plays listed is 'the Sophy'. (Nicoll, *History of Restoration Drama*, 3rd ed. [1940], pp. 314–15.)

1667, 19 Aug. S.R. Henry Herringman entered for his copy by virtue of an assignment from Anne Moseley, widow and executrix of Humphrey Moseley, several books including: '[9] And also, One Booke or Copie, Intituled, Coopers Hill, a Poem. The Sophie, A Tragedy. The Destruccõn of Troy. . . .' (Ibid., p. 71.)

1667/8, 9 Feb. S.R. Henry Herringman entered for his copy 'A Copie or Booke Intituled Poems and Translations wth the Sophy. written by the Honorable Sr Iohn Denham knight of the Bath'. (Ibid.)

1668. Poems And Translations, With The Sophy. Written by the Honourable Sir *John Denham* Knight of the *Bath* . . . 1668.

1671. Poems And Translations, With The Sophy . . . 1671.

1684. Poems And Translations, With The Sophy . . . 1684.

In his account of Sir John Denham, Anthony à Wood says of this play:

> In the latter end of the year 1641 he published the tragedy called *The Sophy*, which took extremely much and was admired by all ingenious men, particularly by Edm. Waller of Beaconsfield, who then said of the author, that he broke out like the Irish rebellion, threescore thousand strong, when no body was aware, or in the least suspected it. (*Athenæ Oxonienses*, Bliss ed. iii. 824.)

If Wood was using 'published' in its usual sense, he was wrong, for the title-page of the first edition bears the date 1642, and it was not entered in the Stationers' Register until August of that year. It is generally assumed, however, that Wood meant performed, and in this he may have been right, though there is no other evidence to support him. If Waller's remark had special point because of the proximity of the two events which it compared, then Denham's play would have been produced in late October or November of 1641. The fact that *The Sophy* does not appear in the list of plays of the King's company protected from the publishers by the Lord Chamberlain on 7 August 1641 (see above, i. 65–66), suggests that on that date the play had not yet come into the possession of the company, or else that they did not value it highly.

A court performance of the play has been claimed on the grounds of the 'Prologue at Court' and 'Prologue at the Fryers', which Banks printed in *The Poetical Works of Sir John Denham*, p. 232 n. He said that the two prologues were found 'In the 1642 edition, between the *dramatis personae* and the text of the play.' (Ibid.) There must be some mistake here. The two prologues are those found in all the copies I have seen of Habington's *Queen of Aragon*, 1640, but they are not in any of the four copies of the 1642 *Sophy* which I have examined. Professor Banks wrote to me saying that the 'Prologue at Court' and 'Prologue at the Fryers' are not found in his own copy of *The Sophy*, 1642, and that he must conclude that they got into his notes through an error.

Various commentators have said that the play is based on the account in Thomas Herbert's *A Relation of Some Years Travel Begun Anno 1626, into Afrique and the Greater Asia*, and J. H. Walter asserts in an article on *Revenge for Honour (R.E.S.* xiii [1937], 425–37) that Denham used the edition of 1634, pp. 100–4. This passage does not resemble the play any more closely than the version in the edition of 1638 (pp. 173–6), but to me the notable fact is the large amount of material used by Denham which is found in neither version. Perhaps he was more fertile than I imagine, but the crowding of material in the play, especially in the swollen fourth and fifth acts, and its rather simple narrative character suggest that Denham may have known some version of the story differing from either of these accounts.

The slight resemblance of the play to *Othello* and in particular of Haly to Iago certainly does not provide the clear indication of imitation which has sometimes been asserted.

There are allusions to the play in the verses by 'Jo. Leigh' before William Cartwright's *Comedies, Tragi-comedies, with Other Poems*, 1651; in Samuel Butler's 'A Panegyric upon Sir John Denham's Recovery from his Madness' (René Lamar, ed., *Samuel Butler: Satires and Miscellaneous Poetry and Prose* [1928], pp. 120–2); in *Scarron's Comical Romance*, 1676 (p. 39); and in the anonymous 'Session of the Poets' (*Poems on Affairs of State, from the time of Oliver Cromwell to the Abdication of King James the Second*, 1697, i. 222). Allusions to Denham as a dramatist, which must be based on *The Sophy*, are found in commendatory verses by Thomas Pestell for Benlowes's *Theophila*, 1652 (H. Buchan, ed., *The Poems of Thomas Pestell*, pp. 83–86), and in *Scarron's Comical Romance*, 1676 (p. 17).

Robert Baron's *Mirza* [1647?, 1655?] uses the same story as
The Sophy, but Baron said that he did not know of Denham's play
until three acts of *Mirza* had been written, and T. H. Banks reports (*Poetical Works of Sir John Denham*, p. 46 n.) that a close
comparison of the two plays shows many plot differences and no
verbal parallels. Baron acknowledged his debt to Jonson's *Catiline*, and Jesse Franklin Bradley has traced the indebtedness
('Robert Baron's Tragedy of *Mirza*', *M.L.N.* xxxiv [1919],
402–3).

SIR KENELM DIGBY
1603–65

There is no evidence that Sir Kenelm Digby, the diplomat,
scientist, author, sailor, and literary patron, was ever a dramatist,
but two of his fragments of translations or proposed translations
have got into play lists. For his career see the *D.N.B.* and Allardyce Nicoll, 'Sir Kenelm Digby, Poet, Philosopher, and Pirate of
the Restoration', *The Johns Hopkins Alumni Magazine*, xxi
(1933), 330–50.

Amyntas (?)
(Lost)

The only trace of a translation of *Amyntas* by Sir Kenelm Digby
is found in the manuscript dedication to the 'lady Mrs. V. S.'
among his papers, once in the possession of Henry Bright. (*Poems
from Sir Kenelm Digby's Papers, in the Possession of Henry A.
Bright*, Roxburghe Club [1877], pp. 1–3.) Sir Kenelm says:

> To obey you (that haue all power ouer me) j send you this rugged
> translation, wch oweth you more of his being then vnto me: for the
> liking that j discouered in you to such compositions, was my first
> motiue to make Amyntas speake English . . . for they [these papers]
> were begotten vpon the sea, when during the tedious expectation of a
> fauourable wind. . . .

The manuscript, from which the signature and date have been
torn off, is endorsed 'The dedication of Amyntas'. The anonymous
translation of *Amyntas* printed in 1628 does not seem, according
to George F. Warner, who annotated the edition of the manuscripts, like the work of Sir Kenelm.

Pastor Fido (?)
(Fragment)

A fragment of a translation of Guarini's *Il Pastor Fido* is found among the papers of Sir Kenelm Digby, once in the possession of Henry Bright. (*Poems from Sir Kenelm Digby's Papers, in the Possession of Henry A. Bright* [1877], pp. 4–5.) The translation, fifty-four lines from II. 5, is signed 'Ken. Digby'. There is no evidence that Sir Kenelm ever completed a translation of the play.

THOMAS DRUE (Drew, Drewe)
fl. 1623

The only certain evidence of a dramatist named Thomas Drue is in the Stationers' Register entry of November 1629 for *The Duchess of Suffolk*, which was published anonymously in 1631. When Sir Henry Herbert licensed the play for the Palsgrave's company in January 1623/4 he called the author 'Mr. Drew'.

The question is, how many Drews were connected with the drama from 1616 to the closing of the theatres? Various answers to this question have been given directly or by implication. Certainly there was an actor named Thomas Drewe who was associated with Queen Anne's company and the Red Bull theatre from about 1613, at least until 1622. (See above, ii. 427–8.) Probably he is the Thomas Drew whose children appear in the registers of St. James's, Clerkenwell, the church of the Red Bull parish (ibid.), but this man was not necessarily the actor, for the St. James's registers do not give occupations. If the Red Bull actor wrote *The Duchess of Suffolk*, as W. J. Lawrence was so sure he did ('Found: A Missing Jacobean Dramatist', *T.LS.*, 23 March 1922, p. 191), he must have transferred his allegiance from the Red Bull company to the Palsgrave's men at the Fortune.

Another Thomas Drewe in this same period translated from the French *Daniel Ben Alexander, the Converted Jew*, 1621. This man could conceivably have written *The Duchess of Suffolk*, but his translation is not the sort of work Jacobean actors are found doing, and it does not seem likely that he was the player at the Red Bull.

A 'Mr. Drew' apparently wrote an unnamed tragedy in September 1624, on the same subject as the lost play by Dekker, Ford, Rowley, and Webster, entitled *A Late Murder of the Son upon the Mother, or Keep the Widow Waking*. In the transcript of Sir Henry

Herbert's office-book in the Folger Shakespeare Library is entered, immediately after the Ford–Dekker–Rowley–Webster play,

The same Trag: writt: M^r. Drew & allowed for the day after theirs because they had all manner of reason. (Halliwell-Phillipps's Scrap-Books, *Fortune*, p. 149.)

Presumably this rather cryptic entry means that two companies had dramatists writing up the same sensational London story at the same time, and that for an unknown reason Herbert gave a one-day head start to the Dekker–Ford–Rowley–Webster play. That play (q.v. under Dekker) was presumably written for the Red Bull theatre, and the Fortune would be a good guess for the Drew play. This 'M^r. Drew' was probably the Thomas Drew who wrote *The Duchess of Suffolk* for the company at the Fortune some eight months before, since Herbert called him Mr. Drew in both instances.

The Woman's Mistaken was entered on the Stationers' Register 9 September 1653 as 'by. Drew, & Dauenport'. (Greg, *Bibliography*, i. 60–61.) This Drew might also have been the author of the play licensed by Herbert in 1624, for his collaborator Davenport (q.v.) was writing plays in 1624. Indeed, it is conceivable that *The Woman's Mistaken* could be the very play which Sir Henry Herbert licensed without giving its name.

The melodrama *The Bloody Banquet* was published in 1639 as by 'T. D.', and Lawrence did not hesitate to announce that 'T. D.' certainly stood for Thomas Drue. (Op. cit.) It may be, but other scholars have had other candidates.

Finally, there was a Thomas Drue who was made a Gentleman Waiter to the King in December 1635. (*M.S.C.* ii. 376.)

Though there are no chronological difficulties involved, it nevertheless seems to me highly improbable that all these records should concern one man. The translator of *Daniel Ben Alexander, the Converted Jew* does not seem likely to have been a Red Bull actor, nor does he seem to me a good candidate for the author of the plays. The gentleman waiter seems to me a possible, but not a likely, translator; I should think it most improbable that he was either an ex-actor or the writer of melodramas; both activities are a little vulgar for such courtly distinction. I'd guess the Thomas Drue sworn waiter to be a man referred to in none of the other records.

The real temptation is to identify the Red Bull actor and the writer of melodrama. Such an identification can be neither proved nor disproved, but Lawrence's intuition may have been right.

The Bloody Banquet (> 1639)

Edition: John S. Farmer, ed., *The Bloody Banquet By T. D.*, Tudor Facsimile Texts (1914).

Cole, George Watson. 'Bibliographical Ghosts', *Papers of the Bibliographical Society of America*, xiii (1919), 98–112.
—— 'The Bloody Banquet', *T.L.S.*, 25 February 1926, p. 142.
Forsythe, R. S. 'The Bloody Banquet', *T.L.S.*, 22 April 1926, p. 303.
Greg, W. W. 'The Bloodie Banquet', *T.L.S.*, 24 December 1925, p. 897.
Lloyd, Bertram. 'The Bloody Banquet', *T.L.S.*, 29 April 1926, p. 323.
McManaway, James G. 'Latin Title-Page Mottoes as a Clue to Dramatic Authorship', *Library*, Fourth Series, xxvi (1945), 28–36.
Oliphant, E. H. C. 'The Bloodie Banquet', *T.L.S.*, 17 December 1925, p. 882.

1620. The frequently alleged edition of this date is a ghost.
1630. The frequently alleged edition of this date is a ghost.
1639, 10 Aug. Among the plays in the repertory of the King and Queen's Young Company at the Cockpit and forbidden to other companies by the Lord Chamberlain is 'The bloody banquett'. (See above, i. 330–1.)
1639. The Bloodie Banqvet. A Tragedie. *Hector adest secumque Deos in proelia ducit. Nos haec novimus esse nihil.* By T. D. . . . 1639.

There are a number of confusions and uncertainties about this play, beginning with the number and dates of editions. Various assertions that there were editions of 1620 and 1630 are mistaken. So far as can be determined now, only one edition—that of 1639— ever existed. The others are erroneous reconstructions of the cropped title-page of the copy of the 1639 edition in the British Museum, a distortion shown very clearly in Farmer's facsimile edition. The confusion was fully exposed by George Watson Cole in his 'Bibliographical Ghosts'. (See above.)

There is also great confusion in the attributions of the play. It has been claimed for Dekker and Middleton (Oliphant, op. cit.), for Davenport (Hazlitt, *Play Collector's Manual*, p. 27, and Mc-Manaway, op. cit.), for Thomas Barker (in some of the seventeenth-century play catalogues), and for Thomas Drue (by Fleay, *Biog. Chron.* i. 162, and others). The case for Dekker and Middleton is based mostly on parallels and repeated words and phrases—the flimsiest kind of 'evidence'—and on the assertion that Archer's attribution of the play in his list of 1656 to Thomas Barker must have been a misreading of Thomas Dekker. Archer made so many irresponsible misattributions in his 1656 list that it seems a little foolish to assume that he had good grounds for his attribution of *The Bloody Banquet* to Dekker which a printer's error made into Barker. I see no reasonable case for Dekker or Middleton.

The attribution to Robert Davenport was apparently first made only because the 'T. D.' on the title-page could have been a mistake for 'R. D.', and later reasserted because in the Cockpit repertory list of 1639 *The Bloody Banquet* follows plays of Davenport's authorship. Neither reason seems very weighty. McManaway noted (op. cit., pp. 34–35) that one of the Latin mottoes on the title-page of *The Bloody Banquet* is the same as that on the manuscript of *Dick of Devonshire* and said:

> I find considerable internal evidence that it [*Bloody Banquet*] and *Dick of Devonshire* are from the same pen, and that the writer was indeed Robert Davenport.

He cites none of the evidence, however, and students must wait for the demonstration. So far, the evidence for Davenport is slight.

Fleay said (*Biog. Chron.* i. 162) that 'there can be little doubt that "T. D.," the author, was Thomas Drue'. Fleay likewise gave no evidence, though it can be said that 'T. D.' were the initials of Drue, as they were not of Davenport, Barker, or Middleton *cum* Dekker. Greg pointed out (*Edinburgh Bibliographical Society Transactions*, ii, Part 4 [1946], 317) that after Archer had attributed the play to Thomas Barker in his list of 1656, Kirkman—a friend of William Beeston, who asserted his ownership of the prompt manuscript in 1639—returned to the initials 'T. D.' in his own lists of 1661 and 1671.

The play is dramaturgically very crude and old-fashioned. It is difficult to imagine Middleton or Dekker or even Davenport producing anything so unskilled, even bathetic. In iv. 2 (E_4^v), the Tyrant, after announcing that he is about to burst with torment, delivers himself of the immortal lines,

> Tis spring-tyde in my Gall, all my blood's bitter,
> Puh, lungs too.

Such stuff might have been produced at the Red Bull when Drue was acting with Queen Anne's men there. (Several of the plays in Beeston's 1639 list were more than twenty years old, and at least one in this list, as well as others known to have been performed at the Phoenix, had been originally written for Queen Anne's men.)

The evidence for Thomas Drue's authorship, then, is meagre, but this attribution seems to me to raise fewer difficulties than any of the others which have been proposed.

No significant evidence for dating the play has been found. Since it was in the Cockpit repertory in 1639, it must have been either composed for that theatre or brought to it by one of the companies who came to the Cockpit from other theatres, like Queen Anne's from the Red Bull, or Prince Charles's (I) from the same theatre. The latter alternative seems more likely because of the crude and unsophisticated character of the play. No companies came to the Cockpit from other theatres after the early twenties.

The play is shorter than most—about 1,900 lines—and this fact led McManaway (op. cit., p. 35) to suggest that it was printed in a bad quarto. I have not examined the quarto closely for dislocations, but it might repay investigation.

The Duchess of Suffolk (1623/4)

Mann, Francis Oscar, ed. *The Works of Thomas Deloney* (1912), pp. 389–93, 587–8.

Neill, J. K. 'Thomas Drue's *Dutches of Suffolke* and the Succession', *M.L.N.* xlviii (1933), 97–99.

1623/4, 2 Jan. 'For the Palsgrave's Company; *The History of the Dutchess of Suffolk*; which being full of dangerous matter was much reformed by me; I had two pounds for my pains: Written by Mr. Drew.' (Adams, *Herbert*, p. 27.)

1623/4, 2 Jan. 'For the Palsgraves company.   Ianuary
The history of the Dutchess of Suffolk by M^r [Drewe being full of dange]rous matter was much reformed & for my [paines this 2^d Jan. 1623 I had 2 *li.*]' (From a transcript in a nineteenth-century hand, possibly that of Craven Ord, of Sir Henry Herbert's office-book. The extracts have been cut out and pasted into Halliwell-Phillipps's Scrap-Books, now at the Folger Shakespeare Library. This one is in *Kemp*, p. 153.)

1629, 13 Nov. S.R. Jasper Emery entered for his copy 'vnder the handes of Sr Hen: Herbert and mr Purfoote warden, A play Called The Duches of Suffolke written by Tho. Drue'. (Greg, *Bibliography*, i. 37.)

1631. The Life Of The Dvtches Of Svffolke. As it hath beene divers and sundry times acted, with good applause. . . . 1631.

This is one of the spate of plays licensed by the Palsgrave's men

after their opening at the new Fortune, following the disastrous
fire which burned the theatre and the plays of their repertory in
December 1621. (See above, i. 141 and 149–51.) From 27 July 1623
to 3 November 1624 the Palsgrave's men brought to the Master of
the Revels the largest number of plays licensed by him for any
company in a similar period during his entire incumbency. The
company was struggling to build up a new repertory. Most of the
plays were probably poor things, for of the fourteen plays licensed
in this period of fifteen months, only *The Duchess of Suffolk* is now
extant.

The character of the 'dangerous matter' which Herbert 'much
reformed' is not apparent. It was not matter touching on the
succession, as Miss Albright thought (*Dramatic Publication in
England, 1580–1640*, p. 188), for, as Mr. Neill pointed out (op. cit.),
the Duchess of Suffolk, who is the protagonist of the play, is not
the one concerned in the succession, but her stepmother, the widow
of Charles Brandon, who later married Richard Bertie and became
a fugitive from religious persecution on the Continent. The play
concerns her marriage with her servant, Richard Bertie, her long
and pitiful flight from religious persecution by Gardiner and
Bonner, and her triumphant return to England on the accession
of Queen Elizabeth. The story appears to have been popular, for it
was told by Foxe (*Acts and Monuments*, ed. 1641, iii. 926–30), by
Holinshed (*Chronicles of England, Scotland, and Ireland*, ed. 1587,
iii. 1142–5), and in a ballad by Thomas Deloney called 'The
Dutchesse of *Suffolkes* Calamatie', printed in his *Strange Histories*,
1602 (Mann, ed., pp. 389–93), and often reprinted. (Roxburghe and
Pepys collections.) Though Drue may well have known these
accounts, they cannot be called, individually or collectively, his
principal source. His details, emphasis, and proportions are quite
different from those of Foxe and Deloney. Holinshed simply reprints Foxe's account.

Possibly some interest in Drue's play is indicated by the entry
in the Stationers' Register 14 December 1624 of a ballad called
'*Duchesse of SUFFOLKE*', with a number of others. This might be
a new ballad or a renewal of Deloney's old one.

In April 1600 Henslowe was paying for a play by William
Haughton called *The English Fugitives*. Collier guessed (*The Diary
of Philip Henslowe* [1845], p. 168, n. 2) that this lost—and apparently uncompleted—play concerned the Duchess of Suffolk, and
his conjecture has sometimes been accepted (e.g. E. M. Albright,
op. cit., p. 188 n.). Collier's assertion, of course, was a pure guess,
for the Duchess was not unique as an English fugitive, but it

might be significant that Drue wrote his play for the Palsgrave's men, the successors of the Admiral's men, who owned Haughton's manuscript—if it was ever completed.

Unknown Play (1624)

1624, Sept. 'A new Trag: call: a Late Murther of the sonn upon the mother writt: by Mr Forde Webster & this   Sept. 1624. 2^{li}.
    'The same Trag: writt: M^r. Drew & allowed for the day after theirs because they had all manner of reason.' (Halliwell-Phillipps's Scrap-Books, *Fortune*, p. 149, Folger Shakespeare Library.)

The above entry comes from an independent transcript of Sir Henry Herbert's office-book in a nineteenth-century hand—perhaps that of Craven Ord—which has been cut into strips and pasted into his scrap-books by J. O. Halliwell-Phillipps. The play here called 'a Late Murther of the sonn upon the mother' was actually by Dekker, Webster, Ford, and Rowley (see above, under Dekker), and is now lost, but it is rather well known from a lawsuit concerning its sub-plot. The second part of the entry, concerning Drue's play, was not copied by Malone or Chalmers and is therefore not to be found in Professor Adams's edition of the office-book. Herbert's entry is somewhat cryptic, but I should interpret it to mean that two different London companies, one playing at the Red Bull (where the Dekker–Webster–Ford–Rowley play was acted) and the other probably at the Fortune (the Red Bull's principal rival and the theatre for which Drue had written *The Duchess of Suffolk* some eight months before), had commissioned plays on the same sensational London murder and had brought them to be licensed at about the same time. Because the second company 'had all manner of reason', Herbert allowed both plays but gave the Red Bull troupe a one-day advantage. Both plays are lost.

It is possible that the unnamed play of Drue's which Sir Henry licensed in September 1624 is to be identified with *The Woman's Mistaken* (q.v.), entered in the Stationers' Register as by Drue and Davenport in 1653 and also lost. This, however, is pure speculation.

The Woman's Mistaken (?)
with Robert Davenport

See Robert Davenport.

WILLIAM DRUMMOND of Hawthornden
1585–1649

Joly, A. *William Drummond de Hawthornden* (1934).

Laing, David. 'A Brief Account of the Hawthornden Manuscripts in the possession of the Society of Antiquaries of Scotland; with Extracts containing several unpublished Letters and Poems of William Drummond of Hawthornden', *Transactions of the Society of Antiquaries of Scotland*, iv (1857), 57–72.

Masson, David. *Drummond of Hawthornden: The Story of His Life and Writings* (1873).

Simpson, Percy. 'The Genuineness of the Drummond Conversations', *R.E.S.* ii (1926), 42–50.

The Scottish poet of Hawthornden can scarcely be called a dramatist or even a man of notable theatrical interests, though he did preserve much theatrical information in his records of his famous conversations with Ben Jonson. He is included here as the author of at least part of the entertainment with which the city of Edinburgh welcomed Charles I in 1633.

William Drummond was born at Hawthornden 13 December 1585, son of the first laird of Hawthornden. He was sent to Edinburgh High School and the new University of Edinburgh, whence he received his M.A. in 1605. Shortly after, he was sent to the Continent to study law at Bourges and Paris; he returned to Scotland in 1609. (Masson, *Drummond of Hawthornden*, pp. 7–15.) In 1610 his father died, and he became laird of Hawthornden, never to return to his legal studies or to practise law. The rest of his life was spent mostly in quiet retirement at Hawthornden. His first published work was an elegy on the death of Prince Henry entitled *Tears on the Death of Mœliades*, 1613. Shortly after, appeared his *Poems*, 1616, and *Forth Feasting*, 1619, the latter a panegyric to King James on the occasion of his visit to Edinburgh in 1617. (Masson, op. cit., pp. 15–60.)

In 1618 Ben Jonson made his famous walking tour to Edinburgh, where he was banqueted by the city and made an honorary burgess and guild brother by the Town Council. (See *Ben Jonson*, i. 233–4.) About Christmas Jonson spent two or three weeks with Drummond at Hawthornden, and the Scottish poet recorded many of the remarks and opinions of his famous guest in a series of notes published in the 1711 edition of his *Works* (pp. 224–7) as '*Heads of a Conversation betwixt the Famous Poet* Ben Johnson, *and* William Drummond *of* Hawthornden, January, 1619'. (See *Ben Jonson*, i.

128 ff.) Four years later, in 1623, Drummond issued his collection of short religious poems and essays entitled *Flowers of Sion.*

Late in 1627 Drummond was granted patents for three years on a series of mechanical inventions, most of them for military purposes. (Masson, op. cit., pp. 156 ff.) There seems to be no other evidence of the workshop activities of this literary gentleman. More compatible with his known interests was his gift, in the same year, of 500 volumes from his library to the University of Edinburgh. (Masson, op. cit., pp. 166–71.)

When Charles I came to Edinburgh for his long-deferred coronation in 1633, the city prepared elaborate pageantry for the King's entry into his northern capital. This entertainment was set forth in some detail in the anonymous *Entertainment of the High and Mighty Monarch Charles, King of Great Britain, France, and Ireland into his Ancient and Royal City of Edinburgh, the fifteenth of June, 1633.* Since the speeches of this *Entertainment* were reprinted in Drummond's *Poems* of 1656 and his *Works* of 1711, it is commonly assumed that the *Entertainment* is his work.

During the troubled years of the Covenant and the Bishops' Wars, Drummond was cautiously sympathetic with the King and circulated various pieces of pro-Royalist verse and prose. (Masson, op. cit., pp. 228–322.) After the war began he became more anti-clerical, but seems not to have been seriously persecuted by the Covenanters. (Ibid., pp. 322–408.) He died on 4 December 1649 and was buried in the church of Lasswade, near Hawthornden. (Ibid., pp. 455–6.)

Drummond's *History of Scotland from the Year 1423 until the Year 1542* was published posthumously in 1655. In this volume was included a large selection of Drummond's letters and miscellaneous prose.

Collected Editions

Poems, By That most Famous Wit, William Drvmmond of Hawthornden (1656).

The most Elegant And Elabovrate Poems Of that Great Court-Wit, Mr William Drummond (1659). [Another issue of the 1656 edition.]

The Works Of William Drummond, Of Hawthornden. Consisting of Those which were formerly Printed, And Those which were design'd for the Press. Now Published from the Author's Original Copies (1711).

The Poems of William Drummond of Hawthornden (1790).

[Another issue] (1791).

The Poems of William Drummond of Hawthornden [Edited by Thomas Maitland and David Irving for the Maitland Club] (1832).

The Poems of William Drummond, of Hawthornden. With Life by Peter Cunningham (1833).

[Another issue] (1852).

The Poetical Works of William Drummond of Hawthornden. Edited by William B. Turnbull. (*Library of Old Authors*) (1856).

[Another issue] (1890).

The Poems of William Drummond of Hawthornden. Edited with a Memoir and Notes by Wm. C. Ward. (*Muses' Library.*) 2 vols. (1894).

The Poetical Works of William Drummond of Hawthornden with 'A Cypresse Grove'. Edited by L. E. Kastner. 2 vols. (1913).

The Entertainment of King Charles at Edinburgh (1633)

1633. The Entertainment Of The High And Mighty Monarch Charles King of *Great Britaine, France,* and *Ireland,* Into his auncient and royall City of Edinbvrgh, the fifteenth of *Iune,* 1633 . . . 1633.

1656. Poems, By That most Famous Wit, *William Drvmmond* Of Hawthornden . . . 1656. [Includes 'Speeches To The High And Excellent Prince, Charles, King of Great *Brittaine, France,* and *Ireland,* at His Entring His City of *Edenbvrgh:* Delivered from the Pageants the 15th of *June,* 1633'.]

1711. The Works Of William Drummond, Of Hawthornden . . . 1711. [Includes '*An intended SPEECH at the West Gate of* Edinburgh *to King* CHARLES I. Anno 1633'.]

The full entertainment given King Charles, 15 June 1633, on his entrance into Edinburgh for his Scottish coronation is found only in the anonymous edition of 1633. In the *Poems,* 1656, appear only the speeches to the King, all the descriptions—perhaps a third of the whole—being omitted. In the *Works* of 1711 the descriptions are also omitted, as well as a prose speech by a nymph which is included in *Poems.* (See Kastner, ed., *The Poetical Works of William Drummond of Hawthornden,* ii. 113–36.)

The anonymity of the 1633 publication and the fact that the editors of 1656 and 1711 reprint only the speeches suggest that Drummond did not devise the entire entertainment, or even write the descriptions, but that he wrote only the speeches, perhaps only the speeches in verse. This interpretation would accord with Drummond's position as a landed gentleman who seems to have lived rather a retired life. Except for this occasion of national celebration, there is no evidence that he ever had anything to do with pageants, shows, or plays.

WILLIAM DRURY

fl. 1616–41

Drury's plays were neither performed nor printed in England, and they do not properly fall within our province. Since he was an Englishman, however, a simple identification of the man and his plays is provided.

William Drury was an English Catholic who seems to have been in prison about the middle of the reign of James I. He indicates that he was released through the efforts of the influential Spanish ambassador, Gondomar, to whom *Alfredus* is dedicated. In 1618 he is found teaching poetry and rhetoric in the college for English Catholics at Douai. It was for the students at Douai that his three Latin plays were written. The date of his death is not known, though he is said to have died abroad. (*D.N.B.*)

Collected Editions

1628. Dramatica Poemata, Avthore D. Gvilielmo Drvræo Nobili Anglo. *Editio secunda ab ipso authore recognita, & multo quam prima auctior reddita.* Dvaci . . . 1628.

1641. Dramatica Poemata . . . Editio Ultima ab Ipso Auctore Recognita . . . *Antverpiæ,* 1641.

Alvredus sive Alfredus (1619)

1620. Alvredus sive Alfredus, Tragi-Comœdia ter exhibita in seminaris Anglorum Auaceno ab ejusdem collegii Juventute, Anno Domini M.DC.XIX. Douay, 1620.

1628. In *Dramatica Poemata,* 1628, *Alfredus* is the first of Drury's three Latin plays.

1641. Alvredvs sive Alfredvs Tragicomoedia. (Head-title in 1641 collection.)

The play concerns the history of Alfred the Great.

Mors (> 1620)

1620. Mors comœdia.

1628. In *Dramatica Poemata* of 1628, *Mors Comoedia* is the second of Drury's three Latin plays.

1641 Mors Comoedia. (Head-title in 1641 collection.)

The comedy is an allegorical farce of Death and the Devil. (See Francis Douce, ed., *The Dance of Death*, 1858, p. 156.)

Reparatus, sive Depositum (> 1628)

1628. *Reparatvs, sive Depositum Tragicocomoedia* is printed third in *Dramatica Poemata*, 1628.

1641. Reparatvs. sive. Depositvm Tragicomedia. Prima Pars. (Head-title in 1641 collection.)

JOHN EDWARDS (Edwardes)
1599/1600–<48

Edwards was born 27 February 1599/1600. He was admitted to the Merchant Taylors' School as a Londoner in 1613 and in 1617 was awarded a Merchant Taylors' scholarship to St. John's College, Oxford, where he matriculated 24 April 1618. He received degrees of B.A. 30 April 1621, M.A. 4 May 1625, and B. and D. Med. 13 June 1639. From 1632 to 1634 he was Headmaster of the Merchant Taylors' School, but in 1635 he was back at Oxford as one of the Proctors of the University. In 1636 he became Sedleian Professor of Natural Philosophy, a post from which he was ejected by the Parliamentary Visitors 26 May 1648. (Simmonds, *Merchant Taylor Fellows*, pp. 17–18, and *Alumni Oxon.* ii. 448.)

Saturnalia (?)
(Lost)

The play is known only from Mark J. Simmonds's statement in his account of Edwards that he 'wrote a comedy *Saturnalia*'. (Op. cit., p. 18.) This cannot have been the *Saturnalia* which was part of *The Christmas Prince* at St. John's in 1607, since Edwards was only seven at that time. Simmonds does not indicate the source of his information.

MILDMAY FANE, Second Earl of Westmorland

1601/2–1665/6

Harbage, Alfred. 'An Unnoted Caroline Dramatist', *Stud. Phil.* xxxi (1934), 28–36. (Condensed in his *Cavalier Drama* [1936], pp. 198–202.)

Leech, Clifford, ed. *Mildmay Fane's Raguaillo D'Oceano, 1640, and Candy Restored, 1641 (Materials for the Study of the Old English Drama)* (1938), pp. 4–59. (Leech corrects Harbage.)

Mildmay Fane, son of Francis, first Earl of Westmorland, was born 24 January 1601/2, according to the statement in his manuscript Latin autobiography (Leech, op. cit., p. 9) and a manuscript note in his copy of his own *Otia Sacra*, which was once owned by Thorn-Drury. (See G. Thorn-Drury, *A Little Ark*, p. 18.) In 1616, according to his autobiography, but according to the Cambridge records in 1618 (*Alumni Cantab.* ii. 120), he entered Emmanuel College, Cambridge, where he took an M.A. in 1619. The following year he is found in the Parliamentary returns as a member for Peterborough, but this seems not to have interfered with the young nobleman's years abroad, for he says in his autobiography that he left England for two years' travel in the same year. (Leech, op. cit., pp. 9–10.)

After his return Fane was admitted to Lincoln's Inn 7 August 1622. (*Records of the Honourable Society of Lincoln's Inn*, i. 191.) Three years later, in 1625, he was elected a Knight of the Shire and served in the Parliaments of 1625–6 and 1627–8, having been knighted by King Charles at the time of his coronation. (Leech, op. cit., p. 10.)

The discussion of his marriages in the autobiography makes it apparent that in 1626 Fane must have married Grace, daughter of Sir William Thornhurst of Herne, Kent. By this lady he had six children—the last of whom had the King for godfather—before she died in or about 1636. On 23 March 1628/9, about two years after his marriage, Fane succeeded his father as Earl of Westmorland. Leech records a number of his activities in public affairs in the fourteen years before the wars began. (Op. cit., pp. 10–13.)

The Earl's plays, all existing only in manuscript, were written between 1640 and 1650, all of them evidently intended to be produced in his own household, and two of them including elaborate directions and sketches for staging and scenery. Two plays have casts (ibid., pp. 31, 50); another is introduced by a statement that it was prepared to be presented 'at Apthorpe by the youth and Servants their'. (Ibid., p. 42.) Evidently the Earl had some sort of a private theatre at Apthorpe in which—for a time, at any rate —he was greatly interested. The staging he planned in at least two of the plays was unusually elaborate, and one of his sketches provides the first known instance of flat revolving wings in England. It is not known where he got his ideas or experience, but Leech (op. cit., p. 56) notes his extraordinary use of Italian names and suggests an untraced familiarity with Italian writing. Possibly he knew something of Italian staging as well.

Westmorland was active in the King's cause for a number of months before and immediately after the outbreak of hostilities, but late in August 1642 he was arrested and confined to the Tower by the Lords. For at least a year and a half the Earl was in the Tower or restricted to London. From 1643 onwards, there are a number of petitions from him requesting his liberty or concerning his fines and sequestration. (Ibid., pp. 13–17.)

In 1648 he published a book of verse under the title *Otia Sacra*, and thereafter Leech found no significant records of his activities until he was made Lord-Lieutenant of Northamptonshire at the Restoration. He died 12 February 1665/6. (Ibid., pp. 17–18.)

According to Leech (op. cit., pp. 19–23), Westmorland's works consist of *Otia Sacra*, 1648, his only published volume; an incomplete prose translation of an Italian treatise, *Of the Art of Well gouerning A people*, in MS. Add. 34251 at the British Museum; his short Latin autobiography in MS. Add. 34220 at the British Museum, apparently composed about 1662; a manuscript volume entitled *Fugitive Poetry*, once in the Westmorland library but not traceable now; four pieces of short miscellaneous verse; and the plays noted below.

Candia Restaurata, or Candy Restored (1640/1)

MSS.: 'Candia Restaurata Presented in a Shewe at Apthorpe the 12th of February 1640 to the Lord and lady of that place by some of their owne Children and famely', Huntington Library MS. H.M. 771; 'Candia Restaurata. Presented in a shew at Apthorpe the 12th of ffebruary 1640 to the Lord and Lady of that place, by some of their owne Children and famelie', B.M. MS. Add. 34221, fols. 1v–18v.

Edition: Clifford Leech, ed. *Mildmay Fane's Raguaillo D'Oceano,*

1640, and Candy Restored, 1641 (Materials for the Study of the Old English Drama) (1938), pp. 30–41, 99–136, 145–58, and 170–84.

Harbage, Alfred. 'An Unnoted Caroline Dramatist', *Stud. Phil.* xxxi (1934), 30–31.

The Huntington MS. contains *Candia Restaurata, Don Phoebo's Triumph*, and some correspondence of the Earl. The B.M. MS. contains the six plays. The two manuscripts of plays reported in the Earl of Westmorland's collection at Apthorpe by the Historical Manuscripts Commission in 1885 (Report X, Appendix, Part iv, p. 58) were apparently those now at the Huntington. The B.M. MS. was purchased at Christie's 18 July 1892. (Leech, op. cit., p. 7.) Though the two versions of *Candia Restaurata* are very close, the Huntington MS. includes two rough drawings of the scenery and is the earlier in date, with many corrections and additions in the Earl's hand. Some of these additions have not been copied by the scribe of the B.M. MS., hence Mr. Leech prints the Huntington MS., though recording all variants in the other. (Op. cit., pp. 7 and 30–32.)

The scenic arrangements for the play are most interesting, consisting of three flats on each side which were revolved to change the set, and at the back a traverse which was drawn, concealing an elaborate painted scene. This scene was revealed by the drawing of the traverse—apparently when the flats were reversed at the beginning of Scene x. (See Leech, op. cit., pp. 32–33.)

The play is an incongruous combination of more or less realistic scenes of English troubles 1628–41 and an allegory of those troubles and their cure. Perhaps the Earl had been unduly impressed by the method of Jonson's *Staple of News* and *Magnetic Lady*. Leech points out (op. cit., pp. 39–40) a resemblance between Scene ix of *Candia Restaurata* and v. 1 of Francis Quarles's *The Virgin Widow* (q.v.), and suggests that Fane was the imitator. I find no verbal imitations in the two scenes, and though the idea is the same, I doubt if it was original with either man, and therefore see no reason to think that one imitated the other.

The date of 12 February 1640 on the manuscript evidently means 1640/1 and not 1639/40, since a number of allusions to events or situations in the play would have little point before the meeting of the Long Parliament. Harbage (op. cit., p. 30) was right in his selection of date, but wrong in his reasons, since his assumptions about the wives and children of the Earl are erroneous. (See Leech, op. cit., pp. 10–11 and 30–31.)

The names of the members of his household who played the parts have been added by the Earl in the Huntington MS.; in the B.M. MS. they have been copied by the scribe, though sometimes in a different form.

Candy Restored

See *Candia Restaurata*.

The Change (1642)

MS.: 'The Change. A Showe written in December—1642', B.M. Add. MS. 34221, fols. 50ʳ–68ᵛ.

Harbage, Alfred. 'An Unnoted Caroline Dramatist', *Stud. Phil.* xxxi (1934), 32–33.
Leech, Clifford, ed. *Mildmay Fane's Raguaillo D'Oceano, 1640, and Candy Restored, 1641 (Materials for the Study of the Old English Drama)* (1938), pp. 45–47.

The play is another moral allegory reflecting contemporary political affairs, though not very specifically. Fane had been arrested and sent to the Tower late in August 1642 (Leech, op. cit., p. 14), and was apparently still there when this play was written, for the Prologue is spoken in the person of the author, a prisoner:

> . . . what I hau' spun here onely to preuent
> The Languishments of an Imprisonment
> And to beguile tyme that standes still alone
> To such as be in like Condition
> Buildinge this Comfort to my selfe hereby
> That when all's Chang'd I shall haue Libertye.
> (Leech, op. cit., p. 8.)

There is no indication that *The Change* was ever acted.

De pugna animi

See *Φ[Ψ?]yxomaxia id est de pugna animi*.

Don Phoebo's Triumph (1645)

MS.: Huntington Library MS. H.M. 770.

Leech, Clifford, ed. *Mildmay Fane's Raguaillo D'Oceano, 1640, and Candy Restored, 1641 (Materials for the Study of the Old English Drama)* (1938), pp. 50–54.

This piece is not found in the collection of Mildmay Fane's plays at the British Museum, but only in a manuscript with his *Candia Restaurata* and some of his letters at the Huntington Library. The hand is the Earl's, and various characteristics of the alterations and corrections give Leech (op. cit., p. 50) reason for thinking that it is a first draft. At the head of the 'Dramatis Person:' appears the date 1645, presumably the year of composition and performance. All the roles have the names of actors attached; seven of them—Waller, Harry Stapleton, Michell, Hind, Dauis, Haythorn, and Watkinson—are names which also appeared in Fane's cast for his *Candia Restaurata*, which was given at Apthorpe 12 February 1640/1. Presumably they were members of his household at Apthorpe.

Don Phoebo's Triumph is an elaborate masque-like show in five short acts with scenery and spectacle. It concerns the pursuit of Primavera, daughter to the Spring, by Signor Calldo, son and heir to the Summer. Other obscurely related characters are Dame Flavia, daughter to the Autumn, Signor Freddo, grandchild to Winter, and Beauty, Innocency, Love, Pride, Inconstancy, Dissimulation, Ambition, Bacchus, Ceres, Silvanus, Pan, &c.

Leech notices that Primavera's fear of ravishment by Signor Calldo in her woodland walk suggests familiarity with *Comus* and that a song at the beginning of the play is another imitation of Jonson's popular stanza, 'Have you seen but a bright lily grow'. (Op. cit., pp. 51–52.)

Ladrones, or The Robbers' Island (1640–50?)

(Lost)

This piece is known only from the record of its sale at Sotheby's 17 July 1888. Hazlitt noted the entry:

Ladrones; or, The Robbers Island: An opera in a Romansike Way, by Mildmay Fane, Earl of Westmoreland. Unpublished MS. of the seventeenth century, with a map drawn in pen and ink.

Sotheby's, July 17, 1888, No. 1054. Among the *dramatis personae* occur Magellan, Drake, Cavendish, etc. (Hazlitt, *Manual*, p. 127.)

Though there is no record of the date of this opera, Fane's seven other known dramatic productions are all dated in the manuscripts from 1640 to 1650. The material of this composition is near enough to that of Fane's *Raguaillo D'Oceano* to make his authorship seem likely. None of his other known dramatic compositions is in the form of an opera.

Φ[Ψ?]yxomaxia id est de pugna animi (1650)

MS.: B.M. MS. Add. 34221, fols. 124ᵛ–147ʳ.

Harbage, Alfred. 'An Unnoted Caroline Dramatist', *Stud. Phil.* xxxi (1934), 33–34.

Leech, Clifford, ed. *Mildmay Fane's Raguaillo D'Oceano, 1640, and Candy Restored, 1641 (Materials for the Study of the Old English Drama)* (1938), pp. 54–56.

This play, dated 1650 in the manuscript, and therefore apparently the last of the Earl of Westmorland's dramatic productions, is another moral allegory. Like several of the others, it contains a key to the significance of the various characters, and their names are presented in columns to emphasize their relationships. Leech notes that at the end of the key the number '23' has been written, and he suggests that this may have been intended as the number of actors who could perform the thirty-five roles, but there is no evidence that the piece was ever acted. (Op. cit., p. 54.)

Lord Mens, the central character, takes an expedition to the island of Microcosmus in Acts III and IV and part of V, where there are fights involving the five senses and various symbolic characters. Harbage (loc. cit.) noted the resemblance of the name and the allegorical action of these scenes to Nabbes's *Microcosmus*, which had been in print for thirteen years by 1650. Leech suggests (op. cit., p. 56) that Fane may also have been influenced by *Pathomachia*, which is based on a similar idea and is also allegorical in character.

Raguaillo D'Oceano (1640)

MS.: 'Raguaillo D'Oceano　　This Show was written & prepared to be acted in Añ. 1640.' B.M. MS. Add. 34221, fols. 107ᵛ–123ʳ.

Edition : Clifford Leech, ed. *Mildmay Fane's Raguaillo D'Oceano, 1640, and Candy Restored, 1641 (Materials for the Study of the Old English Drama)* (1938), pp. 23–30, 61–98, 139–45, and 159–70.

Harbage, Alfred. 'An Unnoted Caroline Dramatist', *Stud. Phil.* xxxi (1934), 29–30.

The date of composition and presumably of performance is given immediately below the title in the B.M. MS. The piece is really a deformed masque, and Leech points out (op. cit., p. 26) that it belongs to the same genre as Shirley's *Cupid and Death*, which was also prepared for private performance. The masque, which concerns the search for Terra Australis Incognita, is prosaic, prolix, and a bit obscure, but Fane seems to suggest that the unknown lands might better be left to Oceanus. Fane's use of Italian names and Italian forms suggested to Leech (op. cit., p. 23) that the piece may have been translated or adapted from the Italian, but he was unable to find a source.

The greatest interest of *Raguaillo D'Oceano* lies in its directions for staging and scenery and in the full costume descriptions. Fane's opening chart, reproduced by Leech (op. cit., p. 62), together with his later directions, indicates a rather elaborate production.

The manuscript is written in the hand of a scribe, but the last few leaves and numerous corrections and additions throughout are in the hand of the author. (Leech, op. cit., p. 7 and n. 3.)

Time's Trick upon the Cards (1641/2)

MS.: 'Tymes trick vpon the Cards, prepared to be represented at Apthorpe by the youth and Servant[es] their the 22th of ffebruary—1641.' B.M. MS. Add. 34221, fols. 19v–49v.

Harbage, Alfred. 'An Unnoted Caroline Dramatist', *Stud. Phil.* xxxi (1934), 31–32.
Leech, Clifford, ed. *Mildmay Fane's Raguaillo D'Oceano, 1640, and Candy Restored, 1641* (*Materials for the Study of the Old English Drama*) (1938), pp. 42–45.

The piece is an allegory in twelve scenes, which breaks into two parts after the sixth scene. The two parts are not closely related, and often the intent is very obscure, though Fane provides a key at the end which purports to give the moral significance of most of the characters and places. Leech, who has given more attention to Fane than anyone else, can make little of the play.

The date '1641' probably refers to 1641/2, rather than 1640/1, since Fane had used the old calendar in his date for *Candia Restaurata* and since one passage (Leech, op. cit., p. 43) seems to refer to the Bishops' Exclusion Bill, which was not passed by the Lords until early in February 1641/2.

Time's Triumph

See Anon.

Virtue's Triumph (1644)

MS.: 'Vertues Triumph. This Comedy was writt in Ann—1644.'
B.M. MS. Add. 34221, fols. 69ᵛ–106ᵛ.

Harbage, Alfred. 'An Unnoted Caroline Dramatist', *Stud. Phil.*
xxxi (1934), 33.
Leech, Clifford, ed. *Mildmay Fane's Raguaillo D'Oceano, 1640, and
Candy Restored, 1641 (Materials for the Study of the Old English
Drama)* (1938), pp. 47–50.

Virtue's Triumph is another political allegory, longer than
Fane's other pieces but equally deficient in action. The statement
at the beginning indicates date of composition only, and there is
no indication that the comedy was ever acted. Leech thinks it is
probably the best of Fane's plays, but its virtues are by no means
startling.

NATHAN FIELD
1587–1619 or 1620

Brinkley, Roberta Florence. *Nathan Field, the Actor-Playwright*,
Yale Studies in English, vol. lxxvii (1928).
Chelli, Maurice. *Étude sur la collaboration de Massinger avec
Fletcher et son groupe* (1926), pp. 121–39.
Greg, W. W. 'Nathan Field and the Beaumont and Fletcher Folio
of 1679', *R.E.S.* iii (1927), 337–8.
Oliphant, E. H. C. *The Plays of Beaumont and Fletcher* (1927),
pp. 78–81, 348–401.
Peery, William, ed. *The Plays of Nathan Field* (1950).
—— 'Nid Field Was Whose Scholar?', *Shakespeare Association
Bulletin*, xxi (1946), 80–86.
Sykes, H. Dugdale. 'Nathaniel Field's Work in the "Beaumont
and Fletcher" Plays', *Sidelights on Elizabethan Drama* (1924),
pp. 200–19.
Verhasselt, Eliane. 'A Biography of Nathan Field, Dramatist and
Actor', *Revue belge de philologie et d'histoire*, xxv (1946–7),
485–508.

All Field's independent dramatic work and most of his acting
career had been completed before 1616, but the majority of his
collaborations and all his association with the King's company
came after the beginning of our period.

Nathan Field was baptized in the parish of St. Giles, Cripplegate, 17 October 1587, the son of John Field, the rabid Puritan

minister and theatre-hater. He was the brother of Theophilus
Field, later Bishop of Llandaff, and of Nathaniel Field, the printer, with whom he has often been confused. (Brinkley, op. cit.,
pp. 1–15.) Young Nathan Field became a student of Richard
Mulcaster at St. Paul's School. While a St. Paul's boy he was
seized by the patentees of the Blackfriars theatre and impressed
as a boy player for the company of the Children of the Chapel,
later called the Children of the Queen's Revels. His impressment
is mentioned by Henry Clifton in a complaint to the Star Chamber
about the similar impressment of his own son about 13 December
1600. (See Fleay, *Stage*, pp. 127–32.)

The young Field was a leading actor of the company under its
various names and organizations until it was amalgamated with the
Lady Elizabeth's company in 1613. (Brinkley, op. cit., pp. 18–29.)
A few of the plays in which he performed have been recorded, and
others can be guessed from the information given on their title-
pages. (See Peery, *Plays of Nathan Field*, p. 14.) That Field
became the friend and possibly the protégé of dramatists is
indicated by his verses for *Volpone* in 1607, *Catiline*, 1611, and
Fletcher's *Faithful Shepherdess*, 1609 or 1610, and by Jonson's
statement to Drummond that ' Nid field was his Schollar & he had
read to him the Satyres of Horace & some Epigrames of Martiall'.
(Herford and Simpson, *Ben Jonson*, i. 137.) Jonson's continued
friendliness is indicated by the lines he wrote into *Bartholomew
Fair* in 1614, where Cokes asks, '. . . which is your *Burbage* now?
. . . Your best *Actor*. Your *Field*?' (Ibid. vi. 119–20.)

Field played for about three years for the Lady Elizabeth's company in its various forms, and he became the leader of the troupe,
sometimes negotiating for them with Henslowe, and apparently
active in the acquisition of plays. (Brinkley, op. cit., pp. 29–35,
38–40; Peery, *Plays of Nathan Field*, pp. 16–21.) At the end of this
period he became a member of the King's company, and he remained with them, so far as we know, until his death in 1619 or
1620. By 1619 Field had become one of the housekeepers at the
Globe theatre. (C. W. Wallace, 'Shakespeare and his London
Associates', *University Studies of the University of Nebraska*, x
[1910], 323.) The date of his transfer to the leading London company is not certain, but Professor Baldwin thinks that he succeeded to Shakespeare's share in 1616 and played joint leads with
Burbage for the next three years. (*Organization and Personnel*,
pp. 51 and 204–7.) About the time of his transfer to the King's
company Field brought out a letter of remonstrance against the
incumbent at St. Mary Overy's, who had been preaching against

players. Field seems to have established himself as a well-known London figure in these years, and there are a number of allusions to him as a player and a favourite of the ladies. (See Brinkley, op. cit., pp. 41–43, and Peery, op. cit., pp. 22–25.) The number of anecdotes attached to Field's name is a striking indication of his popularity, whether or not the same stories were also told of others. Brinkley and Peery note several, and there is another in Josiah Dare's *Counsellor Manners His Last Legacy to His Son*, 1673, G₅. Field's importance in the ensemble of the King's company is suggested by Henry Vaughan's lines on Fletcher's plays:

> Thou doest but *kill*, and *Circumvent* in *Jest*,
> And when thy anger'd Muse *swells* to a blow
> 'Tis but for *Field*'s, or *Swansteed*'s overthrow.

(L. C. Martin, ed., *The Works of Henry Vaughan* [1914], i. 55, from *Olor Iscanus*, 1651.)

The precise date of Field's death is unknown, but his elder sister, Dorcas Field Rice, was granted the administration of his estate 2 August 1620. (Brinkley, op. cit., pp. 43–44 and 153.) Miss Brinkley notes that Field's name does not appear among those of the actors of *Sir John van Olden Barnavelt* in August 1619, though he had been included in the livery list of 19 May 1619 (see above, i. 72–74), and she concludes that he had probably dropped out of the company before the casting of *Barnavelt*. Perhaps she is right, but the evidence is not good. The roles assigned in the manuscript of *Sir John van Olden Barnavelt* (q.v.) are all minor ones—as usual in prompt manuscripts. By 1619 Field was a major actor in the company, and none of the major roles, such as Barnavelt, the Prince of Orange, Leidenberch, Vandort, Bredero, or Modesbargen, is assigned. Nor do the names of other major actors in the King's company in 1619—John Lowin, Nicholas Tooley, John Underwood, Robert Benfield, or William Eccleston—appear in the manuscript.

Since the letters of administration were granted for 'Nathan Field late of the parish of Saint Giles in the Fields' (Brinkley, p. 153), the burial may well be recorded in the registers of that parish, but unfortunately the burial registers for 1610–36 are lost. (See *R.E.S.* vi [1930], 149–51.)

Field's unaided plays, *A Woman Is a Weathercock* and *Amends for Ladies*, were acted before the death of Shakespeare, and there seems to be some likelihood that in this early period he collaborated with John Fletcher in *Four Plays in One* and *The Honest Man's Fortune*. (Brinkley, pp. 101–10 and 131–6.) His later

collaborations, though several of them are uncertain, were all prepared for the King's company. The number of these collaborations, together with Field's high reputation as an actor, suggests
that the last three or four years of his life was very busy indeed,
and that the company suffered a loss at his death only a little less
serious than the loss of Burbage.

There is a portrait of Field in the gallery at Dulwich College. It
is reproduced by Sir Edmund Chambers (*William Shakespeare*, i.
82) and as a frontispiece by Peery.

Collected Edition

The Plays of Nathan Field, Edited from the Original Quartos
with Introductions and Notes by William Peery (1950).

Amends for Ladies

See *The Elizabethan Stage*, iii. 313–14, and Peery, ed., *The Plays
of Nathan Field*, pp. 143–58.

The Fatal Dowry
with Philip Massinger

See Massinger.

Four Plays in One

See *The Elizabethan Stage*, iii. 231, and Brinkley, *Nathan Field,
The Actor-Playwright*, pp. 101–10.

The Honest Man's Fortune

See *The Elizabethan Stage*, iii. 227, and Brinkley, *Nathan Field,
The Actor-Playwright*, pp. 131–6.

The Jeweller of Amsterdam, or the Hague
(Lost)
with John Fletcher and Philip Massinger

See Fletcher.

The Knight of Malta
with John Fletcher and Philip Massinger?

See Fletcher.

The Laws of Candy

See Fletcher. Field's participation is very doubtful.

The Queen of Corinth
with John Fletcher and Philip Massinger?

See Fletcher.

Thierry and Theodoret
with John Fletcher

See *The Elizabethan Stage*, iii. 230, and Oliphant, *The Plays of Beaumont and Fletcher*, pp. 274–88.

A Woman Is a Weathercock

See *The Elizabethan Stage*, iii. 313, and Peery, *The Plays of Nathan Field*, pp. 57–65.

JASPER FISHER
1591– < 1639

Jasper Fisher was born in Carleton, Bedfordshire, in 1591, the son of William Fisher, deputy-auditor for the county of York. (*D.N.B.*) On 13 November 1607 he matriculated at Magdalen Hall, Oxford, and was admitted B.A. 28 January 1610/11, M.A. 27 January 1613/14, and D.D. in 1639. (Clarke, *Registers*, Part ii, 298, and Part iii, 300.) Anthony à Wood says that he was 'Divinity or Philosophy Reader of *Magd.* Coll.', and that about 1631 he became rector of Wilden in Bedfordshire. (*Athenæ Oxonienses*, 1721 ed., i. 619.) According to Miss Bradley in the *D.N.B.*, he married Elizabeth, daughter of the Reverend William Sams, of Burstead, Essex. Oldys, in his manuscript notes on Langbaine, says that Fisher was blind. (*D.N.B.*)

Wood says: 'This person, who was always esteemed an ingenious Man while he lived in *Magd.* Coll. as those that knew him have divers times informed me, lived several years after this, (1636.) but when he died, or what other things he hath published, I cannot learn.' (*Op. cit.* i. 620.) Besides *Fuimus Troes* his only known works are sermons.

Fuimus Troes, or The True Trojans (1611?–33)

Edition: Robert Dodsley, ed., A Select Collection of Old Plays (1744), vol. iii; also in later editions of Dodsley.

1633, 1 Aug. S.R. Entered to Allott 'a Tragedy called ffuimus Troes or the true Troians represented by the gentlemen Students of Magdalen Colledge in Oxford'. (Greg, Bibliography, i. 42.)

1633. Fvimvs Troes Æneid. 2. The Trve Troianes, Being A Story of the Britaines valour at the Romanes first invasion: Publikely represented by the Gentlemen Students of Magdalen Colledge in Oxford. Quis Martem tunicâ tectum adamantinâ Dignè scripserit? . . . 1633.

1637, 1 July. S.R. In the list of sixty-one books transferred from Mrs. Allott to Legatt and Crooke, 'True Trotians [sic] a Tragedy' was forty-second. (Ibid., p. 46.)

There is no available information about this play outside the first quarto and Anthony à Wood's statement that Jasper Fisher was the author. The title-page assertion of a Magdalen College performance fits well enough with the character of the play and the college affiliations of Jasper Fisher. Not enough is known of Fisher's career to suggest a date: any time between 1611 and 1633 would accord with what is known of him.

The copy of the 1633 quarto in the Huntington Library has on the title-page, written in an old hand, 'By W. Rider'. Presumably the author of The Twins (q.v.) is intended. I can see no reason for giving serious consideration to the attribution, since the author of Fuimus Troes must have been connected with Magdalen College, and no W. Rider is so connected in the reigns of James I or Charles I.

In the dramatis personae the author lists the sources from which his characters are drawn: two from Livy, eleven from Caesar's Commentaries, ten from Galfridus's Monumetensis, and five 'names feigned'. One distinctive feature of the play is the second song after the third act. Each act closes with a song or two by the chorus of bards, but this particular one is written in the Scottish dialect, for no reason indicated in the play. From this fact it has been suggested that the play was performed, or was intended to be performed, before James I.

In Rogers and Ley's list of plays printed at the end of their edition of The Careless Shepherdess, 1656, Fisher's play wears the most amusing of the many disguises in that irresponsible list. The printer has unconsciously combined it with Heywood's Fortune by

Land and Sea to make 'Fuimus tries the true Trojans fortune both by Land and Sea'. (See W. W. Greg, 'Authorship Attributions in the Early Play-Lists, 1656–1671', *Edinburgh Bibliographical Society Transactions*, ii, Part 4 [1946], 305–29.)

JOHN FLETCHER
1579–1625

Bald, R. C. *Bibliographical Studies in the Beaumont & Fletcher Folio of 1647.* Supplement to the Bibliographical Society's Transactions, No. 13 (1938).

Dyce, Alexander, ed. *The Works of Beaumont & Fletcher*, 11 vols. (1843–6), i, pp. v–xc.

Ellis-Fermor, U. M. *The Jacobean Drama* (1936).

Fellowes, E. H., ed. *Songs & Lyrics from the Plays of Beaumont and Fletcher with Contemporary Musical Settings* (1928).

Gayley, Charles Mills. *Beaumont, the Dramatist: a Portrait. With Some Account of His Circle, Elizabethan and Jacobean, and of His Association with John Fletcher* (1914).

Gerritsen, Johan. 'The Printing of the Beaumont and Fletcher Folio of 1647', *Library*, Fifth Series, iii (1949), 233–64.

Hatcher, O. L. *John Fletcher: A Study in Dramatic Method* (1905).

Lindsey, Edwin S. 'The Music of the Songs in Fletcher's Plays', *Stud. Phil.* xxi (1924), 325–55.

Makkink, H. J. *Philip Massinger and John Fletcher, A Comparison* (1927).

Maxwell, Baldwin. *Studies in Beaumont, Fletcher, and Massinger* (1939).

McKeithan, D. M. *The Debt to Shakespeare in the Beaumont-and-Fletcher Plays* (1938).

Oliphant, E. H. C. *The Plays of Beaumont and Fletcher: An Attempt to Determine Their Respective Shares and the Shares of Others* (1927).

Sprague, A. C. *Beaumont and Fletcher on the Restoration Stage* (1926).

Tannenbaum, Samuel A. *Beaumont and Fletcher (A Concise Bibliography)* (1938).

—— and Dorothy R. Tannenbaum. *Supplement to Beaumont and Fletcher, A Concise Bibliography* (1946).

Wallis, Lawrence B. *Fletcher, Beaumont, & Company. Entertainers to the Jacobean Gentry* (1947).

Wilson, John Harold. *The Influence of Beaumont and Fletcher on Restoration Drama* (1928).

Considering his social position and his flourishing reputation from about 1620 to the end of the century, the paucity of information about the career of John Fletcher is very curious, much more unaccountable than the obscurity of Shakespeare which the anti-Stratfordians find so satisfactorily mystifying.

John Fletcher was baptized at Rye, in Sussex. Dyce quotes the baptismal register: '1579. December. The xx^th daie John the son of Mr. Richard Flecher mynister of the word of god in Rye.' (Dyce, op. cit. i, p. xviii, n.) His father had formerly been President of Bene't College [Corpus Christi], Cambridge, and subsequent to his incumbency at Rye he became Chaplain to the Queen, Dean of Peterborough, Bishop of Bristol, Bishop of Worcester, and, in 1594/5, Bishop of London. (Ibid., pp. vii–ix.) Nothing is known of the dramatist's early life. There are various John Fletchers in the registers of Oxford and Cambridge, none of whom can be unquestionably identified as the son of the bishop. The most likely one is 'John Fletcher of London', who was admitted pensioner to Bene't College on 15 October 1591. (Ibid., p. xviii.) As Chambers notes (*Eliz. Stage*, iii. 314), this date seems early for the dramatist, but other boys, including Francis Beaumont, were entered at that age. Bishop Fletcher had many connexions with the college, which sent him letters of thanks for gifts in 1591 and 1592. (Dyce, op. cit. i, p. xviii, n., from Masters, *History of the College of Corpus Christi* [1753], Appendix, p. 64.) Furthermore, in 1594 the Bishop said that he commonly resided in London (Dyce, op. cit. i, p. ix), so that the John Fletcher of London entered at Corpus Christi in 1591 might plausibly be assumed to be his son. Masters, followed by Dyce, was uncertain whether it was this John Fletcher or Edward Fletcher who became B.A. in 1594/5 and M.A. in 1598, but *Alumni Cantab.* (ii. 149) assigns both degrees to the poet without question.

While the dramatist was presumably still at Cambridge his father fell from the Queen's favour because of an ill-advised marriage; he died a little more than a year later, in June 1596. The fact that his father died heavily in debt and in his will directed his executors to divide his estate among nine children (Dyce, op. cit. i, pp. lxxxviii–lxxxix) offers a possible reason for John Fletcher's early obscurity.

Gayley suggested (*Beaumont, the Dramatist*, pp. 68–69) that young Fletcher came under the protection of his uncle, Giles

Fletcher, the diplomat, after his father's death, and this is possible. Perhaps it was at this time that his association with the Earl of Huntingdon began. In Massinger's 'Copie of a Letter . . .' written to the Earl of Pembroke some time after 1615, he says:

> I know
> That Iohnson much of what he has does owe
> To you and to your familie, and is neuer
> Slow to professe it, nor had Fletcher euer
> Such Reputation, and credit wonne
> But by his honord Patron, Huntington.

(Quoted by Percy Simpson, *The Athenæum*, 8 September 1906, p. 273, from the MS. at Trinity College, Dublin. See also ibid., p. 303.)

The association with Huntingdon is again recorded in a verse letter now in the Huntington Library, which was addressed 'To the most Excelent and best Lady the Countess of Huntington' and signed ' John fletcher '; in it Fletcher wishes himself at Ashby, the Huntingdon seat. (Tannenbaum, 'A Hitherto Unpublished John Fletcher Autograph', *J.E.G.P.* xxviii [1929], 35–40.) Unfortunately the letter is not dated, nor is Massinger's reference, so it may be that the Huntingdon association did not begin until after Fletcher had become a playwright.

Though John Fletcher was a very common name, Dyce was tempted by one of the marriage entries which Collier noted for him in the registers of St. Saviour's, Southwark: '1612. Nov. 3. John Fletcher and Jone Herring', and by the baptismal record: ' John the son of John Fletcher and Joan his wife was baptised 25 Feb. 1619.' (Dyce, op. cit. i, p. lxxiii.) As Chambers points out in his account of Fletcher, this accords with Oldwit's speech in Shadwell's *Bury-Fair*, I. I:

> I knew *Fletcher*, my Friend *Fletcher*, and his Maid *Joan*: Well, I shall never forget him, I have Supp'd with him, at his House, on the *Bankside*: He lov'd a fat Loyn of Pork of all things in the World: and *Joan*, his Maid, had her Beerglass of Sack; and we all kiss'd her, i'faith, and were as merry as pass'd. (1689 ed., B₃ᵛ.)

In the St. Saviour's manuscript records I noted the marriage entry, but I did not see the baptismal entry, and I strongly suspect it, for it is not in the form used for baptisms in that parish in the first three decades of the seventeenth century. Even the marriage record is less suggestive of the dramatist when one notes that in the St. Saviour's baptismal registers—the only ones which note occupations—there are recorded between 1607 and 1620 John

Fletcher, waterman, John Fletcher, silkweaver, John Fletcher, silkthrostler, and John Fletcher, brewer's servant.

Neither the date of the beginning of Fletcher's dramatic career nor of his association with Beaumont is known, but it is generally conjectured that the two dramatists had begun to work together by 1607 or 1608. By this time Fletcher was a disciple of Jonson and probably one of the Sons of Ben, for Jonson wrote verses for the undated (1609 or 1610?) quarto of *The Faithful Shepherdess*, and in 1618/19 he told Drummond that 'Chapman and Fletcher were loved of him'. Richard Brome, Jonson's former servant and disciple, wrote of Fletcher in his verses for the 1647 Folio:

> *I knew him in his strength; even then, when* He
> *That was the Master of his Art and Me*
> *Most knowing* Johnson (*proud to call him* Sonne)
> *In friendly Envy swore, He had out-done*
> His very Selfe.

The early collaborations of Beaumont and Fletcher seem all to have been prepared for boy companies at the private theatres, often for the Queen's Revels company, from whose repertory a number of them probably passed to the Lady Elizabeth's company, thence to Queen Henrietta's company, and eventually to Beeston's Boys. (See above, i. 194, 250, and 337.) Their later compositions are almost all King's men's plays, and it seems likely to me that the King's men secured their services when the company began acting at the Blackfriars late in 1609 or early in 1610. (See 'Shakespeare and the Blackfriars Theatre', *Shakespeare Survey*, i [1948], 41–46.) The collaboration cannot have been a long one, for Beaumont married a Kentish heiress about 1612 or 1613, and he died 6 March 1615/16. (Chambers, *Eliz. Stage*, iii. 215–17.)

Beaumont's retirement and death coincide almost exactly with Shakespeare's, and as a consequence the King's men must have been seriously concerned at this time about their future repertory. It seems likely that they entered into some sort of a contract with Fletcher. There is no known record of it, and Fletcher—according to the extant company lists—never became a patented member of the troupe as Shakespeare had been. But it is a striking fact that none of the plays of Fletcher which can be dated after 1613 can be shown to have been the property of any other company, and the great majority of them can be definitely shown to have been owned by the King's men.

There is an interesting iteration of this association of Fletcher with the King's men in the Beaumont and Fletcher Folio of 1647, in which the dedication to the Earl of Pembroke and Montgomery, formerly the Lord Chamberlain, is signed by the ten actors who were in 1647 the remaining patented members of the King's company. This is a striking analogy to an earlier collection of plays from the repertory of the King's company, the Shakespeare Folio of 1623, which is dedicated to the then Lord Chamberlain, the Earl of Pembroke, and to his brother, the Earl of Montgomery, by the then leading members of the King's company, Henry Condell and John Heminges.

In his preparation of plays for the King's company Fletcher was frequently assisted—or his plays were later revised—by Philip Massinger, who succeeded him in 1625 as principal dramatist for the company. Less frequently Fletcher was assisted by Nathan Field, and occasionally by William Rowley. The horde of other poets who have been claimed as Fletcher's collaborators by one or another earnest investigator can be generally dismissed. Two or three instances of revision by Shirley or plagiarism from or by Jonson can be demonstrated from external evidence or literal transcription of long passages, but most of the other attributions involve a solemnly irresponsible use of evidence. For the collaboration of Massinger (q.v.), Field (q.v.), and Rowley (q.v.), there is external evidence in the office-book of Sir Henry Herbert, in the Stationers' Register, on title-pages, or in the comments of Sir Aston Cokayne. Moreover, these three all had close connexions with the King's company, for which the plays were written: Massinger as their regular playwright in succession to Fletcher, and Field and Rowley as patented actors of the company.

There is a tradition that Massinger was a close personal friend as well as a collaborator of Fletcher's. It is most definitely stated by Sir Aston Cokayne in a poem printed in the section called *Epigrams* in his *A Chain of Golden Poems*, 1658:

> *An Epitaph on Mr.* John Fletcher, *and Mr.* Philip
> Massinger, *who lie buried both in one Grave in*
> *St.* Mary Overie's Church *in* Southwark.
>
> In the same Grave *Fletcher* was buried here
> Lies the Stage-Poet *Philip Massinger*:
> Playes they did write together, were great friends,
> And now one Grave includes them at their ends:
> So whom on earth nothing did part, beneath
> Here (in their Fames) they lie, in spight of death.
>
> (N_5^v)

Since Fletcher died nearly fifteen years before Massinger, the 'one Grave' possibly means the same church or churchyard. Cokayne should not have been uninformed, since he knew Massinger well enough to write commendatory verses for two of his plays and called him 'my good friend Old *Philip Massinger*' in his poem '*To my Cousin Mr.* Charles Cotton' in *A Chain of Golden Poems*, 1658.

No events besides the succession of his plays have been discovered for the last decade of Fletcher's life. Aubrey says of his death:

in the great plague, 1625, a knight of Norfolk (or Suffolke) invited him into the countrey. He stayed but to make himselfe a suite of cloathes, and while it was makeing, fell sick of the plague and dyed. This I had (1668) from his tayler, who is now a very old man, and clarke of St. Mary Overy's. (*Brief Lives*, ed. A. Clark, i. 254.)

The several burial entries at St. Mary Overy's (now St. Saviour's) are recorded by Rendle, the Southwark antiquarian:

As to John Fletcher,—there are three distinct entries as to his death, and this notwithstanding the fearful number of deaths in 1625 in this parish, so many that numbers were not entered by name at all. ... The entries I refer to are ' John Fletcher, gentleman, in the church, 20*s* gr.' [grave]; ' John Fletcher, a poet, in the church, 21*s*'; and in the register proper, 'Augt 29, 1625, Mr. John ffletcher, a man, in the church'. ('The Graves at St. Saviour's, Southwark', *Athenæum*, 21 August 1886, p. 252.)

The great seventeenth-century reputation of Beaumont and Fletcher (commonly treated as one because of the indiscriminate collection of their plays in the folios of 1647 and 1679) is familiar to most readers of the literature of the time. I have noted without any particular search some 300 allusions to them or their work. With Shakespeare and Jonson, they formed the great triumvirate of the English drama in the estimate of their successors of the seventeenth and early eighteenth centuries. (For further material on their reputation, see Bentley, *Shakespeare and Jonson*, i. 67–70, and ii. 274–8.)

Collected Editions

1646, [4] Sept. S.R. Thirty Beaumont and Fletcher plays and eighteen by other dramatists (presumably all of them the property of the King's company) were entered to Robinson and Moseley. (Greg, *Bibliography*, i. 56–57.)

1647. Comedies And Tragedies Written by Francis Beavmont And Iohn Fletcher Gentlemen. Never printed before, And now published by the Authours Originall Copies . . . for *Humphrey Robinson* . . . and for *Humphrey Moseley* . . . 1647.

The volume contains: Portrait of Fletcher by Marshall; dedicatory epistle to Philip, Earl of Pembroke and Montgomery, signed by the ten patented members of the King's company, Lowin, Robinson, Swanston, Clark, Hammerton, Taylor, Benfield, Pollard, Allen, and Bird; epistle to the reader signed by the regular dramatist to the company at the time of the closing of the theatres, James Shirley; the stationer's address to the readers, dated 14 February 1646[/7] and signed by Humphrey Moseley; thirty-seven sets of commendatory verses; postscript [from the publisher]; and thirty-four plays and a masque: *The Mad Lover, The Spanish Curate, The Little French Lawyer, The Custom of the Country, The Noble Gentleman, The Captain, Beggars' Bush, The Coxcomb, The False One, The Chances, The Loyal Subject, The Laws of Candy, The Lover's Progress, The Island Princess, The Humorous Lieutenant, The Nice Valour or the Passionate Madman, The Maid in the Mill, The Prophetess, The Tragedy of Bonduca, The Sea Voyage, The Double Marriage, The Pilgrim, The Knight of Malta, The Woman's Prize or the Tamer Tamed, Love's Cure or the Martial Maid, The Honest Man's Fortune, The Queen of Corinth, Women Pleased, A Wife for a Month, Wit at Several Weapons, The Tragedy of Valentinian, The Fair Maid of the Inn, Love's Pilgrimage, The Masque of Gray's Inn and the Inner Temple, Four Plays or Moral Representations in One.* These are the thirty plays of the S.R. entry, except for *The Wild-Goose Chase*, which could not be found, with the five plays and a masque of the 1660 S.R. entry added.

1660, 29 June. S.R. *The False One, Wit at Several Weapons, The Nice Valour or the Passionate Madman, The Fair Maid of the Inn, The Masque of Gray's Inn and the Inner Temple,* and *Four Plays in One* entered to Robinson and Moseley. All had been published in F_1 but had not appeared in the S.R. entry of [4] September 1646. (Greg, *Bibliography*, i. 68.)

1679. [F_2] Fifty Comedies And Tragedies. Written by Francis Beaumont And John Fletcher, Gentlemen. All in one Volume. Published by the Authors Original Copies, the Songs to each Play being added. . . . for *John Martyn, Henry Herringman, Richard Marriot,* MDCLXXIX.

The volume contains: Portrait of Fletcher by Marshall; the booksellers' address to the reader; a selection from the commendatory verses of the first Folio; and fifty-two plays and the masque, i.e. all the plays of the first Folio plus eighteen which had been printed individually. Dramatis personae have been added, and casts, presumably the original ones, for twenty-five plays, all but two of which are casts of King's men.

1711. *The Works of Mr. Francis Beaumont, and Mr. John Fletcher; in seven volumes. Adorn'd with cuts. Revis'd and corrected: with some account of the life and writings of the authors.* 7 vols. (1711).

1750. *The Works of Mr. Francis Beaumont, and Mr. John Fletcher. . . . Collated with all the former editions, and corrected. With notes critical and explanatory. By the late Mr. Theobald, Mr. Seward . . . and Mr. Sympson.* 10 vols. (1750).

1778. *The Dramatick Works of Beaumont and Fletcher; collated with all the former editions, and corrected; with notes, critical and explanatory, by various commentators.* [Edited by George Colman the elder.] 10 vols. (1778).

1812. *The Works of Beaumont and Fletcher, in fourteen volumes: with an introduction and explanatory notes, by Henry Weber, Esq.* 14 vols. (1812). (Includes *The Faithful Friends*, printed for the first time from manuscript.)

1840. *The Works of Beaumont and Fletcher.* George Darley, ed. 2 vols. (1840).

1843–6. *The Works of Beaumont and Fletcher; the text formed from a new collation of the early editions.* Alexander Dyce, ed. 11 vols. (1843–6).

1854. [Another edition of the above, published in Boston by Phillips, Sampson and Company, in New York by J. C. Derby. 2 vols. (1854).]

1866. [Another edition of the George Darley edition of 1840. 2 vols. (1866).]

1904–12. *The Works of Francis Beaumont and John Fletcher.* Variorum Edition; A. H. Bullen, general editor. (Twenty plays were individually edited; no more appeared.) 4 vols. (1904–12).

1905–12. *The Works of Francis Beaumont and John Fletcher.* Arnold Glover and A. R. Waller, eds. 10 vols. (1905–12).

Beggars' Bush (> 1622)
with Philip Massinger?

MS.: Folger Shakespeare Library. Bound in with other plays in the so-called Lambarde volume.

Editions: P. A. Daniel, ed., in *The Works of Francis Beaumont and John Fletcher*, Variorum Edition, ii (1905), 339–453; C. F. T.

Brooke and N. B. Paradise, eds., in *English Drama, 1580–1642* (1933), pp. 837–73.

Bald, R. C. *Bibliographical Studies in the Beaumont & Fletcher Folio of 1647*, Supplement to the Bibliographical Society's Transactions, No. 13 (1938), pp. 50–52, 61–64, 75–76, 81–83.

Briggs, W. D. 'First Song in *The Beggar's Bush*', *M.L.N.* xxxix (1924), 379–80.

—— 'The Influence of Jonson's Tragedy in the Seventeenth Century', *Anglia*, xxxv (1912), 326–7.

Elson, J. J., ed. *The Wits or Sport upon Sport* (1932), pp. 78–84 and 372–3.

Lawrence, W. J. *Those Nut-Cracking Elizabethans* (1935), pp. 194–205.

Oliphant, E. H. C. *The Plays of Beaumont and Fletcher* (1927), pp. 256–65.

Rulfs, Donald J. 'Beaumont and Fletcher on the London Stage 1776–1833', *P.M.L.A.* lxiii (1948), 1255.

Sprague, A. C. *Beaumont and Fletcher on the Restoration Stage* (1926), pp. 274–5, *et passim*.

Ward, A. W. *A History of English Dramatic Literature to the Death of Queen Anne* (1899), ii. 725–7.

1622, 27 Dec. 'Upon St. Johns daye at night was acted *The Beggars Bush* by the kings players.' From Sir John Astley's list of 'Revels and Playes performed and acted at Christmas in the court at Whitehall, 1622'. (Adams, *Herbert*, p. 49.)

1630, 30 Nov. 'The 30 of November   . Beggers Bushe.' appears in a bill of the King's company for plays presented at court in 1630 and 1630/1. (See above, i. 27–28.)

1636, 19 Nov. '6 The 19th of November at Hampton Court   . beggers bush.' From a bill of the King's company for plays acted before the King and Queen in 1636. (See above, i. 51.)

c. 1637/8. The elaborate and formal manuscript of *Beggars' Bush* in the Lambarde volume of manuscript plays at the Folger Shakespeare Library is in the same hand as that of the B.M. MS. of Suckling's *Aglaura*, which was apparently prepared for presentation to the King shortly before 7 February 1637/8. (See Bald, op. cit., p. 52.)

1638/9, 1 Jan. 'At Richmount on newyeares day ⎱ .... beggers bush'
and our day lost at our house ⎰

From a bill of the King's company for plays acted at court

before the King and Queen in 1638 and 1638/9. (Adams, *Herbert*, pp. 76–77.)

1641, 7 Aug. 'Beggars' is in a list of plays belonging to the King's company which the Lord Chamberlain forbade the printers to publish without the company's consent. (See above, i. 65–66.) Presumably 'Beggars' is an abbreviated title standing for *Beggars' Bush*.

1646, [4] Sept. S.R. 'Beggars Bush' 'by m^r Beamont & m^r fflesher' appears in a long list of plays licensed by Robinson and Moseley, apparently all from the repertory of the King's company. (Greg, *Bibliography*, i. 56–57.)

1647. 'Beggars Bvsh' is the seventh play of the Beaumont and Fletcher Folio of 1647.

1659 or 1660. Pasted on the last page of *Beggars' Bush* excerpted from the 1647 Folio is a memorandum 'in an early hand' giving the cast: 'At ye Red Bull, 1659 or 1660. Florenz by Char. Hart. Hubert by Burt. Van Dunk by Cartwright. Higgon by Shatterel. Prig by Clun. Woolfort (I think) by Old Theop. Byrd.' (Catalogue No. 87 of Dobell, Tunbridge Wells [1945], Item 21.)

c. 1660. 'Beggars Bushe' is found in a list of the stock plays of Killigrew's company which was furnished to Sir Henry Herbert, probably shortly after the Restoration, and found among his papers by Malone. (Adams, *Herbert*, p. 82.)

1660, 7 and 20 Nov. 'Wensday the 7. No. The Beggers Bushe' and 'Tusday the 20. No. The Beggars Bushe' appear in a list of performances of plays acted by 'the Kings Companie at the Red Bull and the new house in Gibbon's Tennis Court near Clare Market' 1660–2. (Ibid., pp. 116–18.)

1660, 20 Nov. '. . . and I to the new play-house near Lincoln's-Inn-Fields (which was formerly Gibbon's tennis-court), where the play of "Beggar's Bush" was newly begun; and so we went in, and saw it well acted.' (Diary of Samuel Pepys.)

1660/1, 3 Jan. '. . . to the Theatre, where was acted "Beggars' Bush," it being very well done; and here the first time that ever I saw a woman come upon the stage.' (Ibid.)

1661. The Beggars Bush. Written by *Francis Beavmont* And *John Fletcher* Gentlemen . . . 1661.

1661. [Another issue.]

1661, 8 Oct. Pepys saw the play. (Ibid.)

1662. A droll entitled 'The Lame Common-Wealth' made from II. 1 of *Beggars' Bush* appeared in *The Wits*, and a picture of Clause with other droll characters appeared in the frontispiece. (See Elson ed., pp. 78–84.)

1662[-3 ?]. Edward Browne paid 1s. to see 'Beggars bush' 'At the New Theatre in Lincolnes Jnne fields', by the 'Kings players'. (W. W. Greg, 'Theatrical Repertories of 1662', *Gentleman's Magazine*, ccci [1906], 69–72; from B.M. MS. Sloane 1900.)

<1663. Downes notes that 'The Beggars Bush' was one of the old stock plays acted by Killigrew's company after their opening at Drury Lane in the spring of 1663. (*Roscius Anglicanus*, Summers ed., pp. 3 and 8–9.)

1668, 24 Apr. Pepys saw the play at the King's playhouse. (Diary of Samuel Pepys.)

1672/3, 30 Jan. S.R. Humphrey Robinson, executor of Humphrey Robinson, transferred a half-interest in 'Beggers Bush' with a number of other titles to John Martin and Henry Herringman. (Greg, *Bibliography*, i. 72–73.)

1674, 26 Mar. In a warrant for payment for plays performed before royalty by the Theatre Royal company is 'March 26: The Beggers Bush'. (Nicoll, *A History of Restoration Drama*, 3rd ed., p. 307.)

1679. 'Beggars Bush, A Comedy' is the ninth play in the Beaumont and Fletcher Folio of 1679.

<1682. Among the plays revived by the United Companies after their union in 1682, Downes lists 'The Beggars Bush'. (*Roscius Anglicanus*, Summers ed., pp. 39–40.)

1683, 21 Aug. S.R. Sarah Martin, executrix for John Martin, transferred a fourth interest in 'Beggars Bush' and a number of other plays to Robert Scott. (Greg, *Bibliography*, i. 75–76.)

1686, 1 Dec. In a warrant for payment for plays performed before royalty by the United Companies is 'Dec: 1. The Beggars at Whitehall.' (Nicoll, *A History of Restoration Drama*, 3rd ed., p. 313. Professor Sprague [op. cit., p. 54, n. 3] noted that this title might refer to Brome's *The Jovial Crew or the Merry Beggars*. It seems to me more likely that it belongs here, however, since apparently it was this play which was previously referred to as 'Beggars' in the 1641 list of the King's men's plays. See above, i. 65–66.)

1687/8, 13 Feb. In a warrant for payment for plays performed before royalty by the United Companies is: 'February 13 The Beggars Bush at Whitehall.' (Nicoll, *A History of Restoration Drama*, 3rd ed., p. 313.)

1691. Langbaine said of *Beggars' Bush*: 'This Play I have seen several times acted with applause.' (*Account of the English Dramatick Poets*, p. 207.)

There is no reliable evidence for dating the play except Herbert's record of the performance at court in December 1622. This performance has led Weber, Darley, Dyce, Lawrence, and others to date the play 1622, on the ground that it must have been new when performed at court in that year. Such reasoning is absurd, for many plays no longer new were performed at court; witness the performances of this play itself in 1630, 1636, and 1638/9. Moreover the performance of December 1622 is not necessarily the first court performance; there could easily have been a performance of this play by the King's men at court in years when the company was paid for a number of command performances of unspecified plays—years like 1615–16, 1616–17, 1617–18, 1618–19, 1619–20, and 1620–1. (See above, i. 94.)

Fleay said (*Biog. Chron.* i. 199) of the date of the play: 'As there is no actor-list, I have no doubt that the original performance was by the L. Elizabeth's men at the Hope *c.* 1615', and this fine offhand declaration has been accepted by a surprising number of scholars. Apparently he assumed—as have others—that the actor lists preceding certain plays in the second Folio of 1679 were made for all plays originally acted by the King's company and first appearing in the first Folio of 1647. He then further assumed that the absence of such a list for any play first published in 1647 is proof that the play was not originally acted by the King's company but was first produced by some other company, and that therefore it came early in Fletcher's career. These assumptions, which have been frequently made but seldom discussed, will not bear close scrutiny. Nothing is known of the origin of these lists, T. W. Baldwin to the contrary notwithstanding. (See *Organization and Personnel of the Shakespearean Company*, pp. 392–3.) Except for a few instances, there is nothing to indicate that the lists printed are inaccurate, but the absence of a list from the second Folio cannot be taken as evidence of anything until much more is learned about the origin of these casts. (See Baldwin Maxwell, *Studies in Beaumont, Fletcher, and Massinger* [1939], pp. 7–13.)

Koeppel denies (*Quellen Studien . . . Beaumont's und Fletcher's* [1895], p. 110, n. 2) that the play shows any influence of Cervantes's *La Fuerza de la Sangre*, but he is non-committal concerning Ward's remark that Fletcher, like Middleton and Rowley in *The Spanish Gipsy*, 'may have taken the first suggestion of the beggars from the gipsies of Cervantes'—i.e. in *La Gitanilla*. (*History of English Dramatic Literature*, ii. 726 and 508.) Oliphant (op. cit., p. 258) thought the slang terms and the knowledge of the manners of the beggars were taken from Dekker's *Bellman of*

London. Perhaps a close comparison of *The Spanish Gipsy* and *Beggars' Bush* would be fruitful.

Most of the style analysers have thought they recognized work of Massinger as well as of Fletcher in the play, and Oliphant, who gives the most complete summary (op. cit., pp. 256–65), thought that *Beggars' Bush* represents a revision by Fletcher and Massinger of an earlier play written perhaps by Beaumont as well as by Fletcher. His evidence for revision (op. cit., pp. 261–4) is not wholly convincing, but his impressionistic identification of Massinger's work receives some very slight support from Lawrence's observation of Massinger's odd punctuation of his stage directions. (Lawrence, op. cit., pp. 202–3; Bald, op. cit., pp. 62–63.)

The quarto of 1661 was printed from the Folio of 1647 with a few trivial alterations and the addition of a dramatis personae, according to Dyce (*Works*, ix. 2) and Daniel (Variorum ed., ii. 342), who have edited the play most carefully. The prologue and epilogue for *The Captain*, which were printed between that play and *Beggars' Bush* in the Folio of 1647, are mistakenly taken over for *Beggars' Bush* in the quarto. In such an edition the attribution of the play to Beaumont as well as to Fletcher has no significance. The text of the 1679 Folio appears to have come from an independent manuscript. (Greg, *Bibliography*, ii. 772–3.)

The manuscript of the play in the volume sometimes called the Lambarde collection at the Folger Shakespeare Library is most fully discussed by Bald. (Loc. cit.) He finds that it is in the same hand as that of Suckling's *Aglaura* in the B.M. MS., a manuscript which was apparently prepared for presentation to the King at the time of the court performance of that play early in 1637/8. Though a formal manuscript, the transcript in the Lambarde volume appears to have been copied from a prompt copy and seems to carry over some of the characteristics of the King's men's scribe ' Jhon ', most of whose known work belongs to the period 1625–30. Its text generally, though not invariably, agrees with that of the Folio of 1647. Bald noted five omissions of from four to fourteen lines which he took to be theatrical cuts.

The play, with alterations and added songs, was set forth in 1768 by Thomas Hull as *The Royal Merchant: an Opera.* Douglas Kinnaird's alteration entitled *The Merchant of Bruges: or, The Beggars' Bush* appeared at Drury Lane in 1815. It is discussed by Rulfs. (Op. cit., p. 1255.)

Allusions from the third quarter of the seventeenth century suggest that the play was fairly well known then. The lines in Henry Tubbe's poem, ' On the Dominical Nose of O[liver] C[romwell] ':

A bonny Nose! a Nose for Sweet Pig-wiggin!
An eloquent Nose! a Nose for Oratour Higgin!

refer to Higgin in II. 1 of the play, as Professor Bensly pointed out
to Tubbe's editor, G. C. Moore Smith. (*Oxford Historical and
Literary Studies*, v [1915], 96 and 113–14.) '*The Sowgelder's Song,
in the* Beggers-Bush' is printed in *Wit Restor'd*, 1658, M_8v–N_2v.
And Francis Kirkman, in a poem prefixed to Richard Head's *The
English Rogue*, 1669, writes of

> Fletcher the King of Poets of his age,
> In all his writings throughout every page
> Made it his chiefest business to describe
> The various humours of the Canting-Tribe:
> His Beggars-bush, and others of his Playes
> Did gain to him (deservedly) the Bayes.

The Birth of Merlin, or The Child Hath Found His Father

See *The Elizabethan Stage*, iii. 474–5; William Wells, '*The Birth
of Merlin*. 1608', *M.L.R.* xvi (1921), 129–37; E. H. C. Oliphant,
The Plays of Beaumont and Fletcher (1927), pp. 402–14; R. C.
Bald, ed., *Hengist King of Kent; or The Mayor of Queenborough.
By Thomas Middleton* (1938), pp. xxii–xxiii and xxxiv–xxxv.

The Bloody Brother

See *Rollo, Duke of Normandy*.

Bonduca

See *The Elizabethan Stage*, iii. 228.

The Captain

See *The Elizabethan Stage*, iii. 226.

Cardenio, or The Double Falsehood
with William Shakespeare?

See Chambers, *William Shakespeare*, i. 538–42.

The Chances (c. 1617? and c. 1627?)

Edition: E. K. Chambers, ed., in *The Works of Francis Beaumont and John Fletcher*, Variorum Edition, iv. 435–531.

Chambers, E. K. 'The Date of Fletcher's "The Chances"',
M.L.R. iv (1909), 512–14; and v (1910), 210.

Elson, J. J., ed. *The Wits or Sport upon Sport* (1932), pp. 210–18
and 388–9.

Hatcher, O. L. *John Fletcher: A Study in Dramatic Method* (1905),
pp. 49–53.

Koeppel, Emil. *Quellen-Studien zu den Dramen Ben Jonson's, John
Marston's und Beaumont's und Fletcher's* (1895), pp. 92–94.

Macaulay, G. C. 'The Date of "The Chances"', *M.L.R.* v (1910),
112–13.

Oliphant, E. H. C. *The Plays of Beaumont and Fletcher* (1927),
pp. 114–15 and 135–7.

Powell, William C. 'A Note on the Stage History of Beaumont and
Fletcher's *Love's Pilgrimage* and *The Chances*', *M.L.N.* lvi
(1941), 122–7.

Rulfs, Donald J. 'Beaumont and Fletcher on the London Stage
1776–1833', *P.M.L.A.* lxiii (1948), 1256 and 1262–3.

Sprague, A. C. *Beaumont and Fletcher on the Restoration Stage*
(1926), pp. 221–7, *et passim*.

Wilson, Edward M. 'Did John Fletcher Read Spanish?', *P.Q.* xxvii
(1948), 187–90.

1630, 30 Dec. 'The 30 of December. Chaunces' was presented at
the Cockpit in Court by the King's men, according to a bill
presented by them for 'Playes for the Kinge' given between
30 September 1630 and 21 February 1630/1. (See above, i. 28.)

1638, 22 Nov. 'At the Cocpit the 22th of november . . . Chances.'
From a list of plays acted at court by the King's company
1638–38/9. (Adams, *Herbert*, p. 77.)

1641, 7 Aug. 'Chances' is in the list of King's men's plays which
the Lord Chamberlain forbade any printer to publish without
the consent of the players. (See above, i. 65–66.)

1646, [4] Sept. S.R. 'Chaunces' is one of about fifty plays, apparently all from the repertory of the King's company, entered
to Robinson and Moseley. (Greg, *Bibliography*, i. 56–57.)

1647. 'The Chances' is the tenth play in the 1647 Folio.

1660, 24 Nov. 'Saterday the 24. No. The Chances.' appears in a list
of performances of plays by 'the Kings Companie at the Red
Bull and the new house in Gibbon's Tennis Court near Clare
Market' 1660–2. (Adams, *Herbert*, pp. 116–18.)

1661, 27 Apr. '. . . to the Theatre to see "The Chances"'. (Diary
of Samuel Pepys.)

1662. 'Droll. 23. *The Landlady*, out of *the Chances*.' appears in the collection called *The Wits, or, Sport upon Sport*, 1662. (See J. J. Elson, ed., pp. 210–18.)

1662[–3 ?]. Edward Browne noted in his memorandum book that he paid 2s. to see 'Chances' 'At the Cock Pit in Drewry Lane'. (W. W. Greg, 'Theatrical Repertories of 1662', *Gentleman's Magazine*, ccci [1906], 69–72; from B.M. MS. Sloane 1900.)

<1663. Downes lists 'The Chances' as one of the plays acted by the King's company after the opening of the new Drury Lane Theatre in 1663. (*Roscius Anglicanus*, ed. Summers, p. 8.)

1666/7, 5 Feb. '. . . to the King's house to show them a play, "The Chances." A good play I find it, and the actors most good in it; and pretty to hear Knipp sing in the play very properly, "All night I weepe;" and sung it admirably. The whole play pleases me well.' (Diary of Samuel Pepys.)

1668/9, *c.* 12 Jan. One of the plays in 'A Catalogue of part of His Ma^tes Servants Playes as they were formerly acted at the Black-fryers & now allowed of to his Ma^tes Servants at ye New Theatre' is 'The Chances'. (Nicoll, *A History of Restoration Drama*, 3rd ed., p. 315.)

1672/3, 30 Jan. S.R. John Martin and Henry Herringman were assigned a half-interest in 'Chances' and over one hundred other titles. (Greg, *Bibliography*, i. 72–73.)

1679. 'The Chances. A Comedy' is the twentieth play in the second Beaumont and Fletcher Folio.

1682. The Chances, A Comedy: As it was Acted At The Theater Royal. Corrected and Altered by a Person of Honour [George Villiers, Duke of Buckingham] . . . 1682.

1682, 30 Dec. In a warrant for payment for plays performed before royalty by the United Companies is: 'Decemb^r . . . 30: at ye Chances with ye Q: & a box for ye Maides of hono^r.' (Nicoll, *A History of Restoration Drama*, 3rd ed., p. 311.)

1683, 21 Aug. S.R. In an assignment of 360 titles to Robert Scott, a fourth interest in 'Chances' is included. (Greg, *Bibliography*, i. 75–76.)

1685/6, 27 Jan. In a warrant for payment for plays performed before royalty by the United Companies is: 'Jan: 27: The Chances at Whitehall.' (Nicoll, *A History of Restoration Drama*, 3rd ed., p. 312.)

1685/6, 28 Jan. In a letter to the Duchess of Rutland under this date, Peregrine Bertie said: 'last night was acted, *The Chances* at Whitehall'. (*Hist. MSS. Com.*, Twelfth Report, Appendix, Part v [Rutland MSS. ii. 102], quoted by W. J. Lawrence, *Anglia*, xxxii [1909], 87.)

1692. [Another edition of Villiers's alteration.]

The Chances is one of the most successful of Fletcher's comedies. In addition to the seventeenth-century listings given above, the play was frequently performed and frequently reprinted in the eighteenth and nineteenth centuries.

The source of the play, as first noted by Langbaine (*An Account of the English Dramatick Poets*, pp. 207–8), is Cervantes's *La Señora Cornelia*, which appeared in the *Novelas Exemplares* in 1613 and was published in a French translation in 1615. Because of Fletcher's general tendency to use translations, it seems somewhat more likely that he used the French version, but Edward M. Wilson has noted (loc. cit.) two minor and almost negligible instances in *The Chances* which may indicate that he at least consulted the Spanish version. The story is summarized at length in the editions of the play by Weber, 1812; Dyce, 1843–6; Chambers, 1912, and by Hatcher (loc. cit.), who discusses its use. The appearance of the source provides a *terminus a quo* for the play.

A number of terminal dates for the play have been proposed by Macaulay, Fleay, Bullen, Thorndike, and Schelling. Most of them are discussed and the evidence shown to be negligible by Chambers. (Variorum ed., iv. 437–9.) The absence of a play from Malone's and Chalmers's extracts from Sir Henry Herbert's office-book never proves anything; the lines at the beginning of v. 2, '. . . dost thou think / The Devil such an Asse as people make him?' (Folio, 1679), might be an allusion to Jonson's play, but it is preposterous to make them contrariwise a source for Jonson's title; the stage direction in iii. 2, '*Enter Rowl. with Wine*' (Folio, 1679), probably refers to Rowland Dowle (see above, ii. 425–6), who appears in a similar capacity in other plays of the King's company, but who is not heard of before 1631 and whose name was therefore probably inserted by the prompter for a revival, not the original performance. The allusions to the Pope's Bulls and to the military strength of the Duke of Lorraine in iii. 1, which have sometimes been thought to allude to events of 1609, Chambers shows to be probably allusions to events of 1627 and therefore insertions for a revival after Fletcher's death, a revival also indicated by the lines in the prologue which refer to Fletcher as dead. I have spoken of a revival, but Chambers, though he makes no definite assertions about the date of the play, appears to think it likely that there was no performance until after Fletcher's death.

T. W. Baldwin (*Organization and Personnel of the Shakespearean*

Company, p. 198, chart 1) dates the play in the summer of 1615, apparently because this date fits into the 'lines' of the actors which he has developed. Very few scholars have accepted these 'lines', at least with the rigidity which Baldwin demands, and in the case of *The Chances*, unlike many other Fletcher plays, there is no list of actors from the 1679 Folio, much less of the roles they were assigned. The date of 1615 thus has little support, except Fleay's (*Biog. Chron.* i. 199–200), which is negligible.

Though a performance of about 1627 seems to me to be indicated by the lines about the Pope's Bulls and about the Duke of Lorraine's army, and to be compatible with the prologue reference to Fletcher as dead, I am inclined to think that this was a revival rather than a first performance of a play left incomplete by Fletcher in 1625, for even Oliphant could find no evidence of any hand but Fletcher's in the play. (*The Plays of Beaumont and Fletcher*, pp. 135–7.) I see no evidence in the prologue—as Macaulay did but Chambers did not—that it was written for a first performance.

If the play was revived about 1627, when was it first produced? Presumably after 1615, when the source appeared in a French translation. A date is perhaps suggested by the 'devil is an ass' allusion. The lines following those quoted above in v. 2 seem to me even more suggestive:

> . . . dost thou think
> The Devil such an Asse as people make him?
> Such a poor coxcomb? such a penny foot-post?
> Compel'd with cross and pile to run of errands?
>
> (Folio, 1679)

This description of a familiar picture of the devil is peculiarly apt for Pug, the title character in Jonson's play *The Devil Is an Ass*. Pug is a devil who does run errands and perform other menial services for Fitzdottrell in Jonson's comedy. Moreover both Jonson's play and Fletcher's were in the repertory of the King's company—at least Fletcher's was in 1630, and presumably it had always been. Jonson's play was performed at Blackfriars in the autumn of 1616 (see below), and probably *The Chances* was performed at the same theatre, since most of Fletcher's later plays seem to have been given there. It is under circumstances such as these that allusions from one play to another are most effective, for they catch the same audience, and they do not advertise the attractions of any rival theatre. I should hesitate to press this identification of Fletcher's allusion too far, but if it is correct, then *The Chances* would probably date about 1617, soon enough after *The Devil Is an Ass* to make the reference clear and amusing, and about two years after Fletcher's source had become available in French.

Fleay once identified *The Chances* with the lost play, *A Vow and a Good One* (see under Anon.), which was performed at court by the Prince's men in 1623. (*Biog. Chron.* i. 200.) There is no good reason for connecting the two plays, and even Fleay later identified the lost *Vow* with Middleton and Rowley's *Fair Quarrel.* (Ibid. ii. 98.)

Professor Bald suggests (*Bibliographical Studies in the Beaumont & Fletcher Folio of 1647*, pp. 103–4) that an anticipatory stage direction in III. 1 and an actor's name in III. 2 indicate that the text of 1647 may have been set up from a prompt manuscript of the play.

There has been little disposition among the disintegrators of the plays of the Beaumont and Fletcher folios to find any hand save Fletcher's in *The Chances*. If there were revisions for the revival of 1627, they must have been so slight as to defy all the methods of style analysis.

The later popularity of the play is indicated by the droll made from three of its scenes under the title *The Landlady*, which was published in *The Wits, or, Sport upon Sport*, 1662. (See J. J. Elson's edition, pp. 210–18.) Buckingham's alteration of the play is analysed by A. C. Sprague (loc. cit.), and he records various Restoration performances. Later performances are recorded by Donald J. Rulfs in his *P.M.L.A.* article listed above.

Cleander

See Fletcher, *The Lovers' Progress.*

The Coronation

See James Shirley.

The Coxcomb

See *The Elizabethan Stage*, iii. 223–4.

Cupid's Revenge

See *The Elizabethan Stage*, iii. 225–6, and James E. Savage, 'Beaumont and Fletcher's *Philaster* and Sidney's *Arcadia*', *E.L.H.* xiv (1947), 194–206, and 'The Date of Beaumont and Fletcher's *Cupid's Revenge*', *E.L.H.* xv (1948), 286–94.

The Custom of the Country (c. 1619–20 and 1638?)
with Philip Massinger

Edition: R. Warwick Bond, ed., in *The Works of Francis Beaumont and John Fletcher*, Variorum Edition, i. 475–589.

Elson, J. J., ed. *The Wits, or, Sport upon Sport* (1932), pp. 104–10 and 375.

Keightley, Thomas. 'Fletcher's "Custom of the Country"', *N. & Q.*, Second Series, xi (1861), 7–8.

Koeppel, Emil. *Quellen-Studien zu den Dramen Ben Jonson's, John Marston's und Beaumont's und Fletcher's* (1895), pp. 65–67.

Maxwell, Baldwin. *Studies in Beaumont, Fletcher, and Massinger* (1939), pp. 190–1.

Oliphant, E. H. C. *The Plays of Beaumont and Fletcher* (1927), pp. 224–6, 234–6.

1628, 22 Nov. 'The benefitt of the winters day, being the second daye of an old play called *The Custome of the Cuntrye*, came to 17*l*. 10*s*. 0*d*. this 22 of Nov. 1628. From the Kinges company att the Blackfryers.' (Adams, *Herbert*, p. 43.)

1630, 24 Oct. 'The 24 of October. The Custome of the Contrie' appears in a bill of the King's company for plays presented before the King at Hampton Court. (See above, i. 27–28.)

1638, 27 Nov. 'At the Cocpit the 27th of november. The Costome of the C[ountry]' appears in a bill of the King's company for plays acted before the King and Queen in 1638 and 1638/9. (Adams, *Herbert*, pp. 76–77.)

1641, 7 Aug. 'The Custom o' th Cuntry' appears in a list of plays belonging to the King's company which the Lord Chamberlain forbade the printers to publish without the company's consent. (See above, i. 65–66.)

1646, [4] Sept. S.R. Robinson and Moseley entered 'Custome of ye Country . . . by mr Beamont & mr fflesher' in a group of nearly fifty plays, all apparently of the repertory of the King's company. (Greg, *Bibliography*, i. 56–57, and see above, i. 116, 'Burroughs'.)

1647. 'The Custome of the Countrey' is printed as the fourth play in the first Beaumont and Fletcher Folio of 1647.

1662. 'Droll. 8. *The Stallion*, out of *the Custom of the Country*' appears in Kirkman's collection of drolls entitled *The Wits, or, Sport upon Sport*. (See J. J. Elson, ed., pp. 104–10.)

1664, 25 Sept. Pepys read the play and called it a poor one. (Diary of Samuel Pepys.)

1666/7, 2 Jan. '. . . to the King's House, and there saw "The Custome of the Country," the second time of its being acted, wherein Knipp does the Widow well; but of all the plays that ever I did see, the worst—having neither plot, language, nor anything in the earth that is acceptable; only Knipp sings a little song admirably. But fully the worst play that ever I saw or I believe shall see.' (Ibid.)

1667, 1 Aug. Pepys saw *The Custom of the Country* again and called it 'an ill play'. (Ibid.)

1668/9, *c.* 12 Jan. In 'A Catalogue of part of His Ma^tes Servants Playes as they were formerly acted at the Blackfryers & now allowed of to his Ma^tes Servants at ye New Theatre' occurs 'Custome of ye Country'. (Nicoll, *A History of Restoration Drama*, 3rd ed., p. 315.)

1672/3, 30 Jan. S.R. Humphrey Robinson, executor of Humphrey Robinson, transferred to John Martin and Henry Herringman his rights in a long list of plays, including 'Custom of the Country. halfe'. (Greg, *Bibliography*, i. 72–73.)

1679. 'The Custom of the Country' is the fifth play printed in the second Beaumont and Fletcher Folio.

1683, 21 Aug. S.R. Sarah Martin, executrix of John Martin, transferred to Robert Scott her rights in a long list of plays, including 'Custome of the Country ¼'. (Ibid., pp. 75–76.)

The source for either the main plot or the sub-plot of the play has been variously given as 'one of *Malespini*'s Novels, Deca. 6. Nov. 6' (Langbaine, *An Account of the English Dramatick Poets*, p. 208), Cinthio's *Hecatommithi*, vi. 6 (H. Weber, ed., *The Works of Beaumont and Fletcher* [1812], ii. 270), and Cervantes's *Persiles y Sigismunda*, and there seem to be points of similarity in all three, but Bond has shown in his edition of the play (pp. 480–1) that the immediate source of the main plot was clearly Cervantes. *Persiles y Sigismunda* was printed in Spanish in 1617, in French in 1618, and in English in 1619 (S.R., 22 February 1618/19). Bond notes that not only do the story and many of the names come from Cervantes, but many words and phrases have been taken from the English translation.

Since this English translation was used for the play, the first performance cannot antedate 1619, a date which approximates that suggested by the cast of the King's men for a performance of *The Custom of the Country* printed in the Folio of 1679. This cast is given as follows:

The principal Actors were

Joseph Taylor.	⎫	*Robert Benfeild.*
John Lowin.	⎬	*William Eglestone.*
Nicholas Toolie.	⎬	*Richard Sharpe.*
John Vnderwood.	⎭	*Thomas Holcomb.*

There has been much discussion of these twenty-five casts of Jacobean actors for the performance of Jacobean plays, first published in 1679. There is no good evidence as to the source of the information, but except for a very few instances the names are always consistent with other information about the actors and the plays, and the lists are generally accepted as the work of an informed person. They are also generally assumed to be casts for original performances, though the evidence for this assumption is disturbingly incomplete and occasionally contradicted. (See Maxwell, op. cit., pp. 7–13.)

In the case of *The Custom of the Country*, the cast indicates a date after the death of Richard Burbage, who was buried 16 March 1618/19 (see above, ii. 396), for he was the greatest actor of his time, and the company would scarcely have neglected his drawing power in casting the play, had he been available. Nathan Field, perhaps the next most popular actor of the middle years of King James's reign (see above, ii. 434–6), is also omitted. The precise date of his death is unknown, but it was probably after 19 May 1619, when he appeared in a company list, and certainly before 2 August 1620, when his sister was granted letters of administration of his estate. (Ibid.) Joseph Taylor of the cast had been a member of Prince Charles's company as late as January or February 1618/19, but appears in an official list of the members of the King's company 19 May 1619. (See above, ii. 590–2.) All these facts about the actors of the cast fit with the publication of the English translation of *Persiles y Sigismunda* in indicating a date of 1619 or later for the first production of *The Custom of the Country*.

Nicholas Tooley, an actor who appears in the cast, was buried 5 June 1623 (see above, ii. 602), and this date must be a *terminus ad quem* for the cast of the play. The lines of the prologue:

> *So free this work is, Gentlemen, from offence,*
>
> .   .   .   .   .
>
> *Nor Lord, nor Lady we have tax'd; nor State,*
> *Nor any private person.*   (Folio, 1679)

suggest that the actors disclaim contemporary allusion because they had recently been charged with it. The only known difficulties

of the King's men with the censors in the years 1619–23 arose in
the objections to, and censorship of, *Sir John van Olden Barnavelt*, which had been written by the authors of *The Custom of the
Country*, and which was temporarily suppressed in August 1619.
(See above, i. 7.) The lines of the prologue might well refer to that
difficulty, in which case they would presumably have been written
not more than a year after the censorship. From this evidence a
date of 1619 or 1620 seems likely for the first production of the
play.

The folios print two prologues and two epilogues for *The Custom
of the Country*, one set for a new play and the second set clearly
for a revival. Each prologue uses the plural more than once in
referring to the authors. The prologue for the revival is headed, in
the 1647 Folio, '*For my Sonne Clarke*', presumably referring to
Hugh Clark, an actor who was a member of Queen Henrietta's
company as late as 1635 but who became a member of the King's
company, probably in 1636 or 1637. (See above, ii. 406–7.) The
wording indicates that he also delivered the epilogue for the
revival. Since there was a court performance of the play on
27 November 1638, it may well be that the prologue was written
for Clark at the time of a revival preparatory to the court performance.

The multiple authorship referred to repeatedly in both prologues has been generally taken to refer to Fletcher and Massinger,
since Beaumont died several years before the play could have
appeared. Bond summarizes Boyle's analysis of Massinger's work
in the play. (Variorum ed., pp. 478–80.) Oliphant is in general
agreement. (Op. cit., pp. 224–6.) Their identification of Massinger
as a collaborator is reinforced by W. J. Lawrence's observation of
Massinger's peculiar punctuation of stage directions in the folio
text of the play. (*Those Nut-Cracking Elizabethans*, pp. 194–202.)

Bond found the two folio texts good, and in the second Folio
more corrections of errors than commission of new ones. (Variorum
ed., p. 477.) R. C. Bald pointed out six prompt directions in the
folio text. (*Bibliographical Studies in the Beaumont & Fletcher
Folio of 1647*, p. 105.) Either the manuscript from which the play
was printed had been originally prepared for the theatre, or it had
at least seen some later use as a prompt copy.

The records of performances of the play indicate popularity
despite the demurs of Samuel Pepys. Especially notable is the
record of Sir Henry Herbert's share of the receipts in 1628 when
the play was about eight years old. Sir Henry records his receipts
for ten such performances, and *The Custom of the Country* was

the most profitable, though the other plays included *Othello*, *Richard II*, and *The Alchemist*. Most profitable after *The Custom of the Country* was *The Wild Goose Chase*. (See Adams, *Herbert*, pp. 43–44.)

Popular appeal is also suggested by Colley Cibber's use of part of the plot in his *Love Makes a Man, or the Fop's Fortune*, produced at Drury Lane in December 1700, and frequently revived. (See Allardyce Nicoll, *A History of Early Eighteenth Century Drama*, pp. 307–8, and Gotthardt Ost, *Das Verhältnis von Cibber's Lustspiel 'Love Makes a Man' zu Fletcher's Dramen 'The Elder Brother' und 'The Custom of the Country'* [1897].) Charles Johnson has several times been said to have used *The Custom of the Country* for his popular *Country Lasses, or The Custom of the Manor*, 1715, but Professor Wilson found no resemblance other than the use of the *droit du seigneur*. (*Influence of Beaumont and Fletcher on Restoration Comedy*, p. 59 n.)

Dryden's indignant repudiation of the charge of immorality of the Restoration stage: 'There is more Baudry in one Play of *Fletcher's* call'd *The Custom of the Country*, than in all ours together' (*Fables Ancient and Modern* [1700], Preface, *D$_2$^{v}), and the statement of the anonymous author of *The Stage Acquitted* (1699), 'There has been nothing so lewd as the bringing in *Bawdy-Houses*, and the *Stallions* of *Fletcher*; no not in the Plays in the two late Reigns' (pp. 10–11), scarcely indicate popular avoidance of the play.

Richard Lovelace glossed his verses published in the first Folio by placing the names of four comedies, including *The Custom of the Country*, opposite his lines about Beaumont and Fletcher's graceful disguising of wanton wit.

Demetrius and Enanthe

See Fletcher, *The Humorous Lieutenant*.

The Devil of Dowgate, or Usury Put to Use (1623)
(Lost)

1623, 17 Oct. 'For the King's Company. An Old Play, called, *More Dissemblers besides Women*: allowed by Sir George Bucke; and being free from alterations was allowed by me, for a new play, called, *The Devil of Dowgate, or Usury put to use*: Written by Fletcher.' (Adams, *Herbert*, p. 26, from Chalmers, *Supplemental Apology*, pp. 215–16.)

1623, 17 Oct. 'I . . . subjoin a list of eleven other plays written by Fletcher, (with the assistance of Rowley in one only,) precisely

in the order in which they were licensed by the Master of the
Revels. . . .

1623. . . .

October 17, The Devill of Dowgate, or Usury put to Use.
Acted by the king's servants. This piece is lost.' (Malone,
Variorum, iii. 226.)

Chalmers has clearly run two entries together, and Malone's
version is the correct one. This conclusion is verified by Malone's
second transcription of the entry in some manuscript notes in his
copy of 'the second volume of his Langbaine'. He wrote: '*The Devil
of Dowgate, or Usury put to Use*, by Fletcher, was acted by the King's
Servants, October 27, 1623. See Sr. H. Herbert.' (W. J. Lawrence,
Speeding up Shakespeare [1937], pp. 177–8.) Presumably '27' is
Lawrence's mistake in copying Malone's '17'; in any case, both
Malone and Chalmers read '17' elsewhere. Probably Malone's
statement that the play is lost is correct.

Weber suggested in his general introduction and in the intro-
duction to *The Night Walker* (i, pp. lv–lvi; and xiv. 4, n.) that *The
Night Walker* might be an alteration by Shirley of *The Devil of
Dowgate*. This is highly improbable. As Fleay pointed out (*Biog.
Chron.* i. 197), Queen Henrietta's men owned and performed *The
Night Walker* after it was 'corrected by Sherley'. Following the
Queen's men, Beeston's Boys, their successors at the Phoenix,
owned the play, and it is most unlikely that these companies
would have been able to keep a play which had been licensed for
the powerful King's company. (See below, *The Night Walker*.)
Fleay himself, with his familiar urge to pin down all loose titles,
identified *Wit at Several Weapons* with *The Devil of Dowgate* (*Biog.
Chron.* i. 218), and, not satisfied, went on to say that the play had
still a third name, *The Buck Is a Thief*, under which title it was
acted at court 28 December 1623. This game must have been great
fun, but no one ought to take it seriously.

The Double Marriage (c. 1621)
with Philip Massinger?

Bond, R. Warwick. 'On Six Plays in *Beaumont and Fletcher, 1679*',
    R.E.S. xi (1935), 258–61.
Oliphant, E. H. C. *The Plays of Beaumont and Fletcher* (1927),
    pp. 226–30 and 234–6.
Waith, E. M. 'The Sources of *The Double Marriage* by Fletcher
    and Massinger', *M.L.N.* lxiv (1949), 505–10.

1641, 7 Aug. 'The double marriage' is included in a list of plays belonging to the King's men which the Lord Chamberlain forbade the printers to publish without the company's consent. (See above, i. 65–66.)

1646, [4] Sept. S.R. Robinson and Moseley entered 'Double Marriage' 'by m^r Beamont & m^r fflesher' in a group of nearly fifty plays, all apparently of the repertory of the King's company. (Greg, *Bibliography*, i. 56–57, and see above, i. 116, 'Burroughs'.)

1647. 'The double Marriage' is printed as the twenty-first play in the first Beaumont and Fletcher Folio of 1647.

1668/9, c. 12 Jan. 'The Double Marriage' appears in 'A Catalogue of part of His Ma^{tes} Servants Playes as they were formerly acted at the Blackfryers & now allowed of to his Ma^{tes} Servants at ye New Theatre'. (Nicoll, *A History of Restoration Drama*, 3rd ed., p. 315.)

1672. In '*Covent Garden* Drolery, Or A Colection, Of all the Choice *Songs*, *Poems*, *Prologues*, and *Epilogues*, (Sung and Spoken at *Courts* and *Theatres*)' appears a prologue, apparently for a revival of *The Double Marriage*. (See Sprague, *Beaumont and Fletcher on the Restoration Stage*, pp. 50–51.)

1672/3, 30 Jan. S.R. Humphrey Robinson, executor of Humphrey Robinson, transferred to John Martin and Henry Herringman his rights in a long list of plays, including 'Double marriag. halfe'. (Greg, *Bibliography*, i. 72–73.)

1679. 'The Double Marriage. A Tragedy' is reprinted in the second Beaumont and Fletcher Folio of 1679.

<1682. Among the plays listed by Downes as acted by the United Companies after their union in 1682 is '*The Double Marriage*'. (*Roscius Anglicanus*, Summers ed., pp. 39–40.)

1683, 21 Aug. S.R. Sarah Martin, executrix of John Martin, transferred to Robert Scott her rights in a long list of plays, including 'Double Marriage. $\frac{1}{4}$'. (Greg, *Bibliography*, i. 75–76.)

1687/8, 6 Feb. In a Lord Chamberlain's warrant for payment for plays performed at court appears 'The Double Marriage at Whitehall'. (Nicoll, *A History of Restoration Drama*, 3rd ed., p. 313.)

The cast given for the play in the Folio of 1679 is:

Joseph Tailor,	*John Lowin,*
Robert Benfield,	*Rich. Robinson,*
John Vnderwood,	*Nich. Tooly,*
George Birch,	*Rich. Sharp.*

This cast gives an approximate date for the play, since it does not include the famous Burbage, who was buried 16 March 1618/19, and it does include Nicholas Tooley, who was buried 5 June 1623. (See above, *The Custom of the Country*.) The marked similarity of the material of the sea scenes to that in *The Sea Voyage*, which was licensed for production 22 June 1622, suggests that one play exploited further the sea material which had proved popular in the other, and, since the exploitation is fuller in *The Sea Voyage*, one might reasonably guess that *The Double Marriage* immediately preceded it. R. Warwick Bond (loc. cit.) suggests 1621 as the date because of the fact that Castruccio's kingly disappointments at the beginning of Act v seem to be suggested by those of Sancho in *Don Quixote*, Part II, which was first published in English in 1620.

Bond (loc. cit.) pointed out that the source of the historical action of the play and of a number of the names of the characters was Thomas Danett's translation, *The Historie of Philip de Commines*, 1596. Waith (loc. cit.) agrees with this ascription of source, but adds that the story of Virolet's putting away Juliana and the story of his marriage with Martia come from Declamations 64 and 48 of Lazarus Pyott's translation, *The Orator*, 1596. The similarity of the opening scene of the play to *Julius Caesar*, II. I, has been several times commented upon.

The disintegrators seem fairly well agreed that the play contains the work of Massinger as well as of Fletcher, and there is a rough similarity in their assignment of acts and parts of acts. They are divided, however, as to whether the play was originally a composition of Fletcher later revised by Massinger, or a collaboration of Massinger and Fletcher, later perhaps slightly revised by Massinger. Fleay (*Biog. Chron.* i. 211) thought he saw signs of revision in 1630–1 in the reference to oil in Act I, which he thought pointed to the 'soap-boiling monopoly of 1630'. He also saw in the mentions of 'nightpiece' and 'piety' reason to identify *The Double Marriage* with *The Unfortunate Piety, or The Italian Night-Piece*. This double title is in a Stationers' Register entry of 1653 and probably indicates two plays. *The Unfortunate Piety* was licensed as Massinger's by Herbert on 13 June 1631 (Adams, *Herbert*, p. 33), and there is no reason to think that it was not a new play. I find the oil allusion little more convincing. In the first place, the line in the play refers to the price of oil, not to the prohibition of fish oil, as in the controversy, and in the second place, the soap controversy did not take place in 1630, but went on from 1632 to 1635. (See Gardiner, viii. 72 ff.)

Professor R. C. Bald noticed the unusual specificness of the music directions in the play and thought that this, along with one or two anticipatory directions, suggested that the folio text had been set up from a prompt manuscript. (*Studies in the Beaumont & Fletcher Folio of 1647*, pp. 107–8.)

Charles Johnson's *Love and Liberty* (1709) has several times been said to be based on *The Double Marriage* (Montague Summers, ed., *Covent Garden Drollery*, p. 110; Allardyce Nicoll, *A History of Early Eighteenth Century Drama*, p. 105), but Professor Sprague (*Beaumont and Fletcher on the Restoration Stage*, p. xv, n.) found that the Johnson play contained only minor borrowings from *The Double Marriage*.

The Elder Brother (1625?)
with Massinger?

MS.: B.M. MS. Egerton 1994, fols. 2–29. (See W. W. Greg, *Dramatic Documents*, pp. 334–7.)

Editions: W. W. Greg, ed., in *The Works of Francis Beaumont and John Fletcher*, Variorum Edition, ii. 1–100; William H. Draper, ed., 'Now reprinted with slight alterations and abridgement for use on occasions of Entertainment especially in Schools and Colleges' (1915).

Maxwell, J. C. 'A Dramatic Echo of an Overburian Character', *N. & Q.* cxcii (1947), 277.

Oliphant, E. H. C. *The Plays of Beaumont and Fletcher* (1927), pp. 114–15 and 230–4.

1634/5, Feb. John Greene saw *The Elder Brother*, presumably at Blackfriars, on an unspecified date in February. (E. M. Symonds, 'The Diary of John Greene (1635–57)', *English Historical Review*, xliii [1928], 386.)

1635, 25 Apr. 'To a playe eod: Called the Elder Brother . . . . . 00–01–00' and '. . . after dynner to the Elder Brother att the bla: ffryers & was idle'. (Account Book and Diary of Sir Humphrey Mildmay. See above, ii. 677.)

1636/7, 5 Jan. '*The Elder Brother*, on thursday the 5 Janua.' in Sir Henry Herbert's list of plays performed at Hampton Court 26 December 1636–21 February 1636/7. This performance is also listed in the players' bill. (Adams, *Herbert*, pp. 57 and 76.)

1636/7, 24 Mar. S.R. Waterson and Benson entered 'vnder the hands of M^r. Tho: Herbert Deputy of S^r. Henry Herbert/ & Mr Downes warden a [booke *deleted*] Comedy called the Elder

Brother written by Iohn ffletcher'. (Greg, *Bibliography*, i. 45.)

1637. The Elder Brother A Comedie. Acted at the *Blacke Friers*, by his Maiesties Servants. *Printed according to the true Copie*. Written by *Iohn Fletcher* Gent. . . . 1637.

1637. [Another edition, with title in lower case. Probably printed several years after 1637.]

1646, 31 Oct. S.R. John Benson assigned to Humphrey Moseley 'The Elder Brother. by m^r Flesher. halfe'; and on the same day Waterson assigned Moseley 'The Elder Brother his part . . . by M^r fflesher'. (Ibid., p. 57.)

1650–50/1. The Elder Brother A Comedie. Acted at the private house in *Blacke Fryers*, with great Applause, by His late Majesties Servants. *Printed according to the true Copie*. Written by *Francis Beavmont*, and *John Fletcher*. Gent. The second Edition, Corrected and Amended . . . 1651. [A variant issue is dated 'MDCL'.]

c. 1660. 'Elder Brother' is found in a list of the stock plays of Killigrew's company furnished to Sir Henry Herbert, probably shortly after the Restoration, and found among his papers by Malone. (Adams, *Herbert*, p. 82.)

1660, 23 Nov. 'Friday the 23. No. The Elder Brother' appears in a list of performances of plays by 'the Kings Companie at the Red Bull and the new house in Gibbon's Tennis Court near Clare Market' 1660–2. (Ibid., p. 116.)

1661. The Elder Brother, A Comedy. *Acted* at the *Black Friers* by His Majesties Servants . . . Written by *John Fletcher* Gent. . . . 1661.

1661, 6 Sept. 'I went to the Theatre, and saw "Elder Brother" ill acted.' (Diary of Samuel Pepys.)

1662 [–3?]. In Edward Browne's accounts for plays seen in '1662', under the heading 'At the Cock Pit in Drewry Lane' is the entry 'Elder Brother . . . 15 0'. (W. W. Greg, 'Theatrical Repertories of 1662', *Gentleman's Magazine*, ccci [1906], 69–72; from B.M. MS. Sloane 1900.)

<1663. Downes gives a cast for the performances of the play by Killigrew's company at 'the New Theatre in *Drury-Lane*'. (*Roscius Anglicanus*, Summers ed., p. 6.)

1668/9, *c*. 12 Jan. 'The Elder Brother' appears in 'A Catalogue of part of His Ma^{tes} Servants Playes as they were formerly acted at the Blackfryers & now allowed of to his Ma^{tes} Servants at ye New Theatre'. (Nicoll, *A History of Restoration Drama*, 3rd ed., pp. 315–16.)

1678. The Elder Brother: A Comedy. As it is now Acted at the

Theatre Royal, By His Majesties Servants. Written by *Francis Beaumont & John Fletcher*, Gent. . . . M.DC.LXXVIII.

1679. 'The Elder Brother, A Comedy' is the sixth play in the second Beaumont and Fletcher Folio of 1679.

The clearest evidence for dating the play is found in the prologue and epilogue printed in the quarto of 1637 and reprinted in the second Folio:

> *Y' are all most welcome to no vulgar Play;*
> *And so farre we are confident; And if he*
> *That made it, still lives in your memory;*
> *You will expect what we present to night,*
> *Should be judg'd worthy of your eares and sight.*
> *You shall heare* Fletcher *in it; his true straine,*
> *And neate expressions; living he did gaine*
> *Your good opinions; But now dead commends*
> *This Orphan to the care of noble friends:*
> *And may it raise in you content and mirth,*
> *And be receiv'd for a legitimate birth.*
>   *Your grace erects new Trophies to his fame,*
>   *And shall to after times preserve his name.* (Q 1637, $*_2{}^v$)

The same information about Fletcher is found in the epilogue:

>   *. . . that you freely would*
> *To th' Authour's memory, so farre unfold,*
> *And shew your loves and liking to his wit,*
> *Not in your praise, but often seeing it;*
> *That being the grand assurance that can give*
> *The Poet and the Player meanes to live.*   (Q 1637, $K_2{}^v$)

Obviously Fletcher was dead when this prologue and epilogue were written, but there is no indication that the performance was a revival, as has sometimes been suggested. To me the term '*Orphan*' and the requests that the audience receive the play for '*a legitimate birth*' and erect '*new Trophies to his fame*' and praise the play by '*often seeing it*' are clear indications that the players were presenting the piece as a new and hitherto unacted one. A first production after August 1625 is therefore indicated.

How long before Fletcher's death was the play composed? Various dates have been proposed, but it seems to me that Fleay was quite right in observing a datable allusion to a Jonson masque in the piece, though he was inaccurate in his details. (*Biog. Chron.* i. 229.) In courting Angelina, Charles says, in IV. 3:

Then like blew *Neptune* courting of an Iland,
Where all the perfumes and the pretious things
That waite upon great Nature are laid up,
Ide clip it in mine armes, and chastly kisse it. (Q 1637, G₃)

This is a most unusual figure, but it fits precisely the action in Jonson's *Neptune's Triumph*. This masque, about which Fleay was confused, was prepared for Twelfth Night 1623/4, but it was never acted. Jonson salvaged much of his material—including the scene described in *The Elder Brother*—and worked it into *The Fortunate Isles and Their Union*, which was performed at court 9 January 1624/5 and published about the same time. (See below, under the two masques.) This allusion clearly suggests that Fletcher was composing *The Elder Brother* in January 1624/5, or shortly thereafter, for any masque was of very transient interest.

A play on which Fletcher was working in January 1624/5 might very well have remained unacted until after his death, in spite of his rapidity of composition, for in 1625 the theatres were closed not later than 27 March, and they remained closed until about the first week in December. (See above, ii. 654–7.) Thus if Fletcher had completed *The Elder Brother* as much as five months before his death, the play could not have been acted until at least three months after his burial because of the long plague closing.

These theatrical facts—generally ignored—seem to me to remove the implied reasons for assuming that Fletcher left the play unfinished at his death and that Massinger completed it several years later—'not much before 1637', as Greg suggested. (Op. cit., p. 1.) The newly noted performances of 1634/5 and 1635 show that 1637 is too late for Massinger's work. In any case I find it impossible to believe that so valuable a commodity as a Fletcher play—and one which was to prove so popular as this one—would have been left unexploited for ten years or so by the canny King's men. That Massinger did have a hand in the play, the disintegrators seem agreed, and they are even roughly agreed in assigning Massinger the first and fifth acts and Fletcher the second, third, and fourth. Such a division corresponds to the usual Fletcher–Massinger collaboration and offers no evidence at all that Massinger finished what Fletcher left incomplete.

The manuscript of the play in Egerton 1994 is not a very interesting one. It was apparently made by a scribe and shows no playhouse characteristics. Greg notes that the poems at the end of the play suggest a purely literary origin. (*Dram. Doc.*, p. 334.) The text appears to have no particular significance, agreeing sometimes with one quarto and sometimes with another.

The best discussion of the texts of the play is found in Greg's introduction to the Variorum edition. He notes some reason for thinking that the second quarto of 1637 may be a surreptitious, misdated edition.

Fleay (*Biog. Chron.* i. 228–9) insouciantly identified the lost play entitled *The Orator, or The Noble Choice* as a revision of *The Elder Brother*. Greg has little difficulty in disposing of the identification. (Variorum ed., p. 1.)

No source for the play has been identified, but Weber pointed out clear resemblances to Calderón's *De una causa dos efectos*. Greg (ed. cit., pp. 7–8) found that in spite of the resemblances the differences were too fundamental to suggest that either Calderón or Fletcher saw the other's work; he concluded that there must be a common and undiscovered source. Greg scoffs at Koeppel's assertion of a parallel with Boccaccio.

De Vocht observed certain close resemblances between Simon Baylie's *The Wizard* and parts of *The Elder Brother* and concluded that Fletcher had imitated Baylie's play. It seems to me much more likely that Baylie was the imitator. (See Simon Baylie, *The Wizard*, above.) Another borrower from *The Elder Brother* was Colley Cibber, who used parts of it in his *Love Makes a Man, or the Fop's Fortune*, which was produced at Drury Lane in December 1700 and frequently revived. (See Allardyce Nicoll, *A History of Early Eighteenth Century Drama*, pp. 307–8, and Gotthardt Ost, *Das Verhältnis von Cibber's Lustspiel 'Love Makes a Man' zu Fletcher's Dramen 'The Elder Brother' und 'The Custom of the Country'* [1897].)

The Fair Maid of the Inn (1625/6)

Edition: F. L. Lucas, ed. *The Complete Works of John Webster* (1927), iv. 147–238.

Bald, R. C. *Bibliographical Studies in the Beaumont & Fletcher Folio of 1647*, Supplement to the Bibliographical Society's Transactions, No. 13 (1938), *passim*.

Hart, H. C. ' "The Captain" in Fletcher and Ben Jonson', *N. & Q.*, Tenth Series, ii (1904), 184–5.

Koeppel, Emil. *Quellen-Studien zu den Dramen Ben Jonson's, John Marston's und Beaumont's und Fletcher's* (1895), pp. 117–19.

Lloyd, Bertram. ' "The Juggling Captain" in "The Fair Maid of the Inn" ', *T.L.S.*, 12 January 1928, p. 28.

Lucas, F. L. 'Did Dr. Forman Commit Suicide?', *T.L.S.*, 7 April 1927, p. 250.

Maxwell, Baldwin. 'The Source of the Principal Plot of *The Fair Maid of the Inn*', *M.L.N.* lix (1944), 122–7.

Oliphant, E. H. C. *The Plays of Beaumont and Fletcher* (1927), pp. 463–72.

Sargeaunt, M. J. *John Ford* (1935), pp. 63–66.

Stoll, E. E. *John Webster* (1905), pp. 154–6.

Sykes, H. Dugdale. 'A Webster–Massinger Play. "The Fair Maid of the Inn" ', *N. & Q.*, Eleventh Series, xii (1915), 134–7, 155–6, 175–7, 196–8. Reprinted in *Sidelights on Elizabethan Drama* (1924), pp. 140–58.

1625/6, 22 Jan. '*The Fair Maid of the Inn*, by John Fletcher, licensed; acted at the Blackfriars.' (Adams, *Herbert*, p. 31.)

1647. 'The Faire Maide Of The Inne' is the thirty-second play in the Beaumont and Fletcher Folio.

1660, 29 June. S.R. Humphrey Robinson and Humphrey Moseley entered six plays, including 'The Faire Maid of the Inne . . . all Six Copies written by ffra: Beamont & Iohn ffletcher'. (Greg, *Bibliography*, i. 68.)

1668/9, *c.* 12 Jan. In 'A Catalogue of part of His Ma^tes Servants Playes as they were formerly acted at the Blackfryers & now allowed of to his Ma^tes Servants at ye New Theatre' occurs the title, 'The fayre Mayd of ye Inn'. (Nicoll, *A History of Restoration Drama*, 3rd ed., p. 315.)

1672/3, 30 Jan. S.R. In a long list of titles transferred from the heir of Humphrey Robinson to John Martin and Henry Herringman occurs the title 'The faire Maide of the Inn. halfe'. (Greg, *Bibliography*, i. 72–73.)

1679. 'The Fair Maid of the Inn. A Tragi-Comedy' appears in the second Beaumont and Fletcher Folio.

1683, 21 Aug. S.R. The executrix of John Martin transferred to Robert Scott a long list of titles, including a fourth interest in 'faire Maide of the Inn'. (Ibid., pp. 75–76.)

There are many confused conjectures and very few facts about this play. The disintegrators have found in it at one time or another the work of Beaumont, Fletcher, Massinger, Rowley, Jonson, Webster, and Ford. Lucas, following Sykes (op. cit.), even printed the play in his collected edition of Webster and prepared a table of scene attributions, allowing Fletcher none of the play at all. (Op. cit., pp. 148–52.) For none of these dramatists except

Fletcher is there any external evidence whatever; their proponents have been able to find only parallel passages, favourite words and phrases, dubious reminiscent verse patterns, and similar situations. The best of the evidence cited seems to me only faintly suggestive; much of it consists of strained rationalization of hunches. Most of the conjectural attributions are summarized by Oliphant. (Loc. cit.)

Lucas suggests that the attribution to Fletcher by Herbert was an advertising device (op. cit., p. 148), but it is preposterous to suggest that the Master of the Revels was a publicity agent for the King's company; moreover, there was no publicity value in his entry: his office-book was an official record, not a series of public notices. *The Fair Maid of the Inn* is not a particularly characteristic Fletcher play, and Fletcher may have had collaborators or revisers, but no good evidence for the identification of any— with the possible exception of Massinger—has been cited.

Discussions of the date of the play have generally been confused with questions of authorship. Herbert's licence for performance normally indicates the approximate date of a first production, and there is no indication in the entry for *The Fair Maid of the Inn* that the revision of a previously licensed play is recorded, rather than the first licence of a new one. It is true that the text of the piece shows odd crudities and apparent dislocations (see Lucas ed., II. 4; III. 2; V. I), but the alterations or excisions they suggest could have taken place either in the five months between Fletcher's death and the licensing of the play, or in the thirty-one years between the licence and first publication. I see no significant evidence of a production before the one Herbert licensed.

There are several allusions to contemporary events in the play. The dialogue about the new world in the moon in Act IV sounds like an allusion to Jonson's masque of *News from the New World Discovered in the Moon*, which was performed at court 17 January 1619/20. The reference to butter in the discussion of a news pamphlet in Act IV suggests the famous and frequently noted publisher of newsletters in the early twenties named Nathaniel Butter; and the allusions to a captain connected with newsmongering and at the time recently dead seem intended for Captain Gainsford, whose death was recorded in a letter of 4 September 1624. (H. C. Hart, op. cit.) Later in the same act when Forobosco proposes to send the clown to Amboyna for pepper, the clown exclaims, 'To *Amboyna*? so I might be pepper'd.' He is evidently fearful of Amboyna because of the sensational Dutch massacre of the English there in February 1622/3. The news did not reach

England, however, until May 1624, and was a common subject of allusion in the summer and autumn of 1624 and on into 1625. (See Gardiner, v. 241-4, and *C.S.P., Dom., 1623-25, passim.*) Other allusions in Act v to Ball and Dr. Lamb, though less precisely datable, could easily have been current in 1624 and 1625. These allusions are quite compatible with the assumption that *The Fair Maid of the Inn* was new when Sir Henry Herbert licensed it in January 1625/6.

A number of the allusions in *The Fair Maid of the Inn* are directed to the same individuals and events referred to in Jonson's *Staple of News* (q.v.), which was also performed by the King's company in February 1625/6, one month after Herbert licensed *The Fair Maid*. These similar allusions seem to be the principal reason that several of the disintegrators have attributed part of the play to Jonson. The implied sterility of invention is not characteristic of Jonson as I read him, but the fact that the two plays were acted in the same season by the same troupe at the same theatre suggests a possible transference of material from one play to the other—conceivably by the actors.

Evidently *The Fair Maid of the Inn* was not a popular play, for the King's men did not protect it in their repertory of 1641 (see above, i. 65–66), though it had never been published. There are no records of any performances after the licence, and I have found no allusions to the play. It was not licensed with others for the Folio of 1647, and Bald presents evidence that it came late into the hands of the publishers (op. cit., pp. 34–36), and therefore presumably not from the company, though a few of the stage directions suggest a prompt copy. There are no records of Restoration performances, though rights in the play were recorded. Apparently *The Fair Maid of the Inn* did not seem much more effective in the seventeenth century than it does now.

Various scholars have asserted that *La Ilustre Fregona*, one of Cervantes's *Novelas Exemplares*, is the source of *The Fair Maid of the Inn*. Baldwin Maxwell points out (op. cit.) that this tale if used at all could have suggested a few points in one of the subplots, no more. The main plot is based on the Neri–Bianchi feud in Florence, but Maxwell found no evidence pointing to any particular account of the feud.

The Faithful Friends

See *The Elizabethan Stage*, iii. 232–3.

The Faithful Shepherdess

See *The Elizabethan Stage*, iii. 221–2.

The False One (or *The False Friend?*) (*c.* 1620)
with Philip Massinger?

Edition: Morton Luce, ed., in *The Works of Francis Beaumont
and John Fletcher*, Variorum Edition, iv. 1–90.

Bald, R. C. *Bibliographical Studies in the Beaumont & Fletcher
Folio of 1647*, Supplement to the Bibliographical Society's
Transactions, No. 13 (1938).
Baldwin, T. W. *The Organization and Personnel of the Shakespearean
Company* (1927), pp. 198–9, n.
Maxwell, Baldwin. *Studies in Beaumont, Fletcher, and Massinger*
(1939), pp. 166–76.
Oliphant, E. H. C. *The Plays of Beaumont and Fletcher* (1927), pp.
234–7.
Stoye, Max. *Das Verhältnis von Cibbers Tragödie Caesar in Egypt
zu Fletchers The False One* (1897).
Ulrich, Otto. *Die pseudohistorischen Dramen Beaumonts und
Fletchers 'Thierry and Theodoret', 'Valentinian', 'The Prophetess'
und 'The False One' und ihre Quellen* (1913), pp. 76–98.

c. 1619 or 1620. The title, 'The Falce Frend', appears in a list of
plays on waste paper of the Revels Office, dating about 1619 or
1620. It has been plausibly suggested that the plays of the list
were being considered for court performance. (See Marcham,
Revels, p. 11, and Chambers, *R.E.S.* i [1925], 481 and 484.)
1647. 'The False One. A Tragedy.' is the ninth play in the Beaumont and Fletcher Folio of 1647.
1660, 29 June. S.R. Humphrey Moseley and Humphrey Robinson
entered as their copies six plays, including: 'The false one . . .
all Six Copies written by ffra: Beamont & Iohn ffletcher.'
(Greg, *Bibliography*, i. 68.)
1668/9, *c.* 12 Jan. 'The ffalse One' is one of the plays listed in 'A
Catalogue of part of His Ma^tes Servants Playes as they were
formerly acted at the Blackfryers & now allowed of to his Ma^tes
Servants at ye New Theatre'. (Nicoll, *A History of Restoration
Drama*, 3rd ed., p. 315.)
1672/3, 30 Jan. S.R. In a long list of titles transferred from the
heir of Humphrey Robinson to Martin and Herringman is 'The

safe [*sic*] one, halfe', probably a misreading of *The False One*.
(Greg, *Bibliography*, i. 72–73.)

1679. 'The False One. A Tragedy.' is printed in the second
Beaumont and Fletcher Folio.

1683, 21 Aug. S.R. In a long list of titles transferred from the
executrix of John Martin to Robert Scott is included a fourth
interest in 'false one'. (Ibid., pp. 75–76.)

In the second Folio the following cast for the principal roles is
given:

John Lowin.	*Joseph Taylor.*
John Vnderwood.	*Nicholas Toolie.*
Robert Benfield.	*John Rice.*
Richard Sharpe.	*George Birch.*

This cast, like others in the Folio of 1679, is generally taken to be
that for the first performance of the play and to give certain limits
for the date. Since Burbage, the most popular actor the King's company ever had, is not in the cast, the performance is assumed to be
after his death in March 1618/19. (See above, ii. 396.) Nicholas
Tooley, who is in the cast, was buried in June 1623. (See above, ii.
602.) These limits fit very well with the possibility that *The False
One* is the same as *The False Friend*, a title which is found in a
list of plays of about 1619 or 1620 which were perhaps suggested
for court performance. Septimius, the false one, is several times
in the play associated in the dialogue with the betrayal of friends.

This date of about 1620 and the emphasis in the play on the
falseness of Septimius, a character developed far beyond others of
the classic sources, has led Professor Baldwin Maxwell to suggest
(loc. cit.) that Septimius was elaborated to remind the audience of
Sir Lewis Stukeley's betrayal of Sir Walter Raleigh in 1618. The
popular disgust with Stukeley is clear enough, and there may be
some connexion, though associations of this sort are very decep-
tive for readers 300 years after the events.

Professor Bald (op. cit., p. 110) notes that the text of the play
is one of the few in the Folio of 1647 which reveal no trace at all of
playhouse use and therefore may be assumed to have been printed
from a private transcript. He also points out that the texts of
The False One, The Spanish Curate, The Maid in the Mill, and
less markedly *The Prophetess* exhibit the peculiar bracket punctuation characteristic of the manuscripts of Ralph Crane and concludes that 'one need have little hesitation in claiming that these
four plays were printed from Crane's transcripts'. (Ibid., pp.
113–14.) *The False One* is not found in the Stationers' Register

entry for most of the Folio plays, and Bald presents evidence that the publishers acquired the manuscript very late in their publishing schedule. (Bald, op. cit., pp. 30–36.)

Precise sources used for the familiar classical story have not been identified, except that Dyce in his edition noted certain passages quite close to Lucan's *Pharsalia*. Various episodes are reminiscent of *Antony and Cleopatra*, which the author of the prologue seems to have had in mind in his apologetic statements.

The disintegrators are generally agreed that the two authors of the play indicated by the plurals in the prologue and epilogue are Massinger and Fletcher, and that Massinger's hand is found mostly in the first and last acts and Fletcher's in the other three.

Considering the popularity of Fletcher on the stage, it is odd that there are no performance records for *The False One* at all, only two editions, and no drolls or Restoration adaptations. Cibber used the play for his *Caesar in Egypt*, which was performed—but not for long—at Drury Lane in 1724. (See Nicoll, *A History of Early Eighteenth Century Drama*, pp. 103 and 312.)

Four Plays or Moral Representations in One

See *The Elizabethan Stage*, iii. 231.

Generous Enemies

See Fletcher, *The Humourous Lieutenant*

Henry VIII
with William Shakespeare?

See E. K. Chambers, *William Shakespeare*, i. 495–8; Baldwin Maxwell, *Studies in Beaumont, Fletcher, and Massinger*, pp. 54–73; and A. C. Partridge, *The Problem of Henry VIII Reopened* (1949).

The History of Madon, King of Britain
(Lost)

Attributed to Beaumont only. See *The Elizabethan Stage*, iii. 233.

The Honest Man's Fortune

See *The Elizabethan Stage*, iii. 227.

The Humorous Lieutenant, or Demetrius and Enanthe, or
The Noble Enemy, or Generous Enemies (1619?)

MS.: 'Demetrius and Enanthe. a pleasant Comedie written by Iohn Fletcher gent'.' Lord Harlech's manuscripts.

Editions: R. Warwick Bond, ed., in *The Works of Francis Beaumont and John Fletcher*, Variorum Edition, ii. 455–581; Alexander Dyce, ed., *Demetrius and Enanthe, Being The Humorous Lieutenant, A Play, By John Fletcher: Published from a Manuscript Dated 1625* (1830); Margaret McLaren Cook and F. P. Wilson, eds., *Demetrius and Enanthe By John Fletcher*, Malone Society Reprints (1951).

Bald, R. C. *Bibliographical Studies in the Beaumont & Fletcher Folio of 1647*, Supplement to the Bibliographical Society's Transactions, No. 13 (1938), pp. 64–65, 72, 76–77, 92.

Bradford, Gamaliel. 'An Unnoted Elizabethan Source', *The Nation*, lxxxvii (1908), 573.

Elson, J. J., ed. *The Wits or Sport upon Sport* (1932), pp. 151–8 and 380.

Greg, W. W. *Dramatic Documents from the Elizabethan Playhouses* (1931), pp. 359–60.

Koeppel, Emil. *Quellen-Studien zu den Dramen Ben Jonson's, John Marston's und Beaumont's und Fletcher's* (1895), pp. 83–86.

1625, 27 Nov. Ralph Crane's copy of *Demetrius and Enanthe* for Sir Kenelm Digby is dated 'Nouemb. 27. 1625'. (Cook and Wilson ed., Plate 2.)

1641, 7 Aug. 'The humerous Lieuetennt' appears in a list of plays belonging to the King's company which the Lord Chamberlain forbade the printers to publish without the consent of the company. (See above, i. 65–66.)

1646, [4] Sept. S.R. Humphrey Robinson and Humphrey Moseley entered as their copies a list of about fifty play titles, all apparently formerly of the repertory of the King's company. Included is 'The Noble Enemie or the humerous Leiftenant ... by mr Beamont & mr fflesher'. (Greg, *Bibliography*, i. 56–57.)

1647. The fifteenth play in the first Beaumont and Fletcher Folio is 'The Humorous Lieutenant'.

c. 1660. 'The Humorous Lieutenant' is found in a list of the stock plays of Killigrew's company furnished to Sir Henry Herbert, probably shortly after the Restoration. (Adams, *Herbert*, p. 82.)

1660, 29 Nov. 'Thursday the 29. No. The Humorous Lieutenant.'

appears in a list of performances of plays by 'the Kings Companie at the Red Bull and the new house in Gibbon's Tennis Court near Clare Market' 1660–2. (Adams, *Herbert*, p. 117.)

1661, 20 Apr. 'So back to the Cockpitt. . . . And so saw "The Humersome Lieutenant" acted before the King, but not very well done.' (Diary of Samuel Pepys.)

1661/2, 1 Mar. 'Humorous Lieutenant' appears again in the list of performances of plays by the King's company at the Red Bull and Gibbon's Tennis Court. (Adams, *Herbert*, p. 118.)

1662. The droll, 'Forc'd Vallour', which was made from scenes in the second and third acts of *The Humorous Lieutenant*, was printed in *The Wits or Sport upon Sport*. (See J. J. Elson ed., pp. 151–8 and 380.)

1662[–3?]. Edward Browne noted in his memorandum book that he paid 1s. to see 'Humorous Lievtenant' 'At the New Theatre in Lincolnes Jnne fields'. (W. W. Greg, 'Theatrical Repertories of 1662', *Gentleman's Magazine*, ccci [1906], 69–72; from B.M. MS. Sloane 1900.)

1663, 8 Apr. 'The Company [i.e. Killigrew's King's company] being thus Compleat, they open'd the New Theatre in *Drury-Lane*, on *Thursday* in *Easter* Week, being the *8th*, Day of April 1663, With the Humorous Lieutenant.

   '*Note*, this Comedy was Acted Twelve Days Successively.' The cast follows. (Downes, *Roscius Anglicanus*, Summers ed., p. 3.)

1663, 7 May. 'This day the new Theatre Royal begins to act with scenes the Humourous Lieutenant, but I have not time to see it.' (Diary of Samuel Pepys. On the contradiction of date with Downes's entry above, see Nicoll, *A History of Restoration Drama*, 3rd ed., p. 286, n. 4.)

1663, 8 May. '. . . to the Theatre Royall, being the second day of its being opened. . . . The play was "The Humerous Lieutenant," a play that hath little good in it, nor much in the very part which, by the King's command, Lacy now acts instead of Clun. In the dance, the tall devil's actions was very pretty.' (Diary of Samuel Pepys.)

1666, 20 Dec. In a warrant for payment for plays presented at court appears the entry under this date: 'The Humorous Leiv[t] at the Theatre the Queenes Ma[te] there.' (Nicoll, *A History of Restoration Drama*, 3rd ed., p. 305.)

1666/7, 23 Jan. '. . . thence to the King's house, and there saw "The Humerous Lieutenant:" a silly play, I think; only the Spirit in it that grows very tall, and then sinks again to nothing, having two heads breeding upon one, and then Knipp's singing, did please us.' (Diary of Samuel Pepys.)

1668/9, *c.* 12 Jan. In a 'Catalogue of part of His Ma^{tes} Servants Playes as they were formerly acted at the Blackfryers & now allowed of to his Ma^{tes} Servants at ye New Theatre' occurs the title, 'The Humorous Leiv^t.' (Nicoll, *A History of the Restoration Drama*, 3rd ed., p. 315.)

1672/3, 30 Jan. S.R. Humphrey Robinson, executor of Humphrey Robinson, transferred to John Martin and Henry Herringman rights in a long list of plays, including 'Noble Enimies or Hum: Leifetenant. halfe'. (Greg, *Bibliography*, i. 72–73.)

1679. The tenth play in the second Beaumont and Fletcher Folio is 'The Humourous Lieutenant, A Tragi-Comedy'.

<1682. Downes records that after the union of the two companies, 'The mixt Company then Reviv'd the several old and Modern Plays, that were the Propriety of Mr. *Killigrew*, as . . . The Humorous Lieutenant'. (*Roscius Anglicanus*, Summers ed., pp. 39–40.)

1683, 21 Aug. S.R. Sarah Martin, executrix of John Martin, transferred to Robert Scott her rights in a long list of plays, including 'Noble Enemy or humorous Livetenn^t: ¼'. (Greg, *Bibliography*, i. 75–76.)

1684/5, 2 Jan. 'In a warrant for payment for plays acted by the United Companies at court appears 'Jan: 2^d At ye Leivtenant'. (Nicoll, *A History of Restoration Drama*, 3rd ed., p. 311.)

1685/6, 10 Feb. In a warrant for payment for plays acted at court by the United Companies appears 'The Humorous Lievtenant at Whitehall'. (Ibid., p. 312.)

1686, 24 Nov. In a warrant for payment for plays acted at court by the United Companies appears again 'The Humorouse Leiv^t at Whitehall'. (Ibid., p. 313.)

1687/8, 27 Feb. In a warrant for payment for plays acted at court by the United Companies appears again 'The Humerous Leivetenant at Whitehall'. (Ibid.)

1697. The Humorous Lieutenant, Or, Generous Enemies, A Comedy: As it is now Acted by His Majesties Servants, At The *Theatre-Royal* in *Drury-Lane* . . . 1697.

The first two titles for this play are obvious enough. 'The Humorous Lieutenant' is derived from the chief comic character; it seems to be the title always used by the players, since it is invariably found in their records—more than a dozen of them. 'Demetrius and Enanthe', though used only by Ralph Crane for his manuscript, is also clear enough, since it uses the names of the hero and heroine. 'The Noble Enemy' or 'Enemies' first appears in the Stationers' Register entry of 1646, and all the other examples of this title come from the Stationers' Register. Presumably the title appeared on the manuscript which Robinson and Moseley had and was copied from their list by the subsequent owners of the title. But it is odd, since the title is not appropriate and since it never appears in print. Presumably the 'Generous Enemies' of the 1697 quarto refers to the actions of Demetrius and Seleucus in Acts II and III, but these scenes are a very small part of the play. 'Noble Enemies' of the Stationers' Register entries might also refer to these scenes, I suppose.

Since there are no early references to the play and apparently no clear allusions in the text, the discussions of date have been based on the cast for the play given in the second Folio—presumably the actors in the first production. This cast reads:

Henry Condel.	*Joseph Taylor.*
John Lowin.	*William Eglestone.*
Richard Sharpe.	*John Vnderwood.*
Robert Benfeild.	*Thomas Polard.*

Since Richard Burbage, the most famous actor of the company, does not appear in this list, the play was probably produced after his death in March 1618/19. (See above, ii. 394–6.) Condell is thought to have ceased acting in 1619, though the evidence for this supposition is not so complete as it might be. (See above, ii. 410–12.) These facts suggest a date of 1619 for the first production, a date which is compatible with the known careers of the other actors in the cast. (See their biographies in vol. ii.) Pollard is noted in 1648 as being famous for his acting of the humorous lieutenant; presumably the role was created for him. (See above, ii. 401.)

The manuscript of the play is a literary one prepared by Ralph Crane for Sir Kenelm Digby; it begins with an address to Digby signed by Crane and dated 'Nouemb. 27. 1625'. Crane's transcript contains, besides many minor variants, a little over seventy lines not found in other texts; two passages found only in the manuscript appear to represent material cut by the censor. The manuscript omits the songs of IV. 3, and a few other minor passages. (See Greg, loc. cit., and Bald, loc. cit.)

No comprehensive source for the play has been found. Bond summarizes the various discussions in his edition (pp. 458–60) and adds suggestions of his own, but none seems very convincing.

Oddly enough, none of the disintegrators has found any hand but Fletcher's in the play.

The great Restoration popularity of *The Humorous Lieutenant*, which Langbaine said he had 'often seen acted with Applause' (*An Account of the English Dramatick Poets*, p. 209), is in surprising contrast with the single record indicating performance before the closing of the theatres. The excellence of the comic portions of the play suggest that it should have had some vogue in the Caroline theatre. The same suggestion is made by the author of *A Key to the Cabinet of Parliament*, who mentioned Pollard in his role of the humorous lieutenant as a familiar source of hearty laughter. (See above, ii. 401.) Richard Lovelace used it as one of the seven titles of Beaumont and Fletcher plays with which he annotated his verses for the 1647 Folio. Apparently he meant to cite the play as one of five examples of popular comedy. The inclusion of the play in the King's company list of 1641 is still another indication that *The Humorous Lieutenant* must have been popular before 1642 in spite of the paucity of early records.

Mr. Donald Rulfs notes that the Larpent collection contains an anonymous alteration of the play under the title *The Greek Slave; or, the School for Cowards*, which was unsuccessfully produced by Kemble at Drury Lane 22 March 1791. (*P.M.L.A.* lxiii [1948], 1252.)

The Island Princess, or the Generous Portugal (1619–21)

Koeppel, Emil. *Quellen-Studien zu den Dramen Ben Jonson's, John Marston's und Beaumont's und Fletcher's* (1895), pp. 98–100.

Oliphant, E. H. C. *The Plays of Beaumont and Fletcher* (1927), pp. 139–41.

Sprague, Arthur Colby. *Beaumont and Fletcher on the Restoration Stage* (1926), pp. 137–54.

Stiefel, A. L. 'Über die Quelle von J. Fletchers, "Island Princess"' *Archiv*, ciii (1899), 277–308.

1621, 26 Dec. A warrant of 27 March 1622 authorized payment to John Heminges and the King's players for presentation of six plays at court, including 'The Island Princes vppon St Stephens day'. (Murray, *English Dramatic Companies*, ii. 193, from Inner Temple MS. 515, No. 7.)

1621–21/2. 'The Island Princess, The Pilgrim, and The Wild Goose Chase are found among the court exhibitions of the year 1621.' (Adams, *Herbert*, p. 49. Malone was probably summarizing the

Master of the Revels' record of the same performances listed in the warrant.)

1641, 7 Aug. 'The Island Princes' occurs in a list of plays belonging to the King's company which the Lord Chamberlain forbade the printers to publish without the company's consent. (See above, i. 65–66.)

1646, [4] Sept. S.R. Humphrey Robinson and Humphrey Moseley entered as their copies a list of about fifty titles, all apparently formerly of the repertory of the King's company. Included is 'Island Princes . . . by m^r Beamont & m^r fflesher'. (Greg, *Bibliography*, i. 56–57.)

1647. The fourteenth play in the Beaumont and Fletcher Folio is 'The Island Princesse'.

1668, 6 Nov. In a warrant for payment to the King's company for plays acted before royalty is 'Nov: 6: The Island Princesse King & Queene'. (Nicoll, *A History of Restoration Drama*, 3rd ed., p. 306.)

1668/9, 7 Jan. '. . . to the King's playhouse, and there saw "The Island Princesse," the first time I ever saw it; and it is a pretty good play, many good things being in it, and a good scene of a town on fire.' (Diary of Samuel Pepys.)

1668/9, 7 Jan. In a warrant for payment to the King's company for plays acted before royalty is 'Jan: 7 The Island Princesse King here'. (Nicoll, *A History of Restoration Drama*, 3rd ed., p. 306.)

1668/9, c. 12 Jan. In a 'Catalogue of part of His Ma^{tes} Servants Playes as they were formerly acted at the Blackfryers & now allowed of to his Ma^{tes} Servants at ye New Theatre' occurs the title, 'The Island Princes'. (Ibid., p. 315.)

1668/9, 9 Feb. '. . . to the King's playhouse, and there saw "The Island Princesse," which I like mighty well, as an excellent play.' (Diary of Samuel Pepys.)

1669, 23 Apr. '. . . thence to the King's playhouse, and saw "The Generous Portugalls," a play that pleases me better and better every time we see it.' (Ibid.)

1669. The Island Princess: Or The Generous Portugal. A Comedy. As it is Acted at the *Theatre Royal* by His *Majesties* Servants. With the Alterations and New Additional Scenes . . . 1669.

1672/3, 30 Jan. S.R. Humphrey Robinson, executor of Humphrey Robinson, transferred to John Martin and Henry Herringman rights in a long list of plays, including 'Island Princes. halfe'. (Greg, *Bibliography*, i. 72–73.)

1674, 17 Dec. In a warrant to the King's company for plays

acted before royalty is 'Dec 17 The Island princesse'. (Nicoll, *A History of Restoration Drama*, 3rd ed., p. 307.)

1675, 7 June. In a warrant to the King's company for plays acted before royalty is 'June 7 The Island Princesse at Whitehall'. (Ibid.)

1679. The thirty-ninth play in the second Beaumont and Fletcher Folio is 'The Island Princess: A Tragi-Comedy'.

1683, 21 Aug. S.R. Sarah Martin, executrix of John Martin, transferred to Robert Scott rights in a long list of plays, including 'Island Princesse. ¼'. (Greg, *Bibliography*, i. 75–76.)

1687, 25 Apr. In a warrant for payment for plays performed before royalty by the United Companies is 'Aprill 25 The Island Princes at Whitehall'. (Nicoll, *A History of Restoration Drama*, 3rd ed., p. 313.)

1687. The Island-Princess: As it is Acted At The Theatre Royal, Reviv'd with Alterations. By *N. Tate.* Gent . . . 1687.

1690–2. Downes says that between the operas *King Arthur*, *The Prophetess*, and *The Fairy Queen*, the company acted other plays, including '*Island Princess*'. (*Roscius Anglicanus*, Summers ed., p. 43.)

1699. The Island Princess, Or The Generous Portuguese. Made into an Opera. As it is performed at the Theatre Royal. All the Musical Entertainments and the greatest Part of the Play new, and Written by Mr. *Motteux* . . . 1699.

1699/1700, 12 Mar. Lady Marrow said in a letter of this date to Arthur Kay, 'I have been at a play "The Island Princes" which is mighty fine'. (*Hist. MSS. Com.*, Fifteenth Report, Appendix, Part i [Dartmouth MSS. iii. 145]. Quoted by A. C. Sprague, *Beaumont and Fletcher on the Restoration Stage*, p. 85.)

The latest possible date for the play is set by the record of the court performance in December 1621. A *terminus a quo* date can be derived from the cast, which is printed with the piece in the second Folio of 1679:

John Lowin,	*Joseph Tailor,*
John Vnderwood,	*Robert Benfield,*
William Eglestone,	*George Birch,*
Rich. Sharpe,	*Tho. Polard.*

Richard Burbage, the greatest actor in the history of the company and their most profitable attraction, is not in the cast, as he surely would have been had he been available. Presumably this cast is the one for the first production and Burbage is absent

because the play was first produced after his death in March 1618/
19. (See above, ii. 395–6.) All the members of the cast were available during 1619–21, but there is nothing in any of their careers to
narrow the date limits further. If the recorded court performance
was the first one, the play would probably have been initially produced in 1621, but there is no way of knowing that there had
not been previous court performances in 1619 or 1620.

The story of the play is found in a French novel called *L'Histoire de Ruis Dias, et de Quixaire, Princesse des Moluques, composée
par Le Sr. de Bellan*, 1615, which was published with the first
French translation of the *Novelas Exemplares* of Cervantes. But
this novel seems in turn to be based on Bartolomé Leonardo de
Argensola's *Conquista de las Islas Malucas*, 1609 (see Wilson,
Phil. Quart. xxvii [1948], 188), details from which Stiefel (op. cit.)
found in Fletcher's play and which Macaulay (*C.H.E.L.* vi. 139)
states is the source of *The Island Princess*.

The disintegrators have nearly all found the work of Fletcher only
in the play. Rosenbach thought he saw Massinger's hand, but he
appears to have been influenced by his assumption that the source
was available only in Spanish and by the consequent need to
find a Spanish-reading assistant for Fletcher. (See Maurice Chelli,
Étude sur la collaboration de Massinger avec Fletcher et son groupe
[1926], pp. 94–95.)

The great Restoration popularity of *The Island Princess* was
apparently a popularity of Restoration revisions and not of the
Jacobean original. Though the same title is used throughout the
century, it is notable that in the numerous lists of Jacobean plays
performed 1660–8, *The Island Princess* does not appear. The
recorded performances which begin at the end of 1668 were probably performances of the anonymously altered version that was
published in 1669. The alterations of this version were not extensive, according to Sprague. (Op. cit., pp. 137–9.) Tate's revisions
were much more thoroughgoing. (Ibid., pp. 139–46.) The character
and early eighteenth-century vogue of the opera made from the
play are discussed by Sprague. (Ibid., pp. 82–86.)

The Jeweller of Amsterdam or The Hague (1616–17 ?)
with Field and Massinger
(Lost)

1654, 8 Apr. S.R. Humphrey Moseley entered for his copy 'a Play
called The Ieweller of Amsterdam, or the Hague. by Mr. Iohn

Flesher. Nathan: Field, & Phillip Massinger'. (Greg, *Bibliography*, i. 62.)

The play is known only from the Stationers' Register entry. The title indicates that it concerned the murder of the jeweller, John van Wely, in the household of Prince Maurice in 1616. Fleay noted (*Biog. Chron.* i. 202–3) that a pamphlet on the subject was entered in the Stationers' Register 5 June 1616: '*The true narracon of the Confession of 2 murthers [by]* JOHN DE PARIS *and* JOHN DE LA VIGNE *on the person of* JOHN DE WELY &c' (Arber, iii. 589); and Hazlitt recorded the title of the pamphlet: 'True Recitall of the Confession of the two Murderers John de Paris, and Iohn de la Vigne: Touching the horrible Murder committed vpon the person of Mr. Iohn de Wely, a Merchant-Ieweller of Amsterdam: Together with the sentence giuen against them at the Court of Holland, at the Hage, the 16. day of May, 1616. And Executed vpon them the same day.' (*Second Series of Bibliographical Collections and Notes on Early English Literature, 1474–1700* [1882], p. 709.)

Presumably Fletcher, Massinger, and Field had their play ready while the events in the Netherlands were still fresh in the public mind, as Fletcher and Massinger did two or three years later in the very similar circumstances of *Sir John van Olden Barnavelt* (q.v.). Since about the time of the entry of the pamphlet Field appears to have become a member of the King's company, Fletcher its regular dramatist, and Massinger Fletcher's frequent assistant, it is most likely that the play, like *Barnavelt*, was the property of the King's men.

A King and No King

See *The Elizabethan Stage*, iii. 225.

The Knight of Malta (1616–18)
with Field and Massinger?

Edition: Marianne Brocke, ed., with an introduction and notes. Bryn Mawr MS. Dissertation (1944).

Blühm, Erich. *Über 'The Knight of Malta' und seine Quellen* (1903).
Brinkley, Roberta. *Nathan Field, the Actor-Playwright* (1928), pp. 121–30.
McKeithan, Daniel Morley. *The Debt to Shakespeare in the Beaumont-and-Fletcher Plays* (1938), pp. 158–64.

Oliphant, E. H. C. *The Plays of Beaumont and Fletcher* (1927), pp. 392–8.

c. 1619–20. '. . . ght of Malta' appears in a list of plays on waste paper of the Revels Office, probably dating about 1619 or 1620. It has been plausibly suggested that the plays of the list were being considered for court performance. (See Marcham, *Revels*, p. 33, and E. K. Chambers, *R.E.S.* i [1925], 484.)

1641, 7 Aug. 'The knt of Malta' appears in the list of plays belonging to the King's men which the L.C. forbade the printers to publish without the company's consent. (See above, i. 65–66.)

1646, [4] Sept. 'Knights [*sic*] of Malta' appears in the list of thirty Beaumont and Fletcher plays and eighteen others, all presumably the property of the King's company, which were entered to Moseley and Robinson. (Greg, *Bibliography*, i. 56–57.)

1647. 'The Knight of Malta' is the twenty-third play in the Beaumont and Fletcher Folio.

1668/9, *c.* 12 Jan. In 'A Catalogue of part of His Mates Servants Playes as they were formerly acted at the Blackfryers & now allowed of to his Mates Servants at ye New Theatre' occurs the title, 'The Knights of Malta'. (Nicoll, *A History of Restoration Drama*, 3rd ed., p. 315.)

1672/3, 30 Jan. S.R. A half-interest in 'Knights [*sic*] of Maltha' and 104 other titles, many of them plays, was transferred from Humphrey Robinson, executor of Humphrey Robinson, to John Martin and Henry Herringman. (Greg, *Bibliography*, i. 72–73.)

1679. 'The Knight of Malta' is the thirty-fourth play in the Beaumont and Fletcher second Folio.

The play can be dated from the cast in the 1679 Folio, which reads:

Rich. Burbadge,	*Henry Condel,*
Nathan Field,	*Robert Benfeild,*
John Vnderwood,	*John Lowin,*
Rich. Sharpe,	*Thomas Holcome.*

Since Burbage was buried 16 March 1618/19 (see above, ii. 395–6), the play certainly opened before that date and indeed possibly before the end of 1618, if we are to allow any time for a last illness. Of the other actors, Nathan Field was apparently the last to join the company, and the play must date after his admission. Miss Brinkley (op. cit., pp. 32–35), followed by Miss Brocke, thinks that this event occurred in 1617, but Baldwin (*Organization and Personnel*, pp. 50–52) gives more cogent reasons for thinking that he was admitted in 1616, probably as the successor to Shakespeare. The first performance of the play which was possible with this cast falls, therefore, some time between 1616, when Field became a King's man, and 1618/19, when Burbage died. The same date limitations apply to the composition of the play, since Field is not likely to have written for the King's men until he had broken his connexion with his former troupe. Composition in or after 1616 is also suggested by the apparent allusion in III. 1 to Jonson's *Devil Is an Ass*: 'Prethee devil, if thou be'st the devil, / Do not make an Ass of me.' Jonson's play was acted at Black-friars in the autumn of 1616 by the same company which produced *The Knight of Malta*.

Since Fleay showed the way (*Biog. Chron.* i. 205–6), there has been surprising unanimity among the disintegrators on the author-ship of the play, and even, with minor variations, on the assign-ments of portions. (See Brinkley, op. cit., pp. 121–2.) Oliphant, Miss Brinkley, and Miss Brocke pretty well agree with Fleay that Field wrote Acts I and V; Fletcher, Act II, Act III. 1 and 4, Act IV. 2, and perhaps parts of 1, 3, and 4; Massinger, Act III. 2 and 3, and the parts of Act IV not assigned to Fletcher. Oliphant is some-what uncertain about Field's part and toys with the idea that some of the play may have been written originally by Daborne. There are several signs of possible revision, and Oliphant thinks that Massinger may have revised the play for revivals after Fletcher's death.

The text of the play in the first Folio carries several hints that it was set up from a prompt copy: II. 5, '*The Scaffold set out and the staires*'; III. 4, '*A Table out, two stools*'; IV. 1, '*Discover Tombe*'; and V. 1, '*Altar ready, Tapers & booke*'. (See Bald, op. cit., p. 105.)

Koeppel suggested (*Quellen-Studien zu den Dramen Ben Jonson's, John Marston's und Beaumont's und Fletcher's*, pp. 69–70) the story of the Duchess of Savoy and that of Katherine of Bologna from Painter's *Palace of Pleasure*, as well as *Romeo and Juliet*, as sources for the play. After a detailed comparison of the proposed sources and the play, Miss Brocke concludes that '*The plot of The Knight of Malta is synthetic, taken from folk literature, romance and contemporary drama. Incorporating many separate motifs, it has no close or sustained likeness to any known story. Nor, because of the range and multiplicity of its reminiscence, is it possible to believe that any such story can exist. In that the synthesis has never been made before, the plot is original.*' (Op. cit., p. xxxviii.) It is notable, however, that the names of places and personalities at the siege of Malta by the Turks in 1565,

which is the background of the play, are accurate, as are the details
of the ceremonies of investiture and degradation of the Knights of
St. John which provide the outstanding spectacle of the play.
Miss Brocke suggests that the former probably came from Knolles's
Generall Historie of the Turkes, and the latter surely from the
official *Statuta* of the order. (Brocke, op. cit., pp. xxxix–lx.) Most
of the indebtedness of the play to *Romeo and Juliet, Much Ado
about Nothing, Othello,* and *The Tempest* which McKeithan finds is
extremely dubious, though one or two faint recollections of *Romeo
and Juliet* are possible.

   The Knight of Malta is in the list of plays allotted to Killigrew
by the Lord Chamberlain *c.* 12 January 1668/9. (Nicoll, *A History
of Restoration Drama*, pp. 315–16.) Sprague says (*Beaumont and
Fletcher on the Restoration Stage*, p. 67) that a song of Purcell's seems
to have been associated with Restoration performances of the play.
Donald J. Rulfs notes (*P.M.L.A.* lxiii [1948], 1250) that a lost
alteration of *The Knight of Malta* was revived as a benefit for
John Quick on 23 April 1783.

The Knight of the Burning Pestle

See *The Elizabethan Stage*, iii. 220–1.

The Laws of Candy (1619?)

Edition: E. K. Chambers, ed., in *The Works of Francis Beaumont and John Fletcher*, Variorum Edition, iii. 465–544.

Koeppel, Emil. *Quellen-Studien zu den Dramen Ben Jonson's, John
   Marston's und Beaumont's und Fletcher's* (1895), pp. 72–74.
Oliphant, E. H. C. *The Plays of Beaumont and Fletcher* (1927),
   pp. 472–85.

1646, [4] Sept. S.R. Humphrey Robinson and Humphrey Moseley
   entered as their copies a list of about fifty play titles, all apparently formerly of the repertory of the King's company. Included
   is 'The Lawes of Candy', added later. (Greg, *Bibliography*, i.
   56–57.)
1647. The twelfth play in the first Beaumont and Fletcher Folio
   is 'The Lawes of Candy'.
1668/9, *c.* 12 Jan. In 'A Catalogue of part of His Ma^tes Servants
   Playes as they were formerly acted at the Blackfryers & now
   allowed of to his Ma^tes Servants at ye New Theatre' occurs the

title, 'The Lawes of Candye'. (Nicoll, *A History of Restoration Drama*, 3rd ed., p. 315.)

1672/3, 30 Jan. S.R. Humphrey Robinson, executor of Humphrey Robinson, transferred to Henry Herringman and John Martin rights in a long list of plays, including 'Pilgrim or Lawes of Candia. [*sic*] halfe'. (Greg, *Bibliography*, i. 72–73.)

1679. The fifteenth play in the second Beaumont and Fletcher Folio is 'The Laws of Candy. A Tragi-Comedy'.

1683, 21 Aug. S.R. Sarah Martin, executrix of John Martin, transferred to Robert Scott her rights in a long list of plays, including 'Pilgrim or Laws of Candia ¼ [2 Severall Plays *added*]'. (Ibid., pp. 75–76.)

The cast for the play printed in the second Folio is:

Joseph Taylor.	*John Lowin.*
William Eglestone.	*John Vnderwood.*
Nicholas Toolie.	*George Birch.*
Richard Sharpe.	*Thomas Pollard.*

This cast, presumably the one for the first performance of the play, affords the most reliable evidence of date. Richard Burbage, the famous star of the company, is omitted, probably because the play was produced after his death in March 1618/19. (See above, ii. 395–6.) Joseph Taylor, who does appear, was acting as a member of Prince Charles's company in January or February 1618/19, and seems to have joined the King's men only on the death of Burbage. (See above, ii. 590–8.) Tooley, who had a part, was buried in June 1623. (Ibid., pp. 601–2.) The cast, then, fixes the date between March 1618/19 and June 1623. The absence of a licence for the play from the recorded entries of the office-book of Sir Henry Herbert, whose entries begin in 1622, has sometimes been said to indicate a date before 1622, but the evidence is not significant, for many entries have not been preserved. (See above, i. 101.) Fleay thought (*Biog. Chron.* i. 209) that the references to comets and blazing stars suggested a date shortly after the comet of 1618, and such an allusion is possible, but by no means certain. (See Chambers ed., pp. 467–8.) A date of 1619 has generally been used for the play, though any of the three following years is possible.

The disintegrators are pitifully uncertain in their attempts to assign authors to this play, and their contradictory and changing opinions are an illuminating commentary on their methods and their reliability. (See Oliphant, loc. cit., and Chambers ed., pp. 467–9.) It is quite true that the play has little of Fletcher's normal

dramatic effectiveness or clever manipulation, but such short-
comings are scarcely enough to identify the work of some other
dramatist. There may be some suggestion of revision in the fact
that the play is notably shorter than the Fletcher norm.

The source of the political plot of the play is Cinthio's *Hecatommithi*, x. 9, which is summarized by Weber and Dyce, followed by
Chambers. The romantic plot must come from another source,
but it has not been identified.

The records suggest that this was one of the least popular of the
Fletcher plays—and deservedly so. There is no record of a specific
performance of the play, except that implied by the cast, before
the closing of the theatres, and the King's men apparently did
not think enough of the piece to register it in their list of 1641.
(See above, i. 65–66.) Though the Restoration King's company
recorded their rights to the play, there are no indications that
they performed it.

Lisander and Calista

See Fletcher, *The Lovers' Progress*.

The Little French Lawyer (May 1619 < > May 1623)
with Philip Massinger

Edition: Cyril Brett, ed., in *The Works of Francis Beaumont and
John Fletcher*, Variorum Edition, iv. 91–206.

Evans, G. Blakemore. 'Note on Fletcher and Massinger's *Little
French Lawyer*', *M.L.N.* lii (1937), 406–7.

Koeppel, Emil. *Quellen-Studien zu den Dramen Ben Jonson's,
John Marston's und Beaumont's und Fletcher's* (1895), pp. 60–61.

Lea, Kathleen Marguerite, ed. *The Parliament of Love*, The Malone
Society Reprints (1929), p. xv.

Lucas, F. L., ed. *The Complete Works of John Webster* (1928), iii. 5–9.

Maxwell, Baldwin. *Studies in Beaumont, Fletcher, and Massinger*
(1939), pp. 84–106.

Oliphant, E. H. C. *The Plays of Beaumont and Fletcher* (1927),
pp. 237–9.

Stoll, E. E. *John Webster* (1905), pp. 162–71.

Stork, C. W., ed. *William Rowley, His All's Lost by Lust, and A
Shoemaker, a Gentleman* (1910), pp. 50–51, 62–63.

1641, 7 Aug. 'The litle french Lawyer' is in a list of plays belonging
to the King's men which the Lord Chamberlain forbade the

printers to publish without the company's consent. (See above, i. 65–66.)

1646, [4] Sept. S.R. Robinson and Moseley entered 'Litle french Lawyer . . . by m^r Beamont & m^r fflesher' in a group of nearly fifty plays, all apparently of the repertory of the King's company. (Greg, *Bibliography*, i. 56–57.)

1647. 'The Little French Lawyer' is printed as the third play in the first Beaumont and Fletcher Folio of 1647.

1668/9, c. 12 Jan. In 'A Catalogue of part of His Ma^{tes} Servants Playes as they were formerly acted at the Blackfryers & now allowed of to his Ma^{tes} Servants at ye New Theatre' occurs the title, 'The ffrench Lawyer'. (Nicoll, *A History of Restoration Drama*, 3rd ed., p. 315.)

1669–70. 'To the King's players, for acting "The Little French Lawyer," 20 *li*.' (General Account Book of the Inner Temple, Disbursements, 8 November 1669 to 7 November 1670, as quoted by F. A. Inderwick, *A Calendar of the Inner Temple Records*, iii. 73.)

1672/3, 30 Jan. S.R. Humphrey Robinson, executor of Humphrey Robinson, transferred to John Martin and Henry Herringman his rights in a long list of plays, including 'Littell ffrench Lawyer. halfe'. (Greg, *Bibliography*, i. 72–73.)

1679. 'The Little French Lawyer. A Comedy' is the seventeenth play printed in the Beaumont and Fletcher second Folio.

1683, 21 Aug. S.R. Sarah Martin, executrix of John Martin, transferred to Robert Scott her rights in a long list of plays, including 'Little ffrench Lawer ¼'. (Ibid., pp. 75–76.)

In the Folio of 1679 the cast of King's men printed for this play is the same as that printed for *Women Pleased* and for *The Custom of the Country*. This cast could have been used by the King's company only between May 1619 and the end of May 1623. (See *The Custom of the Country*.) No other reliable dating evidence for the play has been cited. That no licence of Sir Henry Herbert for *The Little French Lawyer* is known has frequently been taken to mean that it was written before May 1622, when the entries which Malone and Chalmers copied from the office-book begin. It could equally well mean simply that Malone and Chalmers failed to copy the licence, as they did in other instances. (See above, i. 101.) Perhaps Cleremont's very conspicuous speech against duelling in the opening scene should be taken as evidence that the play was written not too long after King James's speech against duelling in February 1616/17. (See Maxwell, loc. cit.) But the cast of *The*

Little French Lawyer in the 1679 Folio indicates that more than two years must have elapsed between the speech and the first performance of the play, and if so much, another year or two of delay would not make the compliment to James notably less effective.

The story of the woman who persuaded her lover's friend to sleep with her husband in order to cover her own absence, and who then substituted a young lady for her husband, to the tricked friend's later embarrassment, is found in the *Novellino* of Masuccio Salernitano and later in Mateo Alemán's *Guzman d'Alfarache*, and in Scarron's *Fruitless Precaution* and elsewhere. The story is not so important for *The Little French Lawyer* as has been implied, since little use of it is made outside the latter half of Act III. Koeppel (loc. cit.) thought the comic duel derived from *The Merry Wives of Windsor* and Lamira's Nurse from Juliet's, but comic duels were not unusual, and the two nurses are more alike in their errands and their age than in their characterizations.

Bandello's story of the Countess of Cellant was used by Marston in *The Dutch Courtesan*, Massinger in *The Parliament of Love*, Webster in *A Cure for a Cuckold*, and Rowley in *All's Lost by Lust*. Stoll, Stork, Lucas, and Miss Lea in her Malone Society edition of *The Parliament of Love* have all noted the similar material of all or most of these plays, and Lucas and Miss Lea have more or less agreed with Stoll that Lamira's forcing of Dinant to desert Cleremont in the proposed duel with her brother is a variant of the same story and relates *The Little French Lawyer* to the other plays. The similarity of the stories does not seem so suggestive to me as does the appearance of the names Cleremont, Dinant, Lamira, and Beaupré in both *The Little French Lawyer* and *The Parliament of Love*. Sir Henry Herbert licensed *The Parliament of Love* for production at the Cockpit on 3 November 1624 (Adams, *Herbert*, p. 30), a date later than the latest performance possible for the cast listed for *The Little French Lawyer* in the Folio of 1679. The date suggests that Massinger may have used some of his material for *The Little French Lawyer* in writing *The Parliament of Love*, but a fuller investigation of the relationship of the two plays might be illuminating.

The authors of the play are referred to in the plural once in the prologue and five times in the epilogue. Nearly all the disintegrators have agreed that the two must be Fletcher and Massinger, and they agree reasonably well in dividing the play between them, giving Act I to Massinger, Act II to Fletcher, and finding divided composition in the three later acts.

G. Blakemore Evans points out (loc. cit.) that the play which La-Writ admits to Cleremont he is quoting in Act IV is the anonymous *Nero* (q.v.).

His observation of a single anticipatory stage direction in Act III led Bald to believe that the Folio text of *The Little French Lawyer* had been set up from a prompt copy (*Studies in the Beaumont & Fletcher Folio of 1647*, p. 105), but the play also contains directions of a markedly literary type.

Three different writers of verses for the Folio of 1647 mention *The Little French Lawyer*—Richard Lovelace, Robert Gardiner, and G. Hills. Evidently the play was popularly known, and the absence of recorded performances before the closing of the theatres must be a misleading accident. The 'Wood-Man's Song' from Act IV is reprinted in Beaumont's *Poems* of 1653, and in *Covent Garden Drolleries*, 1672. (See Montague Summers, ed., p. 87.)

Eighteenth-century revivals and adaptations of the play are noted by Brett. (Variorum edition, p. 96.)

The Little Thief

See Fletcher, *The Night Walker*.

The Lovers' Progress, or The Wandering Lovers, or Cleander, or Lisander and Calista (1623, revised 1634)
revised by Philip Massinger

Bald, R. C. *Bibliographical Studies in the Beaumont & Fletcher Folio of 1647*, Supplement to the Bibliographical Society's Transactions, No. 13 (1938), p. 107.

Chelli, Maurice. *Étude sur la collaboration de Massinger avec Fletcher et son groupe* (1926), pp. 148–51.

Koeppel, Emil. *Quellen-Studien zu den Dramen Ben Jonson's, John Marston's und Beaumont's und Fletcher's* (1895), pp. 123–5.

Maxwell, Baldwin. *Studies in Beaumont, Fletcher, and Massinger* (1939), pp. 82–83 and 103–5.

Mills, Laurens J. *One Soul in Bodies Twain: Friendship in Tudor Literature and Stuart Drama* (1937), pp. 323–6.

Oliphant, E. H. C. *The Plays of Beaumont and Fletcher* (1927), pp. 239–45.

Ward, A. W. *A History of English Dramatic Literature to the Death of Queen Anne* (1899), ii. 730–2.

1623, 6 Dec. 'For the King's Company: The Wandring Lovers: Written by Mr. Fletcher.' (Adams, *Herbert*, p. 27.)

1623/4, 1 Jan. 'Upon New-years night, by the K. company, *The Wandering Lovers*, the prince only being there. Att Whitehall.' (Ibid., p. 51.)

1634, 7 May. 'The tragedy of *Cleander*, by Philip Massinger, was licensed for the King's Company.' (Ibid., p. 35.)

1634, 21 May. '. . . after dynner wᵗʰ Sʳ Henry Skipwith My wife, Ned: Boteler, Nann: Mildmay att the play Called Lasander & Callista, beinge a poem.' (Diary of Sir Humphrey Mildmay. See above, ii. 676.)

1641, 7 Aug. 'The Louers Progresse' appears in a list of plays belonging to the King's company which the Lord Chamberlain forbade any printer to publish without the consent of the players. (See above, i. 65–66.)

1646, [4] Sept. S.R. Humphrey Moseley and Humphrey Robinson entered as their copies a list of about fifty play titles, all apparently formerly of the repertory of the King's company. Included is 'The Lovers progresse'. (Greg, *Bibliography*, i. 56–57.)

1647. The thirteenth play in the first Beaumont and Fletcher Folio is 'The Lovers Progres'.

1653, 9 Sept. S.R. In a long list of plays entered as his copies by Humphrey Moseley is 'The Wandring Louers, or yᵉ Painter . . . by Phill: Massinger'. (Ibid., pp. 60–61.)

1668/9, c. 12 Jan. In 'A Catalogue of part of His Maᵗᵉˢ Servants Playes as they were formerly acted at the Blackfryers & now allowed of to his Maᵗᵉˢ Servants at yᵉ New Theatre' occurs the title, 'Loves [*sic*] Progresse'. (Nicoll, *A History of Restoration Drama*, 3rd ed., p. 315.)

1672/3, 30 Jan. S.R. Humphrey Robinson, executor of Humphrey Robinson, transferred to John Martin and Henry Herringman rights in a long list of plays, including 'The Louers Progress, All'. But later in the list there is an entry added after the list was finished, 'The Louers Progress. halfe'. (Greg, *Bibliography*, i. 72–73.)

1679. The twenty-fourth play in the second Beaumont and Fletcher Folio is 'The Lovers Progress. A Tragedy'.

1683, 21 Aug. The S.R. transfer of this date, which includes the other plays of the first Folio, omits *The Lovers' Progress*, presumably in error. (See ibid., pp. 75–76.)

The first problem about the play is: How many of the above entries apply to the piece published in the Beaumont and Fletcher

folios of 1647 and 1679? For once I am inclined to agree with
Fleay (*Biog. Chron.* i. 219–20) and conclude that they all do,
except that *The Painter* of the 1653 entry is probably a different
play which Moseley was slipping in as a sub-title—as he did a
number of times in this list. The identification of *The Wandering Lovers,* licensed as Fletcher's, with *The Lovers' Progress* of
the Beaumont and Fletcher folios is suggested by the fact that
the date of the licence and that of the court performance of the
former fit very nicely the date indicated by the cast for *The Lovers'
Progress* printed in the second Folio (see below), and by the fact
that Lisander, Lidian, and Clarange of *The Lovers' Progress* are
indeed wandering lovers, and that in Act II Lisander says to the
other two:

> then I will part too,
> A third unfortunate, and willing wanderer.

Good reason for a change in the title is indicated in the thorough
rewriting of the piece, so explicitly referred to in the prologue and
epilogue:

Prologue.

A Story, and a known one, long since writ,
Truth must take place, and by an able wit,
Foul mouth'd detraction daring not deny
To give so much to Fletchers *memory;*
If so, some may object, why then do you
Present an old piece to us for a new?
Or wherefore will your profest Writer be
(Not tax'd of theft before) a Plagiary?
To this he answers in his just defence,
And to maintain to all our Innocence,
Thus much, though he hath travell'd the same way,
Demanding, and receiving too the pay
For a new Poem, you may find it due,
He having neither cheated us, nor you;
He vowes, and deeply, that he did nor spare
The utmost of his strengths, and his best care
In the reviving it, and though his powers
Could not as he desired, in three short hours
Contract the Subject, and much less express
The changes, and the various passages
That will be look'd for, you may hear this day
Some Scenes that will confirm it is a play,
He being ambitious that it should be known
What's good was Fletchers, *and what ill his own.*

(Folio, 1679.)

Epilogue.

Still doubtfull, and perplex'd too, whether he
Hath done Fletcher *right in this Historie,*
The Poet sits within, since he must know it,
He with respect desires that you would shew it
By some accustomed sign, if from our action,
Or his indeavours you meet satisfaction,
With ours he hath his ends, we hope the best,
To make that certainty in you doth rest.

(Folio, 1679.)

These verses are much more informative than most such. They tell us that *The Lovers' Progress* is an old play '*long since writ*' by Fletcher, that the company is today presenting it '*for a new*', that the '*profest Writer*' (presumably the one advertised on the playbills) '*sits within*', '*Still doubtfull, and perplex'd too, whether he | Hath done* Fletcher *right*', that the play is so completely revised that this '*profest Writer*' felt justified in '*Demanding, and receiving too the pay | For a new Poem*'.

Now Massinger was the principal playwright for the King's company in the thirties, and therefore the one most likely in those years to have been revising a manuscript which the company owned, and to have been sitting nervously in the tiring-house waiting to see how the play was received. Since the prologue says the play was so thoroughly revised that it was called new and paid for as new, it presumably had a new licence from Sir Henry Herbert and would have been licensed as Massinger's. These facts, with the additional fact that the name of the principal tragic character in the play was Cleander, seem to me sufficient for identifying the revised *Wandering Lovers*, later called *The Lovers' Progress*, with the play entitled *Cleander* which Herbert licensed to the King's company on 7 May 1634. Actually *The Lovers' Progress* is somewhere between a tragi-comedy and a tragedy, but so far as Cleander is concerned it is a tragedy, and it is called a tragedy in the title for the play in the 1679 Folio. These conclusions, which were written before Greg's discussion of the identifications appeared (*Bibliography*, ii. 982–3), are in general—though not in precise—agreement with his.

The most dubious of the identifications is the play which Mildmay saw and called 'Lasander and Callista'. I think it likely, however, that he saw *The Lovers' Progress*, for Lisander and Calista are the principal lovers of the piece, and theirs are respectively the largest and the third largest roles. Furthermore Mildmay saw the play just two weeks after Massinger's revision was licensed, when it would be presumed to be playing at Blackfriars. Though Mildmay does not name the theatre, it was probably the Black-friars, for he lived near that playhouse, and he mentioned it in his diary twice as often as all other London theatres put together. (See above, ii. 680.) One further suggestion that the play Mildmay saw was the same as *The Lovers' Progress* of the Folio is found in his odd designation, 'beinge a poem'. This corresponds with the designation of the piece in the prologue as '*a new Poem*'. Plays were often called poems in authors' addresses or in commendatory verses, but not often in purely theatrical material like prologues. I cannot tell whether Mildmay intended to be respectful or derisive.

The cast given for the play in the second Folio reads:

Joseph Taylor.	*John Lowin.*
Robert Benfield.	*John Vnderwood.*
Thomas Polard.	*Richard Sharpe.*
George Birch.	*John Thomson.*

All the members of this cast were players of the King's company in December 1623, when *The Wandering Lovers* was licensed (see above, vol. ii, under the actors' names), though John Underwood was available for only a few months after that, since he made his will in October 1624. (See above, ii. 651.)

The source of the play is D'Audiguier's *Histoire tragi-comique de nostre temps, sous les noms de Lysandre et de Caliste*, 1615. A translation by W. D., entitled *A tragi-comicall history of our times under the borrowed names of Lisander and Calista*, appeared in 1627 and was reprinted in 1635.

R. C. Bald notes (loc. cit.) that the numerous specific directions about properties in the Folio text make it fairly clear that the play was set up from a prompt copy.

The disintegrators are generally agreed that the play contains the work of Fletcher and Massinger. (See Oliphant, loc. cit.) For once there is external evidence that Fletcher wrote the original play and Massinger gave it a thorough revision—enough (according to the prologue) to afford some reason for calling it a new play.

Love's Cure, or The Martial Maid (? and 1625?)
with Francis Beaumont? revised by Massinger?

Bond, R. Warwick. 'On Six Plays in *Beaumont and Fletcher, 1679*', *R.E.S.* xi (1935), 262–9.
—— 'Three Beaumont and Fletcher Plays', *R.E.S.* xii (1936), 444–5.

Chambers, E. K. *The Elizabethan Stage,* iii. 231–2.

Chelli, Maurice. *Étude sur la collaboration de Massinger avec Fletcher et son groupe* (1926), pp. 76–77, 163–5.

Oliphant, E. H. C. *The Plays of Beaumont and Fletcher* (1927), pp. 414–32.

—— 'Three Beaumont and Fletcher Plays', *R.E.S.* xii (1936), 199–202.

Stiefel, A. L. 'Die Nachahmung spanischer Komödien in England unter den ersten Stuarts', *Archiv,* xcix (1897), 271–310.

1641, 7 Aug. 'The martiall maide' appears in a list of plays belonging to the King's men which the Lord Chamberlain forbade the printers to publish without the company's consent. (See above, i. 65–66.)

1646, [4] Sept. S.R. 'Martiall Maid . . . by m^r Beamont & m^r fflesher' is in a long list of plays entered by Humphrey Robinson and Humphrey Moseley. (Greg, *Bibliography,* i. 56–57.)

1647. The twenty-fifth play in the first Beaumont and Fletcher Folio is 'Loves Cure Or, The Martial Maid'.

1668/9, *c.* 12 Jan. In 'A Catalogue of part of His Ma^{tes} Servants Playes as they were formerly acted at the Blackfryers & now allowed of to his Ma^{tes} Servants at ye New Theatre' occurs the title 'Loues Cure', and several plays later in the same list is 'The Marshall Mayd'. (Nicoll, *A History of Restoration Drama,* 3rd ed., pp. 315–16.)

1672/3, 30 Jan. In a long list of play titles transferred from Humphrey Robinson, executor of Humphrey Robinson, to John Martin and Henry Herringman is 'Martiall Maid. halfe'. (Greg, *Bibliography,* i. 72–73.)

1679. 'Loves Cure, or the Martial Maid A Comedy' is the thirty-fifth play in the second Beaumont and Fletcher Folio.

1683, 21 Aug. In a long list of play titles transferred from Sarah Martin, executrix of John Martin, to Robert Scott is a fourth interest in 'Martiall Maid'. (Ibid., pp. 75–76.)

The external evidence concerning this play is slight for a Fletcher production; there is not even a cast in the second Folio. Since it appears in the list of the King's men's unpublished plays of 1641, it was presumably still in repertory, but there is no record of a production. Nearly everything about the play is in a state of confusion.

The various arguments for an early date depend largely on the assumption that the historic setting of the play, *c.* 1604–8, is the

actual date of the play (see Fleay, *Biog. Chron.* i. 180–1) and on
the assumption of the literal accuracy of the prologue statement,
'At the reviving of this PLAY':

> *Then why should not this dear Piece be esteem'd*
> *Child to the richest fancies that e'r teem'd?*
> *When not their meanest off-spring, that came forth,*
> *But bore the image of their Fathers worth.*
> Beaumonts, *and* Fletchers.   (Folio, 1679.)

Chambers (loc. cit.) thinks the first consideration negligible, but
seems to give more weight to the second. Perhaps at the time of the
revival of the play the names of Beaumont and Fletcher were used
as loosely as they were on the title-pages of the two folios, yet it is
notable that in the prologues and epilogues to revivals which were
printed in the second Folio Fletcher is named as author of the
revived play several times and Beaumont and Fletcher only this
once. Whether the author of the prologue had adequate reason for
thinking the piece a collaboration of Beaumont and Fletcher is
another matter. Bond thinks, however (*R.E.S.* xi [1935], 267),
that this prologue really belongs to *The Queen of Corinth*.

The repeated use of the singular in the epilogue of the play
indicates that the revisions for the revival were by one man:
'*Our Author fears there are some Rebel hearts*', '*such odd things as
these | He cares not for, nor ever means to please*', '*he hath his ends*'.
(Folio, 1679.) The prologue and epilogue, therefore, indicate that
Love's Cure was originally a collaboration by Beaumont and Flet-
cher and was later revised by a single dramatist, presumably
Philip Massinger.

The disintegrators are hopelessly, even ludicrously, at odds
about *Love's Cure*. (See Oliphant, *Plays of Beaumont and Fletcher*,
pp. 414–16.) Some find much Beaumont, no Fletcher; some,
much Fletcher, no Beaumont; and some, neither Beaumont nor
Fletcher; some, no Massinger; some, nearly all Massinger. Perhaps
all this does not discredit their methods as completely as one
suspects, but at any rate it throws no light at all on the play.

The absence of a cast from the second Folio is often taken to
indicate that *Love's Cure* was not written for the King's company,
but this deduction is by no means certain. There are forty-four
plays in the Folio of 1679 which are known to have belonged to
the King's men at some time (see above, i. 109–15), but only
twenty-five plays have casts, and of the twenty-five, two (*The
Coxcomb* and *Honest Man's Fortune*) are for another company.
Often the names of the actors in a cast are revealing, but it seems
to me unsafe to argue anything from the absence of a cast.

The discussions of the source of *Love's Cure* are also contradictory. Stiefel (loc. cit.) thought that the source was *La Fuerza de la Costumbre* of Guillen de Castro, and Bond (*R.E.S.* xi. 262–6) develops the relationship at length, but Macaulay (*C.H.E.L.* vi. 140) denied it. The Spanish play was published in a volume not licensed until February 1624/5 (see Oliphant, *The Plays of Beaumont and Fletcher*, p. 417), and such a date would seem to make it rather improbable that Fletcher exploited the new Spanish piece before his death in August. Bond also contends that part of the play is derived from *Gerardo*, which was translated by Leonard Digges in 1622. (Op. cit., pp. 266–7.) Chambers (*Elizabethan Stage*, iii. 231–2) thought that the lines about Muscovites and a great frost must refer to events of 1621. If the relationship of *Love's Cure* to the Spanish play and the romance is as close as Bond thinks, it seems unlikely that they would have been sources for the reviser only. Perhaps a more detailed examination of the relationship between *Love's Cure* and *La Fuerza de la Costumbre* and *Gerardo* would be illuminating.

Professor Bald thinks that the play was printed from a prompt copy because of a single anticipatory stage direction in Act iii. (*Bibliographical Studies in the Beaumont and Fletcher Folio of 1647*, p. 105.)

Love's Pilgrimage (1616?, revised 1635)

revised by ?

Aronstein, P. 'Fletchers *Love's Pilgrimage* und Ben Jonsons *The New Inn*', *Englische Studien*, xliii (1911), 234–41.

Herford, C. H., and Percy Simpson, eds., *Ben Jonson*, ii. 198–200.

Koeppel, Emil. *Quellen-Studien zu den Dramen Ben Jonson's, John Marston's und Beaumont's und Fletcher's* (1895), pp. 127–8.

Maxwell, Baldwin. 'The Date of *Love's Pilgrimage* and its Relation to *The New Inn*', *Stud. Phil.* xxviii (1931), 702–9, reprinted in *Studies in Beaumont, Fletcher, and Massinger*, pp. 107–15.

Oliphant, E. H. C. *The Plays of Beaumont and Fletcher* (1927), pp. 432–9.

Powell, William C. 'A Note on the Stage History of Beaumont and Fletcher's *Love's Pilgrimage* and *The Chances*', *M.L.N.* lvi (1941), 122–7.

Tennant, George Bremner, ed. *The New Inn or The Light Heart, By Ben Jonson*. Yale Studies in English, xxxiv (1908), pp. lxii–lxxi.

1635, 16 Sept. 'Received of Blagrove from the King's Company, for the renewing of *Love's Pilgrimage*, the 16th of September, 1635,—£1.0.0.' (Adams, *Herbert*, p. 36.)

1636, 16 Dec. In a bill of the King's company for twenty-two plays acted before the King and Queen in 1636 and 1636/7 occurs '10 The 16th of December at Hampton Court . loues pilgrimage'. (See above, i. 51–52.)

1641, 7 Aug. In a list of plays belonging to the King's company which the Lord Chamberlain forbade the printers to publish without the company's consent is 'The Louers [*sic*] Pilgrimage'. (See above, i. 65–66.)

1646, [4] Sept. S.R. Humphrey Robinson and Humphrey Moseley entered as their copies a list of about fifty play titles, all apparently formerly in the repertory of the King's company. Included is 'The Lovers [*sic*] pilgrimage'. (Greg, *Bibliography*, i. 56–57.)

1647. The thirty-third play in the first Beaumont and Fletcher Folio is 'Loves Pilgrimage'.

1668/9, *c.* 12 Jan. In 'A Catalogue of part of His Mates Servants Playes as they were formerly acted at the Blackfryers & now allowed of to his Mates Servants at ye New Theatre' occurs the title, 'Loues Pilgrimage'. (Nicoll, *A History of Restoration Drama*, 3rd ed., pp. 315–16.)

1672/3, 30 Jan. S.R. Humphrey Robinson, executor of Humphrey Robinson, transferred to John Martin and Henry Herringman rights in a long list of plays, including 'The Louers [*sic*] Pilgrimage. All', but this was apparently a mistake, for later in the same list is entered 'The Louers [*sic*] Pilgrimage. [*altered from* Progresse.] halfe'. (Greg, *Bibliography*, i. 72–73.)

1679. The thirty-first play in the second Beaumont and Fletcher Folio is 'Loves Pilgramage, a Comedy'.

1683, 21 Aug. S.R. Sarah Martin, executrix of John Martin, transferred to Robert Scott her rights in a long list of plays, including a fourth interest in 'Lovers [*sic*] Pilgramage'. (Ibid., pp. 75–76.)

The source of the play, as Langbaine noted, is Cervantes's story, *Las dos doncellas*, in his *Novelas Exemplares*, which received its final allowance for publication in August 1613, but was not published in the French translation, which Fletcher seems to have used, until 1615. (See Koeppel and Maxwell, op. cit. A synopsis of Cervantes's story appears in Dyce's *Works of Beaumont and Fletcher*, xi. 218–22.) Maxwell notes allusions in the text of the play which make a production in 1616—probably late in the year —seem likely.

That the play was fairly thoroughly revised in 1635 is made apparent by Sir Henry Herbert's record of the fee paid his assistant, William Blagrave. (See above, ii. 380-1.) The fee is Herbert's usual one at this time for allowing the revisions in an old play. (See the entries of 15 August and 23 November 1633, 16 August 1634, and 12 May 1636.)

Several scholars, beginning with Langbaine (*An Account of the English Dramatick Poets*, p. 211), have noted that certain passages in the first scene of *Love's Pilgrimage* are identical with, or obvious modifications of, passages in II. 2 and III. I (1616 Folio numbering) of Jonson's *New Inn*. The relationship is so close—Oliphant notes that in the second passage twenty-four of seventy-four lines are identical, and only six are peculiar to *Love's Pilgrimage*—that direct copying is obviously involved, and there have been various attempts to determine which dramatist was the borrower. The probabilities seem to me most convincingly set forth by Herford and Simpson—Oliphant and Maxwell to the contrary notwithstanding—that the lines were originally Jonson's and were lifted from his play by some reviser. It was not Fletcher who borrowed, however, for he died four and a half years before *The New Inn* was produced. The suggestions that Jonson collaborated with Fletcher and later reclaimed his own lines for *The New Inn*, or that Jonson started to revise *Love's Pilgrimage* and himself inserted his own lines, both seem to me extremely improbable. Presumably the borrower was the author of the revisions which Blagrave licensed in September 1635.

It has several times been mistakenly asserted that this reviser was James Shirley. The original error was Malone's, who, in ably clearing up one confusion about Jonson's *New Inn*, inadvertently created another about *Love's Pilgrimage*:

The origin of this note, by which *confusion is worse confounded*, was probably this: Langbaine, under the article, *Fletcher*, mentions that a scene in his Love's Pilgrimage was *stollen* from the very play of which we have been speaking; Jonson's New Inn. This scene Fletcher himself could not have stollen from The New Inn, for he was dead some years before that play appeared; but Shirley, who had the revisal of some of those pieces which were left imperfect by Fletcher, (as appears from Sir Henry Herbert's Office-book,) finding The New Inn unsuccessful, took the liberty to borrow a scene from it, which he inserted in Love's Pilgrimage, when that play was revived, or as Sir Henry Herbert calls it, *renewed*, in 1635. (*Variorum*, i. 424.)

As a note on his first citation of Herbert's office-book, Malone quoted Herbert's entry about Shirley's revision of Fletcher's *Night Walker* (q.v.). He later noted (ibid. iii. 226), '. . . it appears from the manuscript [Herbert's] so often quoted that The Night-Walker and Love's Pilgrimage, having been left imperfect by Fletcher, were corrected and finished by Shirley'. It appears that Malone's memory betrayed him in the second quotation and that he was guilty of generalizing from inadequate evidence in the first, for *The Night Walker* is the only example in the office-book—at least so far as the extant extracts of Malone and Chalmers go—of Shirley's revision of Fletcher. Shirley revised *The Night Walker* because that play, unlike most of Fletcher's, was the property of Queen Henrietta's company in 1633, and Shirley was the regular dramatist for the company in that year and several years before and after. He is not known to have had any connexion with the King's company before 1640. Certainly Shirley would not have been working on plays which were the property of the King's company while he was the chief dramatist of the principal rival company, Queen Henrietta's men.

This mistaken suggestion of Shirley's connexion with *Love's Pilgrimage* has sadly misled a number of the disintegrators, who dutifully identified Shirley's style in a number of the scenes of *Love's Pilgrimage*. There is no general agreement among the disintegrators about the hands in the play. (See Oliphant, op. cit., pp. 432–5.) Since Massinger was the principal dramatist for the King's company in the thirties, one would be inclined to guess that he would have revised the play for the company in 1635, but few of the disintegrators have felt that they recognized his hand in the play, though a number have seen Shirley's!

The text of the play in the first Folio was evidently derived from a prompt copy of the play, as Professor Bald pointed out (*Bibliographical Studies in the Beaumont & Fletcher Folio of 1647*, pp. 103–4), for it contains anticipatory stage directions with actors' names. In II. I is '*Enter two Servants, Rowl: Ashton*'; in IV. I, '*Ioh. Bacon ready to shoot off a Pistoll*'; and again in IV. I, '*Enter a Servant, Rowl: Ashton*'. The actors Rowland Dowle and John Bacon are known from other sources as hired men of the King's company in the thirties; Ashton is otherwise unknown. (See above, ii. 425–6, 354, and 351.) It is probable, therefore, that these stage directions date from the revival of the revised play in 1635.

The prologue for the play in the first Folio is one of the few which is particularly appropriate for the play it accompanies. The prologue was apparently prepared for the original performance, since it refers to the play as new. The plural pronouns in it, with one possible exception, refer to the actors, not the authors, as has several times been asserted.

Fleay's contention (*Biog. Chron.* i. 194) that *Love's Pilgrimage* is the lost *Cardenio*, which was licensed as by Shakespeare and Fletcher, seems to have impressed no one. He ignores the later alleged history of *Cardenio* (see Chambers, *William Shakespeare*, i. 538–42) and concentrates on names. Fleay does not try to explain why Moseley, who published *Love's Pilgrimage* and who had paid to register his rights in 1646, should pay again to register the same play under the title of *Cardenio* in 1653.

Loyal Subject (1618, revised? 1633)

Edition: John Masefield and R. Warwick Bond, eds. *The Works of Francis Beaumont and John Fletcher*, Variorum Edition, iii. 221–356.

Koeppel, Emil. *Quellen-Studien zu den Dramen Ben Jonson's, John Marston's und Beaumont's und Fletcher's* (1895), pp. 76–77.
Villarejo, Oscar M. 'Lope de Vega's comedia *El Gran duque de Moscovia* as the main source of Fletcher's *The Loyal Subject* and the partial source of Heywood's *The Royall King and the Loyall Subject* and Fletcher's *The Humorous Lieutenant.*' *Research in Progress, P.M.L.A.* lxiii (1948), Supplement, p. 182 (No. 897*b*).
Waith, Eugene M. 'A Tragicomedy of Humors: Fletcher's *The Loyal Subject*', *M.L.Q.* vi (1945), 299–311.

1618, 16 Nov. The play was licensed for production by Sir George Buc, Master of the Revels. (See the next item.)
1633, 23 Nov. 'The Kings players sent me an ould booke of Fletchers called *The Loyal Subject*, formerly allowed by Sir George Bucke, 16 Novemb. 1618, which according to their desire and agreement I did peruse, and with some reformations allowed of, the 23 of Nov. 1633, for which they sent mee according to their promise 1 *l*. 0. 0.' Malone records (*Variorum*, iii. 234) that in the margin of his manuscript, opposite this entry, Sir Henry Herbert noted 'The first ould play sent mee to be perused by the K. players'. (Adams, *Herbert*, p. 35 and n. 6.)
1633, 10 Dec. 'On tusday night at Whitehall the 10 of Decemb. 1633, was acted before the King and Queen, *The Loyal Subject*, made by Fletcher, and very well likt by the king.' (Ibid., p. 53.)

1636, 6 Dec. In a bill of the King's company for plays presented before the King and Queen in 1636 and 1636/7 occurs the item, '8 The 6th of December at Hampton Court . the loyall subiect'. (See above, i. 51–52.)

1641, 7 Aug. In a list of plays belonging to the King's company which the Lord Chamberlain forbade the printers to publish without the company's consent is 'The Loyall subject'. (See above, i. 65–66.)

1646, [4] Sept. S.R. Humphrey Robinson and Humphrey Moseley entered as their copies a list of about fifty play titles, all apparently formerly of the repertory of the King's company. Included is 'Loyall Subiect . . . by m^r Beamont & m^r fflesher'. (Greg, *Bibliography*, i. 56–57.)

1647. The eleventh play in the first Beaumont and Fletcher Folio is 'The Loyal Subiect'.

<1659/60. In the repertory of Rhodes's company acting at the Cockpit, Downes names first 'The Loyal Subject'. He records that in these performances Betterton played Archas and Sheppy, Theodore. (*Roscius Anglicanus*, Summers ed., pp. 17–19.)

1660, 18 Aug. '. . . after dinner . . . to the Cockpitt play, . . ."The Loyall Subject," where one Kinaston, a boy, acted the Duke's sister, but made the loveliest lady that ever I saw in my life, only her voice not very good.' (Diary of Samuel Pepys.)

1660, 12 Dec. Davenant was granted acting rights for two months in several plays, including 'the Loyall Subject'. (Nicoll, *A History of Restoration Drama*, 3rd ed., pp. 314–15.)

1660/1, Feb. In a list of performances by 'the Kings Companie at the Red Bull and the new house in Gibbon's Tennis Court near Clare Market' 1660–2 is 'Feb. Loyal Subject'. (Adams, *Herbert*, p. 117, n. 1.)

1662[–3 ?]. Edward Browne listed in his memorandum book that he paid 2s. 6d. to see 'Loyal Subiect' 'At the King Playhouse in Covent Garden'. (W. W. Greg, 'Theatrical Repertories of 1662', *Gentleman's Magazine*, ccci [1906], 69–72; from B.M. MS. Sloane 1900.)

1668/9, c. 12 Jan. In 'A Catalogue of part of His Ma^{tes} Servants Playes as they were formerly acted at the Blackfryers & now allowed of to his Ma^{tes} Servants at ye New Theatre' occurs the title 'The Loyall Subject'. (Nicoll, *A History of Restoration Drama*, 3rd ed., p. 315.)

1670, 3 May. 'Tuesday in the afternoon his Excellency went to the Theatre [i.e. in Dublin], where *The Loyal Subject* . . . was acted.' (*C.S.P., Ireland, 1669–70*, p. 123.)

1672/3, 30 Jan. S.R. Humphrey Robinson, executor of Humphrey
  Robinson, transferred to John Martin and Henry Herringman
  his rights in a long list of plays, including 'Loyall subject.
  halfe'. (Greg, *Bibliography*, i. 72–73.)
1679. The thirteenth play in the second Beaumont and Fletcher
  Folio is 'The Loyal Subject, A Tragi-Comedy'.
1683, 21 Aug. S.R. Sarah Martin, executrix of John Martin, transferred to Robert Scott her rights in a long list of plays, including
  'Loyall Subject. ¼'. (Ibid., pp. 75–76.)

Sir Henry Herbert's helpful entry of 23 November 1633 gives
the dates of both the original production and the revival. The cast
given in the second Folio fits the date of first production very
nicely.

Richard Burbadge.	⎞	*Nathanael Feild.*
Henry Condel.	⎟	*John Vnderwood.*
John Lowin.	⎟	*Nicholas Toolie.*
Richard Sharpe.	⎠	*William Eglestone.*

Four months after the play was licensed, Burbage was dead, and a
little more than two years before the licence was granted, Field
was a member of another company. (See above, ii. 395–6 and
434–6.) The other six are all known from other sources to have
been acting in the company's productions at this time.

The wording of Herbert's entry seems to indicate that in 1633
he was merely renewing the licence of an old play in which he
ordered a few reformations, and the marginal note which Malone
recorded implies the same thing. Yet it is odd that he charged the
same fee as for a revised play. Presumably the King's men were
acting dozens of plays in the 1630's which were as old as or older
than *The Loyal Subject*—plays of Jonson, Shakespeare, Fletcher,
and others. The lists of plays acted at court by the King's men in
the thirties show more than a score of such revivals. (See above, i.
96–100.) For none of them, except *The Winter's Tale*, was the
licence renewed, according to Herbert's extant records, and his
marginal note provides the information that *The Loyal Subject*
was 'The first ould play sent mee to be perused by the K. players'.
I hesitate to assume revision, in spite of Herbert's words. Perhaps
'some reformations' means in this case revisions by the company
and not expurgations by Sir Henry.

There seems to be general agreement that the play is by Fletcher
alone (see Oliphant, *The Plays of Beaumont and Fletcher*, p. 141),
and this agreement—for what it is worth—would indicate that
Herbert licensed only a renewal and not a revision. Oliphant's

notice of the play's 'ascription to Fletcher in a Stationers' Register entry of 1632–3' (ibid.) is an error, for I can find no entry of the play in 1632, 1633, or any other year before 1646.

Professor R. C. Bald points out that the anticipatory stage direction, '*Little Trunke ready*', in II. 5, about seventy lines before the property is needed, indicates that the Folio text was set up from a prompt copy. (*Bibliographical Studies in the Beaumont & Fletcher Folio of 1647*, p. 105.)

The prologue in the Folios, written by '*a friend*', clearly belongs to a revival. It speaks of Fletcher as the author, and mourns his death. Neither prologue nor epilogue indicates that the play has been revised or refers to its former reputation.

The source of the play has been said to be Bandello as translated by Painter (II. 4) and perhaps Heywood's *The Royal King and the Loyal Subject*. But though there are obvious similarities in the stories, neither Bandello nor Heywood seems to be used in a characteristically Fletcherian fashion. Presumably Mr. Villarejo (op. cit.) has found the solution in a Spanish source for Fletcher, but so far as I can find, his work has not yet been published.

In addition to the Restoration revivals of the play, there was another in 1705 which Sprague discusses. (*Beaumont and Fletcher on the Restoration Stage*, pp. 86–87.) An alteration of *The Loyal Subject*, 'Written by a Young Lady [M.N.]' and entitled *The Faithful General: A Tragedy*, was acted at the Haymarket and published in 1706. (See Variorum edition, pp. 228–9, and Sprague, op. cit., pp. 212–20.)

The Mad Lover (1616?)

Edition: R. Warwick Bond, ed. *The Works of Francis Beaumont and John Fletcher*, Variorum Edition, iii. 111–219.

Hatcher, O. L. *John Fletcher: A Study in Dramatic Method* (1905), pp. 44–46.

Maxwell, Baldwin. *Studies in Beaumont, Fletcher, and Massinger* (1939), pp. 227–9.

Sprague, Arthur Colby. *Beaumont and Fletcher on the Restoration Stage* (1926), pp. 271–3.

1616/17, 5 Jan. 'Upon the 25th [*sic*] I went into the Court. . . . Supped with my Lord and Lady *Arundel* and after supper I saw the play of the Mad Lover in the Hall.' (V. Sackville-West, ed., *The Diary of the Lady Anne Clifford* [1924], p. 47. The date of the 25th is obviously a mistake for the 5th, since it follows an entry

for the 2nd and is in turn followed by entries of the 6th and 8th.
In the same entry Lady Anne records the creation of George
Villiers as Earl of Buckingham, which occurred on the 5th.)

1630, 5 Nov. In a bill of the King's company for performances
before the King in 1630 and 1630/1 occurs the item, 'The 5 of
November, An Induction for the Howse, And The Madd Louer'.
(See above, i. 27–28.)

1639, 21 May. In the account book of Sir Humphrey Mildmay
appears the entry, 'To the Mad louer: 21 . . . 00–06–00'. (See
above, ii. 678–9.)

1641, 7 Aug. In a list of plays belonging to the King's company
which the Lord Chamberlain forbade the printers to publish
without the company's consent is 'The mad Louer'. (See above,
i. 65–66.)

1646, [4] Sept. S.R. Humphrey Robinson and Humphrey Moseley
entered as their copies a list of about fifty play titles, all
apparently formerly of the repertory of the King's company.
The first title is 'Mad Lover', which has been added after the
others. (Greg, *Bibliography*, i. 56–57.)

1647. The first play in the first Beaumont and Fletcher Folio is
'The Mad Lover'.

< 1659/60. In the repertory of Rhodes's company acting at the
Cockpit, Downes names 'The *M*ad Lover'. (*Roscius Anglicanus*,
Summers ed., pp. 17–18.)

1660, 12 Dec. Davenant was granted acting rights for two months
in several plays, including 'The Mad Lover'. (Nicoll, *A History
of Restoration Drama*, 3rd ed., pp. 314–15.)

1660/1, Feb. 'Feb. Mad Lover' appears in a list of performances of
plays by 'the Kings Companie at the Red Bull and the new
house in Gibbon's Tennis Court near Clare Market', 1660–2.
(Adams, *Herbert*, p. 117, n. 1.)

1660/1, 9 Feb. 'Creed and I to Whitefriars to the Play-house, and
saw "The Mad Lover," the first time I ever saw it acted, which
I like pretty well.' (Diary of Samuel Pepys.)

1661, 2 Dec. '. . . to the Opera, to see "The Mad Lover," but not
much pleased with the play.' (Ibid.)

1664, 25 Sept. 'I spent all the morning reading of "The Madd
Lovers," a very good play.' (Ibid.)

1668/9, 18 Feb. '. . . to the Duke of York's house, to a play, and
there saw "The Mad Lover," which do not please me so well as
it used to do, only Betterton's part still pleases me.' (Ibid.)

1672/3, 30 Jan. S.R. Humphrey Robinson, executor of Humphrey
Robinson, transferred to John Martin and Henry Herringman

his rights in a long list of plays, including 'Madd Lovers, [*sic*] halfe'. (Greg, *Bibliography*, i. 72–73.)

1679. The twelfth play in the second Beaumont and Fletcher Folio is 'The Mad Lover, A Tragi-Comedy'.

1683, 21 Aug. S.R. Sarah Martin, executrix of John Martin, transferred to Robert Scott her rights in a long list of plays, including 'mad Lovers. ¼'. (Ibid., pp. 75–76.)

The cast for the play which is given in the second Folio indicates that the first performance could not long have preceded the one seen at court by Lady Anne (see above, entry of 5 January 1616/17):

> Richard Burbadge.
> Robert Benfeild.
> Nathanael Feild.
> Henry Condel.
>
> John Lowin.
> William Eglestone.
> Richard Sharpe.

Benfield apparently did not join the company until about 1615, and Nathan Field not until 1616. (See above, ii. 374–5 and 434–6.) The play was therefore probably produced for the first time in 1616, perhaps late in the year in preparation for the court performance.

Neither the prologue nor the epilogue printed with the play in the Folios gives any indication that it was prepared for a revival, and none of the disintegrators has claimed to find any hand but Fletcher's in the piece, though it is not true, as Oliphant asserts, that the prologue refers to a single author. (*Plays of Beaumont and Fletcher*, p. 142. Perhaps Oliphant was misled by 'the writer's care' in modern editions. There is no apostrophe in the original.) The prompt manuscript from which the first Folio was set up must have been prepared for a revival, however. Actors' names occur in stage directions in Act II: '*Enter Stremon and his Boy Ed. Hor.*', and in Act IV: '*Enter a Servant and R. Bax, and Stremon at the doore.*' The first actor was Edward Horton, who had a boy's role in a King's men play published in 1629 and is not likely to have been with the company many years before; the second, Richard Baxter, is not known to have been connected with the King's company before 1628 and was certainly performing with another company in 1622. (See above, ii. 360–2 and 479.) These directions may well have been added to the manuscript for the performance of 1630, which was probably a gala one. (See above, i. 28, n. 1.)

Sir Aston Cokayne had a manuscript of the play, but apparently not the one from which Moseley and Robinson printed. Among the commendatory verses for the first Folio is a set by Cokayne entitled 'On The Deceased Authour, Mr John Fletcher, his Plays;

and especially, *The Mad Lover*'. Only two lines really concern the play, and they say little, but in the 'Apology' to his *Chain of Golden Poems*, 1658, in which these verses are reprinted, Sir Aston says:

I have been demanded by some Persons of Quality and judgement, why in my copy of Verses before *Mr. Fletchers* volume of Plaies, I chiefly reflect upon the *Mad Lover*, my noble friend and kinsman Mr. *Charles Cotton*, sent me that single Play in a Manuscript, which I had divers years in my hands: therefore when I found the Players were prohibited to act, I writ those poor Verses with an intention to have had the *Mad Lover* printed single, and them to have waited on it; (which when the large Volume came forth) my Cosin *Cotton* commanded from me, and gave the Printers.

Presumably Cokayne had a private transcript prepared for Cotton, and still had it after most of the Folio had been set up.

It is not surprising that Sir Aston Cokayne had a special fancy for *The Mad Lover*, for the play caught the attention of a number of writers. It is mentioned in the commendatory verses of the first Folio by Lovelace, Robert Gardiner, Herrick, and G. Hills, as well as by Cokayne. In the 1653 edition of *Poems, By Francis Beaumont, Gent.*, which includes a great many pieces not by Beaumont, are both the prologue and the epilogue to *The Mad Lover*, as well as four of the songs from that play. Perhaps the popularity of *The Mad Lover* is the reason that Moseley and Robinson printed it first in the Folio of 1647.

The source for the play is not known, though several have been suggested for names or bits of the action. (See Bond, ed., pp. 114–16.) Such an eclectic method of collecting material as these suggested multiple sources imply does not seem very congenial to Fletcher.

In the first few years of the eighteenth century there seems to have been either an operatic version of *The Mad Lover* or another musical entertainment into which various songs and episodes from the play were worked. (See Sprague, loc. cit.)

The Maid in the Mill (August 1623; revised 1 November 1623)
with William Rowley

Bond, R. Warwick. 'On Six Plays in *Beaumont and Fletcher, 1679*', *R.E.S.* xi (1935), 262.

Elson, J. J., ed. *The Wits, or, Sport upon Sport* (1932), pp. 237–51 and 390–1.

Koeppel, Emil. *Quellen-Studien zu den Dramen Ben Jonson's, John Marston's und Beaumont's und Fletcher's* (1895), pp. 111–14.

McKeithan, D. M. 'Shakespearian Echoes in the Florimel Plot of Fletcher and Rowley's *The Maid in the Mill*', *P.Q.* xvii (1938), 396–8.

Oliphant, E. H. C. *The Plays of Beaumont and Fletcher* (1927), pp. 486–8.

1623, 29 Aug. 'For the King's Players; a new Comedy, called, *The Maid of the Mill*; written by Fletcher, and Rowley.'(Adams, *Herbert*, p. 25.)

1623, 29 Sept. 'Upon Michelmas night att Hampton court, *The Mayd of the Mill*, by the K. company.' (In a list of plays performed at court in 1623 and 1623/4. Ibid., pp. 50–51.)

1623, 1 Nov. 'Upon Allhollows night at St. James, the prince being there only, *The Mayd of the Mill* againe, with reformations.' (Ibid., p. 51, from the same list of court performances.)

1623, 26 Dec. 'Upon St. Stevens daye, the king and prince being there, *The Mayd of the Mill*, by the K. company. Att Whitehall.' (Ibid., from the same list.)

1641, 7 Aug. 'The maid of the Mill' occurs in a list of King's men's plays which the Lord Chamberlain forbade the printers to publish without the company's consent. (See above, i. 65–66.)

1646, [4] Sept. S.R. Humphrey Robinson and Humphrey Moseley entered as their copies a list of about fifty play titles, all apparently formerly of the repertory of the King's company. Included is 'Maid of the Mill . . . by mr Beamont & mr fflesher'. (Greg, *Bibliography*, i. 56–57.)

1647. 'The Maid In The Mill' is the seventeenth play in the first Beaumont and Fletcher Folio.

< 1659/60. In the repertory of Rhodes's company acting at the Cockpit, Downes names 'Maid in the Mill'. He records that in these early performances Kynaston played Ismenia; Nokes and Angel, Florimel; and Betterton, Aminta. (*Roscius Anglicanus*, Summers ed., pp. 17–19.)

1660, 12 Dec. Davenant was granted acting rights for two months in several old King's men's plays, including 'The Mayd in ye Mill'. (Nicoll, *A History of Restoration Drama*, 3rd ed., pp. 314–15.)

1661/2, 29 Jan. Two Dutch travellers recorded seeing 'the maid in the mill' at the Duke of York's playhouse this date. (Ethel Seaton, *Literary Relations of England and Scandinavia in the Seventeenth Century* [1935], p. 333.)

1660/1, 29 Jan. '. . . went to Blackfryers (the first time I ever was there since plays begun), and there after great patience and little expectation, from so poor beginning, I saw three acts of "The Mayd in ye Mill" acted to my great content.' (Diary of Samuel Pepys.)

1661, Apr.? In Sir Henry Herbert's incompletely reconstructed list of performances by 'the Kings Companie at the Red Bull and the new house in Gibbon's Tennis Court near Clare Market' 1660–2, appears:

> 1661. March ⎫
> April   ⎬ . . . The Mayd in the Mill.
> May   ⎭

(Adams, *Herbert*, p. 117, n. 1.)

1662. 'The Surprise', a droll made from *The Maid in the Mill*, was published in *The Wits, or, Sport upon Sport*. (See J. J. Elson, ed. [1932], pp. 237–51.)

1662, 1 Apr. '. . . to the playhouse, the Opera, and saw "The Mayde in the Mill," a pretty good play.' (Diary of Samuel Pepys.)

1662[–3?]. In Edward Browne's accounts for plays seen in '1662', under the heading 'At Salisbury or Dorset Court', is the entry, 'Maid in the Mill . . . 26'. (W. W. Greg, 'Theatrical Repertories of 1662', *Gentleman's Magazine*, ccci [1906], 69–72; from B.M. MS. Sloane 1900.)

1668, 10 Sept. '. . . at the Duke's play-house, and there saw "The Maid in the Mill," revived—a pretty, harmless old play.' (Diary of Samuel Pepys.)

1672/3, 30 Jan. S.R. Humphrey Robinson, executor of Humphrey Robinson, transferred to John Martin and Henry Herringman rights in a long list of plays, including 'Maid of the Mill. halfe'. (Greg, *Bibliography*, i. 72–73.)

1679. The thirty-third play in the second Beaumont and Fletcher Folio is 'The Maid in the Mill. A Comedy'.

1683, 21 Aug. S.R. Sarah Martin, executrix of John Martin, transferred to Robert Scott her rights in a long list of plays, including a fourth interest in 'Maid of the Mill'. (*Ibid.*, pp. 75–76.)

The fact that William Rowley collaborated with Fletcher in *The Maid in the Mill* is recorded by Sir Henry Herbert, and Greg suggests that some knowledge of this fact—though it is not noted in the first Folio—may have prompted Edward Archer to list the play as Rowley's in his catalogue of plays in 1656. (*Edinburgh Bibliographical Society Transactions*, ii, Part 4 [1946], 315.)

Rowley's name is one of those in the actor list for the play in the second Folio—presumably the cast for the first performance, since all the players named were active in 1623:

Joseph Tailor,	*John Thomson.*
John Lowin,	*Robert Benfield,*
John Vnderwood,	*Tho. Polard.*
William Rowly.	

Rowley's characteristic fat-clown role (see above, ii. 555–8) appears in the play, and he probably wrote it for himself shortly after he came to the King's company from Prince Charles's troupe. The disintegrators are pretty well agreed that Fletcher wrote the first act, Rowley the second and fourth, and that each contributed scenes to Acts III and V. (See Oliphant, loc. cit.)

Sir Henry Herbert's record of the second court performance two months after the play was originally licensed shows that the comedy has been revised. Oliphant (loc. cit.) saw evidences of revision in the play, but he was confused about the date, apparently because he had not noted Herbert's record of revision. Revision of a play only two months old, which had been properly licensed by Herbert and sanctioned by a previous court performance, is an odd phenomenon. The recorded facts would seem to eliminate the usual reasons for revision, such as censorship or modernization. One can only conjecture either that certain elements unpleasing to the King were removed or that elements especially pleasing were elaborated. The former possibility seems none too likely, since the play had a most unusual number of court performances in the autumn of 1623.

Langbaine noted that the sources of the play are the twelfth story in Belleforest's *Histoires Tragiques* and the Spanish novel, *Gerardo, The Unfortunate Spaniard.* (*Account of the English Dramatick Poets*, pp. 211–12.) Leonard Digges's translation of the Spanish novel did not appear until 1622 (*S.T.C.* 4919), a date conveniently close to Herbert's licence for the play. Both sources are summarized in the introductions to the play in the editions of Beaumont and Fletcher by Weber and by Dyce. I have not seen Goulart's *Histoires admirables et memorables de nostre temps* (Paris, 1600) which Miss Scott (*Elizabethan Translations*, p. 83) says contains the plot of the play. The alleged indebtedness of *The Maid in the Mill* to *Romeo and Juliet* is dubious, for the similarities cited are mostly similarities to the Spanish novel as well. The reminiscences of *The Winter's Tale* discussed by McKeithan (op. cit.) are possible, but by no means certain; all are fairly common romantic elements.

The anticipatory stage direction, '*Six Chaires placed at the Arras*', at the end of Act I in the first Folio suggests that the play was set up from a prompt copy, and Professor Bald (*Bibliographical Studies in the Beaumont & Fletcher Folio of 1647*, p. 113) thinks that the manuscript must have been in the hand of Ralph Crane. It is notable that the title of the play in the first Folio is *The Maid in the Mill*, whereas all previous records had used '*of the Mill*'. The Folio seems to have fixed the later usage.

The droll called *The Surprise*, which was made from three comic scenes in Acts II, IV, and V of *The Maid in the Mill*, was printed in Kirkman's collection called *The Wits*. The principal character is Bustopha, here called just Miller's Son.

Sprague notes eighteenth-century revivals of the play in 1704 and 1710. (*Beaumont and Fletcher on the Restoration Stage*, pp. 76 and 114.)

The Maid's Tragedy

See *The Elizabethan Stage*, iii. 224–5.

The Martial Maid

See Fletcher, *Love's Cure*.

The Masque of the Inner Temple and Gray's Inn

See *The Elizabethan Stage*, iii. 233–5.

Monsieur Perrolis (?)
(Lost or Ghost)

1646, [4] Sept. S.R. In a list of forty-eight or forty-nine plays entered to Robinson and Moseley, the eighteenth is '[Mounsieur Perrollis *deleted*] mistaken'. (Greg, *Bibliography*, i. 56.)

The title appears only in the Moseley and Robinson list, where it has been deleted and marked 'mistaken'. The first thirty-one plays of the list are bracketed and marked 'by m^r Beamont & m^r fflesher'. All but three of the plays of the list certainly belonged to the King's company, and those three probably did too. Indeed, this list of plays is set down in the same order as the list of the King's company repertory, which the Lord Chamberlain sent the stationers in 1641 (see above, i. 65–66), though each list shows additions to or deletions from the other. Professor Bald has suggested with great plausibility (*Bibliographical Studies in the Beaumont & Fletcher Folio of 1647*, p. 9) that both lists were made from the same inventory of the repertory of the King's company.

Under the circumstances it is notable that *Monsieur Perrolis* comes between *Bonduca* and *The Chances* in the Stationers' Register list, and that the play between *Bonduca* and *The Chances* in the Lord Chamberlain's list is Wilson's *The Inconstant Lady*, a play with a French setting. It may be, therefore, that a French name on the manuscript of *The Inconstant Lady* was misread, and listed as a title, and that the publishers later noted that the play was not by Beaumont and Fletcher—as the seventeen preceding and the thirteen following plays are—and deleted it.

It is also possible that 'Mounsieur Perrollis' is a mistaken title for Shakespeare's *All's Well That Ends Well*. This play, in which Parolles is a chief character and which was owned by the King's company, had already been printed twice in the first two folios, a fact that could account for the deletion in Moseley's list. The strongest evidence for identification is the fact that in the copy of the second Folio once belonging to Charles I and now in the Windsor Castle Library, 'Monsieur Parolles' has been written in at the head of *All's Well That Ends Well*. (See Arthur Quiller-Couch and J. Dover Wilson, eds., *All's Well That Ends Well*, pp. xxiv–xxv, and W. T. Lowndes, *The Bibliographer's Manual of English Literature*, ed. Henry G. Bohn [1869], pp. 2256–7.) If this manuscript note records a title sometimes attached to the play in the thirties, then it is not unlikely that Moseley referred to Shakespeare's play, but it is equally possible that the manuscript note in the Windsor Castle folio simply indicates the writer's interest in a notable character.

Monsieur Thomas, or The Father's Own Son

See *The Elizabethan Stage*, iii. 228.

The Nice Valour, or The Passionate Madman (> 1616? ; revived ?)

Bald, R. C. *Bibliographical Studies in the Beaumont & Fletcher Folio of 1647*, Supplement to the Bibliographical Society's Transactions, No. 13 (1938), pp. 8–10, 30–36, 109–10.

Bensly, Edward. 'Burton and Fletcher', *N. & Q.*, Tenth Series, vi (1906), 464–5; and Eleventh Series, i (1910), 196.

Maxwell, Baldwin. '*Nice Valour, or The Passionate Madman*', *Studies in Beaumont, Fletcher, and Massinger* (1939), pp. 116–37.

Oliphant, E. H. C. *The Plays of Beaumont and Fletcher* (1927), pp. 439–51.

1641, 7 Aug. The Lord Chamberlain forbade the printers to publish any of a list of plays belonging to the repertory of the King's company. One play in the list is 'The Bridegroome & yᵉ Madmã'. (See above, i. 65–66.)

1647. The sixteenth play in the first Beaumont and Fletcher Folio is 'The Nice Valovr, Or, The Passionate Mad-man'.

1660, 29 June. S.R. Humphrey Robinson and Humphrey Moseley entered as their copies six plays, including 'The Nice Valour or the passionate Madman . . . all Six Copies written by ffra: Beamont & Iohn ffletcher'. (Greg, *Bibliography*, i. 68.)

1668/9, *c.* 12 Jan. In 'A Catalogue of part of His Maᵗᵉˢ Servants Playes as they were formerly acted at the Blackfryers & now allowed of to his Maᵗᵉˢ Servants at yᵉ New Theatre' is 'The Nice Valour'. (Nicoll, *A History of Restoration Drama*, 3rd ed., pp. 315–16.)

1672/3, 30 Jan. S.R. Humphrey Robinson, executor of Humphrey Robinson, transferred to John Martin and Henry Herringman all his rights in a number of plays, including 'The Nice valour. halfe'. (Greg, *Bibliography*, i. 72–73.)

1679. The fiftieth play in the second Beaumont and Fletcher Folio is 'Nice Valour. A Comedy'.

1683, 21 Aug. S.R. Sarah Martin, executrix of John Martin, transferred to Robert Scott her rights in a long list of plays, including a fourth interest in 'Nice Valour'. (Ibid., pp. 75–76.)

There seems to be no really reliable evidence of any kind about this play before the closing of the theatres. Sir Edmund Chambers suggested (*M.S.C.* i, Parts iv and v. 365) that in the list of plays in the repertory of the King's men in 1641 'The Bridegroome & yᵉ Madmã', a title not otherwise known, might refer to *The Nice Valour, or the Passionate Madman*; but *The Bridegroom* would not be an appropriate title for the play as we have it, and there is nothing else to connect the current play with the King's company.

There is no actor list for the play in the second Folio, as there is for most of the Beaumont and Fletcher plays belonging to the King's men. Most of the plays published in the first Beaumont and Fletcher Folio of 1647 were entered in the Stationers' Register in a long list on 4[?] September 1646, a list in which the Beaumont and Fletcher entries seem to have been taken from an inventory list of the King's company. (See Bald, op. cit., pp. 8–10.) *The Nice Valour*, however, was not entered until thirteen years after it had been printed, and then appeared in a supplementary list of six plays, most of which appear not to have belonged to the King's company. (Ibid.) Such evidence as we have, therefore, indicates that *The Nice Valour* was not written for the King's company. If not for the King's company, the play is probably not a Fletcher play of the period 1613–25. (See above, Life of Fletcher.) The text of the play in the first Folio shows no evidence that *The Nice Valour* was set up from a playhouse prompt copy, as most of the others in the Folio were. (Bald, op. cit., pp. 109–10.) The play is much shorter than any other in the Folio and shows evidence that it has been extensively cut, or, perhaps, never completed. (See Oliphant, pp. 441–4.)

Professor Maxwell's article on the play presents a great deal of possible dating evidence, but all of it is highly uncertain, except for his demonstration that the reference to '*Fishers* Folly' in v. 3 probably does not refer to the pamphlet of 1624, but to a well-known London house erected in the reign of Elizabeth and frequently referred to as Fisher's Folly in the reign of James. (Op. cit., pp. 116–21.) His suggestion that the action in the play concerning the Duke's insult to Shamont reflects King James's insult to John Gibb seems to me highly improbable. He tentatively accepts a date of late 1615 or early 1616, but he realizes how shaky his evidence is.

The disintegrators are widely at variance in their identification of original work and revisions in the play. One or another of them has found Beaumont, Fletcher, Rowley, and Middleton. Somewhat unusual is the number who have seen the work of Middleton. (See Oliphant, op. cit., pp. 448–51.)

Both the prologue and the epilogue printed with the play in the Folio refer to the author in the singular, and the epilogue—unlike most Folio prologues and epilogues—affords clear evidence that it was written for this play. The prologue is entitled 'THE PROLOGUE *at the reviving* of this Play' and is one of several concerning the fashion of prologues and the dramatists' reluctance to write them. The wording indicates that the writer whom the players requested to write a prologue (presumably this one for the revival) was the author of the play, and consequently implies that this revival was before 1625—if Fletcher was indeed the author.

The song in praise of melancholy, beginning '*Hence all you vaine Delights*', in Act III of the play, is found attributed to William Strode in various manuscripts. Bertram Dobell (*Poetical Works of William Strode*, pp. xxxvii–xxxix) contends that the song is Strode's and was inserted into *The Nice Valour, or The Passionate Madman*, but his evidence is by no means conclusive. The similarity of the song to *Il Penseroso* has attracted comment. Edward Bensly pointed out that if Fletcher wrote the song he could not have been influenced by Burton. Bensly did not know about the Strode attribution, and his evidence would not apply to Strode or to the possibility that Strode's song was worked into the play years after its original composition.

No source for the play has been identified.

The history of *The Nice Valour, or The Passionate Madman* is so uncertain that the possibility that it is not a Beaumont and Fletcher play should not be ignored.

The Night Walker, or The Little Thief (*c.* 1611 ?; revised 1633)
Revised by James Shirley

Bond, R. Warwick. 'On Six Plays in *Beaumont and Fletcher, 1679*', *R.E.S.* xi (1935), 269–71.

Chambers, E. K. *The Elizabethan Stage* (1923), iii. 230–1.

Koeppel, Emil. *Quellen-Studien zu den Dramen Ben Jonson's, John Marston's und Beaumont's und Fletcher's* (1895), pp. 125–7.

Maxwell, Baldwin. 'The Date of Fletcher's *The Night-Walker*', *M.L.N.* i (1935), 487–93. Reprinted in *Studies in Beaumont, Fletcher, and Massinger* (1939), pp. 46–53.

Oliphant, E. H. C. *The Plays of Beaumont and Fletcher* (1927), pp. 488–92.

1633, 11 May. 'For a play of Fletchers corrected by Sherley, called *The Night Walkers*, the 11 May, 1633,—£2. 0. 0. For the queen's players.' (Adams, *Herbert*, p. 34.)

1633/4, 30 Jan. '*The Night-Walkers* was acted on thursday night the 30 Janua. 1633, at Court, before the King and Queen. Likt as a merry play. Made by Fletcher.' (Ibid., p. 54.)

1639, 25 Apr. S.R. Andrew Crooke and William Cooke entered for their copies 'these five playes vidlt Night walters [*sic*], Oportunity. Loues Cruellty, The Coronation   witt without money'. (Greg, *Bibliography*, i. 50.)

1639, 10 Aug. Included in a list of plays protected by the Lord

Chamberlain for the King and Queen's Young Company at the Cockpit is 'The Night Walkers'. (See above, i. 330–1.)

1640. The Night-Walker, Or The Little Theife. A Comedy, As it was presented by her Majesties Servants, at the Private House in *Drury* Lane. Written by *John Fletcher*. Gent . . . 1640.

1661. The Night-Walker, Or The *Little Thief*. A Comedy, As it was presented by her Majesties Servants, at the Private House in Drury-Lane. Written by *John Fletcher*, Gent. . . . Printed for *Andrew Crook*, 1661.

1661, 2 Apr. '. . . so to White-fryars and saw "The Little Thiefe," which is a very merry and pretty play, and the little boy do very well.' (Diary of Samuel Pepys.)

1661/2, 15 Mar. 'The Litle Theefe. 15. March.' appears in a list of performances of plays by 'the Kings Companie at the Red Bull and the new house in Gibbon's Tennis Court near Clare Market', 1660–2. (Adams, *Herbert*, p. 118.)

1662, 31 Mar. 'Thence to the play . . . and there we sat and heard "The Little Thiefe," a pretty play and well done.' (Diary of Samuel Pepys.)

1662, 19 May. '. . . to the Theatre, and there in a box saw "The Little Thief" well done.' (Ibid.)

1662 [–3 ?]. Edward Browne noted in his memorandum book that he paid 1s. 6d. to see 'The little thiefe' 'At the Kings Armes Norwich'. (W. W. Greg, 'Theatrical Repertories of 1662', *Gentleman's Magazine*, ccci [1906], 69–72; from B.M. MS. Sloane 1900.)

1664, 1 Nov. According to the records of the Inner Temple, £20 was paid 'To his Majesty's players, for acting a play on All Saints day last in the Temple called "The Little Thief"'. (F. A. Inderwick, ed., *Calendar of the Inner Temple Records*, iii. 25.)

1679. The thirty-seventh play in the second Beaumont and Fletcher Folio is 'The Night-Walker, Or The Little Thief. A Comedy'.

1691. Langbaine said that *The Night Walker* was 'a Comedy which I have seen acted by the King's Servants, with great Applause, both in the City and Country'. (*Account of the English Dramatick Poets*, p. 213.)

The Night Walker, or The Little Thief is one of the few plays of the second Folio which appear never to have belonged to the King's company. It is in none of their lists; it was revised in 1633 for Queen Henrietta's company by Shirley, then a regular dramatist for that company; it was published as a play of that company; and in 1639 it was protected as the property of the successor to that company. Presumably, then, *The Night Walker* was originally written for one of the antecedents of Queen Henrietta's company—the Queen's Revels company or Lady Elizabeth's men. There is no cast for the play in the second Folio to associate it with one of these early companies, as there is for *The Coxcomb* and *The Honest Man's Fortune*. It is perhaps significant that when Cooke and Crooke licensed the play for publication they licensed with it four other plays belonging to Queen Henrietta's men, three of them by Shirley, who revised this comedy.

Professor Maxwell (loc. cit.) presents evidence that the play was originally composed about 1611, shortly after *The Woman's Prize, or The Tamer Tamed*. While his evidence is by no means conclusive, it seems to me more cogent than the arguments presented for any other date.

The reference in Act III of the play to 'the late Histriomastix' clearly alludes to Prynne's treatise against the theatres which was published in 1633 and indicates that Shirley must have made his revisions shortly before Sir Henry Herbert licensed them, as one would expect. The entry in the office-book clearly suggests that Fletcher's original play was revised by Shirley, not completed by him, as has sometimes been said. Herbert's fee of £2 suggests that the revisions were extensive, for in the last ten years before the closing of the theatres he several times allowed scenes to be added to old plays for a fee of £1 and seems usually to have charged £2 only for the licensing of a new play. (See Adams, *Herbert*, pp. 34–39.) Oliphant points out various indications of revision in the text. (Loc. cit.) The disintegrators are in general agreement that the hands of Fletcher and Shirley and no others are to be seen in the play.

The suggestion that *The Night Walker* is the same as *The Devil of Dowgate*, a lost play by Fletcher, is almost certainly wrong, since *The Devil of Dowgate* (q.v.) was acted by the King's men in 1623, and *The Night Walker* belonged to Queen Henrietta's men.

The source of the play has not been found. Koeppel suggests (loc. cit.), without much conviction, that the device of the heroine awaking from her coffin may have come from Bandello's *Novelle*, Part II, Nov. 41. Miss Scott lists *Decameron*, Dec. iii, Nov. 8, as a source for *The Night Walker*, but offers no evidence or comment. (*Elizabethan Translations*, p. 94.)

The Noble Enemy

See Fletcher, *The Humourous Lieutenant.*

The Noble Gentleman (1625/6?)

Bond, R. Warwick. 'On Six Plays in *Beaumont and Fletcher, 1679*', *R.E.S.* xi (1935), 273–5.
—— 'Three Beaumont and Fletcher Plays', *R.E.S.* xii (1936), 444–5.
Lawrence, W. J. *Those Nut-Cracking Elizabethans* (1935), p. 204.
Maxwell, Baldwin. *Studies in Beaumont, Fletcher, and Massinger* (1939), pp. 147–65. (Revised with numerous additions from *M.L.N.* xliii [1928], 22–27.)
Oliphant, E. H. C. *The Plays of Beaumont and Fletcher* (1927), pp. 183–201.
—— 'Three Beaumont and Fletcher Plays', *R.E.S.* xii (1936), 198–9.
Sprague, Arthur Colby. *Beaumont and Fletcher on the Restoration Stage* (1926), pp. 238–44.

1625/6, 3 Feb. '*The Noble Gentleman*, by John Fletcher, licensed; acted at the Blackfriars.' (Adams, *Herbert*, p. 31.)
1641, 7 Aug. In a list of plays belonging to the King's men which the Lord Chamberlain forbade the printers to publish without the company's consent is 'The noble gentleman'. (See above, i. 65–66.)
1646, [4] Sept. S.R. In a list of about fifty plays, all apparently formerly of the repertory of the King's company, entered by Humphrey Robinson and Humphrey Moseley is 'Noble gentleman . . . by mʳ Beamont & mʳ fflesher'. (Greg, *Bibliography*, i. 56–57.)
1647. The fifth play in the Beaumont and Fletcher Folio is 'The Noble Gentleman'.
1661/2, 22 Jan. Two Dutch travellers saw at the Red Bull a play they called 'The New-Made Nobleman [Den nieuw-gemaakten Adelman]'. (Ethel Seaton, *Literary Relations of England and Scandinavia in the Seventeenth Century* [1935], pp. 333–5. See also William Van Lennep, *T.L.S.*, 20 June 1936, p. 523.)
1668/9, *c.* 12 Jan. In 'A Catalogue of part of His Maᵗᵉˢ Servants Playes as they were formerly acted at the Blackfryers & now allowed of to his Maᵗᵉˢ Servants at yᵉ New Theatre' occurs the title 'The Noble Gentlemen [*sic*]'. (Nicoll, *A History of Restoration Drama*, 3rd ed., pp. 315–16.)

1672/3, 30 Jan. S.R. Humphrey Robinson, executor of Humphrey Robinson, transferred his rights in a long list of plays to John Martin and Henry Herringman; included is '[71] Noble Gentleman. halfe'. (Greg, *Bibliography*, i. 72–73.)

1679. The fortieth play in the second Beaumont and Fletcher Folio is 'The Noble Gentleman. A Comedy'.

1683, 21 Aug. S.R. Sarah Martin, executrix of John Martin, transferred her rights in a long list of titles to Robert Scott; included is a one-fourth interest in '[79] Noble Gentleman'. (Ibid., pp. 75–76.)

1688. A Fool's Preferment, Or, The Three Dukes of Dunstable. A Comedy. As it was Acted at the Queens Theatre in *Dorset-Garden*, by Their Majesties Servants. *Written by Mr. D'urfey* . . . 1688.

Sir Henry Herbert's licence of this comedy five months after Fletcher's death, considered with the somewhat confused state of the text, suggests that the play was one of the last of the playwright's productions, possibly completed by another dramatist after his death. Such a conclusion is somewhat unsettled by the prologue for the play which is printed in the Folios:

> WIT *is become an Antick, and puts on*
> *As many shapes of variation,*
> *To court the times applause, as the times dare,*
> *Change several fashions, nothing is thought rare*
> *Which is not new, and follow'd, yet we know*
> *That what was worn some twenty years agoe,*
> *Comes into grace again, and we pursue*
> *That custom, by presenting to your view*
> *A Play in fashion then, not doubting now*
> *But 'twill appear the same, if you allow*
> *Worth to their noble memory, whose name,*
> *Beyond all power of death, live in their fame.*
>
> (Folio, 1679.)

Clearly this prologue was intended for a revival twenty years or so after the first production, that is, approximately 1646, if the play was new when Sir Henry licensed it. There was, of course, surreptitious drama after the closing of the theatres, but new prologues for such uncertain performances seem unlikely.

The application of the prologue statements to *The Noble Gentleman* is doubtful, however, for the same prologue is also printed in the 1649 quarto of *Thierry and Theodoret*. It has been thought inappropriate for that play, presumably because the reference to wit is less apt for a tragedy than for a comedy. Actually, like most of

the prologues and epilogues in the Folios, this one is so general in
character that it could be used with any number of plays ; even the
wit reference is not impossible for a tragedy.

The epilogue printed with *The Noble Gentleman* in the Folios
appears also in the 1649 quarto of *The Woman Hater*. It seems to
imply revision in the concluding lines:

> *We'ave done our best, for your contents to fit,*
> *With new pains, this old monument of wit.*
>
> (Folio, 1679.)

Not much weight should be placed on either prologue or epilogue,
since neither makes any allusion to the content of the play, and
both have been printed with other plays.

Mr. Oliphant, none the less, based most of his argument for the
date and authorship of the play on the prologue. (Loc. cit.) Since
there was a revival twenty years after composition, he thought
that the 1625/6 licence of Herbert could not have been for first
performance but must have been for the revival for which the
prologue was prepared, and that the first performance was necessarily about 1606. This date would indicate that the phrase, '*their
noble memory*', in the prologue referred to Beaumont and Fletcher.
Such magnanimous ignoring of numerous alternate possibilities
is unfortunately characteristic of much Beaumont and Fletcher
scholarship. Even if it were certain that the prologue printed with
it in the Folio belonged to *The Noble Gentleman*, the unknown revival cannot thus arbitrarily be set at 1625/6 ; it could have been
staged any time before 1642, for we know from the Lord Chamberlain's list that the play was still in repertory in 1641. No solid
evidence for a date early in Fletcher's career has been cited.

The absence of a cast for the play in the second Folio has
prompted several commentators to conclude that the play cannot
have been originally performed by the King's men. Again, the
evidence about these casts is much too slight and contradictory to
allow such a conclusion. (See above, *The Beggars' Bush*.) There is no
evidence to connect the play with any other company. The various
attempts to identify this comedy with *The Nobleman* or *The Conceited Duke* or *The Woman's Plot* have sometimes been prompted
by a desire to connect it with another company, but there is no
reason to identify *The Noble Gentleman* with any of these other
titles.

Professor Maxwell finds in the play two topical allusions which
seem to him to date 1619–21. (Loc. cit.) They could have been
written in, either at the time of original composition or upon

revision. Professor Maxwell also finds a number of lines which offer notable parallels to the affairs of the unfortunate Arabella Stuart. He seems to think the parallels inadvertent, but so striking that they could never have been allowed on the stage in the years 1610–15 when King James was so acutely fearful of the great political dangers threatened by this poor girl. The play must therefore have been written after Arabella Stuart's death in 1615 or before the King became so fearful of her potential threat in 1609. Maxwell favours the earlier date because he is inclined to accept Beaumont's participation. This choice seems to me perverse. Most of the disintegrators, including Macaulay and Gayley and Maxwell himself, have failed to see any clear evidence of Beaumont's hand in the play; the dubious prologue in the Folio does not refer to Beaumont, as Maxwell and Oliphant indicate, but only to plural authorship. Maxwell's evidence, though inconclusive, seems to me to suggest composition after 1615, and possibly 1619–21, though his allusions might still have been good in 1625.

R. Warwick Bond (*R.E.S.* xi [1935], 273–5) would date the play not earlier than 1612 and not later than 1616. He wants a date early enough to include Beaumont as a collaborator and late enough to allow use of Shelton's 1612 translation of *Don Quixote*. But he seems also to be relying on situations parallel to those of other plays. Such dating evidence is always dubious, but in this case it seems to me utterly inconclusive, inasmuch as the parallels cited are to be found in plays of 1603, 1612, 1615–18, 1618–22, *c.* 1620, and 1624. In such a welter of inadequately supported conclusions and dubious evidence, it seems to me best to rely on the only piece of external evidence concerning the play which we have—Herbert's licence. Possibly the play he licensed was not new, but it seems to me sensible to assume that it was, until better evidence to the contrary is forthcoming.

No comprehensive source for *The Noble Gentleman* has ever been noted.

The disintegrators are completely at odds about the play. We have already noted that Macaulay, Gayley, and Maxwell found no Beaumont in it, though Oliphant, Bond, and Wells did. Macaulay and Bullen thought that Fletcher wrote none of the play. Others have found the hands of Fletcher, Rowley, Shirley, and Middleton; and W. J. Lawrence noted (loc. cit.) some of the characteristic punctuation of Massinger. One can only assume that Sir Henry Herbert knew what he was talking about when he licensed the play as Fletcher's, but that he would not necessarily have known of a collaborator or reviser.

Professor Bald points out that *The Noble Gentleman* is one of the few plays in the first Folio which show no evidence at all of having been set up from a prompt book; presumably it came from a private transcript. (*Bibliographical Studies in the Beaumont & Fletcher Folio of 1647*, pp. 109–10.)

In 1688 Thomas D'Urfey published *A Fool's Preferment, Or, The Three Dukes of Dunstable*. The piece is an adaptation of *The Noble Gentleman*. (See Sprague, loc. cit.)

The Passionate Madman

See Fletcher, *The Nice Valour*.

Philaster, or Love Lies a Bleeding

See *The Elizabethan Stage*, iii. 222–3.

The Pilgrim (1621?)

Koeppel, Emil. *Quellen-Studien zu den Dramen Ben Jonson's, John Marston's und Beaumont's und Fletcher's* (1895), pp. 100–3.

Maxwell, Baldwin. *Studies in Beaumont, Fletcher, and Massinger* (1939), pp. 210–19. Reprinted with additions from *Phil. Quart.* xiii (1934), 350–6.

Oliphant, E. H. C. *The Plays of Beaumont and Fletcher* (1927), pp. 145–6.

Rulfs, Donald J. 'Beaumont and Fletcher on the London Stage 1776–1833', *P.M.L.A.* lxiii (1948), 1254–5.

Sprague, Arthur Colby. *Beaumont and Fletcher on the Restoration Stage* (1926), 51–52, 89–93, 105–6, 110, 116–17, 244–8.

1621/2, 1 Jan. In a warrant of 27 March 1622 for payment to John Heminges of £60 for six plays presented by the King's men at court 5 November 1621 through 5 March 1621/2 is 'The Pilgrim on new yeares day'. (Murray, *English Dramatic Companies*, ii. 193.)

1621–21/2, Christmas. '*The Island Princess, The Pilgrim*, and *The Wild Goose Chase* are found among the court exhibitions of the year 1621.' (Malone's comment [*Variorum*, iii. 225–6] is an indirect quotation, presumably from Herbert's office-book. The reference could well be to the performance of 1 January 1621/2. Adams, *Herbert*, p. 49.)

1622, 29 Dec. 'Upon the Sonday following *The Pilgrim* was acted by the kings players.' (Adams, *Herbert*, p. 49.)

1641, 7 Aug. In a list of King's men's plays which the Lord Chamberlain forbade the printers to publish without the company's consent is 'The Pilgrim'. (See above, i. 65-66.)

1646, [4] Sept. S.R. Humphrey Robinson and Humphrey Moseley entered as their copies a list of about fifty plays, all apparently formerly the property of the King's company. Included is 'Pilgrime . . . by m^r Beamont & m^r fflesher'. (Greg, *Bibliography*, i. 56-57.)

1647. 'The Pilgrim' is the twenty-second play in the first Beaumont and Fletcher Folio.

1668/9, *c.* 12 Jan. In 'A Catalogue of part of His Ma^{tes} Servants Playes as they were formerly acted at the Blackfryers & now allowed of to his Ma^{tes} Servants at ye New Theatre' occurs the title 'The Pilgrim'. (Nicoll, *A History of Restoration Drama*, 3rd ed., pp. 315-16.)

1672. In '*Covent Garden* Drolery, Or A Colection, Of all the Choice *Songs, Poems, Prologues*, and *Epilogues*, (Sung and Spoken at *Courts* and *Theatres*)' appears a prologue for *The Pilgrim* which indicates that the play had been revised. (Montague Summers, ed., p. 10.)

1672/3, 30 Jan. S.R. Humphrey Robinson, executor of Humphrey Robinson, transferred his rights in a long list of plays to John Martin and Henry Herringman. Included is 'Pilgrim or Lawes of Candia. [*sic*] halfe'. (Greg, *Bibliography*, i. 72-73.)

1679. The twenty-fifth play in the second Beaumont and Fletcher Folio is 'The Pilgrim. A Comedy'.

1683, 21 Aug. S.R. Sarah Martin, executrix of John Martin, transferred her rights in a long list of plays to Robert Scott. Included is 'Pilgrim or Laws of Candia $\frac{1}{4}$'. (Ibid., pp. 75-76.)

1700. The Pilgrim, A Comedy: As it is Acted at the *Theatre-Royal*, in Drury-Lane. *Written Originally by Mr*. Fletcher, *and now very much Alter'd, with several Additions*. Likewise *A* Prologue, Epilogue, Dialogue *and* Masque, *Written by the late Great Poet Mr*. Dryden, *just before his Death, being the last of his* Works . . . 1700. (The alterations are by Vanbrugh. See Sprague, op. cit., pp. 89-93.)

1700. [Another issue.]

The play has usually been dated 1621, before the recorded court performance in 1621/2, and after the entry of *The Pilgrim of Castile*, the English version of Lope de Vega's *El Peregrino en su*

Patria, in the Stationers' Register 18 September 1621. (Arber, iv. 59.) The significance of the indebtedness to Lope de Vega was belittled by Macaulay, who said that 'the resemblance is only in trifling details, and there may be no connection'. (*C.H.E.L.,* 1932 ed., vi. 139.) Macaulay was right in denying that the Spanish romance was the comprehensive source of Fletcher's play; on the other hand, two incidents of the play are too close to the romance for chance. Maxwell (op. cit., pp. 218–19) pointed out how closely Fletcher followed *The Pilgrim of Castile* in his mad-house scenes, and it seems to me that Fletcher must have made use of the novel in II. 2, though the method of avoiding the hanging in the comedy is altered to a much more Fletcherian device. The loose and hasty construction of the play is compatible with composition in the short time between the entry of the translation in the Stationers' Register and the court performance. On the other hand, not enough has been made of the fact that D'Audiguier's French translation of Lope de Vega's novel had been available since 1614.

Professor Maxwell (loc. cit.) cites a number of allusions in the play which appear to refer to events of around 1621. Unfortunately the allusions are not specific, and most of the situations they seem to refer to are spread over several years before 1621. The allusions do not prove original composition in 1621, but they are suggestive. Fleay (*Biog. Chron.* i. 215) pointed out that the incident of the Mad Scholar who announces that he is Neptune in III. 6 is derived from *Don Quixote,* and Koeppel noted that the passage is in Part ii, chapter i.

In the 1679 Folio the following cast for the play is published:

Joseph Taylor.	*John Lowin.*
Nicholas Toolie.	*John Vnderwood.*
Robert Benfield.	*George Birch.*
John Thompson.	*James Horn.*

All these actors were performing for the King's company in 1621, though they were also available, with the possible exception of James Horn, both before that date and after, until June 1623, when Tooley was buried. (See above, vol. ii.) The absence of Burbage from the cast is good evidence that the performance recorded— presumably the first—took place after his death in March 1618/19.

The combined evidence, therefore, makes 1621 a probable date for the first performance of *The Pilgrim,* but by no means a certain one.

Weber noted in his edition of the play that Alinda's song in IV. 2, beginning 'He called down his merry men all', is from the ballad

'The Knight and the Shepherd's Daughter', which was licensed in 1624. (See Rollins, 'Analytical Index', Nos. 173, 2420, *Stud. Phil.* xxi [1924], 1–324.)

According to Professor Bald (*Bibliographical Studies in the Beaumont & Fletcher Folio of 1647*, pp. 109–10), *The Pilgrim* is one of only eight plays in the Folio which exhibit no signs of the prompter's work. Presumably, therefore, it was not printed from the copy used for performances by the King's company.

None of the disintegrators has suggested any hand but Fletcher's in the play.

The fact that the play appears in the 1641 repertory list of the King's company suggests that it was being performed in the thirties, but no surviving records of such performances have been found. The repertory list of 1668/9 and the prologue printed in 1672 indicate that there were also Restoration productions, but no specific performance is known until the revision of 1700. This revision was the work of Sir John Vanbrugh, with contributions from John Dryden. Sprague (loc. cit.) discusses the performances and the alterations. Eighteenth- and nineteenth-century revivals of the play are noted by Rulfs. (Loc. cit.)

The Prophetess (1622)

with Philip Massinger?

Adams, John C. *The Globe Playhouse* (1942), pp. 351–6.

Briggs, W. D. 'The Influence of Jonson's Tragedy in the Seventeenth Century', *Anglia*, xxxv (1912), 322–4.

Chelli, Maurice. *Étude sur la collaboration de Massinger avec Fletcher et son groupe* (1926), pp. 106–9.

Koeppel, Emil. *Quellen-Studien zu den Dramen Ben Jonson's, John Marston's und Beaumont's und Fletcher's* (1895), pp. 104–6.

Maxwell, Baldwin. 'The Hungry Knave in the Beaumont and Fletcher Plays', *Studies in Beaumont, Fletcher, and Massinger* (1939), 74–83.

Oliphant, E. H. C. *The Plays of Beaumont and Fletcher* (1927), pp. 245–6.

Sprague, Arthur Colby. *Beaumont and Fletcher on the Restoration Stage* (1926), pp. 69–71, 154–60.

Ulrich, Otto. *Die pseudohistorischen Dramen Beaumonts und Fletchers 'Thierry and Theodoret', 'Valentinian', 'The Prophetess' und 'The False One' und ihre Quellen* (1913), pp. 53–75.

1622, 14 May. 'A new play called *The Prophetess*, licensed May 14, 1622.' (Adams, *Herbert*, p. 23.)

1629, 21 July. 'The benefitt of the summers day from the kinges company, being brought mee by Blagrave, upon the play of *The Prophetess*, comes to, this 21 of July, 1629,—6*l.* 7*s.* 0*d.*' (Ibid., p. 43. See also above, i. 23–24.)

1641, 7 Aug. In a list of King's men's plays which the Lord Chamberlain forbade the printers to publish without the consent of the company is 'The Prophetesse'. (See above, i. 65–66.)

1646, [4] Sept. S.R. Humphrey Robinson and Humphrey Moseley entered as their copies a list of about fifty plays, all apparently formerly the property of the King's company. Included is 'The [Ph *deleted*] Prophetesse . . . by m^r Beamont & m^r fflesher'. (Greg, *Bibliography*, i. 56–57.)

1647 'The Prophetesse' is the eighteenth play in the first Beaumont and Fletcher Folio.

1668/9, *c.* 12 Jan. In 'A Catalogue of part of His Ma^{tes} Servants Playes as they were formerly acted at the Blackfryers & now allowed of to his Ma^{tes} Servants at ye New Theatre' occurs the title, 'The Prophetesse'. (Nicoll, *A History of Restoration Drama*, 3rd ed., pp. 315–16.)

1672/3, 30 Jan. S.R. Humphrey Robinson, executor of Humphrey Robinson, transferred his rights in a long list of plays to John Martin and Henry Herringman. Included is '[14] The Prophetess, All', but later in the same list is another listing, '[76] The Prophetess. halfe'. (Greg, *Bibliography*, i. 72–73.)

1679. The twenty-seventh play in the second Beaumont and Fletcher Folio is 'The Prophetess. A Tragical History'.

1683, 21 Aug. S.R. Sarah Martin, executrix of John Martin, transferred her rights in a long list of plays to Robert Scott. Included in the list is '[84] Prophetesse', which is bracketed with a number of other plays and marked 'a fourth'. (Ibid., pp. 75–76.)

1690. The Prophetess: Or, The History of Dioclesian. Written by *Francis Beaumont* and *John Fletcher*. With Alterations and Additions, After the Manner of an Opera. Represented at the Queen's Theatre, By Their Majesties Servants . . . 1690.

1690. [Another issue.]

1690, 17 Nov. In a warrant for payment for plays acted before royalty is the entry, '1690 . . . Nov. 17th ye Q a Box & a Box for ye Maids Hono^r Prophetess   [£] 30'. (Nicoll, *A History of Restoration Drama*, 3rd ed., p. 314.)

1697, Nov.–Dec.? The *Post-Boy* for 16–18 December 1697 contained this notice: 'We hear that the Marquiss of Carmathen who lately Entertain'd the Great Officer from the *Czar* of Muscovy, at the Opera call'd the Prophetess, has this day Bespoke the Entertainment of the Indian Queen.' (See A. C. Sprague, *Beaumont and Fletcher on the Restoration Stage*, pp. 93–94.)

1697/8, Jan. The *Post-Boy* for 13–15 January 1697/8 announced: ''Tis said that this day will be Acted, at the Theatre in *Dorset-Garden*, the Opera, called *Prophetess* or *Dioclesian*, at the Request of a Nobleman.' (Ibid., p. 94.)

1697/8, Jan. The next issue of the *Post-Boy* noted: ''Tis said that the Czar of *Muscooy* [*sic*], was at the Play-house on *Saturday*, to see the Opera.' (Ibid.)

The date of production of the play is set, probably within a few days, by Herbert's licence, and his considerate inclusion of the word 'new' eliminates the usual arguments that he was licensing only a revision. That the play was licensed for the King's company is shown by Herbert's 1629 entry, by the 1641 repertory list, and by the cast printed in the second Folio:

John Lowin.	*Joseph Taylor.*
Robert Benfield.	*Nicholas Toolie.*
John Shanke.	*George Birch.*
Richard Sharpe.	*Thomas Holcombe.*

All these men were active in the King's company in 1622, though not much later than that, since Nicholas Tooley was buried early in June 1623. (See above, ii. 601–2 *et passim.*)

Sir Henry Herbert's entry of 21 July 1629 shows that the play was in active repertory then, and rather popular. About a year before, the King's company had agreed to give the Master of the Revels twice a year the receipts at the second performance of a revived play. They would deduct only the house charges of about £2. 5s., and Herbert was to select the play himself. One may assume that the Master of the Revels was canny enough to select a play which could be expected to draw. In his records of his receipts for five years under this agreement, *The Prophetess* was the most profitable of the summer plays (i.e. those acted at the Globe), though of course plays acted at Blackfriars were much more profitable. (See above, i. 23–24.)

The disintegrators seem generally agreed that *The Prophetess* displays the work of both Fletcher and Massinger, though they differ in their assignment of particular scenes. (See Oliphant, loc. cit., and Fleay, *Biog. Chron.* i. 216.) Oliphant says:

That the play was founded on one by a sixteenth-century dramatist
I do not doubt; but none of his work was retained outside the choruses.

Presumably he was led to this statement by the naïve and spectacular character of the play and by the crudely sketched action,
depending partly on dumb show and choral summary, in Act IV
and at the beginning of Act V. Parts of the play do seem very unlike the sophisticated Fletcher of *The Custom of the Country* and
The Wild Goose Chase. Possibly he was condescending to the Globe
audience, for which the date of licence and Herbert's record of
1629 suggest that the play was intended. Though the suggested
derivation of *The Prophetess* from a sixteenth-century play is
only a guess, it is a tempting one. It is odd that Fleay suggested
that the lost *Diocletian*, which Henslowe notes was performed on
16 November 1594 (*Henslowe's Diary*, ed. Greg, i. 20), was the
foundation of *The Virgin Martyr* (q.v.) and not of *The Prophetess*,
in which Diocletian is a much more important character. He did
conjecture that the pastoral names of V. 3 might contain contemporary allusions. (*Biog. Chron.* i. 216.)

The revision of the play by Betterton in 1690, with music by
Purcell, dances by Priest, and a prologue by Dryden, is discussed
by Sprague. (Loc. cit.) Downes says that it was 'set out with
Coastly Scenes, Machines and Cloaths . . . it gratify'd the Expecta-
tion of Court and City; and got the Author great Reputation'.
(*Roscius Anglicanus*, Summers ed., p. 42.) The piece continued in
repertory in the eighteenth century. (See Nicoll, *A History of
Early Eighteenth Century Drama* [1925], pp. 132, 134, 226.)

Various classic sources for the familiar story of Diocletian have
been cited, but no thoroughgoing analysis has established precisely
which were used for *The Prophetess*. Koeppel (loc. cit.) notes with
approval Moriz Rapp's comparison of Geta with Sancho Panza.
Koeppel's further suggestion that the 'prophetess', Delphia,
derives from Prospero seems dubious to me.

The 1647 Folio text has several stage directions which suggest—
but not very clearly—that the manuscript used by the printers
contained prompter's additions. (See Bald, *Bibliographical Studies
in the Beaumont & Fletcher Folio of 1647*, p. 108.)

The Queen

In Edward Archer's 'Exact and perfect CATALOGUE of all the
PLAIES that were ever printed', which is appended to his edition
of *The Old Law*, 1656, he lists 'Queen. T. *John Fletcher*'. The
attribution does not occur elsewhere, and Greg says, 'Fletcher's

name has crept in from another entry'. (*A List of Masques, Pageants, &c.*, p. [*c.*]) In any case, there is no reason to think that Fletcher ever wrote such a play. See John Ford.

The Queen of Corinth (1616–17)

with Field and Massinger?

Revised by Massinger?

Briggs, W. D. 'The Influence of Jonson's Tragedy in the Seventeenth Century', *Anglia*, xxxv (1912), 325–6.

Brinkley, Roberta Florence. *Nathan Field, the Actor-Playwright* (1928), pp. 110–20.

Chelli, Maurice. *Étude sur la collaboration de Massinger avec Fletcher et son groupe* (1926), pp. 125–8.

Fenton, Frank L. 'The Authorship of Acts III and IV of *The Queen of Corinth*', *M.L.N.* xlii (1927), 94–96.

Koeppel, Emil. *Quellen-Studien zu den Dramen Ben Jonson's, John Marston's und Beaumont's und Fletcher's* (1895), pp. 74–75.

Maxwell, Baldwin. *Studies in Beaumont, Fletcher, and Massinger* (1939), pp. 76 ff.

Oliphant, E. H. C. *The Plays of Beaumont and Fletcher* (1927), pp. 372–6, 392–3, 398–401.

Schwarz, H. F. 'One of the Sources of the *Queen of Corinth*', *M.L.N.* xxiv (1909), 76–77.

Waith, E. M. 'The Sources of *The Double Marriage* by Fletcher and Massinger', *M.L.N.* lxiv (1949), 508, n. 5.

1641, 7 Aug. In a list of King's men's plays which the Lord Chamberlain forbade the printers to publish without the consent of the company is 'The Queene of Corinth'. (See above, i. 65–66.)

1646, [4] Sept. S.R. Humphrey Robinson and Humphrey Moseley entered as their copies a list of about fifty plays, all apparently formerly the property of the King's company. Included is 'Queene of Corinth . . . by m^r Beamont & m^r fflesher'. (Greg, *Bibliography*, i. 56–57.)

1647. 'The Queene of Corinth' is the twenty-seventh play in the first Beaumont and Fletcher Folio.

1668/9, *c.* 12 Jan. In 'A Catalogue of part of His Ma^{tes} Servants Playes as they were formerly acted at the Blackfryers & now allowed of to his Ma^{tes} Servants at ye New Theatre' occurs the title, 'The Queene of Corinth'. (Nicoll, *A History of Restoration Drama*, 3rd ed., pp. 315–16.)

1672/3, 30 Jan. S.R. Humphrey Robinson, executor of Humphrey Robinson, transferred his rights in a long list of plays to John Martin and Henry Herringman. Included is '[69] Queene of Corinth. halfe'. (Greg, *Bibliography*, i. 72–73.)

1679. 'The Queen of Corinth, A Tragi-Comedy' is the twenty-eighth play in the second Beaumont and Fletcher Folio.

1683, 21 Aug. S.R. Sarah Martin, executrix of John Martin, transferred her rights in a long list of plays to Robert Scott. Included in the list is '[77] Queene of Corinth', which is bracketed with a number of other plays and marked 'a fourth'. (Ibid., pp. 75–76.)

The cast printed before the play in the second Folio is:

Richard Burbadge,	*Nathan Feild,*
Henry Condel,	*John Lowin,*
John Vnderwood,	*Nich. Toolie,*
Thomas Polard,	*Tho. Holcomb,*

This cast, presumably the one for the opening, indicates that the play was performed before Burbage died in March of 1618/19, and after Nathan Field left the Lady Elizabeth's for the King's men, probably in 1616. (See above, ii. 395–6 and 434–6.) A production in this period is also indicated by the allusion in III. 1 to *T. Coriate Traveller for the English Wits; Greeting from the Court of the Great Mogul*, 1616, with its illustration of the author riding on an elephant:

> *Nea.* A plague on him for a fustian Dictionary; on my conscience this is the *Ulissean* Traveller that sent home his Image riding upon Elephants to the great *Mogoll*.
> *Sos.* The same: his wit is so huge, nought but an Elephant could carry him.   (1679 Folio.)

Such a present tense reference to Coryate would not be apt after his death, which occurred in India in December 1617, or at least after news of it reached England. Fleay thought (*Biog. Chron.* i. 206) that the reference in IV. 1 to the burning of Diana's temple with the church-book recording Onos's birth was an allusion to 'the burning of the Palace at Paris with the ancient French records, 1618, Mar. 7', but if any allusion is intended, any church fire in which parish registers were destroyed would have been equally apt, and Paris seems a bit far afield. The cast and the allusions to Coryate seem to me to indicate 1616–17 for date of composition.

No comprehensive source for the play has been cited. Koeppel (loc. cit.) thought that the principal theme derived from *La Fuerza de la Sangre*, one of Cervantes's *Novelas Exemplares*, but Macaulay denied it (*C.H.E.L.*, 1932 ed., vi. 138). H. F. Schwarz (loc. cit.) noted that the story of the double rape and the contrary demands of the two victims are found in the *Gesta Romanorum*, but this seems somewhat remote, and furthermore Waith (loc. cit.) finds the same story in Pyott's translation of *The Orator* (1596), Declamation 61, and strikingly similar ones in Declamations 54 and 68.

The disintegrators have variously found the play to contain the work of Fletcher, Field, Rowley, Massinger, and Middleton. Field is suggested by his presence in the cast, and Miss Brinkley (loc. cit.) follows Sykes in assigning him Acts III and IV, an assignment with which Oliphant agrees but Frank L. Fenton (op. cit.) does not. Several scholars have noted that the traveller is called both Onos and Lamprias, though the uncle is sometimes called Lampree, and they have taken this confusion together with the dumb show in Act IV as evidence of revision, presumably by Massinger.

Professor Maxwell (loc. cit.) includes the role of Onos in the list of hungry-knave parts in the Beaumont and Fletcher plays, roles which he thinks were prepared for John Shank. Unfortunately his case is weaker for *The Queen of Corinth* than for several of the other plays, since Onos is less the hungry knave than most of the others.

The mention of specific properties in several of the stage directions of the Folio text suggests to Professor Bald (*Bibliographical Studies in the Beaumont & Fletcher Folio of 1647*, pp. 108–9) that the play may have been set up from a manuscript which contained prompter's notes, but the evidence is not very extensive.

The inclusion of this tragi-comedy in the list of plays belonging to the King's company in 1641 implies that *The Queen of Corinth* was still in repertory, but there are no records of particular performances either before or after the Restoration as there are for a number of other Fletcher plays.

A Right Woman (?)
(Lost?)

1660, 29 June. S.R. The first two of twenty-six plays entered to Humphrey Moseley are:

The Faithfull Friend. [*sic*] a Comedy.	by ffrancis Beamont &
A right Woman. a Comedy.	Iohn ffletcher/

(Greg, *Bibliography*, i. 68–69.)

Nothing is known of the play save this entry, but one's confidence in its existence is increased by the fact that the other play in the bracket, also omitted from the Beaumont and Fletcher folios, has been preserved in a manuscript now in the Dyce collection at South Kensington. (Greg, *Dramatic Documents*, pp. 324–9.) *The Faithful Friend[s]* was not published until Weber's edition in 1812.

Fleay (*Biog. Chron.* i. 227) identifies *A Right Woman* with Massinger's *The Woman's Plot*, but with no good reason.

Rollo, Duke of Normandy, or The Bloody Brother (1617?; revised 1627–30?)

with Ben Jonson?; revised by Philip Massinger?

Edition: J. D. Jump, ed. *Rollo Duke of Normandy or The Bloody Brother, A Tragedy, Attributed to John Fletcher, George Chapman, Ben Jonson and Philip Massinger* (1948).

Crawford, Charles. 'Ben Jonson and "The Bloody Brother"', *Sh. Jahr.* xli (1905), 163–76.

Elson, John James, ed. *The Wits, or, Sport upon Sport* (1932), pp. 132–8 and 377–8.

Evans, Gwynne Blakemore. *The Plays and Poems of William Cartwright* (1951), pp. 30–32.

Fleay, F. G. *Biog. Chron.* i. 203–4.

Garnett, R. 'Ben Jonson's Probable Authorship of Scene 2, Act IV, of Fletcher's "Bloody Brother"', *Mod. Phil.* ii. (1905), 489–95.

Hensman, Bertha. *John Fletcher's The Bloody Brother, or Rollo Duke of Normandy*. Unpublished dissertation, University of Chicago, 1947.

Herford and Simpson, eds. *Ben Jonson*, x, Appendix xxii, 'Jonson and "The Bloody Brother"', pp. 292–9.

Jump, J. D. '*Rollo, Duke of Normandy*: Some Bibliographical Notes on the Seventeenth-Century Editions', *Library*, Fourth Series, xviii (1937–8), 279–86.

Oliphant, E. H. C. *The Plays of Beaumont and Fletcher* (1927), pp. 457–63.

Sprague, Arthur Colby. *Beaumont and Fletcher on the Restoration Stage* (1926), pp. 76, 108, 122–3.

Wells, William. 'The Bloody Brother', *N. & Q.* cliv (1928), 6–9.

1630, 7 Nov. In a bill for plays presented before the King by the

King's men between 30 September 1630 and 21 February 1630/1 appears the item: 'The 7 of November . Rollo.' (See above, i. 27–28.)

1630/1, 21 Feb. In the same bill is a later item: 'The 21 of februarie . Rollo, and the daie at the howse loste.' (Ibid.)

1633, 23 May. In the accounts of Sir Humphrey Mildmay appears the entry: 'To a play Called Rolloe, & the globe: 23 . . . oo—o1—o6.' (Ibid. ii. 675.)

1636/7, 17 Jan. In a bill of the King's company for plays presented before the King and Queen in 1636 and 1636/7 appears the item: 'The 17ᵗʰ of January at Hampton Court—Rollo.' (Ibid. i. 51–52. In Sir Henry Herbert's records of this court season this performance is dated 24 January, apparently through a mistake which omitted the performance of *Hamlet* on the 24th. See Adams, *Herbert*, p. 57.)

1639, 4 Oct. S.R. 'A Tragedy called The Bloody Brother. by I: B: [sic]' entered for John Crooke and Richard Sergier. (Greg, *Bibliography*, i. 51.)

1639. The Bloody Brother. A Tragedy. By B. J. F. London, Printed by R. *Bishop*, for *Thomas Allott*, and *Iohn Crook*, and are to be sold in Pauls Churchyard, at the signe of the Greyhound 1639.

1640. The Tragœdy of Rollo Duke of Normandy. Acted By His *Majesties Servants*. Written by John Fletcher *Gent*. Oxford, Printed by Leonard Lichfield *Printer to the Vniversity*. Anno 1640.

1648. In the winter of 1648 a troupe made up from members of the old London companies acted at the Cockpit. As they were presenting 'the Tragedy of the *Bloudy Brother*', the theatre was raided by soldiers, and the actors were carried off in their costumes to prison. (*Historia Histrionica*. See above, ii. 695.)

1655. John Cotgrave's *English Treasury of Wit and Language* includes five quotations from this play. (See Bentley, *Stud. Phil.* xl [1943], 186–203.)

c. 1660. 'Rollo Duke of Normandy' is found in a list of the stock plays of Killigrew's company which was furnished to Sir Henry Herbert, probably shortly after the Restoration, and found among his papers by Malone. (Adams, *Herbert*, p. 82.)

1660, 6 Dec. Herbert records a performance by the King's company at Gibbon's Tennis-Court. (Ibid., p. 117.)

1661, 28 Mar. 'Then with Mr. Shepley to the Theatre and saw "Rollo" ill acted.' (Diary of Samuel Pepys.)

1661, 8 Aug. S.R. 'Rollo Duke of Normandy and Rule a wife and

have a wife both written by ffranc: Beamont and Iohn fflesher'
were transferred from Samuel Brown and William Wilson to
Mrs. Anne Moseley. (Greg, *Bibliography*, i. 69.)

1662. 'The Three Merry Boyes', a farce extracted from *The Bloody
Brother*, was published in *The Wits*, edited by F. Kirkman.
(See Elson, ed., pp. 132–8.)

1662[–3 ?]. Edward Browne paid 1s. 6d. to see 'Rollo Duke of
Normandy' 'At the King Playhouse in Covent Garden'. (W. W.
Greg, *Gentleman's Magazine*, ccci [1906], 69–72, from B.M. MS.
Sloane 1900.)

< 1663. Downes gives the cast for the performances of the play
by the King's company at 'the New Theatre in *Drury-Lane*'.
(Summers, ed., *Roscius Anglicanus*, pp. 5–6.)

1667, 17 Apr. '. . . to the King's playhouse . . . and saw a piece of
"Rollo," a play I like not much, but much good acting in it:
the house very empty.' (Diary of Samuel Pepys.)

1668, 17 Sept. '. . . to the King's playhouse, and saw "Rollo,
Duke of Normandy," which, for old acquaintance, pleased me
pretty well.' (Ibid.)

1668/9, *c*. 12 Jan. 'Rollo Duke of Normandy' appears in a list of
plays assigned to Killigrew's company. (Nicoll, *A History of
Restoration Drama*, 3rd ed., pp. 315–16.)

1674, 9 Nov. In a warrant for performances before royalty by the
Theatre Royal company appears the item:

Nov. 9   Rollo Duke of Normandy   10
A box for ye Queene . . . 10   (Ibid.)

1675, 19 Apr. In a warrant for plays acted before royalty by the
Theatre Royal company appears the item: 'Aprill 19 Rollo Duke
of Normandy . . . 10.' (Ibid.)

1678. Thomas Rymer analysed the play at length in *The Tragedies
of the Last Age Considered*, pp. 16–55.

1679. 'The Bloody Brother; Or, Rollo. A Tragedy' is the twenty-
first play in the second Beaumont and Fletcher Folio.

< 1682. John Downes records that after the union of the two com-
panies, 'The mixt Company then Reviv'd the several old and
Modern Plays, that were the Propriety of Mr. *Killigrew*, as . . .
Rollo'. (Summers, ed., *Roscius Anglicanus*, pp. 39–40.)

1684/5, 20 Jan. In a warrant for plays presented before royalty by
the United Companies appears the item: 'Janu: 20 The Queene
at Rolo . . . 05.' (Nicoll, *A History of Restoration Drama*, 3rd
ed., p. 312.)

1685, 28 Apr. In the same warrant appears the item: '1685 Aprill
28 The King & Queene & a Box for ye Maydes of Honor at

Rolo. 15.' (Nicoll, *A History of Restoration Drama*, 3rd ed., p. 312.)

1686. Rollo, Duke of Normandy: Or, The Bloody Brother. A Tragedy, As it is now Acted by His Majesty's Servants. Written by John Fletcher, Gent. Licensed *November* 27. 1685, Roger L'Estrange . . . 1686.

1686/7, 26 Jan. In a warrant for plays acted before royalty occurs the item: 'January 26 Rolo at Whitehall 20.' (Ibid., p. 313.)

1691. Langbaine says of the play, '. . . a Tragedy much in request . . . has still the good fortune to Please: it being frequently acted by the present Company of Actors, at the Queen's Play-House in *Dorset-Garden*'. (*Account of the English Dramatick Poets*, p. 207.)

A great welter of conjectural dates, most of them based on extremely dubious evidence, has been offered for this play by various scholars. (See Jump, ed. cit., pp. xxx–xxxi.) It has been argued, for example, that the play must date before 1622 because it does not appear in our extracts from Sir Henry Herbert's office-book, but such evidence is insignificant, for our list of Herbert's licences is far from complete. (See above, i. 101.) Equally insubstantial is the argument that the play must date after Jonson's *Neptune's Triumph*, 1623/4, because it is thought that Cook's proposals of fortifications made of pastry (II. 2) must surely derive from a similar passage in *Neptune's Triumph*. Other plays had such passages, and apparently many court cooks aspired to such elaborate creations. (See Jump, ed. cit., p. 84, though he himself takes the imitation from Jonson for granted after showing how improbable it is.) One is, in fact, constantly amazed at the repeated assumptions by scholars that men who had enough originality to write successful plays could not observe the ordinary types about them with their own eyes but had to resort to another writer's observation of a given phenomenon. The resemblance of IV. 2, for instance, to the Latin play *Querolus* is no greater than to a dozen other gulling and exposure scenes in a time when gulling was a staple of the drama.

A number of critics have suggested revision of the play in 1636, but though there is evidence of revision, the only reason for assigning it to 1636 has been the fact that there was a court performance of the play in 1636/7. For a long time this was the only recorded Caroline performance, but information of the last few years shows performances in 1630, 1630/1, and 1633, and if a date for revision must be derived from performance records, 1630 or shortly before would be a better one.

The attributions of authorship for *Rollo* have been almost as chaotic as the arguments for a date. Jump records attributions by more or less reputable scholars to at least nine different authors. (Op. cit., pp. xxv–xxix.) Part of this confusion derives from the cryptic 'by I: B:' in the Stationers' Register entry and from the 'By *B. J. F.*' on the title-page of the 1639 edition. The most sensible explanation of these initials is, as usual, Greg's:

> It would be easy to see in '*B. J. F.*' a misprint for '*B. & F.*', were it not for the fact that the entry of 4 October assigns it to '*J: B:*' This I take to be a slip, due to obvious confusion, for '*J: F:*' and the '*B. J. F.*' of the printed title merely a muddled correction. ('Some Notes on the Stationers' Registers', *Library*, Fourth Series, vii [1927], 382.)

In any case, it seems to me most unlikely that esoteric information about the authorship of such a well-known play should be concealed in initials supplied by a printer.

The evidence offered for the attribution of the play to most of the dozen proposed authors is trivial, impressionistic, or plain absurd, and it would be a sheer waste of space to refute them all. Fletcher's connexion with the play can be accepted from the 1640 title-page and the common attribution of the play to him in seventeenth-century allusions, such as Hill's mention of the cook as a Fletcher character in his verses for the 1647 Folio, even though *Rollo* is not included in that volume. Nearly all the disintegrators have seen Massinger's work in the play as a reviser, and at least seven have identified his hand in all of Act I and the first half of v. 1. Since 1905, when Crawford cited his long lists of superficial parallels to the work of Jonson in the play (loc. cit.), most students have agreed that probably Ben did contribute to it, but the more judicious ones have confined his contributions to IV. 1 and 2, the scenes of the cheaters and the preparation for them. The authorship conclusions of J. D. Jump, the most recent editor of the play, coincide with those of Oliphant, but instead of setting forth his evidence he merely notes that 'a large collection of parallel passages and a set of metrical statistics' supporting them have been deposited in the University Library of Liverpool. (Op. cit., p. xxvii.)

By far the most solid and illuminating discussion which I have seen of the date and authorship of the play is that in Miss Bertha Hensman's manuscript thesis. She presents conclusive evidence that in addition to the sources for the play which were pointed out long ago by Langbaine—Herodian, Dio Cassius, and Seneca's *Thebais*—there has also been full and careful use of Gentillet's *Discours sur les moyens de bien gouverner*, translated in 1602 by S. Patericke as *A Discourse upon the Meanes of Wel Governing* . . . *against N. Macchiavell*, with minor use of other sources, including Machiavelli's *Prince*. She makes a full and detailed analysis of the use of all the sources, scene by scene through the play (op. cit., pp. 38–137), showing that several bits of the duelling and astrological and poisoning material apparently refer to events of 1616 and before. She then shows that all the Gentillet material which is scattered through the play is found in scenes which contain characteristic Massinger writing, and that the characteristic Fletcher writing is all found in scenes based on Herodian or alluding to events of 1616 or earlier. Her conclusion, carefully and cautiously worked out, is that Fletcher wrote the play in the summer of 1617, probably with some collaboration by Jonson; that it was later almost completely rewritten by Massinger in terms of the story as told by Gentillet, with ideas from Machiavelli and details and speeches from Dio Cassius and Seneca; and that Massinger also revised or added the characters of Latorch and Aubrey. Miss Hensman shows a number of the details of the revision most convincingly and accounts for many of the omissions and inconsistencies which have puzzled previous critics. She suggests on the basis of her findings that the revision took place 1627–30, a date which neatly accords with the new and marked popularity of the play in and after 1630. Her conclusions about both the original composition and the revision are much the best supported of any that have appeared.

Shakespeare's song, 'Take, oh take those lips away', from *Measure for Measure*, appears in v. 2, with a new second stanza which was apparently written by John Fletcher.

The two Caroline quartos of the play, London 1639, and Oxford 1640, are independent texts with numerous differences; the latter is the better text. Both of them, Miss Hensman shows, probably derive ultimately from prompt copies. Her close and illuminating comparison of the 1640 quarto with the practices in the prompt manuscript of *Believe as You List*—also written by Massinger for the King's company not more than three or four years after his proposed revision of *Rollo*—leave little doubt that Lichfield, the Oxford printer, had a King's men's prompt manuscript of *Rollo*, marked for the prompter in much the same way that *Believe as You List* is, and that Act 1 of this manuscript had been edited for this Oxford edition. (Hensman, op. cit., pp. 196–233.) Miss

Hensman and Mr. Jump both point out that Lichfield's edition of *Rollo* seems to be part of the same enterprise as his printing of the 1640 quarto of *Rule a Wife and Have a Wife*. For the Folio of 1679 the 1639 London quarto was used as copy. This play seems to have been one of the most frequently performed pieces of the seventeenth century. Before the closing of the theatres, an unusual number of performances is recorded. While the theatres were closed, it had at least one performance, as Wright records; it was quoted several times by Cotgrave; and in those years the droll, *Three Merry Boys*, was made from II. 2 and III. 2. After the Restoration the performances were very frequent —Sprague (op. cit., pp. 122–3) says that up to the last decade of the century performances of *Rollo* were more frequent than of any other of the Beaumont and Fletcher plays. Familiarity to Restoration audiences is also implied by Rymer's lengthy treatment of the play and by Langbaine's statement about its popularity. Sprague (op. cit., pp. 76, 108) records two early eighteenth-century performances, but the piece seems to have lost its popularity earlier than some of Fletcher's other stock plays.

Rule a Wife and Have a Wife (1624)

Editions: R. Warwick Bond, ed., in *The Works of Francis Beaumont and John Fletcher*, Variorum Edition, iii. 357–464. There are many reprints of this play in eighteenth- and nineteenth-century collections and in various twentieth-century anthologies of Elizabethan drama.

Bahlsen, Leo. *Eine Komödie Fletcher's, ihre spanische Quelle und die Schicksale jenes Cervantesschen Novellenstoffes in der Weltlitteratur* (1894).

Elson, John James, ed. *The Wits, or, Sport upon Sport* (1932), pp. 98–103 and 374–5.

Grant, R. Patricia. 'Cervantes' *El casamiento engañoso* and Fletcher's *Rule a Wife and Have a Wife*', *Hispanic Review*, xii (1944), 330–8.

Koeppel, Emil. *Quellen-Studien zu den Dramen Ben Jonson's, John Marston's und Beaumont's und Fletcher's* (1895), pp. 115–17.

Leonhardt, Benno. 'Die Textvarianten von . . . *Rule a Wife and Have a Wife*', *Anglia*, xxiv (1901), 311–40.

Rulfs, Donald J. 'Beaumont and Fletcher on the London Stage 1776–1833', *P.M.L.A.* lxiii (1948), 1257–62.

Sprague, Arthur Colby. *Beaumont and Fletcher on the Restoration Stage* (1926), *passim.*

Wilson, Edward M. '*Rule a Wife and Have a Wife* and *El Sagaz Estacio*', *R.E.S.* xxiv (1948), 189–94.

1624, 19 Oct. '*Rule a Wife and Have a Wife*, by John Fletcher, licensed.' (Adams, *Herbert*, p. 29.)

1624, 2 Nov. 'The night after, my Lord Chamberlin had *Rule a Wife and Have a Wife* for the ladys, by the kings company.' (Ibid., p. 52.)

1624, 26 Dec. 'Upon St. Steevens night, the prince only being there, [was acted] *Rule a Wife and Have a Wife*, by the kings company. Att Whitehall.' (Ibid.)

1634/5, Feb. 'Thus . . . we hear . . . in February [1634/5] of visits to Blackfriars Theatre or the Cockpit where John saw *Rule a Wife and have a Wife*.' (E. M. Symonds, 'The Diary of John Greene (1635–57)', *English Historical Review*, xliii [1928], 386.)

1640. Rvle A Wife And have a Wife. *A Comoedy*. Acted By His *Majesties Servants*. Written by John Fletcher *Gent*. Oxford, Printed by Leonard Lichfield *Printer to the Vniversity*. Anno 1640.

< 1659/60. In the list of plays acted by Rhodes's company at the Cockpit, John Downes lists 'Rule Wife and have a Wife'. (Montague Summers, ed., *Roscius Anglicanus*, pp. 17–18.)

1660, 12 Dec. Sir William Davenant was granted acting rights in a number of plays which had been formerly acted at Blackfriars, including two months acting rights in 'Rule a Wife and haue a Wife'. (Nicoll, *A History of Restoration Drama*, 3rd ed., pp. 314–15.)

1661, 1 Apr. 'Then to Whitefryars, and there saw part of "Rule a wife and have a wife," which I never saw before, but do not like it.' (Diary of Samuel Pepys.)

1661, 8 Aug. S.R. Mrs. Anne Moseley entered for her copies by virtue of an assignment from Samuel Brown and William Wilson all their rights in 'Rollo Duke of Normandy and Rule a wife and have a wife both written by ffranc: Beamont and Iohn fflesher'. (Greg, *Bibliography*, i. 69.)

1661/2, 28 Jan. 'Rule a wife and Haue a wife. 28. Jan.' appears in a list of performances of plays by 'the Kings Companie at the Red Bull and the new house in Gibbon's Tennis Court' in 1660–2. (Adams, *Herbert*, pp. 116–18.)

1661/2, 5 Feb. 'I and my wife to the Theatre . . . and there saw "Rule a Wife and have a Wife" very well done.' (Diary of Samuel Pepys.)

1661/2, 11 Feb. Two Dutch travellers saw 'Rule a Wife an [*sic*] have a Wife' in London. (Ethel Seaton, *Literary Relations of England and Scandinavia in the Seventeenth Century* [1935], p. 333.)

1662. 'An Equall Match', made from parts of Acts III and IV of *Rule a Wife and Have a Wife* is the seventh droll in 'The Wits, Or, Sport upon Sport. In Select Pieces of Drollery, Digested into Scenes by way of Dialogue . . . 1662.' (See J. J. Elson, ed., pp. 98–103.)

< 1663. John Downes gives a cast for the performances of *Rule a Wife and Have a Wife* by the King's company in their new theatre in Drury Lane. (Montague Summers, ed., *Roscius Anglicanus*, p. 3.)

1666/7, 14 Feb. Either *Flora's Vagaries* or *Rule a Wife and Have a Wife* was presented before the King at Court. Two lists differ. (See Nicoll, *A History of Restoration Drama*, 3rd ed., p. 305, and Eleanore Boswell, *The Restoration Court Stage* [1932], p. 282.)

1668/9, *c.* 12 Jan. In 'A Catalogue of part of His Ma^tes Servants Playes as they were formerly acted at the Blackfryers & now allowed of to his Ma^tes Servants at ye New Theatre' occurs the title: 'Rule a Wife & haue a Wife.' (Nicoll, op. cit., pp. 315–16.)

1679. 'Rule a Wife, and have a Wife' is the fourteenth play in the second Beaumont and Fletcher Folio.

1682, 1 Nov. According to the records of the Inner Temple, £20 was paid 'To the Duke's players, for a play called "Rule a wife and have a wife," on All Saints' day, before the judges'. (F. A. Inderwick, ed., *A Calendar of the Inner Temple Records* [1901], iii. 183.)

1682, 15 Nov. On 11 November the Lord Chamberlain ordered that *Rule a Wife and Have a Wife* be given on the 15th before the King. (Nicoll, *A History of Restoration Drama*, 3rd ed., p. 318.)

< 1682. John Downes reports that after the union of the companies, 'The mixt Company then Reviv'd the several old and Modern Plays, that were the Propriety of Mr. *Killigrew*, as, *Rule a Wife, and have a Wife:* Mr. *Betterton Acting Michael Perez: Don Leon*, Mr. *Smith: Cacofogo*, Mr. *Cartwright: Margaretta*, Mrs. *Barry: Estiphania*, Mrs. *Cook* . . .'. (Montague Summers, ed., *Roscius Anglicanus*, p. 39.)

1685, 4 Nov. In a warrant for payment for plays acted before the King is 'Nov: 4th Rule a Wife at Whitehall   20.' (Nicoll, *A History of Restoration Drama*, 3rd ed., p. 312.)

1691. Langbaine said that *Rule a Wife and Have a Wife* was 'A Tragi-Comedy which within these few years has been acted, with applause at the Queen's Theatre in *Dorset-Garden'*. (*Account of the English Dramatick Poets*, p. 214.)

1697. 'Rule a Wife, And Have a Wife ... As it is Acted at the New Theatre, in Little Lincolns Inn-fields ... 1697.' (On the cast published in this edition, see Sprague, *Beaumont and Fletcher on the Restoration Stage*, pp. 76–78.)

Rule a Wife and Have a Wife established itself as one of the most popular of Fletcher's plays. In addition to the numerous seventeenth-century records listed, there were many eighteenth- and nineteenth-century performances. R. Warwick Bond prints an incomplete list of eighteenth- and nineteenth-century 'editions' which includes seventeen printings, and there have been a number of others in the twentieth century. Donald J. Rulfs (loc. cit.) discusses a number of the late eighteenth- and early nineteenth-century performances and examines some of the alterations in the text which were made to meet the taste of more prudish audiences.

The date of the first production of the comedy is fixed by Herbert's licence in the autumn of 1624, and this date is confirmed by the prologue for the play printed in the first quarto. This prologue alludes clearly and even boastfully to the spectacular success and subsequent suppression of the company's play, *A Game at Chess*, which had been the talk of the town in August 1624. (See above, i. 9–14.) The two court performances of the play within a few weeks of its licensing suggest that it was popular with more sophisticated audiences from the beginning.

Though the play has occasionally been listed without discussion as Beaumont and Fletcher's, no modern scholar or critic has questioned Fletcher's sole authorship.

The Perez–Estefania plot of the play is found in one of Cervantes's *Novelas Exemplares* called *El Casamiento Engañoso*. Though there was no translation of this tale into English before 1624, there had been a French translation in 1615. There is a full summary of the Spanish story in Warwick Bond's edition of the play. (Op. cit., pp. 361–4.) Miss Grant (loc. cit.) lists a number of details from *El Casamiento Engañoso* which Fletcher has used in his play. The source of the main plot of the play has not been certainly identified, but Mr. Edward M. Wilson (loc. cit.) thinks it is *El Sagaz Estacio, Marido examinado*, by Salas Barbadillo. This comedy or novel was allowed in 1613 14, but there is no trace of publication until 1620. There was no seventeenth-century English translation, though a French version appeared in 1634. (Wilson, op. cit., pp. 189–90.) As Wilson outlines the Spanish novel, there are clear general resemblances to *Rule a Wife and Have a Wife*, but the few common details he cites seem to me sufficiently obvious developments of the situation to have been due to chance. I see no evidence that Fletcher had the text of *El Sagaz Estacio, Marido examinado* before him as he wrote *Rule a Wife and Have a Wife*. He may well have heard the story of the Spanish novel, or he may have used a derivative which has not yet been cited. The frequently mentioned resemblances of Fletcher's comedy to *The Taming of the Shrew* are more a matter of the familiar subject of a tamed woman than any specific indebtedness.

The quarto of 1640 is a companion piece to the Oxford quarto of *Rollo, Duke of Normandy*, which was printed by the same publisher in the same year, and the two copyrights were transferred together to Mrs. Anne Moseley twenty-one years later. It has been suggested that Lichfield acquired his copies when the King's company played in Oxford, but I know of no evidence. Later editors have called the quarto text a good one. The prologue, clearly intended for the first London performance, is printed in the Oxford quarto, but there is no dramatis personae, nor is there any in the Folio of 1679. The Folio prints no cast for this play, as it does for so many of the later Fletcher plays.

The clown part of Cacafogo in the play seems very like the known roles of William Rowley, and it appears not unlikely that Fletcher wrote it for Rowley, who was a member of the King's company when *Rule a Wife and Have a Wife* was licensed. (See above, ii. 555–8.)

The Scornful Lady

See *The Elizabethan Stage*, iii. 229–30; E. H. C. Oliphant, *The Plays of Beaumont and Fletcher*, pp. 207–14; and Baldwin Maxwell, *Studies in Beaumont, Fletcher, and Massinger*, pp. 17–28. The *terminus ad quem* for the composition of the play is not 1617, as Chambers gives it, but 19 March 1615/16, when the play was entered in the Stationers' Register. (See Greg, *Bibliography*, i. 29.)

The Sea Voyage (1622)
revised (?) by Philip Massinger?

Chelli, Maurice. *Étude sur la collaboration de Massinger avec Fletcher et son groupe* (1926), pp. 140–4.
Jacobi, G. A. 'Zur Quellenfrage von Fletchers "The Sea Voyage"', *Anglia*, xxxiii (1910), 332–43.

Koeppel, Emil. *Quellen-Studien zu den Dramen Ben Jonson's, John Marston's und Beaumont's und Fletcher's* (1895), pp. 106–7.

Oliphant, E. H. C. *The Plays of Beaumont and Fletcher* (1927), pp. 246–9.

Sprague, Arthur Colby. *Beaumont and Fletcher on the Restoration Stage* (1926), pp. 66 and 232–8.

Sykes, H. Dugdale. 'Massinger and "The Sea Voyage"', *N. & Q.*, Twelfth Series, xi (1922), 443–6, 484–6.

1622, 22 June. '*The Sea Voyage*. This piece was acted at the Globe.' (Adams, *Herbert*, p. 24.)

1646, [4] Sept. S.R. In a list of about fifty plays, all apparently formerly of the repertory of the King's company, which were entered by Humphrey Robinson and Humphrey Moseley is '[The Sea Voyage *added*] . . . by mr Beamont & mr fflesher'. (Greg, *Bibliography*, i. 56–57.)

1647. The twentieth play in the first Beaumont and Fletcher Folio is 'The Sea Voyage'.

1667, 25 Sept. '. . . I to the King's playhouse. . . . The play was a new play; and infinitely full: the King and all the Court almost there. It is "The Storme," a play of Fletcher's; which is but so-so, methinks; only there is a most admirable dance at the end, of the ladies, in a military manner, which indeed did please me mightily.' (Diary of Samuel Pepys.)

1667, 26 Sept. '. . . then with my wife abroad to the King's play-house, to shew her yesterday's new play, which I like as I did yesterday, the principal thing extraordinary being the dance, which is very good.' (Ibid.)

1667, 27 Sept. In a warrant for payment for performances of plays before the King at court or at the Theatre Royal occurs the item: 'Sept: 27 The Sea Voyage His Mate had two boxes at ye Theatre . . . 20.' In another list the date is the 25th. (Nicoll, *A History of Restoration Drama*, 3rd ed., pp. 305–6.)

1668, 25 Mar. '. . . with my wife to the King's playhouse to see "the Storme," which we did, but without much pleasure, it being but a mean play compared with "The Tempest," at the Duke of York's house, though Knepp did act her part of grief very well.' (Diary of Samuel Pepys.)

1668, 16 May. '. . . I did go forth by coach to the King's play-house, and there saw the best part of "The Sea Voyage," where Knepp I see do her part of sorrow very well.' (Ibid.)

1668/9, c. 12 Jan. In 'A Catalogue of part of His Mates Servants

Playes as they were formerly acted at the Blackfryers & now allowed of to his Ma^tes Servants at ye New Theatre' occurs the title, 'The Sea Voyage'. (Nicoll, *A History of Restoration Drama*, 3rd ed., pp. 315–16.)

1672/3, 30 Jan. S.R. Humphrey Robinson, executor of Humphrey Robinson, transferred his rights in a long list of plays to John Martin and Henry Herringman; included is '[67] Sea voyage. halfe'. (Greg, *Bibliography*, i. 72–73.)

1679. The forty-third play in the second Beaumont and Fletcher Folio is 'The Sea-Voyage. A Comedy'.

1683, 21 Aug. S.R. Sarah Martin, executrix of John Martin, transferred her rights in a long list of titles to Robert Scott; included is '[75] Sea-Voyages. [*sic*] ¼'. (Ibid., pp. 75–76.)

1686. A Common-Wealth Of Women. A Play: As it is Acted at the Theatre Royal, By their Majesties Servants. By Mr. *D'Urfey* . . . 1686.

1690–2. John Downes says that between the operas, *King Arthur, The Prophetess*, and *The Fairy Queen*, the company acted several plays, including '*A Sea Voyage*'. (Montague Summers, ed., *Roscius Anglicanus*, p. 43.)

The licence for the play sets the approximate date of first production, a date which agrees with the one suggested by the cast given in the second Folio:

Joseph Taylor,	*Joh Lowin.*
William Eglestone,	*John Vnderwood.*
Nich. Toolie.	

Such a cast, omitting Burbage, was evidently prepared after his death in March 1618/19, and before the death of Nicholas Tooley in June 1623. (See above, ii. 396 and 602.) This cast lists only five names instead of the usual eight, possibly because the number of adult roles in the play is abnormally small; there are six roles for boys, four of them longer than all but the two leading adult roles. (See Baldwin, *Organization and Personnel*, Chart 3, opposite p. 198.) The other casts usually list one or two boys, but this one has none.

The relation of the play to Shakespeare's *Tempest* has been frequently commented upon. Dryden refers to it—using the title *The Storm*, as Pepys did, and speaking of it as the property of the rival King's company—in the prologue for his and Davenant's version of *The Tempest*:

The Storm which vanish'd on the Neighb'ring shore,
Was taught by Shakespear's *Tempest first to roar.*
That innocence and beauty which did smile
In Fletcher, *grew on this* Enchanted Isle.
But Shakespear's *Magick could not copy'd be.*

(1670 ed., A₄.)

He made further remarks on the relationship in his preface. Certain general situations, like the desert island, the storm, and the woman who had never seen a man, may well have been derived from *The Tempest*, and the first act of *The Sea Voyage* repeatedly reminds one of Shakespeare's comedy, but most of the action in the last four acts shows only occasional reminiscences. No comprehensive source for the play has been noted.

Most of the disintegrators have seen the work of both Fletcher and Massinger in the play, and Chelli and others have thought that Massinger revised the work of Fletcher. (Oliphant, loc. cit.; Chelli, loc. cit.) That there has been some revision seems likely enough from the state of the text, which shows loose ends, contradictions, and omissions; the last scene in particular seems to end with little more than half its business accomplished. Bald points out (*Bibliographical Studies in the Beaumont & Fletcher Folio*, p. 105) that the last act contains two prompter's directions, and this suggests a playhouse copy, but one would expect more such directions if the players' prompt copy had been used by the Folio printers.

The number of references to the play after the Restoration make it somewhat surprising that there are not more before the closing of the theatres. The absence of *The Sea Voyage* from the repertory of the King's men which the Lord Chamberlain protected in August 1641 (see above, i. 65–66)—a list which contained most of the other unpublished Fletcher plays—suggests that *The Sea Voyage* was not then in active repertory.

D'Urfey's revision of the play in 1685, published in 1686 under the title *A Commonwealth of Women*, is examined by Sprague. (Op. cit., pp. 232–8.) Downes's statement about performances in the nineties would seem to indicate that the original play continued to be performed even after D'Urfey's revision. Donald J. Rulfs says that *The Sea Voyage* was one of fourteen Beaumont and Fletcher plays still being steadily presented in 1710 (*P.M.L.A.* lxiii [1948], 1245), but he does not list any specific performances.

Sir John van Olden Barnavelt (14 < > 27 August 1619)
with Philip Massinger?

MS.: B.M. MS. Add. 18653.

Editions: A. H. Bullen, ed., *A Collection of Old English Plays*,
ii (1883), 201–314; Wilhelmina P. Frijlinck, ed., *The Tragedy of
Sir John Van Olden Barnavelt* (1922). (Miss Frijlinck lists another
Dutch edition and a Dutch and a German translation, p. 114.)

Barnouw, A. J. 'The Cartload in the Gate', *M.L.N.* liii (1938),
417–21.
Boyle, R. 'Zur Barnavelt-Frage. Eine Erwiderung auf das Nach-
wort des Herrn Prof. Delius', *Englische Studien*, ix (1886),
153–61.
Briggs, W. D. 'The Influence of Jonson's Tragedy in the Seven-
teenth Century', *Anglia*, xxxv (1912), 329–30.
Chelli, Maurice. *Étude sur la collaboration de Massinger avec
Fletcher et son groupe* (1926), pp. 99–103.
Chew, S. C. '*Lycidas* and the Play of *Barnavelt*', *M.L.N.* xxxviii
(1923), 122.
Frijlinck, Wilhelmina P., ed. *The Tragedy of Sir John Van Olden
Barnavelt* (1922), pp. i–clviii.
Greg, W. W. *Dramatic Documents from the Elizabethan Playhouses*
(1931), pp. 268–74.
Hart, H. C. 'Notes on Bullen's Old Plays: Sir John Barneveldt',
Academy, xxxiv (1888), 171.
Oliphant, E. H. C. *The Plays of Beaumont and Fletcher* (1927), pp.
220–4.
Ward, Adolphus William. *A History of English Dramatic Literature
to the Death of Queen Anne* (1899), ii, 716–18.

1619, 14 Aug. Thomas Locke wrote to Sir Dudley Carleton at The
Hague: 'The Players heere were bringing of Barnavelt vpon the
stage, and had bestowed a great deale of money to prepare all
things for the purpose, but at th' instant were prohibited by my
Lo: of London.' (Sidney Lee, *Athenaeum*, 19 January 1884,
p. 89, from *C.S.P., Dom.*, James I, vol. cx, No. 18.)
1619, 27 Aug. Locke wrote again to Sir Dudley, saying: 'Our
players haue fownd the meanes to goe through with the play of
Barnavelt, and it hath had many spectators and receaued
applause.' (Ibid., from *C.S.P., Dom.*, James I, vol. cx, No. 37.)

There was no seventeenth-century publication of this play.
Indeed, dramatic historians did not know of the existence of such

a play until A. H. Bullen published it from the B.M. MS. in 1883.
Bullen's cursory comments on the manuscript (*A Collection of Old English Plays*, ii. 201–6) were greatly extended by Miss Frijlinck and still further supplemented and corrected by Dr. Greg. (Loc. cit.)

The manuscript of *Sir John van Olden Barnavelt* was written by Ralph Crane (see above, ii. 415–16), who did other work for the King's company, and it was revised for prompt use in the theatre, presumably by the prompter. It was read and censored by Sir George Buc, Master of the Revels, who signed his initials to one of his objections, though his licence does not appear on the manuscript. (See Greg, op. cit., pp. 268–70.) In the prompter's additional directions appear the names, nicknames, or initials of a number of actors who played minor roles. As usual in prompt manuscripts, the actors of the major roles are unnamed. The actors named are George Birche (?), Robert Gough, Thomas Holcomb, G. Lowen, Nicholas Underhill (?), Michael, Thomas Pollard, John Rice, Richard Robinson, and R. T. (See ibid., p. 273, and above, i. 74, and ii, under the actors' names.) Most of these men are known to have been associated with the King's company in 1619, and none is known to have been connected with any other troupe at this time. The play is thus identified as the property of the King's company.

The letters of Thomas Locke fix with unusual precision the date of the opening of the play between 14 August 1619, when he recorded its suppression, and 27 August 1619, when he noted the popularity of the performances. Miss Frijlinck points out that even the date of composition can be roughly fixed, since the dismissal of Barnavelt's son as Governor of Bergen-op-Zoom is recorded in iv. 3, an event which the English ambassador reported to London in a letter of 14 July 1619. (Frijlinck, op. cit., p. xix.) A summer performance is also indicated by the censored lines about the number of whores in London:

> ay they abound Sir,
> and yo^u fight in the shade to those that serve there
> I meane in the tearme time, for now ther's a [Tearme] Truce S^r,
> the Somer's their vacation.
>
> (Frijlinck, ed., lines 215–18.)

Presumably a performance at this time of year would have taken place at the Globe, and the lines following those above bout the conduct of the whores in the theatres may be intended to allude to conditions at that playhouse.

The downfall of the Dutch patriot was a matter of great interest in London at this time. Several pamphlets concerning the man, his trial, and his execution are known to have been published in London, and probably others now lost were translated from the Dutch. (See Frijlinck, op. cit., pp. xxiv–xxix.) Not only was the execution of a great Dutch patriot a matter of sensational interest, but the conflict between Calvinism and Arminianism of which it was a part cannot have been without interest in England. One wonders if the Jacobean audience was expected to see analogies between the affairs of Barnavelt and those of Sir Walter Raleigh, who had been executed the previous year. Miss Frijlinck traces at some length the probable sources of the play and its historicity. (Op. cit., pp. xxiv–lviii and cxxvi–cliv.)

No external evidence of the authorship of *Sir John van Olden Barnavelt* has been discovered, but all who have examined the play have seen the work of Fletcher and of Massinger. (See Oliphant, loc. cit., and Frijlinck, op. cit., pp. lix–xcvi.) There is no complete agreement on the distribution of their work, but most have seen Massinger in I. 1, 2; II. 1; III. 2; and IV. 4, 5; and Fletcher in I. 3; III. 1; IV. 1, 2, 3; and V. 2 and 3.

The controversial character of the subject makes it understandable enough that the Bishop of London (not the Lord Mayor, who had no power to prohibit plays in the regular theatres) should have stopped the first performance. It is not at all surprising that the players should have been eager to capitalize on the popular interest in such a subject, but it is a little curious that they were eventually allowed to do so. Perhaps the press censors were more timid than the Master of the Revels. *Barnavelt* is not a great play, as some of its earliest readers thought, but it is an interesting one, and one would have expected a quarto to sell even after the play had lost its timely appeal in the theatres of the King's company.

The Spanish Curate (1622)
with Philip Massinger?

Edition: R. B. McKerrow, ed., *The Works of Francis Beaumont and John Fletcher*, Variorum Edition, ii. 101–228.

Bald, R. C. *Bibliographical Studies in the Beaumont & Fletcher Folio of 1647* (1938), pp. 104–5 and 110–11.

Chelli, Maurice. *Étude sur la collaboration de Massinger avec Fletcher et son groupe* (1926), pp. 117–21.

Elson, John James, ed. *The Wits or Sport upon Sport* (1932), pp. 85–89 and 373.

Klein, Emmo. *Fletchers 'The Spanish Curate' und seine Quelle* (1905).

Koeppel, Emil. *Quellen-Studien zu den Dramen Ben Jonson's, John Fletcher's und Beaumont's und Fletcher's* (1895), pp. 107–9.

Oliphant, E. H. C. *The Plays of Beaumont and Fletcher* (1927), pp. 250 and 535–6.

Rulfs, Donald J. 'Beaumont and Fletcher on the London Stage 1776–1833', *P.M.L.A.* lxiii (1948), 1253–4.

1622, 24 Oct. '*The Spanish Curate*. Acted at Blackfriars.' (Adams, *Herbert*, p. 24.)

1622, 26 Dec. 'Upon St. Steevens daye at night *The Spanish Curate* was acted by the kings players.' (Ibid., p. 49.)

1638, 6 Dec. In a bill of the King's company for plays acted before the King and Queen in 1638 and 1638/9 occurs the item: 'At the Cocpit the 6th of desember......The spanish Curatt.' (Ibid., pp. 76–77. For a note on the present location of this bill, see Bentley, *T.L.S.*, 8 December 1932, p. 943.)

1638/9, 7 Jan. In the same bill is a later item:

At Richmount the 7th of Janeuarye⎞
and our day lost at our house   ⎠. The spanish Cura[tt]

(Adams, *Herbert*, pp. 76–77.)

1641, 7 Aug. In a list of King's men's plays which the Lord Chamberlain forbade the printers to publish without the consent of the company is, 'The spanish Curat'. (See above, i. 65–66.)

1646, [4] Sept. S.R. Humphrey Robinson and Humphrey Moseley entered as their copies a list of about fifty plays, all apparently formerly the property of the King's company. Included is 'Spanish Curate . . . by mr Beamont & mr fflesher'. (Greg, *Bibliography*, i. 56–57.)

1647. 'The Spanish Curat' is the second play in the first Beaumont and Fletcher Folio.

1653. In the 1653 edition of the fraudulent 'Poems, By *Francis Beavmont*, Gent.' appear the prologue and epilogue which were printed with *The Spanish Curate* in the two Folios.

< 1659/60. In the repertory of John Rhodes's company acting at the Cockpit, John Downes names 'The *Spanish* Curate'. (Montague Summers, ed., *Roscius Anglicanus*, pp. 17–18.)

1660, 12 Dec. Sir William Davenant was granted acting rights for two months in several plays, including 'the Spanish Curate'. (Nicoll, *A History of Restoration Drama*, 3rd ed., pp. 314–15.)

1660/1, 16 Mar. '. . . so to Whitefriars and saw "The Spanish Curate," in which I had no great content.' (Diary of Samuel Pepys.)

1661, 20 Dec. In a list of performances of plays by 'the Kings Companie at the Red Bull and the new house in Gibbon's Tennis Court near Clare Market', 1660–2, appears the entry, 'The Spanishe Curate.   20. Decemb.' (Adams, *Herbert*, p. 118.)

1661/2, 1 Jan. '. . . seeing that the "Spanish Curate" was acted . . . we went by coach to the play, and there saw it well acted, and a good play it is, only Diego the Sexton did overdo his part too much.' (Diary of Samuel Pepys.)

1662. The fifth droll in *The Wits or Sport upon Sport* is 'The Sexton, or The Mock-Testator', made from IV. 5 of *The Spanish Curate*. (See J. J. Elson, ed., pp. 85–89.)

1662[–3 ?]. In Edward Browne's accounts for plays seen in '1662', under the head 'At Salisbury or Dorset Court' is the entry, 'Spanish curate......10.' (W. W. Greg, 'Theatrical Repertories of 1662', *Gentleman's Magazine*, ccci [1906], 69–72, from B.M. MS. Sloane 1900.)

1668/9, *c.* 12 Jan. In 'A Catalogue of part of His Ma^tes Servants Playes as they were formerly acted at the Blackfryers & now allowed of to his Ma^tes Servants at ye New Theatre' occurs the title, 'The Spanish Curate'. (Nicoll, *A History of Restoration Drama*, 3rd ed., pp. 315–16.)

1669, 17 May. '. . . to the King's playhouse, and saw "The Spanish Curate" revived, which is a pretty good play, but my eyes troubled with seeing it, mightily.' (Diary of Samuel Pepys.)

1672/3, 30 Jan. S.R. Humphrey Robinson, executor of Humphrey Robinson, transferred his rights in a long list of plays to John Martin and Henry Herringman. Included is '[54] Spanish Curate. halfe'. (Greg, *Bibliography*, i. 72–73.)

1675/6, 2 Feb. 'To the King's players, for acting a play called "The Spanish Curate" in the Inner Temple Hall on Candlemas day, 1675–6, 20 *li*.' (F. A. Inderwick, ed., *A Calendar of the Inner Temple Records*, iii. 108.)

1679. The seventh play in the second Beaumont and Fletcher Folio is 'The Spanish Curate, A Comedy'.

1683, 21 Aug. S.R. Sarah Martin, executrix of John Martin, transferred her rights in a long list of plays to Robert Scott. Included is '[61] Spanish Curate ¼'. (Greg, *Bibliography*, i. 75–76.)

1687, 11 Apr. Included in a bill of the United Companies for plays presented by them before royalty is: 'Aprill 11 The Spanish

Curate at Whitehall   20.' (Nicoll, *A History of Restoration Drama*, 3rd ed., p. 313.)

1691. Langbaine said that *The Spanish Curate* was 'a comedy frequently reviv'd with general Applause'. (*Account of the English Dramatick Poets*, pp. 214–15.)

The approximate day of first performance is set by the Master of the Revels' licence of 24 October 1622, and the cast is given in the second Folio:

Joseph Taylor.	*William Eglestone.*
John Lowin.	*Thomas Polard.*
Nicholas Toolie.	*Robert Benfeild.*

The licence indicates that the play was intended for Blackfriars performance, as would have been expected at this time of year, and the date suggests that it may have been planned for Michaelmas term, as the company's principal new offering for the termers.

Composition of the play was not begun before the preceding spring or summer, for it is derived from Leonard Digges's translation of *Poema trágico del Español Gerardo*, by Gonzalo de Cespedes y Meneses. Digges's translation, entitled *Gerardo the Unfortunate Spaniard*, was published in 1622, having been entered in the Stationers' Register 11 March 1621/2. An abridgement of the translation was printed by Dyce (*The Works of Beaumont and Fletcher*, viii. 373–92) and is reprinted by McKerrow (op. cit., pp. 107–20) with modifications to make it conform to the edition of 1622. That the authors of *The Spanish Curate* did use the translation and not the original is shown by the wording of the letter in II. 1, as Dyce and McKerrow point out.

There has been fairly general agreement that the play displays the writing of both Fletcher and Massinger and that the work has been divided according to the two main plots of the comedy, Massinger writing up the more serious story of Don Henrique, Jacintha, Violante, and Ascanio, and Fletcher writing up the story, taken from a later section of *Gerardo the Unfortunate Spaniard*, concerning Bartolus, Amaranta, Leandro, and Lopez the Curate. (See especially Chelli, loc. cit.) Except for one or two scenes in each plot, the dramatists seem to have kept each to his own story, and most of the disintegrators agree in giving to Massinger 1; III. 3; IV. 1, 4; V. 1, 3; and to Fletcher II; III. 1, 2, 4; IV. 2, 3, 5, 6, 7; and V. 2. Fleay observed that the two dramatists use different forms of some of the names of characters. (*Biog. Chron.* i. 217; corrected by Oliphant, op. cit., p. 536.) McKerrow (op. cit., p. 106) shows that Angelo Milanes appears to be one character, not two, as in the folios and a number of later editions.

The text of the play in the first Folio was clearly set up from a prompt copy, as is indicated by the unusual number of specific property directions and anticipatory stage directions. (Most, but not all, are noted by Bald, op. cit., pp. 104–5.) Professor Bald pointed out that the text of the play in the first Folio is characterized by the peculiar bracket punctuation found in the work of Ralph Crane, who several times did transcriptions of plays of the King's company. He concluded that the prompt manuscript from which *The Spanish Curate* was set had been copied by Ralph Crane. (Ibid., p. 113.)

The court productions of *The Spanish Curate* in 1638 and 1638/9 and the inclusion of the play in the repertory list of 1641 probably indicate that it continued to be performed with some regularity. This same suggestion that the play was a familiar one to late Caroline audiences is reiterated by the list of comedies which Lovelace printed beside the 'Mirth' passage in his verses to the authors in the 1647 Folio. This list of popular comedies consists of *The Spanish Curate, The Humorous Lieutenant, The Tamer Tamed, The Little French Lawyer*, and *The Custom of the Country*. The number of Restoration performances recorded shows that the play must have been as generally successful with audiences in the time of Charles II as it had been in the reigns of his father and grandfather.

Rulfs (loc. cit.) notes an adaptation of the play in 1811 by a coal merchant named Stephen Clarke. This piece used Fletcher's part of the original play and entitled it *The Kiss; or, the Lawyer Outwitted*.

McKerrow (op. cit., p. 105) lists the editions of the play up to 1905.

The Tragedy of Thierry, King of France, and His Brother Theodoret

See *The Elizabethan Stage*, iii. 230, and Oliphant, *The Plays of Beaumont and Fletcher*, pp. 274–82.

The Triumph of Honour, The Triumph of Love, The Triumph of Death, The Triumph of Time

See *The Elizabethan Stage*, 'Four Plays in One', iii. 231.

The Two Noble Kinsmen

See *The Elizabethan Stage*, iii. 226–7, and *William Shakespeare*,
i. 528–32.

Valentinian

See *The Elizabethan Stage*, iii. 229.

A Very Woman

See Philip Massinger.

The Wandering Lovers

See *The Lovers' Progress*.

The Widow

See Thomas Middleton.

A Wife for a Month (1624)

Koeppel, Emil. *Quellen-Studien zu den Dramen Ben Jonson's, John
Marston's und Beaumont's und Fletcher's* (1895), pp. 114–15.
Oliphant, E. H. C. *The Plays of Beaumont and Fletcher* (1927),
p. 148.
Sprague, Arthur Colby. *Beaumont and Fletcher on the Restoration
Stage* (1926), pp. 95–98, 202–12.

1624, 27 May. 'For the King's Company, A Comedy, called,
A Wife for a Month: Written by Fletcher.' (Adams, *Herbert*,
p. 28.)
1636/7, 9 Feb. '*A Wife for a Monthe*, by the K. players, at St.
James, the 9 Febru.' appears in Sir Henry Herbert's record of
plays performed at court. (Ibid., p. 58.)
1636/7, 9 Feb. In the bill presented by the players of the King's
company for plays acted before the King and Queen in 1636 and
1636/7 appears the item, '20 The 9th of ffebruary at St James.
the wife for a moneth'. (See above, i. 51–52.)
1641, 7 Aug. In a list of plays which belonged to the King's men
and which the Lord Chamberlain forbade the printers to publish without the company's consent appears the title, 'A wife
for a moneth'. (See above, i. 65–66.)
1646, [4] Sept. S.R. Humphrey Robinson and Humphrey Moseley

entered a list of about fifty plays, all apparently formerly belonging to the repertory of the King's company. Included in the list is 'Wife for a Month . . . by m͏ʳ Beamont & m͏ʳ fflesher'. (Greg, *Bibliography*, i. 56–57.)

1647. The twenty-ninth play in the first Beaumont and Fletcher Folio is 'A Wife for a Moneth'.

< 1659/60. In his list of plays acted by Rhodes's company at the Cockpit, John Downes lists 'A Wife for a Month'. (Summers, ed., *Roscius Anglicanus*, pp. 17–18.)

1661, May < > Dec. In his list of plays acted by the King's company at the Red Bull and at Gibbon's Tennis Court, 1660–2, Sir Henry Herbert lists under 1661, 'A wife for a monthe'. (Malone's transcription is given inaccurately in Adams, *Herbert*, p. 117, n. 1. See Sprague, op. cit., p. 16, n. 2, and Malone's *Variorum* [1790], i, Part ii, p. 266.)

1668/9, *c.* 12 Jan. In 'A Catalogue of part of His Ma͏ᵗᵉˢ Servants Playes as they were formerly acted at the Blackfryers & now allowed of to his Ma͏ᵗᵉˢ Servants at y͏ᵉ New Theatre' occurs the title, 'A Wife for a Moneth'. (Nicoll, *A History of Restoration Drama*, 3rd ed., pp. 315–16.)

1672/3, 30 Jan. S.R. Humphrey Moseley, executor of Humphrey Moseley, transferred to John Martin and Henry Herringman his rights in a long list of plays including '[57] Wife for A month. halfe'. (Greg, *Bibliography*, i. 72–73.)

1679. The twenty-third play in the second Beaumont and Fletcher Folio is 'A Wife for a Month; A Tragi-Comedy'.

1683, 21 Aug. S.R. Sarah Martin, executrix of John Martin, transferred her rights in a long list of plays to Robert Scott. Included is '[64] A wife for the Month. ¼'. (Ibid., pp. 75–76.)

1697. The Unhappy Kindness: Or A Fruitless Revenge. A Tragedy, As it is Acted at the Theatre Royal . . . Wrirten [*sic*] by Mr. Scot . . . 1697.

Sir Henry Herbert's entry of his licence for the play fixes the approximate date of first performance. The list of actors for the play in the second Folio is one of the very few which do not confirm the external date of first performance. This cast reads:

> *Joseph Taylor.* ⎫   *Robert Benfield.*
> *Richard Robinson.*⎬   *John Vnderwood.*
> *Nicholas Toolie.* ⎭   *George Birch.*

Nicholas Tooley cannot have appeared in *A Wife for a Month*, in spite of his appearance here, because he was buried on 5 June

1623 (see above, ii. 601–2), almost a year before Herbert's licence. It has also been noted that John Lowin, who was a principal actor in the company at this time and who appears in most of the casts immediately before and after 1624, is missing. (See above, ii. 499–506.) Finally, Professor Baldwin thinks (*Organization and Personnel*, p. 391, n.) that William Rowley must have had a leading role in the play because the role of Tony in *A Wife for a Month* is strikingly similar to others which Rowley is known to have played in the period 1620–4, or which have been written into Fletcher plays, 1620–5. (See above, ii. 555–8.) The cast for *A Wife for a Month* which was printed in the second Folio is thus clearly confused. Whether it is the wrong cast entirely or merely one which omits two or three names and includes a wrong one is not clear, though both views have been presented.

Though Archer listed *A Wife for a Month* as by Beaumont and Fletcher in his catalogue of plays of 1656, none of the disintegrators has doubted Fletcher's sole authorship. The prologue, which seems to be for an original production, speaks of the author in the singular.

The performance of the play at court in 1636/7 and its inclusion in the list of the plays of the King's company in 1641 suggest that it remained in repertory until the closing of the theatres. There are fewer evidences of Restoration performance, however, than for a number of other Fletcher plays.

The repetition of a speech at the end of III. 2, and the omission of speeches for First Citizen when there are speeches for Second and Third Citizen in II. 4, have been suggested as evidence of revision of the text, but they are so slight that they may indicate nothing more than a compositor's confusion. The addition of the phrase 'and a Chaire' at the end of the stage direction before Act III suggests to Professor Bald (*Bibliographical Studies in the Beaumont & Fletcher Folio of 1647*, p. 109) the prompter's hand in the manuscript from which the play was set. The addition is highly characteristic of a prompter, but if the copy was indeed a prompt manuscript, it is very odd that more such evidence is not found in the text.

The source of the play is not known, though Langbaine noted that:

The Character and Story of *Alphonso*, and his Brother *Frederick's* Carriage to him, much resembles the History of *Sancho* the Eighth, [*sic*] King of *Leon*. I leave the Reader to the perusal of his Story in *Mariana*, and *Louis de Mayerne Turquet*. (*Account of the English Dramatick Poets*, p. 216.)

Thomas Scott's revision of *A Wife for a Month* under the title, *The Unhappy Kindness*, is discussed by Sprague (loc. cit.). It was for this piece that the comedian Joe Haynes wrote his popular epilogue, 'written, and spoke, by Mr. *Haynes*, in the Habit of a *Horse Officer*, mounted on an *Ass*', and which he later used for other plays.

The Wild Goose Chase (1621?)

Editions: Though there is no elaborate modern edition of the play, it is printed with explanatory notes and brief introductions in several anthologies: William Allan Neilson, ed., *The Chief Elizabethan Dramatists* (1911), pp. 625–55; Harold Reinoehl Walley and John Harold Wilson, eds., *Early Seventeenth-Century Plays 1600–1642* (1930), pp. 704–77; Hazelton Spencer, ed., *Elizabethan Plays* (1933), pp. 881–923; G. E. Bentley, ed., *The Development of English Drama* (1950), pp. 310–55.

Griffith, Herbert. 'The Wild-Goose Chase', *The Observer*, London, 26 July 1925, p. 9. (Review of a performance.)

Heldt, W. 'Fletcher's *Wild-Goose Chase*, and Farquhar's *Inconstant*', *Neophilologus*, iii (1917), 144–8.

Koeppel, Emil. *Quellen-Studien zu den Dramen Ben Jonson's, John Marston's und Beaumont's und Fletcher's* (1895), pp. 103–4.

Oliphant, E. H. C. *The Plays of Beaumont and Fletcher* (1927), pp. 149–50.

Sprague, Arthur Colby. *Beaumont and Fletcher on the Restoration Stage* (1926), pp. 98–100, 248–55.

1621–21/2, Christmas. '*The Island Princess, The Pilgrim*, and *The Wild Goose Chase* are found among the court exhibitions of the year 1621.' (Adams, *Herbert*, p. 49.)

1621/2, 24 Jan. In a book, probably a copy of some part of the books of the Lord Chamberlain of the Household, is a series of licences and warrants for payments to players. One, dated 27 March 1622, is 'A warrant for allowance of lx^{li} to John Hemmings and his fellowes the Kings Ma^{ts} Players for 6 plaies vizt . . . The Wildgoose Chase the xxiiii of Januarie'. (J. T. Murray, *English Dramatic Companies*, ii. 193, from Inner Temple MS. 515, No. 7. This record possibly, but not necessarily, indicates the same performance as the Master of the Revels' record above.)

1632, 6 Nov. 'Received for the summer day of the kings company ye 6 Novemb. 1632,—1 *l.* 5 *s.* 0 *d.*
Received for the winter day upon *The Wild Goose Chase,* ye same day,—15 *l.* 0 *s.* 0 *d.*' (Adams, *Herbert,* p. 44.)

1641, 7 Aug. In a list of King's men's plays which the Lord Chamberlain forbade the printers to publish without the company's consent appears the title, 'The wild goose chase'. (See above, i. 65–66.)

1646, [4] Sept. S.R. Humphrey Robinson and Humphrey Moseley entered a long list of plays, all apparently from the repertory of the King's company. Originally the first play in the list was 'Wild goose chase . . . by m^r Beamont & m^r fflesher'. (Greg, *Bibliography,* i. 56–57.)

1647. In the address to the readers for the first Beaumont and Fletcher Folio, Humphrey Moseley says that he has included all unpublished plays of the two dramatists, but 'One only Play I must except (for I meane to deale openly) 'tis a COMEDY called the *Wilde-goose Chase,* which hath beene long lost, and I feare irrecoverable ; for a *Person of Quality* borrowed it from the *Actours* many yeares since, and (by the negligence of a Servant) it was never return'd ; therefore now I put up this *Si quis,* that whosoever hereafter happily meetes with it, shall be thankfully satisfied if he please to send it home'.

1652, 12 Apr. S.R. Humphrey Moseley entered as his copy 'A Play called The Wild-Goose Chase Written by Fra: Beaumont & Iohn Fletcher Gent.' (Greg, *Bibliography,* i. 60.)

1652. The Wild-Goose Chase. A Comedie. As it hath been Acted with singular Applause at the *Black-Friers*: Being the Noble, Last, and Onely *Remaines* of those Incomparable *Drammatists, Francis Beavmont,* And *John Fletcher,* Gent. Retriv'd for the publick delight of all the Ingenious; And private Benefit Of *John Lowin,* And *Joseph Taylor,* Servants to His late Majestie. By a Person of Honour . . . 1652.

<1659/60. In the repertory of Rhodes's company acting at the Cockpit, John Downes lists 'The Wild Goose Chase'. (*Roscius Anglicanus,* Summers, ed., pp. 17–18.)

1660/1, Feb. In a list of plays performed by the King's company 'at the Red Bull and the new house in Gibbon's Tennis Court near Clare Market', 1660–2, appears 'Feb. The Wild-goose Chase'. (Adams, *Herbert,* p. 117, n. 1.)

1667/8, 11 Jan. '. . . to the King's house, there to see "The Wild-goose Chase," which I never saw, but have long longed to see it, being a famous play, but as it was yesterday I do find that where

I expect most I find least satisfaction, for in this play I met with nothing extraordinary at all, but very dull inventions and designs.' (Diary of Samuel Pepys.)

1668/9, c. 12 Jan. In 'A Catalogue of part of His Ma^tes Servants Playes as they were formerly acted at the Blackfryers & now allowed of to his Ma^tes Servants at ye New Theatre' occurs the title, 'The Wyd Goose-Chase'. (Nicoll, *A History of Restoration Drama*, 3rd ed., pp. 315–16.)

1672/3, 30 Jan. S.R. Humphrey Robinson, executor of Humphrey Robinson, assigned to John Martin and Henry Herringman all his rights in a long list of plays, including '[51] Wild Goose Chase, halfe'. (Greg, *Bibliography*, i. 72–73.)

1679. The twenty-second play in the second Beaumont and Fletcher Folio is 'The Wild-Goose Chase; A Comedy'.

1683, 21 Aug. Sarah Martin, executrix of John Martin, transferred her rights in a long list of plays to Robert Scott. Included is '[58] Wild Goose Chase ¼'. (Ibid., pp. 75–76.)

The first production of the play presumably took place some time before the court performance at Christmas, 1621–21/2, but there is no evidence as to how long before. It is generally assumed that the play was new when it was performed at court, but there is no assurance that this is true or that the 1621–21/2 performance was the first at court. The year 1621 is a plausible date for the first production of the play in the absence of evidence to the contrary.

Moseley's statement in his address to the readers in the Folio of 1647 gives the reason for the play's omission from that volume. A manuscript was found later and published in folio in 1652 by Moseley for the benefit of the former leaders of the King's company, John Lowin and Joseph Taylor. This publication is one of the most handsome and elaborate issues of a single play in the time. It has commendatory verses by Richard Lovelace, Norreys Jephson, W. E., H. Harington, and James Ramsey. The dedication by Lowin and Taylor includes a valediction to the Caroline theatre:

And now Farewell our *Glory*! Farewell your *Choice Delight*, most noble Gentlemen! Farewell th' *Grand Wheel* that set *Vs* smaller Motions in Action! Farewell the Pride and Life o' th' Stage! Nor can we (though in our Ruin) much repine that we are so little, since *He* that gave us being is no more.

The cast published in this edition is one of the most complete of the time and much the most elaborate.

DRAMMATIS PERSONÆ.

DE-GARD, A Noble stayd Gentleman that being newly lighted from his Travells, assists his sister *Oriana* in her chase of *Mirabell* the *Wild-Goose*. } Acted by Mr. *Robert Benfield.*

LA-CASTRE, the Indulgent Father to *Mirabell*. } Acted by Mr. *Richard Robinson.*

MIRABELL, the *Wild-Goose*, a Travayl'd Monsieur, and great defyer of all Ladies in the way of Marriage, otherwise their much loose servant, at last caught by the despis'd *Oriana*. } Incomparably Acted by Mr. *Joseph Taylor.*

PINAC, his fellow Traveller, of a lively spirit, and servant to the no lesse sprightly *Lillia-Bianca*. } Admirably well Acted by Mr. *Thomas Pollard.*

BELLEUR, Companion to both, of a stout blunt humor, in love with *Rosalura*. } Most naturally Acted by Mr. *John Lowin.*

NANTOLET, Father to *Rosalura* and *Lillia-Bianca*. } Acted by Mr. *William Penn.*

LUGIER, the rough and confident Tutor to the Ladies, and chiefe Engine to intrap the *Wild-Goose*. } Acted by Mr. *Hilliard Swanston.*

ORIANA, the faire betroth'd of *Mirabell*, and wittie follower of the *Chase*. } Acted by Mr. *Steph. Hammerton.*

ROSALURA } the Aërie Daughters of *Nantolet*. } { *William Trigg.*
LILLIA-BIANCA } { *Sander Gough.*

PETELLA, their waiting-woman. Their Servant Mr *Shanck.*

MARIANA, an English Courtezan.

A young FACTOR. by Mr. *John Hony-man.*

PAGE.

SERVANTS.

SINGING-BOY.

TWO MERCHANTS.

PRIEST.

FOURE WOMEN.

THE SCENE PARIS.

It has several times been pointed out that this cast cannot have been the one for the original production in 1621 or earlier. William Penn was still a member of Prince Charles's company as late as 1625 (see above, ii. 523–4); Swanston did not become a King's man until 1624 (ibid., pp. 584–5); Stephen Hammerton is unknown before 1632, but, since he was acting boys' roles then, it is unlikely that he was performing at all in 1621 (ibid., pp. 460–1); Trigg was also still acting boys' roles in 1631 (ibid., pp. 604–6);

Alexander Gough was not baptized until August 1614, and it does not seem likely that he would have been acting at seven (ibid., pp. 446–7); and John Honeyman, who was baptized in February 1612/13, was not old enough in 1621 to have played the adult role of the young Factor (ibid., pp. 476–7). All twelve members of the cast were performing for the King's company in 1632 and in roles similar to those assigned them in *The Wild Goose Chase*, but they could not have performed them much later than that date, for Shank died in 1635/6 (ibid., p. 567); Penn disappears after 1636; and Trigg and Gough were hired men—i.e. no longer boys—in 1636. It has generally been assumed, therefore, that the elaborate cast printed in the 1652 edition of *The Wild Goose Chase* applies to a revival of 1632, the year in which Sir Henry Herbert records his receipts from a performance of the play.

This record of Sir Henry is one of several which list his receipts under an agreement with the King's company according to which he was to receive the profits of the second performance of a revival each summer and another each winter. Since he was allowed to select the play, it can be assumed that he selected a popular one. The £15 which he received for the second day of the revival of *The Wild Goose Chase* was the remainder of the receipts after the daily charge of the house-keepers had been deducted. This sum was the second largest he recorded, exceeded only by the 1628 revival of *The Custom of the Country*. (See Adams, *Herbert*, pp. 43–44.) Of course the receipts from winter performances at Blackfriars were much greater than those from summer performances at the Globe. (See above, i. 30, n. 6.) The fact that Sir Henry received the summer payment and the winter payment on the same day and that he does not name the summer play does not indicate that the summer play was *The Wild Goose Chase*. Sir Henry left unnamed the three plays on which his receipts were least (see above, i. 24), evidently finding no reason to remember them. The date of 6 November 1632 is probably not the date of the winter performance, but only that of the payment.

The popularity of *The Wild Goose Chase* before the closing of the theatres is suggested, as we have seen, by Sir Henry Herbert's selection of it for his winter's benefit and by the large sum he realized. It is further suggested by the verses for the 1652 folio edition and by Lowin and Taylor's statement in the dedication:

The Play was of so Generall a receiv'd Acceptance, that (he *Himself* a *Spectator*) we have known him un-concern'd, and to have wisht it had been none of His; He, as well as the *throng'd Theatre* (in despight of his innate Modesty) Applauding this *rare issue of his Brain*.

Pepys's designation of *The Wild Goose Chase* as a famous play indicates that the echoes of its popularity were still heard after the Restoration, but Pepys's own opinion of it is more in agreement with the records of Restoration performances, which are fewer than for a number of other Fletcher plays.

No source for *The Wild Goose Chase* has been discovered.

Fletcher's sole authorship of the play is generally accepted, but Fleay thought (*Biog. Chron.* i. 216) that the text showed evidences of abridgement, and both he and Oliphant (loc. cit.) noted the confusion about the names of Lugier and Leverduce or Leverdure. Revision for the 1632 revival (not 1631, as Fleay and Oliphant state, following Malone's error; see Adams, *Herbert*, p. 44, n. 2) is not impossible, but Oliphant is reluctant to postulate one because he can find no hand but Fletcher's. He speculates about revision before Fletcher's death. The confusions cited seem to me insufficient to require the assumption of a revision; they could be simply evidence of Fletcher's carelessness.

Farquhar's *The Inconstant, or The Way to Win Him*, published in 1702, is a rewriting of *The Wild Goose Chase*. Heldt (loc. cit.) and Sprague (loc. cit.) trace the relationship of the two plays.

Wit at Several Weapons

See *The Elizabethan Stage*, iii. 232, and Oliphant, *The Plays of Beaumont and Fletcher*, pp. 451–7.

Wit without Money

See *The Elizabethan Stage*, iii. 229.

The Woman Hater, or The Hungry Courtier

See *The Elizabethan Stage*, iii. 219–20, and Oliphant, *The Plays of Beaumont and Fletcher*, pp. 214–20.

The Woman's Plot

See Philip Massinger.

The Woman's Prize, or The Tamer Tamed

See *The Elizabethan Stage*, iii. 222, and Oliphant, *The Plays of Beaumont and Fletcher*, pp. 151–6.

Women Pleased (revised [?] 1619–23)

Kiepert, Willy. *Fletcher's 'Women pleased' und seine Quellen* (1903).

Maxwell, Baldwin. *Studies in Beaumont, Fletcher, and Massinger* (1939), pp. 74–83.

Oliphant, E. H. C. *The Plays of Beaumont and Fletcher* (1927), pp. 156–60 and 430–1.

Vogt, George McGill. '*The Wife of Bath's Tale, Women Pleased, and La Fée Urgele*: A Study in the Transformation of Folk-Lore Themes in Drama', *M.L.N.* xxxvii (1922), 339–42.

1646, [4] Sept. S.R. Robinson and Moseley entered 'The Woemen pleased . . . by mʳ Beamont & mʳ fflesher' in a group of nearly fifty plays, all apparently of the repertory of the King's company. (Greg, *Bibliography*, i. 56–57.)

1647. 'Women pleas'd' is printed as the twenty-eighth play in the Beaumont and Fletcher Folio of 1647.

1668, 20 Aug. 'Woemen pleas'd' is found in a list of plays allowed to be acted by the Duke of York's company. (Nicoll, *A History of Restoration Drama*, 3rd ed., p. 315.)

1668, 26 Dec. At the Duke of York's house Pepys saw the play, 'which we had never seen before; and, though but indifferent, yet there is a good design for a good play'. (Diary of Samuel Pepys.)

1672/3, 30 Jan. S.R. Humphrey Robinson, executor of Humphrey Robinson, transferred to John Martin and Henry Herringman his rights in a long list of plays, including 'The Woman [*sic*] Pleased. halfe.' (Greg, *Bibliography*, i. 72–73.)

1679. 'Women Pleas'd A Tragy-Comedy' is the thirty-sixth play in the second Beaumont and Fletcher Folio.

1683, 21 Aug. S.R. Sarah Martin, executrix of John Martin, transferred to Robert Scott her rights in a long list of plays, including 'The woman [*sic*] Pleased. ¼'. (Ibid., pp. 75–76.)

Kiepert discusses at length Fletcher's use of his sources: Juan de Flores's *La Historia de Grisel y Mirabella* (translated as *Historie of Aurelio and of Isabell*); Chaucer's *Wife of Bath's Tale*; and three of the tales in the *Decameron*. Since all, or nearly all, were available in English in the sixteenth century, they give no clue to the date of composition of the play.

An allusion in *The Taming of the Shrew* appears to refer to Soto,

the clown in *Women Pleased*, and his design to woo Belvidere.
The allusion has puzzled many commentators.

> *Lord.* With all my heart. This fellow I remember
> Since once he play'd a farmer's eldest son.
> 'Twas where you woo'd the gentlewoman so well.
> I have forgot your name; but sure that part
> Was aptly fitted and naturally perform'd.
> *Player.* I think 'twas Soto that your honour means.
> *Lord.* 'Tis very true. Thou didst it excellent.
> (Kittredge, ed., Induction, Sc. 1, lines 83–89.)

The question is whether the lines were in the original version of
Shakespeare's play and therefore indicate a sixteenth-century
version of *Women Pleased*, whether the lines are a late insertion
into *The Taming of the Shrew* and therefore an allusion to the
Fletcher play as we have it, or whether the allusion does not refer
to the Fletcher play at all. Pertinent for these considerations is
the fact that in the 1623 Folio text an actor's name has slipped
in, and the compositor has set 'Sincklo' instead of 'Player'.
This actor, John Sincler, Sinklo, or Sincklo, appears in minor
capacities in quite a few plays of the nineties and as late as the
Induction of Marston's *Malcontent* in 1604. (See Nungezer, *A
Dictionary of Actors*, pp. 326–7.) There is no record of him after
1604, however, and no evidence that he ever had a major role.
These facts suggest that the actor's name and the allusion to his
playing of Soto were probably written into the manuscript of
The Taming of the Shrew not later than 1604 and that therefore
they do not allude to Fletcher's play in its present form. Wilson
and Quiller-Couch note (New Cambridge ed., pp. 131–3) that in
Fletcher's play Soto does not woo the gentlewoman, as Shakespeare's Lord remembers, but only plans to do so, and this suggests
to them that *Women Pleased* is a revision of the play to which the
Lord alludes. This explanation seems to me not unlikely, for
Women Pleased is a curiously ill-constructed play, with various
elements which seem too old-fashioned for the latter part of
Fletcher's career. Oliphant (op. cit., pp. 156–9) thinks that the
play is a revision, but claims the original version for Fletcher
about 1603 or 1604. It seems to me that an original version by
some other dramatist in the nineties is much more likely.

In the Folio of 1679 the play has a cast identical with those for
The Little French Lawyer and *The Custom of the Country* (q.v.),
which must date May 1619–May 1623. It must, therefore, be the
cast for a revival of the play—perhaps for the first performance of
Fletcher's revision.

The role of Penurio in *Women Pleased* is one of the most developed of Fletcher's 'hungry knave' roles. Professor Baldwin Maxwell, who has commented most extensively on these roles (loc. cit.), thinks that they were written for John Shank, a principal comedian of the King's company and a notoriously lean man. In general his case seems a good one, but in this play Shank does not appear in the cast. In other plays his absence from the cast may be attributed to the small number of his lines, but the part of Penurio in *Women Pleased* has 324 lines and is the second largest in the play. (Baldwin, *Organization and Personnel*, p. 198, Chart 2.) Either Maxwell or the cast must be wrong.

The disintegrators seem pretty well agreed that the play is the work of Fletcher alone.

It is unusual that a Beaumont and Fletcher play should leave no records at all before the closing of the theatres, not even in the list of the plays of the King's men in 1641. Apparently *Women Pleased* had little or no vogue.

The inclusion of two stage directions for entrances with lights, and another direction which seems to indicate one character added as an afterthought, led Professor Bald to think that the play may have been set up from a prompt manuscript, but the evidence is scanty. (See Bald, *Bibliographical Studies in the Beaumont & Fletcher Folio of 1647*, pp. 108-9.)

JOHN FORD (Foard, Foarde, Foord, Forde)
1586- <1639

Babb, Lawrence A. *John Ford and Seventeenth Century Psychology*. Unpublished dissertation, Yale (1934).

Bacon, Wallace A. 'The Literary Reputation of John Ford', *Huntington Library Quarterly*, xi (1948), 181-99. [Impressionistic criticism; not a reputation study.]

Cochnower, M. E. 'John Ford' in *Seventeenth Century Studies*, ed. Robert Shafer (1933).

Eliot, T. S. 'John Ford' in *Elizabethan Essays* (1934).

Ellis-Fermor, U. M. 'John Ford' in *The Jacobean Drama* (1936).

Ewing, S. Blaine. *Burtonian Melancholy in the Plays of John Ford* (1940).

—— 'Burton, Ford, and *Andromana*', *P.M.L.A.* liv (1939), 1007-17.

Koeppel, Emil. *Quellen-Studien zu den Dramen George Chapman's, Philip Massinger's und John Ford's* (1897).

Lloyd, Bertram. 'An Inedited MS. of Ford's *Fames Memoriall*', *R.E.S.* i (1925), 93–95.

—— 'An Unprinted Poem by John Ford (?)', ibid., pp. 217–19.

Pierce, Frederick E. 'The Collaboration of Dekker and Ford', *Anglia*, xxxvi (1912), 141 ff. and 289 ff.

Sargeaunt, M. Joan. *John Ford* (1935).

—— 'John Ford at the Middle Temple', *R.E.S.* viii (1932), 69–70.

—— 'Writings Ascribed to John Ford by Joseph Hunter in *Chorus Vatum*', *R.E.S.* x (1934), 165–76.

Sensabaugh, George F. *The Tragic Muse of John Ford* (1944).

Tannenbaum, Samuel A. *John Ford* (*A Concise Bibliography*) (1941).

Ward, Adolphus William. *A History of English Dramatic Literature to the Death of Queen Anne* (1899), iii. 71–89.

Most of our information about Ford's life is derived from his career at the Middle Temple. Considering his reputation in the nineteenth and twentieth centuries, there are surprisingly few contemporary references to him as a dramatist; most of them are found in the usual entries in Sir Henry Herbert's office-book, in the Stationers' Register, and in the front matter of the early editions of his plays.

There are a few others. William Heminges mentioned him with twenty-odd other Jacobean and Caroline writers in his *Elegy on Randolph's Finger*:

> Deep In a dumpe Iacke forde alone was gott
> W^th folded Armes and Melancholye hatt.
> (G. C. Moore Smith edition, lines 81–82.)

And he may have had Ford in mind also in the lines:

> More worthyes Like to thes I could Impart
> but that wee are troubled wth a broken hart.
> (Ibid., lines 91–92.)

Thomas May is alleged to have written four lines '*To my worthy friend, John Ford*' (*Variorum*, i. 405), but Malone presents good reasons for believing that these lines are an eighteenth-century forgery (ibid., pp. 426–9); Thomas Heywood, in noting the nicknames of various contemporary poets, observes that Ford was called '*Iacke Foord*' (*Hierarchie of the Blessed Angels*, 1635, p. 206 [S₁ᵛ]); Thomas Bancroft has a two-line punning epigram to him in his *Two Bookes of Epigrammes, and Epitaphs*, 1639 (No. 192, E₃ᵛ); and there is a conventional epigram to him in the mis-

cellany called *Wits Recreations*, 1640 (No. 56, B₈ᵛ). This is a far
smaller number of allusions than is extant for Caroline dramatists
whom we now consider lesser lights, like Randolph, Cartwright,
Suckling, or Davenant.

Since various writers of commendatory verses for his plays, as
well as Ford himself, note that he was of the Middle Temple, he can
probably be identified with the John Ford, second son of Thomas
Ford of Ilsington, Devonshire, who was admitted 16 November
1602. (Sargeaunt, *John Ford*, p. 212, n. 9.) The Fords were an
old Devonshire family. John, son of Thomas and Elizabeth, was
baptized at Ilsington on 17 April 1586. The dramatist's mother
was a niece of Lord Chief Justice Popham, a member of the Middle
Temple. Miss Sargeaunt thinks that the dramatist may have been
the John Ford of Devon, age 16, who matriculated at Exeter
College, Oxford, 26 March 1601, but there were many Devonshire
Fords. (Ibid., pp. 1–2.)

In the Hilary Term, 1605/6, Ford was expelled from the Middle
Temple for failure to pay his buttery bill, and he was not reinstated until 10 June 1608. (Sargeaunt, *R.E.S.* viii. 69–70.) His
first publications come in this period, and it is possible that the
expulsion strengthened the literary urge. *Fame's Memorial* and
Honour Triumphant, or The Peers' Challenge were both published
in 1606. The first is an elegy on the death of the Earl of Devonshire, dedicated to the Countess, formerly Penelope Rich, and is a
dull poem but a suggestive anticipation of Ford's later attitude
toward lovers. (See S. P. Sherman, ed., *'Tis Pity She's a Whore
and The Broken Heart*, pp. ix–xi.) The second is a pamphlet on the
general subject of love and beauty, dedicated to the Countesses of
Pembroke and Montgomery. It seems to have been suggested by
one of the entertainments for the King of Denmark in 1606.

According to the will of Ford's father, who died in 1610, the
poet's elder brother received the reversion of the principal estate
and his two younger brothers an annual £10, but the poet himself
received only a total bequest of £10. This testamentary discrimina-
tion suggests paternal disapproval, but nothing more is known of
the situation.

Miss Sargeaunt thinks Ford was the author of the religious
poem *Christes Bloodie Sweat, Or the Sonne of God in His Agonie*
(1613), which, though published anonymously, has a dedication
to the Earl of Pembroke which is signed 'I. F.', and of *The Golden
Meane* (1613 and 1614), a moral pamphlet. (*R.E.S.* x. 165–76.)
On 25 November 1615 'A booke called, *Sir THOMAS OVERBURYes
Ghost contayneinge the history of his life and vntimely death* by

JOHN FFORD gent.' was entered in the Stationers' Register, but it is not now known.

By the will of his elder brother, Henry, dated 17 September 1616, John Ford was left £20 per annum on the condition that he surrender to Henry's children his estate in two tenements. (Sargeaunt, *John Ford*, pp. 13–14.) This proposal again suggests the poet's impecuniousness, though there could be other reasons for the transaction.

In 1617 Ford's name was on a list of forty members of the Middle Temple admonished by the Benchers on 30 May for wearing hats instead of the traditional lawyers' caps in and about the Inn. Though there is no record that Ford ever became an utter barrister or was called to the Bar, these and later allusions indicating his long residence in the Middle Temple suggest to Miss Sargeaunt that he must have been engaged in some legal activity other than that of barrister. (Ibid., pp. 14–16.)

The beginnings of Ford's dramatic activities are obscure. If he really was the author of *An Ill Beginning Has a Good End* and if that play was the same as *A Bad Beginning Makes a Good Ending* (see below), then he had written a play for the King's company as early as 1612, but the identifications are not certain. *Beauty in a Trance*, *The London Merchant*, *The Royal Combat*, and *The Queen* are undatable, and any or all of them could have been composed before Ford's first datable play.

We are not on certain ground until we come to *The Witch of Edmonton*, 1621, *The Sun's Darling*, 1623/4, *The Late Murder of the Son upon the Mother*, 1624, *The Fairy Knight*, 1624, and *The Bristow Merchant*, 1624. All five of these earliest dated plays are collaborations with Thomas Dekker, though in *The Witch of Edmonton* there was a third collaborator, and in *The Late Murder* a third and fourth. Evidently Ford, like Webster, went through a period of Dekker's tutelage, though it is possible that he had had still earlier dramatic experience. Dekker in the early twenties had been recently released from a long period of imprisonment and seems to have been in poverty. (See above.) The fact that Ford collaborated with Dekker five times in three or four years suggests that Ford may also have been feeling the pinch of poverty. Miss Sargeaunt, noting that Nathaniel Finch, the lawyer who signed Dekker's deposition in the suit arising from *The Late Murder of the Son upon the Mother*, is one of the two dedicatees of *The Lover's Melancholy*, suggests that Finch was the connecting link between Dekker and Ford. (Sargeaunt, *John Ford*, p. 20.)

For the dating of Ford's later and more distinguished plays the evidence is exasperatingly meagre. All the extant plays except *The Queen* are assigned to acting companies: three of them were the property of the King's company and the other five the property of Christopher Beeston's companies at the Phoenix in Drury Lane. Two of the plays for the King's men, *The Lover's Melancholy* and *Beauty in a Trance*, are dated 1628 and >1630, and the third, *The Broken Heart, c.* 1627–31, certainly not later than 1632/3. There is not much to date the Phoenix plays, but all of them—with the possible exception of *Perkin Warbeck*— seem to me to date after 1630. Possibly Ford wrote for the King's men in the first four or five years of Charles's reign and for Beeston thereafter.

Ford's London friends are probably to be found among the authors of the commendatory verses for his plays—Edward Green- field, George Donne, William Singleton, Humphrey Howorth, James Shirley, Ralph Eure, George Crymes, John Brograve, John Ford (his cousin), and Thomas Ellice—and among those dedicatees of whose friendship he boasts—John Wyrley and his wife, Nathan- iel Finch, John Ford, Henry Blunt, Robert Ellice (the last four all of Gray's Inn), and the Earl of Peterborough. Ford himself wrote verses for Barnaby Barnes's *Four Books of Office*, 1606, Overbury's *The Wife*, 1616, Henry Cockeram's *English Dictionary*, 1623, Web- ster's *Duchess of Malfi*, 1623, Shirley's *Wedding*, 1629, Massinger's *Roman Actor*, 1629, Brome's *Northern Lass*, 1632, Massinger's *Great Duke of Florence*, 1636, and *Jonsonus Virbius*, 1638. It is perhaps significant that Ford's last known set of verses was published in 1638 and that the last play to be published with front matter by the dramatist—*The Lady's Trial*—appeared early in 1639 (Stationers' Register, 6 November 1638). The evidence sug- gests that he left London or died in 1639, for there is no certain later record of him.

Bertram Lloyd thought the dramatist was the 'J. Foord' who some time before 1645 signed manuscript verses celebrating the marriage of Sir Erasmus de la Fountaine and Mary Noel, but the name is a common one. ('An Unprinted Poem by John Ford (?)', *R.E.S.* i. 217–19.) A writer to *Notes & Queries* (Fourth Series, xi [1873], 403) reports an inscription in a copy of *The English Secretorie*, signed 'Johne Ford Middle Tempil 15 Jully 1641', but Miss Sargeaunt notes that a John Ford of Chewford was admitted to the Middle Temple on 11 November 1616. (*John Ford*, p. 29.)

Gifford reported in his edition of Ford a faint tradition that the dramatist retired to his home in Devonshire (i, p. xliv), but one wonders what leading questions elicited such a tradition after

nearly 200 years. Miss Sargeaunt finds a possible connexion between
this tradition and the appearance of commendatory verses signed
'Jo: Ford' prefixed to *Dia Poemata*, 1655, by Edmund Elys,
the son of the rector of East Allington, Devonshire, a village about
seventeen miles from Ford's Ilsington. (*John Ford*, pp. 30–31.)
But again, one remembers the frequent occurrence of the name,
especially in Devonshire.

Collected Editions

The Dramatic Works of John Ford, ed. Henry Weber, 2 vols.
(1811).

The Dramatic Works of John Ford, ed. William Gifford, 2 vols.
(1827).

*The Dramatic Works of John Ford: with an Introduction and Notes
Critical and Explanatory*, ed. Anon., 2 vols. (1831).

The Dramatic Works of Massinger and Ford, ed. Hartley Coleridge
(1840).

The Works of John Ford, ed. William Gifford and Alexander
Dyce, 3 vols. (1869 and 1895).

John Fordes Dramatische Werke, ed. W. Bang and H. De Vocht,
Materialien, xxiii (1908) and N.S. i (1927).

A Bad Beginning Makes a Good Ending

See *An Ill Beginning Has a Good End*.

Beauty in a Trance (> 1630)
(Lost)

1630, 28 Nov. 'Beauty in a Traunce' was presented by the King's
company in the new court theatre, the Cockpit in Whitehall,
according to the bill presented by the company. (See above, i.
28.)

1641, 7 Aug. 'Beauty in a Trance' is one of a list of plays in the
repertory of the King's company which the Lord Chamberlain
ordered the Stationers' Company not to allow to be printed
without the consent of the King's men. (See above, i. 65–66.)

1653, 9 Sept. S.R. 'Beauty in a Trance. by M^r. In^o. Ford' is one
of forty-one plays entered in the S.R. by Humphrey Moseley.
(Greg, *Bibliography*, i. 60–61.)

c. 1710–50. 'Beauty in a Trance A C. Jo^n. Forde' appears in
Warburton's list of manuscript plays. (See Greg, *Library*, Third
Series, ii [1911], 230–2.)

This play is known only from the above records. Presumably the manuscript passed from the repertory of the King's company to Moseley, but there is no assurance that Warburton ever had it. Dr. Greg presents evidence (op. cit.) that Warburton may well have copied much of his famous list from the Stationers' Register and thus may never have seen the manuscripts.

Only three of Ford's plays are known to have been performed by the King's company—*The Lover's Melancholy* in November 1628, *Beauty in a Trance* > November 1630, and *The Broken Heart* at a date not later than its entry in the Stationers' Register in March 1633. Since the five later plays acknowledged to be his were all performed by Beeston's companies at the Cockpit in Drury Lane, it seems possible that Ford wrote two sequences of plays—an earlier series of three for the King's men in the late twenties and a second series for Beeston's companies at the Cockpit in the thirties.

The Bristow Merchant
with Thomas Dekker

See Thomas Dekker.

The Broken Heart (c. 1627–31?)

Editions: Edited with Notes and an Introduction by Clinton Scollard, 1895; with a Preface, Notes, and Glossary by Oliphant Smeaton, 1906; *'Tis Pity She's a Whore and The Broken Heart*, ed. S. P. Sherman (1915).

Baskervill, C. R. 'Bandello and *The Broken Heart*', *M.L.N.* xxviii (1913), 51–52.

Davril, R. '*The Broken Heart*, étude critique, texte anglais et traduction française, notes.' Announced, *Research in Progress*, *P.M.L.A.* lxiii (1948), Supplement, p. 183, No. 900.

Ewing, S. Blaine. *Burtonian Melancholy in the Plays of John Ford* (1940), pp. 26–28, 55–64.

Koeppel, Emil. *Quellen-Studien zu den Dramen George Chapman's, Philip Massinger's und John Ford's* (1897), pp. 175–8.

Lamb, Charles. *Specimens of English Dramatic Poets* (1808), pp. 253–65.

Sherman, S. P. 'Stella and the *Broken Heart*', *P.M.L.A.* xxiv (1909), 274–85.

1633, 28 Mar. S.R. 'Hugh Beeston   Entred for his Copy vnder the
hands of S^r. Henry Herbert & m^r Aspley Warden a Tragedy
called The broken heart by Iohn fford.' (Greg, *Bibliography*,
i. 42.)

1633. The Broken Heart. A Tragedy. *Acted* By the Kings Majesties
Seruants at the priuate House in the Black-friers. *Fide Honor*
... 1633.

Ford's name does not appear on the title-page of this play, but
his anagram, *Fide Honor*, is there, and the dedication to Lord
Craven is signed '*Iohn Ford*'. The dedication reveals nothing about
the play or the author, except Ford's usual implications of digni-
fied, studious aloofness. There are no commendatory verses. The
most curious piece of front matter is the dramatis personae,
headed 'The Speakers names, fitted to their Qualities', e.g.

> Ithocles, *Honour of louelinesse*,
> Orgilvs, *Angry*,
> Bassanes, *Vexation*.

The prologue and epilogue are conventional and unrevealing
except for one couplet in the former:

> *What may be here thought a* fiction, *when Times youth*
> *Wanted some riper yeares, was knowne A Truth*

This statement implies a source which Ford took to be historical.
Professor Sherman suggested (op. cit.) that Ford planned his play
to reflect the relationship between Sir Philip Sidney and Penelope
Rich; it is clear enough that *The Arcadia* was often in the author's
mind, but the indebtedness of the play to the details of Sir
Philip's life is much more dubious.

There is very little to suggest a date for *The Broken Heart*
beyond the entry in the Stationers' Register. W. J. Lawrence
(*T.L.S.*, 12 July 1923, p. 472) would like to date the play by a
reference in IV. 2:

> *Gran.* O sweet man!
> Thou art the very hony-combe of honesty.
> *Phul.* The garland of good-will.   (1633 4°, H₁.)

Lawrence thought this must refer to T[homas] D[eloney]'s *The
Garland of Good Will*, which was published in 1631. He did not
note, however, that Nashe had referred to Deloney's collection
in 1596, that it had appeared in the Stationers' Register in 1593,
1596, and 1629, and that there is some evidence of an edition of

1604. (See F. O. Mann, *The Works of Thomas Deloney*, pp. xii and 562–3, and *S.T.C.*)

S. Blaine Ewing (*Burtonian Melancholy in the Plays of John Ford*, pp. 26–28) suggests late 1632 for three reasons, all dubious: (1) There seems to be an allusion to the play in the couplet in William Heminges's *Elegy on Randolph's Finger*:

> More worthyes Like to thes I could Impart
> but that wee are troubled wth a broken hart.
>
> (Moore Smith ed., lines 91–92.)

But this allusion certainly does not suggest composition late in 1632, for Heminges's poem was written about 1632, or perhaps earlier (see G. C. Moore Smith's edition, pp. 4–6); furthermore, *The Broken Heart* need not have been recent to be mentioned, for other plays referred to by Heminges in his elegy are *The Duchess of Malfi, Sejanus, Catiline, Aristippus, The Alchemist*, and *A Game at Chess*, all dating before 1627 and four of them before 1616. (2) The title-page of *The Broken Heart* mentions performance at Blackfriars only, whereas that of *The Lover's Melancholy* mentions both Blackfriars and the Globe. Mr. Ewing, placing an unwarranted confidence in the meticulousness of publishers, takes this as evidence that *The Broken Heart* had been acted *only* at Blackfriars, and therefore not in the summer, and deduces that it must therefore have been composed *after* the summer of 1632! Such reasoning—whatever may be said of its logic—ignores the prestige of Blackfriars at this time (see above, i. 30, n. 6) and ignores also the dominant motive of publishers—to sell books. (3) Crashaw's couplet,

> Thou cheat'st us *Ford*, mak'st *one* seeme two by Art.
> What is *Loves Sacrifice*, but *The broken Heart*.

supports the interpretation that *The Broken Heart* was composed before *Love's Sacrifice*. If Crashaw's exercise in wit (published in *Delights of the Muses*, 1646) can be made to bear any chronological testimony, it might suggest the order in which he had read the plays, or possibly the order in which they had been published, but nothing about composition. In any case, the date of composition of *Love's Sacrifice* is unknown.

I can offer little more than a suggestion for the date of this tragedy. Twelve of Ford's seventeen known plays can be assigned to acting companies on the basis of external evidence. Eliminating the collaborations with Dekker, we find that three plays were performed by the King's company and five by Beeston's companies at the Phoenix. None of the plays for Beeston can be shown to be before 1630, but of the three for the King's company *The Lover's Melancholy* was licensed by Herbert 24 November 1628, *Beauty in a Trance* was acted at court 28 November 1630, and the third is *The Broken Heart*. It seems to me that the few facts we have suggest that, after he ceased to collaborate with Dekker, Ford wrote three or more plays for the King's company; then, at least a year or so before 1633 (since the Queen's play, *Love's Sacrifice*, was licensed 21 January 1632/3, and both it and *'Tis Pity* were published as Queen's plays in 1633), he made some sort of agreement with Christopher Beeston and wrote all the rest of his plays for the management of the Phoenix. If this is the case, *The Broken Heart* must have been close in date to *Beauty in a Trance* and *The Lover's Melancholy*, or about 1627–31.

The Excellency of Her Sex

See Ford, *The Queen*.

The Fair Maid of the Inn

See Fletcher for Ford's alleged contributions to the play.

The Fairy Knight
with Thomas Dekker

See Thomas Dekker.

The Fancies Chaste and Noble (1631?, 1635–6)

Ewing, S. Blaine. *Burtonian Melancholy in the Plays of John Ford* (1940), pp. 28–32 and 47–54.
Koeppel, Emil. *Quellen-Studien zu den Dramen George Chapman's, Philip Massinger's und John Ford's* (1897), pp. 184–5.

1637/8, 3 Feb. S.R. Entered for 'M^r. Seile' 'a Play called the ffancies by Io: fford'. (Greg, *Bibliography*, i. 47.)
1638. The Fancies, Chast and Noble: Presented by the Queenes Maiesties Servants, At the Phoenix in *Drury-lane*. Fide Honor ... 1638.

This prurient and confused comedy adds nothing to Ford's reputation, and one wonders what *Beauty in a Trance, The Royal Combat, An Ill Beginning Has a Good End,* and *The London Merchant* must have been if he chose to publish this play and to allow them to go unprinted. That the play was published with

the author's consent is demonstrated by the dedication to the
Earl of Antrim which is signed 'IOHN FORD'. This dedication
throws no light on the play or on the author. In the single set
of commendatory verses addressed to Master John Ford of the
Middle Temple, 'Edw. Greenfield' sneers at university and court
playwrights in a fashion familiar in the late thirties and commends
Ford's comedy as an academy for the young and fair. What
curious educational principles Master Greenfield must have held!

Fleay noted (*Biog. Chron.* i. 234) that since the title-page recorded performance of the play by Queen Henrietta's men at the
Phoenix, it must date before May 1636, when that company
ceased to act at the Phoenix. (See above, i. 236 ff.) Fleay also
noted that the barber's remark,

a gelding was lately seene to leape an old Mare; and an old man of one
hundred and twelve stood in a white sheet for getting a wench of
fifteene with childe, here hard by (v. 2, I₄ᵛ),

must refer to Old Parr. This old man, reputed to be 152 years old,
was brought to court by the Earl of Arundel in September 1635;
he died in London 14 November 1635 and was buried in Westminster Abbey. John Taylor's pamphlet about him which was
entered in the Stationers' Register three weeks later, on 7 December, records the story of the old man standing in a sheet in Alder-
bury parish church as a punishment for lechery at the age of 105,
one of the very few anecdotes about the old man in Taylor's
uninformative catch-penny pamphlet. (See John Taylor, *The Old,
Old, Very Old Man*, 1635.) Ford may not have taken the incident
from Taylor's pamphlet, for Taylor was evidently retailing one of
the few specific incidents he could discover about Old Parr, and
if Taylor knew it, the penance-in-a-sheet story must have been
fairly common knowledge. Whatever the source of Ford's knowledge of the incident, he must have expected his audience to recognize the allusion to the old man who had been a two months'
wonder in London and had been buried in the Abbey. If so, the
allusion could not have been made before the old man came to
London in September 1635, and it must have been made before
the talk of him died out, and at any rate before the Queen's men
ceased to act at the Phoenix at the plague-closing in May 1636.

Reyher (*Les Masques anglais*, p. 329) thought he saw further
evidence of a date of 1636 in the masque with which *The Fancies
Chaste and Noble* concludes. This masque of the influence of love
on 'Soldier, Gentry, foole, scholler, Merchant man, and Clowne' he
thought derived from the second antimasque in Davenant's

Triumphs of the Prince D'Amour, which was entered in the Stationers' Register 19 February 1635/6 and performed at the Middle
Temple 23 or 24 February. (See above, under Davenant.) If Reyher
is correct, the imitation indicates a date of February–May 1636, for
the first performance of *The Fancies*, and this would agree with
the date suggested by the Old Parr allusion. It is likely enough
that Ford, himself a member of the Middle Temple, who probably
had to help pay for the production of Davenant's masque, was
familiar with the second antimasque of *The Triumphs of the Prince
D'Amour*, and probably even knew many of the masquers. Yet
there is no description of the actions of the masquers in Ford's
play, and his six masquers were not inevitably suggested by
Davenant's Spanish, Italian, French, Dutch, and English lovers.

This evidence for 1636 seems to be contradicted by a further
note of Fleay's, greatly elaborated by Ewing (op. cit., pp. 28–32).
Fleay noted apparent ridicule of *The Fancies* and of Ford in
Shirley's *Changes*, which was licensed for performance 10 January
1631/2. Ewing thinks, moreover, that the prologue for *The Fancies* was written for publication, not performance, and contains a
reply to Shirley. Though Ewing's analyses of the allusions in *The
Changes* are not entirely convincing, they are highly suggestive.
It is perhaps significant—though Ewing fails to note it—that
Shirley had been a regular writer for the company for which *The
Fancies* was written, but that *The Changes* was written for a
rival company at the Salisbury Court theatre. It is more likely
that Shirley would ridicule a Queen Henrietta's playwright in
The Changes than that he would make such an attack in one of his
long series of plays written for that company.

I cannot confidently reject Shirley's satire as intended for Ford,
yet it seems to me less evident than the Parr allusion and about as
convincing as the indebtedness to Davenant. It is possible, though
it does not seem to me too likely, that there was an original performance of the play in 1631 and that revisions were made in
1635–6.

A Good Beginning May Have a Good End

See *An Ill Beginning Has a Good End*.

An Ill Beginning Has a Good End (?)
(Lost)

Parrott, T. M. 'A Note on John Ford', *M.L.N.* lviii (1943),
247–53.

1612–13. On 20 May 1613 John Heminges was paid for 'Sixe severall playes, viz: one play called a badd beginininge [*sic*] makes a good endinge, . . . ' performed the previous winter before the King. (*Eliz. Stage*, iv. 180, and Cunningham, *Revels*, p. xliii.)

1660, 29 June. S.R. Entered to Humphrey Moseley in a list of twenty-six plays, most of them otherwise unknown, are:

The Royall Combate. a Comedy.
An ill begining has a good end, & a bad begin- } by Iohn fforde.
ing may have a good end. a Comedy
The London Merchant. a Comedy

(Greg, *Bibliography*, i. 68–69.)

c. 1710–50. 'A good beginning may have A good end by Jon. Ford' appears in Warburton's list of MS. plays. (See Greg, *Library*, Third Series, ii [1911], 230–2.)

The confusion about the title of this play is no greater than the other uncertainties about it. The 1613 title makes sense; the 1660 title seems foolishly redundant; Warburton's title seems pointless. Warburton may be ignored, since it seems not unlikely that he simply miscopied the Stationers' Register and had not seen the manuscript. (See Greg, op. cit.) Moseley is the only considerable authority for assigning the play to Ford, yet this particular list of Moseley's, in which he assigns to Shakespeare *Duke Humphrey*, *The History of King Stephen*, and *Iphis and Iantha*, and to Marmion *The Soddered Citizen*, has not inspired much confidence. The 1613 and 1660 titles are so similar that the same play must surely be intended. Ford was old enough to write plays in 1612, but the date is nine years before his first certain dramatic composition. Fleay's suggestion (*Biog. Chron.* i. 234–5) that *A Bad Beginning* was the same as *The London Prodigal* is based on one proverbial line in *The London Prodigal* and is not convincing.

It is possible, as Sir Edmund Chambers suggests (*Eliz. Stage*, iii. 315–16), that Ford may have revised the play of 1612–13 and thus got his name on the manuscript in Moseley's possession, but there seems little point in conjecture among so many uncertainties.

Professor Parrott attempts to prove (op. cit.) that Ford *could not* have written the play. It is true enough that the evidence for Ford's authorship is contradictory and inconclusive, but Professor Parrott's objections are based on a reconstruction of Ford's life into which *An Ill Beginning* will not fit. Unfortunately the reconstructed life is an imaginative one into which the facts are fitted, but other imaginative reconstructions into which *An Ill Beginning* could be fitted are equally possible—even tempting.

The Lady's Trial (1638)

Ewing, S. Blaine. *Burtonian Melancholy in the Plays of John Ford* (1940), pp. 88–91.
Koeppel, Emil. *Quellen-Studien zu den Dramen George Chapman's, Philip Massinger's, und John Ford's* (1897), pp. 185–7.
Sargeaunt, M. Joan. *John Ford* (1935), pp. 87–92, 148–52.

1638, 3 May. 'One of the leaves of Sir Henry Herbert's Manuscript, which was missing, having been recovered since the remark in the text was made, I find that the *Ladies Trial* was performed for the first time at the Cockpit theatre in May, 1638, on the 3d of which month it was licensed by the Master of the Revels.' (Adams, *Herbert*, pp. 37–38, from *Variorum*, i. 424.)
1638, 6 Nov. S.R. 'Hen: Sheapard' entered 'a Play called The Ladies triall. by Iohn fford gent'. (Greg, *Bibliography*, i. 49.)
1639. The Ladies Triall. Acted By both their Majesties Servants at the private house in *Drvry Lane*. Fide Honor . . . 1639.
1668/9, 3 Mar. '. . . to the Duke of York's playhouse, and there saw an old play, the first time acted these forty years, called "The Lady's Tryall", acted only by the young people of the house; but the house very full. But it is but a sorry play.' (Diary of Samuel Pepys.)

As usual, Ford's anagram but not his name appears on the title-page of the first edition. His name is signed, 'IOHN FORD', to the dedicatory epistle to John Wyrley, Esquire, and Mistress Mary Wyrley, his wife, an epistle in which Ford says, 'I have enjoyed freely acquaintance, with the sweetnesse of your dispositions', but nothing else of a revealing nature.

The play has a prologue at the close of which in some copies (not in the Folger copy) appears, apparently as a signature, 'Mr. Bird'. This man must have been the actor Theophilus Bird, son-in-law of the manager of the Cockpit theatre and regularly associated with the companies at that theatre from about 1625 until about 1640. (See above, ii. 377–9.) His name appears attached to the prologue, epilogue, or dedication of three plays, all of them in whole or in part by Ford—*The Witch of Edmonton*, *The Sun's Darling*, and *The Lady's Trial*. Signatures to prologues and epilogues are most unusual, and one can only guess that Bird was the author rather than the speaker of those to which his name is attached, and that some special friendship with Ford made the dramatist want to acknowledge the actor's composition when the play was published. The verse form of the prologue for *The Lady's Trial* is an unusual one for Jacobean or Caroline prologues, and it is duplicated in the epilogue. Possibly Bird wrote that too.

The company which performed the play was the successor at the Cockpit or Phoenix under Christopher Beeston's management to Queen Henrietta's company, for which Ford's plays for the last several years had been written. (See above, i. 324 ff.) Christopher Beeston died in October 1638, and was succeeded as manager of the theatre by his son, William. (See above, ii. 363–74.) The fact that Ford wrote another play for the Cockpit or Phoenix after Queen Henrietta's men ceased to act there, but wrote no more, so far as we know, after Christopher Beeston's death, suggests some special relationship—possibly a contract—between Ford and Christopher Beeston.

Dr. Charles Lacy Lockert suggested that Ford took the basic situation for *The Lady's Trial* from Massinger and Field's *The Fatal Dowry*, acted as early as 1619 and published in 1632 (ed. *The Fatal Dowry. By Philip Massinger and Nathan Field*, 1918, pp. 39–40). The initial situation is similar, and Lockert has an interesting hypothesis that Ford developed *The Lady's Trial* as a reinterpretation of characters found in the situation of Act III of *The Fatal Dowry*. The hypothesis is worth consideration and it might be susceptible of further development.

The Late Murder of the Son upon the Mother, or Keep the Widow Waking
with Webster, Rowley, and Dekker

See Dekker.

The London Merchant (?)
(Lost)

1660, 29 June. S.R. Entered to Humphrey Moseley in a list of
   twenty-six plays, most of them otherwise unknown, are:
The Royall Combate. a Comedy. ⎫
An ill begining has a good end, & a bad begin-   ⎬ by Iohn fforde.
   ing may have a good end. a Comedy   ⎪
The London Merchant. a Comedy. ⎭
   (Greg, *Bibliography*, i. 68–69.)

c. 1710–50. 'The London Marchat [*sic*] A Com̃. by Jo^n Ford' appears in Warburton's list of manuscript plays. (See Greg, *Library*, Third Series, ii [1911], 230–2.)

The play is known only from the entry in the Stationers' Register, for Warburton's record of it may well be only a copy of the register entry and no evidence that he had ever seen the manuscript. (See ibid.)

Fleay pointed out (*Biog. Chron.* i. 234–5) that *The London Merchant* was the title on the board during the Induction to *The Knight of the Burning Pestle* and asserted with astonishing literalmindedness that it was the original title of the Beaumont and Fletcher play. There is no reason for thinking that the title on the board in the Induction was anything more than a straw man for *Citizen* to shoot at. In any case, Moseley certainly could not in ignorance have licensed *The Knight of the Burning Pestle* under this title in 1660, for the play had been printed three times before. Moseley as the publisher of the folio of 1647 was familiar with the plays of Beaumont and Fletcher, and he himself advertised *The Knight of the Burning Pestle* in his own play-list of 1660. (See Greg, *Bibliography*, i. 459.)

Chambers suspected (*Eliz. Stage*, iii. 316) that *The London Merchant* was a mistake for *The Bristow Merchant*, which Sir Henry Herbert licensed for the Palsgrave's company in 1624 as by Ford and Dekker. This is possible, but since nothing is known of either title except a licensing entry, speculation on the possibility seems idle.

The Lover's Melancholy (1628)

Bouchier, Jonathan. 'John Ford: François Coppée', *N. & Q.*, Seventh Series, xii (1891), 85.

Eliot, T. S. 'John Ford' in *Elizabethan Essays* (1934).

Ewing, S. Blaine. *Burtonian Melancholy in the Plays of John Ford* (1940), pp. 32–46.

Koeppel, Emil. *Quellen-Studien zu den Dramen George Chapman's, Philip Massinger's, und John Ford's* (1897), pp. 172–5.

Sargeaunt, M. Joan. *John Ford* (1935), *passim*.

Sensabaugh, G. F. 'Burton's Influence on Ford's *The Lover's Melancholy*', *Studies in Philology*, xxxiii (1936), 545–71.

——'Ford's Tragedy of Love-Melancholy', *Englische Studien*, lxxiii (1939), 212–19.

—— *The Tragic Muse of John Ford* (1944), pp. 35–78 *et passim*.

1628, 24 Nov. 'Ford's play [*The Lover's Melancholy*] was ex-
hibited at the Blackfriars on the 24th of November, 1628, when
it was licensed for the stage, as appears from the office-book of
Sir Henry Herbert, Master of the Revels to King Charles the
First, a manuscript now before me.' (Adams, *Herbert*, p. 32,
from Malone, *Variorum*, i. 421.)

1629, 2 June. S.R. 'Hen: Seile   Entred for his Copie vnder the
hand[*es*] of Sr Hen: Herbert and m^r Weaver Warden, The
lovers Melanchollye by Iohn fford gent.' (Greg, *Bibliography*,
i. 37.)

1629. The Lovers Melancholy. *Acted* at the Private Hovse in the
Blacke Friers, and publikely at the Globe by the Kings Maiesties Seruants . . . 1629.

1629. [A variant issue has 'H. Seile' instead of 'H. S.' in the imprint.]

This is the only one of Ford's major unassisted plays for which
we have a definite date, a fact which has generally led to a hud-
dling of his dramatic development into the short period between
1628 and 1633 when *'Tis Pity She's a Whore, The Broken Heart,*
and *Love's Sacrifice* were all published. The argument has been
that, since *The Lover's Melancholy* is inferior to those three
tragedies, it must of course have been written before them. The
absurdity of an argument which assumes unchecked progress in
the development of any artist is so thoroughly demonstrated by the
known chronology of so many writers, painters, and musicians,
that it is not worth considering. Ford collaborated on four plays
in 1624; three of his five best plays were in print in 1633, and the
fourth in 1634. Given these facts, it is rather unlikely that he
wrote none of his considerable plays in 1625, 1626, 1627, or early
1628, and then wrote his five best between 1628, when *The Lover's
Melancholy* was licensed for the stage, and February 1633/4,
when *Perkin Warbeck* was licensed for the press.

That *The Lover's Melancholy* was acted by the King's company
is indicated not only by Herbert's licence and the title-page of the
1629 quarto, but by the list, which was printed in the quarto, of
the seventeen actors of the King's company who took part in the
original performance. (See above, i. 82–83.) Such attention to the
actors, though commoner in Caroline than in Elizabethan or
Jacobean dramatic publication, was still most unusual, and may
indicate some pride on the author's part in the auspices under
which his play had appeared (but see below, Massinger's *The
Roman Actor*).

Though neither Ford's name nor his anagram appears on the title-page of the quarto, his name is signed to the dedicatory epistle. This epistle, directed to Nathaniel Finch, John Ford, Henry Blunt, Robert Ellice, 'and all the rest of the Noble Society of *Grayes Inne*', calls the play his first publication and hints that it may be his last:

> This Piece, *being the* first, *that euer courted Reader; and it is very possible, that the like complement with Me, may soone grow out of fashion.*

Further indication of Ford's selfconsciousness in preparing his first dramatic publication is seen in the four sets of commendatory verses prefixed to the play, signed by George Donne, William Singleton, Hum. Howorth, and 'Ο φίλος. The verses are the usual sort, saying little, though they are not so excessive in their phrases as commendatory verses often are. Even so, some contemporary seems to have thought their praise too high, for Hazlitt noted (*Manual*, p. 140) a copy of the play which has an added couplet in a contemporary hand:

> Jack Ford, these youngsters shew, methinks, great folly,
> In commending thy Lovers' Melancholy.

All commentators have noted the detailed and frank dependence of the play upon Robert Burton's *Anatomy of Melancholy*. The significance for Ford's thought in general of certain of Burton's conceptions has given this play a more central position in modern criticism of Ford than it otherwise would have had. (See Ewing, op. cit., *passim*.)

Some unscrupulous advertising of the eighteenth century has confused the literary history of this play. A performance of *The Lover's Melancholy* was proposed as a benefit for Mrs. Macklin at Drury Lane, 22 April 1748, though postponed until 28 April. Apparently as a puff for this performance, the verses about Ford and Shakespeare, signed 'Thomas May', were composed, as well as the poem about Ford, Randolph, Jonson, and Shakespeare, signed 'Endymion Porter', and extracts from an alleged pamphlet called *Old Ben's Light Heart Made Heavy by Young John's Melancholy Lover*. These were published in two letters sent by the actor Charles Macklin to the *General Advertiser* in April 1748, and they have had no little part in building up the myth of Jonson's hostility towards Shakespeare. There can be no doubt that Macklin's verses and quotations are eighteenth-century forgeries and that his pamphlet was imaginary (see the original letters and Malone's discussion of them, *Variorum*, i. 402–35), though they still obtain occasional credence, e.g. the verses are reprinted in *The Jonson Allusion-Book* (pp. 141 and 189). The forgeries are sufficiently skilful to make one wonder if Macklin did not have the assistance of a more learned man.

Love's Sacrifice (1632?)

Koeppel, Emil. *Quellen-Studien zu den Dramen George Chapman's, Philip Massinger's, und John Ford's* (1897), pp. 182–4.
Sargeaunt, M. Joan. *John Ford* (1935), pp. 132–41.

1632/3, 21 Jan. S.R. 'Hugh Beeston. Entred for his Copy vnder the hands of S^r. Henry Herbert & m^r Aspley warden a Tragedy called Loues sacrifice by Iohn fford.' (Greg, *Bibliography*, i. 42.)
1633. Loues Sacrifice. A Tragedie Receiued Generally Well. Acted by the Qveenes Majesties Seruants at the *Phœnix* in *Drury-lane* . . . 1633.
1639, 10 Aug. 'Loues Sacrifice' is one of a list of forty-five plays which William Beeston said belonged to the repertory of the King and Queen's Young Company at the Phoenix, and which the Lord Chamberlain accordingly forbade any other London company to act. (See above, i. 330–1.)

The title-page of the quarto omits Ford's name, as usual, but 'IOHN FORD' is signed to the dedication to his cousin, John Ford of Gray's Inn. That the front matter for this quarto was written during the rising excitement about Prynne's *Histriomastix* is indicated by lines in both Ford's dedication and James Shirley's commendatory verses. Ford says to his cousin:

> The contempt throwne on *studies of this kinde*, by such as dote on their owne singularity, hath almost so out-fac'd *Inuention*, and pre-scrib'd *Iudgement*; that it is more safe, more wise, to be *suspectedly silent*, then *modestly confident* of opinion, herein. Let me be bold to tell the seuerity of *censurers*, how willingly I neglect their practice, so long as I digresse from no becomming thankfulnesse.

Though the title-page of *Histriomastix* bears the date 1633, it had been issued late in 1632, and Prynne had his first hearings before the Star Chamber late in January 1632/3, and was committed to the Tower in February. (Ethyn W. Kirby, *William Prynne A Study in Puritanism* [1931], pp. 20–25.) The cautious tone of Ford's remarks indicates that they were probably made before the initiation of the actions against Prynne, but James Shirley, who wrote the only set of commendatory verses for the play, was much more outspoken; his contempt suggests that he wrote at a time when he was aware of the probability of severe punishment for Prynne:

> *Looke here* Thov *that hast* malice *to the Stage,*
> *And* Impudence *enough for the whole Age;*
> Voluminously-Ignorant! *be vext*
> *To read this Tragedy, and thy owne be next.*

Shirley's violence is an interesting anticipation of his ironic dedication of his own *Bird in a Cage* (Stationers' Register, 19 March 1632/3) to William Prynne in the Tower.

Fleay thought (*Biog. Chron.* i. 233–4) that the reference to 'women-antics' in III. 2 was an allusion to the actresses of the French company which had performed publicly in London in November 1629, and accordingly dates the play *c.* 1630, but a closer examination of the passage, of the reception of the French actresses, and of the activities of Queen Henrietta Maria, suggests to me that Fleay misinterpreted the allusion. The passage in the play is as follows:

> *Duke.* . . . *Ferentes,*
> Be it your charge to thinke on some deuice
> To entertaine the present with delight.
>   *Fer[nando].* My Lord, in honour to the Court of *Pauy,*
> I'le ioyne with you: *Ferentes,* not long since,
> I saw in *Bruxils,* at my being there,
> The Duke of *Brabant* welcome the Arch-bishop
> Of *Mentz* with rare conceit, even on a sudden,
> Perform'd by Knights and Ladies of his Court,
> In nature of an Anticke; which, me thought,
> (For that I ne're before saw women Anticks)
> Was for the newnesse strange, and much commended.
>   *Bian[ca].* Now good my Lord *Fernando* further this
> In any wise, it cannot but content.
>   *Fior[monda].* If she intreat, 'tis ten to one the man
> Is won before hand.
>   *Duke.* Friend, thou honour'st me:
> ▪ But can it be so speedily perform'd?
>   *Fern[ando].* I'll vndertake it, if the Ladies please
> To exercise in person onely that:

Now this passage, though it notes the novelty of actresses, by no means condemns them, whereas such records as we have of the French troupe indicate strong disapproval in at least one instance. (See above, i. 25.) Furthermore, the proposal which meets with approval in *Love's Sacrifice* is for court ladies to act, and the performers whom Fernando reports seeing in Brussels were not actresses but court ladies. Considering these facts, I can see little likelihood that Ford was asking his audience to recall the unfortunate French women of the autumn of 1629.

There may well be, however, another allusion intended in the lines. It should be remembered that this play was written for Queen Henrietta's company, a troupe almost as popular at court and with the private-theatre audience in the early thirties as the King's men were. (See above, i. 222–9.) Its principal dramatist was James Shirley, who on the title-page of *The Bird in a Cage*, published in the same year as *Love's Sacrifice*, was called 'Servant to Her Majesty' and who in that year was chosen to write the great Inns of Court masque to be performed before the King and Queen by the lawyers in demonstration of their loyalty after Prynne's alleged attack on the Queen as an actress in *Histriomastic*. (See Shirley, *Triumph of Peace*.) We have seen that Shirley attacked Prynne in the commendatory verses he wrote for *Love's Sacrifice*. In the light of the relationships of the acting company and its principal dramatist—the play's commender—to the Queen and the courtly audience, is it not likely that the allusion in question was intended to remind the Phoenix audience of the Queen and the ladies of her court, who had acted in court performances like the one proposed in III. 2? The Queen and her ladies had performed a French pastoral at court as early as 21 February 1625/6, at which there was some murmuring (see Harbage, *Cavalier Drama*, pp. 10–12), but the court seems to have become accustomed to the idea of court ladies in theatricals, and there was much interested discussion of the preparations of the Queen and her ladies for performance of Walter Montague's *Shepherd's Paradise* (q.v.). As early as 20 September 1632, Mr. Pory was writing to Sir Thomas Puckering about the rehearsals. (Birch, *Charles I*, ii. 176.) The polite tone of Ford's allusion seems to me much more likely to refer to these activities of the patroness of the company than to the dubious French actresses of 1629. If so, the lines in question were presumably composed after there was some talk of the Queen's proposed performance, i.e. in the late summer or early autumn of 1632.

An adaptation of *Love's Sacrifice*, entitled *The Duchess of Pavy*, by S. A. Eliot Jr., was published in *Little Theater Classics*, vol. iii (1921).

Perkin Warbeck (1622–32 ?)

Editions: *The Chronicle History of Perkin Warbeck. A Tragedy. A Strange Truth.* Ed. Anon., 1714; *A Critical Edition of Ford's Perkin Warbeck*, ed. Mildred Clara Struble, 1926. But see also the review by R. A. Law, *J.E.G.P.* xxvi (1927), 128–32.

Babb, Lawrence. 'Abnormal Psychology in John Ford's *Perkin Warbeck*', *M.L.N.* li (1936), 234–7.

Brereton, J. Le Gay. 'The Sources of Ford's Perkin Warbeck', *Anglia*, xxxiv (1911), 194–234.

Gehler, Victor. *Das Verhältnis von Fords Perkin Warbec kzu Bacons Henry VII* (1895).

Koeppel, Emil. 'John Fords "Chronicle History of Perkin Warbeck" und Thomas Gainsfords "History of Warbeck"', *Anglia, Beiblatt*, xxii (1911), 212–16.

—— *Quellen-Studien zu den Dramen George Chapman's, Philip Massinger's, und John Ford's* (1897), pp. 187–94.

Sargeaunt, M. Joan. *John Ford* (1935), pp. 113–17.

Struble, Mildred C. 'The Indebtedness of Ford's "Perkin Warbeck" to Gainsford', *Anglia*, xlix (1925), 80–91.

1633/4, 24 Feb. S.R. 'Hugh Beeston. Entred for his Copy vnder the hands of Sʳ. Henry Herbert & mʳ Aspley warden (observing the Caution in the License) a Tragedy called Perkin Warbecke by Io: fford.' (Greg, *Bibliography*, i. 43.)

1634. The Chronicle Historie *Of* Perkin Warbeck. A Strange Truth. Acted (some-times) by the Queenes Maiesties Servants at the *Phœnix* in *Drurie* lane. *Fide Honor* . . . 1634.

c. 1700 ? 'Perkin Warbeck, an historical play', Bodleian MS. Rawl. poet. 122.

1745, 19 Dec. *Perkin Warbeck* was revived at Goodman's Fields. (Genest, iv. 197.)

The quarto, like most of Ford's, omits his name from the title-page, though it does, like three of the others, exhibit his anagram, *Fide Honor*. His name is signed to the dedication to the Earl of Newcastle, and three of the five sets of commendatory verses are addressed to him by name. These commendatory verses are signed by George Donne, Ra[lph] Eure, George Crymes, John Brograve, and the poet's cousin, John Ford of Gray's Inn. Neither the verses nor the dedication throws any light on the play.

Perkin Warbeck, one of the last and most interesting of the chronicle history plays, derives its material largely from Bacon's

Historie of the Raigne of King Henry the Seventh, 1622, and from
Thomas Gainsford's *The True and Wonderfull History of Perkin
Warbeck,* 1618. (See Brereton, op. cit., and Struble, *Anglia,* loc.
cit.) It is presumably to Bacon that Ford refers in the opening
statement of his dedication to the Earl of Newcastle.

Ovt of the darknesse of a former Age, (enlighten'd by a late, both
learned, and an honourable pen) I haue endevoured, to personate a
great Attempt, and in It, a greater Daunger.

Evidence for dating the play is negligible. In a speech in IV. 4
(not III. 5, as Fleay gives it), King Henry asserts that the Bishop
of Durham deserves to be appointed Archbishop of Canterbury
when Archbishop Morton dies. Fleay (*Biog. Chron.* i. 234) thought
he saw in this speech Ford's subtle recommendation to King
Charles I that on the expected death of Archbishop Abbot (whom
Fleay inadvertently calls Bishop of London) *Thomas* Morton
would be a better candidate for the archbishopric than Laud.
This interpretation would date the play after Morton's translation
to the see of Durham in 1632 (Le Neve, *Fasti Ecclesiae Anglicanae,*
iii. 296), but surely not even Ford was naïve enough to make
ecclesiastical recommendations in a Phoenix play. Moreover, the
fifteenth-century Bishop of Durham is a fairly important character
in the play, to whom King Henry VII has good reason to be grateful at the time of the speech. The fact that the historical Henry
VII did not later make the appointment suggested by Ford's
character is fantastically irrelevant. Fleay was led astray by the
fortuitous identity of the names of the fifteenth-century Archbishop of Canterbury and the seventeenth-century Bishop of
Durham.

Miss Struble makes no specific statement on the date of the play,
but she seems to assume 1633. (Ed. *Perkin Warbeck,* pp. 31, 34,
37.) Her superficial and naïve analysis of the Caroline political
situation leads to her contention that Ford deliberately contrasted
the conceptions and policies of James IV with those of Henry VII
in order to present the advice of the lawyers to Charles I. This
contention is wholly unjustified by the evidence cited from the
play and most improbable in the light of the recorded actions of
Sir Henry Herbert, of the licensers for the press, and of the attitude of Ford and his friend James Shirley to the reforming lawyer,
William Prynne, as set forth in 1632/3 in the front matter for
Love's Sacrifice (q.v.).

The only suggestion of a date for the play I can see is in
the odd statement about performance on the title-page: 'Acted

(some-times) by the Queenes Maiesties Servants.' All seven of Ford's unassisted plays which were published before the closing of the theatres carried dedications, which show that he had something to do with the publication, and all have statements about the performing company on their title-pages. Two printed in the preceding year (*Love's Sacrifice* and *The Broken Heart*) were published by Hugh Beeston, the publisher of this play. Yet none of them uses the statement 'Acted (some-times)'. In the circumstances the special statement would seem to mean that *Perkin Warbeck* was not often or not recently acted, and therefore that 1633 was too late for a composition date. Possibly, however, there is some unknown connexion between the '(some-times)' of the title-page and the equally unusual '(observing the Caution in the License)' of the Stationers' Register entry of the play under the hands of Sir Henry Herbert and Mr. Aspley. The Stationers' Register note could be simply an observation of one of the forms of Herbert's licence for performance on the manuscript containing the words '(the Reformacons observ'd)'. (See Adams, *Herbert*, p. 37.) But it is conceivable that the '(some-times)' means that performances had been suppressed and that the Stationers' Register comment indicates a press censor's caution in consequence of the suppression. Such an interpretation raises many difficulties and is no doubt fanciful, but the two unusual statements about performance and licensing of the play are puzzling. I have sometimes wondered if there could be any connexion between this play, prepared for Queen Henrietta's men, and another play concerning a royal pretender which was prepared in January 1630/1 for the King's men, chief rival of the Queen's company, and heavily censored, though later allowed to be acted—Massinger's *Believe as You List* (q.v.).

The Bodleian manuscript of *Perkin Warbeck* is a rather heavily cut copy of the 1634 quarto—I noted about 23 lines cut from the first scene and about 180 from the second—presumably prepared for production but with little if any marking for the stage. The hand looks like a late seventeenth- or early eighteenth-century one. The odd summary which precedes the play is more a summary of historical events than a synopsis of the play and sounds a bit like a play-bill or advertisement. The possible relationship of the manuscript to the edition of 1714 or the performance of 1745 might be worth investigating.

The Queen, or The Excellency of Her Sex (?)

Edition: Ed. W. Bang, 'Nach der Quarto 1653 in Neudruck herausgegeben', *Materialien*, 1906.

Ewing, S. Blaine. *Burtonian Melancholy in the Plays of John Ford* (1940), pp. 79–88. Synopsis.

Sargeaunt, M. Joan. *John Ford* (1935), Appendix I.

Sherman, S. P. 'A New Play by John Ford', *M.L.N.* xxiii (1908), 245–9.

Sykes, H. D. *Sidelights on Elizabethan Drama* (1924), pp. 173–82.

1653. The Queen, or The Excellency of Her Sex. *An Excellent old Play.* Found out by a Person of Honour, and given to the Publisher, Alexander Goughe . . . 1653.

The play was published anonymously, and there had been little notice of it until Bang claimed it for Ford in his edition of 1906. All subsequent Ford students of any standing have agreed with Bang's attribution, though none has been able to find any external evidence of authorship. Ford's interests, methods, and style are so clear in the play, however, that it may be accepted as his until evidence of its composition by a very clever imitator is forthcoming. For Archer's mistaken attribution of the play to John Fletcher, in 1656, see Fletcher.

Apparently the publisher, Gough (who preserved the manuscript), and the writers of the commendatory verses were all unaware of—or at least unconcerned with—the authorship of the play. The front matter of the quarto—Gough's dedication to Lady Catherine Mohun and the commendatory verses of R. C., Edmond Rookwood, and T. C.—is concerned with the fate of plays in general during the interregnum rather than with this particular play. Alexander Gough, a former member of the King's company (see above, ii. 446–7), seems to have had some access to the old repertories, for in the early fifties he brought to publication four plays: *The Queen, The Passionate Lovers*, I and II, and *The Widow*. (Ibid.) Since the last three plays belonged to the repertory of Gough's former company, the King's men, it might be guessed that *The Queen* did too, but on the other hand Gough put the company's name on the title-pages of the editions of the other plays he sponsored, and the fact that he omitted it from the 1653 edition of *The Queen* suggests rather that that play did *not* belong to his former company. Gough was evidently concerned in the surreptitious acting which was carried on after the closing of the theatres (see above, ii. 446–7), and it seems likely that it was from this period of his activities that the acquisition of the manuscripts dates.

Langbaine noted (*An Account of the English Dramatick Poets*, p. 335) that part of the play is derived from Belleforest's *Histoire tragique*, tom. i, Nov. 13, and that the Belleforest incident is also used in the second act of Machin's *Dumb Knight*.

No evidence for the date of the play has been cited save for Bang's impression that the style would place it near Ford's major tragedies.

The Royal Combat (?)
(Lost)

1660, 29 June S.R. Entered to Humphrey Moseley in a list of twenty-six plays, most of them otherwise unknown, are:

The Royall Combate. a Comedy. ⎫
An ill begining has a good end, & a bad begin- ⎬ by Iohn fforde.
   ing may have a good end. a Comedy ⎪
The London Merchant. a Comedy. ⎭

(Greg, *Bibliography*, i. 68–69.)

c. 1710–50. 'The Royal Combate A C. by Jo^n. Forde' appears in Warburton's list of manuscript plays alleged to have been burned by his cook. (See Greg, *Library*, Third Series, ii [1911], 230–2.)

The play is known from only one reliable record, for Warburton's listing of it may well be simply a copy of the Stationers' Register entry and not evidence that he had ever seen the manuscript, much less owned it. (See Greg, op. cit., pp. 225–59.) Even this particular list of Moseley's has not inspired the greatest confidence, since in it he assigns to Shakespeare *Duke Humphrey*, *The History of King Stephen*, and *Iphis and Iantha*, and to Shakerley Marmion *The Soddered Citizen*. No doubt Moseley had the manuscripts he paid to license, but one would like to have corroborative evidence of more of his attributions of authorship.

The Spanish Duke of Lerma

See Alfred Harbage, 'Elizabethan-Restoration Palimpsest', *M.L.R.* xxxv (1940), 297–304, for his contention that Ford, not Henry Shirley (q.v.), wrote *The Spanish Duke of Lerma* and that much of Ford's original play is extant in Sir Robert Howard's

The Great Favourite, or The Duke of Lerma. His case is a very interesting one, and his contention that Sir Robert revised a Caroline play is most persuasive; less convincing is his argument that Ford and not Henry Shirley wrote the lost original.

The Spanish Gipsy

For arguments that the title-page attribution of this play to Middleton (q.v.) and Rowley is incorrect and that Ford was at least part author, see H. Dugdale Sykes, 'John Ford, the Author of "The Spanish Gipsy"', *M.L.R.* xix (1924), 11–24, and M. Joan Sargeaunt, *John Ford,* pp. 41–57.

The Sun's Darling (1623/4, 1638–9)
with Dekker

Greg, W. W. 'The Authorship of the Songs in Lyly's Plays', *M.L.R.* i (1905), 49–51.

Halstead, William L. 'Dekker's "Phaethon"', *N. & Q.* clxxv (1938), 380–5.

Hinman, Charlton. 'Principles Governing the Use of Variant Spellings as Evidence of Alternate Setting by Two Compositors', *Library,* Fourth Series, xxi (1941), 78–94.

Koeppel, Emil. *Quellen-Studien zu den Dramen George Chapman's, Philip Massinger's, und John Ford's* (1897), pp. 194–5.

Lawrence, W. J. 'The Problem of Lyly's Songs', *T.L.S.,* 20 December 1923, p. 894.

—— 'The Origin of the Substantive Theatre Masque', *Pre-Restoration Stage Studies* (1927), pp. 325–39.

Moore, John Robert. 'The Songs in Lyly's Plays', *P.M.L.A.* xlii (1927), 623–40.

Pierce, F. E. 'The Collaboration of Dekker and Ford: the authorship of the Sun's Darling', *Anglia,* xxxvi (1912), 141–68.

Russell, H. K. 'Tudor and Stuart Dramatizations of the Doctrines of Natural and Moral Philosophy', *Stud. Phil.* xxxi (1934), 1–27.

Sargeaunt, M. Joan. *John Ford* (1935), pp. 57–63.

1623/4, 3 Mar. 'For the Cockpit Company; *The Sun's Darling*; in the nature of a masque by Deker, and Forde.' (Adams, *Herbert,* p. 27.)

1639, 10 Aug. 'The Sunnes Darling' is one of a list of forty-five plays which William Beeston said belonged to the repertory of the King and Queen's Young Company at the Phoenix, and which the Lord Chamberlain accordingly forbade any other London company to act. (See above, i. 330–1.)

1656. The Sun's-Darling: A Moral Masque: As it hath been often presented at *Whitehall*, by their Majesties Servants; and after at the Cock-pit in *Drury Lane*, with great Applause.

$$\text{Written by} \left\{ \begin{array}{c} \textit{John Foard} \\ \text{and} \\ \textit{Tho. Decker} \end{array} \right\} \text{Gent.}$$

. . . 1656.

1657. [Another issue.] As it hath been often presented by their Majesties Servants; at the Cock-pit in *Drury Lane*, with great Applause.

The quarto has a dedication signed by Theophilus Bird and Andrew Pennycuicke, both former actors (see above, ii. 377–9 and 524–5) and both concerned in one way or another with other plays published during the interregnum. Neither their dedication, however, nor the commendatory verses by John Tatham gives any information about the play. The dedicatee differs in different copies; I have noted the Earl of Southampton, the Earl of Kingston, and Lady Newton, and perhaps there are others.

It has frequently been said that the masque is a work of Dekker's which was revised by Ford. (Fleay, *Biog. Chron.* i. 232; Ward, *History of English Dramatic Literature*, ii. 470; Pierce, *Anglia*, xxxvi, 168; Greg, *Henslowe's Diary*, ii. 190.) But there is no considerable evidence for such a conclusion. Dekker did write a lost play called *Phaethon* for Henslowe in 1598 (*Henslowe's Diary*, i. 83), but any identification of lost plays is hazardous in the extreme, and this masque is not about Phaethon or the Phaethon myth, though Raybright, the protagonist and the title character, is said to be grandson to the sun. (See Halstead, op. cit.) There is no real internal evidence of early date: the reference to *Tamburlaine* (III. 2) certainly does not suggest that *The Sun's Darling* was a play near in date to *Tamburlaine*, for such references are common in Jacobean and Caroline literature. See, for instance, Benjamin Spenser, *Vox Civitatis*, 1625, F_1; R. M., *Micrologia*, 1629, D_6^v; Randolph's *Praeludium*, 1630 (*The Poems and Amyntas of Thomas Randolph*, ed. Parry, p. 227); R. H., *The Arraignement of the Whole Creature*, 1631, p. 240. I can see no reason for not accepting Herbert's licence date as an indication of recent composition and intention of immediate first production.

But though there is no evidence that *The Sun's Darling* was

composed before 1623, there is evidence that additions to it were
made long after 1623. The last three lines of Act IV and the first part
of Act V break sharply from the character of the rest of the play and
refer almost unmistakably to the Scottish troubles and the preparations for the Bishops' Wars in 1638 or perhaps early in 1639.
(See W. J. Lawrence, *T.L.S.*, 20 December 1923, and Moore,
op. cit.) Since the King's *proposed* journey to the north is mentioned, the passage must have been written in 1638 or 1639. This
journey was evidently attractive to the company at the Phoenix,
for in May 1640 the company was suppressed for treating the
same subject in an unlicensed new play. (See above, i. 332–3.)

The song in II. 1 seems at first glance to be a debased version
of the cuckoo song in Lyly's *Alexander and Campaspe*, v. 1, but
the cuckoo song did not appear in any edition of Lyly's play
until 1632, and Moore (op. cit.), following Greg (*M.L.R.*, loc. cit.),
makes a good case for thinking it is more thoroughly integrated
into *The Sun's Darling* than into *Alexander and Campaspe*. Whatever the origin of the songs in Blount's 1632 edition of Lyly's
plays, it does not seem probable that the cuckoo song was copied
from Lyly's play into Dekker and Ford's.

The masque as a whole is an odd piece for a London theatre.
In its present form it certainly required scenery and quite a bit
of the spectacle ordinarily associated with the court masques.
To the modern reader it seems confused and somewhat pointless,
but the fact that Beeston wanted it protected for the Phoenix in
1639 indicates that the actors did not think it negligible. Possibly
the odd character of the masque is in some way related to the
unusual statement on the title-page of the 1656 (but not the 1657)
edition: 'As it hath been often presented at *Whitehall*, by their
Majesties Servants; and after at the Cock-pit in *Drury Lane*.'
This statement reverses the usual order of production, and certainly the original play was licensed by Herbert for the Cockpit
theatre. Is it possible that the revisions of 1638–9 were for court
performance, that these revisions included new staging effects, as
well as the passage about the Scottish troubles, and that the
whole new production was transferred as something of a feat to
the Phoenix? Such a sequence of events would fit the new passage,
the curiously elaborate staging, and the title-page statement,
but one would expect an event of this nature to have attracted
some contemporary comment.

462 PLAYS AND PLAYWRIGHTS

'Tis Pity She's a Whore (1629?–33)

Editions: *Annabella* (*'Tis pity she's a whore*). *Drame en cinq actes de John Ford, Traduit et adapté pour le Théâtre de l'Œuvre par Maurice Maeterlinck* (1895); S. P. Sherman, ed. (with *The Broken Heart*), The Belles-Lettres Series (1915); *John Ford: Dommage qu'elle soit une prostituée, suivi de Le sacrifice d'amour. Traduit de l'anglais par Georges Pillement* (1925).

Ewing, S. Blaine. *Burtonian Melancholy in the Plays of John Ford* (1940), pp. 70–76.

Koeppel, Emil. *Quellen-Studien zu den Dramen George Chapman's, Philip Massinger's, und John Ford's* (1897), pp. 178–82.

Sargeaunt, M. Joan. *John Ford* (1935), pp. 21–24, 168–75, *et passim*.

1633. 'Tis Pitty Shee's a Whore Acted by the *Queenes* Maiesties Ser*uants, at the Phœnix in Drury-Lane* . . . 1633.

1639, 10 Aug. 'Tis pitty shee's a Whore' is one of a list of forty-five plays which William Beeston said belonged to the repertory of the King and Queen's Young Company at the Phoenix, and which the Lord Chamberlain accordingly forbade any other London company to act. (See above, i. 330–1.)

1662[–3?]. Edward Browne's 'Memorandum Book, 1662' (B.M. MS. Sloane 1900, fols. 65–60 [*sic*]), contains a list of plays and sums which presumably represent plays which Browne saw and the amounts he paid for seats. Under the heading, 'At the Kings Armes Norwich', is: 'Tis pity Shee is a whore . . . . 1 6.' (W. W. Greg, 'Theatrical Repertories of 1662', *Gentleman's Magazine*, ccci [July, 1906], 69–72.)

'Tis Pity She's a Whore, with *The Broken Heart*, has been the most widely esteemed of Ford's plays in the present century, and *'Tis Pity* has had modern performances in 1894, 1923, and 1934. (See Sargeaunt, *John Ford*, pp. 171–3.) This recent attention is largely accounted for by Ford's marked interest in the individual and by his reiteration of a kind of scientific determinism (see Sensabaugh, *The Tragic Muse of John Ford, passim*); there is no evidence that this or any other of his tragedies attracted much attention in the seventeenth century. None of his plays went through more than one edition; most of them are never alluded to outside the commendatory verses; and such allusions as there are to the others are rare, casual references, not praise. (See above.)

    Ford's name does not appear on the title-page of the first edition of *'Tis Pity She's a Whore*, but 'IOHN FORD' is signed to the dedication to the Earl of Peterborough. This dedication is made up of the usual empty forms except for one sentence:

Your Noble allowance of These *First Fruites* of my leasure in the Action, emboldens my confidence, of your as noble construction in this Presentment: especially since my Seruice must euer owe particular duty to your Fauours, by a particular Ingagement.

What Peterborough had done for Ford is unknown and has not even been speculated upon, but '*First Fruites* of my leasure' has been much discussed. Fleay (*Biog. Chron.* i. 233) interpreted it to mean 'his first play without a coadjutor', which would place it before *The Lover's Melancholy*, and Fleay guessed the probable date of composition to be *c.* 1626. Ward (*History of English Dramatic Literature*, iii. 77–78) chose to consider '*First Fruites*' and 'leasure' inexplicable, and to order the plays according to his conception of Ford's dramatic development. Professor Sherman (op. cit., pp. 127 and xxxvi–xxxvii) gives no indication that he has considered the claim of *'Tis Pity* to be Ford's first play, but he was much impressed by the possibility that the theme had been suggested to Ford by the trial of Sir Giles Allington in 1631 for marrying the daughter of his half-sister. Miss Sargeaunt (op. cit., pp. 20–23), though she is troubled by the fact that *An Ill Beginning Makes a Good End* is apparently an unassisted play of Ford's whose existence in 1612–13 would date Ford's '*First Fruites*' in 1612 or earlier, is inclined to accept Fleay's argument and the date of 1625–8.

None of this evidence seems to me to carry much weight. Why should '*First Fruites* of my leasure' refer only to dramatic composition, and then only to unassisted dramatic composition? The simple meaning of the phrase would seem to me to be either that *'Tis Pity* was Ford's first composition and therefore written before 1606, when *Fame's Memorial* and *Honour Triumphant* were published; or that the play was the product of some newly acquired leisure—conceivably a leisure connected with the 'particular Ingagement' Ford owed to Peterborough. The first alternative is most unlikely since it would have Ford acknowledging Peterborough's 'Noble allowance' of the play 'in the Action' twenty-seven years or more after the performance. The second, which seems to me the most likely interpretation, affords us no help in placing the play in Ford's development, since the new leisure itself cannot be dated. I can only fall back on the suggestion made before (see above, *The Broken Heart*) that Ford's plays for the

Phoenix were written after his plays for the King's men at Black-friars, and that therefore this one would date 1629?–33.

Some slight support for a performance date shortly before publication seems to me to be afforded by the fantastically irrelevant printer's apology at the end of the quarto:

The generall Commendation deserued by the Actors, in their Presentment of this Tragedy, may easily excuse such few faults, as are escaped in the Printing:

If this apology has any relation to facts at all—which it may not—it would seem to refer to a fairly recent production which the reader of the newly printed quarto was expected to recall.

The single set of commendatory verses for '*Tis Pity She's a Whore*, signed by Thomas Ellice (possibly a connexion of the Robert Ellice of Gray's Inn who was one of the dedicatees of *The Lover's Melancholy*), is missing from many copies of the play. The verses have been mounted and set into the Huntington Library copy. The transcript in Dyce's *Ford* (i, p. lxxiv) is roughly accurate.

Professor Sherman thought (op. cit., pp. xliv–liii) that Ford's source, or at least a considerable influence in his composition of this play, was Sperone Speroni's play, *Canace è Macareo*, first published in an authentic edition in 1546 and the subject of considerable discussion in Italy. Sherman contended not so much for similarity of plot, as for a strikingly similar attitude towards the incestuous love of brother and sister.

A copy of the quarto of 1633 with extensive manuscript prompt notes was offered for sale by Rosenbach in his catalogue, *English Plays to 1700* (1940), No. 204. One statement in the description of these notes, 'The notes of scenic changes and off-stage noises are similarly marked', suggests that the prompt notes may have been prepared for a Restoration rather than a Caroline performance—perhaps the one Pepys saw.

The Witch of Edmonton
with Thomas Dekker and William Rowley

See Thomas Dekker.

SIR CORNELIUS FORMIDO
? – ?

The only reference to a dramatist of this name is found in Humphrey Moseley's entry in the Stationers' Register in 1653 of

'The Gouernour. by S^r. Cornelius Formido'. No other records of a man of this name have been found.

The Governor (?)

MS.: B.M. Add. MS. 10419.

Greg, W. W. 'The Bakings of Betsy', *Library*, Third Series, ii (1911), 225–59.
Harbage, Alfred. *Cavalier Drama* (1936), p. 225.
—— 'Notes on Manuscript Plays', *T.L.S.*, 20 June 1936, p. 523.

1636/7, 16 Feb. In a bill presented by the King's company for 'Playes acted before the kinge and Queene this present yeare of the lord. 1636' occurs the item, '21 The 16th of ffebruary at St James . the Governour'. (See above, i. 51–52.)
1636/7, 17 Feb. '*The Governor*, by the K. players, at St. James, the 17 Febru. 1636.' (Adams, *Herbert*, p. 58. Sir Henry was surely referring to the same performance as that recorded in the players' bill. I know no way to determine which date is correct.)
1653, 9 Sept. S.R. In a long list of plays entered by Humphrey Moseley as his copies is: 'The Gouernour. by S^r. Cornelius Formido.' (Greg, *Bibliography*, i. 60–61.)
c. 1710–50. 'The Governer T. S^r. Corñ. Fermido' appears in Warburton's list of manuscript plays. (Greg, 'The Bakings of Betsy', p. 230.)

There is some uncertainty as to whether one, two, or possibly three plays are indicated in the above entries. It would be natural to assume that the play Moseley licensed in 1653 was the one the King's company acted in February 1636/7, for after the closing of the theatres Moseley licensed as his copies literally scores of plays which are known to have belonged to the repertory of that company (see his entries of 4 September 1646, 31 October 1646, 9 September 1653, and 29 June 1660), and in the case of the plays of the Beaumont and Fletcher Folio and *The Wild Goose Chase* he had the co-operation of the remaining responsible members of the troupe. As to the last item, the play which John Warburton owned was surely the play Moseley licensed, for Warburton gives the same author. Here confusion sets in.

Many of the titles Warburton set down in his famous list were probably copied from the Stationers' Register and may never have been owned or even seen by him at all. (See Greg, loc. cit.) Yet he did have some play manuscripts, for the manuscript containing his list contains also *The Queen of Corsica, The Second Maiden's Tragedy, The Bugbears,* and a fragment of Wild's *Benefice,* and a manuscript of *The Tyrant* was sold in Warburton's sale. (See Greg, loc. cit.) A manuscript of a play called *The Governor* was sold in Heber's sale, and the catalogue carried this curious statement (vol. iv, Part xi, p. 135):

> The Governor, A Tragi Comedy, 1656. This play is one of the very few which Warburton's Servant spared. It is to be regretted that instead of being by Sir Corn. Formido, it was one of those written by our older dramatists.

This is the manuscript now in the British Museum. On the fly-leaf among notes or scribbles too dim to be read is the inscription:

1744

Nº. 81

> This Play formerly belonged to [?] John
> Warburton, Somerset Herald
> Supposed in Jones's Biographia Dram. to be
> destroyed by the servant.

The date seems to be in one hand, the first sentence and possibly the number in a second, and the second sentence in a third. Dr. Greg said that the sentence about Warburton was 'possibly in Heber's own hand-writing'. (Op. cit., p. 257.)

So far the evidence seems to indicate that all the entries concern the same play, which was perhaps, but not certainly, written by Sir Cornelius Formido. But the first page of manuscript is headed:

The Governor
A Tragi Comedy 1656—
Scene Barcellona
Samuel

Some writing on this page seems to have been obliterated. The name 'Samuel' is still legible, and Harbage (*T.L.S.,* loc. cit.) thought it the first name of the author, but Greg (*Bibliography,* ii. 981) noted that the hand was childish and thought it arbitrary to assume that an author had been intended. I have seen only a photostat, but I should agree with Greg. He noted also the remains of what might have been a name: 'W . . . . . we.'

The '1656' on the manuscript is another source of confusion. If it indicates date of composition, the play cannot be that belonging to the King's men in 1636/7 or the one entered by Moseley in 1653, and Harbage concludes, accordingly, that the

manuscript is not that of the Caroline play. (*T.L.S.*) The date
could, however, indicate the date of transcription of the manuscript, in which case we might have the Caroline play, but not
the manuscript which the King's men had or the one which
Humphrey Moseley licensed.

Certain aspects of the play lend weight to the latter possibility.
For example, various allusions to the wars in the Low Countries
suggest a date much earlier than 1656. In the dramatis personae,
Olanzo is called 'a low Country Collonell'; Jago is recommended
to go into the Low Countries and 'trayle a pike' (fol. 3^v); Olanzo
is asked for news from Holland and responds, 'Troth none but
that the warres continue still' (fol. 6); Olanzo hears that the disguised Facundo comes from the Low Countries and asks,

> Pray how stands the warr   what did you
> this sumers service what: any battells fought
> or any townes taken of either side.

The desperate Facundo replies with what he can remember from
a pamphlet on the siege of Ostend, and Olanzo, disgusted, rebukes
him for

> this yor story out oth penny booke
> I knowe the affaires better then those records.   (fol. 25^v)

References to Puritans also sound much earlier than the forties
and fifties. Vigetto says: 'I have lost as little of this story as a
Puritan does of a sermon when he writes short hand' (fol. 37^v);
and at the close of the play Abbot says: 'Now may I turne
preacher in Scotland and that I had almost as good be hang'd as
do' (fol. 48).

These allusions are not enough to set the date of such a confused
play (though Ostend sounds like 1601–4), but they seem to me to
refute the arguments for 1656 as a composition date.

In both prologue and epilogue the author says that he does not
write for gain, but the references to the players in the epilogue
seem to indicate that a commercial production was expected. The
stage directions are sufficiently specific for the commercial theatre:
'The Curtaines drawne & Nicholais & Sabina discovered on a seat
togeather' (fol. 8); 'shee peepes att the hangings' (fol. 10^v); 'enter
Vigetto & Olivia above' (fol. 10^v); 'enter Sabina thrust in in her
bead' (fol. 23); 'Facundo peeps in att the hangins' (fol. 25).

The evidence, indeed, seems to be inadequate not only to establish a date but to prove definitely that the B.M. MS. is either
Formido's play or the one the King's men presented at court, or
both. The identification still seems to me possible, however, for

on the one hand composition in 1656 is contradicted by lines in the play, and on the other, since the name 'Samuel' seems to me not intended for the first name of an author, I am dubious about the candidacy of Samuel Holland. (See Harbage, *T.L.S.*)

SIR RALPH FREEMAN
c. 1590–1667

D.N.B.

Gumm, Charles Clayton. 'Sir Ralph Freeman's *Imperiale*', in *Studies in English Drama*, First Series, edited by Allison Gaw (1917), pp. 105–15.

Sir Ralph Freeman was a wealthy London man of business who turned to literature in his leisure hours. There is some uncertainty about his career because of the confusion with his namesake who was Lord Mayor of London. The author of *Imperiale* appears to have been the son of Martin Freeman and the nephew of Ralph Freeman, the Lord Mayor (from both of whom he inherited estates), and of William Freeman. (Gumm, op. cit., pp. 106–8.)

The date of Freeman's birth is unknown, but it is probably within a few years of 1590; he was admitted to the Middle Temple in 1606 and received his first known public appointment, that of Master of Requests, in 1618; his namesake uncle was born in 1560. Before he was made Master of Requests—an office which he held for the rest of his life—Freeman had married a relative of Buckingham, probably Catherine, daughter of William Brett of Rotherby. (*D.N.B.*) In 1619 he was a member of a starch commission, and in or about 1622 he received grants in reversion of the auditorship of imprests in the exchequer and the auditorship of the mint. In 1623 he became one of the commissioners of the King's house, and in the following years a number of records attest his standing with the King. In 1623 and 1624 he was a candidate for the vacant posts of Provost of Eton and Master of the Rolls. (Gumm, op. cit., pp. 108–10.) He was M.P. for Winchelsea in 1625 and again in 1628–9. (*D.N.B.*)

In the first decade of the reign of Charles I, Gumm finds Freeman active as master worker of the mint, serving on several royal commissions, and engaged in a long dispute with Sir Giles Mompesson. (Gumm, op. cit., pp. 110–11.) Sir Ralph's extensive private interests included the manufacture of alum, the reclamation of public lands, and the development of the Newcastle coalfields. (Ibid., p. 115.)

After the outbreak of hostilities Sir Ralph must have seen active service, though confirmation comes only from a late and indirect reference when, in a petition of 1661, he speaks of his service in England, Ireland, and the Scilly Isles, and of his threatened execution and flight. He was in repeated difficulties with the new government over his estates and, according to Gumm, paid fines seven times in sequestration proceedings. (Ibid., pp. 112–13.)

After the Restoration, Freeman was restored to a number of his offices, and there are several Restoration records of his activities at the mint. (Ibid., p. 114.) He died between April and July 1667. (*D.N.B.*)

In addition to his original Senecan tragedy, *Imperiale*, Sir Ralph Freeman published two translations of Seneca:

> *L. A. Seneca, the Philosopher, his Booke of Consolation to Marcia. Translated into an English Poem.* 1635. [The S.R. entry assigns the translation to 'Sir Ra: ffreeman'.]
>
> *Lucius Annæus Seneca, the Philosopher: his Booke of the Shortnesse of Life. Translated into an English Poem.* 'Second Edition', 1663.

Imperiale (> 1638/9)

Gumm, Charles Clayton. 'Sir Ralph Freeman's *Imperiale*', in *Studies in English Drama*, First Series, edited by Allison Gaw (1917), pp. 115–29.

1638/9, 1 Mar. S.R. Thomas Harper entered for his copy 'a booke called A tragedy called Imperiale &c.' (Greg, *Bibliography*, i. 50.)

1639. Imperiale, A Tragedie, . . . Printed by *Thomas Harper*. *M.DC.XXXIX*.

1640. Imperiale, A Tragedy . . . Printed by Thomas Harper. *M.DC.XL*.

1655. Imperiale, A Tragedy . . . Printed by *Thomas Harper*, and are to be sold by *Robert Pollard*, at his Shop behind the Old Exchange, at the signe of *Ben: Jonson*. *MDCLV*.

The first two issues of the play are what W. W. Greg calls 'private and anonymous', but the 1655 edition has a dedication to John Morris which is signed '*R. F.*', and in their 'exact and perfect Catologue of all *Playes* that are Printed', which was appended to the 1656 edition of *The Careless Shepherdess*, Rogers and Ley attribute it to '*Freeman*', and Kirkman in his list of 1661 assigns the play to '*Sr. Ralph Freeman*'. (Greg, 'Authorship Attributions in the Early Play-Lists', *Edinburgh Bibliographical Society Transactions*, ii, Part 4 [1946], 308 and 325.) Langbaine discussed the play under the heading, *Sir* Ralph FREEMAN' in 1691. (*An Account of the English Dramatick Poets*, pp. 226–7.) The attribution to Sir Ralph has been generally accepted.

Imperiale has all the characteristics of closet drama: it is lurid, static, and stilted. There is no evidence that it was ever performed, and there is little likelihood that it would have had a London performance in the seventeenth century, though a university performance is not inconceivable. Actually *Imperiale* is simply another form of Senecan exercise to be considered with Sir Ralph's two translations of Seneca. (See Gumm, op. cit., pp. 120–9.) Sir Ralph says in the dedication of the authorized edition of 1655 that the play is now permitted to appear abroad 'chiefly to prevent a surreptitious publication intended from an erroneous Copy. . . . I never design'd it to the open World.'

Langbaine noted that the familiar story on which *Imperiale* is based is found in various accounts, including Bandello's *Novelle*, Beard's *Theatre of God's Judgments*, and Goulart's *Histoires admirables et mémorables de nostre temps*. Gumm, though he notes that Bandello's account is the one which would have given the most of his material to Freeman, offers no analysis of the prose accounts in relation to the play. (Op. cit., pp. 117–19.)

PRINTED IN
GREAT BRITAIN
AT THE
UNIVERSITY PRESS
OXFORD
BY
CHARLES BATEY
PRINTER
TO THE
UNIVERSITY